CW01432749

EDUCATION
AND
THE LAW

*For my late parents
Albert and Margaret King
and for my husband Harry*

EDUCATION
AND
THE LAW

by

DYMPNA GLENDENNING

BA, H Dip in Ed, M Ed, PhD, BL

Butterworths

Ireland	Butterworth (Ireland) Ltd, 26 Upper Ormond Quay, DUBLIN 7
United Kingdom	Butterworths a Division of Reed Elsevier (UK) Ltd, Halsbury House, 35 Chancery Lane, LONDON WC2A 1EL and 4 Hill Street, EDINBURGH EH2 3JZ
Australia	Butterworths, a Division of Reed International Books Australia Pty Ltd, Chatswood, NEW SOUTH WALES
Canada	Butterworths Canada Ltd, Markham, ONTARIO
India	Butterworths India, NEW DELHI
Malaysia	Malayan Law Journal Sdn Bhd, KUALA LUMPUR
New Zealand	Butterworths of New Zealand Ltd, WELLINGTON
Singapore	Butterworths Asia, SINGAPORE
South Africa	Butterworths Legal Publishers (Pty) Ltd, DURBAN
USA	Lexis Law Publishing, Charlottesville, VIRGINIA

© Butterworths Ireland Ltd 1999

All rights reserved. No part of this publication may be reproduced or transmitted in any form or by any means, including photocopying and recording, without the written permission of the copyright holder, application for which should be addressed to the publisher. Such written permission must also be obtained before any part of this publication is stored in a retrieval system of any nature.

A CIP Catalogue record for this book is available from the British Library.

ISBN 1 85475 8411

ISBN 1-85475-841-1

9 781854 758415

Printed and bound by Bookcraft (Bath) Ltd, Midsomer Norton, Avon

Visit us at our website: http//www.butterworthsireland.com

Foreword

Little did I realise the treat that was in store for me when I agreed to write the foreword to this book. In fact, to be perfectly honest, the thought of reading through a book of many hundreds of pages on the topic of education and the law did not enthuse me very much.

Before I was presented with the proofs of the book I was of course aware of the very informal way in which the Irish system of education has operated since 1922. I anticipated that the work would treat of seemingly endless administrative circulars and memoranda from the Department of Education which have been such a feature of the educational system in this country. I was also aware of the criticisms of this method of operation which had been voiced by Costello P in the case of *McCann v Minister for Education*. These circulars, which were issued at regular intervals from the Department of Education, were turgid, ambiguous, uncertain and written in a style which would do credit to Sir Humphrey of "Yes Minister" fame. I wrongly assumed that a book that would have to deal with such documents might very well share some of their characteristics. I was wrong.

No doubt many people would pity someone who admits that a legal textbook constitutes compelling reading. But that is precisely what I am prepared to admit to in the case of Dr Glendenning's book.

The historical outline which introduces the book gives a fascinating and panoramic view of the topic both before and after the attainment of independence. That chapter whets the appetite for an insight into the ideological background which played such a part in the drafting of the 1937 Constitution and in particular those articles which deal with education. That background in turn casts light upon the most interesting analysis of the drafting process concerning Articles 42 and 44. The research done on the de Valera papers, the involvement of Alfred O'Rahilly (as he then was), Father Edward Cahill SJ, Father J C McQuaid CSSp (as he then was), Joseph P Walsh and Cardinal Pacelli (as he then was) make for a most interesting narrative.

The book goes on to deal with the constitutional provisions dealing with education and how they have been construed and applied by the Courts over the years. This is so, not merely in relation to education in general but also deals with special education provision which has to be made from time to time. The Education Act of 1998 is fully considered and the author then goes on to consider education in a European Community context as well as from a human rights point of view.

The chapters dealing with the teacher's duty of care in the context of both negligence in schools and school discipline will prove to be both invaluable and topical. A further bonus is the author's treatment of the employment law which relates to teachers.

Finally, Dr Glendenning treats in a most readable way another topical subject, namely freedom of information insofar as it applies to school records.

This book is a most valuable contribution to both education and the law. Dr Glendenning deserves to be praised for both the breadth and quality of her scholarship. The fact that she is able with such ease to translate those into a most readable and interesting text is a magnificent achievement.

I congratulate her on this excellent work which I have no doubt will be of great use and benefit not merely to those who are directly involved in the field of education and the law but even to those who have no more than a passing interest in the subject.

Peter Kelly
The High Court
St Romauld's Day 1999.

Preface

The past decade has seen an unprecedented reassessment and evaluation of this education system, its curriculum and upholding structures. Scarcely a day passes without some innovation in education. As this book goes to press, the reserved Supreme Court judgement in *DPP v Best*, which deals with the constitutional right of parents to educate in the home, is awaited with much interest. During the 1990s, educational jurisprudence has developed rapidly and this complex branch of law is likely to continue to expand.

As Ireland enters a new era of legal regulation of education, it builds upon an inherited informal denominational system which has evolved over the centuries. Currently, decisions are being taken with a view to preserving what is best in the system, to ensuring its relevance to current needs and with a view to securing a worthy inheritance for future generations. As Black J reminds us in his dissenting decision in *Tinker v Des Moines Community School* 393 US 503 21 L Ed 731, 89 S Ct 733 at 740, "Change has been said to be truly the law of life but sometimes the old and the tried and true are worth holding".

Irish education law does not respect inter-disciplinary boundaries drawing as it does on history, education, social science, law and canon law. This book considers the structures within which the education system operates. It discusses historical developments, relevant constitutional provisions, human right instruments, European Community law and recent legislation including the Education Act 1998 and the Education (Welfare) Bill 1999 which has now passed through the Seanad. Many of the more practical issues, relating to school management are considered in later chapters, such as the legal principles upholding the teacher's duty of care, negligence in schools, school discipline, statutory rights to information and employment law for teachers.

Recent reforms in education have been guided by a consensus distilled from the partners in education and the main developments in this sphere are detailed. The implementation of such reforms has been influenced significantly by material emanating from the Department of Education and Science and elsewhere. While the various circulars, memoranda, guidelines, information sources of law, they are important information sources and guides to good practice. Accordingly reference is made to these documents when relevant.

In attempt to state the law as clearly as possible, as of 22 June 1999, I hope that this book will prove useful to lawyers interested in education and to educators interested in the growing interface of education and law. Hopefully, it will also be of interest to school inspectors, boards of management, centres of education, students and parents. This book explores and discusses the legal principles which uphold education in Ireland. However, it is not intended as a "do it yourself" guide to legal problems which arise in schools and advice on specific problems arising must necessarily remain with the lawyers retained for that purpose.

I am most grateful to Butterworths for publishing this book and in particular I would like to express my sincere thanks to my editor Louise Leavy for her friendly but firm guidance and encouragement and to Ciara Fitzpatrick for her patient and thorough editing of the final text.

A book such as this builds what has gone before and relies on the assistance of colleagues and the support of friends and family. In this regard, special thanks is due to the following who each read a chapter of the book and made recommendations, Professor Áine Hylands of Cork University, James O'Reilly SC, Niamh Hyland BL, Eileen Barrington BL, Teresa Blake BL, John O'Donnell BL Mary Honan BL and Carol Fawsitt, Solicitor, Fawsitt and Co, Solicitor. Any errors or omissions, however are entirely the author's.

In the collection of material for this book, I was greatly assisted by former teacher colleagues and teacher unions, insurance companies, the Department of Education and Science and in particular its Press Office staff and by various libraries and archives. My special thanks is due to the staff of the Law Library, the Franciscan Library, Dun Mhuire, Killiney for allowing access to the De Valera Papers, the National Archives, the State Paper Office, Trinity College Libraries and to the Catholic Central Library, Merrion Square. Other most useful and helpful sources of information were the Offices at the Ombudsman, the Data Protection Commissioner, the Freedom of Information Commissioner. I would also like to acknowledge the kind assistance of the Educate Together organisation and the Gaelscoileanna organisation.

A special word of thanks is also due to the supervisors of my earlier academic work in the faculties of education and law in Trinity College. In this regard, I am grateful to Professor WN Osborough, Doctor Seamus McGuinness and Mr Gerry Whyte BL for fostering my interest in education law. Mr Justice Costello, former President of the High Court, read a draft of this book at the early stages and I am deeply grateful to him for his encouragement and for the recommendations he made. My particular thanks is due to Mr Justice Peter Kelly for finding time, in his very busy schedule, to read the final draft and for writing such a kind and interesting foreword.

Finally, I would also like to extend my thanks to Maurice Moynihan for granting me an interview relating to the drafting of Article 42 and 44 of the Constitution and to the internationally-known author John McGahern for an interview which shed light on his dismissal from his post as a primary teacher. This book would not have been completed without the support and encouragement of my husband Harry to whom I am deeply grateful.

As Ireland strives to find a judicious balance between the old law and the new, between the informal and the formal and between the right of parties in education, one is reminded of Cardinal Newman's statement in his University Lectures: "I look towards a land both old and young; old in its Christianity, young in the promise of its future; a nation which received grace before the Saxon came to Britain and which has never quenched it. I contemplate a people which have had a long night and who must have an inevitable day."

Dympna Glendenning
11 June 1999

Contents

Chapter 4   Educational Provision and the Constitution

Chapter 5   Educational Provision for Children with Disability

Chapter 6   The Education Act 1998

Chapter 7   European Community Competence in Education

Part I: The Legal Basis for Community Intervention in Education in the Member States Prior to the TEU

Part II: The Legal Basis for Community Legislation on Education Following the Treaty on European Union

Chapter 8 Human Rights and Education

Chapter 9 The Teacher's Duty of Care: Negligence

Chapter 10 The Teacher's Duty of Care: School Discipline

Chapter 11 Employment Law Relating to Teachers

Chapter 12 Freedom of Information: Access to Records in Schools

Appendices

Abbreviations

ASTI	Association of Secondary Teachers in Ireland
CEEP	European Centre for Public Enterprises
CIE	Coras Iompair Éireann
CPSMA	Catholic Primary Schools' Managers' Association
CRC	The Convention on the Rights of the Child 1989
DVPs	De Valera Papers
EAT	Employment Appeals Tribunal
EC	European Community
ECHR	European Convention on Human Rights
ECJ	European Court of Justice
EHB	Eastern Health Board
EPTs	Eligible Part-time Teachers
ERSI	Economic and Social Research Institute
ETUC	European Trade Union Confederation
EU	European Union
FOI	Freedom of Information
Gov Pubs	Government Publications
HEA	Higher Education Authority
HSA	Health and Safety Authority
IBEC	Irish Business and Employers Federation
ICCPR	International Covenant on Civil and Political Rights 1966
ICESCR	International Covenant on Economic, Social and Cultural Rights 1966
ICTU	Irish Congress of Trade Unions
IDEA	The Individuals with Disabilities Education Act 1990
IEP	Individualised Education Plan
INTO	Irish National Teachers Organisation
LEA	Local Education Authority
MBC	Metropolitan Borough Council
MOSA	Medical Officers of Schools Association
NCCA	National Council for Curriculum and Assessment
NETCB	National Education and Training Certification Board
NPC	National Parents' Council
NRB	National Rehabilitation Board
PCW	Programme for Competitiveness and Work

PESP	Programme for Economic and Social Progress
PNR	Programme for National Recovery
RCRG	Report of Constitution Review Group
RECs	Regional Education Councils
SAO	School Attendance Officer
SIPTU	Services Industrial Professional Technical Union
SPOs	State Paper Office
UDAs	Unfair Dismissals Acts (1977-1993)
UN	United Nations
UNICE	Union of Industrial and Employer's Conference of Europe
VEC	Vocational Education Committee

Table of Cases

H

I

M

S

X

Y

Table of Statutes

Constitution of Ireland

United Kingdom

International Conventions and Treaties

EU Directives and Regulations

Statutory Instruments

Chapter 1

Introduction[1]

[1.01] In the not too distant past, many European countries sought to retain their homogenous character by restricting the freedom of thought and action of citizens by imposing the values of the majority on all persons. It is now commonly accepted in the western world that human society is fissile[2] and that diverse opinions need to be reflected in society generally. By adopting a pluralist approach, it is argued, tolerance and diversity is fostered resulting in a fruitful interaction between people which permits freedom to "the questing nature of the human soul".[3] Thus, a pluralist[4] outlook, which respects and formally accommodates the beliefs and values of a diversity of cultures and individuals, is a common feature of most western societies which is reflected in many dimensions of life including education.

Pluralism and Education

[1.02] The provision of education in most developed countries echoes this pluralist outlook in that denominational schools exist alongside, albeit separate from, the public school system. By contrast, in Ireland, State schools are few and the vast majority of schools are denominational. In the past two decades, significant social changes have introduced greater diversity and complexity into the provision of schools generally. In 1995, the White Paper on Education (1994)[5] recognised pluralism as one of its central tenets. Yet, as the Irish system moves towards pluralism, other countries increasingly appreciate the advantages inherent in denominational education.[6]

---

[1]   In this work, the Department of Education (recently named the Department of Education and Science) will be referred to as "the Department" while the Minister for Education and Science will be referrred to as "the Minister", unless otherwise indicated "national school" and "primary school" will be used interchangeably as will the terms "student" and "pupil". The term "second level teachers" will apply to all teachers who teach at second level. The term "secondary schools" will denote voluntary secondary schools only (ie those schools run by religious orders and diocesan authorities) and a "secondary teachers" will mean one who teaches in a secondary school.

[2]   Cassell's English Dictionary defines this word as from the Latin word *fissilis* from *findere*, that may be cleft or split especially in the direction of grain, as wood or along natural planes of cleavage, as rock.

[3]   See further O'Donnell, *Wordgloss*, (1990), Institute of Public Administration.

[4]   Deriving from the Latin word *plus, pluris* denoting more than one.

[5]   *Charting our Education Future*, Gov Pubs, p 6.

[6]   England and Wales are striving to foster grant-maintained schools that reflect specific religions and philosophical beliefs as these schools appear to provide a sound education. See Mooney, 'A Lesson from Church Schools', The Times, 22 January 1999, p 41 in which the writer cites research which indicates that Roman Catholic schools in England provide a sound education.

The Challenge Facing Ireland

[1.03] As a country on the cusp of change, Ireland is attempting to forge a *via media* between its traditional system of informal denominational education and the excesses of rigid formality. While striving to accommodate the needs of all creeds and none, it desires to protect its existing denominational system on behalf of the majority of parents. As it searches for an appropriate balance in these pivotal issues, this relatively young State[7] draws on an ancient and honourable tradition in education. Essentially, the contemporary challenge lies in adapting that system, without suffering the loss of its inherent character, to the exigencies of the present. The approach to educational change in Ireland may be seen as distinctive to that prevailing in most other Member States in the European Union (EU) in that negotiation is the keynote rather than prescriptive imposition.[8] This position arises by virtue of the largely State-aided nature of the system which derives from its historical legacy. Change that emanates in this manner may be slow and tortuous but it may also be more fruitful as it derives from the multitude, so to speak.

[1.04] As is frequently the case with social change, law must be in the vanguard of educational reform[9] for law alone can devise the structures within which education can be equitably delivered. Writing in the 1960s, the late Charles McCarthy, a significant educator, stated "... when a society is at the brink of great developments, many people are themselves quite unaware of what is moving in their midst".[10] More than thirty years later, Ireland is finally seeing the fruits of that earlier stirring. The quality of educational policy formulation, the equity of the new structures for education and the decisions now being taken will be of historical significance as they lay down the legislative basis for education in the next century.

Accommodation

[1.05] For centuries, it has been argued that the mingling of fellow countrymen of different religions is more necessary in Ireland than in any other country in the world,[11] a contention which can scarcely be denied in view of the experience of the past three decades euphemistically referred to as "The Troubles". In its

---

[7] The franchise was given to a small number of Ireland's mainly Catholic population in 1793. However, the right to sit in parliament was denied them until 1829.

[8] *Report on the National Education Convention*, Coolahan, ed, (1994), Gov Pubs, p 9.

[9] See Quinn, McDonagh and Kimber, *Disability Discrimination Law in the United States, Australia and Canada*, (1993), Oak Tree Press, p 3.

[10] McCarthy, *The Distasteful Challenge*, (1968), Institute of Public Administration, p 113.

[11] Redmond-Howard, *The New Birth of Ireland* (1913), Collins Press, citing O'Donnell, *History of the Irish Parliamentary Party*, p 382.

current educational reforms, Ireland has much to learn from the experience of other countries and much to contribute to the general educational debate.[12]

The Changing Nature of Irish Education

[1.06] In 1960, a visiting American professor, Doctor Eoin MacTiarnáin, pointed to the fact that the absence of "a native virile philosophy" was a serious defect in Irish education which, in his opinion, may have caused "the appalling lack of self-confidence this nation exhibits."[13] Chapter 3 below shows Ireland has a very definite philosophy of education which is frequently unspoken but nonetheless present. One author remarks that the Irish system of education in the 1960s, was, more or less, the system which has been imposed on the country by the British Government.[14] Very little had changed structurally and "the work of creation", so desired by Pearse[15] had not come about.

[1.07] In 1991, the OECD in its *Reviews of National Education Policies for Education: Ireland* criticised the centrality of the Irish education system as one of its main weaknesses and advocated devolution to an intermediate tier.[16] The Report concluded that "The face that the Irish school presents to the world is quite recognisably that of previous generations."[17] Indeed, few structural changes had occurred in Irish education for more than a century and a half.

Transfer of Powers

(i) Law

[1.08] While an attempt to break with the common law tradition was considered prior to the Anglo-Irish Treaty of 1921, the weight of three centuries of common law tradition made such a change quite impracticable.[18] Finally, it was decided that, subject to certain exceptions, the existing body of pre-1922 law would form the foundation of the law in the new Irish State. Changes occurred, however, in the administration of law and in legal institutions and personnel.

---

[12] For one of the most interesting books on Irish education see Akenson, *The Irish Education Experiment,* Routledge and Keegan Paul 1970.

[13] 'An American looks at Irish Education', address to AGM of Conference of Convent Secondary Schools, 23 June 1960. Published in *Report of CCSS 1959-1960*, pp 32-45 cited in Randles, pp 57.

[14] Sr Randles, *Post Primary Education in Ireland 1957-1970*, (1975), Veritas, see generally Ch 1.

[15] Pearse, *The Murder Machine*, in O'Buachalla, 'The Educational Writings of PH Pearse, A significant Irish Educationalist', *Collected Works of Pearse*, (1980), Mercier, pp 374-376.

[16] At p 41 of the Report.

[17] At pp 55, 61 of the Report.

[18] Boyle and Greer, *New Ireland Forum: The Legal Systems North and South*, (1983), Gov Pubs, pp 14-15. This document draws attention to the impulse to break with the common law system and to the difficulties encountered.

The Courts Act 1924

[1.09] The new legislature and courts system inherited the whole *corpus* of case law and statute law in force throughout the country immediately prior to the partition of Ireland. Nevertheless, the practice of law continued virtually undisturbed as many of the changes were of form rather than substance. While diverging to such degree as was required to meet Irish policy needs, there was a strong tradition of following British legislative precedent.[19] Further and more profound divergence ensued as constitutional law influenced on Irish jurisprudence as will be seen in later chapters below.

(ii) Education

[1.10] Under British rule, the predecessors of the Department of Education were "the Commissioners of National Education". Their successors in the Irish Free State were "the National Commissioners of Education", an important distinction. Following the Treaty of 1922, all the jurisdictions, powers and duties of the Commissioners of National Education in Ireland were transferred to a new board entitled the National Education Board.[20] Subsequently the Minister and Secretaries Act 1924 vested the business and administration of primary education in the Department of Education with the Minister as executive authority.[21] Unlike its predecessor, the new board was not a corporate body but a department of State. Teachers would have the same relationship with the Minister as they previously had with the earlier board of education.[22] However, the administrators of the Irish Free State inherited in 1922 educational administrative structures which were unaltered since their inception. These structures have remained unco-ordinated until 1998.

[1.11] Yet, the past quarter of a century has witnessed dramatic changes in Irish education,[23] which have contributed collectively to the demand for supporting structural change. Closer contacts with other countries and their systems of education through information technology together with Ireland's membership of the EU have profoundly influenced education. Currently, a quiet revolution is taking place as the powerbase of education is shifting from Church to State. Formal structures are being put in place for a system of education conceived and nurtured in informality. It has fallen to this generation to establish a legislative

---

[19] Boyle and Greer, pp 6, 15 and 16.
[20] By order of the Executive Council, 16 August 1923.
[21] There was also a Transfer of Functions Order (No 264 of 1925) in favour of the Minister.
[22] *McEneaney v Minister for Education* [1941] IR 470.
[23] See *Irish Education Documents*, Hyland and Milne, eds, (1987), Church of Ireland College of Education, Vol 1 p 2.

framework for education which is capable of accommodating the diverse needs of all the people on this island for the next century.

Educational Reform and the Role of the Law

[1.12] The law has a crucial role to play in this restructuring of education:

(a) in drafting appropriate legislative structures for education;

(b) in upholding the constitutional framework for education within which all legislation must be necessarily be accommodated;

(c) in ensuring that such legislation is fairly implemented;

(d) in advancing social justice and equality in all matters pertaining to education.

[1.13] Education is normally perceived as a national obligation falling on the State and the right to education is perceived as one of the social rights the State undertakes to vindicate on behalf of the citizen.[24] By contrast, in the Constitution of Ireland 1937, the State is accorded a subsidiary role in education although it bears most of the financial burden for education which is provided, for the most part, in Church-owned schools, Thus, the provision of education is shared between Church and State although many shifts in the upholding powerbase of the system have occurred since its establishment.[25] While much greater parliamentary control is envisaged for education, this can only build on a negotiated consensus with the partners in education which imposes a restraint on the State's forward thrust in education.

The Partners in Education

[1.14] The system of education has evolved from a large number of interest groups, collectively referred to as the partners in education. The partners generally include school patrons, national associations of parents, recognised school management organisations, recognised trade unions and staff associations representing teachers. Some of these partners are long established and are directly implicated in policy formulation and administration while others have a more broadly based involvement deriving from their participation in various dimensions of contemporary life.[26] At the heart of the system is the pupil who has an implied constitutional right to free primary education while

---

[24] *The Educational Structures in the Member States of the European Community*, (1989), Luxembourg, Office for Official Publications of the EC, p 101; Alastair Macbeth, *Studies*, 'The Child Between', Luxembourg, (1984), Office for Official Pubs, p 11.

[25] Osborough, 'Education in the Irish Law and Constitution', (1978) Ir Jur, (ns) pp 145-180 at 151.

[26] See generally, *Charting our Education Future*, White Paper on Education, (1995), Gov Pubs, p 213.

constitutional recognition is expressly accorded the family as the primary and natural educator of the child. The complexity of the system necessitates the need for all the partners to work harmoniously as part of an interdependent structure.

The Meaning of Education

[1.15] When debating the issue of school discipline in *Campbell and Cosans*,[27] the European Court of Human Rights pointed out that the education of children is:

> "the whole process whereby, in any society, adults endeavour to transmit their beliefs, culture and other values to the young, whereas teaching or instruction refers in particular to the transmission of knowledge and to intellectual development."

[1.16] In *Ryan v AG*,[28] Kenny J in the Irish High Court considered education, in the context of Article 42 of the Constitution, to be scholastic in nature. When that case reached the Supreme Court, O'Dálaigh CJ expanded the definition as follows:

> "Education essentially is the teaching and training of a child to make the best possible use of his inherent and potential capacities, physical, mental and moral."

[1.17] The obligation falling on the State to provide for the education of children with mental and physical disability had not been considered by the Irish courts until *O'Donoghue v Minister for Health*.[29] In that case O'Hanlon J broadened the scope of the term "education" in Article 42.4 considerably so as to encompass State provision of education for those persons with severe and profound disability. This landmark decision was later affirmed by the Supreme Court subject to certain variations and conditions which are discussed later in Chapter 5.[30] with regard to the provision of education by the State under Article 42.4 of the Constitution, the trial judge O'Hanlon J stated:

> "I conclude, having regard to what has gone before that there is a constitutional obligation imposed on the State by the provisions of Article 42, s 4 of the Constitution to provide for free basic elementary education of all children and that this involves giving each child such advice, instruction and teaching as will enable him or her to make the best possible use of his or her inherent and potential capacities, physical, mental and moral, however limited these capacities may be, or to borrow the language of the United National Convention and Resolution of the General Assembly - 'such education as will

---

[27] (1982) 4 EHRR 293 at 303.
[28] [1965] IR 294.
[29] [1996] 2 IR 20.
[30] See below, para **[5.64]**.

be conducive to the child's achieving the fullest possible social integration and individual development; such education as will enable the child to develop his or her capabilities and skills to the maximum and will hasten the process of social integration and reintegration'."[31]

Growing Interface of Education and Law

[1.18] No substantive legislation relating to first- and second-level general education was enacted in Ireland in this century until the enactment of the Education Act 1998.[32] Following a gestation period of almost a decade, the Education Act 1998 passed into law on 23 December 1998. At the time of writing, only some sections of the Act are in operation.[33] Other provisions of the Act may come into effect on different days, thereby giving time for the establishment of support services. However the Act must be fully operational by 23 December 2000.[34]

[1.19] The Education (Welfare) Bill 1999 is a legislative landmark which has the potential to transform the Irish system of education for the coming century as it marks a new departure in Irish life. The Bill aims to provide for a comprehensive national system which would ensure that children between six to sixteen years attend school, or, if they do not do so, that they receive a minimum education otherwise. One of the aims of this urgently needed Bill is to address the root causes of truancy by assisting children and their families in this regard and by identifying, at the early stages, children at risk of developing truancy problems.

[1.20] The Bill places an obligation on schools to adopt a more pro-active policy to truancy matters and puts in place a procedure for facilitating liaison and coordination between the relevant publicly funded agencies which deal with school attendance matters. The statutory duty, which currently obliges parents to send their children to a recognised school, is retained and where children are educated outside that system, the Minister may prescribe minimum standards of education following consultation with the National Council for Curriculum and Assessment (NCCA) and other bodies, if any, as he considers appropriate but clearly such a minimum may differ reflecting the age and capacities of different children. All children who are to be educated outside the recognised school system, will be required to register following an assessment of the capacity of the home, or outside body, to provide minimum standards of education.

---

[31] At p 65 of the judgment.
[32] In regard to vocational education, see VEC Acts 1930-1970.
[33] These are ss 2-6 inclusive, ss 13, 25, 26 36, 37 and Parts VIII and IX, Education Act 1998, Commencement Order 1991 (SI 29/1999).
[34] Section 1(3).

Provision is made in the Bill for on-going assessment, subject to registration, of education provision outside the recognised school system.

[1.21] A new body is to be established, entitled the National Educational Welfare Board, which will carry overall responsibility, subject to Ministerial policy, for the implementation and operation of the Act, when enacted. The functions of the Board extend to advisory powers, research powers and direct involvement in the enforcement of school attendance. Existing school attendance legislation will be repealed and procedures will be established which will monitor school attendance. Schools will be required to prepare a code of behaviour in accordance with s 23. One of the most hopeful aspects of the Bill is that it addresses the employment of young children, which appears to be adversely impacting on education, and s 24 imposes sanctions for breaches in that regard.

[1.22] There is little doubt that the provisions outlined in this courageous and enlightened Bill would remedy many of the existing deficits in the contemporary provision of education as identified in this book. The Bill is likely to have a controversial passage through the Oireachtas and may he the subject of a presidential referral.

Chapter 2

The Structure of Irish Education: an Historical Outline

Introduction

[2.01] In the Member States of the European Union (EU), education is perceived as a national obligation falling upon the Member States and the right to education is viewed as one of the social rights the State undertakes to vindicate on behalf of the citizen.[1] Prior to appraising the constitutional provisions on education and religion in the Constitution of Ireland 1937, this chapter summarises the main historical events which have shaped Irish education with the aim of abstracting the legislative and administrative structure of the system to date.

[2.02] Ireland is heir to a singular tradition in education,[2] which the OECD *Reviews of National Policies for Education: Ireland* (1991) concluded can only be understood in the light of history.[3] History alone enables the abstraction of the structure which remains permanent through a succession of events.[4]

PART I: EDUCATIONAL DEVELOPMENTS PRIOR TO 1922

Education in Ireland

A Church-State Alliance

[2.03] Since 1831, the provision of education in Ireland has been a partnership between Church and State although many changes have occurred in this relationship over time. Throughout the centuries, the powers inherent in this unique partnership have ebbed and flowed, almost imperceptibly, adding considerable complexity to the system of education. However, Ireland's informal

---

[1] *The Educational Structures in the Member States of the European Community*, (1989), Luxembourg, Office for Official Publications of EC, p 101; Alastair Macbeth, *Studies*, 'The Child Between', (1984), Office for Official Publications p 11.
[2] For a summary of the upholding ideology of Irish education, see McNeill, 'Guidelines for an Irish Educational Policy' (1979) 14 Ir Jur (ns) 378.
[3] OECD, 1991, Paris, pp 6-7.
[4] See Levi-Strauss, *Structural Anthropology*, (1969), translated by Jackson and Grundfest, Penguin, p 22.

9

education structures are now being recast in legislative form and the lengthy process of formalisation and transformation is described later in Chapter 6.

Tradition of Informality

[2.04] Informality has been a singular characteristic of the Irish system of education since 1922. Until the enactment of the Education Act 1998, the system was highly reliant on rules, regulations, memoranda and circulars, a fact which has not escaped judicial censure.[5] In *McCann v Minister for Education*[6] Costello P criticised informal administrative methods in education, which affect the rights and livelihood of those to whom they are addressed, because of their uncertainty, their ambiguity and their inaccessibility.

[2.05] The law, he stated, should be certain and clearly accessible, and this principle applies equally to non-statutory administrative measures. While Costello J considered that it was not normally part of the judicial function to suggest how other organs of government should execute their duties, in exceptional instances, where case law manifests defects in the law or in its administration which may lead to injustice, then the judiciary could properly draw attention to such defects. More recently, in an unprecedented decision *DB (A Minor) SB v The Minister for Justice, The Minister for Health, The Minister for Education, Ireland, the Attorney General and the Eastern Health Board,*[7] the High Court has directed the Minister for Health to carry into effect his decided policy regarding children who require secure accommodation with treatment for their own welfare. This case is further discussed in Chapter 4.

Growing Formality

[2.06] With the passing into law of the Education Act 1998, Ireland has taken its first step in the enactment of a legislative framework for its informal, denominational system of education. Further legislation is currently being planned. New school types are emerging in response to parental demands and a new curriculum is being introduced into schools. Not only is the character of Irish education changing, its upholding jurisprudential base also appears to be in a state of flux. Recent case law indicates that the lack of appropriate educational facilities, as well as specific legislative obligation, is adversely affecting on the rights of a number of children who have being deprived of their constitutional

---

[5]   *O'Callaghan v Meath VEC* High Court, unrep, 20 November, 1990, p 2, Costello P.

[6]   [1997] ILRM 1, in which judicial review proceedings were instituted by the plaintiff, who had pursued a general course in teacher training in Leicester University. The plaintiff failed in her attempt to quash the two decisions of the Minister refusing her credit under the payment of incremental salaries in Ireland.

[7]   High Court, unrep, 29 July 1998, Kelly J.

educational and care rights. Thus, the scope and extent of the State's obligation in educational provision is gradually becoming clearer.

The Role of the Law

[2.07] In the restructuring of education the law has a pivotal role to play in upholding the constitutional framework for education and in ensuring that it adapts to the needs of contemporary society; in vindicating the constitutional right of the child to education and care; in achieving an equitable social balance in educational provision; and in ensuring the constitutionality of educational legislation. No education system can be fully understood in isolation from its background. Hence, it is now proposed to summarise the principal historical features which coloured and contoured the system of education in Ireland.

The Historical Legacy

[2.08] O'Curry,[8] Dowling[9] and Auchmuty[10] give an account of the Bardic schools that existed in Ireland after 1475. While Auchmuty holds that these schools retained all that was best in ancient Irish culture, it was through the influence of the monastic schools in the eight and ninth centuries that Ireland acquired the title of "Island of Saints and Scholars."[11] Hyland and Milne trace the evolution of these schools leading up to the eighteenth century.[12]

[2.09] From the twelfth century conquest onwards, Ireland had been a "lordship" of the English crown. In 1541, King Henry VIII of England, having previously proclaimed himself "King of Ireland" and "Supreme Head of the Church of Ireland", enacted two statutes to give effect and substance to these claims.[13] As Foster points out, this change of title denoted effective and total rule.[14] With the dissolution of the monasteries in 1537,[15] new plans for Irish education were formulated which would be implemented by the legislative method.

---

[8]   *Manners and Customs of the Native Irish*, (1873), Dublin.

[9]   Dowling, *A History of Irish Education: a Study in Conflicting Loyalties*, (1971), Mercier, Ch 1, p 9.

[10] Auchmuty, *Irish Education: an Historical Study*, (1937), Hoggis Figgis.

[11] Auchmuty, pp 10-11.

[12] *Irish Educational Documents* Hyland and Milne, eds, (1987), Church of Ireland College of Education, Vol 1, Ch 1.

[13] An Act that the King of England, his Heirs and Successors be Kings of Ireland 1542 (33 Henry 8 c 3); An Act authorising the King, his heirs and successors to be Supreme Head of the Church of Ireland (28 Henry 8, c 3).

[14] Foster, *Modern Ireland 1600-1972*, (1989), Penguin, p 3.

[15] An Act for the Suppression of the Abbies (28 Hen 8 c 27).

Early Legislation

[2.10] The Tudors were the first to employ legislation to promote education in Ireland with a view to fostering the influence of the Reformation.[16] State interventions of the sixteenth, seventeenth and eighteenth centuries significantly influenced education in Ireland. Government plans for education included the establishment of a range of parish schools, diocesan schools and one university.[17] However, these initiatives found scant favour with the native Irish as they were repressive of both nationality and language.

[2.11] The earliest Irish schools established under statute were Henry VIII's "parish schools" founded under the provisions of An Act for the English Order, Habite and Language 1537.[18] These schools were established with the objective that "the said English tongue, habite and order may be henceforward continually ... used by all men ... and shall ... procure his children to use and speak [it]".[19] It seems a considerable number of these parish schools existed in the diocese of Kildare and Leighlin in 1824, the majority being supported by grants from the Educational Societies.[20]

[2.12] During the following two and a half centuries, legislation was used to implement the dual government policy of fostering the production of English speaking children of the Protestant faith in Ireland.[21] Subsequently, Elizabeth I set up "diocesan schools" under An Act for the Erection of Free Schools 1670[22] while James II continued this policy by establishing royal schools[23] by Decree of the Privy Council in 1608. In 1612 formal racial distinctions between the English and the Irish were ended,[24] and from then onwards, religion became the primary mark of distinction between the two races.[25] Following the Battle of the Boyne in 1690, a Protestant ascendancy dominated Ireland for approximately a century and a half.[26]

---

[16] Auchmuty, *Irish Education: a Historical Study*, (1937), Hoggis Figgis, p 50, points out that, with the exception of Kilkenny College, no Irish school can find its origin in the Elizabethan reign.

[17] Auchmuty, *Irish Education: a Historical Study*, (1937), Hoggis Figgis, pp 38-9.

[18] (28 Hen 8 c 26); *cf* the first statutory provision for Scottish education, An Act for Settling Schools 1696.

[19] See Corcoran, *State Policy in Irish Education 1536-1836*, (1916), Dublin, pp 42-43.

[20] See Brennan, *Schools of Kildare and Leighlin AD 1775-1835*, (1935), Gill and Son, p 108.

[21] Auchmuty, *Irish Education: a Historical Study*, (1937), Hoggis Figgis, p 42; Foster, *Modern Ireland 1600-1972*, (1989), Penguin, p 3.

[22] (12 Elizabeth 1 c 5).

[23] See further *Irish Educational Documents* Hyland and Milne, eds, (1987), Church of Ireland College of Education, Vol 1, p 46 *et seq.*

[24] Statute (2 James 1 c 5).

[25] See Daniel O'Connell, MP, *Memoir on Ireland*, (1844), Dublin, pp 2-4.

[26] Auchmuty, *Irish Education: a Historical Study*, (1937), Hoggis Figgis, p 49.

The Penal Laws

[2.13] During the seventeenth and early eighteenth centuries, England relied upon a comprehensive series of repressive legislative measures, (the Penal Laws), to implement its policies in Ireland thereby affecting four crucial areas of Catholic life; property; religion; personal disabilities and education.[27] Catholic education was proscribed by An Act to Restrain Foreign Education 1695[28] and Catholic teachers were prohibited by law from teaching or running a school. If teachers disobeyed these laws, they were singled out, like the clergy, for exceptionally punitive treatment. Fines for those found teaching in Catholic schools were rank-ordered under the provisions of An Act for Explaining and Amending an Act entitled An Act to Prevent Further Growth of Popery 1709:

(a) £50 for a dean, monk, friar or Jesuit;

(b) £20 for a regular clergyman; and

(c) £10 for a schoolteacher.[29]

The authors of *Hall's Ireland* (1843) believed that the Penal Laws fostered a servile, dependant mentality among the native Irish[30] leading in time to complex disguises for educational, religious and political activities.[31]

Hedge Schoolmasters

[2.14] While the Penal Laws were in force, the more prosperous Catholics were educated on the continent.[32] Sporadic schooling for the poorer classes was provided secretly by travelling teachers in so-called "hedge schools" (or payschools) in the open air or in cabins in return for fees or lodgings.[33] Despite allegations against them of immoderate drinking, harsh discipline[34], the promotion of revolutionary ideas and the demise of the Irish language,[35] the hedge schoolmasters had in general achieved a relatively high social status by

---

[27] See An Act for the Uniformity of Public Prayers and Administration of Sacraments, 1665 (17 and 18 Charles 2 c 6); An Act to Prevent the Further Growth of Popery, 1703 (2 Anne c 6); An Act for Explaining and Emending an Act entitled An Act to Prevent the Further Growth of Popery, 1709 (8 Anne c 3).

[28] (7 William III c 4).

[29] (8 Anne c 3 1709).

[30] See *Halls' Ireland* (1843), London, p 266.

[31] Foster, *Modern Ireland 1600-1972*, (1989), Penguin, pp 206-7.

[32] Moody, *A New History of Ireland*, III, zlvl; *Irish Educational Documents* Hyland and Milne, eds, (1987), Vol 1, Church of Ireland College of Education, pp 49-51.

[33] Carleton, *Traits and Stories of the Irish Peasantry*, (1843/44) Dublin, Curry, pp 293-302, pp 14-8; Dowling, *A History of Irish Education: a Study in Conflicting Loyalties*, (1971), Mercier, pp 86-100.

[34] Porter, *The Life and Times of Henry Cooke*, (1871), London, pp 3-4; Little, *Malachi Horan Remembers*, (1976), Dublin, p 52.

[35] Dowling, *A History of Irish Education: a Study in Conflicting Loyalties*, (1971), Mercier, pp 93-97 citing Croker, *Researches in the South of Ireland*, (1824), London.

the end of the eighteenth century.[36] The poet Spenser (1552-1599), however, had some reservations regarding their moral influence.[37]

[2.15] Against this background of legislative proscription, it is not surprising that the priest-teacher alliance in education prospered, in an unofficial capacity, until it became the object of State suspicion and concern. Even when the provisions of the Catholic Relief Act 1782 permitted Catholics to teach school, the unofficial system of education, which had evolved during the Penal Laws, continued to receive the support of the native people. It was this system which continued to operate throughout the early decades of the nineteenth century. Even in the face of increased State support for the Educational Societies,[38] this unofficial system of education continued, albeit in dwindling numbers, until approximately 1870.[39]

Establishment of Religion

[2.16] The Church of England and the Church of Ireland "as by law established", were united by the Acts of Union 1800, which set up the United Kingdom of Great Britain and Ireland, into one United Church of England and Ireland whose doctrinal essence, discipline and government would be the same as "are by law established for the Church of England." Between 1800-1869, the Established Church in Ireland (the Church of Ireland) had a monopoly of State funds in education while Catholics were precluded in conscience from receiving grant-aid by the conditions imposed. Suspicions of proselytising persisted in the State supported charter schools[40] and to a somewhat lesser degree in the schools of the Educational Societies.[41] The Catholic Relief Act 1782 allowed Catholics to teach school and repealed certain laws relating to the guardianship of children of Catholics. From 1787 onwards a consensus was emerging for some form of State intervention in "united or mixed education" which would cater for all religions in one school.[42]

---

[36] Coolahan, *Irish Education: History and Structure*, (1981), Institute of Public Administration, p 30; *Irish Educational Documents,* Hyland and Milne, eds, (1987), Church of Ireland College of Education, Vol 1, pp 69-73.

[37] Edmund Spenser, *View of the State of Ireland*, (1809), Dublin, p 121.

[38] *Irish Educational Documents* Hyland and Milne, eds, (1987), Church of Ireland College of Education, Vol 1, p 69.

[39] Coolahan, *Irish Education: History and Structure*, (1981), Institute of Public Administration, p 8.

[40] See *First Report of the Commissioners of Irish Education Enquiry*, HC 1835 (400) xii, p 5.

[41] Sister de Lourdes Fahy, *Education in the Diocese of Kilmachduagh in the Nineteenth Century*, (1972), Convent of Mercy, Gort, Ch 4.

[42] Thomas Orde, (Chief Secretary for Ireland), placed his plan for education before Parliament in 1787; *Report of the Commissioners of Irish Education Enquiry* (1791) Vol II, HC 1857-58 (2336) XXII, Pt III, pp 341-79; Henry Grattan's letter in *Fourteenth Report of the Commissioners of the Board of Education in Ireland* HC 1812-13 (21) VI, p 230.

The National School System: State Initiative

[2.17] It was not until 1831, two years after Catholic Emancipation, that this plan was implemented by the establishment of the National School System nationwide.[43] As Professor Ó Buachalla points out, very few countries had similar State-supported systems providing universal elementary education in 1831.[44] Only Prussia and France, after the Guizot Law of 1833, had similar elaborate systems[45] and it was not until 1902 that a full State-supported system of primary education had evolved in England.[46]

[2.18] One striking facet of the system was the degree to which the Catholic clergy participated in education. That their educational skills and organisational experience would be utilised in education seemed a natural development following their earlier involvement in the unofficial system of education during the Penal laws. In reality, there was little else to build on.[47] While the clergy had never been in the forefront of politics, they could promote their interests in spheres where a consensus existed between the clergy and the laity. As Corish observes, however, "the clergy dared not lead where the laity would not necessarily follow."[48]

[2.19] Following the establishment of State-funded primary education in 1831, Catholic teachers formed a closer official alliance in education with the clergy of the parish becoming their employees and co-adjutors; a relationship which has largely continued to the present day. The teacher's appointment or approbation came from the priest and was dependant upon his or her teaching of the Catholic faith in the school.[49] In this manner, the priest became the employer of the teacher thus securing the ethos or characteristic spirit of the school.

[2.20] England's concern for basic education in Ireland, it appears, was not totally altruistic. It was possible, through the medium of education to advance English culture, to foster loyal Irish subjects, to use Ireland for social experiments, such as universal State-aided education, which might be unacceptable to the English public at that time.[50] Given the experimental nature

---

[43] See Hyland, 'National Education' in *Irish Educational Documents,* Hyland and Milne, eds, (1987), Church of Ireland College of Education, Vol 1, Ch 3, p 98.

[44] Ó Buachalla, *Educational Policy in Twentieth Century Ireland,* (1988), Wolfhound, p 19.

[45] Ó Buachalla, p 19.

[46] See further Jarman, *Landmarks in the History of Education,* (1963), London, p 256.

[47] Corish, *The Irish Catholic Experience: a Historical Survey,* (1985), p 229.

[48] See Corish, p 229.

[49] See Brennan, *Schools of Kildare and Leighlin AD 1775-1835,* (1935), Gill and Son, p 108, p 61 citing Lewis Mills, Schools' Inspector in *Report from the Select Committee of the House of Lords on the New Plan of Education in Ireland,* (1837), Pt 1 pp 618-9.

[50] See Coolahan, *Irish Education: History and Structure,* (1981), Institute of Public Administration, pp 4-5.

of this initiative, statutory provision of education was perceived as inappropriate. Structural flexibility, on the other hand, was the ideal vehicle for Stanley's fragile, interdenominational educational experiment.[51]

[2.21] In 1831, the Chief Secretary of Ireland, Lord Stanley, established a voluntary unpaid board, the Board of National Education in Ireland, for the superintendance of a system of national education. In his letter[52] (generally referred to as the "Stanley letter") to the Duke of Leinster, Stanley informed him of the government's initiative and outlined the main features of the system. He further invited the Duke to become president of the new board.

[2.22] State funds were withdrawn from the schools of the Educational Societies and transferred to the Board. Stanley invited the Duke of Leinster to become chairman of the Board of Commissioners of National Education (the Commissioners). Thus, Stanley's letter became the genesis of the managerial system of primary education which has continued in operation to the present day.[53] This system, *inter alia*, was given a legislative base when the Education Act 1998 was enacted.

The Role of the Patron

[2.23] The patron was the person (or body) at the apex of control in national school management from 1831 onwards. It was the patron who requested recognition of the school in the first instance and it was he who activated the local initiative in establishing a school. Accordingly, he remained at the pinnacle of managerial authority in national schools although he generally delegated powers to a manager to act on his behalf in school management.[54] In 1975, when voluntary boards of management were introduced in national schools, as a result of financial incentives, the boards assumed managerial control of the schools with the former manager acting as chairperson of the board.

---

51 Akenson, *The Irish Education Experiment*, (1970).

52 Lord Stanley to His Grace the Duke of Leinster, HC 1831-32 [196] XXIX, 345 in *Royal Commission of Enquiry into Primary Education* (Irl) Vol I, Pt I, pp 22-26 (C 6) HC 1870, XXVIII pt 1. Two forms of this letter exist, see Akenson, pp 392-402; The text of the Stanley Letter is also published in *Irish Educational Documents* Hyland and Milne, eds, (1987), Vol 1, pp 98-103, see Appendix 1. This is the version published in the *Report of the Select Committee on Irish National Education 1837*. A number of letters explaining the system are also contained in this volume.

53 For a detailed account of the managerial system see O'Connell, *A History of the INTO: 100 Years of Progress*, (1968), INTO, Ch 2.

54 See definition of the term "patron" in Education Act 1998, s 8(1) and its extension to include second level schools.

The "Mixed Education Principle"

[2.24] A central pillar of Stanley's plan was that it would:

> "afford combined literary and moral, and separate religious instruction, to children of all persuasions, as far as possible, in the same school, upon the fundamental principle that no attempt shall be made to interfere with the peculiar religious tenets of any description of Christian pupil."[55]

Thus, all creeds would be educated together in secular subjects, with separate religious instruction being provided in accordance with the wishes of the various denominations. This concept, which is generally referred to as "the mixed education principle", was pivotal to the system and was expressly laid down as "the object of the system of National Education" in the lease to trustees.[56]

Royal Charters: Corporate Bodies

[2.25] In 1845 and again in 1861, Royal Charters were granted under which the Commissioners were incorporated as a corporate body. Under the 1845 charter,[57] the Commissioners were empowered as a corporate body to:

    (a) hold lands;

    (b) make leases;

    (c) erect and maintain schools;

    (d) sue and be sued in their corporate name; and,

    (e) have a common seal.

These charters were merely a framework for the system.[58] As the century moved forward, the national schools gradually moved towards denominationalism, so that by the end of the century, it had become a full denominational system. Osborough succinctly summarises:

> "The fact that the majority of people in Ireland viewed, or were persuaded to view, the problem of elementary education in denominational terms ensured that there emerged, long before the Powis Commission of 1870 extended to it their imprimatur, a nation of denominational schools, for this was what by then the "national" schools had become, and, is indeed, to a very large extent, what in the modern Republic, they remain".[59]

---

[55] At p 2 of the letter.

[56] See *Rules for National Schools*, (1898), HMSO, p 226.

[57] A Copy of Charter of Incorporation granted by Her Majesty to the Board of Education in Ireland, HC 1846 (193) XIII.

[58] See further *Leyden v Minister for Education* [1925] IR 334 at 371, Johnston J; Part IX of the Education Act 1998 provides for the establishment of corporate bodies to provide services in relation to education.

[59] Osborough, 'Irish Law and the Rights of the National Schoolteachers' (1979) 15 Ir Jur 36 at 37.

Accordingly, although the State carried the main financial burden, including the payment of the teachers, control remained largely with the churches.

The Lease of National Schools

[2.26] In the National School System, the lease (usually for a 99 year period) is the instrument by which the State's legal interests in the school are safeguarded. The lease establishes a legal relationship between the Patron and the Commissioners of National Education (the predecessors of the Minister for Education and Science). The lease secures control over the use of the school property and a degree of control over the State's financial investment in the school. Where the site of a new national school is in the ownership of a diocesan trust, the legal instrument is termed "a declaration of trust." The parties to the lease or as the case may be, the declaration of trust, are the lessor (owner of the site, generally the patron), the lessees (the trustees), and the Minister for Education and Science.[60]

The lease constitutes an agreement between the parties under which the trustees undertake:

    (a) to retain the property for the purpose of operating a national school for the 99 year term;

    (b) to insure the premises and contents against fire and tempest;[61]

    (c) to comply with the Rules for National Schools;

    (d) to raise the local contribution towards the cost of the building and the furnishing of the school; and

    (e) to pay to the Minister an agreed sum of money in default of due execution and performance of duty.

As well as the national schools, other types of school existed at this time including the remaining "hedge schools", the schools of the Irish Christian Brothers and those of the Church Education Society[62] which was established by the Protestant Church following its withdrawal from the National School System.

---

[60] See further Commission on School Accommodation, *Report of the Technical Working Group*, Gov Pubs, 1998, p 69 and generally Ch 7 referred to hereafter as the *Report of the Technical Working Group*.

[61] See *The Rules for National Schools*, (1898), Her Majesty's Office, Appendix 'Form of Lease to Trustees'.

[62] Mr and Mrs Hall spoke glowingly of the Newport-Mayo schools funded by the Church Education Society. These two schools accommodated 226 children of which more than 50% were Catholic although there was a national school nearby, *Hall's Ireland*, (1843), Vol 3, London, Jeremiah How, pp 385-389; *cf* Hall's less than enthusiastic account of the "Protestant Colony" in Achill administered by the Reverend Edward Nangle at pp 394-401 of the same volume.

Early Church-State Tensions

Teacher Formation

[2.27] As Akenson observes, conflicting perspectives were manifest in the outlook of the churches and the State[63] as the former viewed the school as a spiritual trust while the latter perceived it as a national investment. From the beginning, the Catholic Church, in particular, considered its religious ethos or characteristic spirit to be an integral part of education permeating the entire school day. The State, on the other hand, was determined that religion should be strictly time-tabled like any other subject. As will be seen in the following chapters, this pivotal tension has constitutional implications which have not been fully reconciled even to this day. Furthermore, Church and State perceived teacher formation as strictly their own prerogative, and this issue became a matter of considerable controversy as the century progressed.

[2.28] While the early teachers learned "on the job" so to speak, it was envisaged by the State in 1831 that a Central Training College would operate in Dublin with thirty two local model schools nationwide which would cater for pupil teachers.[64] Marlborough Training College, Dublin was established in 1838 by the State and the first model school opened its doors in 1849. However, Catholic student-teachers were forbidden by the bishops to attend either the Model schools or the State Training College.[65] Meanwhile pressure increased for State funding for denominational training colleges which was finally conceded in 1883.[66]

State-Aided Ab Initio

[2.29] In the Stanley plan for national schools, the State neither provided schools directly or employed the teachers. Rather, it undertook to grant-aid such provision in response to local initiative. Usually the patron was the person who took up the local initiative in school establishment and he was generally the bishop or ecclesiastical authority of the relevant area. The patron sought State-aid for a school and undertook to comply with the stipulated conditions including the "mixed education principle." He could undertake the duties of manager himself, or appoint a manager who was generally the local clergyman. The State funded a large portion of the building costs and of the teachers' salaries and controlled, to a degree, the choice of managers and teachers.[67] At

---

63 Akenson, *The Irish Education Experiment*, (1970).
64 Corish, *The Irish Catholic Experience: a Historical Survey*, (1985), p 206.
65 This ban was later removed when State funding was acheived for denominational Teaching Training Colleges in 1883.
66 See further *Irish Educational Documents*, Hyland and Milne, eds, (1987), Church of Ireland College of Education, Vol 1, p 138.
67 Saorstát Éireann Report 1924, pp 7-10.

first, the majority of the Roman Catholic bishops tolerated the national system. The archbishop of Dublin, Dr Murray, sat on the national board. Bishop Doyle of Kildare and Leighlin considered that the terms of Stanley's letter were not the very best which could be devised although they were "well suited to the special circumstances of this distracted country".[68] However, being desirous of securing State funding, the churches generally participated in the "mixed education system".[69] Teachers were obliged to take the oath or make a solemn declaration of allegiance to the English monarch before a magistrate in the presence of the Commissioners.[70]

Growing Denominationalism

[2.30] As a result of the demographic pattern in Ireland, the schools catered almost entirely for pupils of one faith. With the passage of time, therefore, each denomination stamped its individual character on the body of schools under its jurisdiction.[71] From 1840 onwards, the churches, and in particular the Catholic church, became more assured in their educational role. As the system became more denominational, the controlling power of the manager in schools increased. Gradually the balance of power moved towards the churches who achieved control over the two main pillars of the system, ownership of individual schools, and control of teacher education or training.

By the end of the nineteenth century Stanley's high-minded but unrealistic vision of non-denominational education had failed as the Sadler Special Report (1897) illustrates:

> "Walking down King's Inn Street (Dublin) the passenger may see, divided by a narrow lane, two separate buildings both bearing the inscription of National school. On the one side of the lane is a school under the management of the ladies of a convent; on the other side is the school of a Presbyterian church. Not a single Protestant child attends the one; not a single Roman Catholic child the other. Yet in both religious education is fetterred and controlled ... In the narrow

---

[68] *Irish Educational Documents,* Hyland and Milne, eds, (1987), Church of Ireland College of Education, Vol 1, p 107 citing a circular sent by Bishop Doyle to his clergy upon the first announcement of the national system of education and dated 26 December 1831.

[69] In 1839 the Church of Ireland denounced the national system and established its own system, See further Akenson, *A Mirror to Kathleen's Face: Education in Independent Ireland 1922-1960,* (1975), London, p 3; The Presbyterians opposed the national system in 1841, see Appendix to *Eighth Report of the Commissioners of National Education in Ireland, 1841.*

[70] The Rules for National Schools included in the *Fifth Report of the Commissioners of National Education in Ireland,* Vol 1 which covers 1834-51, HMSO, 1865, s 111(3), p 68.

[71] *Report of the commissioners appointed to enquire into the nature and extent of the instructions afforded to the several institutions in Ireland for the purpose of elementary education; also into the practical working of the system of national education in Ireland* (Powis) Vol 1, Pt 1 HC 1870 (c 6) XXVIII, 1; Pt III, Vols 1-VIII, HC 1870, XXVIII, Pts 2-5; (Powis) 1870, I, 70; House of Lords Reports, 1837, p 94.

compass of that lane, about four yards wide, any observer may estimate the reality of the system of united education and the deep practical wisdom of its rules."[72]

[2.31] In short, the *de jure* system of non-denominational education had become a *de facto* denominational system by the end of the nineteenth century.[73]

Official Regulation and the Mixed Education Principle

[2.32] The governing rules, the Rules for National Schools (the Rules), indicate that from 1898 onwards the Commissioners were painstaking in their efforts to ensure that the "mixed education principle" was upheld and that their conscience clause was implemented.[74]

[2.33] The Rules of 1898 are even more specific as they introduce, in respect to the conscience clause a certificate book in which a parent could consent to his child receiving religious instruction from a teacher of a different denomination to that of his child, or from a teacher giving any religious instruction different from the creed of his child. This document required the certification of both the teacher and the inspector.[75] Even towards the end of the nineteenth century, when schools were becoming mainly denominational, National Archive material testifies to the sustained efforts of the Commissioners to uphold "the mixed education principle" in practice.[76]

Early Public Education Eschewed

[2.34] A general system of public education was introduced in England by the Elementary Education Acts (England) 1870-1909 and in Scotland by the Elementary Education Act (Scotland) 1872 incorporating local authority education control. Gladstone had similar plans for Irish education[77] but these met with strong opposition from the Catholic bishops and the plans were abandoned by 1873.[78] Because of the lack of local authority financial support,

---

[72]   At p 227 of the Reports. Cited in Balfour, *The Educational Systems of Great Britain and Ireland,* (2nd ed, 1903), Oxford, Clarendon Press.

[73]   Akenson, *Kathleen's Face,* p 4.

[74]   *Fifth Report of the National Commissioners of Education in Ireland,* Vol 1, s 11, p 67 covers 1834-1851; Vol 11 covers 1852-1865 inclusive.

[75]   *Rules and Regulations of the Commissioners of National Education in Ireland with Appendix,* September 1898, Dublin, HMSO, (1898), s 111, p 13-15.

[76]   Education, File 9, No 2690, complaint against King's Inns Street Convent NS, Dublin 1884/85, failing to remove the crucifix during secular instruction; File No 4349, Co Down, 1887, pupils given secular instruction during RE time; File No 4593, Co Antrim, 1887/88, violation of Rule 90, in which Roman Catholic pupils were present at RE class.

[77]   See *Irish Educational Documents,* Hyland and Milne, eds, (1987), Church of Ireland College of Education, Vol 1, p 133.

[78]   *The Powis Report* did not recommend such a measure but rather more definite recognition of the denominational character of Irish schools, *Report of the Commissioners (Powis)* 1870 (c 6) XXVIII.

funds for Irish schools were derived from some unlikely and uncertain sources such as the Poor Law Unions[79] and Custom and Excise whiskey duties popularly known as "whiskey money".[80]

Legislative Provision

[2.35] Legislation was used, however, for certain matters related to education:

(a) to secure school leases;[81]

(b) to secure school loans;[82] and

(c) for the provision of teachers' residences.[83]

No substantive educational legislation was enacted, however, and the system was administered by the non-statutory Rules for National Schools.

School Attendance Legislation

[2.36] At common law a parent was not under a legal duty to educate his or her child. England, however, had legislated for compulsory education in 1880. In Ireland a minimalist and unsatisfactory form of compulsory school attendance was introduced by the Education (Ireland) Act 1892 which required parents in cities and large towns to send their children (6-14 years) to school for a minimum of 75 days annually. This Act abolished school fees at primary level and provided for free primary education by introducing *in lieu* of fees a parliamentary grant for education.

Local Authority Control: General Education

[2.37] The final attempt, under British rule, to legislate for education in the whole island of Ireland failed when the highly controversial Education Bill 1919,[84] was defeated. The Bill, which provided for the establishment of a local co-ordinating education authority to liaise with local democratic education bodies, was strongly resisted by the Catholic church fearing the loss of control in education, but it was favoured by the Protestant church.[85] It appears that political

---

[79] The National School Teachers (Ireland) Act 1875 enabled Poor Law Unions to make optional annual contributions to national teachers employed in their areas; see also National School Teachers (Ireland) Act 1879 and rules thereunder; National School Teachers Amendment (Ireland) Act 1884.

[80] Local Taxation (Custom and Excise) Act 1890.

[81] Leases for Schools Act 1881.

[82] Loans for Schools and Training Colleges (Ireland) Act 1884.

[83] National Schoolteachers' Residences (Ireland) Act 1875.

[84] See further *Irish Educational Documents,* Hyland and Milne, eds, (1987), Church of Ireland College of Education, Vol 1, pp 186-189.

[85] See further Ó Buachalla, *Educational Policy in Twentieth Century Ireland,* (1988), Wolfhound, p 52.

instability contributed significantly to the withdrawal of the Bill in 1920. Consequently, by contrast with Northern Ireland, popular elected control of education was not introduced south of the border with the exception of the vocational education initiative of 1930 which is discussed later.

[2.38] The recent attempt in the Education Bill 1997 to legislate for the introduction of ten regional education boards nationwide failed to pass into law. Until the enactment of the Education Act 1998, the structure of the education experiment initiated by Stanley's letter remained essentially the same, the introduction of boards of management in 1975 being the sole structural change.

Structures for Education

Second Level Education: Voluntary Denominational Initiative

[2.39] Although there was a small number of secondary schools in Ireland from about 1570, they did not receive State funding until 1878. Following the passing of the Catholic Relief Act 1782, the expansion of Catholic secondary education commenced. After Catholic Emancipation (1829), this system of education flourished and by the nineteenth century the religious teaching orders had established a network of denominational schools nationwide without the financial assistance of the State. These voluntary schools, which were owned and administered either by the religious orders or by the diocese in which the school was situated, made a pivotal contribution to Irish education which is well documented.[86]

Duality of Aims

[2.40] The religious orders had a dual interest in the control and management of schools as they were involved in the academic education of their students and their religious formation. Being established without State aid or intervention, these schools, once they complied with certain mainly regulatory controls, retained until very recently considerable autonomy in their internal affairs, and a high degree of discretion in the matter of appointment and retention of teachers[87] once they were appropriately qualified. Although the voluntary schools were highly cost-effective, the State favoured exchequer funding for them only on the basis of the "mixed education principle" which underpinned the national school system. The emergence of legislative control of education in this context was inevitably slow, narrow in scope and chiefly concerned with funding.[88]

---

[86] Akenson, *Education Experiment*, (1970); Titley, *Church, State and the Control of Schooling in Ireland 1900-1944*, (1983), Gill and MacMillan; Sr Randles, *Post-Primary Education in Ireland 1957-1970*, (1975), Dublin; Fahey, 'Nuns in the Catholic Church in Ireland in the Nineteenth Century', *Girls Don't Do Honours*, Cullen, ed, (1987), Women's Bureau, pp 7-30.

[87] Saorstát Éireann Report 1924, p 6.

[88] See *Irish Educational Documents,* Hyland and Milne, eds, (1987), Church of Ireland College of Education, Vol 1, Ch 4.

State Funding

[2.41] Having experienced almost fifty years of intermittent Church-State conflict in the national schools, the State reluctantly agreed to fund second level denominational education in 1878. The exchequer funds which arose from the disestablishment of the Protestant Church in Ireland[89] provided the necessary finance for this initiative. It was the Intermediate Education (Ireland) Act 1878 (the 1878 Act)[90] which provided for State funding of voluntary secondary schools on the basis of the confirmed success of students in public examinations (the "Results System"). An enabling State Board (the Intermediate Education Board), which was a body corporate, was established under the Act to administer the system. When contrasted with the broad scope of the Elementary Education (England) Act 1870,[91] it becomes evident that the 1878 Act was merely a method of facilitating State funding of denominational secondary education without apparent loss of face on the part of the State. Section 7 of the 1878 Act provided:

> The Board shall not make any payment to the managers of any school unless it be shown to the satisfaction of the Board that no pupil attending such school is permitted to remain in attendance during the time of any religious instruction which the parents or guardians of such pupil shall not have sanctioned, and that the time for giving such religious instruction is so fixed that no pupil not remaining in attendance is excluded directly or indirectly from the advantages of secular education given in the school.[92]

Similar provisions are found in s 8 of the Elementary Education (England) Act 1870, in s 68 of the Elementary Education (Scotland) Act 1872, in the Government of Ireland Act 1920, in the Free State Constitution 1922, in the Constitution of Ireland 1937 and in more recent educational statutes.[93] In order to allow the Board to carry over its surplus income from year to year, the 1878 Act was amended in 1882[94] while in 1890 the Board received a substantial residual grant from the surplus proceeds of the "whiskey money" mentioned earlier.[95]

---

[89] By the Disestablishment Act 1869.
[90] An Act to Promote Intermediate Education in Ireland, 16 August 1878, Law Reports, *Statutes*, Vol XIII 1878.
[91] Which provided for teacher tenure, dismissal, residences, management and maintenance by school boards and conditions of parliamentary grants, see ss 14, 86 and 97.
[92] Intermediate Education (Ireland) Act 1878, s 7.
[93] Education (Scotland) Act 1962, s 9; Education (Scotland) Act 1980, s 9; Education Reform Act 1988 c 40, s 9 (England).
[94] The Intermediate Education (Ireland) Act 1882.
[95] Local Taxation (Customs and Excise) Act 1890.

[2.42] The State adopted a *laissez-faire* approach to secondary education while the churches attempted to preserve education from State intrusion. In this setting, legislative control of secondary education was inevitably tardy and tentative. The 1878 Act was amended by the Intermediate Education Amendment Act 1900 which enabled adjustments in the general operation of the secondary education. In 1914, with the purpose, *inter alia*, of making the registration of all secondary teachers mandatory, the Intermediate Education (Ireland) Act 1914 was enacted and the Teachers' Registration Council was placed on a statutory footing for the first time.

Technical Education

[2.43] This system, which is essentially distinctive in character from both primary and secondary education, involved a blending of central and local popular control which has statutory origins. The Local Government (Ireland) Act 1898 set down the framework for a systematic local authority structure and provided for the levying of rates for technical instruction. One year later the Agriculture and Technical Instruction (Ireland) Act 1899[96] provided for a system of technical education under the Department of Agriculture and Technical Instruction.[97] This system later flourished becoming, in turn, the genesis of the 1930 vocational education system.

PART II: EDUCATIONAL PROVISION AFTER 1922

Partition: Divergence

[2.44] The partition of Ireland meant that the two parts of Ireland proceeded along different paths including that of educational development.[98] Because of partition, innovation in the North of Ireland became an imperative as most of the administration of the Catholic elementary school system was centered in Dublin. In Northern Ireland, the managerial system [of education] was replaced by local control of education, a change effected by the Education Act (NI) 1923. It was envisaged that, henceforward, no public money would be spent on religious instruction in State-aided schools.[99] However, the 1923 Act was amended in 1925 and this amendment made provision for religious instruction and permitted

---

[96] (52, 53 Vict c 41).

[97] See generally Coyne, *Ireland: Industrial and Agricultural*, (1902), Brown and Nolan.

[98] See *County Council of Londonderry v McGlade* [1929] NIR 47 at 55 for Wilson J's explanation. See further Akenson, *Education and Enmity: The Control of Schooling in Northern Ireland, 1920-1950*, David and Charles, Newtown Abbot, 1973; Birrell and Murie, *Policy and Government in Northern Ireland: Lessons of Devolution*, (1980), Gill and Macmillan, Barnes and Noble, Ch 10; Corkey, *Episode in the History of Protestant Ulster*, 1923-47 History of the Struggle of the Protestant Community to Maintain Bible Instruction in their Schools, Privately Published, Belfast, and Murray, 'Educational segregation "Rite" or Wrong', in *Ireland: A Sociological Profile*, Clancy, Drudy, Lynch and O'Dowd, eds, (1986), Institute of Public Administration, pp 244-264.

[99] See Government of Ireland Act 1920, s 5; Osborough, 'Education in the Irish Law and Constitution', (1978) 13 Ir Jur (ns) 145 at 152-155; and *County Council of Londonderry v McGlade* [1929] NIR 47 at 55.

the religious beliefs of candidates, for teaching posts, to be taken into account by the employing body.[100] Three kinds of school emerged in Northern Ireland:

    (a) Controlled or State schools;[101]

    (b) Maintained schools;[102] and

    (c) Voluntary schools.[103]

State funding of these schools was in proportion to the degree of State representation on their management committees. Initially, the Catholic population generally opposed any governmental interference in their schools and so they became and remained voluntary schools until 1967 when an amendment Act introduced better funding which was contingent upon increased State representation on the management committees. By the mid 1970s most Catholic schools had become maintained schools.[104] By contrast, apart from some minor structural changes and the renaming of certain institutions, the administrators of the Free State, continued with the existing non-statutory system whose structures had not altered since 1831.

Education in the Free State

A Denominational System

[2.45] In closing the non-denominational training college in Marlborough Street in 1922, and in transferring its student-teachers to denominational colleges, the Free State indicated that its educational policy would be denominational. Further movement towards denominationalism is apparent also from the Rules for National Schools as from 1922 onwards the Rules relating to the protection of the rights of religious minorities in schools became less precise.[105]

[2.46] The Department of Education was established by the Minister and Secretaries Act 1924 and the three systems of education, already under the control of the Minister for Education, were assigned to that Department.[106] One

---

[100] Birrell and Murie, *Policy and Government in Northern Ireland: Lessons of Devolution*, (1980), Gill and Macmillan, Barnes and Noble, p 236 *et seq.*

[101] Those schools established by Local Authorities or the State or handed over to the State by previous managers.

[102] Those schools with management committees comprising four representatives of the former managers and two of the local government authorities, Murray, 'Educational Segregation "Rite" or Wrong', in *Ireland: A Sociological Profile*, Clancy, Drudy, Lynch and O'Dowd, eds, (1986), Institute of Public Administration, p 249.

[103] Those schools who wished to remain independent of the local government authorities.

[104] Murray, 'Educational Segregation "Rite" or Wrong', in, *Ireland: A Sociological Profile*, Clancy, Drudy, Lynch and O'Dowd, eds (1986), Institute of Public Administration, pp 249-250.

[105] See Hyland 'The Multi-Denominational Experience in the National School system' *Irish Educational Studies* Vol 8, No 1(1).

[106] Saorstát Éireann Report 1924, p 6.

factor common to all sectors[107] was that the newly established, under-resourced State neither established the schools or employed the teachers.

Legal System

[2.47] A decision was made, subject to certain exceptions, that the existing body of pre-1922 law would become the basis of the law in the Irish Free State.[108] The Courts Act 1924 set up the courts system in accordance with the Constitution of 1922 (Articles 64-66). This system continued until 1961 when an identical courts system was established in accordance with the 1937 Constitution (Article 34).[109]

Informality in Education Continues

[2.48] The Free State's preference for informal administrative methods facilitated policy changes with a minimum of attention and expense. The distrust of State control of education, manifest in the writings of Pearse[110] and the other revolutionaries, carried over into the 1922 Constitution. Perhaps Alfred O'Rahilly,[111] Eoin McNeill, later to become the first Minister for Education in the Free State government, and George O'Brien, who advised the Constitution Committee, best exemplify the general antipathy to statism in education.[112] McNeill warned of the hypertrophy of the State in a series of articles in the Irish Review and the Irish Statesman[113] and promulgated the view that the principles of education in the historic practice of the Catholic church were the trusted guidelines for an Irish education policy:

> "Catholic teaching regards education as a right and duty of parentage. Statism regards education as a right and duty of the State ie for the government of the time being ... The State notion of education corresponds to a materialistic view of humanity. In this view the individual ends with death ... In the Christian teaching, the individual is immortal, the particular community to which he belongs, and its political organ, the State are transitory. Therefore, the interest

---

[107] With the exception of the model schools.

[108] Article 73 of the 1922 Constitution.

[109] See further Boyle and Greer, *New Ireland Forum: The Legal Systems, North and South*, (1993), Gov Pubs, p 37.

[110] 'The Murder Machine', *The Educational Writings of PH Pearse*, O'Buachalla, ed, (1980), Mercier pp 371-385 at p 372.

[111] Who assisted in the drafting of the 1922 and 1937 Constitutions. O'Rahilly's Draft C was rejected by the drafters of the 1922 Constitution.

[112] Farrell, 'The Drafting of the Irish Free State Constitution: IV' (1971) Ir Jur 347, 350, n 5.

[113] Irish Review, (28 October 1922), pp 3-4; (October-January 1922/23), p 1; 'Education - the Idea of the State'; (25 November 1922), p 27; 'Irish Educational Policy', Irish Statesman, Pt I (24 October 1925), p 202; 'Irish Educational Policy', pt 2, Irish Statesman, (7 November 1925); 'The Control of Education', An Claidheamh Soluis, 5 (23 May 1903), no 11, pp 5-6; 'The Servile School' New Ireland, 5 (23 March 1918), p 322.

of the community and of the State is subordinate to the interest of the individual."[114]

It will be shown in Chapter 3 below that this entrenched anti-statist philosophy deeply influenced the constitutional provisions on education and religion which are grounded on the principle of State subsidiarity in education. Almost thirty years later Alfred O'Rahilly, whose impact on Article 42 is observed later,[115] articulated this ideology in a European setting:

"... For when the State starts to be schoolmaster, it ceases to be neutral and liberal, it begins to inculcate a creed and to suppress all cultural rivalry and diversity, it becomes a monopolistic Church backed by physical force and overwhelming economic pressure. We in Ireland-Catholic, Protestant, or Jew - are determined to resist any State imposed ideology."[116]

When viewed against the background of earlier proscriptive legislation, which sought to suppress both language and religion,[117] it comes as no surprise to find the churches becoming the main partners in the educational enterprise in the Irish Free State.

[2.49] In his memoirs,[118] written in 1986, the late Sean O'Connor, who was Secretary to the Department of Education for many years, states that the alliance of priest and teacher, though disturbed by occasional differences and hostilities, was a very successful one which extended beyond school affairs into other parochial activities. One unhappy result of the alliance, he observes, was that the lay people in the community were excluded from all responsibility for the direction of the school,[119] a position which has changed substantially in recent years.[120] O'Connor's criticism implies a lack of democracy and dynamism in Irish education at that time. He observes that the placing of vocational education under the jurisdiction of local authorities in 1930 had not been followed by the transfer of responsibility of any other sector of the system to a local authority. Furthermore, he submits that of the four potentially great powers in education, (the parents, the Church, the teachers and the Minister) only the Church had exercised any decisive influence on the system. However, in view of the great expansion in political and economic contacts with Europe,[121] he envisaged that

---

[114] See McNeill, 'Guidelines for an Irish Educational Policy' (1979) 14 Ir Jur (ns) 378 at 380 with an introductory note by Osborough at 378.

[115] See below, para **[3.26]**.

[116] O'Rahilly, 'The Republic of Ireland', in European Yearbook 1951, p 354.

[117] See above, para **[2.10]**.

[118] O'Connor, *A Troubled Sky: Reflections on the Irish Educational Scene 1957-1968,* (1968), Dublin, Drumcondra Teachers' Centre, pp 5-6.

[119] O'Connor, pp 5-6.

[120] See below Ch 6.

[121] Among other matters.

the ferment in education being experienced there would surely create "some stir in the placid - some would say stagnant - pool of Irish education."[122] That O'Connor's words were quite prophetic is clear from the ferment in Irish education in the past decade which is discussed in Chapter 6 below.

School Attendance Legislation

[2.50] In the discharge of its constitutional obligations, the Free State enacted the School Attendance Act 1926[123] which obliged children between six and fourteen years to attend school unless it could be established that they were receiving "a certain minimum education" in the home. The loss of the School Attendance Bill 1942[124] by the Department of Education in 1942, which is discussed in Chapter 3,[125] was significant in that it was the first Bill to fall in independent Ireland and no further attempt to legislate for education ensued until the 1990s.

[2.51] The School Attendance (Amendment) Act 1967 was enacted with the purpose of expediting the serving of warning notices on parents of children who were absenting themselves from school, of facilitating the production of the child before the court, and increasing certain fines imposed by the 1926 Act. This amendment raised the upper age-limit for compulsory schooling to fifteen years, which is the upper age legislative requirement at the time of writing but is shortly to be raised to sixteen years under the Education (Welfare) Bill 1999.

[2.52] Although the Education Act 1998 applies to national schools,[126] the non-statutory Rules for National Schools[127] ("the Rules" hereafter) still apply to the management and conduct of these schools. The Rules, which were last published in 1965, have been considerably amended and supplemented by circulars. The Rules which are unpublished and have been judicially considered in a number of cases.[128]

[2.53] As will be seen in following chapters, the courts have expressly recognised the denominational ethos of these national schools and the State has

---

[122] O'Connor, *A Troubled Sky: Reflections on the Irish Educational Scene 1957-1968,* (1968), Dublin, Drumcondra Teachers' Centre, p 12.

[123] Section 17 of the School Attendance Act 1926 was amended by the Child Care Act 1991, s 75.

[124] *Re Article 26 and the School Attendance Bill 1942* [1943] IR 334.

[125] See below para **[3.90]**.

[126] See below Ch 6.

[127] (1965) Gov Pubs; The Rules and Constitution of the Boards of Management (as amended) are also relevant since 1975 when boards of management were introduced into primary schools.

[128] *Mulloy v Minister for Education and the AG* [1975] IR 88; *Leyden v AG* [1925] IR 334; *Ryan v Madden* [1944] IR 157; *McKeown v Flynn* (1935) 69 ILTR 61; *Maunsell v Minister for Education* [1940] IR 214, 236; *Cotter v Ahern* HC [1976-7] ILRM 248; *Crowley v Ireland* [1980] IR 102.

formally recognised the integration of all subjects, including religious education in the 1971 curriculum. No alternative educational provision was made for parents who did not wish their children to be educated in a specifically religious ethos until 1978.

A. Primary Education

[2.54] The primary education sector is comprised of primary schools, special schools and non-aided private primary schools which in all cater for approximately 500,000 children. In 1995, these schools comprised:

    (a) 3,200 primary schools;

    (b) 115 special schools; and

    (c) 79 private primary schools.[129]

(i) Primary Schools

The vast majority (98%) of children receive their education in primary schools and these schools employ in excess of 20,000 teachers. More than 50% of these schools have four or less than four teachers. While the preponderance of the primary schools are privately owned by the churches, there are exceptions to this general rule.

(ii) State Schools

[2.55] The small number of State schools comprise:

    (a) the nine remaining model schools;

    (b) *circa* 60 schools which are vested in the Minister for Finance (which were transferred from the pre-independence Commissioners of National Education); and

    (c) *circa* 30 newly established gaelscoileanna that are vested in the Minister for Education and Science.

    (d) some State-owned special schools.[130]

Thus, it may be concluded that the system of national schools is a State-aided system by contrast with a State-owned and administered system.[131] In latter years, however, there is a growing diversity of school provision in response to parental demands.

---

[129] White Paper on Education (1994), Gov Pubs, 1994, p 18.

[130] Report of the Technical Working Group: Commission on School Accommodation, Department of Education and Science, 1998, p 69.

[131] See Report, p 69.

(iii) Special Schools

[2.56] These schools provide for children with special educational needs for whom a variety of provision is in place. The Department owns the site and buildings of four of the special centres for young offenders; the Office of Public Works owns at least one special school while others are owned by Health Boards or by religious orders or voluntary bodies. In instances where the sites are privately owned, the State usually defrays 95% of the cost of the buildings.[132]

Diversity of Provision in Latter Decades

[2.57] The General Register Office indicates that there are thirty three religious denominations with a building or buildings in Ireland for the purpose of the solemnisation of marriages.[133] Increases in minority denominations and multi-denominational schools mirrors the trend in the population as presented by the Census of 1991.[134] The substantial increases in the categories of "other stated religions", "no religion" and "not stated" in the period 1981-1991 illustrates the growing diversity of the population. While one inter-denominational (Catholic-Protestant) school has been founded, no non-denominational school has been established since the foundation of the State. Some submissions to the Report on School Accommodation indicated a belief that a growing number of parents are voicing their desire for a non-denominational school.[135] If parents make such a demand and they comply with the requirements in this regard, then, it would seem incumbent on the State to meet this need with due respect. Realistically, the State will be unable to meet all minority needs, however, and this brings to the fore the sensitive issue of the inclusivity of mainstream primary schools in meeting the needs of children of other faiths which is discussed in the following chapter.

(i) Multi-Denominational Schools

[2.58] With the aim of addressing the need for multi-denominational education, a group of parents came together in the 1970s. They founded the first multi-denominational school in Dalkey, County Dublin in 1978 (the Dalkey School Project hereafter). This school was placed under the management of a limited company without share capital. The establishment of this school was a landmark in Ireland as it was the first time in more than a century that a State-funded

---

[132] See Report, p 70.
[133] See Report, p 80.
[134] Central Statistics Office, Census 1991, Vol 5, Religion, which is included in the Report of the Technical Working Group: Commission on School Accommodation, Department of Education and Science, 1998, p 80.
[135] See Report, p 83.

school had been set up independently of church control and management other than a special school for the mentally handicapped.[136]

[2.59] Following the establishment of the Dalkey School Project, an over-arching representative body was founded, entitled "Educate Together" with a view to setting up a national patronage body for multi-denominational schools nationwide. However, the Department refused to sanction the nationwide patronage body so that each school established was obliged to form a limited company without share capital with the board of directors as their patrons. Subsequently, it was arranged that each school would become a member of Educate Together, reserving a veto over policy decisions to each individual school. The power conferred by this veto has led to difficulties both for Educate Together and the Department.[137]

[2.60] Currently, the number of multi-denominational schools stands at sixteen. When the new proposals for the capital funding and ownership of all new schools come into effect,[138] earlier obstacles to the establishment of this category of school will disappear, and so expansion in this sphere is likely to be considerable. These schools cater for children of many different faiths and those children with no faith. They provide a core religious education programme for all pupils and they facilitate those parents who desire to ensure religious instruction (in one particular faith) for their children.[139]

(ii) Gaelscoileanna

[2.61] Gaelscoileanna have evolved from parental initiative.[140] Unlike mainstream national schools, the former are not parish schools and so they do not have access to a local school site in the parish or to local contributions. The Department buys the site and provides 100% of the capital building programme. In contrast with denominational and multi-denominational schools, the State is the owner of the gaelscoileanna but it is not their patron.[141] By 1997, the number

---

[136] St Michael's House had established a special school for mildly mentally handicapped children whose manager was a lay person and it was recognised and funded by the Department. Later other special schools with lay managers were established throughout the country.

[137] The author is grateful to Ms Jacqueline Ní Fheargúsa of Gaelscoileanna for providing this information.

[138] See Ch 4, para **[4.69]**.

[139] Report of the Technical Working Group: Commission on School Accommodation, Department of Education and Science, 1998, pp 81 and 82.

[140] In 1973 a group of parents organised with the aim of ensuring a united voice in the education system for schools teaching through the medium of the Irish language. Shortly afterwards they established Gaelscoileanna, as the co-ordinating body for Irish medium schools with the dual objective of assisting parents to set up new Gaelscoileanna, and the safe-guarding of existing Irish medium schools. This voluntary body, which has been in receipt of grant-aid from Bord na Gaeilge since 1978, has facilitated parents wishing to establish further schools.

[141] Cf the Model schools where the State owns the schools and the Minister is the patron.

of gaelscoileanna had risen to 112 schools. Initially, all gaelscoileanna were under the patronage of the bishop of the diocese. Since 1993, however, these schools may opt for diocesan patronage, or that of a nationwide patronage body termed *An Foras Patrunachta na Scoileanna Lán-Ghaeilge* (*An Foras*) which is a limited company under the Companies Acts 1963-1990. At the time of writing, the breakdown of the 24 schools under the patronage of *An Foras* is:

    (a) 20 schools having a Catholic ethos;

    (b) 3 multi-denominational schools;

    (c) 1 inter-denominational school (Catholic-Protestant).

Currently, 125 gaelscoileanna exist at primary level of which 108 are in the Republic. The demand for these schools is increasing rapidly.[142] Some unrecognised schools, it appears, also exist.

[2.62] The Minister's proposed arrangement for new gaelscoileanna will bring capital grants for these schools into line with other mainstream schools. In the case of new buildings and renovations, the patron must provide 5% of the capital cost subject to a ceiling of £50,000. However, in the case of gaelscoileanna with either permanent or temporary recognition, current arrangements will apply, ie the State will pay fully for the site and the building and the school will be owned by the State.[143]

Patronage of gaelscoileanna

[2.63] In 1993, *An Foras Pátrúnachta na Scoileanna LánGhaeilge* (*an Foras* hereafter) was established as an independent patronage system for gaelscoileanna. This body initially governed only multi-denominational gaelscoileanna and this was accepted by the Department. Subsequently, some denominational gaelscoileanna pressed for independent patronage under *An Foras* and this was also sanctioned by the Department. From 1994 onwards, all new gaelscoileanna were given the option of going under the patronage of *An Foras* or the patronage of the Catholic bishops. The legal status of these schools is discussed in greater detail in Chapter 4.[144]

B. Second Level Education

(i) Secondary schools: private ownership

[2.64] The secondary schools, earlier referred to as intermediate schools, continued to be the main providers of second level education from 1922-1960.

---

[142] Report of the Technical Working Group: Commission on School Accommodation, Department of Education and Science, 1998, pp 25-26.

[143] Press Release, Minister for Education and Science, 10 January 1999.

[144] See below para **[4.62]**.

They prepared students for the Intermediate (now Junior Certificate) and Leaving Certificate examinations introduced by the Intermediate Education Act 1924. These schools were and continue to be in the private ownership of:

(a) religious orders or communities;[145]

(b) diocesan authorities;[146]

(c) boards of governors;[147] or

(d) private individuals.[148]

While State funding for these schools first derived from the provisions of the Intermediate Education Act 1878, financial aid was quite restricted initially.

[2.65] The Intermediate Education (Amendment) Act 1924 provided for the payment of capitation grants for each recognised secondary pupil. However, the majority of pupils also paid a fee to the school at the individual school's discretion.[149] No State funds were expended on the building and contents of these schools until 1964. With increased State funding came tentative State control,[150] although school ownership and the appointment[151] and retention of teachers remained with the school authorities.[152]

[2.66] From the late 1950s onwards, the power of the State increased gradually in these schools as a consequence of a number of factors including the extended role of various Ministers for Education,[153] the payment of State capital grants,[154] and the introduction of free secondary education. It is the Education Act 1998, however, which marks the first substantive legislative intervention in secondary education. Its main provisions are summarised in Chapter 6 below. However, the Intermediate Education (Ireland) Act 1878,[155] and the Intermediate Education (Amendment) Act 1924 are still germane to these schools which currently educate approximately 61% of all second level students.[156] Under this

---

[145] In the case of Catholic schools.

[146] In the case of some Catholic schools.

[147] In the case of Protestant managed schools.

[148] In some instances where schools are in private ownership.

[149] Less well-off pupils frequently paid little or nothing.

[150] See generally Coolahan, *The ASTI and Post-Primary Education in Ireland, 1909-1984,* (1984), Association of Secondary Teachers in Ireland.

[151] Subject to teacher registration after 1918 under the provisions of the Secondary Teachers' Registration Council Act 1918.

[152] Randles, *Post-Primary Education in Ireland 1957-1970,* (1975), Dublin, p 19.

[153] O'Connor, *A Troubled Sky: Reflections on the Irish Educational Scene 1957-1968,* (1968), Dublin, Drumcondra Teachers' Centre.

[154] Coolahan, *Irish Education: History and Structure,* (1981), Institute of Public Administration, pp 133, 194.

[155] As amended by the Education Act 1998, s 35.

[156] *Report of the Constitution Review Group* (RCRG), (1996), Gov Pubs, p 340.

legislation, the Rules and Programmes for Secondary Schools are issued usually on an annual basis. The Teachers' Registration Council, which was established under the Secondary Teachers' Registration Council Act 1918,[157] governs the recognition and registration of secondary teachers whether nationals or EU members.

(ii) Vocational schools: state ownership; local authority administration

[2.67] The emergence of a new administrative framework for technical or vocational education in the twentieth century, had its origin in the two previous centuries. Technical education, however, was not placed under either of the education boards but was transferred to the Department of Agriculture and Technical Instruction. Consolidation of the existing system of technical education was achieved and fundamentally altered by the Vocational Education Act 1930 (the 1930 Act).

[2.68] The State owns the schools having provided the full cost of the school site and the buildings. It also defrays the full costs of new buildings and renovations. However, the schools are administered by the VECs under the 1930 Act as amended. It was envisaged that these schools would provide facilities for students entering local industry. Hence, they would provide "continuation education"[158] in general subjects for students leaving primary school at fourteen years. Certain guarantees were given by the Minister for Education at that time (John Marcus O'Sullivan) to the Catholic bishops that general education would not be provided in these schools.[159]

[2.69] Until the mid 1960s, VEC schools prepared students for the Group Certificate but not for the more academic Intermediate or Leaving Certificate examinations. Thus, in effect, students in vocational schools could not sit the Intermediate and Leaving Certificate examinations in their schools from 1930 until the mid-1960s.[160] The 1963 plan for post-primary education included a common Intermediate Certificate for vocational and secondary schools. Although VEC schools are technically non-denominational, these schools include religion as part of the curriculum. Furthermore, the VEC must ensure that the schools under its jurisdiction have a sufficient number of teachers of religion, who are appointed subject to the approval of the relevant religious authority to provide religious instruction. In common with other teachers, these

---

[157] See further RCRG, pp 340-341.
[158] See VEC Act 1930, para 3.
[159] Ó Buachalla, *Educational Policy in Twentieth Century Ireland*, (1988), Wolfhound, p 64.
[160] Ó Buachalla, *Educational Policy in Twentieth Century Ireland*, (1988), Wolfhound, p 19.

teachers are paid by the State.[161] It is estimated that these school currently educate approximately 26% of all second level students in the State.[162]

[2.70] The Apprenticeship Act 1959[163] had wide-ranging effects on vocational education as it enabled An Cheard Chomhlaire to control the qualifications of aspiring apprentices. The Vocational Education (Amendment) Act 1970 provided for the extension of the ambit of VEC activities including the sharing of costs and resources with other schools subject to joint ownership and management by the VECs and other educational bodies. This Act facilitated the introduction of community colleges in the past decade which are also under the control and management of the VECs and these schools are discussed below.

(iii) Comprehensive schools: a State initiative

[2.71] By the 1960s the growing perception of education as an economic investment and the facilitating of equal opportunity, resulted in State involvement in the provision of second-level education. The findings of the OECD Report, *Investment in Education*,[164] impelled State involvement in second level education which resulted in the establishment of comprehensive schools.[165] Trusts for education were set up and three new comprehensive schools were opened. These schools are built and maintained totally out of State funds. While they are vested in the State in fee simple, they are leased to trustees under a deed of trust for educational purposes.

[2.72] In establishing these schools, statutory provision was avoided in favour of equity which gives indirect assistance to the advancement of education generally by recognising a trust for public education as charitable.[166] Currently there are 16 comprehensive schools in existence. These schools have proved particularly attractive to the Protestant church because of their resourcing implications as they do not have the backing of the religious orders to finance their schools. The establishment of comprehensive schools was not unattended by controversy. Fears were expressed regarding the lack of public debate and consultation attending their establishment which was overtaken, to a significant degree, by the introduction of free second level education in 1966-67. Draft deeds of trust for these schools were drawn up in 1966 which *inter alia* established board of management structures for these schools. Further controversy arose from the

---

[161] Farry, *Vocational Teachers and the Law* (1998), Blackhall Publications, p 34 and generally.
[162] RCRG, p 341.
[163] Which replaced the Apprenticeship Act 1931.
[164] OECD, *Investment in Education Report*, Gov Pubs, 1965.
[165] See further O'Flaherty, *Management and Control in Irish Education: The Post-Primary Experience*, (1992), Drumcondra Teachers' Centre, Ch 2.
[166] 15 *Halsbury's Statutes* (4th ed), p 3.

fact that these boards of management excluded parents and teachers.[167] Negotiations are ongoing in this regard and shortly, it seems, this democratic deficit will be remedied. The establishment of comprehensive schools heralded the introduction of community schools in 1972.[168]

(iv) Community schools: a Church/State compromise

[2.73] Community schools were a significant landmark in Irish education. Essentially, their introduction was quite a radical measure which proposed to fuse a private denominational educational sector (voluntary secondary schools) with a public non-denominational one (vocational schools). Not surprisingly, this proposal was attended by many difficulties chiefly those of control and ownership. Some existing schools would amalgamate to form a community school while new schools would be opened in other areas (referred to as green field schools). Such a plan could come about only through negotiation and progress was slow and frequently emeshed in controversy. O'Flaherty states that:

> "What emerged was essentially a Catholic post-primary school where the Church authorities had obtained what was legally a minority interest, but as the schools were to be almost exclusively used by Catholic children, the bishops could claim that they were Catholic schools and could demand and get reserved places, conditions safeguarding religion, and paid Catholic chaplains for at most a five percent contribution to the initial building cost".[169]

[2.74] Constitutional issues would have arisen if the State withdrew recognition from existing secondary schools in an amalgamation scheme of vocational and secondary schools in a single comprehensive or community school.[170] Though the Minister's plans met with much contention and even animosity, they were not challenged in the Irish courts by contrast with the English situation.[171]

[2.75] Case law has established that the "deed of trust", the operative instrument by which the trusts for these schools were established, is a binding legal instrument which sets up a public charity for education.[172] It would fall to the Attorney General to enforce the deed of trust in so far as these duties relate to a public charity.[173] The deed of trust vests the control and management of the

---

[167] See O'Flaherty, *Management and Control in Irish Education: The Post-Primary Experience* p 41 for the two kinds of structure provided.
[168] See O'Flaherty, Ch 3.
[169] O'Flaherty, *Management and Control in Irish Education: The Post-Primary Experience*, (1992), Drumcondra Teachers' Centre, p 73.
[170] Article 42.3.1
[171] *Wood v Ealing* LBC [1967] 3 ALL ER 514; *Tameside Case* [1976] 3 WLR 641.
[172] *O'h-Uallacháin v Burke*, High Court, unrep, 7 August, 1987.
[173] *O'h-Uallacháin v Burke*, High Court, unrep, 7 August, 1987.

school in the board of management which operates under Articles of Management specified in the trust deed.

[2.76] In contrast to other schools, community and comprehensive schools have been allocated a budget annually by the State. These schools educate approximately 13% of all second level students.[174]

[2.77] Where the community school resulted from an amalgamation of existing schools, a contribution towards the building was traditionally required from the existing school authorities. This contribution was generally dispensed with, however, in the case of green field (new) schools.

(v) Community colleges: a local authority concession

[2.78] With the establishment of community schools, VEC authorities became solicitous for the continuation of their role in the provision of non-denominational vocational education. A compromise was achieved whereby a number of new schools, community colleges, would be set up under the control of the VECs but run on similar lines as community schools.[175] Certain existing vocational schools were also restructured as community colleges. The board of management, which manages each college, is in effect a sub-committee of each VEC. While there is no standard model as in the community schools, three broad models for boards of management exist reflecting the origin and aims of the schools.[176] Local preference is a key factor in relation to the type of school to be established and the slow and painful process of negotiation leading to consensus meant that the establishment of these schools was unattended by any legal challenge.

Proposed Changes in School Ownership

[2.79] The State did not generally become involved in school ownership in the past as the traditional model of school ownership was followed. With the emergence of diverse school types, the *Report of the Technical Working Group*[177] has recommended a new approach to future school ownership.[178] It points to the fact that of the 80 schools recognised between 1986-1997:

(a) 56 are gaelscoileanna;

(b) 13 are multi-denominational schools; and

(c) 9 are special schools[179]

---

[174] RCRG, (1996), Gov Pubs, p 342.

[175] O'Flaherty, *Management and Control in Irish Education: The Post-Primary Experience*, (1992), Drumcondra Teachers' Centre, Ch 4.

[176] See further O'Flaherty, pp 92, 136.

[177] 1998.

[178] At pp 70-73 of the Report.

[179] Some of these schools are under the patronage of the Health Boards.

Alongside the growth in new school types has come new forms of patronage, mainly parent groups or parent-teacher groups, who have combined to form corporate bodies with charitable status, having little interest or capacity for school ownership.[180] Significant changes in the ownership of new schools have been recently been announced by the Minister[181] and these changes are discussed in Chapter 4 below. Recently the Minister announced substantially increased State funding for new first and second level schools which will be owned by the State.[182]

Universities

[2.80] The University of Dublin (Trinity College) was founded in 1591 as a reformation foundation being a branch of the Tudor's policy of colonization.[183] It was established by Charter of Queen Elizabeth I in 1592 and was "to endure forever".[184] Maynooth College, on the other hand, was set up in 1795 for the training of Catholic priests in Ireland as the French Revolution had resulted in the closure of the continental seminaries which were attended by many Irish priests. It was established by Act of Parliament and became exclusively a seminary after 1817 and it remained so until modern times.[185]

[2.81] The establishment of the three Queen's Colleges in Cork, Galway and Belfast led to controversy as they were to be undenominational and not subject to any religious group. Furthermore, all professorial appointments were to be made by the Crown.[186] In 1851, the Synod of Catholic bishops at Thurles, having condemned the Queen's Colleges, decided to establish a Catholic university and they invited the well known Oxford scholar and convert, John Henry Newman,[187] to become its Rector. Despite Newman's vision of a great Catholic

---

[180] O'Flaherty, *Management and Control in Irish Education: The Post-Primary Experience*, (1992), Drumcondra Teachers' Centre, p 71.

[181] See Appendix E.

[182] The White Paper *Charting our Education Future*, (1995), p 32 had already identified school ownership-related problems and provided for a situation where education boards would "own new school buildings and properties for leasing to different groups of patrons and trustees." The *Report of the Commission on Technical Working Group* (1998) recommended that, in the absence of education boards, the Department of Education and Science should now implement this recommendation.

[183] See further Parkes, 'University Education', in *Irish Education Documents*, Hyland and Milne, eds, (1987), Vol 1, pp 302-363.

[184] See Dublin University Callendar, 1833, pp 26-9.

[185] Parkes, p 305.

[186] Atkinson, *Irish Education*, (1969), Allen Figgis, pp 126-127 citing *Hansard 3*, lxxx 356.

[187] See Beales, 'John Henry Newman' in *Pioneers of English Education*, Judges, ed, (1952), Faber and Faber.

university,[188] he encountered grave difficulties with the Irish bishops and resigned his position in 1858.

[2.82] In 1908, the Irish Universities Act 1908[189] gave birth to two new universities, which were *de jure* non-denominational:

(a) the National University of Ireland; and

(b) Queen's University, Belfast which had evolved from Queen's College Belfast.

The National University of Ireland was comprised of three constituent colleges, Cork, Galway and University College Dublin, which was to be *de facto* a university for Catholics, being closely associated with Cardinal Newman, while Queen's College, Belfast retained its Protestant identity. These colleges proved controversial as they were to be State funded and *de jure* non-denominational. No religious tests were allowed in them and the public funding of religious instruction or chapels was prohibited.[190] The staff of the colleges was to be appointed by the Queen of England and their objective was "the better advancement of learning among all classes of Her Majesty's subjects in Ireland."[191] Maynooth College was affiliated to the National University while Magee College, which had been founded as a Presbyterian college, became affiliated to Trinity College, Dublin.[192]

[2.83] Subsequent to the establishment of the National University of Ireland, Parkes points out that the Gaelic League, in its campaign led by Douglas Hyde and Professor Eoin Mac Néill, gained the backing of the County Councils to have Irish made a compulsory subject for the matriculation for the university. Eventually in 1910, the university senate concurred and in 1913 Irish became a compulsory subject for entrance to the university.[193]

The Modern Universities

[2.84] The newer universities such as Dublin City University and the University of Limerick were established by the Dublin City University Act 1989 and the

---

[188] "... I dimly see the island I am gazing on, become the head of passage and union between two hemispheres, and the centre of the world. I see its inhabitants rival Belgium in populousness, France in vigour, and Spain in enthusiasm; and I see England taught by advancing years to exercise on its behalf that good sense which is her characteristic towards everyone else". This passage is cited by Woodlock, *Catholic University Education*, p 18.

[189] An Act to make further provision with respect to university education in Ireland 1908 (8 Edw 7, c 38).

[190] Parkes, 'University Education', p 358.

[191] The Colleges (Ireland) Act 1845.

[192] Parkes, p 358.

[193] Parkes, 'University Education', pp 360-361.

University of Limerick Act 1989. The Universities Act 1997 is the first comprehensive university legislation since 1908. This much amended Act:

(a) reconstitutes the three colleges of the National University of Ireland as full universities;

(b) provides for the updating of the universities governing structures; and

(c) redefines the relationship between the State and the universities.

While the universities are theoretically autonomous, the Higher Education Authority (HEA), which largely funds them, acts as an arm of State control.

Conclusion

[2.85] It seems that early legislative initiatives, which strove to change the character of Irish education, led ultimately to a bias against legislative methods and statism in education; a bias which became more entrenched with the legislative prescription of Catholic education. These factors impacted on education leading in time to the growth of an informal, denominational system of education in which legislation played only a minor role. By contrast with the educational direction taken by England, Scotland, Wales and Northern Ireland, Ireland eschewed local authority control of general education and continued to concede to the churches and religious orders the right to act on behalf of the people in education. Accordingly, education, with the exception of VEC education, was provided almost exclusively in privately owned institutions until the 1960s.

[2.86] While it is undisputed that the churches and religious orders made an inestimable contribution to Irish education, the democratic process normally associated with the enactment of substantive educational legislation was largely by-passed. Even after independence, suspicions of formal State involvement in education persisted as is apparent from the subsidiary role accorded the State in education in the 1937 Constitution. When the State discharged most of the financial burden in independent Ireland, clear reluctance to allow full State control of education persisted. Yet, despite the primacy accorded the family and parents in education by the 1937 Constitution, the lay community were virtually excluded from responsibility for the direction of the school until the 1970s and 1980s. No broadly based reappraisal of this system ensued until the 1990s.

[2.87] Until then, there was scant formulation of a consensus on a native educational philosophy, there was limited devolution of responsibilities in education to local authority bodies and no recasting of the structures which upheld the system of education.

[2.88] With increased prosperity in the 1990s came greater investment in educational provision and a degree of public interest in education that has been unprecedented in our history. Calls for the reappraisal, restructuring and greater democratisation of the system of education came from the EC and from national sources. Standards of education rose significantly and gradually, the homogeneity of Irish society began to fragment. With the decline in religious vocations came greater secularity in life generally. National confidence increased and the State tentatively, at first, began to move to the fore in education.

[2.89] It is against this background that Ireland faces the challenge of enacting a legislative framework for education which will, hopefully, dispense social justice, accord with constitutional requirements and meet the needs of an increasingly diverse population. Neither can educational reforms ignore the realities of the peace initiatives in Northern Ireland. Taking account of this background, these reforms must necessarily accommodate the needs of all the people on this island. At the same time, the system of denominational education, which is the preferred system of the majority of people, must be adequately safeguarded.

[2.90] On 13 December 1998 the Education Act 1998 (the 1998 Act) was enacted. At the time of writing the following sections are in operation: ss 2-6 inclusive, ss 13, 25 26, 26 37 and Parts VIII and IX.[194] This legislative measure, which is the first of a number of Acts envisaged for education, is discussed in detail in Chapter 6 below.

---

[194] Education Act 1998 (Commencement) Order 1999 (SI 29/1999).

Chapter 3

Education and the 1937 Constitution: Ideological Background and Case Law

Introduction

[3.01] As in many other countries of the world, religion plays a significant role in Irish life. This fact is particularly manifest from the inter-linked provisions of the 1937 Constitution, Article 42 (Education) and Article 44 (Religion). These Articles, which recite the broad principles underpinning education, have combined to stamp their character on Irish education and on educational policy making. As Keane J stated in *Campaign to Separate Church and State Ltd v Minister for Education*,[1] even if such provisions were absent from the Constitution, courts could not disregard, at least in a relevant context, the fact that religious beliefs and practices are interwoven through the fabric of Irish society.[2]

[3.02] With a view to extracting the philosophy and legal principles underpinning education in Ireland, this chapter considers the current approach of the Superior Courts to fundamental rights and the natural law generally. It then examines the drafting of Articles 42 and 44 and some of the case law emanating from those Articles. Echoes of this chapter and the discussion of the implied constitutional right to education will be found in Chapter 8[3] in which the right to education is also perceived as a fundamental right albeit from the international law perspective.[4]

PART I: THE 1937 CONSTITUTION

Ideological Background

Democratic Rights

[3.03] There is a growing consensus internationally as to the principal rights necessary for full membership of a democratic society including, among others the right to:

---

[1] [1996] 2 ILRM 241 SC.

[2] In an article written at the express request of the editor of a newspaper (Revista Xaveridna, Bogota, Columbia) in December 1937, the Irish Constitution is described as "probably unique among modern written constitutions".

[3] Entitled "Human Rights and Education".

[4] References to the Papal Encylicals are taken from *The Papal Encylicals 1740-1878*, Claudie Carlen Ihm, ed, (1981) and from *Education: Papal Teachings* compiled by the Benedictine Monks of Solesmes translated by Rev Rebeschina.

(a) equality before the law;

(b) inviolability of every citizen's dwelling in accordance with the law;

(c) personal liberty in accordance with the law;

(d) security of persons or groups under the law;

(e) education;

(f) freedom of association;

(g) freedom of expression, of conscience and religion; and

(h) freedom of assembly.

(These rights will be referred to as democratic rights hereafter).

Democratic Rights in the Irish Constitution

[3.04] The Constitution of Ireland 1937[5] guarantees the above rights and manifests a deep commitment to liberal democracy.[6] During the Dáil Debates of 25 May 1934, de Valera indicated the existence of a Cabinet consensus[7] for the inclusion in the Constitution of a number of Articles which would guarantee certain democratic rights which, he stated, "we are not willing to have made easily changeable".[8] There was a clear understanding that, such rights, which in the 1937 Constitution are referred to as "bunchearta", or fundamental rights, predated the 1937 Constitution and that they would be immune from change by a simple majority in the Oireachtas. A number of legal cases refer to the fact that certain rights, guaranteed by the Constitution, do not spring from the Constitution,[9] being superior to and antecedent to positive law. A significant distinction is made, between these latter rights and other rights, which are expressly conferred by the Constitution and derive from positive law.[10]

---

[5] Enacted by the People on 1 July 1937 and came into operation on 29 December 1937.

[6] Being influenced by the English Bill of Rights (1689), the American Constitution and its amendments, *Declaration des Droits de l'Homme et du Citoyen* and other fundamental rights concepts expressed in Western European Constitutions. Clearly other constitutions were studied, a reference to *Select Constitutions of the World*, Shiva, ed (1934), Madras, was noted by the author in the official files relating to the drafting of Articles 42 and 44 in the *De Valera Papers* (*DVP*), Archives of the University College Dublin.

[7] Although many voices in government were raised against this.

[8] *Dáil Debates*, Vol 52, 25 May 1934, cols 1876-8, col 1201, cols 1218-20, cols 1192-4, cols 1180-81, cols 1167-72.

[9] *Finn v AG* [1983] IR 154, Barrington J; *McGee v AG* [1974] IR 284, 310, Walsh J; *Doyle v Murphy and the PMPA Insurance Co* [1978] ILRM 25, 30, Doyle J; *Northampton County Council v ABF* [1982] ILRM 164, 166, Hamilton J; see further Whyte, 'Natural Law and the Constitution', ILT Vol 14 (ns), 8.

[10] Walsh, 'The Judicial Power, Justice and the Constitution of Ireland', in *Constitutional Adjudication in European and National Law*, (1992), Butterworths, pp 145-157, 149.

[3.05] With regard to the protection of fundamental rights, there are those who view the Constitution as making a break with the positivist character of the common law.[11] As there are many natural law theories running from the ethics and rhetoric of Aristotle to the ancient Romans;[12] to the Scholastics; and on to the American Revolution (1776) and the French Revolution (1789), the question here is "which theory of natural law is to be applied?"[13]

Aquinian Natural Law

[3.06] In Irish jurisprudence, the theory or concept of natural law most frequently invoked is that promulgated by St Thomas Aquinas (1225-1274).[14] In the hands of the scholastics and canonists, natural law became identified with the law conferred by God on Adam and Eve, which derived from the general and primitive law of mankind.[15] Aquinas's theory of natural law is merely part of a much wider body of philosophy. For the purposes of this book, it is sufficient to state that the central principles of Aquinas's theory of law are as follows:

    (a) the existence of God;

    (b) the concept of a Divine Reason controlling the universe;

---

[11] Henchy, (1962) 25 MLR 544 at 557; in *Essays in Memory of Alexis Fitzgerald* (1987), Costello P states: "It has more than once been judicially observed that it can clearly be inferred that the Constitution rejects legal positivism and suggests instead a theory of natural law from which those rights can be derived. There are strong arguments to support that conclusion". In support of his thesis, Costello P relies on the Preamble, and on Article 6, Article 41, Article 42 and Article 43; see 'Natural Law, the Constitution and the Courts' in *Essays in Memory of Alexis Fitzgerald*, (1987), Incorporated Law Society, p 104 at 109-110; for an interesting discussion on justice and natural law see de Blacam, 'Justice and Natural Law', (1997), Ir Jur, Vol 32 p 323.

[12] Apart from the contributions of Hebrew law, one of the greatest achievements of natural law is that, through the impact of the Romans, borrowed from the Greeks, it gave rise to the establishment of a system of law of universal validity. The Romans considered that they were governed partly by their own particular laws and custom and partly by those laws which are common to all mankind. The latter laws were referred to by various names such as The Law of Nations, The Law of Nature, Natural Law or *Jus Naturale* because it is that part of the law which natural reason appoints for all mankind, see Maine, *Ancient Law,* (1961) London, Routledge, pp 37-8 citing the *Institutional Treatise* published under the authority of the Emperor Justinian. See also *Corpus Iuris Civilis* written by Byzantine lawyers in 534 AD.

[13] Professor Clarke points out the ambiguities that may arise between the natural law theories propounded by Aquinas, Suarez, Locke and Rousseau and in contemporary philosophy between Nozick and Finnis, see Clarke, *Church and State*, Chs 2, 47-68, 49; for some natural law theories, see Maritain, *The Rights of Man and Natural law,* (1944), London; Maine, *Ancient Law,* (1961), London, Routledge; d'Êntrevès, *Natural Law: An Introduction to Legal Philosophy,* (1970), Hutchinson; Crowe, *The Changing Profile of the Natural Law,* (1977), The Hague; Finnis, *Natural Law and Natural Rights,* (1980), Clarendon Press.

[14] *Summa Theologica*, Blackfriars (1963).

[15] d'Êntrevès, *Natural Law: An Introduction to Legal Philosophy,* (1970), Hutchinson p 35.

(c) the concept of practical reason;

(d) that the will of the governor or sovereign has the force of law only so long as it accords with reason:

(e) that law must be directed by the common good; and

(f) that law must be formulated by some person in authority; and

(g) that law must be promulgated.[16]

Natural Rights Philosophy

[3.07] By the seventeenth and eighteenth centuries, the medieval concept of natural law (with God as its source) was rejected by many modern democracies who returned to the secular vision of the State as enunciated earlier by the Greek and Roman philosophers. In Europe generally, a new image of the State came to the fore which was essentially at odds with the traditional Christian viewpoint.[17] In mainly Catholic Ireland, there are those who believe that Aquinian natural law became embodied in certain fundamental Articles of the 1937 Constitution.

[3.08] The medieval and modern concepts of natural law differ profoundly as to the origin of political authority;[18] the former viewing God as the origin of all political authority while the latter perceive man himself as the source of political powers. This latter philosophy, generally referred to as "the natural rights philosophy," posits the view that natural law retains its validity even if God does not exist.[19] Possibly, the most critical period in the evolution of the natural rights philosophy was that introduced by Rousseau between 1749-1762.[20]

Democratic Rights in a Religious Setting

[3.09] In the Constitution of 1937,[21] the democratic rights, are incorporated in a Constitution imbued with respect for religion, which acknowledges God as the source of its authority.[22] As Ireland moves irrevocably towards greater plurality and secularity, these democratic rights are at the core of an ongoing debate.

---

[16] d'Êntrevès, *Medieval Contribution to Political Thought*, (1939), Oxford.

[17] d'Êntrevès, *Medieval Contribution to Political Thought*, (1939), Oxford, p 62.

[18] Maine, *Ancient Law*, London, (1961), Routledge, Chs 3 and 4.

[19] See *Declaration des Droits de l'Homme et du Citoyen.*

[20] In the drafting papers relating to these Articles, Fr McQuaid's submission to de Valera on the origin of civil authority is not without significance in that he rejects outright Rousseau's theory of Civil Authority stating: "His purpose is to find a juridical basis for society, and in that search he ends by basing his whole theory on human liberty." *DVP,* File 1091.

[21] See Farrell, 'A Note on the Dáil Constitution 1919' (1969) 4 Ir Jur (ns) 127-38; Farrell, 'The Drafting of the Irish Free State Constitution: I' (1970) 5 Ir Jur, 115-40; Farrell, 'The Drafting of the Irish Free State Constitution: II' (1970) 5 Ir Jur, 342-55; Farrell, 'The Drafting of the Irish Free State Constitution: III' (1971) 6 Ir Jur 111-36; Farrell, 'The Drafting of the Irish Free State Constitution: IV' (1971) Ir Jur, 345-59.

[22] Preamble, Article 6, Article 44.1, Article 44.2.5° and Article 44.2.6° while it concludes with the dedication: "*Dochum Glóire Dé agus Onóra na h-Éireann*" (for the glory of God and in honour of Ireland).

[3.10] Speaking extra-judicially, Walsh J stresses that as a law, the Constitution speaks always in the present tense, embracing both social and political objectives, though as a document it may be regarded as being of another generation.[23] Reflecting contemporary life, which has diverged substantially from Aquinian ideals, the courts have legalised artificial contraception, divorce and abortion information. Against this background, is it possible to still regard Aquinian law as the basis of Irish constitutional law? Or to put the question in a different form - can constitutional law be divorced from the political process and from the realities of contemporary life?

[3.11] This was in essence the dilemma faced by the courts in *McGee v Attorney General*[24] in which the Supreme Court vindicated the plaintiff's right to marital privicy thereby holding unconstitutional a statutory provision which criminalised the importation of contraceptives, despite the Catholic Church's teaching that artificial contraception breached the natural law. In the High Court, Walsh J stated:

> "In a pluralist society such as ours, the courts cannot as a matter of constitutional law be asked to choose between the differing views, where they exist, of experts on the interpretation by the differing religious denominations of either the nature or extent of ... natural rights as they are to be found in the natural law."[25]

[3.12] Nonetheless, Walsh J goes on to confirm the existence of fundamental rights antecedent to positive law and states and acknowledges the importance of natural law theory for constitutional interpretation.

Mr Justice O'Hanlon's Theory

[3.13] O'Hanlon J, however, took the matter much further when he posited the view that the right of the people to amend the Constitution in Article 46 is restricted to amendments which are compatible with natural law theory.[26] While various accounts have been given of natural law in human reason, he states that Article 6 of the Constitution and the Preamble unambiguously identify "the Most Holy Trinity" as the source of this higher law against which all human positive law may be measured. In a later article,[27] O'Hanlon J refers to natural law as interpreted by the Roman Catholic bishops and archbishops of Ireland

---

[23] Walsh, 'The Constitution and Constitutional Rights' in *The Constitution of Ireland 1937-1987*, Litton, ed, (1988), Institute of Public Administration, p 86.

[24] [1974] IR 284.

[25] *Re Article 26 of the Constitution and in the Matter of the Reference to the Court of the Regulation of Information Bill 1995* [1995] 2 ILRM 81.

[26] See O'Hanlon, 'Natural Rights and the Irish Constitution' (1993) 11 ILT 8.

[27] 'The Judiciary and the Moral Law', (1993) 11 ILT (ns), 129, 132.

and Great Britain and by a professor of canon law in Maynooth College thereby making it quite clear that he equates natural law with the teachings of the Roman Catholic Church.

[3.14] Possibly the most serious objection to O'Hanlon J's hypothesis is that, if implemented, it would permit judges to set aside constitutional amendments adopted by the people if they conflicted with Aquinian natural law,[28] thereby striking at the core of democracy upon which the Constitution is grounded.[29] Murphy strongly disputes O'Hanlon J's theory and argues that the Constitution "does not endorse a uniform objective standard of morality based on the theological doctrine of any one religion's interpretation of natural law."[30] He points to the fact that conflicting views as to what constitutes natural law exist within, as well as between, the theocratic and secular traditions of natural law. In the Irish context, Murphy also points to the divergence between the Catholic and Protestant traditions in regard to the theocratic natural law theories. Since these two Christian churches adopt different positions on what the divine law actually is, he states, they take up opposing natural law positions on contraception, sterilisation and abortion. In conclusion, he believes, that in terms of any debate on natural law, the question will always remain: "whose natural law?"

[3.15] In his response to the O'Hanlon thesis,[31] Clarke submits that it is *a reductio ad absurdum*[32] as it justifies the judiciary relying on their own philosophical or religious convictions to rule that an amendment to the Constitution is unconstitutional. This would be the case, he states, even when the amendment was expressly enacted by the people in accordance with Article 46.1 following widespread public debate, on the basis that it conflicts with the provisions of an unwritten law which was implicitly enacted into the Constitution by those who voted by a relatively small majority,[33] for the original text of the Constitution in 1937.

---

28 See Whelan, 'Constitutional Amendments in Ireland: The Competing Claims of Democracy', Quinn, Ingram and Livingstone, eds, *Justice and Legal Theory in Ireland*, (1995), p 45.

29 Article 6. This principle is acknowledged in the *DVP,* file 1055 'Deirimid-ne gur Stát Daonfhláthach an Stát so ...' and written in at the side "The Constitution is frankly based on the democratic principle." Again under the heading of "National Parliament" is written "Every elector who casts his vote in favour of the adoption of this Constitution will in effect be subscribing his name to the proposition that in this country the people and the people alone are the masters."

30 Murphy, 'Democracy, Natural Law and the Irish Constitution', (1996) ILT Vol 14, 81 at 83.

31 'The Constitution and Natural Law: A Reply to Mr Justice O'Hanlon', (1993) 11 ILT (ns) 177.

32 de Blácam, 'Justice and Natural Law', (1997), Ir Jur, Vol 32, 333 points out that a natural lawyer might argue that the natural law does not depend for its validity on the fact that it was enacted in the Constitution or upon any enactment.

33 On 1 July 1937, the Constitution was approved by plebiscite by 685,105 votes to 526,945.

The Abortion Information Bill 1995

[3.16] The controversial issue raised by O'Hanlon J, in an academic journal, was essentially the same argument which came before the Supreme Court in *Re Article 26 of the Constitution and in the Matter of the Reference to the Court of the Regulation of Information (Services outside the State for Termination of Pregnancies) Bill 1995*[34] (the Abortion Information Bill hereafter).[35] Counsel for the unborn[36] submitted that, on the grounds of natural law any constitutional or statutory provision which permitted the communication of information which amounted to assistance in the destruction of the life of the unborn, breached the natural law right to life of the unborn. Counsel also claimed that the natural law was superior to the Constitution and that accordingly no such constitutional or legislative provision could lawfully be enforced. If this theory was accepted, it would mean that the 1995 Bill, whose objective was to protect the right to communicate information relating to abortion services outside Ireland, was repugnant to the Constitution on the grounds that it breached natural law.[37]

[3.17] In view of the crucially important issue before the court, which goes right to the core of the Constitution, one would have expected a very deep and sensitive analysis of natural law principles as they apply in the Irish setting. However, having revisited the relevant sections of the Constitution[38] and some selective case law, the court flatly rejected this argument. Hamilton CJ, delivering the sole judgment of the court, referred in particular to Articles 5[39] and 6[40] of the Constitution, stressing the supremacy of the Constitution. He emphasised that the courts were and are bound to recognise the fundamental law of the State "to which the organs of the State were subject and at no stage recognised the provisions of the natural law as superior to the Constitution."

---

34 [1995] 2 ILRM 81.

35 After the 13th and 14th amendments of the Constitution were adopted, which amended Article 40.3.3°, thereby guaranteeing freedom of travel and freedom of information, the 1995 Bill was passed by the Dáil and the Seanad to establish a legal structure for the regulation of information relating to abortion services available outside Ireland. When the Bill came before the President for signature, it was referred by the President to the Supreme Court under Article 26 of the Constitution for a decision on its constitutionality.

36 In this case the court appointed two teams of counsel to put forward the argument against the Bills' constitutionality. One of these teams presented the arguments based on the rights to life of the mother while the other presented arguments on behalf of the right to life of the unborn, see further de Blacam, 'Justice and Natural Law', (1997), Ir Jur, Vol 32, 334.

37 For a more detailed discussion of this case, see Whyte, 'Natural Law and the Constitution' (1996) 4 ILT (ns), 10.

38 Articles 5, 6, 15, 26.2, 34.1, 35.2.

39 Which states "Ireland is a sovereign, independent, democratic state."

40 Which states "All powers of government, legislative, executive and judicial, derive, under God, from the people, whose right it is to designate the rulers of the State and, in final appeal, to decide all questions of national policy, according to the requirements of the common good."

[3.18] The Court ruled that the people are entitled to amend the Constitution in accordance with the provisions of Article 46 and the judges are obliged to interpret the law in accordance within the guidelines laid down in the Constitution. With regard to fundamental rights, the Supreme Court considered that responsibility falls finally upon the judges to make their decisions in accordance with their ideas of prudence, justice and charity. The comprehensive reliance by the court on the judgment of Walsh J in *McGee v AG*[41] seems incongruous in view of what can only be interpreted as Walsh J's staunch support of the existence of fundamental rights which are antecedent to positive law in that case.[42]

Criticism of the Supreme Court's Decision

[3.19] Hamilton CJ's judgment has been the subject of some criticism.[43] Binchy has stated that the significance of this Supreme Court decision lies in its rejection of the very concept of the existence of a fundamental principle of law.[44] Whyte observes that one of the serious weaknesses in the judgment is that the term "Constitution" appears to be understood exclusively in a positive law sense without making clear how this "refined understanding of the Constitution, from which any natural law influence has been expurged" was deduced.[45] Whyte admits that the argument submitted by counsel for the unborn was not without its difficulties and he does not contend that it was necessarily correct. It was, nonetheless, he states, a serious argument which drew on "an ideology which undeniably influenced the drafting and interpretation of the Constitution."[46] The author concurs with this view and believes that this judgment required a much deeper analysis and more circumspective treatment than it received in the Supreme Court.

[3.20] Of course, this decision does not mean the end of the natural law as a theory of justice, which one lawyer sagely suggests, is "so embedded in our law as to require a shift of massive proportions to dislodge it."[47] If we examine education, we find that one particular theory of natural law has impacted profoundly on Irish education.

---

41   [1974] IR 284.
42   See also *G v An Bord Uchtála* [1980] IR 32, Walsh J.
43   Twomey, 'The Death of the Natural Law?' (1995) ILT (ns) 270; Whyte, 'Natural Law and the Constitution' (1996) 14 ILT (ns) 8.
44   Binchy, 'Abortion Ruling one of the most significant legal decisions since foundation of the State', Irish Times, 15 May 1995, p 12.
45   Whyte, 'Natural Law and the Constitution' (1996) 14 ILT (ns) 10.
46   See Whyte, p 12.
47   de Blácam, 'Justice and Natural Law', (1997), Ir Jur, Vol 32, 335.

Education and the Natural Law

[3.21] Chapter 2 has shown that Irish education had assimilated Catholic social principles long before the Constitution embodied their essence in Articles 42 and 44. Article 44 built largely on Article 8 of the 1922 Constitution which conformed broadly with Article 16 of the Treaty of 1921. Article 8 of the 1922 Constitution had merely stated: "All citizens of the Irish Free State have the right to free elementary education."

[3.22] In Ireland in the 1920s, the Catholic Social Movement presented an alternative to socialism in Europe and this movement gradually grew in importance prior to 1937.[48] The Papal encyclical *Quadragesima Anno* (1931) viewed State activity in education with suspicion, and promulgated the principle of subsidiarity[49] which perceives the State as playing a restricted role in family life and in the education of children. This doctrine became one of the main principles of Catholic social teaching which later emerged as a political doctrine. While the Catholic Church states that it does not contest the educational role of the State in relation to its citizens, it clearly views such role as subsidiary;[50] its duty being to protect the rights of the child only in cases of parental default, incapacity or misconduct.[51] These principles became the upholding pillars of Articles 42 and 44 as the system of education envisaged would be a State-aided system in which the State's role would be subsidiary and the family/parents would be the primary educators.

The Family and Education

[3.23] With regard to the family and education, Catholic social principles derive mainly from Papal encyclicals and from canon law[52] which draw deeply on the teachings and philosophy of St Thomas Aquinas. The basic principles, relating to the family and education, which are extracted largely from these sources, are echoed in the provisions of Articles 42 and 44:

---

[48] Breen, Hannan, Rottman and Whelan, *Understanding Contemporary Ireland*, (1990), Gill and Macmillan, p 26.

[49] The principle of subsidiarity, which owes its genesis to the ancient Greeks is also reflected in the European context, see *Subsidiarity and Education: Aspects of Comparative Educational Law*, De Groof, ed, (1994), Acco, Leuven.

[50] *Non Abbiamo Bisogno*, 'On Catholic Action in Italy', 29 February 1931, p 45. The State's role in Articles 42 and 44 is a subsidiary role.

[51] Pope Pius XI, *Divini Illius Magestrii*, (1929), p 19; this principle is embodied in Article 42.5.

[52] *The Papal Encyclicals 1903-1939*, (1981), Raleigh, McGrath Pubs, see in particular Pius XI "On the Reconstruction of the Social Order", 15 May 1931; *Education: Papal Teachings*, compiled Benedictine Monks of Solesmes, translated by Rev Rebeschini, see in particular, Pope Pius XI 'The Vocation of the Educator', p 437: Canon 1113 on Education.

(a) that the family derives directly from the Creator the right to educate the young, a right inalienable and anterior to any power on earth;[53]

(b) that the child is not the mere creature of the State; and that through the agency of Catholic families, Catholic education belongs pre-eminently to the Church;[54]

(c) that the State's duty is to protect, through legislation, the prior rights of the family through whom children become part of the civil society;[55]

(d) that Catholic families ought to prevent any invasion of this natural right;[56]

(e) that the State, through its aiding role, should make provision for parental deficiencies in conformity with the natural rights of the child and the supernatural rights of the Church;[57]

(f) that State monopoly of education which forces families to make use of government schools, contrary to their lawful preferences and Christian consciences, is unlawful and unjust;[58]

(g) that denominational education is the ideal for Catholics;[59] and

(h) that the school is a necessary social institution as the family may be unequal to the task of educating their children but that it is, by its nature, subsidiary and complimentary to the family and to the Church;[60]

(i) that the voluntary school is the ideal school model;[61]

(j) that teachers are parental delegates, being *in loco parentis* in the course of their professional duties in school;[62]

(k) that Catholic teachers ought to protect their rights by insisting on just educational laws and on the achievement of a standard of living in keeping with their needs and the dignity of their work as educators;[63] and

---

[53] *The Papal Encyclicals 1903-1939*, 1981, pp 5, 13, 14, 15, 33 citing St Thomas Aquinas and Pope Leo XIII; see also Canon 1113; this concept is embodied in Article 42.1.

[54] *Libertas* 24, *cf* no 123.

[55] PopeLeo XIII, *Rerum Novarum*, (1891), p 266.

[56] Pope Leo XIII, *Sapientiae Christinae*, (1890), p 15.

[57] Pope Leo XIII, *Sapientiae Christinae*, (1890), p 15; see Article 42.5.

[58] Pope Leo XIII, *Rerum Novarum*, (1891), pp 268-69; see Article 42.3.1°.

[59] Articles 42 and 44 impliedly protect denominational schools, see Art 44.2.3°, 44.4 and 44.6.

[60] Pope Leo XIII, *Sapientiae Christinae*, (1890), pp 15, 36 and *Principes Catholique d'Action Civique*, p 147.

[61] Pope Leo XIII, *Spectata Fides*, (1885), p 121; approximately 61% of all second level schools are voluntary schools.

[62] The common law incorporated this principle which was upheld by the Supreme Court in *Murtagh v Board of Management of St Emer's National School* [1991] 2 ILRM 549.

(l) that it is not only important to teach religion to children at specified times, but that religion should be integrated with other subjects of the curriculum.[64]

This final aim was achieved in 1971 when the integration of all subjects including religious instruction was given official recognition by the Department of Education in the Curriculum of 1971.[65]

The Drafting Process: Articles 42 and 44

[3.24] Natural law theories were of assistance to the drafters of the Constitution in considering what democratic rights were to be guaranteed in the Constitution but not enumerated by it. The drafters of the 1922 Constitution had been keenly conscious of European developments and they had prepared a digest of 80 constitutions which was most likely available to the drafters of the 1937 Constitution.[66]

[3.25] From the *De Valera Papers*[67] and some State Papers, it seems that Catholic social principles entered the 1937 Constitution through its drafters, a small, select group of civil servants,[68] under the direction of John Hearne,[69] with de Valera retaining personal control. Hearne's centrality in the drafting process was confirmed by Maurice Moynihan in an interview given to this author[70] when he stated: "John Hearne gave him [de Valera] the material and benefit of his own thinking," while adding, "John's draft was completed under Dev's eyes".[71] This fact is confirmed by de Valera's inscription on the draft Constitution,[72] in which he described Hearne as "Architect in chief and Draughtsman of this Constitution ..." De Valera also sought the assistance of three significant non-civil servants in

---

[63] *Education: Papal Teachings*, compiled by Benedictine Monks of Solesmes, translated by Reverend Rebeschini, and in particular Pope Pius XI 'The Vocation of the Educator', p 437.

[64] Pope Leo XIII, *Militantis Ecclesiae*, (1897), pp 141, 421.

[65] See *Curraculum na Bunscoile: Primary School Curriculum*, Teachers' Handbook, Part 1, pp 19 and 23. A new curriculum has been drafted and is currently being implemented

[66] See *Select* Constitutions of the World, (1922), Dublin mentioned in *State Paper Office*, File 2979, p 26.

[67] *DVP*, File 1054 of the contains the essence of *Divini Illius Magestrii*.

[68] John Hearne, Maurice Moynihan, Michael McDunphy, Philip O'Donoghue and Arthur Matheson. The latter was a member of the Church of Ireland and according to Moynihan was "a brilliant draftsman under whom Hearne worked".

[69] Hearne, a legal adviser in the Department of External Affairs, had been a student priest in Maynooth College and was well versed in philosophy and theology. Hearne was, it seems, influenced by Jacques Maritain, a leading French Catholic philosopher of the 19th century, see Coughlan, Irish Times, 18 November 1987.

[70] On 14 October 1991.

[71] 14 October 1991.

[72] National Library, MS section, *Hearne Papers*, MS 23508.

the drafting process: Alfred O'Rahilly, Father Edward Cahill SJ, and Father JC McQuaid CSSp, President of Blackrock College, as he was then.

Alfred O'Rahilly

[3.26] O'Rahilly made a significant contribution to the political life of his era and played an important role in the drafting of the 1922 Constitution.[73] He later became a pro-Treaty deputy in Dáil Éireann. Later, perhaps having grown weary of the pace of the Cosgrave administration, O'Rahilly joined forces with de Valera in promoting constitutional change[74] and the two maintained a close life-long relationship.[75] The Attorney General invited O'Rahilly's assistance on constitutional issues, and requested him to formulate a memorandum summarising his view on the Oath and the Statute of Westminster.[76]

[3.27] O'Rahilly forwarded, *inter alia* a copy of Draft C of the 1922 Constitution to de Valera. Some two years later (27 March 1934), there was a letter from de Valera in which he returned "the drafts for the Constitution which you were so kind enough to lend me some time ago".[77] The *De Valera Papers* contain a booklet by O'Rahilly entitled *Thoughts on the Constitution*[78] which covers the same ground as Draft C,[79] written by O'Rahilly which include many of the central concepts of Articles 42 and 44 such as:

(a) that the family based on marriage, as the fundamental unit group of society, should be protected from attacks on the purity, health and sacredness of that institution;

(b) parental priority in education;[80]

(c) no State monopoly of education;

(d) the teaching of religion is obligatory, except for those pupils whose parents or guardians express dissent therefrom;

(e) children deprived of parental care have the right to the help and protection of the State in the limits fixed by the law;

(f) there is no established or State-endowed Church.

---

73 Farrell, 'The Drafting of the Irish Free State Constitution: 1' (1970) 5 Ir Jur 119.

74 Farragher, CSSp *Dev and His Alma Mater*, (1984), Dublin, p 207.

75 Farragher, p 176.

76 Maguire to O'Rahilly, *O'Rahilly Correspondence*, 23 May 1932, p 112 cited in Farrell, at 112.

77 *O'Rahilly Correspondence* cited in Farrell.

78 (1937), Dublin, Brown and Nolan, in *DVP,* File 1045.

79 O'Rahilly, *Thoughts on the Constitution* (1937), Dublin, Brown and Nolan, p 52 written in a desire, as O'Rahilly states, to help de Valera "to secure a more concise and effective formulation."

80 "Mr de Valera and I agree that the primary responsibility for educating children falls on the parents, and that the State is merely subsidiary".

While O'Rahilly's influence on the Constitution goes beyond marriage, the family and education, it is in these areas that he exercises the most important influence.[81] Draft C, it seems to the author, contained the embryonic Articles 42 and 44. Another influence on constitutional drafting was that of a Jesuit priest, Father Cahill.[82]

Father Edward Cahill SJ

[3.28] The *De Valera Papers*[83] contain correspondence between de Valera and Fr Cahill written between 22 March 1932 and 26 August 1940. Included is a letter from de Valera to Fr Cahill returning a manuscript[84] which the latter had sent to de Valera at his request.[85] At this point, little detailed constitutional drafting had been done[86] and there is no evidence that the issue of fundamental rights had been seriously considered.[87] Like O'Rahilly, Fr Cahill stressed the primary educational role of the family and the Church and the subsidiarity of the State's role in the interests of the public good.[88] In his reply to Cahill, de Valera acknowledged that some of his principles could be included in the Preamble but that his submission included little material suited to the body of the Constitution. However, he invited Cahill to draft a Preamble and some draft Articles for the Constitution.[89]

[3.29] Fr Cahill was assisted in his work by a committee of the Jesuit Order[90] who recommended, *inter alia*, compulsory primary education in State-aided,

---

81   *DVP*, File 1045.
82   For greater detail on the drafting of Articles 42 and 44 see Glendenning, 'The Role of the State in First and Second Level Education in Ireland: Retrospect and Prospect', Ph D dissertation, Law School, Trinity College, Dublin 1996, Ch 3.
83   *DVP*, File 1096; *SPO* s 9902.
84   "Suggestions regarding the general or fundamental principles of the Constitution".
85   *DVP*, File 1095/1, 19 September 1936.
86   *DVP*, File 1095 2A.
87   See further Faughnan, 'The Jesuits and the Drafting of the Irish Constitution' *Irish Historical Studies*, No 101 (May 1988) citing *DVP*, File 1095 2A.
88   *DVP*, File 1095/1, de Valera to Cahill, 19 September 1936. Cahill's submission refers to the Polish Constitution (1921), the Portuguese Constitution (1933) and the Austrian Constitution (1934).
89   *DVP*, File 1095/1, de Valera to Cahill, 19 September 1936.
90   Keogh, 'The Irish Constitutional Revolution: An Analysis of the Making of the Consitution in *The Constitution of Ireland 1937-1987*, Litton ed, (1988), 11-19, found evidence which established the existence of a committee which met five times, between 24 September and 18 October 1936 with the consent of the Jesuit Provincial. De Valera does not appear to have been fully appraised of this fact; there appears to be no reference in the official biography of de Valera, by Longford and O'Neill, to the establishment of a formal Jesuit committee, to formulate a consensus on the proposed submission, Longford and O'Neill, *Eamon de Valera*, pp 295-97.

denominational single-sex schools. They further advised that religion be taught during school hours as a part of the curriculum under the direction of the relevant religious body.[91] This committee had the aim, it seems, of censoring Fr Cahill whose views could be extreme.[92] The second document, sent by Cahill to de Valera, entitled *Suggestions for a Catholic Constitution*[93] appears to be the work of this committee.[94] Cahill apparently tendered this document to de Valera as his own work but, in fairness to him, admitted obtaining "the advice and assistance of three or four others who have made a special study of these matters ...".[95] Nonetheless, de Valera seems to have been under the impression that the later work was Fr Cahill's own contribution.

The Jesuit Committee's Submission

[3.30] The Jesuit committee's submission ("the submission")[96] contains a draft Preamble which opens with the words of the Constitution's Preamble: "In the name of the Most Holy Trinity.... we, the people of Ireland ...". In the latter document the word Ireland was changed to Éire and paragraph 1 is distilled to read "who sustained our fathers through centuries of trial".[97] It appears that the Polish, Austrian and Portuguese Constitutions were the predominant influences in the submission, together with certain Papal encyclicals.[98] The submission's preamble is followed by six articles on religion, marriage, the family, education, private property liberty of speech and of the press. The article on religion recommends:

(a) freedom of religious worship;

(b) that the Catholic faith be accorded "a unique and preponderant position";

(c) that religious associations recognised by the State be allowed to freely manage their own affairs including those providing for educational and charitable purposes;

(d) compulsory primary education in State-aided denominational, single-sex schools for adolescents;

---

[91] Longford and O'Neill, *Eamon de Valera*, p 84.
[92] Keogh, pp 11-19.
[93] *DVP*, File 1095/2B.
[94] Keogh, p 16.
[95] Cahill to de Valera, *DVP*, File 1095/2B, October 1936.
[96] It comprises eight type-written sheets, marked with the name of Fr Cahill, and dated 21 October 1936.
[97] De Valera to Cahill, 19 September 1936, *DVP*, 1095/I.
[98] *Casti Connubii*, Pope Pius XI, (1930); *Arcanum Divine*, Leo XIII, (1880); *Rerum Novarum*, Leo XIII, (1891); *Divini Illius Magestri*, Pius XI, (1929).

(e) the primacy of the family in education and the principle of State subsidiarity in education;

(f) freedom for parents to freely choose teachers for their children, and freely select the schools to which their children's education is to be entrusted;

(g) the teaching of religion within school hours, and as a part of the curriculum, to be obligatory in all schools maintained or subsidised by the State and that this teaching shall be under the direction of the relevant religious body.[99]

It is difficult to ascertain the impact of the submission on the family and educational provisions of the Constitution. It clearly influenced on the Preamble and Article 44 as the similarities are many. Longford and O'Neill state that when de Valera read it, he decided to adapt the Articles to a form better suited to Irish conditions[100] and this may well be the case.

[3.31] However, Fr Cahill's influence and that of the Jesuit submission pale in comparison to the profound influence of Fr John Charles McQuaid. Keogh concurs with Longford and O'Neill that Fr McQuaid was particularly influential in the drafting of what ultimately became Articles 40-45[101] and McQuaid's letters to de Valera, discussed below, put this beyond doubt.[102]

The Drafting of Article 44

[3.32] In a letter to Cullins, who was a member of *Marie Duce*, a body which sought the inclusion of an Article in the Constitution which would acknowledge the Catholic Church as "the one true church", de Valera admitted that the drafting of Article 44 (then 45) caused him "more anxiety than anything else in the Constitution".[103] The influence of de Valera's friend and mentor, Fr John Charles McQuaid, on the Constitution appears seminal as it goes right to the origin of civil authority.[104] Nowhere is Fr McQuaid's impact more evident than in Article 42 (education) and to a lesser degree in Article 45 (religion, later to become Article 44).

---

[99] Cahill to de Valera, *DVP*, File 1095/2B.

[100] Longford and O'Neill, *Eamon De Valera*, p 296.

[101] Keogh, p 19.

[102] McQuaid to De Valera, *DVP*, File 1091, 25 March 1937 which states "Herewith I send with great pleasure the remaining dossier, point by point, for the family, education and private property ...".

[103] De Valera to Cullins, *DVP*, File 1089/1, 4 July 1949.

[104] See *DVP*, File 1091 which contains "Rousseau's theory of Civil Authority" together with those of Vitoria, Zigliara and Thomas Aquinas: it is worthy of note that these documents are also contained in the *State Paper Files* (SPO) of the period, see *SPO* File s 9715B which contain Fr McQuaid's memo filed under 'Principles of Political Authority'.

The influence of Fr McQuaid

[3.33] If one examines the drafting of Articles 42 and 44, it becomes clear that these Articles draw deeply on the version of natural law as articulated by St Thomas Aquinas in the thirteenth century and later promulgated in various papal encyclicals and in canon law. The *De Valera Papers* contain at least 22 letters from Fr McQuaid[105] to de Valera written between 16 February 1937 and 3 January 1938. One file refers to the rights of the family as "superior to all positive law".[106] Five other pages contain an examination of the relationship between natural law and human law which cite the teachings of Leo XIII and other Popes. In the final two pages, Fr McQuaid examines the meaning of natural law relying largely on the teachings of St Thomas Aquinas.[107]

[3.34] Fr McQuaid clearly believed in the sovereignty of Aquinian natural law which teaches that all public power must proceed from God as the sovereign ruler and not from the multitude.[108] For him, natural law equated with Catholicity and his sincere wish was that the new State would respect Aquinian natural law and legislate accordingly,[109] and that the new Constitution would confer a special place in law on the Holy Catholic Apostolic and Roman Church. In these twin objectives, Fr McQuaid was supported by certain leading churchmen and by a number of lay persons.[110]

[3.35] Pragmatically, de Valera could not take this route, as he cautiously traversed the fragile, taut tightrope of Church-State relations at this crucial juncture.[111] At least five major churches needed to be appeased. While the

---

[105] Later to become Archbishop of Dublin, see further *DVP*, Files 1078, 1052, 1079, 1095; Maurice Moynihan, one of the drafters informed this author that McQuaid's influence on de Valera's thinking commenced much earlier than the date of the first letter as they took frequent long walks together long before that date.

[106] *DVP*, File 1979/2.

[107] At the top of one page, McQuaid cites his own definition of natural law - "God's design evident in his words and in the nature and his(tory) of man."

[108] See the references in the McQuaid documentation to *Immortale Dei*, (1885), pp 107-8 and to *Romans* 13.1.

[109] One undated letter to de Valera in File 1091 states "Hence the Society and the Government ought *per se* to profess the true faith and legislate in accordance with it ..." That letter concludes "And when the State legislates according to natural law, of necessity, it legislates according to Catholicity, because the latter is the guardian of the natural law". See also File 1095 in which McQuaid, referring to personal rights, religion, the family (including marriage and education), private property and the obligation of social justice, states "The manifest aim of these provisions is to reform gradually the social and economic organisation of the country in accordance with the principles laid down in the great encyclicals of Leo XIII and Pius XI."

[110] Such as those persons in *Maria Duce*.

[111] *DVP*, File 1995/2F which details the many sensitive Church-State difficulties involved in a document which was taken by Joseph Walshe to Rome.

Catholic Church was the church of the vast majority of the people, the Church of Ireland[112] comprised about one-fourth of the population of the total island and it was closely linked to its sister churches in Great Britain and Northern Ireland. If the new Constitution embodied the full Catholic ideal, it would, most likely, alienate the other churches and a bitter religious controversy could ensue.[113] In this fraught situation, de Valera had to find a judicious balance so that the Constitution would be adopted by a majority of the people in a plebiscite.

[3.36] Because of his absolutist views, de Valera withdrew Article 45 (later to become 44) from Fr McQuaid. He also omitted the Article on religion from the Draft Constitution and proceeded to draft that Article alone. This treatment, it seems, was the subject of Fr McQuaid's "disappointment" and apology to de Valera expressed in a letter dated 15 April 1937.[114] Subsequently, de Valera, fearing that the Vatican would be inadvertently embroiled in Irish political matters and side with his opponents, dispatched Joseph P Walsh, Secretary of the Department of Foreign Affairs to Rome, to meet Cardinal Pacelli[115] so as to convince the Pope of his orthodoxy.

Walsh's journey to Rome

[3.37] Walsh was instructed to convey the message, through Cardinal Pacelli, that while the proposed Articles were not the ideal as expressing the relationship that should exist between Church and State, in the conditions pertaining in Ireland, it was not possible to go further due to the conditions prevailing in the country.[116] Walsh was to secure general approval for the religious section; to get the official name of the Catholic Church; and to get the Pope's permission to phrase Article 3 so as to include the following:

> "The State also recognises the other Christian Churches, namely Church of Ireland etc as well as the Jewish congregations and the other religious bodies existing in Éire at the time of the coming into operation of this Constitution."[117]

Following negotiations, the Cardinal, having met the Pope conveyed the message to Walsh: "I do not approve or disapprove; we shall remain silent".[118] The Pope

---

[112] Being until 1869 the State Church and the Protestant religion the State religion.

[113] *DVP*, File 1995 2F.

[114] *DVP*, File 1091, which includes two letters written on the same day, in one of which he concludes: "Should I be able to serve, now or in the future, even to a small degree, I should like to think that you will not hesitate to ask me and to believe that I bow willingly to those who are placed above and who give their decisions", see further Faughnan, *Irish Historical Studies* XXVI 101 100.

[115] Secretary of State and later Pope Pius XII.

[116] *DVP*, 16 April 1937.

[117] *DVP*, File 1995 2 F.

[118] *Ni approvo ni non disapprovo; taceremo.*

took the middle position and remained silent. That was all that was necessary to enable de Valera to proceed with his plans, for his opponents were, for the time being, silenced. Copies of the documents were shown to the heads of the main churches[119] and they seemed reasonably content with the contents.[120]

Revision and Circulation of Draft Constitution

[3.38] The First Official Draft, with the exception of the religious article (then Article 45), was circulated to most State Departments for comment on 16 March 1937.[121] The Departments of Local Government and Finance, *inter alia*, expressed reservations over the envisaged direct provision of free primary education by the State. They feared that it could be construed so as to include the full cost of education including text-books and school requisites. The Secretary of the Department of Education had already expressed similar concerns in writing to de Valera three years earlier.[122] On 1 April, the First Revise was circulated and was followed on 7 April by the Second Revise.[123] Section 5 provides: "The State shall provide (for) free primary education and shall give reasonable aid to private and corporate educational initiative ..." The word "for" is written in what appears to be de Valera's hand. The addition of the proposition "for" at the eleventh hour resulted from the pressure of the State Departments of Finance,[124] Local Government;[125] and Education, as they feared direct provision of primary education by the State would be both litigious and costly as against the State. This is borne out by O'Neill's letter and by the State Papers. De Valera, an astute and pragmatic politician, seems to have feared the rejection of his Constitution by the State Departments and in particular the Department of Finance. With the substitution of the word "regard" for "respect" this provision was enacted as Article 42.4 of the Constitution. The Third Revise (23 April) became the final version of the Constitution as enacted.

[3.39] In the light of the above, it can scarcely be argued that the provisions for education and religion are grounded in any theory of natural law other than that

---

[119] *DVP*, File 1995 2 E.

[120] In his book, *Ireland and the Vatican*, (1995), Cork University Press, p 132 *et seq*, Dermot Keogh has documented this in a fascinating manner, so it is not intended to replicate it here, see also Keogh, *The Vatican, the Bishops and Irish Politics, 1919-1939* 1986, Cambridge; Keogh, 'The Irish Constitutional Revolution: The Making of the Constitution: an Historical Analysis' in Frank Litton, ed, *The Constitution of Ireland 1937-1987, Administration*, (1988), Vol 35, no 4 pp 4-85; Keogh 'The Jesuits and the Making of the 1937 Constitution', *Studies* (Spring 1989), pp 82-92.

[121] *SPO*, 9715/B (Moynihan's memo).

[122] See Appendix F.

[123] Formulated from the contents of *DVP*, File 1079.

[124] *SPO* 9715/B.

[125] *SPO* 9715/B.

of Aquinas. It would take much more than one decision of the Supreme Court, it is respectfully submitted, to alter the character and foundation of Irish education, which, of course, was never intended by that court in the Abortion Information Bill. That decision, nevertheless, weakens the basis which supports education and leaves its position vulnerable to jurisprudential change.

PART II: TENSIONS IN CONTEMPORARY EDUCATION

[3.40] Concerns have been expressed that the difficulties in education are, in some measure, due to our acceptance of a formal and static version of democracy in which control of education has been ceded away from the people and given to an authority that does not seek its mandate from the public will but rather invokes a transcendental authority.[126] Increased demands for democracy, pluralism and partnership in educational structures have been expressed in the White Paper on Education.[127]

[3.41] Against this background, Aquinian natural law theory as the foundation of constitutional law is not without its difficulties. Some fear its affinity with Catholic doctrine[128] while others suspect its influence on judicial interpretation.[129] Because of the many and varied theories of natural law, and the distinctions between the Christian churches, it is difficult to ascertain its precise content, its ambit or its requirements in a specific situation. In constitutional litigation, the judges identify the salient issues and endeavour to strike a balance between the policies upholding the broad statements of principle embodied in Articles 42 and 44.[130] In the education context, this process requires rational analysis and perceptive balancing of the intersecting rights and duties arising from broadly stated constitutional principles such as parental primacy, the natural and imprescriptible rights of the child, the political doctrine of State subsidiarity and the role of the State in education, in a manner which reflects the needs and realities of a changing society. There is an enormous responsibility cast on the Supreme Court, as chief arbiter of the Constitution, to find an equitable equilibrium between these rights. Undue constitutional buttressing of family/parental rights may cloak inadequate State support for children whose parents fail them or who lack parents. Failure to define the concept and failure to

---

[126] Michael D Higgins, in Preface to Alvey, *Irish Education: The Case for Secular Reform*, (1991), Church and State Books, p 5; see also McCarthy, *The Distasteful Challenge*, (1968), Institute of Public Administration.

[127] *Charting our Education Future*, (1995), pp 6-7.

[128] See Clarke, 'The Role of Natural law in Irish Constitutional Law' (1982) 17 Ir Jur (ns) 187.

[129] Whyte, 'Constitutional Adjudication, Ideology and Access to the Courts' in Whelan, ed, *Law and Liberty in Ireland* (1993), Dublin.

[130] See generally, Duncan, 'The Constitutional protection of Parental Rights' in *Report of the Constitution Review Group*, (1996), Gov Pubs, p 612.

identify the components of "a certain minimum education" add to the
difficulties encountered by the courts in attempting to vindicate the
constitutional rights of children to basic educational rights. Case law displays a
somewhat puzzling number of approaches when applying constitutional rights or
interpreting the Constitution. Hogan[131] and Whyte[132] have classified the most
common approaches as:

   (a) historical;[133]

   (b) literal;[134]

   (c) the natural law approach;[135] and

   (d) the harmonious approach.[136]

If the judicial reasoning in the Abortion Information Bill decision were applied
to education, it would demolish the Aquinian natural law foundations which
embodied education as a fundamental right antecedent to positive law. As will be
seen, a number of the recommendations of the *Report of the Constitution Review
Group* (RCRG) indicate that some movement in that direction may be necessary
if the Constitution is to remain relevant to societal needs and demands.

The Non-Endowment Principle

[3.42] Philosophical conflict is also apparent in Article 44.2.2° in which the
State guarantees not to endow any religion. The principle of non-endowment of
religion by the State was mentioned briefly in the Supreme Court in *McGrath
and O'Ruairc v Trustees of Maynooth College*,[137] which, to some extent,
foreshadows the decision in the *Campaign to Separate Church and State Ltd v
The Minister for Education*,[138] which is discussed below.

---

[131] Hogan, 'Constitutional Interpretation' in Litton, ed, *The Constitution of Ireland 1937-1987*, *Administration* (1988), p 173.

[132] Whyte, 'Education and the Constitution,' in *Religion, Education and the Constitution*, Lane, ed, (1992), The Columba Press, pp 103-4.

[133] For example when the Constitution is interpreted in the light of public opinion and legal developments in 1937 as in *Crowley v Ireland* [1980] IR 102.

[134] When plain words are given a plain meaning.

[135] The natural law approach is exemplified by a consideration of the principles of natural law as outlined earlier.

[136] When various Articles are read in the light of one another, the approach is usually termed harmonious; Casey adds purposive interpretation, see Casey, *Constitutional Law in Ireland*, (1987), Sweet and Maxwell, pp 304-5.

[137] [1979] ILRM 166.

[138] [1996] 2 ILRM 241; Supreme Court, unrep, 25 March 1998. The other defendants were the Attorney General and the State. Four metropolitan Catholic Archbishops were sued later on foot of an application to the Master of the High Court in which it was successfully argued that they would suffer substantial financial loss if the plaintiff succeeded. The defendant's counsel was also instructed on behalf of the Church of Ireland.

[3.43] In the *McGrath* case, the plaintiffs alleged that the statutes of Maynooth College violated Article 44.2.3° which provides that "the State shall not impose any disabilities or make any discrimination on the ground of religious profession, belief or status".[139] The argument advanced by the plaintiffs[140] was that as Maynooth was receiving substantial public funding, they were being discriminated against on the grounds of status, under the statutes, for breaches of clerical discipline that were inapplicable to lay persons.

[3.44] In the Supreme Court, Kenny J held that the prohibition imposed by Article 44.2.3° is confined to the State and that extending the constitutional prohibition to institutions which receive public moneys leads to ludicrous results.[141] Henchy J was of the view that a literal interpretation was not appropriate in this instance:

> "To construe the provision literally, without due regard to its underlying objective, would lead to a sapping and debilitation of the freedom and independence given by the Constitution to the doctrinal and organisational requirements and proscriptions which are inherent in all organised religions. Far from eschewing the internal disabilities and discriminations which flow from the tenets of a particular religion, the State must on occasion recognise and buttress them. For such disabilities and discriminations do not derive from the State; it cannot be said that it is the State that imposed or made them; they are part of the texture and essence of the particular religion; so the State, in order to comply with the spirit and purpose inherent in this constitutional guarantee, may justifiably lend its weight to what may be thought to be disabilities and discriminations deriving from within a particular religion."[142]

[3.45] This *dictum* indicates that, given the freedom and independence that the Constitution has conferred on organised religion, the spirit and purpose of the liberal provisions in Article 44 must be read in terms of their underlying objectives and the State may support and even occasionally buttress what appear to be disabilities and discriminations deriving from a particular religion.

The Campaign to Separate Church and State Ltd v The Minister for Education: High Court

[3.46] The *McGrath* case was approved by Costello P in the *Campaign to Separate Church and State Ltd v The Minister for Education*.[143] While the plaintiff conceded that the payment of salaries of teachers of religion is constitutionally permissible, it alleged that payment of salaries of chaplains out

---

[139] See also *Molloy v Minister for Education* [1975] IR 88.
[140] Who were laicised priests.
[141] [1979] ILRM 166.
[142] [1979] ILRM 166.
[143] [1996] 2 ILRM 241.

of State funds is unconstitutional as it breaches Article 44.2.2° in which the State guarantees "not to endow any religion."[144] Chaplains were appointed *ab initio* in these schools to provide religious instruction and they were paid salaries by the State in common with other teachers. It was contended at the outset that the plaintiffs lacked *locus standi*. However, Costello P, at the request of the parties, agreed to deal with that issue only in the event of the plaintiff being successful.

[3.47] The State argued that the plaintiff's claim was non-justiciable, there being no express statutory authority for the establishment of community schools, and that the court lacked jurisdiction to grant constitutional declaratory relief in what was essentially a matter of private contract. Conceding the non-statutory origin of the schools, but not their private contractual basis, or a lack of jurisdiction in the matter, the judge pointed out that the authority to make the payment of salaries of chaplains was authorised by the annual adoption by the Dáil of departmental estimates and by the enactment of the annual Appropriation Act.[145] Costello P distinguished between "endowment of religion" and "establishment of religion" noting the absence of a prohibition against "establishment of religion" in Irish constitutional law.

[3.48] A detailed analysis of community schools, their trust deeds, and the role of their chaplains, as established in evidence, was conducted by the judge. Although built largely by State funds, these schools, he stated, are not in the legal ownership of the State or any State authority, or in the legal ownership of any religious order or the diocese or of any church. Rather, he continued, these schools are vested in trustees[146] who together with the board of management, the principal teacher and the Minister, are under a legal obligation to ensure that the school is managed according to the trust deed; the Minister's powers extending to supervision of its curriculum and the school's expenditure.

[3.49] The "Instrument of Management" and the "Articles of Management" (the Articles), Costello P noted, are part of the said trusts, subject to which the trustees hold the property upon trust for the purposes of the school which include "the purpose of contributing towards the spiritual, moral, mental and physical well-being and development of the said Community ..." (Clause 2).[147] So, the judge continued, the board's general discretionary power in Clause 10 of the Articles is subject to the specific provisions of Clause 11. Hence, the trustees and the board, he concluded, are legally obliged to provide religious worship and

---

[144] In 1996, this scheme cost £1.2 million.
[145] [1996] 2 ILRM 241.
[146] [1996] 2 ILRM 241.
[147] Of the Model Lease.

religious instruction for the pupils in the school with the exception of pupils whose parents request, in writing, that their children be withdrawn from religious worship and/or from religious instruction.[148] Furthermore, Costello P stated that the teacher of religion may be a priest.

[3.50] Interpreting the Articles further, the judge observed that religious instruction and religious worship within the school are to accord with the rites, practice and teaching of the religious denomination to which the pupils belong and is to comprise two hours per week. With reference to the position of chaplain, the judge referred to Clause 11(x) of the Articles, specifically authorising the competent religious authority to appoint a chaplain as an ex-quota, full-time member of staff who shall be paid a salary equivalent to that of a teacher in the school.

[3.51] Costello P considered that the Irish Constitution has developed the significance of certain human rights instruments[149] and has imposed additional duties on the State in respect of them. In this regard, he cited the inalienable right of the family/parents to provide, *inter alia,* religious education for their children and the State's guarantee to respect that right. In particular, he noted the State's obligation in respect of the provision of "a minimum education, moral intellectual and social"[150] and when providing educational facilities the obligation to have due regard for parental rights, "especially in the matter of religious and moral formation".[151] The judge distinguished between religious education and religious formation:

> ".... broadly speaking the religious *education* of a child is concerned with the teaching of religious doctrine, apologetics, religious history and comparative religions, whilst the religious *formation* of a child involves familiarising the child not just with religious doctrine but with religious practice (by attendance at religious services) and developing the child's religious and spiritual life by prayer and bible reading and I think the Constitution should be construed so as to reflect this meaning."[152]

Costello P stated that one of the important reasons why chaplains, as well as teachers of religion, are appointed to the staff of community schools is for the purpose of aiding the religious and moral formation of the pupils. He observed that Article 42.4 enjoined the State when providing educational facilities to have regard to these two distinct rights. As to the purpose and effect of the payment of chaplains, the judge considered, that it was in practice "having regard to the

---

[148] Clause 10 (ii) of the Articles.
[149] See below Ch 8.
[150] Article 42.3.2°.
[151] Article 42.4.
[152] [1996] 2 ILRM 241.

rights of parents *vis-à-vis* the religious formation of their children and enabling them to exercise their constitutionally recognised rights".[153]

[3.52] Echoing Henchy J's statement in *McGrath v Trustees of Maynooth College*,[154] Costello P considered that if the purpose of State financial funding is to facilitate the protection of constitutionally recognised rights, or to aid in their exercise by right-holders or to fulfil the State's obligation to respect them, that it cannot be constitutionally invalid to confer such aid. The spirit and purpose of the liberal guarantees contained in Article 44, he continued, must be read in conjunction with Article 42. Thus, he concluded, the prohibition against endowment of religion in Article 44.2.2° must be interpreted so as to permit State aid to assist in the religious formation of children in accordance with the wishes of their parents.

[3.53] Accordingly, Costello P ruled that the payment of salaries of teachers of religion (including ministers of religion and members of religious orders) out of public funds is constitutionally permissible and does not constitute "endowment of religion" as prohibited by Article 44.2.2°. Taking the matter one step further, the judge held that, if the payment of salaries of teachers of religion out of public funds does not constitute "endowment" of religion, then this must apply whether the teacher is in a denominationally managed school or in primary or secondary schools not so managed.

[3.54] By holding that the spirit and purpose of the liberal provisions must be read in the light of Article 42, Costello P indicated that he viewed education as resting firmly on Aquinian natural law principles.[155]

[3.55] Tensions are apparent between this decision and the jurisprudence of the Supreme Court as expressed in the Abortion Bill decision. Many commentators believed the positivist approach apparent in that decision had severed the Catholic control inherent in the theistic concept of natural law which underpins the Constitution. This fundamental change in the jurisprudence of the Supreme Court contrasts sharply with Costello P's vigorous support of the theistic natural law tradition as it applies to education. It seems that the radical departure of the Supreme Court into the realm of legal positivism may have been perceived by Costello P as a corruption of law as traditionally interpreted.[156]

---

[153] [1996] 2 ILRM 241.

[154] [1979] ILRM 166. Henchy J's statement in this case was, however, confined to matters dealing with "disabilities and discriminations which flow from the tenets of a particular religion." On the facts of the case, the Supreme Court did not deal with the principle of non-endowment *per se*.

[155] See an earlier article written by the trial judge, Costello, 'The Natural Law and the Irish Constitution' *Studies* (1956) 45, 403-14.

[156] *Ryan v AG* [1965] IR 294; *McGee v AG* [1974] IR 284; *Finn v AG* [1983] IR 154; Barrington, 'Article Forty-Four-1', *Studies* 80 (1952), p 379; Walsh J 'The Constitution: a View from the Bench' in Farrell, ed, *De Valera's Constitution and Ours*, p 188.

*The Campaign to Separate Church and State Ltd v The Minister for
Education: Supreme Court*

[3.56] This case was appealed by the plaintiff to the Supreme Court where
judgment was delivered by Keane J on the 25 March 1998.[157] Interpreting
Article 44.2.3°, Article 42.4, and Article 44.2.4° harmoniously, the Court found
that the State is permitted to provide aid to schools of different religious
denominations and that they may include religious instruction as a subject in
their curricula. Turning to the specific issue of endowment, the court noted that
there was no question of a direct subvention by the State to any religious
denomination. What required to be determined, it considered, was whether the
payment to chaplains from the Exchequer was *prima facie* in breach of the
guarantee given in Article 44.2.2°. If it was not, the plaintiff's case failed. If it
was in breach, then it had to be determined whether, although *prima facie* an
endowment, it was still sanctioned either expressly or impliedly by Article 42.4.

[3.57] The Court focused on Article 44.2.2°, its language, content and intent. It
considered the etymological derivation of the term "endow" which originated
from the French word "douer" originally meaning dowry or marriage portion
given to the wife or "dower" to a widow. It noted its wider application over time
and its definition in the recent *Oxford English Dictionary*:[158] "to enrich with
property; to provide (by bequest or gift) a permanent income for (a person,
society or institution)".[159]

[3.58] When used in the context of religion, the Court stated, the term "endow"
had to be distinguished from the word "establish" and other cognate words in
this case. While observing the express prohibition of any law "respecting an
establishment of religion ..." in the first amendment of the Constitution of the
United States of America which Thomas Jefferson construed as creating "a wall
of separation" between Church and State, the Court agreed with the trial judge
that the US authorities cited were of no assistance in construing Article 44.2.2°.

[3.59] With regard to Article 44.2.2° and Article 44.2.3° of the 1937
Constitution, (prohibiting religious discrimination), the Court traced their
genesis from the various Home Rule measures initiated in the Westminster
Parliament, between 1886 and 1920, to the Anglo-Irish Treaty of 1921,[160] and
thence to the 1922 Constitution and subsequently to the 1937 Constitution. It
observed the general aiding nature of the State's constitutional obligation in

---

[157] [1998] 2 ILRM 81.
[158] Vol 4, (2nd ed, 1991).
[159] The same volume defines "endowment" as the action of endowing, in various sences, and
secondly "The property or fund with which a society, institution, etc is endowed.
[160] Section 16.

education (to provide for free primary education) as established by the Supreme Court in *Crowley v Ireland*.[161] As to the intent of Article 44.2.2°, the Court considered that Article 44.2.2° was thus intended to render unlawful the vesting of property or income in a religion *as such* in perpetual or quasi-perpetual form. It was not designed to render unlawful the comprehensive system of aid to denominational education which had become so central a feature of the Irish schools system and the validity of which was expressly acknowledged by the Constitution.

[3.60] The Court noted that Article 44.2.2° was further intended and originally prompted to outlaw in any form the "concurrent endowment" proposed by the House of Lords during the stormy debate on the disestablishment of the Church of Ireland lest the Catholic faith be endowed in preference to the others.[162] In fact, the Supreme Court had already made it clear in *Re Article 26 of the Constitution and the Employment Equality Bill (1997)*,[163] that this form of endowment was outlawed by Article 44.2.2°.

[3.61] Having established that the *raison d'être* of Article 44.2.2° was as stated, the Court ruled that the payment of salaries of chaplains in community schools is not even *prima facie* an endowment of religion within the meaning of Article 44.2.2°. However, even if these payments were *prima facie* an endowment within the meaning of Article 44.2.2°, the Court indicated that it would hold that they had constitutional sanction.

[3.62] Thus, the Supreme Court upheld the decision of the trial judge although it arrived at that decision by a different route.

[3.63] Because of the anti-discrimination guarantee in Article 44.2.4°, it seems that all religions will be entitled to have their chaplains or teachers of religion remunerated out of public funds which will result in a huge drain on public finances.[164] In this context, the question of what constitutes "religion" could prove problematic as a number of sects may assert constitutional protection and State funding for their chaplains or teachers of religion.

Parental Rights in Education

[3.64] While parents are theoretically at the apex of the pyramidal constitutional structure supporting education, in practice, they were excluded from responsibility for the direction of the school until 1975.[165] The family seldom

---

[161] [1980] IR 102.

[162] See Keogh, *Twentieth Century Ireland: Nation and State*, (1994), Gill and Macmillan.

[163] [1997] 2 IR 321.

[164] In 1996 State funding of comprehensive and community schools amounted to £1.2 million.

[165] When boards of management were introduced in primary schools. See *Dáil Debates*, Vol 207, col 408, 15 February 1964 where a reference to parents as "interlopers" in education is made by the late George Colley TD: O'Connor, *A Troubled Sky*, (1986), Education Research Centre, Dublin, pp 5-6.

educated directly[166] and so the churches generally participated in education on its behalf. While Article 42 does not expressly mention the churches, this provision can scarcely be read in isolation from Article 44 which supports the position of the religious denominations in education.[167] The evolution of the centralist character of the Department of Education also contrasts sharply with its perceived subordinate constitutional role which builds on the subsidiarity principle. These factors contributed to bring about the subordinate position of parents in Irish education by comparison with the more central role of the school owners and the State. In these two respects, educational policy and practice appears to have diverged from the constitutional plan for education as envisaged. It is submitted that it was the informality of the system and the absence of legislative constraints which permitted these divergences from the constitutional "blueprint".

[3.65] Fragmentation of the homogenous mould of Irish life has resulted in changes in this pattern and the premise that full parental support exists for denominational education can no longer be accepted.[168] As the *Report on the National Education Convention* (1994) observes, now that parents are more educated, the old model of patron acting "on behalf of" parents is coming under challenge,[169] a matter which is evident from the pattern of school establishment since 1990.[170]

The Family

[3.66] In Article 41.1, the State recognises the family as "the natural primary and fundamental unit group of society." Case law indicates that the rights referred to in this instance are the rights of the family as a unit recognised in marriage rather than the rights of the individual within that unit.[171] Parental rights have a fundamental status in Article 42 being described as "inalienable" indicating that they can never be totally transferred to the State.[172] In the setting of the enormous changes in contemporary family arrangements, such an approach seems unduly restrictive.

[3.67] The *RCRG* has recommended that all family rights, including those of unmarried mothers or fathers and children born of unmarried parents should be

---

[166] No firm figures are available for home education but it is estimated that approximately 200 families currently educate their children at home.

[167] See Articles 44.2.4°, 44.2.5°, 44.2.6°.

[168] See *Report on the National Education Convention*, (1994), Ch 5; *Report of the Constitution Review Group*, Coolahan, ed, (1996) Gov Pubs, p 345.

[169] *Report on the National Education Convention* (1994), p 25.

[170] See above Ch 2.

[171] *Murray v Ireland* [1985] IR 532; *L v L* [1992] 2 IR 77.

[172] This was also the meaning given to this word by de Valera, see *DVP*, File 1042; *Ryan v AG* [1965] IR 294 at 350.

protected in Article 41.[173] Pragmatically, the Report takes the view that any revision of Article 41 should be consistent with the relevant family-related sections of Articles 42 and 44. In Article 42.1, in which the family is acknowledged as "the primary and natural educator of the child ...", the *RCRG* recommends that Article 42.1 be amended to apply to all non-marital parents, provided they have appropriate family ties and connections with the child in question. Such changes seem necessary as otherwise an increasing number of non-marital families/parents will be excluded from the full ambit of constitutional protection.

Parental Choice of School

[3.68] Parents may exercise their right to educate their children at home,[174] as a small number of families have opted to do,[175] or they may send their children to private schools or to schools recognised or established by the State, if these exist. As we have seen, parents have traditionally exercised their constitutional right to educate through the agency of the churches who did not, until recently, include parents in their management bodies.[176] While constitutional theory bestows a wide choice of school on parents, in practice, parental choice is extremely narrow as few alternatives exist to the traditional denominational school. Evidence is now emerging that some parents are seeking alternatives to the traditional denominational schools for their children.[177]

Family Autonomy and the Rights of the Child

[3.69] The constitutional doctrine of family autonomy has significantly influenced Irish education and its social function resulting in a remarkable reluctance in Irish law to permit State control of parental powers in education. Children's rights to education have traditionally been perceived as vested in their parents and courts have upheld the primacy of parental choice in primary education, subject only to the State's right to require minimum standards of education.[178]

---

[173] At p 336.

[174] The right to educate children in the home has been asserted by several international Conventions, General Assembly of the UN, 16 December 1966, res 2200, Article 13, s 3; European Social Charter, 1961; UN Convention on the Rights of the Child, 1989, Articles 5, 14, 18, the right to educate at home has also been upheld by the Irish High Court In the Matter of the Courts (Supplemental Provisions) Act 1961; *DPP v Best* [1998] 2 ILRM 549.

[175] Approximately 200 Irish families were involved in home education in 1995, 'Home Schooling: What's gained, what's lost when parents educate children themselves?' Irish Times, EL, 4 April, 1995.

[176] See O'Connor, *A Troubled Sky: Reflections on the Irish Educational Scene 1957- 1968*, (1986), Education Research Centre, Dublin.

[177] *Report on the National Education Convention,* (1994), p 25; *RCRG*, Gov Pubs, 1996, p 345.

[178] *Re Article 26 and the School Attendance Bill 1942* [1943] IR 334.

[3.70] This approach was notable during the drafting of Protocol 1(2) of the European Convention on Human Rights in the early 1950s when Ireland entered a reservation to the effect that the right to education in the Protocol was not sufficiently explicit in protecting parental choice of schools and the right to educate at home.[179] It has been alleged that Article 42, with its emphasis on the doctrine of parental autonomy, has indirectly consolidated the power of the churches within the educational system.[180] Possibly, the chief advantage of such a constitutional doctrine has been the protection it has afforded against the excesses of State orthodoxy in education.

[3.71] On the other hand, excessive conservatism in this regard has impacted adversely on the educational rights of individual children within the family unit.[181]

[3.72] While Article 42.4 imposes an obligation on the State to provide for free primary education, Article 42.1, Article 42.2 and Article 42.3 emphasise much more strongly the rights of parents in the education of their children. Remarkably, this constitutional doctrine of parental primacy did not translate into parental involvement in school administration. In recent years, parents have achieved consultative status in education and they will acquire a number of important statutory rights when the Education Act 1998 becomes fully operational.[182] Parents have also become more assertive in the establishment and management of schools.

[3.73] In 1955 the Supreme Court upheld the principle of parental priority in *Doyle v Minister for Education*[183] when it ruled that s 10(1)(d) and s 10(1)(e) of the Children Act 1941 infringed parental rights under Article 42. The court considered the Act deprived a parent, whose child had been sent to an industrial school, the right to resume control of the child and to provide for the child's education once that parent was willing and capable of doing so.

[3.74] Having examined the underlying common law principle, that parents not alone have the right to control the education of their children but that they cannot surrender this right, the Court concluded that by the provisions of Article 42, the framers deliberately preserved this common law principle and have put it beyond the reach of ordinary legislation. However, Part III of the Child Care Act 1991 has made provision for the protection of children in emergencies.

---

[179] [1954] Ir TS, No 3, see Ch 8.
[180] Duncan, 'The Constitutional Protection of Parental Rights' *RCRG*, (1996), Gov Pubs, p 618.
[181] See Ch 5.
[182] See Ch 6.
[183] Supreme Court, unrep, 21 December 1955.

[3.75] In *Comerford v The Minister for Education*,[184] which dealt with the problems posed by a dysfunctional family, McGuinness J remarked that the Eastern Health Board could have acted with greater alacrity in taking the children of the family into care. However, the judge noted the constitutional constraints under which the Health Board acted in these circumstances as the powers of the State as against the parents in the sphere of education are strictly limited:[185]

> "…. in approaching this situation the Health Board had to bear in mind the extremely strong rights given to parents and the family in the Constitution and the comparative lack of express constitutional rights for the child as against the parents."[186]

It appears that undue emphasis on the autonomy of the family has delayed the emergence of a judicial balancing approach to the constitutional rights of parents and children in education and this may have cloaked the underfunding of child-protection by the State. Fears of trespassing on parental rights has impeded legislators from enacting educational legislation[187] and adequate child protection laws thus delaying much needed reforms. The writer concurs with the recommendation of the *RCRG* that the right and duty of educating children should remain vested in parents but that this right ought to be subject to two further rights:

(a) the best interests of the child; and

(b) the right of the State to ensure that children receive a certain minimum education "as may be determined from time to time by law" provided that the State shall at all times have due regard to the right of parents to make decisions concerning the religious and moral education of their children.[188]

The Rights of the Child: Lack of Statutory Protection

[3.76] Possibly the major disadvantage of the constitutional bias towards parental autonomy has been the resultant lack of statutory protection for the child's right to education. Recent case law indicates that the main categories affected by this singular omission have been those pupils who frequently find themselves outside of mainstream schools such as those children suffering severe or profound disability, disruptive and emotionally disturbed children and

---

[184] High Court, unrep, 20 December 1996, p 20. This case is dealt with in greater detail in Ch 5.

[185] *Comerford v The Minister for Education* High Court, unrep, 20 December 1996, p 11 referring to *Re Article 26 and the School Attendance Bill 1942*.

[186] *Comerford v The Minister for Education* [1997] 2 ILRM 134.

[187] See submission of the Department of Education to the *RCRG*.

[188] *RCRG*, p 350.

those whose parents have failed in their care and educational duties towards their children.

[3.77] Other groups of pupils who have been adversely affected by the legislative lacuna in education have been weaker pupils in mainstream schools who have been deprived of adequate support services, eg remedial education, assessment, counselling and psychological services and pupils who are suspended or expelled from schools in circumstances where no alternative education is provided and traveller children. Few parents can afford the investment in time and money required to vindicate the right of their children to education in a constitutional action. Consequently, educational provision for many of these categories has been uneven, inadequate and in some cases non-existent. Educational provision for these children is discussed in Chapter 4.

School Attendance: The State's Right and Obligation to Prescribe a Minimum Standard of Education

[3.78] It has been argued that the function of the law in ensuring school attendance is the removal of obstacles or the "hindering of hindrances" to the development of personalities. Ignorance is such a hindrance and its removal by law, it has been argued, is justified.[189]

The Minimum Constitutional Standard

[3.79] Article 42.3.2° attempts to strike a balance between the rights of the State, children and the public interest in promoting an educated populace by permitting the State "as guardian of the common good"[190] to intervene in education to a limited degree. Thus, it may require "in view of actual conditions that the children receive a certain minimum education, moral, intellectual and social."[191] It follows that in order to implement this right, the Oireachtas must legislate for school attendance.[192] The existence of this duty laid upon the State indicates that parental rights in this regard are subject to the State's right to require that all children attain a certain minimum of education either in school or at home.

[3.80] Case law has held that this latter right vests a corresponding right in every child to receive a minimum education, moral, intellectual and social, and the State must make arrangements to have this minimum education provided free of

---

[189] See Ginsberg, *On Justice in Society*, (1965), Penguin, p 118 citing Green, *Principles of Political Obligation*, paras 208-9.
[190] For an interesting discussion on the common good, see Costello, 'Natural Law, The Constitution and the Courts', *Essays in Memory of Alexis Fitzgerald*, (1987), Incorporated Law Society, pp 104-117, 115.
[191] Article 42.3.2°.
[192] *Re Article 26 and the School Attendance Bill 1942* [1943] IR 334 at 335.

charge.[193] What are the constituents of this "certain minimum education" which the State may require that all children receive?

[3.81] This certain minimum education has not been defined either constitutionally or in statute. It will be recalled that in *Re Article 26 and the School Attendance Bill 1942*[194] the Supreme Court ruled that the State, acting through the Oireachtas, had power to define this phrase although no attempt to do so has ensued.

[3.82] In their recent submission to the *RCRG*, the Department expressed concerns that the absence of a more precise definition of "a certain minimum education" might leave the State open to a charge that the level of education as required by the State was either lesser or greater than the minimum envisaged by the Constitution. These fears were well grounded as the High Court, in *DPP v Best*,[195] has since upheld the right of a parent to educate at home provided the minimum constitutional standard is met. This case was appealed to the Supreme Court and a reserved judgment is awaited.

Constitutional Protection for Families/Parents

[3.83] The doctrine of constitutional protection for family/parents in education has influenced judicial interpretation of statutes contributing to the loss of a number of statutes. Article 42 embodies a principle of the common law that if a parent or guardian delivers a child up to another for the purposes of education, he has a right to retake the child.[196] Perhaps the failure of the School Attendance Bill 1942[197] to pass into law best exemplifies the constitutional doctrine of parental autonomy in education. While the Bill contained some worthy objectives,[198] it included a "hidden agenda" which can only be fully understood in the light of two preceding cases which will next be briefly outlined.

The School Attendance Act 1926

[3.84] Section 4 of the School Attendance Act 1926 (the 1926 Act) made provision for the attendance of children at primary school generally but any of the following was a reasonable excuse for failing to comply with that section:

---

[193] *Re Article 26 and the School Attendance Bill 1942* [1943] IR 334, O'Higgins CJ; *Crowley v Ireland* [1980] IR 102 at 108, 126, McMahon J.

[194] [1943] IR 334.

[195] [1998] 2 ILRM 549.

[196] *Barnado's Case* [1890] QB 194 discussed in *Cases and Materials on the Irish Constitution*, 1980, ILS; see also *Reg v Clarke* 7 E & B 186; *Yearbook* (Mich 8 Edward IV fol B 2).

[197] *Re Article 26 and the School Attendance Bill 1942* [1943] IR 334.

[198] Such as provision for traveller children and the prohibition of employment of children under twelve years of age.

(a) that the child had been prevented from attending by the sickness of the child;

(b) that the child was receiving suitable elementary education in some manner other than by attending a national or other suitable school;

(c) that there was not a national or other suitable school accessible to the child which the child could attend and to which the parent of the child did not object on religious grounds to send the child;

(d) that the child had been prevented from attending school by some other sufficient cause.[199]

The Act did not require a child to have a knowledge of Irish as a component of a minimum education, so the State resolved in 1934 to alter this situation by ministerial intervention. Firstly, it required all schools, desirous of being deemed "suitable schools" under the 1926 Act, to apply to the Department for certification by a school inspector.

[3.85] Schools were notified accordingly and it was made clear to them that no certification would issue to any school whose curriculum did not include the teaching of the Irish language.

Carberry v Yates[200]

[3.86] Among the schools notified was a tiny private school in Enniscorthy with an otherwise impeccable academic record.[201] This school, however, could not comply with this notification as neither the principal or her assistant had any knowledge of the Irish language. Subsequently, one of the parents of an eight year-old pupil attending the school, received a warning notice from the Department requiring him to enrol his daughter, Hazel, in a school which complied with the 1926 Act, or to furnish a reasonable excuse for not doing so.

On failing to comply with either option, the parent was prosecuted under the 1926 Act and convicted in the District Court.

[3.87] The appeal in *Carberry v Yates*[202] was heard in the Circuit Court in 1935. Devitt J ruled that a school, giving otherwise suitable education, complied with the Act even when Irish was excluded from the curriculum. In the absence of a statute or statutory regulation requiring the compulsory teaching of Irish in all

---

[199] Until 1936, there was a ten day seasonal exception (between 17 March-15 May) for children over twelve years who were engaged in light agricultural work for a parent on a parent's land.

[200] (1935) 69 ILTR 86.

[201] In the words of Devitt J in the Circuit Court, the school "... seemed to be perfect in every other way in regard to education but did not teach Irish," see (1935) 69 ILTR 86 at 87 and 88.

[202] (1935) 69 ILTR 86.

primary schools, the judge acted on the existing law rather than on the opinion of one man:

> "I do not think I can send a man to gaol or fine him because a Minister says that no child will be educated unless taught the Irish language. When Parliament says that a thing must be done I am bound to see that it is done, but compulsion is a hard thing, and I am not going to exercise it unless I must ... It would be the greatest despotism if the Minister could rule out every school in the country unless Irish were taught."[203]

Thus, this pre-Constitution attempt to promote the Irish language by ministerial intervention had fallen foul of the law.[204]

"Closing the Gap on Irish"

[3.88] As has been seen, the compulsory teaching of the Irish language in all primary schools did not become a constitutional principle although this was included in early constitutional drafts.[205] Neither does the Constitution include any specific national policy or aim in respect to the restoration of the Irish language. Articles 42 and 44 are silent on the Irish language issue in education. However Article 8.1 confers the status of "national language and first official language" on the Irish language and states:

> Provision may, however, be made *by law* for the exclusive use of either of the said languages for any one or more official purposes, either throughout the State or any part thereof.[206]

Thus, the only lawful avenue for[207] ensuring that Irish became part of the content of education required by the State for the purposes of school attendance lay in enacting this measure in legislation. However, there was no certainty that this would be acceptable to the people. Discussions took place in the Dáil on informally "closing the gap on Irish",[208] as de Valera termed it, and clearly he felt there was nothing unconstitutional in so doing.[209] Another attempt to promote the Irish language by ministerial intervention ensued. Although unrelated to school attendance, the case of *McEneaney v Minister for Education*[210] is relevant to the context in which the School Attendance Bill

---

[203] (1935) 69 ILTR 86 at 88.
[204] See also *Re Westby Minors* (No 2) [1934] IR 311.
[205] See *DVP*, Document No 4, *Summary of Draft Heads of the Constitution*, Part 1X 2.
[206] Author's emphasis.
[207] See discussion on this issue in *Dáil Debates*, Vol 88, cols 2122-3, November 1942.
[208] *Dáil Debates*, Vol 88, cols 2122-3, November 1942.
[209] *Dáil Debates*, Vol 88, cols 2122-3, November 1942.
[210] [1941] IR 430.

1942[211] is set as it most likely contributed to judicial suspicion of the Department of Education's motivation in moving the 1942 Bill.

McEneaney v Minister for Education

[3.89] Prior to 1932, the Rules for National Schools ("the Rules") were those published in 1917 as amended. Under these latter rules, teachers were required to have a certificate to teach Irish as a subject of the curriculum and they were entitled to increments provided no adverse reports were made on them by an inspector of schools. In 1932 new rules were implemented which made the grant of increments conditional on the teacher having acquired a bilingual certificate which would certify the teacher's ability to give instruction in Irish and English in all subjects of the curriculum. Many teachers failed to achieve the bilingual certificate and so had their increments withheld. This unilateral alteration of the conditions of employment of existing teachers led to the High Court challenge in *McEneaney v Minister for Education*[212] in which the court found for the Minister. On appeal, this finding was reversed by the Supreme Court which ruled that the Department was not entitled to alter unilaterally the terms and conditions of an existing teacher's contract of employment. Subsequently, all money withheld from the teachers who had failed to achieve the bi-lingual certificate was repaid by the Department. Referring to the motivation behind this case, the Court held that:

> "while the object of the Department to promote the use of the Irish language was indeed a laudable one, the methods adopted to promote this object must not be contrary to the rules of law."[213]

This salutary warning, however, did not deter further invasions of parental rights by the State in regard to the Irish language as the following case illustrates.

The School Attendance Bill 1942

[3.90] Under the School Attendance Act 1926 the option of organising "other suitable elementary education" lay entirely in the hands of parents. Section 4 of the School Attendance Bill 1942 provided that:

> A child shall not be deemed for the purposes of this Act to be receiving suitable education in a manner other than by attending a national school, a suitable school, or a recognised school unless such education and the manner in

---

[211] *Re Article 26 and the School Attendance Bill 1942* [1943] IR 334. The Bill was entitled An Act to make further and better provision for ensuring school attendance by children to whom the School Attendance Act 1926, applies and for that and other purposes to amend the said School Attendance Act.

[212] [1941] IR 430.

[213] *McEneaney v Minister for Education* [1941] IR 430.

which such child is receiving it, have been certified under this section by the Minister to be suitable.

If this Bill passed into law, the Minister, through the agency of the school inspectorate, would have power to specify what constituted "a suitable education" and to decide the manner in which such education would be given.[214]

[3.91] Political opposition to the Bill intensified when it became clear in the Dáil that the Minister, under the guise of an amendment to improve school attendance, was seeking to include a knowledge of the Irish language not only as part of a "suitable education" but was also proposing to control the manner by which such education would be acquired. Thus, if a child's education did not receive the Minister's *imprimatur*, it fell outside the ambit of s 4[215] thereby leaving certain parents open to prosecution under the amended Act. In practice, the implementation of s 4 would conflict significantly with parental choice of schools/education as it would prevent numbers of Irish parents from educating their children abroad[216] and would preclude some 500 children from crossing the border daily to attend schools in Northern Ireland as they did in 1942.[217]

[3.92] The ensuing controversy which surrounded the Bill in the Dáil and the Seanad centred upon the primacy of parental rights in Article 42. Professor O'Sullivan reminded the Minister of the status of education as a natural right vested in parents and of the safeguards erected by de Valera around Article 42 so as to protect that natural right targeted by s 4 of the Bill:

> "I refer to the right not because it is in the Constitution; I think it is higher than the Constitution. I think it is a natural right, and it is a natural right which many people have insisted on for many centuries."[218]

[3.93] James Dillon also vociferously condemned s 4 of the Bill as an impermissible intrusion by the State into the family which has rights precedent to the State.[219] School attendance, he asserted, was a matter for parents who, under the law of God, are invested with the duty of rearing the children.[220] In seeking to claim a pre-emptive right of control over children, as s 4 of the Bill proposed, Dillon alleged that the State was now taking itself into the very centre of the home and "eating at the foundations of the house." Opposition to the Bill intensified in the Seanad where Professor Tierney vehemently opposed s 4:

---

[214] See further *Dáil Debates*, Vol 88, col 1559, November, 1942.

[215] By excluding a knowledge of the Irish language.

[216] See Osborough, 'Education in the Irish Law and Constitution' (1978) 13 Ir Jur (ns) 145-180, at pp 157-58.

[217] See further *Seanad Debates*, 1942, Vol 27, cols 780, 228.

[218] *Dáil Debates*, Vol 88, col 1558.

[219] *Dáil Debates*, Vol 88,, col 1570.

[220] *Dáil Debates*, Vol 88, col 1569.

"Why should the State take on such powers? It [the State] wants to penalise people who do not like to see their children subjected to compulsory Irish. That is what the whole thing boils down to, as far as I can see."[221]

[3.94] A number of amendments were moved and either defeated or withdrawn and finally the Bill passed through both houses of the Oireachtas. President Douglas Hyde referred the Bill to the Supreme Court to test its constitutionality under Article 26. In considering whether the provisions of s 4 of the Bill were repugnant to any provision of the Constitution, the Supreme Court dealt mainly with the scope of the State's powers to require a minimum education under Article 42.3.2°.

[3.95] The next question was whether the State, in assuming such additional powers, had exceeded the limitations imposed upon it by Article 42.3.1°. The Court considered that the dominant rights in education were vested in parents and that the State could interfere only to the extent that Article 42.3.2° permitted it. While it is quite likely that the term "certain minimum education" was intentionally left undefined by the Constitution, the Court held that the State acting in its legislative capacity, through the Oireachtas, had power to define this phrase.[222]

[3.96] In delivering the judgment of the Court, O'Sullivan CJ was of the opinion that a definition of the phrase "certain minimum education" should give effect to Article 42.3.2° without violating any other constitutional provision. As to the meaning of the phrase "certain minimum education", the Court held that it indicated "a minimum standard of elementary education of general application" which might be regarded as "the lowest standard appropriate to the attainment of the common good."[223]

[3.97] Thus, the Court concluded that, if the State operated within the above constraints, it was free to legislate provided it did not require more than "a certain minimum education" and provided that in the manner of its application, school attendance legislation did not conflict with parental rights. While recognising the State's rights to require that children receive a certain minimum education, the Court held that the State is not entitled to require that such education be given in any specific manner. Accordingly, as the standard envisaged in s 4 of the Bill exceeded the above limits, it could not be justified under the Constitution. The court's objections to s 4 of the Bill were four-fold:

---

[221] *Seanad Debates*, 1942, Vol 27, cols 228, 247-5, 780.
[222] *Re Article 26 and the School Attendance Bill 1942* [1943] IR 334 at 345.
[223] *Re Article 26 and the School Attendance Bill 1942* [1943] IR 334 at 335.

(a) That if s 4(1) passed into law, a higher standard might be required by such law than that which was prescribed by the Constitution as a minimum standard (Article 42.3.2°).

(b) The standard contemplated by the section could vary from pupil to pupil and would not therefore constitute "a standard of general application" as envisaged by the Constitution.

(c) Parents of children over six years, who were being educated at home or in private schools, could be subject to penalties during the intervening period prior to certification by the Minister.

(d) The court found no constitutional authorisation for sub-s (1) which provided that not only the education but "the manner in which such child is receiving it" required certification by the Minister.[224]

Confirming the principle of a presumption of constitutionality in favour of a Bill or Act,[225] the court advised the President that s 4(1) of the Bill was repugnant to the Constitution. An attempt to redraft the legislation was abandoned, as serious problems arose in ascertaining the full implications of the Supreme Court's decision.

Presumption of Constitutionality

[3.98] The restricted meaning of the presumption of constitutionality has expanded since 1942.[226] In *Loftus v AG*[227] the Supreme Court held this presumption to mean:

"When legislation which has been passed by the Oireachtas is impugned on the grounds of unconstitutionality, a meaning which is consistent with the constitutionality of the legislation ought to be sought. If such a meaning can be found which does no violence to the language used and which is consistent with the object and purpose of the legislation then it is to be assumed that the Oireachtas acting within its constitutional powers meant the words to be used in that sense. But such presumption bears with it not alone the presumption that the constitutional interpretation or construction is the one intended by the Oireachtas, but also that the Oireachtas intended that the proceedings, procedures, discretion, and adjudications which are authorised, provided for, or

---

[224] [1943] IR 334 at 345.

[225] *Re Article 26 and the Offences against the State (Amendment) Bill* [1940] IR 470; *Ryan v AG* [1965] IR 294; Kelly, *Fundamental Rights in the Irish Law and Constitution*, (1967), Allen Figgis, pp 33-4.

[226] *Re Offences against the State (Amend) Bill 1940* IR 470; *Ryan v AG* [1965] IR 294: *McDonald v Bord na gCon* [1965] IR 217 at 239; *East Donegal Co-Operative v AG* [1970] IR 317 at 340-341; *Loftus v AG* [1979] IR 221; *Article 26 and the Regulation of Information Bill 1995, Re* \[1995] 2 ILRM 81, pp 16-17.

[227] [1979] IR 221.

prescribed by an Act of the Oireachtas are to be conducted in accordance with the principles of constitutional justice."

[3.99] Given the failure of the *Oireachtas* to define that pivotal phrase "a certain minimum education," it may be concluded that the Supreme Court's decision in the School Attendance Bill still stands as the recent case *DPP v Best*,[228] which is dealt with below, illustrates.

Home Education and Parental Rights

[3.100] Parents have a constitutional right to educate their children at home although this right is subject to the State's right, "as guardian of the common good" to require that the children receive a "certain minimum education moral, intellectual and social" which has not been defined in the Constitution, in statute or otherwise. The High Court has recently clarified some elements of this hitherto uncertain sphere.

[3.101] In *DPP v Best*,[229] which was a consultative case stated from the District Court, Geoghegan J determined a question arising in a prosecution under the School Attendance Act 1926 (the 1926 Act) as amended. The respondent had been charged with an offence under s 17 of the 1926 Act for failing to cause her three children to attend school. As has been seen, one of the four instances which constitute a "reasonable excuse" for non-attendance at school under this section is "that the child is receiving suitable elementary education in some manner other than by attending a national or other suitable school." In short, the respondent contended that she was educating her child at home and that she had a constitutional right to do so once she met the constitutional minimum requirement. The respondent outlined to the High Court her programme of home teaching for her three children which included:

- (a) daily "lessons" on weekdays;
- (b) Maths and English on a daily basis;
- (c) history and geography;
- (d) nature;
- (e) arts and crafts one or twice a week;
- (f) cooking;
- (g) weekly swimming;
- (h) library visits;
- (i) ballet lessons for the girl; and
- (j) some intersocial mingling with children and adults.

---

[228] [1998] 2 ILRM 549.
[229] [1998] 2 ILRM 549.

She reiterated her constitutional right to educate at home citing Article 42.2 and stated that she had informed the Department by letter the previous year of her intention to implement that right in regard to her children.

[3.102] With the encouragement of the respondent, the District Court judge arranged that an assessment be made by an inspector of the Department of Education and Science as to whether the home education given to the respondent's children amounted to "a certain minimum education" which is the only germane qualification which the Constitution imposes in regard to the parents' right to educate at home. In his report, the inspector found some aspects of the home education praiseworthy although he was critical of others. He noted, *inter alia,* that no provision was made for studying Irish although a trained primary teacher gave a weekly French lesson of one hour's duration.

[3.103] Geoghegan J concluded that it would seem to follow that an education that comes within the description of "a certain minimum education moral, intellectual and social" must necessarily be considered "a suitable elementary education" within the meaning of the 1926 Act. He was of the view that the concept of "a certain minimum education" was an evolving one and that the use of the word "minimum" did not indicate "some lowest common denominator" in regard to education. However, Geoghegan J considered that any reasonable standard of elementary education, which might be set down by the State would be considered as equating with the expression "a certain minimum education" used in the Constitution. With regard to the meaning and extent of Article 42.3.2°, and in particular the phrase "a certain minimum education," Geoghegan J noted it had not been defined by the Constitution and that accordingly he considered that the State, acting in its legislative capacity, has power to define it and that the phrase "a certain minimum education" should be defined in such a way as to effectuate the general provisions of the clause without contravening any other provisions of the Constitution. Subject to these limitations, the State, he held, was free to act, so long as it does not require more than a "certain minimum education" which in the view of the court indicates a minimum standard of elementary education of general application.

[3.104] All of this had already been established by the Supreme Court in *Re Article 26 and the School Attendance Bill 1942.*[230] Almost six decades later, the State has not statutorily defined "a certain minimum education" nor has it included such a definition in the Education Act 1998. However s 14(1) of the Education (Welfare) Bill 1999, provided that the Minister following consultation with the NCCA, may prescribe a minimum education to be provided to each

---

[230] [1943] IR 334.

child and that different minimum standards of education in respect of children of different ages and of different capacities may be so prescirbed.

[3.105] Geoghegan J noted the express constitutional provision permitting home education,[231] which is qualified by the State's supervisory right in Article 42.3.2° and the statement of non-interference implicit in Article 42.3.1°. He next referred to a pre-Constitution (1937) case, *Carberry v Yates,*[232] discussed above,[233] in which a Circuit Court judge held that the teaching of the Irish language was not a necessary component of a "suitable education" for the purposes of the 1926 Act. In his decision, Geoghegan J found that in the absence of statutory or other formal definition by the State of "a certain minimum education", it would be wrong for a District Court judge to go into fine details of teaching methods as different judges nationwide might form different views on its content and meaning and parents would lack security in supplying home education to their children.

[3.106] Such a regime, he held, can scarcely be viewed as properly vindicating the *prima facie* constitutional right of the parent to educate his or her children at home as, he added, "There is no vindication of that right if there is gross uncertainty". On the particular facts of the case before him, Geoghegan J ruled that the District Court judge would not be entitled to form an opinion beyond reasonable doubt that a suitable elementary education was not being provided by the respondent having regard to Article 42 of the Constitution.

[3.107] Finally, Geoghegan J stated that it was implicit in his judgement that he agreed with the late Judge Devitt in *Carberry v Yates*[234] that the inclusion of the Irish language in the curriculum, at least in the case of children not living in the Gaeltacht areas, is not essential to comply with the constituional minimum. It would seem, he stated, that what was contemplated by the Constitution as a minimum education incorporated basic reading and writing skills, basic skills in arithmetic and such other basic knowledge as might be universally taught.

[3.108] In addition, the judge stated:

> "Even if some educationalists might believe that there should be some teaching of another language before the completion of primary education, the respondent in this case has arranged for some limited teaching of French. Obviously if I am wrong in the view that Irish is not essential then there would be ample evidence before the District Judge to enable her to convict but for the reasons indicated I have held otherwise."

---

[231] Article 42.2.
[232] (1935) 69 ILTR 86.
[233] See above, para **[3.86]**.
[234] (1935) 69 ILTR 86.

Significantly, as the alleged offence was of criminal nature, the judge noted, the burden of proof falling on the District Court would be beyond reasonable doubt.

Implications of the Decision in DPP v Best

[3.109] In view of the earlier cases and in particular the *Re Article 26 and the School Attendance Bill 1942*,[235] Geoghegan J's decision in *DPP v Best*[236] seems well founded. Meanwhile, an appeal has been lodged to the Supreme Court. If the trial judge's decision is upheld, it will permit parents to educate at home without the necessity to include Irish as part of their education, provided such education meets the minimum standard to be prescribed by the Minister.[237]

[3.110] The minimum education issue should not be confused with the State's right and obligation to promote and foster the Irish language in schools generally and to require that teachers in recognised schools have some expertise in the Irish language.

[3.111] If the *Best* case is upheld in the Supreme Court, clearly it will be established that the State, in the past, has exceeded its brief, so to speak, by requiring Irish as part of "a certain minimum education".

The State and the Irish Language

[3.112] There can be little doubt, however, that the State has important obligations relating to the Irish language. When referring to Article 4 of the 1922 Constitution, in *O'Foghlúdha v McClean*,[238] O'Kennedy CJ held that the State has duties in education to establish and maintain the Irish language in its status as the national language and to recognise it for all "official purposes" as the national language.

[3.113] In *O'Murchú v Registrar of Companies and Minister for Industry and Commerce*,[239] O'Hanlon J stated that he was of the opinion that Article 8 of the 1937 Constitution was stronger still in giving recognition to the Irish language than was Article 4 of the 1922 Constitution. However, the inclusion of the words *by law*, (le dlí), in Article 8 indicate that this provision may be implemented by legislation only.

[3.114] Article 8 is merely declaratory. It is not formulated as a right nor is it placed alongside the fundamental rights but among the early descriptive Articles of the Constitution.[240] It is scarcely arguable, therefore, that Article 8.3 confers

---

[235] [1943] IR 334.

[236] [1998] 2 ILRM 549.

[237] See s 14 of the Education (Welfare) Bill 1999.

[238] [1934] IR 469.

[239] High Court, unrep, 20 June 1988.

[240] See generally O'Máille, *The Status of the Irish Language: A Legal Perspective*, (1990), Bord na Gaeilge.

any authority on the State to include Irish as part of the "certain basic minimum education" it may require the children to receive under Article 42.2.2°. Whether it permits the State to discriminate on the grounds of language in the provision of funds for the establishment of schools, is another matter entirely which is debated in Chapter 4.[241]

Parental Priority

Crowley v Ireland: High Court

[3.115] Even as late as 1980, the Supreme Court, in *Crowley v Ireland*[242] championed the primacy of parental rights in education to a degree that required only minimalist provision from the State during strike action by teachers. This case evolved from strike action over the appointment of a primary principal by a manager, who claimed to be acting on the instructions of the patron of the school.[243] State involvement in the case arose from the Department's supervisory role in teacher appointment.

[3.116] From 1 April 1976, all the teachers, except one, withdrew their services from the three primary schools in Drimoleague parish as a protest against a breach of the "Rules for National Schools"[244] by the manager in appointing a principal who did not have the requisite period of experience at the date of his initial appointment. Despite the protestations of the teachers' union, the appointee was retained in the post as a temporary principal and was finally sanctioned by the Department when he had the requisite period of experience.

[3.117] As a result of this action, formal schooling in Drimoleague parish was suspended until January 1978 when the Department provided buses to convey the affected pupils to outlying schools following successful injunctive action[245] by the pupils' parents. Following unsuccessful negotiations, the INTO issued a directive, on 1 August 1976, to its members in schools in neighbouring parishes not to enrol pupils from Drimoleague parish. Although the union withdrew this directive in June 1977, the plaintiffs, being unhappy with the alternative schooling provided by the State,[246] sought an order from the High Court directing the provision of free primary education in the parish of Drimoleague

---

[241] See below, para **[4.62]** *et seq.*
[242] [1980] IR 102.
[243] Doctor Lucey, then Bishop of Cork and Ross. See judgment of O'Higgins CJ in *Crowley v Ireland* [1980] IR 102 at 116; see further Farry, *Education and the Constitution*, (1996) Roundhall, Sweet and Maxwell, p 13.
[244] Rule 76 (2).
[245] Mandatory injunction granted by McWilliam J.
[246] Bus transport to outlying schools provided by the Department.

and as against the INTO damages for conspiracy to deprive them of their constitutional right to education after 1 January 1978.[247]

[3.118]The plaintiffs made no claim based on the educational facilities provided for them between March 1976 - 31 December 1977. Nonetheless, McMahon J, ruled on both periods:

(a) From March 1976 - 31 December 1977, when no buses were being provided by the State, and

(b) From January 1978 onwards when buses were provided by the State to convey the children to schools in outlying parishes.

In respect of period (a), the judge held that there was *prima facie* evidence of a breach of duty on the part of the State that it had failed to provide for free primary education for the plaintiffs and that the State had not displaced this inference.[248] Regarding period (b), the judge ruled that there was no constitutional right to have primary education provided within the parish of Drimoleague where the children lived once the education provided was reasonably accessible.[249] Thus, O'Hanlon J concluded that in the circumstances of strike action, after January 1978, the State had discharged its constitutional duty under Article 42.

[3.119] Turning to the allegations against the INTO, the judge ruled that both the action of the union in issuing the directive to its members in outlying schools and the action of the teachers in obeying this circular were unlawful.[250]

[3.120] The INTO did not appeal against this finding to the Supreme Court.[251] As the case against the union falls under employment law, that aspect of the *Crowley v Ireland* case will be discussed more fully in Chapter 11. The remarkable result of the High Court decision was that the manager,[252] who had breached the State's non-statutory rule on teacher appointment avoided liability, having received State sanction for his irregular decision, while the State was held *prima facie* liable only in a sphere in which it was not sued.

---

[247] *Crowley v Ireland* [1980] IR 102 at 112.

[248] *Crowley v Ireland* [1980] IR 102 at 112.

[249] *Crowley v Ireland* [1980] IR 102 at 113-114.

[250] See further *Hayes v Ireland, the Minister for Education, AG, the INTO* [1987] ILRM 651 *per* Carroll J.

[251] However, the union unsuccessfully appealed the amount of damages and the exemplary damages.

[252] And later the board of management.

Crowley v Ireland: Supreme Court

[3.121] Faced with the verdict of liability in the period from March 1976-December 1977, the three other defendants appealed to the Supreme Court which reversed the High Court decision. Kenny J was of the view that the Irish translation distinguished more clearly than the English between the duty "to provide for" free primary education and a duty to provide it. This distinction enabled the court to decide that the duty laid upon the State was an indirect aiding duty. Accordingly, it held in a 3:2 decision,[253] that:

(a) the provisions of Article 42.4 bestowed on the plaintiffs a right to receive free primary education;

(b) that the relevant duty laid upon the State under Article 42.4 was "to provide for" such education and not to supply it;

(c) that the absence of primary education in a district for a considerable period of time indicates *prima facie* evidence that the State is failing to perform its constitutional duty in that area.

(d) that the totality of the evidence in this case indicated that the State had not failed to provide for free primary education in Drimoleague.[254]

Given the opportunity to identify, balance and update the policies which underpin the broad statements of principle in Article 42, the Court delivered a remarkably minimalist interpretation of the State's constitutional obligations in education:

"However the State is under no obligation to educate. The history of Ireland in the 19th century shows how tenaciously the people resisted the idea of State schools. The Constitution must not be interpreted without reference to our history and to the conditions and intellectual climate of 1937 when almost all schools were under the control of a manager or of trustees who were not nominees of the State. That historical experience was one of the State providing financial assistance and prescribing courses to be followed at the schools; but the teachers, though paid by the State, were not employed by and could not be removed by it: this was the function of the manager of the school who was almost always a clergyman. So s 4 of Article 42 prescribes that the State shall provide for free primary education. The effect of this is that the State is to provide the buildings, to pay the teachers who are under no contractual duty to it but to the manager or trustees, to provide means of transport to the school if this is necessary to avoid hardship, and to prescribe minimum standards."[255]

---

[253] Kenny J, Henchy J, Griffin J, O'Higgins CJ, and Parke J.

[254] *Crowley v Ireland* [1980] IR 102 at 130, O'Higgins CJ and Parke J dissenting.

[255] *Crowley v Ireland* [1980] IR 102 at 126, Kenny J.

By directing its focus mainly on the past, the court sanctioned the inactivity of the Department of Education during strike action. As Casey has observed, with the exception of providing buses to outlying parishes, it was not considered mandatory on the State that during strike action it should provide substitute teachers, or remunerate teachers employed by parents or ameliorate the educational deficit suffered by the pupils.[256] The influence of the *Crowley* decision on the education system was quite profound for it seemed somehow to confer constitutional *sanction* on the State's *laissez-faire* approach to education generally and on existing informal arrangements for education, thereby delaying much-needed educational reform.

Analysis of the Crowley *Case*

[3.122] At a time when the provision of education was being recognised internationally as a national obligation falling on the State, the Irish Supreme Court concluded that the State was under "no obligation to educate".[257] Rather, the court ruled, the State must act directly to do so only when assistance to the church schools is not possible, or when the church schools cannot succeed in providing the necessary means.[258]

[3.123] Such a minimalist interpretation of the State's obligation in educational provision is difficult to reconcile with Murnaghan J's *dictum* in the Supreme Court in *McEneaney v Minister for Education*[259] almost 40 years earlier: "For now more that a century it has been recognised that the provision of primary education is a national obligation ..." .

[3.124] With the introduction of free secondary education in the 1960s, the focus of State provision had moved to second level education, a transition which took place outside the parliamentary process envisaged by Article 44.2.4°. At that time a number of spheres of primary education, which had not been statutorily protected, such as remedial teaching for weaker pupils and support structures for these children, were receiving sparse provision. A clear contemporary statement of the State's pivotal role in respect of primary education could have re-adjusted the focus of public attention and State provision on that pivotal sphere of education. Regrettably, the Supreme Court merely buttressed the *laissez-faire* approach of the State in education generally.

[3.125] Hence, it is strongly arguable that in *Crowley*, the Court upheld the principle of the primacy of parental powers in education, through the agency of the churches, to a degree that adversely affected childrens' rights. For, despite

---

[256] Casey, *Constitutional Law in Ireland* (1987), Sweet and Maxwell, p 519.
[257] *Crowley v Ireland* [1980] IR 102 at 126, Kenny J.
[258] *Crowley v Ireland* [1980] IR 102 at 123, O'Higgins CJ.
[259] [1941] IR 430 at 438.

the statutory enshrinement of the welfare principle in Irish law,[260] the Court failed to strike a realistic balance between the State's rights, parental rights and childrens' rights to education. This was particularly pernicious in view of the lack of statutory protection for childrens' rights to education.

[3.126] It was scarcely foreseeable in 1980 that the State's victory in *Crowley* would become the albatross it would fail to dislodge in the 1990s when it sought comprehensive reform of the education system. For it is in the contemporary debate on the ownership and management of schools that the *Crowley* decision has stamped its most indelible mark in that it imposed a crucial curb on substantive educational reform in the sphere of school ownership and school governance. The *Crowley* decision conferred constitutional recognition on the existing organisation of primary schools, on denominational school authorities and their boards of management;[261] and on the State's subsidiary role in education:

> "Thus the enormous power which the control of education gives was denied to the State; there was interposed between the State and the child the manager or the committee or board of management."[262]

Paradoxically, despite constitutional constraints on State action in education, the State had in practice acquired substantial control in education largely through the use of informal administrative measures. Indeed, the Irish system of education was considered by the OECD *Reviews of National Education Policies: Ireland (1991)* to be one of the most centralised systems in Western Europe.

[3.127] By bestowing constitutional recognition on non-statutory boards of management, the *Crowley* decision also sanctioned the existing minimalist parliamentary control of education. As Buckley points out, in the absence of statutory controls, it now seemed possible to construe this decision in a manner that could afford constitutional protection to individual managers or boards of management,[263] which could result in decisions taken by school authorities

---

[260] Section 3 of the Guardianship of Infants Act 1964 which provides that the court shall regard the welfare of the infant as the first and paramount consideration; also s 3(2)(b) of the Child Care Act 1991, which provides that the Health Board in exercising its function in the care and protection of children, shall "have regard to the rights and duties of parents, whether under the Constitution or otherwise and shall regard the welfare of the child as the first and paramount consideration."

[261] *Crowley v Ireland* [1980] IR 102 at 126-7. These voluntary non-statutory boards, which were introduced into primary schools in 1975 have no originating authority.

[262] *Crowley v Ireland* [1980] IR 102 at 126-7.

[263] Buckley, 'The Administration of National Schools-aspects of the legal and constitutional background' in *A Proposal for Growth; The Administration of National Schools*, (1980), INTO, p 78.

falling outside the control of the Oireachtas. Against this background, the necessity for a legislative base for education was self evident.

[3.128] It is submitted that these criticisms of the *Crowley* case should not eclipse its pivotal significance. The Supreme Court clarified the following points:

    (a) that the imposition of the duty under Article 42.4 of the Constitution conferred a right on citizens to receive free primary education;

    (b) that the State's general obligation in education was an indirect one;

    (c) that it was only when assistance to the church schools was impossible, or when they could not succeed in providing the necessary means, that the State must provide directly for education.

Thus, the seeds of future judicial developments in education were sown in the *Crowley* case, seeds which would take more than a decade to germinate.

The Right of the Child to Education

Report of the Constitutional Review Group

[3.129] It is generally accepted that the need to adjust the focus of constitutional reform on childrens' rights is long overdue. The *Report of the Constitutional Review Group* (RCRG) considered that conferring on the family unit rights which are described as "inalienable or imprescriptible," even if they are interpreted as not being absolute rights, potentially places undue emphasis on the rights of the family as a unit as compared with the rights of the individual within that unit. Accordingly, it recommends the removal of certain key adjectives such as "inalienable," "natural" and "imprescriptible" from Articles 41 and 42.[264]

[3.130] While this recommendation, if implemented, will permit much needed State intervention on behalf of the child, some may perceive these changes as a dismantling of natural law safeguards erected by de Valera around education as a fundamental right and around the family as constituted in marriage. The challenge lies in striking a judicious legal balance between the rights of individual family members and those of the family as the unit group of society.

[3.131] Such alterations seem necessary in order to achieve an equilibrium between the educational rights of parents, children and the State. By adding the phrase "in view of actual conditions" to the minimum education requirement, it seems the drafters intended that such education should adjust and adapt to the needs of a changing society. In a lecture delivered in the late 1960s, Professor

---

[264] At p 465 of the Report.

John Kelly argued that the standard and content of this "certain basic minimum education", in Article 42.3.2° must be resolved "in view of actual conditions" of society.[265]

[3.132] The *RCRG* recommends that the words "in view of actual conditions be deleted from Article 42.3.2°. If this matter is to be determined "from time to time by law" as that body suggest elsewhere, then the words "in view of actual conditions" become superfluous.[266]

[3.133] A further recommendation of the *RCRG* is that, notwithstanding the legislative protection of the child welfare principle, it would be desirable to include in the Constitution an express obligation to treat the best interests of the child as of paramount consideration in any action in relation to children.[267] This change, the author believes, is long overdue. The *RCRG* considers that Article 42.3.2° should refer to education only and that the various aspects of education should not be itemised. Moral education, however, is essentially concerned with character formation and conduct as regard the distinction between right and wrong and it is expressly within the State's educational brief. It cannot be regarded as wrong for the State to require a child to receive a particular type of moral education. The omission of the word "moral," the author believes, would be a mistake.

A Constitutional Right to Education

[3.134] Although Mill was of the view that governments should not interfere with individuals for their good, he was of the view that education was an exception to this rule as there are things of the mind the want of which is felt least where the need is greatest.[268] The right to education is expressly recognised in many international human rights instruments and conventions[269] and in the constitutions of many countries.[270] In South Africa, the recent constitutional negotiations leading up to the formulation of the right to education in the new constitutional text[271] were the most difficult of all the negotiations threatening at one stage to cause a constitutional stalemate.[272]

---

[265] See Kelly, 'Education and the Irish State', Ir Jur 1993, Vols XXV-XXVII, (ns) 1990-1992, p 81 at 84, 85.

[266] *RCRG*, p 466.

[267] At p 329 of the Report.

[268] Ginsberg, *On Justice in Society*, (1965), Penguin, citing Mill at p 118.

[269] The UN Declaration of Human Rights (1948); the UN Declaration of the Rights of the Child (1959); the UN Convention of the Rights of the Child (1989).

[270] In the constitutions of: Greece, (Article 16.4); Spain (Article 27); Denmark (Article 76); Finland (Article 13); the Netherlands (Article 23); Italy (Article 33, 34); the Russian Federation (Article 43); the Czech Republic (Article 33).

[271] Article 29.

[272] See further Potgieter, 'The Right to Education and the Protection of Minorities in South Africa: a Preliminary Perspective' in *The Legal Status of Minorities in Education*, de Groof and Fiers, eds, (1986), Acco, Leuven, p 423 at 428.

[3.135] Article 10 of the 1922 Constitution provided expressly for the citizen's right to free elementary education[273] rather that for the State's duty. This right was never fully invoked so the scope of the duty it imposed is unclear.[274] By contrast, the 1937 Constitution does not expressly provide for a right to education although the *De Valera Papers (DVP)* clearly show the original intention of the drafters to confer a right to free primary education.

Early Drafting Documents

[3.136] Preliminary drafts of the Constitution up to the First Official Revise, which was circulated to State Departments for comment on 16 March 1937, included an express right to free primary education.[275] *DVPs*, File 1066/9, undated, states in Article 38.1: "All citizens have the right to free elementary education." *DVP*, File 1078, dated 5 February 1937, states in Article 37(8), s 2: "Primary education is compulsory, and the right to free primary education is guaranteed." What appears to be the penultimate Irish text stated: "In a theannta sin, ní foláir don Stát cabhrughadh agus cur le tionnscnamh oideachais ... *agus go hairithe cuirfigh sé ar fagháil phriomh-oideachas in aisce ...*"[276]

[3.137] The question requiring an answer here is what impelled the drafters to exclude the express right to education, a change wrought by the inclusion of the phrase "provide for" *in lieu* of the word "provide" so late in the drafting process? It appears that de Valera's linguistic compromise[277] came about as a result of pressures exerted on him by the State Departments. The First Official Draft, with the exception of the religious article (then Article 45), was circulated to most State Departments for comment on 16 March 1937.[278] The Departments of Local Government and Finance expressed reservations over the envisaged direct provision of free primary education by the State. They feared that it could be construed so as to include the full cost of education including text-books and school requisites.[279] The Secretary of the Department of Education had already

---

[273] "All citizens of the Irish Free State (Saorstát Éireann) have the right to free elementary education".

[274] Letter from Seosamh O'Néill, Secretary to The Department of Education, dated 2 July 1994 contained in *DVP*, File No 1074 and in *SPO* File s 2979.

[275] *Cf* the views expressed in Farry, *Education and the Constitution*, (1996), Round Hall, Sweet and Maxwell, p 11.

[276] *DVP*, File 1073, Irish text, Alt 39.5, author's emphasis, which broadly translates "Moreover, the State must assist and provide for educational facilities and in particular it will provide basic education free of charge".

[277] Included in Article 42.4 on the 7 April 1937. *DVP*, File 1078, Article 38.1 (later 37.1) in which the words "provide for" are written in pen on the margin in what appears to be de Valera's handwriting.

[278] *SPO*, 9715/B (Moynihan's memo).

[279] *SPO*, 9715/B (Moynihan's memo).

expressed concerns in his letter of 1934 that the inclusion of a right to free primary education would be both litigious and costly as against the State.[280] On 1 April, the First Revise was circulated and was followed on 7 April by the Second Revise.[281] Section 5 provides: "The State shall provide (for) free primary education and shall give reasonable aid to private and corporate educational initiative ..." The word "for" is written in what appears to be de Valera's handwriting. The draft Constitution then read:

> The State shall provide for free primary education and shall endeavour to supplement and give reasonable aid to private and corporate educational initiative and when the public good requires it, provide other educational facilities or institutions with due respect, however, for the rights of parents, especially in the matter of religious and moral formation.[282]

The Third Revise (23 April) substituted the word "regard" for "respect" and this revise was enacted as Article 42.4 of the Constitution.

Judicial Interpretation of Educational Rights

[3.138] Articles 42 and Article 44 of the 1937 Constitution establish an intricate division of powers in education between the family/parents, the State and the child. Even though no express right to free primary education is articulated in Article 42, case law has held that such a right is implicit in that Article. The Supreme Court held in *Crowley v Ireland*[283] that Article 42.4 vests in each citizen a right to education:

> "However, the imposition of the duty under Article 42, s 4, of the Constitution creates a corresponding right in those in whose behalf it is imposed to receive what must be provided. In my view, it cannot be doubted that citizens have a right to receive what it is the State's duty to provide for under Article 42, s 4."[284]

The many changes in society since 1937, including the gradual withdrawal of the religious orders from education, increased marital breakdown and long-term unemployment, have influenced Irish life so that the circumstances in which the State must make provision for education have increased substantially. Recent case law mirrors this reality. The landmark case of *O'Donoghue v Minister for*

---

[280] In researching the *De Valera Papers* in the early 1990s the author noted the letter of Seosamh O'Néill in that file and also in the SPO file. See Glendenning, 'The Role of the State in Education in First and Second Level Education in Ireland', PhD Dissertation, Law School, Trinity College, 1996, unpublished; see also *Report of the Constitution Review Group*, May 1996, pp 342-345.

[281] Formulated from the contents of *DVP*, File 1079.

[282] *DVP*, File 1079/3.

[283] [1980] IR 102. See above paras **[3.115]** *et seq.*

[284] *Per* O'Higgins CJ.

Health[285] and other cases have expanded the right to education considerably. A discussion of these cases is contained in Chapters 4 and 5 below.

Constitutional Protection for Denominational Education

[3.139] Early drafts of the Constitution show that it was originally intended that only denominational schools would be constitutionally protected.[286] Following the abandonment of this approach, an edifice of implied protection was erected around denominational education in the Constitution which includes guaranteed property rights. In *Crowley v Ireland*,[287] the Supreme Court held that Articles 42 and 44 conferred tacit support on denominational education, a position that has recently been confirmed by the Supreme Court in *The Campaign to Separate Church and State v Minister for Education*.[288]

[3.140] Article 42 expressly recognises the right and obligation of parents to provide, according to their means for the religious and moral education of their children either in their homes, in private schools or in schools established by the State. Further denominational safeguards may be implied into Article 42.3.1° which guarantees that the State may not coerce parents "in violation of their conscience and lawful preference" to send their children to State schools or to any specific type of school designated by the State. Article 42.4 places a duty on the State in respect of funding for schools generally[289] and specifically for denominational schools while Article 44.1 acknowledges Catholic social principles, by recognising the homage due to God and by undertaking to respect and honour religion.[290] Finally, Article 44.2.6°, which is reminiscent of s 2 of the Maynooth Agreement,[291] copperfastens the property rights of religious denominations in that it guarantees such property "shall not be diverted save for necessary works of public utility and on payment of compensation."[292] This provision is, of course, an addition to the general private property rights in Article 43. Given this constitutional background, the question which next comes

---

[285] [1996] IR 1.

[286] *DVP*, File 1050/4, Summary Draft Heads of Constitution, Part IV, 4.

[287] [1980] IR 102; see also *McGrath and O'Ruairc v Trustees of Maynooth College* [1975] ILRM 166.

[288] [1996] 2 ILRM 241 (HC); Supreme Court, unrep, 25 March, 1998.

[289] See below, Ch 4.

[290] The *RCRG* have suggested the deletion of this Article or, if that is not deemed desirable or politic, its reformulation as follows: "The State guarantees to respect religion."

[291] First drafted in 1894 and redrafted in 1927, see Appendix F; see O'Connell, *A History of the INTO*, (1968), INTO, pp 44-5, 68-9.

[292] The *RCRG*, at p 468, recommends the substitution of the word "diverted" by the words "compulsorily acquired".

to the fore is, "do the voluntary schools have a right in law to insist on the protection of their schools' characteristic spirit or ethos?"

The Religious Ethos of Catholic Voluntary Schools

[3.141] One of the spheres which best exemplifies the difficulties in reconciling the tensions in education is reflected in areas where Church and State interests intersect. The owners of Catholic voluntary secondary schools[293] have recently reiterated that their legal and constitutional rights to the ownership of their schools severely limits the power of the Minister to introduce changes in their powers and duties, or to alter the fundamental nature of the school, except on a voluntary basis.[294] Because of the demise of the Education Bill 1997,[295] it was not necessary to challenge these matters legally.

Canon Law

[3.142] Central to the contemporary debate on ownership and control of schools, was the right of the school owners to retain, free from State intrusion, the school ethos or characteristic spirit of the school.[296] Canon law[297] specifies that the bishop of the diocese has the right "to watch over and inspect Catholic schools in his territory" and "to issue directives concerning the general regulation of Catholic schools."[298] A central feature of the trustee role is, therefore, the attempt to ensure that the school remains true to the intention for which it was founded.[299]

[3.143] As we have seen, there is firm support for denominational schools in Articles 42 and 44 and in the *Crowley v Ireland*[300] decision with its finding of implied constitutional protection for denominational education. Furthermore,

---

[293] Voluntary schools draw on Canon Law, Papal encyclicals, conciliar decrees and publications of the Vatican Congregation for Catholic education. See *The Catholic School*, (1977), the Sacred Congregation for Education, Rome.

[294] *Report on the National Education Convention,* Coolahan, ed, (1994), Gov Pubs, pp 131-132.

[295] This Bill, which proposed, *inter alia*, the establishment of ten Regional Education Boards nationwide, did not pass into law as the 27th Dáil had completed its term. Following a general election, a new government took up office and drafted the Education (No 2) Bill 1997 which was enacted as The Education Act 1998.

[296] See further the *Declaration on Christian Education* of the Second Vatican Council; Abbott, ed, *The Documents of Vatican II*, (1966), New York, p 639; the *Declaration on Religious Freedom of the Second Vatican Council.*

[297] The present Code of Canon Law, drawn up in 1983, includes a separate title (Title 111) on Catholic education, comprising 29 Canons, 10 of which deal specifically with schools.

[298] Code of Canon Law, Canon 806.

[299] Code of Canon Law, p 13. The school trustee shares a duty to ensure that policy and practice in their schools are informed by the distinctive religious and educational philosophy of the congregations they represent.

[300] [1980] IR 102.

Costello P held in *Campaign to Separate Church and State v Minister for Education*[301] that a Catholic ethos is not solely concerned with religious instruction but embraces religious formation which is best exemplified by a pervasive Christian atmosphere throughout the school.

[3.144] It is well settled in English,[302] New Zealand[303] and Canadian law,[304] that Catholic voluntary secondary schools differ from secular schools because of the doctrinal mission for which they were established which confers on them a distinctive character. Courts in those countries have recognised that, apart from its academic aims and objectives, the mission of the Catholic school is evangelisation and the Catholic school is one of the means by which the church works towards its goal of evangelisation. In the New Zealand case, *Rich v Christchurch Girls' School Board of Governors (No 1)*,[305] the Court of Appeal held that "the secular clause" in the Education Act 1964 (NI) did not apply to a voluntary secondary school. Thus the Board of Governors was held to be been justified in including or approving a form of religious observance during the daily school assembly.

[3.145] The ethos of a voluntary aided English school was recognised in *Choudhury v Governors of Bishop Challoner Roman Catholic Comprehensive School*[306] in 1992. The court accepted that this school had been established to provide education on Christian and specifically Roman Catholic principles. Thus, the court ruled that, in circumstances where the number of parental preferences for application exceeded the number of places available, the school in its admission policy was lawfully entitled to discriminate in favour of Christians and specifically Roman Catholics. Such a policy was considered reasonable in view of the fact that the school was established to foster and maintain a Roman Catholic ethos. Hence, it was not unlawful to have it in mind as a reason for refusing to facilitate the parental preferences of Muslim and Hindu parents under the Education Act 1980, s 6.[307] This case also indicates that religious discrimination, as opposed to racial discrimination, is allowed in certain English denominational schools so that they may retain their character and provide the specific type of education for which they were instituted.

---

[301] [1996] 2 ILRM 241.

[302] See *R v Lancashire County Council, ex p Foster*, DC, 16 May, 1994; *Choudhury v Governors of Bishop Challoner Roman Catholic Comprehensive School* [1992] 3 All ER 277.

[303] *Rich v Christchurch Girls' School Board of Governors (No 1)* 1 NZLR CA 1 at 16 *per* White J.

[304] *Caldwell v Stuart*, Canadian SC, 1984, Vol 2, 603-630.

[305] 1 NZLR CA, 1 at 16 *per* White J.

[306] [1992] 3 All ER 277.

[307] Section 6(6) of this Act, enables the Governing bodies of Roman Catholic (RC) schools to agree with the Local Education Authority (LEA) a limit of the non-RC children who may be admitted and some others provide that no non-RC children may be admitted.

[3.146] Other germane cases are dealt with in the context of employment law,[308] when discussing difficulties faced by some teachers, when their private lives conflict with the requirement to support the religious ethos of the employing school.

The Integrated Curriculum in Primary Schools

[3.147] There appears to be no objection to State provision of facilities for religious education when it is acting as the agent of parents who desire such education for their children. Indeed, Costello P, in *The Campaign to Separate Church and State Ltd v Minister for Education,*[309] held that there is a positive duty on the State when providing educational facilities to have regard both to religious education and religious formation of children. When such provision is made by the State, however, the Constitution requires that it does not conflict with certain liberal provisions in Article 44.[310]

The Integrated Curriculum

[3.148] As has been observed, Catholic educators maintain their right to have their religious values and attitudes permeate the full school day. Accordingly they do not draw a rigid separation between religious and secular subjects in the curriculum but rather integrate all subjects including religious instruction. This concept is generally referred to as "the integrated curriculum" and it was officially adopted as an upholding principle of the 1971 curriculum.[311] It has been alleged, that if the integrated curriculum is implemented in primary schools, it permits a religious ethos to permeate other subject-areas thus depriving numbers of children of other religious faiths, or none, of their constitutional right[312] to attend schools receiving public money without attending religious instruction at that school.[313]

[3.149] In 1991, a legal challenge to the concept of "the integrated education" was initiated by the Campaign to Separate Church and State with a view to having religious instruction in State-aided primary schools confined by time-tabling to one separate subject.[314] In view of the promised reforms in the White

---

[308] See Ch 11.
[309] [1996] 2 ILRM 241.
[310] Article 44.2.1°, Article 44.2.2°, Article 44.2.3° and Article 44.2.4°.
[311] *Curracalam na Bunscoile*, Cuid 1, Ch 1V.
[312] Article 44.2.4°.
[313] Alvey, *Irish Education: The Case for Secular Reform*, (1991), Church and State Books, Chs 1 and 2.
[314] Walsh, 'Legal Challenge to integration of Religious Studies', Irish Times, 17 September 1991, p 1.

Paper on Education, it seems, this case was abandoned. The human rights dimension of this difficulty is addressed in Chapter 8 below.

The Conscience Clause

[3.150] It will be recalled that the concept of "the conscience clause" has an ancient and honourable tradition in Irish education being one of the central tenets of State-aided elementary education in 1831 deriving from the "mixed education principle".[315] Subsequently, the Intermediate Education (Ireland), Act 1878[316] and the Government of Ireland Act 1920[317] incorporated "a conscience clause" to protect this specific right. When self-government was achieved, even though the State supported denominational education, both the 1922 Constitution of 1922[318] and the 1937 Constitution[319] continued the liberal protection clauses for children of different faiths in State-funded schools. Regrettably, this principle was not included in legislation in independent Ireland until 1998 (Education Act 1998, s 30(2)(e)). This latter provision is wider than previous "conscience clauses" as it extends to "any subject which is contrary to the conscience of the parent of the student or in the case of a student who has reached the age of eighteen years, the student". This "conscience clause" was regulated in the Rules for National Schools.

[3.151] As schools became almost exclusively denominational, this liberal protection clause was gradually diluted or overlooked. The 1947 Rules required the separation of "combined secular and separate religious instruction to children of all religions". However, intimations of change are apparent in the Preface of the 1965 Rules, which amended Rule 68 which deals with Religious Instruction:

> In the pursuance of the provisions of these Articles [42 and 44.2.4] the State provides for free primary education for children in national schools and gives explicit recognition to the denominational character of these schools.

The 1965 Rules, which at the time of writing, still apply,[320] omitted the earlier provision that teachers were required to be "careful in the presence of children of different religious beliefs not to touch on matters of controversy." As Hyland points out, this small clause had protected minority interests for close on fifty years.[321] In 1971, the State clearly sided with denominational interests when it

---

[315] See generally, Ch 2.
[316] Section 7.
[317] Section 5.
[318] Article 8.
[319] Article 44.2.4°.
[320] With a number of amendments effected mainly by Department Circulars.
[321] 'The Multi-Denominational Experience' in Alvey, *Irish Education: The Case for Secular Reform*, (1991), Church and State Books, App 3, p 124.

gave official sanction to the "integrated teaching"[322] of religious studies in the primary school curriculum[323] for the first time. Although, this measure was a significant achievement for church interests, it left State interests constitutionally vulnerable if educational legislation was enacted.

[3.152] Paradoxically, while the State acknowledged that the prescribing of religious instruction, its syllabus and its supervision were "outside its competence", it articulated a set of principles by which religious instruction is animated and incorporated in the curriculum of 1971.[324] With regard to the separation of religious and secular instruction, the 1971 Curriculum makes it clear "That the separation of religious and secular instruction into differentiated subject compartments serves only to throw the whole educational function out of focus ...".[325] By taking an overt stance in favour of denominationalism and by entering the realm of religious instruction, which is the domain of the churches,[326] it is strongly arguable that the Department exceeded its constitutional brief and that it also breached, at least, the spirit, if not the letter, of Article 44.4.[327]

[3.153] While the majority of parents, it seems, desire to and are entitled to secure denominational education for their children, there are other groups of parents who are exercising their constitutional right to have other models of education provided for their children.[328] It is incumbent on the State to reflect such parental demands in educational provision in a balanced and equitable manner, a matter which is discussed more fully in Chapter 4.

Philosophical Objections to the Predominantly Denominational System

[3.154] Clarke has raised ideological objections to the almost exclusively denominational education system.[329] Writing in 1985, he argues that a system in which denominational schools hold a monopoly in educational provision is by its very nature unconstitutional. His argument is not against religious schools *per se,* but rather against a monopoly of religious schools nationwide.[330] In making available religious schools exclusively in most parts of the country, he avers, the rights of children of non-believers or of parents who disapprove of

---

[322] It will be recalled that this was one of the suggestions in 'The Jesuit Submission' forwarded by Fr Cahill SJ to de Valera, see para **[3.30]** above.

[323] Which cites Rule 68 of the 1965 Rules.

[324] *Curracalam na Bunscoile,* Cuid 1, p 23.

[325] *Curracalam na Bunscoile,* Cuid 1, p 23

[326] *Cf* the role of parents in Article 42.1 and that of the State in Article 42.3.2° and Article 42.4.

[327] See also *European Convention on Human Rights,* Protocol 1(2) and Ch 8 below.

[328] *Report of the National Education Convention,* Coolahan, ed, (1994), Gov Pubs, pp 152-153.

[329] Clarke, *Church and State* (1984), Cork University Press, Ch 8.

[330] Clarke, p 219.

church schools are being obstructed by Church-State collusion in policy and planning.[331] Clarke contends that the fundamental inspiration of pluralist legal systems is that the rights of minorities are valued just as highly as the rights of majorities and that the legal system should refrain, as far as possible, from enforcing values which are patently religious.[332] He further avers that the only consistent principle, already explicit in the Constitution, is for the State to remain strictly neutral in regard to religious belief.[333]

[3.155] Due to the growing secularity of Irish life, the author believes that it will be necessary to find a more equitable balance between the constitutional protection of denominational rights in education and the safeguarding of the rights of those who profess other religious faiths or who profess no religion.

[3.156] Alvey expresses dissatisfaction with the State's policy of providing almost exclusively denominational schools and observes that though the Constitution places a legal duty on parents to educate their children according to their conscience, the State is under no legal obligation to help particular parents whose beliefs do not fit neatly into the two major categories allowed for in education, to meet their duties or assert their rights. That, he asserts, is a central question that needs to be addressed in legislation.[334] Tensions in this sphere of Irish education are unlikely to disappear.

The Constitutionality of Redeployment or Redundancy Panels

Primary Schools

[3.157] Non-statutory, redundancy or redeployment schemes have been established for primary and secondary teachers and the issue of the constitutionality of these schemes arises.[335] A redundancy system commonly known as "the panel" has operated for fully qualified teachers in Catholic managed primary schools for more than sixty years. This agreement was negotiated by the Catholic bishops and the INTO in 1937 and was later endorsed by the Department, assimilated into the "Rules for National Schools"[336] and extended to include teachers in Church of Ireland schools. An annual Circular is issued by the Department setting down the arrangements for each year.[337] As a result of this arrangement, a teacher whose post is suppressed due to insufficient

---

[331] Clarke, p 19.
[332] Clarke, p 17.
[333] Clarke, p 226.
[334] Alvey, *Irish Education: The Case for Secular Reform*, (1991), Church and State Books, p 19.
[335] The Republic of South Africa has also adopted similar redeployment arrangements.
[336] See Rule 97.
[337] See further Circular 4/95.

enrolment in one school has his or her name placed on a list termed "the panel" which acquires priority above all other teachers in the employment market.

[3.158] If any primary school authority has a vacancy for a permanent post, it must choose from "the panel" until it has been cleared. The "redundant" teacher continues to work in the original school until he or she secures a post in another school requiring an extra teacher. In this manner, continuity of service and protection is secured for the teacher. In the six decades of its existence, no legal challenge to "the panel" at primary level has ensued. Special panels also exist for members of religious orders and for special schools, multi-denominational schools and "temporary" teachers.

Redeployment in Voluntary Secondary Schools

[3.159] In the 1980s there was concern among secondary schoolteachers regarding school closures or amalgamation which was adversely influencing their career prospects. In order to give some continuity and security to these teachers, a redeployment scheme ("the scheme") for lay teachers in Catholic secondary schools under religious or clerical management was agreed between the Catholic school authorities and the ASTI and this arangement was endorsed by the Department. This panel is commonly known as "the main panel". The object of the agreement, which has been established on principles broadly analogous to those governing "the panel" in primary schools, is to secure continuity of service for lay permanent teachers in such schools.

[3.160] One distinguishing feature of the secondary teachers' scheme is that it is governed by an agreed administrator with whom, it has been judicially established, the teacher does not have a contractual relationship, when offered a position on behalf of a school authority.[338] The scheme lays down agreed procedures by which lay teachers may be redeployed to permanent teaching positions in the circumstances of school closure or where a teaching post is suppressed due to insufficient enrolment. The operation of the scheme, which was amended in 1995, is subject to annual review by the parties.

[3.161] Some time later, another panel was set up which gave similar rights to teachers who wished to be redeployed in other schools and this was also endorsed by the Department. Finally, a third panel was established known as "the supplementary panel" which was established with a view to assisting young teachers who were desirous of teaching in Catholic secondary schools. This panel would establish a priority system so that as vacancies occurred, those disappointed teachers, subject to suitability and qualification, would acquire the first offers of a position in order of seniority.

---

[338] *Fee v Meehan and Hyland* High Court, unrep, 31 July 1991.

[3.162] Criteria were then formulated for choosing teachers who would be entitled to be on this panel. As this arrangement meant that Catholic schools would be, on occasion, compelled to appoint a specific teacher, the school authorities wished to ensure that some arrangement was put in place to protect the Catholic ethos of the school. One of the mechanisms, among others,[339] which sought to protect the ethos was that, in order to qualify for the Supplementary Panel, a teacher must have taught for a minimum of two years in the same Catholic school, or taught for a minimum of three years in different Catholic schools. In order to gain access to this panel a teacher had to fulfil the conditions and achieve the requisite teaching experience in a Catholic school or in Catholic schools.

[3.163] In *Greally v The Minister for Education, The AG and the ASTI*,[340] a constitutional challenge was taken by a second level teacher, and a practising Roman Catholic against the supplementary panel. The plaintiff had not succeeded in fulfilling the conditions above as he was unable to gain access to temporary positions which would qualify him for access to that panel. Counsel for the plaintiff challenged the supplementary panel on the following grounds:

(a) that there is no power to establish the scheme;

(b) that the scheme infringes Article 44.2.3° of the Constitution;

(c) that the panel system is hapazard, arbitrary and unfair;

(d) that the Minister has infringed the constitutional right to earn a livelihood and has done so without statutory authority.

Having heard evidence from a senior official from the Department of Education and Science, Geoghegan J considered that, in all the circumstances of the case, the arrangement put in place by the supplementary panel was "a reasonable compromise arrangement which does not infringe the Constitution". He pointed out that if the Catholic headmasters had been compulsorily forced to accept the supplementary panel system, without having any control over the kind of teacher that would emerge from that panel, then the Minister would have been open to constitutional challenge as effectively undermining the right to denominational education.

[3.164] Geoghegan J alluded to the fact that secondary schools were not State schools but rather privately owned schools that are State funded. Hence, he was of the view that the conditions laid down by the supplementary panel are not unfair and had the merits of objectivity. He further observed that qualification

---

[339] For the full conditions required see *Greally v The Minister for Education, The AG and the ASTI* High Court, unrep, 29 January 1999 *per* Geoghegan J at p 5 of the judgment.

[340] High Court, unrep, 29 January 1999 *per* Geoghegan J.

for membership of such panel does not involve any enquiry into an individual's private beliefs or as to whether they practice their religion. Rather, all that is required is that they prove satisfactory service as a teacher for specified periods in Roman Catholic schools.

[3.165] Counsel for the plaintiff made the further point that, under the supplementary panel system an exception is made whereby a clerical teacher may be replaced by another clerical teacher and may effectively bypass the panel arrangements. Geoghegan J considered that this was a further compromise arrangement and an intrinsic part of the overall concern of the Catholic Headmasters Association to maintain the religious identity of the schools.

[3.166] The plaintiff's next contention was that the supplementary panel scheme infringed Article 44.2.3° of the Constitution which provides "The State shall not impose any disabilities or make any discrimination on the ground of religious profession, belief or status". Turning to this argument, the judge ruled that Article 44.2.3° cannot be read in isolation from Article 42 which preserves the parental right to have their children educated in denominational schools. He had already made it clear, he stated, that the scheme was not grounded in religious profession, belief or status. Neither, he believed was the panel haphazard, arbitrary or unfair. With regard to the challenge to the panel as infringing the plaintiff's right to earn a livelihood, Geoghegan J stated that because a person has a right to a particular livelihood, that does not mean that he has a right to receive employment from any particular employer:

> "The conditions in the Supplementary Panel system are conditions laid down
> by those employers in consideration of their agreement to honour the system
> and in assertion of the right to maintain denominational schools."[341]

[3.167] Furthermore, the judge pointed out that the plaintiff's livelihood was in no way affected as he had since acquired an excellent post with excellent prospects in the community school sector. As to the plaintiff's contention that his pension entitlement had been adversely affected, Geoghegan J was not satisfied that this was the case. He noted that the plaintiff was at all material times eligible to apply for a post in a Catholic school openly advertised.

[3.168] Summing up, Geoghegan J stated that the general thrust of this decision, based on the totality of Article 42, is that the State could not adopt a funding scheme for secondary teachers which effectively would destroy the denominational character of the schools requiring funding. Accordingly, it was, for that reason, reasonable that balancing conditions should be attached to the

---

[341] High Court, unrep, 29 January 1999 *per* Geoghegan J, p 11.

supplementary panel system. Thus, he considered that the plaintiff's claim was ill-founded and must be dismissed.

Redundancy in Other Schools

[3.169] In vocational schools, the right to transfer a teacher to any school within the jurisdiction of the relevant VEC is expressly within the powers of the vocational education committees.[342] Such transfers, of course, come within the scope of equality legislation and may be challenged on those grounds.[343] The Department has agreed to the setting up of redeployment schemes for teachers in community and comprehensive schools but at the time of writing no agreement has yet been negotiated. In practice, these schools are mainly in a developing situation. Where redundancies have occurred in the past, teachers have frequently been retained as ex-quota teachers. In a recent unsuccessful claim for unfair dismissal a part-time comprehensive teacher was granted redundancy.[344]

[3.170] These redundancy arrangements are not unique to Ireland as similar schemes exist in Belgium, the Netherlands and in the Republic of South Africa.[345]

---

[342] A VEC teacher who is an officer may be transferred to any school within the jurisdiction of the VEC. See further Farry, *Vocational Teachers and the Law*, (1997) Blackhall Press, p 76.

[343] One successful challenge was that of *Limerick VEC v Cotter* EE 11/1989 in which a single male teacher proved discrimination under s 3 of the Employment Equality Act 1977.

[344] 'X case author loses job appeal', Irish Independent, 6 March 1994, p 4.

[345] For a fine description of the South African system generally, see Beckmann, 'Creating a legal framework to support the provision of high quality education in South Africa', *Education and the Law* 9 (1997) 2 123.

Chapter 4

Educational Provision and the Constitution

Introduction

[4.01] This chapter and Chapter 5 consider current educational provision in the light of Articles 42 and 44 of the Constitution. The focus of these two chapters, therefore, is not the quality of education but rather the system of educational provision. Education has been a significant priority of the Irish State for many decades. Major improvements have occurred in the education system since the 1960s in terms of access and quality.[1] The proportion of total government expenditure on education rose from 16% in 1965 to 20% in 1993, while the number of students in the system rose by approximately 50%.[2] Despite the fact that Ireland has a much higher number of pupils relative to the working population than the OECD average, public expenditure in 1995 was only slightly above the OECD average indicating an efficient use of resources in education.[3] Indeed, this country's current economic success is frequently linked to the quality of its general education and the calibre of its teachers.[4]

[4.02] At the same time, respected international bodies have consistently noted the social and economic dimensions of failure in the system of educational provision. The OECD *Economic Surveys: Ireland (1995)* points to the fact that the Irish education system still falls behind the most advanced countries in a number of respects. Virtually one quarter of all students do not achieve a full second level education. Consequently, children from lower socio-economic backgrounds are almost five times as likely to leave school with low qualifications and face a 50% probability of being unemployed one year after leaving school.[5]

Identifying the Problem

[4.03] One of the primary objectives of free secondary education in 1966 was the abatement of socio-economic inequalities. Nonetheless, Hannan in 1992

---

[1] See *Irish Educational Documents*, Hyland and Milne, eds, (1987), Church of Ireland, College of Education, Vol 1, p 2.

[2] *OECD Economic Surveys: Ireland 1995*, p 70.

[3] *OECD Economic Surveys: Ireland 1995*, p 103.

[4] *OECD Economic Surveys: Ireland 1995*, p 104; see further Burke, *Teaching: Retrospect and Prospect*, (1992), Gov Pubs, p 8.

[5] *OECD Economic Surveys, Ireland 1995*, p 104.

found the outcomes of education to be "highly inequitable in social class terms ... class inequalities in educational failure are now so pronounced and so serious that a gross injustice exists in the educational provision for such children".[6]

[4.04] Some three years later, the OECD *Economic Surveys: Ireland* (1995) indicated that the quality of the education system, especially for pupils at the lower end of the ability scale was "not up to international standards".[7] One year later the *Social Fund: Evaluation Report "Early School Leavers"* (1996) found that the education system had not effected a parallel shift in quality and equity across the spectrum. This report further cautioned that if the system did not alter so as to accommodate the longer term education and training needs of early school leavers, this group would, in all probability, resort to anti-social behaviour the ultimate cost of which would far outstrip pro-active investment in the shorter term.[8]

[4.05] These salutary warnings combined to focus official attention on early school leavers in Ireland and since 1996 these problems have been addressed more seriously. A number of non-statutory initiatives have been established by the government in recent years to alleviate educational disadvantage.[9] At a time when the educational system is being re-cast in legislative form, full cognisance needs to be taken of upholding legal and constitutional principles so that educational policy and practice accords with social justice and with fundamental law.

Educational Disadvantage: Targeting the Problem

[4.06] The extent of educational disadvantage in Ireland is clear from the data for the period 1993-1995 (annual averages) based on Department of Education data which found that:[10]

(a) up to 1,000 students did not progress to second level school at all;

(b) 7,600 students left school having completed Junior Certificate only;

(c) 3,000 students left second level with no qualification whatever;

(d) approximately 7,000 students did not achieve 5 passes in the Leaving Certificate examination.[11]

---

6   Hannan, *Poverty Today*, July/September 1992, p 2; since then however, class inequalities at Leaving Certificate level and among third level entrants have begun to decline.

7   *OECD Economic Survey: Ireland* 1995, p 90.

8   *Social Fund: Evaluation Report "Early School Leavers"*, (1996), pvi at p 171.

9   'The Home-school Liaison Programme, Early Start, Breaking the Cycle'.

10   See Economic and Social Research Institute (ERSI) *School Leavers' Survey* (1996).

11   Figures taken from *Early School Leavers and Youth Unemployment*, Forum Report, No 11, National Economic and Social Forum, (1997), Gov Pubs, p 39.

Traveller children appear to among the most educationally disadvantaged as they comprise, it seems, the vast majority of the *circa* 1,000 who fail to attend any second level school.[12]

The Constitutional Framework for Educational Provision

Indirect State Provision of Education: The Norm

[4.07] As has been seen in earlier chapters, it was envisaged by a number of Government Departments that the enshrining in the Constitution of an indirect duty of educational provision on the State would inure the State from the full expense of provision, maintenance and equipment of schools and from the expense of providing school books, school requisites and school transport.[13] Traditionally, the cost of school books, school uniforms and school requisites has been borne almost entirely by parents.[14] Hence, the aiding character of the system enabled the State to generally share the provision of education with the religious orders and the dioceses.[15] In this manner, many benefits in education accrued to Irish society during the years when the State was grossly under-resourced and relied heavily on church participation in education. With the advent of a more prosperous society has come a more assertive State role in education which in turn implies greater State responsibility for education.

Educational Provision: State Obligations

[4.08] Article 42.4 lays down the core principles by which the State is to be guided in providing funds for education in what appears to be a pyramidical plan of diminishing obligation. At the base of that pyramid is primary education in regard to which Article 42.4 provides: "The State shall provide for free primary education ...". When construing these words in *Crowley v Ireland*,[16] the Supreme Court held that they impose a duty on the State which is of general application to all citizens and that the imposition of that duty vests a right to free primary education in all citizens.[17]

[4.09] The Court ruled that the State's obligation in education is normally an indirect duty albeit a continuing one. Taking account of both the English and Irish texts of Article 42.4, O'Higgins CJ considered that, in the case of primary

---

[12] *Early School Leavers and Youth Unemployment*, p 55.
[13] See Ch 3.
[14] Apart from a small grant towards the cost of school books, or of the cost of rental of school books for necessitous children.
[15] There are a few instances in which the State provides directly for education as in the six remaining model schools inherited from the nineteenth century system.
[16] [1980] IR 102 at 121, O'Higgins CJ.
[17] [1980] IR 102 at 122.

education, these words oblige the State "to see that machinery exists under which and in accordance with which such education is in fact provided".[18] He held that the State discharged this obligation by paying teachers in the national schools, making grants available for repairs and renovation, school buildings, making grants available for heating costs, school books and providing a proper curriculum and appropriate supervision in schools.

[4.10] Clearly the State's obligation does not end here, as O'Higgins CJ continued "it is only when such assistance to the church schools is not possible, or cannot succeed in providing what is required, that the State must act directly to do so".[19] In summary, the *Crowley* decision indicated that the State must act directly to provide for education in the following circumstances:

(a) if it is impossible to make provision through existing church-owned schools; or

(b) when such schools cannot succeed in providing what is required by way of provision; or

(c) when existing provision within such schools becomes ineffective or unworkable.

Even the discharge of these duties by the State, O'Higgins CJ stated, does not relieve the State or Minister of the further duty of pursuing "alternative or other means or methods" in order to provide the education which is constitutionally guaranteed to children.[20] The hierarchy for educational provision as laid down by Article 42.4 indicates that, in the context of limited resources, State initiatives seeking to secure the right to "a minimum education" for all citizens should be accorded priority in any national plan for the provision of education. Because, *inter alia,* of the dwindling numbers of religious in life generally and specifically in education, the circumstances in which the State must provide directly for education appear to have increased considerably since 1980.

[4.11] While the State is not constitutionally obliged to establish or administer schools, neither is it precluded from doing so. Article 42.2 envisages that State schools would be an option for parental choice. If a viable number of parents require the establishment of State schools, then, it seems, the State must provide them directly and fully defray the cost of such education. It is not inconceivable that State schools will become an option for parental choice in the future.

---

[18] [1980] IR 102 at 122.

[19] [1980] IR 102 at 123.

[20] [1980] IR 102 at 124, hence the injunctive relief accorded the Drimoleague children when the High Court required the State to provide buses to outlying schools.

[4.12] Since 1980, a statutory structure for the education system has been planned and the first educational legislation of general application since 1922, the Education Act 1998, has been enacted under which the State has important functions in education.

Priorities in Provision

[4.13] It seems pivotal to society that the State, as guardian of the common good, would set priorities in educational policy and practice. As a point of departure, the rights of the casualities of the existing system of education to "a certain minimum education"[21] require urgent attention. That this obligation is not just desirable or concessionary is clear as it derives from constitutional law,[22] equity and human rights law.[23] It is strongly arguable, therefore, that such an obligation should receive precedence over other less pressing forms of education. In the context of limited resources, initiatives to secure the right to "a minimum education" for clearly identified needy groups must gain priority over matters such as free third level fees and ensuring parental preference for alternative school types, where adequate provision already exists. Otherwise, the State may stand accused of discriminating in favour of certain classes of children while denying others their basic constitutional right (to a minimum education).

[4.14] Applying O'Higgins CJ's *dicta* in the *Crowley* case, it appears that the State must act directly to provide for education for those students who have already been identified as educationally disadvantaged.[24] Other groups who may fall into that grouping are:

    (a) those children who have been unable to gain access to mainstream schools or special schools because of severe or profound disability;

    (b) the unknown number of children whom schools have felt obliged to suspend or expel in recent years.[25]

    (c) children whose parents have failed in their duty towards them for physical or moral reasons.[26]

On the broad front, however, little progress can be made unless some definition of "a certain minimum education" is formulated.

---

21 Article 42.3.2°.

22 And the hierarchy which Article 4.2.4° appears to establish.

23 See the priority accorded primary education and those who drop out of that system in human rights law, *post*, Ch 8.

24 See below Ch 3, para **[3.115]**.

25 Of whom a recent Departmental Report stated "It is not possible at present to give any reliable measure of this phenomenon," see *School Attendance/Truancy Report*, Department of Education, 1994, at p 14.

26 Article 42.5.

Definition of Minimum Education

[4.15] During submissions to the Constitution Review Group, the Department raised the issue of the definition of "a certain minimum education". It expressed its concern that the absence of a more precise definition could leave the State vulnerable, in enacting any new school attendance legislation, to a charge that it is seeking to impose a standard which is greater than the minimum as envisaged by the Constitution,[27] or alternatively that it might be argued that the level of education as set by the State was too low. The Department's submission indicates that a provision in the Constitution to the effect that it is for the Oireachtas to determine the level of education required as a minimum may avoid these potential problems.[28] No such definition has been included in the Education Act 1998, or in any secondary legislation to date.

The Rights of the Child to Education

[4.16] Article 42.3.2° attempts to balance the educational rights of the family/ parents, children and the people in promoting an educated populace by permitting the State "as guardian of the common good" to intervene in education to a limited degree. Although parental rights are clearly the dominant rights in the Article, they are subject to the State's right to "require in view of actual conditions that the children receive a certain minimum education, moral, intellectual and social".[29] It follows that in order to implement the latter right, the State must legislate for such requirement[30] and the Oireachtas has sought to discharge this duty by enacting the School Attendance Acts 1926-1967[31] which require children, between 6 and 15 years, to attend school unless an exemption is secured under Article 42.2.[32] Section 14(1) of the Education (Welfare) Bill 1999 (the 1999 Bill), which was published on 28 April 1999, provides that the Minister, following consultation with the NCCA and others, may prescribe a minimum education to be provided to each child, to be referred to as the "prescribed minimum education". Regulations made by the Minister, under s 14(1) may prescribe different standards of education in respect of children of different ages or of different capacities (including physical, mental and emotional capacities).

---

[27] On this point see *DPP v Best* [1998] 2 ILRM 549.

[28] *RCRG*, (1996), Gov Pubs p 355.

[29] Article 42.3.2°.

[30] *Re Article 26 and the School Attendance Bill 1942* [1943] IR 334 at 335.

[31] Child Care Act 1991, s 25 amends the School Attendance Act 1926, s 17 thereby providing for the making of a care order by the relevant health board.

[32] See *DPP v Best* [1998] 2 ILRM 549.

[4.17] This provision is closely linked to s 15 which includes a set of provisions which aim to ensure that children, educated outside the recognised school system, are identified and that they receive at least a minimum education in order that the State can discharge its constitutional duty in this regard. This cohort of children will be identified through the mechanism of a registration system and early assessment of the education being provided to such children will be put in place so as to ensure that it meets minimum standards.

[4.18] The National Education Welfare Board (NEWB), which will be established under Part II of the 1998 Act will set up and maintain a register of children, of 6 to 16 years, who are receiving education outside the recognised school system. Following parental application, a child will be entered on the register provided the NEWB is satisfied that the level of education being provided is adequate. Parents must be consulted during the assessment; further, they may put forward representations and appeal the outcome under an independent appeal's committee.

[4.19] The reforms proposed in the Bill are praiseworthy, urgently required and long overdue. If implemented, they will address many of the existing deficits in the education system. However, the Bill deals with highly sensitive issues such as home education, parental rights, childrens' rights and the State's right to monitor the education received by its citizens. Accordingly, it is likely to have a controversial passage and may well be the subject of a Presidential referral to the Supreme Court under Article 26. Hopefully, the Bill will not be revisited by the "ghost" of the School Attendance Bill 1942, which is discussed earlier in this book.[33]

[4.20] Given this background, the recommendation in the *Report of the Constitution Review Group*[34] (*RCRG*), that the right of every child to free primary education should be explicitly stated in the Constitution, is timely. Regarding the Report's further recommendation, that the Oireachtas should seriously consider extending this right to second level education as this may be defined by law,[35] it is submitted that any express constitutional right to second level education should end at Junior Certificate level, thus ensuring priority for early education. This approach would:

  (a) broadly coincide with the upper age limit in proposed school attendance legislation (sixteen years);

  (b) target early school leavers;

---

[33] See para **[3.90]** above.
[34] (1996), Gov Pubs, p 465.
[35] *RCRG*, p 465.

(c) enable the redirection of national resources towards primary and early secondary education; and

(d) facilitate the realignment of contemporary practice in educational provision with the hierarchical plan for such provision as envisaged by Article 42.4.

The writer concurs with the recommendation of the *RCRG* that the rights and duty of educating children should remain vested in parents but that this right ought to be subject to the best interests of the child and to the right of the State to ensure that children receive a certain minimum education as may be determined from time to time by law.

The Constitutional Right to Education

[4.21] Prior to 1980,[36] there was scant recognition of the concept of free primary education as a constitutional right. It is only in latter decades that individual parents began to vindicate their childrens' constitutional right to education in the absence of supporting legislation, as was the case, prior to the enactment of the Education Act 1998. A body of recent High Court decisions, only one of which has been appealed to the Supreme Court, has obliged the State to make provision for the education of individual children mainly under the provisions of Article 42.4 or Article 42.5. In *O'Donoghue v Minister for Health*,[37] the Supreme Court ruled, *inter alia*,[38] that the State was obliged, under Article 42.4, "to provide for" the education of the applicant who suffered from severe and profound disabilities. This case and other related cases are discussed in Chapter 5.

Parental Choice of School

[4.22] A further dimension of the State's duty in education is that of pursuing "alternative or other means or methods"[39] of education in meeting the demands of parental choice. This obligation has been discharged by the establishment of new school types such as multi-denominational schools and gaelscoileanna. If the applicants comply with the required criteria for establishing schools, and no appropriate model of school already exists, then the State may act to respond to such demands either by providing a State-aided school or a State school. However, such initiative is subject to the phrase "when the public good requires it". The priorities of national policy and the constraints on public monies must necessarily set limitations to any such development.

---

[36] *Crowley v Ireland* [1980] IR 102.
[37] [1996] 2 IR 20.
[38] See the full order of the Supreme Court, Ch 5 para **[5.64]**.
[39] *Crowley v Ireland* [1980] IR 102 at 123.

Constitutional Constraints on Educational Legislation

[4.23] Legislation which provides for the funding of schools by the State, such as the Education Act 1998, may not discriminate between denominationally-managed schools unless, as case law indicates, the purpose of such funding is to facilitate the protection of constitutionally recognised rights or to permit the State to fulfil its obligation to respect such rights.[40]

[4.24] Section 12 of the Education Act 1998, which makes provision for the determination annually of criteria by which recognised schools or centres of education are to be funded, is subject to two conditions by virtue of Article 44.2.4°. Such legislation must not discriminate between schools under the management of different denominations, or prejudice the right of any child to attend a State-aided school without attending religious instruction at that school.

[4.25] It is notable that Article 44.2.4° prohibits only discrimination between schools managed by different religious denominations. As Walsh J observed in *Quinn's Supermarket v AG*,[41] although the Constitution reflects the firm conviction that we are a religious people, it does not prefer one denomination to another nor does it confer any privilege or impose any disability or diminution of status upon any religious denomination. Neither does it permit the State to do so. Arguably, Article 44.2.4° does not stand alone but is buttressed by Article 44.2.3° which further prohibits the State from imposing any disabilities or any discriminations grounded in religious belief or status. This provision has seldom been litigated in the context of education[42] but, with the increasing secularisation of society, this situation may change. One case which was grounded in Article 44.2.3° was *Mulloy v Minister for Education*[43] which will now be discussed.

Mulloy v Minister for Education

[4.26] In *Mulloy v Minister for Education*[44] an incremental salary scheme for secondary teachers, drawn up by the Department of Education was the subject of a successful legal challenge following its amendment by the Minister for Education. The amendment provided that specific teaching services overseas by "a lay secondary teacher" would be considered as qualifying for teaching service under the scheme. However, members of religious orders, such as the plaintiff, who had similar teaching services to the lay teachers, were not included in the scheme. On returning to Ireland from Africa, the plaintiff successfully challenged his exclusion from specific incremental increases. The trial judge

---

[40] See *McGrath v Trustees of Maynooth College* [1979] ILRM 166 referring to Article 44.2.4°.
[41] [1972] 1 IR, SC; see para **[4.85]**.
[42] See *McGrath v Trustees of Maynooth College* [1979] ILRM 166, Ch 3, paras **[0.00]**.
[43] [1975] IR 88.
[44] [1975] IR 88.

held that a discrimination had been introduced into the scheme by the amendment with regard to the plaintiff on the grounds of religious "status" and as such it was repugnant to Article 44.2.3° in that it had created a distinction based on religious status.

[4.27] On appeal to the Supreme Court, Walsh J stated that the reference to religious status, in both the Irish and English texts of the Constitution, related clearly to the position or rank of a person in terms of religion in respect to others, either of the same religion or of another religion, or to those of no religion at all. The Court approved *Quinn's Supermarket v AG*,[45] which was concerned with the constitutionality of an exemption granted to proprietors of shops which sold only meat killed and prepared by the Jewish ritual method.[46] In that case, the Court ruled that it was not permissible to create differences between persons or bodies or to distinguish between them on the ground of religious profession, belief or status, irrespective of whether the difference is to their advantage or disadvantage, except where it is necessary to do so for the implementation of the constitutional right to the full and free practice of religion as expressed in Article 44.2.1°. The court further held that Article 44.3.2° must also be read in the light of Article 44.3.5° which provides that "Every religious denomination shall have the right to manage its own affairs, acquire and administer property, movable and immovable, and maintain institutions for religious and charitable purposes". Dismissing the appeal from the High Court in the *Mulloy* case, the Supreme Court held the incremental scheme in question clearly violated Article 44.2.3° in that it created a discrimination grounded in religious status and accordingly it could not be allowed to stand.

Constitutional Protection for Non-Believers

[4.28] There is no express provision in Article 42 and Article 44 that protects those persons who profess no religion although in the *Mulloy* case the Supreme Court ruled that Article 44.2.3° contains an implied protection for such persons. Further support for such rights may be found in Articles 42.1, 42.2, 42.3.1°, 44.2.1° and 44.2.4°. As has been seen, case law has tended to interpret these latter rights against the backdrop of Article 42 which confers implied protection on denominational education. It may be concluded, therefore, that the general tenor of Articles 42 and 44 favours some form of religious belief.[47] In a

---

[45] [1972] 1 IR SC.

[46] It was alleged that Shops (Hours of Trading) Act 1938, s 25 was unconstitutional as it infringed Article 40.1 of the Constitution.

[47] In this regard, the Constitution seems to concur with Edmund Burke who stated: "we know, and what is better, we feel inwardly, that religion is the basis of civil society and the source of all good and of all comfort," see *The Works of the Right Honourable Edmund Burke* (1815), Rivington, Vol 5, p 173.

democratic society, this raises questions of justice and equity for non-believing citizens and for the establishment of schools which accord with their parental preferences.

[4.29] Clarke argues that constitutional protection for the rights of non-believers in Article 44.2.4° is inadequate since it only comes into force if and when legislation provides State funds for private (national) schools. The most obvious implication of the guarantee in Article 44.2.4°, he avers, is that is that the State should equitably fund a variety of religious schools,[48] if it funds them at all; its less obvious implication being that the State should equally fund non-religious schools which are managed by private groups of citizens.[49] There can be little argument with the fact that the State is required to respond equitably to the requirements of groups of parents who comply with the necessary criteria for the establishment and funding of schools whether they are religious or secular schools. Recently, parents and pupils at the Steiner school at Coolenbridge, County Clare, failed in their constitutional action against the State[50] seeking, *inter alia,* State funding for the school in accordance with parental choice. Only one of the teachers in the school had a qualification entitling her to recognition under the Rules for National Schools and so the school had been refused recognition by the Minister. Further difficulties were encountered regarding the teaching of Irish in the school.[51] The plaintiffs also sought a declaration that the Rules for National Schools, which delimited their right to provision for free primary education, were void and unconstitutional and that the rejection of their application for recognition of the school by the Minister was in breach of their constitutional rights under, *inter alia,* Article 42.4.

[4.30] With regard to teacher recognition, Laffoy J stated:

> "While the plaintiffs did not overtly suggest that there should be no prescribed standard at all, by seeking the relief they claim in these proceedings on the basis of the evidence adduced, in essence that is what they are doing."[52]

Turning to the teaching of Irish, she considered Article 8 of the Constitution and in particular the position of Irish as "the national language and the first official languages".

---

[48]   Clarke, *Church and State* (1985) Cork University Press, Ch 8 generally.
[49]   Clarke, *Church and State,* p 213.
[50]   *O'Shiel and Coolenbridge Ltd v The Minister for Education and Science and the AG*, High Court, unrep, 16 April 1999, *per* Laffoy J.
[51]   See further p 17 of the judgment.
[52]   At p 49 of the judgment.

She distinguished *Carberry v Yates*[53] and *DPP v Best*,[54] both of which dealt with school attendance issues. In line with what she considered to be the State's constitutional obligation under Article 42.4, the judge examined the issue of whether the prescription of Irish as a compulsory curriculum subject in primary schools, under the Rules, is a proper criterion for eligibility for recognition of schools in accordance with the purpose of Article 42 and the provisions of the Constitution generally. Laffoy J held that a duty to provide for the education of the children of the State, at their first stage of formal teaching and instruction, must involve an obligation to provide for education in the constitutionally recognised first official language of the State. Hence, she concluded that the requirement of the Rules, that teachers who teach in recognised primary schools should have proficiency in Irish, is a valid provision under the Constitution.

[4.31] Furthermore, Laffoy J held that it is a valid requirement under European law and in application to the facts of the instant case, and that applying the test laid down in *Groëner v Minister for Education*,[55] it is neither disproportionate nor discriminatory.

[4.32] With regard to the evidence, Laffoy J considered that the treatment of Irish in the curriculum of the Coolenbridge School, details of which were sent to the Department in 1994, was "totally inadequate" and accordingly, the Minister was justified in withholding recognition from the school.[56] Neither did the plaintiffs succeed in establishing that, in the prevailing circumstances, they had the right to require the State to fund Coolenbridge School in the manner in which recognised schools are funded and so they were not entitled to any of the reliefs they claimed.

[4.33] The judge regretted that the Court had been unable to provide any solution for this particular school and commended the strong commitment of the parent plaintiffs. She expressed a hope that some solution to the recognition difficulty would be achieved by the parties and subsequently awarded costs to the plaintiffs. The Minister has recently announced a new funding initiative for all new primary and post-primary schools, which is described later in this book.[57]

The Integrated Curriculum

[4.34] The *RCRG* does not recommend the inclusion of express protection of the rights of persons with no religion in the Constitution but states that "broadly

---

[53] (1935) 69 ILTR 86.
[54] [1998] 2 ILRM 549.
[55] [1990] ILRM 335.
[56] At p 55 of the judgment.
[57] See para **[4.69]**.

speaking, the existing provisions of Article 44 are satisfactory and have worked well."[58] However, the Report later contradicts that statement when it goes on to state with reference to the integrated curriculum:

> "In summary, therefore, the present reality of the denominational character of the school system does not accord with Article 44.2.4°. The situation is clearly unsatisfactory. Either Article 44.2.4° should be changed or the school system must change to accommodate the requirements of Article 44.2.4°."[59]

[4.35] The Report does not make suggestions as to how the school system might change so as to accord with Article 44.2.4°. It states that, because of the growing diversity of religious beliefs and secular opinions, this particular Article has, in the context of an integrated curriculum, the potential to be problematic.

[4.36] The legal principles of non-discrimination and the protection of the rights of children of other faiths or none to be withdrawn from religious instruction in State-funded schools, which are embodied in that Article, are time-honoured principles which have a long tradition in Irish law and in the jurisprudence of many European countries. It was observed in Chapter 2 that the latter right in particular was safeguarded by regulation in primary education from 1831-1971[60] and in secondary education in the Intermediate Education (Ireland) Act 1878.[61] Moreover, the White Paper on Education (1996) incorporated the ideal of pluralism as one of its fundamental principles and the Education Act 1998 (the 1998 Act hereafter) undertakes to respect the diversity of "values, beliefs and traditions in Irish society". Against this background, any notion of altering Article 44.2.4° in contemporary Ireland is quite unrealistic.

[4.37] In 1937, when the Constitution was adopted by the people, the periods of formal religious instruction were fixed so as to facilitate children of other faiths or none who wished to withdraw from this subject. Article 44.2.4° mirrors this practice and the Rules for National Schools further endorse it. The current rules (1965) state in Rule 69(2):

(a) No pupil shall receive, or be present at, any religious instruction of which his parents or guardian disapprove.

(b) The periods of formal religious instruction shall be fixed so as to facilitate the withdrawal of pupils to whom paragraph (a) of this section applies.

Rule 69(5) states that the periods of formal religious instruction shall be indicated on the timetable.

---

58 *RCRG*, (1996), Gov Pubs, p 369.
59 *RCRG*, p 375.
60 When a new *Curraculum na Bunscoile*, 1971 was introduced, see p 19 s(d).
61 See para **[2.41]**.

[4.38] Even though these Rules still govern schools, *Curraculum na Bunscoile* (1971) gave official sanction to the decision to construct an integrated curriculum which moved away from the rigid separation of different subjects. It stated that the integration of the curriculum may be seen "in the religious and civic spirit which animates all its parts."[62] One of the central tenets of this approach was "That the separation of religious and secular instruction into differentiated subject compartments serves only to throw the whole education function out of focus ...".[63]

[4.39] The fact that the rigid time-tabling of religious instruction was apparently no longer officially required gave rise to concerns among certain commentators[64] that religious instruction could occur in schools at any time thereby trespassing on the right of the dissenting child under Article 44.2.4°.

[4.40] If s 12 of the 1998 Act is to provide State funds for schools, it follows that the right of any child to attend a school without attending religious instruction at that school must not be prejudiced. This right, it seems, would be prejudiced by any *formal* religious instruction which occurs during the school day from which any child to which s 12 applied, would not be free to withdraw. Accordingly, the time-tabling of formal religious instruction appears necessary so as to facilitate any child who wishes to withdraw from such instruction.

[4.41] This is the position as set down in the Rules for National Schools (1965)[65] and it would appear to satisfy the requirements of Article 44.2.4° in this regard.

[4.42] Reflecting the fact that the Education Act 1998 provides for mainly denominational State-aided schools, s 30 of the Act confers power on the Minister, subject to consultation with the parties in education, to prescribe the curriculum for recognised schools, including the subjects to be offered and the amount of instruction time to be allotted to each subject.[66] It further provides that the Minister shall have regard to the characteristic spirit of a school or class of school in exercising his or her functions under this section.[67]

---

[62] *Curraculum na Bunscoile*, 1971 at p 19, s (d).

[63] Section (b).

[64] Whyte, 'Education and the Constitution: Convergence of Paradigm and Praxis', (1990/92) 25-27, Ir Jur (ns) 69; *RCRG*, Gov Pubs (1996), p 375; Alvey, *Irish Education: The Case for Secular Reform*, Part Two, p 36.

[65] Rule 69, in particular Rule 69(2)(b) and Rule 69(5).

[66] *Cf* the position of the Secretary of State in England who has power to prescribe the subjects to be studied in schools (10 in England and 11 in Wales) but is prohibited by statute from prescribing the amount of time to be spent on each subject. However, he/she may prescribe the attainment targets, the programmes of study and the assessment procedures at the end of four stages between 5-16 years of age, see Education Act 1996, Part V, previously in Education Act 1988, Part 1.

[67] Section 30(b).

[4.43] Accordingly, s 30(2)(d) provides that, without prejudice to the generality of subs (1), the Minister:

(c) shall ensure that the amount of instruction time to be allotted to subjects on the curriculum as determined by the Minister in each school day shall be such as to allow for such reasonable instruction time, as the board with the consent of the patron determines, for subjects relating to or arising from the characteristic spirit of the school and

(e) shall not require any student to attend instruction in any subject which is contrary to the conscience of the parent of the student or in the case of a student who has reached the age of 18 years, the student.

This provision envisages curricular areas which are likely to be sensitive or constitutionally vulnerable such as religious instruction[68] or sex education.[69] The sensitivity of some parents in the face of school-based sex education programmes was underscored by the threat of injunctive action against the Department and school principals which preceded the proposed introduction of the Staysafe Programme[70] into North Kerry national schools in 1993. Such "reasonable instruction time" in s 30(c), it seems, may include assembly, daily religious instruction, preparation time for the sacraments and other religious observances and practices.[71]

[4.44] Unlike the Rules for National Schools (1965), the Act does not provide that the periods of formal religious instruction shall be fixed or indicated on a timetable[72] so as to facilitate the withdrawal of pupils from religious instruction[73] as required by Article 44.2.4°. In short, with regard to the integrated curriculum *per se*, the Act is silent.

[4.45] Schools will shortly be required by law to publish, in such manner as the board with the agreement of the patron considers appropriate, the admission policy of the school.[74] This document will require careful drafting as any refusals to admit to the school must accord with such policy published under s 15(2)(d) of the Education Act 1998. Unlike most other countries, Ireland does not have a State system of schools or a secular body of schools running alongside the denominational schools and so, the denominational school may be

---

68 See Article 44.2.4°.
69 See *Kjelsden v Denmark* (1979) 1 EHRR 711, for further discussion of this case, see Ch 8 para **[8.35]** *et seq.*
70 A basic sex and relationships programme education.
71 On this see the *dicta* of Costello P in *Campaign to Separate Church and State v The Minister for Education* [1996] 2 ILRM 241; [1998] 2 ILRM 81 (SC) 25 March 1998.
72 Rule 69(5).
73 Rule 69(2)(b).
74 See Education Act 1998, s 15 (2)(d), also Education (Welfare) Bill 1999,s 19(1).

the only alternative available to pupils of other faiths, or none, in an area. Article 44.2.4° seems to imply that a school which is funded from public finances cannot simply confine its admission policy to pupils of one religion.

[4.46] Hence, it appears that a recognised school's admissions policy may not restrict its pupil intake to pupils of one religion only. Otherwise children of other faiths or none could be deprived of their constitutional right to education. However, there is a point at which a school may have a constitutional right, by virtue of Article 44.2.5°, to depart from its normal "open door" admissions policy, for example if its characteristic spirit is under a real threat of serious undermining, extinction or dilution as a result of a major influx of pupils of other denominations, or none, into the school.

[4.47] With regard to the right of pupils of other faiths or none, further difficulties arise from the implementation of the integrated curriculum in schools. The *RCRG* admitted that it was unable to find any satisfactory answer to the conflict of rights in Article 44.2.4° It stated:

> "The conflict lies between the right of the child (exercised through its parents) not to be coerced to attend religious instruction at a publicly funded school and the right of denominational schools, in receipt of such public funding to provide for the fullness of denominational education through the medium of an integrated curriculum and other measures designed to preserve the religious ethos of a particular school."[75]

[4.48] The *RCRG*, however, did not recommend the amendment of Article 44.2.4°, particularly in the context of Northern Ireland, as any such amendment "would send the wrong signal concerning pluralism in this State".[76] The author fully concurs with the *RCRG*'s recommendations. If Article 44.2.4° is to remain as it stands, a recognised schools' admissions policy and practice must accord with it. One significant step in that direction would be the time-tabling of formal religious instruction, at a time of the school day which would facilitate the withdrawal of pupils of other faiths and none, if their parents make such a request to the school in writing. Against the background of an increasingly pluralist and rights-conscious society, denominational schools will be required to strike a reasonable balance between protecting their ethos and respecting the religious and philosophical beliefs of diverse groups of parents and adult students. It will be for the judiciary to find an equitable balance in these issues when they come before the courts.

---

[75] *RCRG*, Gov Pubs, (1996), p 386.
[76] *RCRG*, p 387.

Facilitating Parental Choice of School

[4.49] In providing for education under Article 42.4, part of the State's obligation is to provide other educational facilities or institutions "when the public good requires it". In its response to this demand, the State is expressly required to have regard to parental rights particularly "in the matter of religious and moral formation". However, the implications of the parental freedoms in Article 42 and of the liberal guarantees in Article 44, would, it appears, require the State to respond equitably to the demands of a group of parents seeking to establish a non-denominational school provided the applicants comply with the criteria for the establishment of schools including the teaching of Irish and the requirements for teacher recognition.

Provision for School Accommodation in Practice

Traditional Arrangements

[4.50] Arising out of the arrangements in Stanley's letter (1831)[77] and consolidated by the principle of subsidiarity underpinning the 1937 Constitution, a percentage of capital and current expenditure of schools must be met from local sources (known as the local contribution). As already observed, the State pays the teachers' salaries in all recognised schools.

A. Capital Funding

[4.51] Denominational schools and multi-denominational schools have traditionally had one common funding criterion: the patron must provide the site of the school or the full cost of the site together with up to 15% towards building and furnishing costs. Should a vacant school become available, then the patron buys the site and provides up to 15% of the costs of the building and of refurbishment. In return for this commitment, the patron owns the school.

[4.52] In special schools, the patron must provide the full cost of the school site and normally 5% of building costs as a result of which the patron owns the school. In the case of gaelscoileanna, the State, which owns the schools, has provided from their inception for, the full cost of the site, the new building and furnishings. However, approximately 75% of these schools are in temporary accommodation and the State pays the rental costs. The *Report of the Technical Working Group*[78] shows that the level of capital funding for primary schools declined consistently from £34.26 million in 1985 to £16.71 million in 1990 and rose gradually to £30.70 million in 1996. Since 1990, however, there has been

---

[77] For Stanley's Letter see Appendix F.
[78] *Report of the Technical Working Group* (1998), Gov Pubs, Appendix 5, p 165.

virtually no demand for new denominational schools, the last such school being the Islamic school established in 1990.[79]

B. Current Funding

[4.53] Most of the current and capital costs of primary schools, including the full cost of teachers' salaries, are discharged by the State although it is supplemented by local contributions. Special funding arrangements are also made towards officially designated disadvantaged schools and for schools catering for children with special needs.[80] The 79 or so private primary schools receive no State funding.

[4.54] Provided a local contribution is paid into the school account, the State pays a capitation grant (currently £60) per student annually. At the time of writing, the local contribution is £8.50 for ordinary national schools and £5.50 for disadvantaged schools. Frequently, the total amount does not meet the needs of the school and further funds have to be raised by the parish. Much depends on the wealth of the supporting parish which is generally reflected in the physical resources in the school. Despite more favourable funding for disadvantaged schools, considerable distinctions in school resourcing persist.[81] The abolition of the local contribution which would bring much needed equity into the system.[82]

Permanent Recognition: Provisional Recognition

[4.55] Recognition of schools and the withdrawal of recognition is now covered by ss 10 and 11 of the Education Act 1998 as discussed in Chapter 6 below.[83]

[4.56] However, in the past new denominational schools and special schools have been granted permanent recognition by the Department at the point of establishment. Permanent recognition confers an entitlement on a school to capital funding immediately. In 1987 the Department introduced provisional recognition, for minority denominational schools, gaelscoileanna and multi-denominational schools, at the point of their establishment, which entitled those schools to the payment of teachers' salaries but not to capital funding. As soon as a school received permanent recognition, (normally from two-four years), it became entitled to capital funding. Due to restrictions on capital funding for primary schools, it could take up to fifteen years from the date of establishment for these "new" schools to acquire permanent accommodation.

---

[79] *Report of the Technical Working Group* (1998), Gov Pubs, p 154.

[80] *Report of the Technical Working Group* (1998), Gov Pubs.

[81] See further *RCRG*, Gov Pubs (1996), p 340.

[82] In her budget speech of Spring 1996, the Minister at that time, Niamh Bhreathnách, indicated that the local contribution would be phased out.

[83] *Post*, para **[6.52]** *et seq*.

[4.57] Because new denominational schools received recognition from their inception, provisional recognition was commonly viewed as discriminatory as against new school projects other than those promoted by the main religious denominations.[84] Furthermore, the *Report on the National Education Convention* confirmed that there was "unanimous agreement among participants at the Convention that the rights of parents to multi-denominational education should be respected and facilitated."[85]

[4.58] The Minister set up a Commission on School Accommodation to report and make recommendations on appropriate criteria and procedures for the consideration of applications for school recognition at primary level. The report of that Commission will now be considered.

Report of the Commission on School Accommodation in Primary Schools: Report of the Technical Working Group

[4.59] The *Report of the Commission on School Accommodation*[86] (the 1998 Report) by the Technical Working Group gathered information on current practice and experience over the past decade in the recognition of new primary schools. It concluded that the summary of documents on current practice by the Department of Education and Science reveals the urgent need for equality, consistency and validity in criteria and procedures for the recognition of new primary schools[87] and drew attention to the many anomalies in the existing system.[88] It observed a changing pattern in the establishment of contemporary schools pointing to the fact that of the 80 schools recognised between 1986-1997:

(a) 56 are gaelscoileanna;

(b) 13 are multidenominational schools;

(c) 9 are special schools;[89] and

(d) 1 is a Muslim school.[90]

[4.60] The diversity of the eight applicants, who were refused recognition, is apparent from the spread of applicants and school types: Catholic, Tridentine, three gaelscoileanna, one Seventh Day Adventist[91] and two private schools.[92]

---

[84] White Paper, *Charting our Education Future* (1995), p 32.

[85] 1998 Report , p 31.

[86] Department of Education and Science, (1998).

[87] 1998 Report, p 21.

[88] See generally Ch 3 of the Report.

[89] Some of these schools are under the patronage of the Health Boards.

[90] See Appendix N of the 1998 Report, pp 170-172.

[91] On the grounds that the teachers concerned were not qualified to teach in Ireland.

[92] 1998 Report, p 21.

While the 1998 Report noted that the main obstacle to the recognition of gaelscoileanna was achieving the necessary number of pupils for enrolment, the chief obstacle in the case of the multi-denominational schools was the difficulty of finding suitable accommodation.

[4.61] The 1998 Report observed new forms of patronage, mainly parent groups or parent-teacher groups, who have combined to form corporate bodies with charitable status, having little interest or capacity for school ownership.[93] The White Paper (1995)[94] had already identified school ownership-related problems and provided for a situation where education boards would "own new school buildings and properties for leasing to different groups of patrons and trustees". The 1998 Report recommended that, in the absence of education boards, the Department of Education and Science should implement this recommendation.[95]

Gaelscoileanna

[4.62] The creation of a distinct network of designated all-Irish schools, in areas where national schools already existed which are capable of satisfying the linguistic requirement, was questioned by the CPSMA in their submission to the *Commission on School Accommodation*.[96] The Catholic managers also queried the justification of additional funding and staffing concessions to this category of school and argued that the level of funding they enjoy (100%) should be extended to all schools. At the same time, the CPSMA reiterated its commitment to the promotion of the Irish language and suggested that Irish should be supported and widely used in all primary schools. There can be little argument with this last statement which has recently been upheld by the High Court in the Steiner school case[97] as discussed above.[98]

[4.63] In gaelscoileanna the State has provided the site of the schools, full building costs, maintenance, special pupil-teacher ratios and free transport. Extra grants are also paid to the teachers who teach in these schools. As both denominational, minority denominational, and multi-denominational gaelscoileanna exist, the State, in making such provision, does not discriminate between the denominations. Neither does it impose any disabilities or make any discrimination on the grounds of religious profession, belief or status.

---

[93] 1998 Report, p 71.

[94] White Paper *Charting our Education Future*, (1995), p 32.

[95] 1998 Report, pp 70-73.

[96] 1998 Report, p 29.

[97] *Shiel and Coolenbridge Ltd v The Minister for Education and Science and the AG*, High Court, unrep, 16 April 1999 *per* Laffoy J.

[98] See above para **[4.29]** *et seq*.

[4.64] In establishing gaelscoileanna, it can be argued that the State is discharging its obligation under Article 42.4 to "provide other educational facilities or institutions ..." in response to parental demands and with due regard for parental freedom (Article 42.1.2°) and parental choice of school (Article 42.3.1°). O'Higgins CJ, in the *Crowley* case, spoke of the State's duty to provide "alternative or other means or methods"[99] of educational provision when, *inter alia*, the church schools cannot succeed in providing what is required.[100] It is, of course the position that all national schools are capable of teaching the Irish language.

[4.65] Gaelscoileanna are owned by the State but, unlike the position in the model schools, the State is not their patron.[101] The legal status of these schools has not yet been judicially considered. Whether State provision for gaelecoileanna is constitutional or not seems to depend on the legal status of these schools. If these are State schools, then it seems, there could be no constitutional bar to their favourable funding or treatment as they would be on an equal footing with the model schools. If, on the other hand, the gaelecoileanna are State-aided schools, then the State appears to be discriminating in the funding of schools (under Article 42.4) which may well be unconstitutional. It is scarcely arguable that the protection of Article 8 extends to the provisions of Article 42 and relates to school funding provisions. It is conceivable that the favourable treatment and funding of gaelscoileanna may be surrounded by a degree of judicial suspicion arising from earlier cases involving State machinations in relation to the Irish language which are discussed in Chapter 3. Whatever the constitutional implications, there remains the disquieting fact that gaelscoileanna are more generously State funded than mainstream schools, than special schools and even than officially designated "disadvantaged" schools and so a question-mark also hangs over such provision from a social justice perspective. Yet, prior to s 12(4) of the Education Act 1998, which carries over certain existing funding arrangements, no law or constitutional provision expressly supported this funding initiative.

Differences in Enrolment Requirements

[4.66] It is reasonable for the State to require that new schools have a sufficient enrolment of pupils so as to ensure that public funds are not dissipated on non-viable and non-sustainable schools. However, the 1998 Report observed the differences in enrolment requirements between denominational, multi-denominational schools and minority denominational schools. In this regard, the

---

[99] A reference to O'Higgins CJ's statement in *Crowley v Ireland* [1980] IR 102.
[100] [1980] IR 102 at 123.
[101] See above, Ch 2, para **[2.63]**.

State can point to the fact that it is generally impossible to predict enrolments in minority denominational, multi-denominational schools and gaelscoileanna so as to ensure their viability and sustainability while projected figures for denominational school enrolments are readily accessible from parish baptismal certificates.

[4.67] It seems discriminatory that no requirement has been set down for a minimum total enrolment or minimum of junior infants in multi-denominational schools while in minority denominational schools, a minimum enrolment of not less than 24 pupils (of 4 years and over) on opening is required. Once again the requirement in gaelscoileanna to have an enrolment of 20 pupils on opening (who have not previously attended school) seems discriminatory.

[4.68] With regard to the constitutionality of the more favourable arrangements for special schools,[102] the State can show that the spirit and purpose of the favourable funding and enrolment is to facilitate parental rights under Article 42 in regard to the education of these special category children.

New Funding Initiatives: Ownership of New Schools

[4.69] The Minister announced on 10 January 1998, what he described as "the most significant change in the State funding of school capital projects since independence"[103] which is to become effective immediately. With the assent of the Minister for Finance, the State will offer:

(a) to provide the full costs for all new schools at both primary and second level.

(b) to reduce the contribution to the costs of new schools to 5% and to cap this figure at £50,000; and

(c) to reduce the cost of renovations, including extensions to 10% and to cap this figure at £25,000.

---

[102] Nine special schools were recognised between 1986 and 1997 as follows:

    (a) one residential school for young offenders;

    (b) one residential school for children at risk;

    (c) three schools in residential care units for children at risk;

    (d) one school for children with a specific learning disability;

    (e) two schools for emotionally disturbed children; and

    (f) one school for severely and profoundly mentally handicapped children.

Source: Commission on School Accomodation, (1988) Department of Education and Science, p 20.

[103] Press Release, 'Historic Move in State Funding for School Buildings', 10 January 1999, p 2, see Appendix E.

[4.70] Further benefits accrue to special schools and to officially designated disadvantaged schools where the local contribution for building work will be set at 5% and capped at £10,000.[104] One change of major importance in the new arrangements is that the schools thus provided will be in the ownership of the State and will be leased to the patrons under a lease or deed of trust. These arrangements make it clear that gaelscoileanna, apart from those already having permanent or temporary recognition, will be subject to the same conditions as denominational and multi-denominational schools. However, current arrangements still apply to all gaelscoileanna with either permanent or temporary recognition ie the State will provide the full cost of site and buildings.

[4.71] The denominational school authorities remain free to avail of the new arrangements for school ownership or they may continue to establish schools under the traditional arrangements as outlined above. While the churches will, no doubt, welcome the new financial arrangements, they may be likely to view the change in school ownership as a breach of the subsidiarity principle and a further attempt by the State to secure the ownership of all new schools.

Current Expenditure in Education

The Division of National Resources in Education

[4.72] In 1995, educational expenditure per pupil in Ireland was approximately two thirds the simple average of such a ratio in other OECD countries[105] despite the fact that approximately one third of State expenditure on higher education came from EU funds.[106] In apportioning the £2,196 billion[107] allocated to education in 1996:

    (a)   primary education received 32.3%;

    (b)   second level education received 39.1%;

    (c)   third level education received 23.7% and

    (d)   the Minister's office received 4.9%.[108]

[4.73] The £2,212,312 voted as Current Expenditure for Education for the year 1998 was allocated as follows:[109]

---

[104] 'Historic Move in State Funding for School Buildings'.
[105] *OECD Economic Surveys: Ireland (1995)*, p 72, (Diagram 21).
[106] *OECD Economic Surveys: Ireland (1995)*, p 110, n 31.
[107] Approximately 2.8 billion punts in 1998.
[108] Education & Living, Irish Times, 20 February 1996, p 16.
[109] Source, *Estimates of Receipts and Expenditure*, (1999), Department of Finance, Gov Pubs, p 7. The percentages have been rounded off by the author.

Level	1998		1999	
	Expenditure £	%	*Expenditure £*	%
First Level	1751.575,000	34%	778.163,000	33%
Second Level	861.391,000	39%	906.702,000	38%
Third Level	496.386,000	22%	568.725,000	24%
Ministers Office	102.960,000	5%	116.695,000	5%

Total Voted Current
Expenditure :   **3,212,312,000**   **2,370.285,000**

[4.74] The Official Estimates for Education for the year ending 31 December 1998 are as follows:[110]

Level	Expenditure (£)	%
First Level	774,353,000	32.7%
Second Level	864,092,000	36.5%
Third Level	531,072,000	22.5%
Minister's Office	196,973,000	8.3%

Total Amount of Estimate   **2,366,490,000**

[4.75] Despite the universality of primary education and its special constitutional position, the State contributes more generously to second level education than to primary education despite the fact that only children in the 6-15 year age group are statutorily obliged to attend school. The *National Economic and Social Forum Report No 11* (1997), using 1995 per capita costs for different levels of education, states:

> "the £11,400 spent by the education system on a child who leaves after primary school and the £15,850 incurred on behalf of a child who leaves after two years of secondary school, is in sharp contrast to the £37,525 spent by the State on behalf of a student who completes a four year programme at third level."

[4.76] Expenditure per student, according to level, for the year 1996-1997 were as follows:[111]

Level	Expenditure per student (£)
First Level	1,576
Second Level	2,483
Third Level	4,830

---

[110] Source, Department of Education and Science.
[111] Source: Department of Education and Science. The *Combat Poverty Fact Sheets on Poverty in Ireland* cite the per capita annual costs for the three levels of education in 1995 as follows: Primary Education: 1,425; Secondary Education: 2,225; Third Level Education: 3,750 Cited in *National Economic and Social Forum Report No 11*, 1997, p 56.

Third level education is, by its nature, more expensive than either of the other two levels. However, in view of the clearly identified deficits persisting in primary education, this apportionment of State resources can scarcely be compatible with constitutional provisions or with the common good of society.

[4.77] The OECD *Economic Surveys: Ireland (1995)* noted that participation in higher education varies according to income level.[112] This report found that between 1991-1993, children from higher level economic backgrounds showed an average participation rate of 57% in higher education[113] while the percentage of pupils from lower-status backgrounds who achieve the highest level of qualifications is extremely low with an even higher disparity apparent at university level.[114] Hence, it recommended that resources be concentrated on poorly-performing schools and pupils and on facilitating access to education for disadvantaged groups.[115] Significantly, the report did not recommend the abolition of university fees. Rather, its whole tenor suggested that the pattern of educational provision in Ireland, as it stood then, needed urgent re-adjustment in the direction of the disadvantaged in primary schools and in the lower levels of second level schools. While the State has begun to address this problem, it has been dilatory in taking these remedial steps.

The Primacy of Primary Education

[4.78] It seems that post 1966 developments, such as the introduction of free secondary education and the abolition of university fees became the focus of educational reform and provision to a degree that has influenced adversely on primary education. Apart from the function of the Appropriation Acts, major changes in the apportionment of national resources came about in a non-statutory manner despite the fact that the Constitution envisaged that legislation would be used for this purpose.[116]

[4.79] Against this background, it is not surprising to find that pivotal deficits arose in State provision for primary education which for many years remained

---

[112] *National Economic and Social Forum Report No 11*, (1997), p 65.

[113] This disparity, which was even wider among those students in universities, arose from three factors: (a) nearly 90% of children from higher status families complete second level education as against 68% of the remainder of the population; (b) in secondary schools, the academic results from lower-status families are poorer; and (c) the proportion of pupils from lower status groups who go on to higher education is lower than is the case for those with equivalent results from higher status backgrounds (except those very able students who progress to high education regardless of background). See pp 65-67 of the survey and diagram 17, p 66.

[114] *National Economic and Social Forum Report No 11*, (1997), pp 65 and 80 citing P Clancy, 'Participation of the Socially and Economically Disadvantaged', UCD and the HEA.

[115] *National Economic and Social Forum Report No 11*, (1997), p 68.

[116] Article 44.2.4°.

cloaked by the informality of the system and the absence of statutory redress. Crucial educational supports for less able pupils such as remedial education, counselling, assessment and treatment were frequently absent or grossly inadequate. Likewise, the social response to the enormous difficulties inherent in school absenteeism and truancy, especially among disadvantaged children, was totally inadequate and this issue is discussed more fully in Chapter 4.[117]

[4.80] Clarke argues that, from the perspective of justice alone, that those pupils in primary education should be favoured over others in the context of limited financial resources.[118] Writing prior to the abolition of university fees he considered the educational scheme in Ireland to be unjust in that the case for highly subsidised third-level education had not been established by arguments grounded in equality of opportunity. Accordingly, he continues, if education cannot be provided for everybody, then it should be paid for by those who benefit from it.[119] Identifying the main objection to the system in the 1980s, he stated:

> "the status of those who enjoy social and natural advantages in society is further enhanced at the expense of those who share the cost of the system but are prevented from using it."[120]

[4.81] The above factors appear to have contributed, in no small way, to the social phenomenon of the early school leaver which is considered in Chapter 5.

[4.82] Two dimensions of second level educational provision will next be considered from a constitutional perspective; first, the block grant for Protestant schools and second, the practice of reserving places for church nominees in community schools.

Second Level Provision

(i) The "block grant" for Protestant schools

[4.83] As Protestant children comprise a widely dispersed, dwindling population, in order to secure appropriate denominational education in accordance with parental wishes, they must attend boarding schools. The "block grant" which facilitates this education, currently amounts to approximately 3 million pounds and it is disbursed annually by a special committee.[121] In view of the prohibition against discrimination in Article 44.2.4°, the "block grant" to

---

[117] See the *Truancy Report*, (1994), Department of Education; see further O'Mahony, 'Punishing Poverty and Personal Adversity' in *Crime and Poverty in Ireland*, (1998), Bacik and O'Connell, eds, Round Hall, Sweet and Maxwell, p 49.

[118] Clarke, *Church and State* (1984), p 19.

[119] Clarke, p 195.

[120] Clarke, p 195.

[121] The "block grant" amounted to 3 million pounds in 1997/98 and the estimate for the year 1998/99 is 3.1 million pounds.

enable the provision of boarding school facilities for Protestant children is *prima facie* unconstitutional. However, a consideration of its underlying objective indicates otherwise.

[4.84] In this instance, a conflict arises between Article 44.2.3° which prohibits discrimination between schools managed by different religious denominations and certain rights guaranteed to parents in Article 42 such as the free profession and practice of religion and parental freedom to choice of schools. This situation is somewhat analogous to the position which arose in the *Quinn's Supermarket*[122] case in which Walsh J found the decision of Brennan J in *Abington School District v Schempp*[123] and other American cases,[124] most helpful.

[4.85] While the special funding accorded the Protestant schools is discriminatory on its face, the matter does not end there. As Walsh J observed in the *Quinn's Supermarket*[125] case, if the implementation of the guarantee of free profession and practice of religion requires that a distinction should be made so as to facilitate persons professing or practising a particular religion their guaranteed right to do so, then such a distinction is not invalid having regard to the provisions of the Constitution:

> "It would be completely contrary to the spirit and intendment of the provisions of Article 44.2 to permit the guarantee against discrimination on the ground of religious profession or belief to be made the very means of restricting or preventing the free profession or practice of religion."[126]

[4.86] Again in *McGrath v Trustees of Maynooth College*[127] the Supreme Court indicated that the spirit and purpose of the liberal provisions in Article 44 must necessarily be read in terms of their underlying objectives.[128] Approving the *McGrath* case, in *Campaign to Separate Church and State v Minister for Education*,[129] Costello P considered that if the purpose of State financial funding is to facilitate the protection of constitutionally recognised rights or to aid in their exercise by right-holders or to fulfil the State's obligation to respect them, then it cannot be constitutionally invalid to confer such aid.

---

[122] [1972] IR 1.
[123] (1963) 374 US 203, see particularly p 294.
[124] *McGowan v Maryland* 336 US 420 (1961); *Two Guys from Harrison Allentown Inc v McGinley* 366 US 582 (1961); *Sherbert v Verner* 374 US 498 (1963) and *Braunfeld v Brown* 366 US 599 (1961).
[125] [1972] IR 1.
[126] [1972] IR 1.
[127] [1979] ILRM 166 *per* Kenny J.
[128] *Post*, Ch 3, para **[3.44]**.
[129] [1996] 2 ILRM 241.

[4.87] Costello P's decision was upheld by the Supreme Court although it followed a different line of reasoning. Applying these well established principles to the implementation of the "block grant", it seems that the purpose, effect and spirit of this measure would be read by a court in the light of the inalienable right of the family/parents to provide religious education and religious formation for their children[130] and of the State's guarantee to respect that right. It is strongly arguable that in this instance, the State discriminates in funding between the denominations in order to vindicate parental choice of school as required by Article 42.1.2°. Furthermore, the State can argue that Article 42.3.1° precludes it from designating any particular type of school for these children and that it is through the medium of the "block grant" that the State discharges its obligation with regard to a minimum education as "guardian of the common good." Thus, the State can argue convincingly that the operation of the "block grant" is necessary for the implementation of the constitutional right to the full and free practice of religion as guaranteed by Article 44.2.1°.

(ii) Reserved places for church nominees in community schools

[4.88] The constitutionality of the practice set down in the Articles of Management of Community Schools,[131] which permits religious superiors, who were parties to the deed of trust, to nominate a number of their members[132] for appointment as teachers, provided they were qualified and approved by the selection committee,[133] has been questioned by some writers.[134] This measure, which became commonly known as "the reserved places clause" was highly contentious in the 1960s but became less so as the numbers of religious in post-primary education diminished.[135]

[4.89] While *prima facie* this initiative discriminates on the grounds of religious status under Article 44.2.3°,[136] it is most likely that the underlying objective, effect and spirit of the measure would be examined by the court. It will be recalled that when community schools were being established, many religious orders ceded their constitutionally protected property rights[137] and the goodwill of their schools in order to facilitate the new structures.[138] Given this context, a

---

[130] Article 42.

[131] See Draft Deed of Trust for Community School, Articles of Management, Clause 7 B.

[132] If one religious order was involved, the Mother Superior was entitled to appoint four such members; if two religious orders were involved that number was increased to six teachers.

[133] Under Clause 7A(c)(ii).

[134] See O'Flaherty, *Management and Control in Irish Education,* (1992) Drumcondra Teachers' Centre, pp 59, 67, 69-73, 134.

[135] O'Flaherty, p 59.

[136] See *Mulloy v Minister for Education* [1975] IR 88.

[137] Article 44.2.5°.

[138] Many schools evolved from the amalgamation of voluntary schools with other school(s) while others were new schools (greenfield schools).

court would probably view the "reserved places clause" as a compensatory measure which was necessary for the safeguarding of the denominational property interests and ethos of the voluntary schools and as such, it was required for the implementation of the right to the full and free practice of religion. Furthermore, the implementation of the "reserved places" measure would probably be viewed by a court as necessary for the full and free practice of religion and as facilitating the protection of denominational education in the light of Article 42.

Addendum

[4.90] Recently, the Minister, Micheál Martin, has announced significant funding and other measures to address educational disadvantage which will be phased in over a two year period.[139] These include the employment of 450 new teachers for remedial and other disadvantage uses, a major increase in adult literacy funding and almost £7 million to promote access to third level education. Capitation grants for primary schools are to increase by £10 per pupil while capitation grants to voluntary secondary schools will increase by £7 per pupil. The opposition spokesperson[140] pointed out that the biggest increase in the package generally was in higher education and that primary education was still "the poor relation".[141]

---

[139] Press Release, 'Martin Details £57 Million Plan to Tackle Educational Disadvantage' 3 December 1998, Martin, Minister for Education and Science. Detailed funding allocations involve:

    (a) £13.9 million for new teachers;

    (b) £12.2 million for issues affecting children with special needs;

    (c) £1.5 million for schools psychological service;

    (d) £3 million for other school disadvantage initiatives;

    (e) £1.2 million for early education particularly for children with disabilities;

    (f) £1.5 million for a stay in school programme;

    (g) £3.2 million for adult literacy;

    (h) £6.9 million for disadvantage schemes at third level;

    (i) £13.8 million for a range of other initiatives.

[140] Richard Bruton TD.

[141] See Walshe, Education Editor, 'Education spending to get extra 220m', Irish Independent, 12 December 1998.

Chapter 5

Educational Provision for Children with Disability

Introduction

[5.01] As Ireland is at a crucial stage in reassessing education, this chapter examines special educational provision from a comparative perspective. It will contrast and compare elements of such provision with that of a number of countries which have already legislated for the education of children with special needs. In the past, there has been a tradition in society to segregate persons with disabilities. Regrettably, the law has not only permitted such segregation, but has frequently buttressed it. Accordingly, the experience of many persons with disability has been one of exclusion from many meaningful spheres of life.

[5.02] In latter decades, however, the law has redeemed itself somewhat by playing a significant role in social reforms in many countries and in particular by enacting anti-discrimination legislation to safeguard the rights of persons with disabilities. While equality and participation lie at the core of law reform in this sphere, education holds the key to empowerment as it alone has the potential to unlock the door to equality and participation.

[5.03] The term "disability" in this chapter is used in the broader sense[1] so it includes those categories of children whose disabilities and/or circumstances prevent them from benefitting adequately from the education which is normally provided for pupils of similar age[2] as well as those children who suffer from behavioural disabilities or disorders.

Segregation of Children with Disabilities: The Wider Context

[5.04] Segregation of children with disability became a notable feature of the public system of education in the USA. Cook charts the laws enacted in certain American states which imposed segregation of, and discrimination against, persons with disabilities.[3]

---

[1]   *Cf* the narrow definition of "special educational needs" in the Education Act 1998.
[2]   See a somewhat similar definition of 'Special Education Needs' in *Report of the Special Education Review Committee* (1993), p 18.
[3]   Cook, *The Americans with Disabilities Act: The Move to Integration*, 64 Temple L Rev (1991) 393 at 400.

[5.05] He points out that children with disabilities were classified as "unfit for citizenship" under Mississippi law, "unfit for companionship with other children" under Washington law[4] and "ineducable" or "untrainable" under Pennsylvania law.[5] Between 1944-1970, English law also classified one category of children with disabilities as "ineducable".[6] Indeed, as late as 1993, Ireland's Department of Education argued in *O'Donoghue v Minister for Health*,[7] that children suffering from severe and profound disabilities were "ineducable" within the meaning of Article 42 of the 1937 Constitution.

Integration: The Way Forward?

[5.06] Latterly, a discernible worldwide movement towards the integration of children with disabilities into mainstream schools (mainstreaming) is apparent. It has been established globally for many years that children with profound mental handicap can benefit from formal education and this finding has become the corner-stone of international policies in education for this category of child. Since the 1970s, it has been the stated aim of EC policy to encourage such integration[8] although primary responsibility for the implementation of this aim rests with the Member States. Of course, the introduction of a policy of integration in any country presupposes that realistic pupil-teacher ratios are in place and that reasonable support structures are provided for this category of child from early primary schooling onwards.

Legislative Provision in Europe

[5.07] Some European countries such as Finland[9] and Portugal[10] expressly protect the right to special education in their constitutional provisions. Other countries, and this appears to be the norm, have made statutory provision for the

---

4 Cook, pp 400-401.

5 See *Pennsylvania Association for Retarded Children (PARC) v Pennsylvania* (1971) 343 F Supp 279 (ED Pa 1972).

6 See below, para **[5.21]**.

7 [1996] 2 IR 20.

8 See Council Resolution of 27 June 1974 which outlines an early Community Action Programme for the vocational training of handicapped persons, OJ C 09.06.74, 80/30; Council Decision 88/231/EEC (Helios) of 18 April 1988 which set up a second community action programme for the disabled, OJ L 23.04.88, 104/38; Council Decision 93/136/EEC (Helios 2) of 25 February 1993 establishing a second community action programme for the disabled.

9 Article 13 of the Finnish Constitution provides that free elementary schooling shall be available to all people and that the government shall also provide for special education according to the ability or special needs of the students.

10 The Portuguese Constitution permits positive discrimination on behalf of handicapped children; see Barbas Homen, 'Right to Education and Minorities, Portuguese Report' in *The Legal Status of Minorities in Education*, de Goof and Fiers, eds, (1996) Acco, Leuven, p 273 at p 281.

education of such children. International experience generally has shown that separate disability legislation is necessary for effective change in this sphere.[11] Separate legislation has been enacted in the USA (Americans with Disabilities Act 1990), Australia (Disability Discrimination Act 1992)[12] and Canada (The Act to amend Certain Acts with respect to Persons with Disability 1992, commonly known as the Omnibus Act).[13]

[5.08] Following a long and controversial debate, Austria has legislated for the integration of children with disabilities into mainstream primary schools in the School Organisation Act 1993. Under the Compulsory School Act, parents are required to register these children at the local primary school as soon as they are of school age when the principal decides whether he is capable of attending a primary school.

[5.09] An administrative appeal lies from that decision to both district and provincial education authorities.

[5.10] Under the law, a mainstream primary school class may not accommodate more than four pupils with special needs. Such classes have a favourable pupil-teacher ratio and frequently have a second teacher.[14]

[5.11] The integration of all handicapped pupils in mainstream education is also part of Norwegian education policy where all children have a statutory right to special education if they are deemed to require such, following a medical examination. In Norway, children classified as in need of special education also have a statutory right to free transporation to school or a right to be housed in or at their school. Pre-school children in Norway, with a specific need, also have a statutory right to special education.[15]

---

[11] See generally Quinn, McDonagh and Kimber, *Disability Discrimination Law in the United States, Australia and Canada*, (1993) Oak Tree Press in Association with the National Rehabilitation Board.

[12] Section 22 prohibits discrimination in respect of admission of students, denial of benefits, expulsion and subjection of the student to any detriment; see further McDonagh, 'Disability Discrimination Law in Australia' in *Disability Discrimination Law*, (1993), pp 119-162.

[13] See Kimber, 'Disability Discrimination Law in Canada' in *Disability Discrimination Law*, (1993), pp 165-219.

[14] See further Fankhauser, 'Development of education law on schools in Austria (1993-1996), Part 1: Schools', in *European Journal for Education Law and Policy*, (1997) Kluwer Law International, Vol 1-2, 101 at 103.

[15] See Dahl, 'The Right to Education: The Legal Position of Minorities in Education in Norway' in *The Legal Status of Minorities in Education*, de Groof and Fiers eds, (1996) Acco, Leuven, pp 349-355.

Provision in the United States of America

Background

[5.12] There is no specific "right to education" in the United States Federal Constitution. In time, however, the courts became a pivotal agent in the process which placed special education on the federal agenda. It was the celebrated case of *Brown v Board of Education*[16] which placed the Supreme Court at the centre of the education policy debate. Racial inequality, arising from legally sanctioned segregation of students, was at issue in the *Brown* decision, but its influence escalated and in time encompassed matters of equity in public education.[17] By articulating the view that it is doubtful that any child may reasonably be expected to succeed in life if he or she is denied the opportunity of an education and by holding that separate education facilities conflicted with the Fourteenth Amendment's equal protection guarantee, the court laid the foundations on which subsequent rights-seekers built including separately schooled children with disability. It was as a result of the *Brown* decision that the concept of rights and due process procedures were introduced into schools that had earlier relied upon the discretion of teachers and school administrators.[18]

[5.13] Some twenty years later, the case of *Pennsylvania Association for Retarded Children (PARC) v Pennsylvania*[19] applied similar reasoning to that of *Brown* to the circumstances of children with disabilities. By linking their educational needs to the equal protection safeguards embodied in the Fourteenth Amendment, the court drew the attention of Congress to the urgent need for comprehensive legislation for this group of children. The final court order prohibited the defendants from applying statutes excluding mentally retarded students from public education and it further obliged them "to provide every retarded child [with] access to a free public programme of education and training appropriate to his or her learning capacities". Further detailed provision was made in the court order outlining the procedures necessary for classifying mentally retarded children together with a full range of due process procedures requirements. Shortly afterwards, a Federal district court, in *Mills v Board of Education of District of Columbia*,[20] affirmed the rights established in the *PARC* case and extended them to all handicapped children.

---

[16] (1954) 347 US 483, 495.

[17] See further Kirp, 'Introduction: The Fourth R: Reading, Writing, 'Rithmetic and Rules'; in Kirp and Jensen, eds, *School Days, Rule Days, The Legalization and Regulation of Education,* (1986) The Falmer Press, p 1.

[18] See Neal and Kirp, 'The Allure of Legalization Reconsidered: The Case of Special Education' in *Law and Contemporary Problems*, (1985), Vol 48 1, p 61.

[19] 343 F Supp 279 (ED Pa 1972).

[20] (1922) 348 F Supp 866 (DDC 1972).

From Test Case to Legislative Provision

[5.14] Widespread publicity concerning the unequal treatment of those with disabilities resulted in the protection of the handicapped in the Rehabilitation Act 1973.[21] The following year the Education of the Handicapped Amendments Act 1974 provided for a statutory "right to education" for children with disabilities together with grants for the integration of children with disabilities into mainstream schools (mainstreaming). However, there can be little doubt that the most important statute was and remains, the Education for All Handicapped Children Act 1975 later retitled the Individuals with Disabilities Education Act 1990 (IDEA).[22] The latter Act confers a right on all children with disabilities, no matter how profound or severe their handicap, to a "free and appropriate public education" in publicly funded schools thus taking the concept of mainstreaming another step further. In *Board of Education v Rowley*,[23] the US Supreme Court stated that the purpose of the IDEA was more to make public education accessible to children (with disabilities) on appropriate terms than to guarantee any particular level of education once inside.[24]

[5.15] Once a child is categorised as handicapped within the meaning of the IDEA, they are entitled to services thereunder. The 1990 Act also entitles parents to a free independent determination as to whether their child falls into the category of handicapped as classified under the IDEA. Such classification is widely drafted[25] and includes children with serious emotional disturbance and specific learning disabilities. When a child is identified as falling within the ambit of the IDEA, a specialist team meet to draft a written Individualised Education Plan (IEP)[26] and the child is then placed in an appropriate educational environment. If unhappy with either the determination, the procedures followed or their outcome, parents who are central to all such decisions, may initiate administrative or judicial review proceedings.

---

[21] Section 504.

[22] Effected by the Education of the Handicapped Amendments Act 1990.

[23] (1982) 458 US 176.

[24] (1982) 458 US 176 at 192.

[25] It includes children with (a) mental retardation, hearing impairments, visual impairments, speech or language impairments, blindness, serious emotional disturbance, orthopedic impairments, autism, traumatic brain injury, other health impairments, specific learning disabilities and (b) who, by reason thereof need special education and related services, 20 USC 1401 (a)(1) (A)-(B).

[26] See Neal and Kirp, 'The Allure of Legalization Reconsidered: The Case of Special Education' in *Law and Contemporary Problems*, Vol 48 1 (1985), p 71; Quinn *et al*, *Disability discrimination Law in the United States, Australia and Canada*, (1993) Oak Tree Press in association with the National Rehabilitation Board, p 29.

[5.16] Although the IDEA requires public school districts to implement the concept of mainstreaming to the maximum extent appropriate, not all pupils are suited to mainstreaming. Clearly, these requirements have to be weighed against the legitimate educational needs of other pupils in the school together with the budget of programme administration and resources.[27] In one instance, a pupil who was suffering from severe behavioural difficulties, due to Downs Syndrome, was held by the court as not requiring mainstreaming.[28] Another 17 year-old boy with autism, who required a different educational pace of learning pattern, was considered as requiring provision other than a mainstream classroom.[29]

Provision of "Related Services"

[5.17] Further statutory duties under the IDEA fall on public school districts to make provision for "related services" for children with disabilities in schools. Such services include transportation and support services such as speech pathology and audiology, psychological services, physical and occupational therapy, recreation, early identification and assessment of disabilities in children, counselling and medical services for diagnostic or evaluation purposes, school health services, social work services and parent counselling and training.[30]

A Legislative Landmark: The Americans with Disabilities Act 1990

[5.18] Progress in education remains limited, however, unless discrimination in the wider life is addressed. Political demands for major reform of the growing body of discrimination legislation finally bore fruit when the landmark Americans with Disabilities Act 1990 was enacted. This comprehensive statute prohibits discrimination against individuals with disabilities, in education, housing, public accommodation, communication, transportation, recreation, institutionalisation, health services, voting and access to public services and employment.

[5.19] The Act also prohibits discrimination in employment against qualified persons with disabilities where employers have 15 or more employees. Rather than imposing quotas, it seeks to ensure that persons with disability, who are capable of working, are not excluded from the labour market.

---

[27] See Lane, 'The Use of the Least Restrictive Environment Principle in Placements Decisions Affecting School-Age Students with Disabilities', (1992) 69 Univ of Detroit, Mercy L Rev 291.

[28] *David D v Dartford School Committee* (1985) 775 F 2d 411.

[29] *De Vries v Fairfax Co Field Board* (1988) 882 F 2d 876.

[30] 34 CFR 300 13 (a).

Provision in England

[5.20] In England, education for children with disabilities has had a legislative base for more than fifty years. It was the Education Act 1944 (the 1944 Act) which provided the legal base for educational provision for such children until the coming into force of the Education Act 1981. The 1944 Act identified and provided for ten categories of children with disability and these categories became the responsibility of the Local Education Authority (LEAs). These children were generally educated separately in special schools but this was not a requirement of the 1944 Act.

[5.21] With regard to one particular category of children, the LEAs were empowered to classify them as "ineducable," following a medical examination and these children were placed under the care of the Health Boards. This position continued in place until the Education (Handicapped Children) Act 1970 came into force. In the 1970 Act, the LEA's power to categorise children as unsuitable for mainstream schools was abolished and these children were returned to the care of the LEA's.[31] The Education (England) Act 1971 extended educational facilities to include all categories of mental handicap, including severe and profound handicap.

The Warnock Report

[5.22] In 1978 the *Warnock Report*[32] was published and it became the "blueprint" for future legislation. This seminal report proposed the abolition of the ten categories in the 1944 Act and the introduction of a more broadly based, flexible concept of "special needs". It considered that any child who needed help, temporarily or permanently, should be classified as a child with a special need which should be catered for, in so far as possible, in mainstream schools. However, the Report still envisaged the retention of the special school as a provider of education for those children with complex or severe disabilities.

Legislation for Children with Special Needs

[5.23] Acting on the recommendations of the *Warnock Report*, the Education (England) Act 1981[33] established a framework for assessment and provision for special education which continued until 1993 when the Education Act 1993 came into force.[34] The 1981 Act provided for the right of disabled children to be

---

[31] Special educational needs in England are considered in detail in Ch 5 of *The Head's Legal Guide*, (1998), Croner. This is a looseleaf volume which is updated annually.

[32] *Special Educational Needs: Report of the Committee of Enquiry into the Education of Handicapped Children and Young People*, (1978).

[33] Which became effective in 1983.

[34] The Disabled Persons (Services, Consultation and Representation) Act 1986 makes further provision for the improvement of the effectiveness and the co-ordination of resources, in the provision of services for people with mental or physical handicap and for those with mental illness, to make provision for their needs and for connected purposes.

educated in mainstream schools in so far as this was possible.[35] It required LEAs to identify children with special education needs, to "determine" provision, where necessary, to formulate multi-disciplinary assessments and to issue statements of their special educational needs.

[5.24] Although the 1981 Act had significantly improved the lot of children with disabilities, by the early 1990s problems were escalating. Not the least of these difficulties was the growth in the number of pupils being excluded[36] from mainstream schools many of whom were pupils with special needs, the increasing number of parental challenges taken by way of appeal or by judicial review and the lack of clarity regarding the role of mainstream schools in regard to pupils with special needs.[37]

[5.25] Part III of the Education Act 1993 (amended in 1996), contains the provisions relating to special education needs.[38] It applies to any child under 19 years who is registered at a school. The Act retains the broad definition of "special educational needs" introduced by the 1981 Act. With regard to special needs education, the 1993 Act provides for the duties and powers falling on LEAs, school governors and the head teacher. Section 161(4) of the 1993 Act provides that all those involved in making special educational provision for a child in mainstream schools have a duty to ensure that the child becomes involved in the activities of the school together with children who do not have special needs as far as practicable and where compatible with the provisions of s 160. An appeal structure was established under the 1993 Act whereby parents aggrieved by LEA decisions could appeal to local appeal committees and thence to the Secretary of State. However, this appeal system, it seems, has not been very satisfactory as the local committees were viewed as not fully independent of the LEAs while the latter frequently were dilatory in their response.[39]

[5.26] The establishment of the Special Educational Needs Tribunal under the Education Act 1993 signifies a most significant reform of the law. The Tribunal, replaces the structure established under the 1993 Act while it is independent of the LEAs and its decisions are binding, subject to an appeal to the High Court on a point of law. One perceived defect in the Tribunal is that the right of appeal is vested in the parent and not in the child, a matter which considerably limits the

---

[35] The Education Reform Act 1988 governs the curriculum in maintained schools and in special schools.

[36] Under the Education England (No 2) Act 1986.

[37] See further *The Head's Legal Guide*, (1998), Croner, para 5.4.

[38] See ss 156-190.

[39] See Meredith, 'Education Legislation in England and Wales', in European Journal for Education Law and Policy, (1997), Kluwer Law International, London, Vol 1, 175 at 178.

availability of legal aid, which might otherwise be available, to finance appeals to the High Court.[40]

[5.27] The Special Educational Needs Tribunal Regulations 1995[41] make provision in regard to the establishment and regulation of the Special Educational Needs Tribunal set up by the Education Act 1993, s 177. They also revoke the Special Educational Needs Tribunal Regulations 1994 and they re-enact the provisions together with amendments. Among the most significant features of the 1993 Act is the Code of Practice offering practical advice and guidance to LEAs and schools on the implementation of the Act. Both schools and LEAs are under a statutory obligation to take account of the Code of Practice which is considered in detail in the *Head's Legal Guide.*[42]

Provision in Northern Ireland

[5.28] The Education (Northern Ireland) Order, 1996 and the Education (Special Educational Needs) Regulations (Northern Ireland) 1997 govern special education provision in Northern Ireland. These Regulations revoke and replace, with some modifications, the Education (Special Educational Needs) Regulations (Northern Ireland) 1985. The 1996 Regulations apply to the assessment of special educational needs and to statements of such needs. They provide that Education and Library Boards, in making an assessment of a child's special educational needs, are obliged to seek parental advice, educational advice, psychological advice, advice from health and social services and any other advice which they consider suitable in order to make a satisfactory assessment. Detailed provision is also made as to the persons from which such advices are sought.

[5.29] Further provision is made for the form and content of a notice to be served on a parent with a draft statement of special educational needs and a statement of special educational needs. Detailed provision is also made for reviewing of statements and for the transfer of a statement from one Education and Library Board to another, the duties of the old Board being transferred to the new Board. Restrictions are imposed on the disclosure of statements and steps are taken to avoid unauthorised persons having access to them.

---

[40] Meredith, 'Education Legislation in England and Wales' in European Journal for Education Law and Policy, (1997), Kluwer Law International, London, Vol 1, 175 at 178; see further Robinson, 'Special Educational Needs, the Code and the New Tribunal' in *Education and the Law,* (1996); Harris, 'Special Educational Needs and Access to Justice,' (1997), Jordans.
[41] SI 1995/3113.
[42] (1998), Croner, p 5-7 *et seq.*

Provision in Ireland

[5.30] Irish education has a long and worthy tradition of informal provision for children with special needs. As with general education, the religious orders were the innovators in the provision of services for these children.[43] Voluntary bodies have also played a significant role in such provision. Early initiatives on behalf of children who could neither hear nor speak were undertaken by the Christian Brothers and Dominican Sisters in the mid-nineteenth century and by the Irish Sisters of Charity in the 1870s and these were assimilated into the national school system in the following century. Schools for the blind were also established and run by the Irish Sisters of Charity and by the Carmelite Brothers in the 1870s. However, these schools only entered the national school system *circa* 1918.[44]

[5.31] Official recognition was conferred on schools for the mentally handicapped in 1955. St Michael's House was established in the 1950s by parents. It was later assimilated into the national school system and was the first school in Ireland to have a lay person as manager. By 1968, 62 special schools were in existence. One significant feature of this provision was that it was all non-statutory and contained a high degree of voluntary input. Another less than satisfactory feature of this provision was the lack of official support and provision for the group of children who were profoundly or severely disabled.

[5.32] While the State has responded reasonably generously to the educational needs of moderately and mildly mentally and physically disabled children, it fell behind many developed countries in its provision for the small but most seriously disabled group of all, ie those children with severe and profound disability[45] whose parents have had to cope alone.

[5.33] The position of children with autism was also regrettably overlooked or ignored until recently.[46]

---

[43] See generally Cullen, ed, *Girls Don't Do Honours: Irish Women in Education in the 19th and 20th Centuries*, (1987) Women's Educational Bureau.

[44] I am indebted to Ms Ann O'Gara for this information; Atkinson has charted the singular contribution of Nano Nangle (1728-1784), the Presentation Sisters, Catherine McCauley (1787-1841), the Mercy Sisters, Mother Ball and the Loreto Sisters, Edmund Ignatious Rice (1762-1844) to general education in Ireland; Atkinson *Irish Education*, (1969) Allen Figgis, pp 73-80.

[45] See O'Hanlon J's criticism of the State on this point in *O'Donoghue v Minister for Health* [1996] 2 IR 24 at 65.

[46] See John and Mary Hanlon, *A Journey with Gavan: coping with autism*, (1996) published by the authors at 225 Ryevale Lawns, Leixlip, Co Kildare.

Official Response

[5.34] In 1965 a Commission of Enquiry into Mental Handicap recommended that a network of schools be established for pupils with mild and moderate mental handicap and this recommendation was implemented. A Working Party was set up in 1983 which produced a report commonly known as the *Blue Report*. It recommended that the severely and profoundly mentally handicapped should be given as much training and education as possible, that all centres providing for such children should have education and training programmes and teachers accredited and paid by the State. A decade later, the *Report of the Special Education Review Committee* (1993) recommended the gradual phasing in of education for the severely and profoundly handicapped. Two years later, approximately 200 such children were receiving education, on a pilot scheme basis, provided by the Department, out of approximately 2,000 children.

[5.35] Following the *O'Donoghue v Ireland*[47] decision, State provision for these children appears to have improved considerably. Pupil-teacher ratios were reduced to 6:1, extra teachers were allocated to this sector and "special needs assistants" were appointed to work with these teachers.[48] While the Education (Welfare) Bill 1999 opens the door of State support for, *inter alia*, children with "special educational needs," much remains to be done in this sphere. The Minister has established a Commission to study this important area with a view to making further provision.

Numbers of Children in Special Education

[5.36] The *Report on the Status of People with Disabilities* (1996) indicates that approximately 4% of the school-going population have a disability. The existing 114 Special Schools cater for around 8,000 of these children while approximately 3,800 children with a variety of disabilities are catered for in special classes in mainstream primary schools. A further 8,000 or so children with "specific disabilities" are in ordinary classes in mainstream primary schools.

[5.37] In second level education, 48 special classes cater for approximately 2,300 students while 1,000 students with disability participate in third level education. These statistics, of course, do not include the considerable number of children who drop out of school early or who never attend any secondary school. The *School Attendance/Truancy Report*[49] stated that "Indications are that up to 8% of primary school leavers may not transfer to second level schools at all".[50]

---

[47] [1993] 2 IR 20.
[48] I am grateful to the Department of Education and Science for this information.
[49] Department of Education 1994.
[50] At p 8 of the report.

This is a disquieting and somewhat alarming statement in view of the State's constitutional obligation in respect of "a certain minimum education" and in view of the fact that these under 15 year old pupils are within the ambit of the School Attendance Acts 1926-1967.

[5.38] It appears that school principals and schools are no longer being required, under s 15 of the 1926 Act, to make returns containing prescribed particulars on every child who is absent from school and the prescribed particulars of such absences to the enforcing authorities under s 8 of the 1926 Act. In this regard the *School Attendance/Truancy Report* states:

> "This practice has fallen into disuse at primary level, and may be said never to have been applied in other schools. Where School Attendance Officers pay frequent visits to schools, such information is readily available; in areas outside the jurisdiction of the School Attendance Committees, however, such information may be passed to the Gardaí only in respect of children with persistent attendance problems."[51]

This could conceivably leave the State open to suit in particular instances, where parents have failed their children in this regard and their childrens' right to free primary education has not been vindicated. However, the Education (Welfare) Bill 1999 will address many of the most urgent issues relating to this area of life.

Care and Education

[5.39] It is commonly accepted that one of the major difficulties in the sphere of child-care arises from the fragmentation of responsibility between three Government Departments: Health, Justice and Education.[52] The Department of Education has statutory duties in respect of residential provision for deprived and delinquent children, for reformatory and industrial schools and for school attendance. The Department of Justice has responsibilities for probation and juveniles under detention[53] while the Department of Health is concerned with welfare services and with certain categories of children in care.

[5.40] In the past, the absence of a statutory framework to meet the needs of children with behavioural problems and/or learning disabilities, who attend mainstream schools, has placed them at a huge disadvantage. Likewise, the serious educational plight of Traveller children is highlighted in the recent *Report of the Task Force on the Traveller Community*.[54] It became extremely

---

[51] Department of Education 1994, pp. 19-20.

[52] McCarthy, Kennedy and Matthews, *Focus on Residential Child Care in Ireland*, (1996) Focus Ireland.

[53] Saint Patrick's Institution, (previously known as Borstal), accommodates young offenders between 16-19 years of age.

[54] (1995) Gov Pubs, Dublin. This report found that 800 Traveller children are not enrolled in any school and those who are enrolled are generally erratic attenders. It cites the findings of a 1993 Report which found that, out of a cohort of 2,000 Travellers in the 12-15 year age group, only 100 children attended school.

difficult for many parents to secure alternative access to education for such children when they are suspended or expelled from their national school. In the past decade, parents are increasingly seeking to enforce their childrens' constitutional right to education in the courts. At the time of going to press these cases are ongoing.

Constitutional Litigation and Special Education Needs

[5.41] In Ireland, the courts have, since 1980, played a pivotal role in securing rights for children with disabilities. While the legislative lacuna has effectively deprived a small, but growing, body of children of constitutionally enshrined educational and care rights, the courts seem prepared to take a firm stance on the State's duty to vindicate the constitutionally enshrined rights of such children.[55] In 1980, Finlay J considered the constitutional rights of the child in *G v An Bord Uchtála*[56] in which he upheld the parental right to custody and control of the upbringing of a child:

> "In my view, her daughter likewise has a constitutional right to bodily integrity and has an unenumerated right to an opportunity to be reared with due regard to her religious, moral, intellectual, physical and social welfare. The State, having regard to the provisions of Article 40, s 3, sub-s 1, of the Constitution must by its laws defend and vindicate these rights as far as practicable."[57]

[5.42] This decision was later affirmed by the Supreme Court. It is under the aegis of Article 42.5 that the State is given authority to enact "care and protection" measures and to establish and maintain institutions for young offenders. The duties laid upon the State in this Article appear more onerous than those under Article 42.4 as they include all the parental duties expressed in Article 42.1. Arguably, the State when discharging Article 42.5, is acting in *loco parentis* to these special category children. Moreover, the scope of the State's intervention under Article 42.5 must be read in the light of the total Article and, as shown in *G v An Bord Uchtála*,[58] this duty may be further re-enforced by Article 40.3, in which the State guarantees in its laws to respect, as far as practicable, and to defend and vindicate the personal rights of the citizen some of which are unenumerated.[59]

---

[55] *MF v Superintendent of Ballymun Garda Station* [1991] 1 IR 189; *L v Ireland* High Court, unrep, 24 March 1995; *T v Minister for Education* High Court, unrep, 24 March 1995; *N v Minister for Education* High Court, unrep, 23 March 1995; *GL v Minister for Justice, Minister for Health* High Court, unrep, 24 March, 1995, Geoghegan J.

[56] [1980] IR 32.

[57] [1980] IR 32 at 44.

[58] [1980] IR 32.

[59] *Ryan v AG* [1965] IR 294.

[5.43] In 1995, Barr J upheld the right of a ten year old boy, whose mother and others had failed to control him, to have his case judicially reviewed so that his constitutional right to religious, moral, intellectual, physical and social education would be vindicated by the State, including a right to secure accommodation.[60]

[5.44] In *FN v Minister for Education, Minister for Health*,[61] an application for judicial review on behalf of a child with hyperkinetic conduct disorder who required a period of time in a secure unit, Geoghegan J stated:

> "I would take the view that where there is a child with very special needs which cannot be provided by the parents or guardian there is a constitutional obligation on the State under Article 42 s 5 of the Constitution to cater for those needs in order to vindicate the constitutional rights of the child."[62]

[5.45] For such care to be effective in the applicant's case, the judge considered an element of detention was necessary. Rejecting counsel's submission that the State was not obliged to provide for the specialist requirements of a child such as the applicant, Geoghegan J relied on *G v An Bord Uchtála*[63] which held that a child having been born has the right to be fed and to live, to be reared and educated and that these rights must equally be protected and vindicated by the State. While normally these duties are carried out by the parents, in exceptional circumstances, the State must take on the obligation.

[5.46] Geoghegan J concluded that the State was under a constitutional duty to establish, as soon as reasonably practicable,[64] "suitable arrangements of containment with treatment for the applicant". He was, however, of the view that the State's duty was not an absolute one as some very exceptional circumstances might arise in which some quite exceptional need of the child might fall outside the constitutionally required State provision. However, he considered that the provision of such accommodation, services and arrangements as were necessary to meet the needs of the applicant in the instant case, were not so impractical or prohibitively expensive as to come within any notional limitation on the State's constitutional obligations. He observed that other children with similar requirements to the applicant were in urgent need of special treatment, attention and education.

---

[60] Irish Times, 13 April 1995, p 11; see also McCarthy, Kennedy and Matthews, *Focus on Residential Child Care in Ireland,* (1996), Dublin, Focus Ireland.

[61] [1995] 2 ILRM 297.

[62] [1995] 2 ILRM 297.

[63] [1980] IR 32.

[64] Either by use of the Children Act 1908, s 58(4) or otherwise.

[5.47] The judgment in *DT v Eastern Health Board, Ireland and the AG, Minister for Education and Minister for Health*,[65] which was delivered on the same day as the *FN* decision by Geoghegan J, was concerned with the plight of a 12 year-old girl with suicidal tendencies. The girl been placed under the care of the Eastern Health Board which sought an element of confinement in order to secure her care and control. The judge indicated that his observations in *FN v Minister for Education*,[66] applied equally to this case but noted that the remedy under the Children Act 1908, s 58(4) was not available to the girl because no certified industrial school for girls existed in the State at that time. As the court was under pressure in this case because of the girl's suicidal proclivity, the judge made an interim order empowering a member of the Garda Síochána to detain the applicant and convey her to Oberstown House[67] where she would be detained and receive appropriate care. In making this order, Geoghegan J relied on constitutional provisions and on the Supreme Court's decision in *MF v Superintendent Ballymun Garda Station*.[68] While the above-mentioned decisions made a crucial contribution to the evolution of childrens' education and care rights,[69] it was *O'Donoghue v Minister for Health*,[70] which placed the courts at the centre of the education policy debate in Ireland.

The O'Donoghue *Case: The High Court*

[5.48] In 1993 the State was providing for children with moderate disabilities in separate special schools.

[5.49] Approximately 200 children with severe or profound disabilities were in education with teachers while others attended centres with no teachers. On 24 February 1992, the applicant, a boy with, *inter alia*,[71] profound mental handicap, was granted leave in the High Court to apply by way of judicial review for the following reliefs:

   (a) an order of *mandamus* to compel the respondents to provide for free primary education for him the applicant;

   (b) a declaration against the respondents that in failing to provide for free primary education for the applicant and in discriminating against him as compared with other children, the respondents had deprived the

---

[65] High Court, unrep, 24 March 1995.
[66] High Court, unrep, 23 March 1995.
[67] Under the aegis of the Health Board.
[68] [1991] IR 189, O'Flaherty J.
[69] *Brown v Board of Education* (1954) 347 US 483, 495.
[70] [1996] 2 IR 24.
[71] He was diagnosed as having Reye's Syndrome and later on as suffering from residual spastic quadriplegia and profound mental handicap.

applicant of constitutional rights under Articles 40 and Article 42 of the Constitution of 1937; and

(c) damages for breach of his constitutional rights.

Following the commencement of proceedings, a claim for interim relief was met by the offer of day-care and educational facilities at the Cope Foundation[72] in Cork.

[5.50] It was submitted on behalf of the respondents that the applicant was in effect "ineducable" within the meaning of Article 42.4 and that the constitutional guarantee of free primary education is the conventional type of primary education, scholastic in character as exemplified in the curriculum of the national schools and that such education cannot benefit the applicant. They argued that any such training as could be given to him was not really "education" and could not be construed as "primary education" within the meaning of Article 42. Moreover, as the applicant had already acquired a placing in the Cope Foundation, they contended that he had already achieved the essential relief sought and so the instant proceedings were no more than a moot.

[5.51] Observing that Kenny J's definition of education within the meaning of Article 42 in *Ryan v AG*[73] considered such education to be of a scholastic nature, O'Hanlon J was of the view that Kenny J's real purpose was to state that "education" was not sufficiently wide in that context to include "rearing and nurturing". Turning to O'Dálaigh CJ's definition of education when *Ryan v AG*[74] reached the Supreme Court, he found it was more in harmony with the dramatic advances made to alleviate the lot of the mentally handicapped through education since 1965 and with the whole momentum in the human rights area generally. He considered O'Dálaigh CJ's wider definition of education more acceptable as it permitted him to conclude that the applicant, though severely handicapped, was educable within the meaning of Article 42. Accordingly, he stated:

> "I am of the opinion that it is not sufficient for the respondents to grant as a matter of grace and concession, educational benefits which the applicant is entitled to claim as of right."[75]

[5.52] O'Hanlon J next considered the decision in *Crowley v Ireland*[76] and noted, *inter alia*, the Supreme Court's statement that the provisions of Article 42.4

---

[72] A State-funded voluntary body in Cork.
[73] [1965] IR 294.
[74] [1965] IR 294.
[75] *O'Donoghue v Minister for Health* [1996] 1 IR 20 at 68.
[76] [1980] IR 102 at 108, 122 and 126.

conferred a right to receive free primary education which imposed an obligation on the State which is of general application to all citizens.[77]

[5.53] Having established the universality of the State's constitutional obligation, the judge next analysed a number of Irish[78] and US precedents,[79] certain international instruments,[80] Vatican documents, a Papal Encyclical[81] and current provision for mentally handicapped children in the United Kingdom, the USA and Ireland.[82] He noted that the Irish State had responded generously to its obligations in respect of virtually all categories of handicapped children but that it lagged behind many other developed countries in regard to the most seriously handicapped of all. O'Hanlon J stated that it had been established on a worldwide basis for many years that the conventional school environment can be of real benefit to children with severe and profound physical and mental handicap. He concluded that the evidence given in the case before him gave rise to "a strong *conviction* that primary education for this category, if it is to meet their special needs, requires a new approach ...".[83]

[5.54] O'Hanlon J then proceeded to outline the parameters of such an approach[84] including the age of commencement (of education),[85] the duration of education[86] and the continuity of such education.[87] Taking these factors into account, he considered that the existing provision for the applicant in the Cope Foundation was insufficient to discharge any claim he might have under the Constitution to have free primary education provided for his benefit. The judge expanded the scope of the definition of "education" as follows:

---

[77] [1980] IR 102 at 121 citing O'Higgins, CJ.

[78] *Ryan v AG* [1965] IR 294; *Landers v AG* (1973) 109 ILTR 1; *Murphy v Roche* [1978] IR 106; *McDaid v Judge Sheehy* [1991] IR 1; *Crowley v Ireland* [1980] IR 102.

[79] *Brown v Board of Education* (1954) 347 US 483; *Pennsylvania Association for Retarded Children v Commonwealth of Pennsylvania* (1971) 334 F Supp 1257; *Mills v Board of Education of District of Columbia* (1972) 348 F Supp 866; *Honig v Doe* (1988) 484 US 305.

[80] The Universal Declaration of Human Rights, The UN Declaration on the Rights of the Child, Article 23 and the General Assembly Resolution 3447 (xxx) of 9 December 1975, which includes 'Declaration on the Rights of Disabled Persons'.

[81] *Aposltolicam Actuositatem.*

[82] Both the UK and the USA have State systems of education by contrast with Ireland's State-aided system.

[83] At p 70 of the judgment, author's emphasis.

[84] At p 70 of the judgment.

[85] Early intervention and assessment being of vital importance.

[86] The process should, ideally continue for as long as the ability for further development is discernible.

[87] The teaching process should, so far as practicable, be continuous throughout the entire year including the lengthy holiday breaks.

"I conclude, having regard to what has gone before, that there is a constitutional obligation imposed on the State by the provisions of Article 42 s 4 of the Constitution to provide for free basic elementary education of all children and that this involves giving each child such advice, instruction and teaching as will enable him or her to make the best possible use of his or her inherent and potential capacities, physical, mental and moral, however limited these capacities may be. Or, to borrow the language of the United Nations Convention and Resolution of the General Assembly, - 'such education as will be conducive to the child's achieving the fullest possible social integration and individual development; such education as will enable the child to develop his or her capabilities and skills to the maximum and will hasten the process of social integration and reintegration'."[88]

[5.55] Finally, O'Hanlon J decided in favour of the applicant and made orders in the following terms:

"(1) I make an order declaring that the respondents, in failing to provide for free primary education[89] for the applicant and in discriminating against him as compared with other children, have deprived him of constitutional rights arising under Article 42 of the Constitution, with particular reference to Article 42, s 3 subs 2, and Article 42, s 3, subs 4 thereof. I do not find it necessary to deal with the further claims made in reliance on Article 40 of the Constitution.

(2) I award the sum of £7,645.71 by way of damages in favour of the applicant."

The judge stated that the claim for damages was very modest in the particular circumstances of this case.[90] Although the whole thrust of the judgment indicates a remedy under Article 42.4, it is omitted from paragraph 1 of the order. One can only conclude that this is a typographical error as there is no Article 42.3.4°

Analysis of the O'Donoghue *Case: High Court*

[5.56] The *O'Donoghue* case is distinctive from earlier cases in its approach, its rationale and its findings. It seems that O'Hanlon J deliberately eshewed reliance on Article 42.5 with the purpose of bringing the right of the applicant to free primary education within the ambit of the mainstream educational provision (Article 42.4) which was in itself a singular achievement. The first step in the

---

88 At p 65 of the judgment.
89 Author's emphasis.
90 Recently the Ombudsman, Kevin Murphy, recommended that a mother, whose child had been denied the school transport service offered by the Department, be awarded £6,800 in compensation for the inadequate transport service he was offered, Press Release, 11 February 1998, see Appendix E. Ombudsman's recommendations. While the complainant has been paid £6,800 compensation, the transport scheme for children with special educational needs has not yet been published as the Ombudsman required.

judgment, which found that the applicant was educable within the meaning of Article 42.4 and had accordingly a constitutional right to education, follows logically from the judicial argument. However, the second step of the judgment, that it is the State's obligation to provide for such education, displays a much less disciplined approach. Applying a natural law interpretation, O'Hanlon J refers to Papal encyclicals and Vatican documents[91] which are not usual or anticipated sources of law in reserved judgments of the Superior courts.[92] Furthermore, the reference and reliance upon the Papal Encyclical on Education, *Apostolicam Actuositatem,* was a matter relied upon solely by counsel for the applicant.

[5.57] Furthermore, some of the judicial language employed indicates a degree of subjectivity which is not generally found in reserved judgments of the Superior Courts. It is unusual the way O'Hanlon stated that the evidence given in the case before him "gives rise to a strong *conviction* that primary education for this category, if it is to meet their special needs, requires a new approach ...."[93] the parameters of which he proceeded to outline in some detail.

[5.58] With regard to the duration of such education, O'Hanlon J was of the view that the process of education for this category of child should ideally continue "as long as the ability for further development is discernible". Furthermore, O'Hanlon J was of the view that if one is to deal adequately with the needs of the severely or profoundly handicapped children, this appears to require that the teaching process should, so far as practicable, be continuous throughout the entire year including the lengthy holiday breaks.

[5.59] Arguably, the details of a programme of this nature might more properly be considered a matter for the Executive. Finlay P, as he was then, in *Frawley v Ireland,*[94] held that it is not the function of the court to recommend to the Executive what is desirable or to fix the priorities of its health and welfare policy. By analogy, it could be argued that it is not the function of the courts to formulate educational policy for the Executive.

[5.60] By holding that the content of the education guaranteed under Article 42 includes advice, instruction and teaching for all children according to their potential capacities "however limited these capacities may be," O'Hanlon J expanded the definition of "education" as judicially interpreted. The term "advice" in this context seems to imply counselling skills, guidance, psychological and perhaps psychiatric advice in certain instances. The word

---

[91] *Cf* the German Basic Law (Grundgesetz) Article 4GG, which obliges judges to remain ideologically and religiously neutral.

[92] Although a passing reference was made to a Papal Encyclical in *Ryan v AG* [1965] IR 294.

[93] At p 70 of the judgment.

[94] [1976] IR 365.

"instruction" is generally linked to the learning of skills, which could be provided by a teacher's aid or other person as opposed to "teaching" *per se*. The reference to "teaching" might include the ordinary class teacher, a remedial teacher or team teacher or a speech therapist. If children with disability are integrated into mainstream primary schools and such services are not provided, it seems that these rights are there to be litigated again in order to secure those services. Clearly, these measures can only be implemented through a legislative programme of sweeping reform which will have huge resource implications.

[5.61] It is conceivable that the trial judge could have achieved a more assured decision by relying solely on the Supreme Court judgment in *Crowley v Ireland*.[95] It will be recalled that the court in *Crowley* ruled that it was only when assistance to the denominational schools was impossible, or when they could not succeed in providing the necessary means, that the State must act directly to provide education.

[5.62] Because of the severity of the applicant's disabilities in the *O'Donoghue* case, the denominational schools were incapable of providing the necessary means to provide for the applicant's education. Likewise, the applicant's parents were unable to provide the necessary skills and means for his education. It strongly arguable, therefore, that the applicant fell into the category for which the State must necessarily *provide education directly* under Article 42.4. This approach could also have dislodged the "albatross" personified by the preposition "for" in the phrase "to provide for" at least for one child with disability.

[5.63] While this case vindicates the rights of one child only, it is relevant to all those children who can prove that they have suffered loss or damage at the hands of the State as a consequence of deprivation of their constitutional right to education as the judge stated:

> "... I am satisfied from the evidence in the case that the respondents have failed for some years past to carry out a duty imposed on them by the Constitution to provide for free primary education for his benefit, and for this breach of his constitutional rights that they are liable in damages for any loss and damage thereby caused to the applicant."[96]

This statement has enormous implications for those children who are currently being denied their constitutional right to free primary education and for other children who can establish in evidence, that their constitutional rights have been denied or ignored in the past.

---

[95] [1980] IR 102.
[96] At p 70 of the judgment.

The O'Donoghue *Case: The Supreme Court*

[5.64] The respondents appealed to the Supreme Court and on 6 February 1997 that court made an order in the following terms:

> "The appeal on the part of the respondents pursuant to notice of appeal dated the 23 July 1993, from the judgment and order of the High Court (Mr Justice O'Hanlon) given and made on the 27 May 1993, coming on for hearing this day.
>
> Whereupon and upon opening and debate of the matter, this Court being informed by counsel for the applicant and by counsel for the respondents that the State is now providing for the infant applicant education appropriate to his current condition, this Court substitutes for the declaration in the High Court a declaration that the infant applicant is entitled to free primary education in accordance with Article 42, s 4 of the Constitution and the State is under an obligation to provide for such education.
>
> And this Court notes the statement of counsel for the respondents that the said respondents are not to be taken as accepting the manner in which the learned trial judge interpreted the said obligation.
>
> And this Court notes the statement of counsel for the applicant that he is not to be taken as acknowledging any error in the manner in which the learned trial judge interpreted the said obligation.
>
> IT IS ORDERED that the Order of the High Court do otherwise stand affirmed and that the respondents do pay the applicant the costs of this appeal, the said costs to be taxed in default of agreement."[97]

Critical Comment on the O'Donoghue *Decision*

[5.65] The Supreme Court in substituting its declaration for that of the High Court relied upon Article 42.4 solely, thereby vindicating the right of the applicant to free primary education under the general provision as was envisaged by the trial judge. Subject to this alteration and to the acknowledgment of counsels' reservations, the Court affirmed the order of the High Court. The Court made it clear, however, that this decision vindicated only the right of Paul O'Donoghue to free primary education under Article 42.4. Nonetheless, the right is there to be litigated again by those children who can prove that they have suffered loss or damage at the hands of the State as a consequence of deprivation of their constitutional right to primary education. It is necessary to take a constitutional action to vindicate this right and few parents can afford this investment in time and money. It is notable, that although the Supreme Court held that the State was obliged to act directly in order to make provision for the education of the applicant, it still retained the phrase *to provide for education.*

---

[97]   [1996] 2 IR 70, editor's note.

Provision for Autistic Children

[5.66] As yet, there is no school specifically for autistic children in Ireland. In 1996 McGuinness J approved a settlement in which a child, who was diagnosed as having Asperges Syndrome in 1986, sought an order, *inter alia,* directing the Minister to provide him with free education appropriate to his needs. The applicant alleged he had been placed in a special school where he was subject to repeated bullying. The Minister acknowledged that the applicant, as a child with special needs, had not had the benefit of a continuous school environment and that this had an adverse impact on him. She also agreed to provide a tutor specially trained in educating a child with autism together with a sum of £30,000 damages and the costs of the proceedings.[98]

[5.67] Parents of autistic children have been increasingly before the courts demanding rights for their children and a recent initiative, announced by the Minister for Education and Science, indicates that their position, and that of other children with special educational needs will improve considerably.[99]

A Dysfunctional Family

[5.68] In *Comerford v The Minister for Education,*[100] which came on for hearing on the same day as the latter settlement, McGuinness J considered the case of an eleven year-old boy who was suffering from attention deficit disorder and had effectively been abandoned by his dysfunctional family and was seeking a number of reliefs by way of judicial review. The parents, who were known to the Eastern Health Board (EHB) from at least 1988, finally left the jurisdiction abandoning their five children who were taken into the care of EHB on 9 September 1996.[101] The applicant sought by way of judicial review, *inter alia,* a declaration that in failing to provide for his education, the respondents had deprived him of constitutional rights under Article 40 and 42 of the Constitution and an order of *mandamus* requiring the respondents to provide forthwwith for his religious, moral, intellectual, physical and social education. At the date of hearing the notice party (the EHB) had provided the applicant with a long term placement in a residential care facility.

[5.69] Evidence was given that the applicant was "out of control" in the primary school, that he constituted a threat to himself and to others and that the school authorities could not ensure that he would remain in school once he arrived

---

98 Ryan, 'Mum who educated autistic son gets £30,000', Irish Independent, 16 November 1996.
99 See Press Release, "Major Initiative in Special Education Services: 'Moves marks breakthrough for integrated education and children with autism'," 5 November 1998.
100 [1997] 2 ILRM 134.
101 Interim Care Orders pursuant to the Child Care Act 1991 having been obtained in the District Court.

there.[102] The School Attendance Officer (SAO) intervened during 1995 and it was agreed, at a case conference, in October 1995 to seek an assessment of the applicant, with parental consent, in order to determine suitable educational provision for him.

[5.70] Difficulties ensued and in order to expedite the assessment, the SAO initiated legal proceedings under the School Attendance Act 1926 which came on for hearing in the Children's Court on 29 November 1995. The SAO applied under s 17(4)(a) of the 1926 Act for a remand to St Michael's Assessment Centre for a three week assessment placement. This was agreed and the case was then adjourned to 20 December 1995. In St Michael's Assessment Centre, the applicant was the subject of a full three week assessment. Detailed reports followed including a number of recommendations for placements for the applicant but none of these proved fruitful.

[5.71] McGuinness J observed that the EHB might have moved earlier to take the applicant and his siblings into care. However, she noted the constraints both constitutional and statutory[103] under which the EHB operated. She considered the reference to the rights of the child contained in *G v An Bord Uchtála*,[104] and the germane sections of *Crowley v Ireland*[105] and concluded that the tenor of the Supreme Court's judgments in the latter case is that the child has a right to free primary education and that the State must "provide for" that education.[106] McGuinness J also took account of two other High Court decisions, *FN v Minister for Education*[107] and *O'Donoghue v Ireland*.[108] Observing that a number of subsequent cases had followed the principles set out by Geoghegan J in the former case, the judge accepted those principles together with those set out by O'Hanlon J in the latter case. McGuiness J, in granting the declaration held, *inter alia*, that the Constitution imposed a duty on the State to provide for free primary education, it also confirmed rights and concomitant duties on parents in regard to the education of their children. While the applicant was largely under the control of his parents, his educational deprivation had to be viewed in the light of their behaviour which culminated in the abandonment of all the children in 1996. Nonetheless, the State had vailed to vindicate the applicant's constitutional rights in that it had made no proper effort to cater for

---

[102] Evidence of school Principal, Brother Dundon, at p 4 of the judgment.

[103] Child Care Act 1991, s 3(2) states "In the performance of this function (the promotion of the welfare of children) a health board shall ... (c) have regard to the principle that it is generally in the best interests of a child to be brought up in his own family."

[104] [1980] IR 32.

[105] [1980] IR 102, at 121-123.

[106] *Crowley v Ireland* [1980] IR 102.

[107] [1995] 2 ILRM 297.

[108] [1996] 2 IR 24.

the applicant's special educational needs from the date of the assessment in December 1995, at which time psychiatric diagnosis and educational recommendations had been made until the date of the hearing. The judge granted the declaration relief sought, but as appropriate educational arrangements had been made for the applicant as of the date of hearing, no further order was made.[109]

The Separation of Powers and the Care, Custody and Control of Certain Children

[5.72] While judicial intervention has vindicated individual rights and focused attention on the deficiencies of the child care system, this cannot be regarded as an entirely welcome development. The Constitution envisages independent and separate legislative, executive and judicial functions. Article 15.2.1° provides that the sole and exclusive power of making laws for the State is vested in the Oireachtas; no other legislative authority has power to make laws for the State. Worthy though individual cases may be, there is a danger inherent in the courts assuming what in effect amounts to legislative and executive powers. However, there comes a time when the discretion of the executive is exhausted and the courts must act to vindicate constitutional rights. That this point has now been reached is clear from the landmark decision of Kelly J in *DB v The Minister for Justice and Ors.*[110]

[5.73] The 15 year-old applicant had already succeeded in having the court exercise its original jurisdiction by making directions for his custody, care and control by the respondent Health Board. In his new application, he requested the Court to become involved in the enforcement of his and other persons' constitutional rights in a much more direct manner than had been the case up to this point. Thus, he sought an order directing the Minister for Health "to provide sufficient funding to allow the Eastern Health Board to build, open and maintain a 24 bed high support unit at Portrane in the County of Dublin". He also sought an order compelling the Minister for Health "to do all things necessary to facilitate the building, opening and maintenance of that unit at Portrane".

[5.74] It will be recalled that Geoghegan J in *FN v Minister for Education, Minister for Health*[111] ruled that the State was under a constitutional duty to establish, as soon as reasonably practicable,[112] "suitable arrangements of containment with treatment for the applicant". Hence, Kelly J considered that

---

[109] [1997] 2 ILRM 134 at 135, 136.
[110] High Court, unrep, 29 July 1998.
[111] [1995] 2 ILRM 297.
[112] Either by use of the Children Act 1908, s 58(4) or otherwise.

the State was on notice for six years as to its duty to minors exhibiting problems of the character which existed in that case and which existed in the case before the court. He expressed the frustration of the Superior Courts which were being asked to make orders, in favour of applicants who require secure containment for their welfare, only to find that no facilities are available.

[5.75] Because the State had failed to take timely and effective steps to meet the needs of these young persons with special needs, Kelly J felt obliged to ensure that this position was addressed. He summed up the dilatory approach of the State towards addressing the rights of persons such as the applicant which he described as "a scandal" and as appearing to be "bogged down in a bureaucratic and administrative quagmire". Kelly J concluded that the time had come to progress to the next step required of it under the Constitution so as to ensure that troubled minors who require placement of the kind envisaged are met. Accordingly, he granted the injunction against the Minister which the applicant sought. In doing so, the judge stressed that he was not interfering in policy. Rather, he stated, he was merely ensuring that the Minister who had already formulated the policy would carry it into effect.

[5.76] From the date of the granting of this injunction by the High Court, the Minister for Health is no longer free regarding the approach to be adopted towards solving the problem of young persons such as the applicant, as the developments proposed must be executed within the timescale set by the court. Furthermore, any proposed alterations to the policy would have to be submitted to the Court seeking a variation of the injunction which the court indicated would not be granted lightly. In his final comment, Kelly J indicated that he would adopt a firm stance in the future with analogous cases stating: "I therefore reserve the right to intervene by way of injunction if necessary to ensure the provision of a short term solution in any case that requires it".

[5.77] While the Irish courts have made a remarkable contribution by focusing public attention on the deficits in educational provision and by pressing for specific action in certain instances, it would be regrettable if they were obliged to continue to compensate for legislative inertia in this sphere.

[5.78] As the most recent press release demonstrates, the Minister has responded by setting up informal support structures which will considerably improve the situation for children with special needs. However, if reform in this sphere is to be worthwhile and enduring, long term policy and practice on educational provision in special education needs to be formulated and separate legislation to meet those needs requires to be enacted as a matter of urgency. Nothing short of specific legislation in this sphere will meet the needs of these children.

[5.79] Article 45 of the Constitution comprises a number of principles of social policy intended for the general guidance of the Oireachtas. The application of these principles in the making of laws is stated to be "the care of the Oireachtas exclusively, and shall not be cognisable by any court ...". The State is required to promote the welfare of the whole people by securing and protecting a social order in which justice and charity informs all the institutions of national life. Furthermore, the State must direct its policy towards securing that the ownership and control of material resources are distributed amongst private individuals and the various classes as best to subserve the common good. These are the principles which must guide the State when legislating for, *inter alia*, education.

[5.80] In Ireland, there is convincing evidence which indicates a clear link between severe socio-economic disadvantage and educational disadvantage.[113] O'Mahony's research (1997)[114] into the characteristics of prisoners in Mountjoy prison found that 80% had left school by the age of 16 while one third had not gone beyond primary school or special school level.

[5.81] While there are, of course, many factors which contribute to educational failure, the *European Social Fund Evaluation Report: Early School Leavers* (1996) observed a lack of systematic follow-up and commitment on investment in early school leavers and

> "a distinct imbalance in the concentration of resources that is not explained as between the investment in those who progress through the mainstream system and those who have exited before the end of the senior cycle."[115]

[5.82] The report stated "the failure of the current system to cater to the needs of early school leavers must be openly acknowledged by the system itself". It observed that approximately 14,500 young persons leave the school system each year without having finished the senior cycle of second level education and concluded that the level of provision available to meet the needs of these young people is inadequate.[116]

[5.83] Stressing the crucial and significant role that can be played by the education system in terms of establishing *a more equitable social balance* in Ireland, the report recommended a reassessment of the balance of education and training investment as between those marginalised in society and those who are relatively more advantaged. It stressed the need for a more co-ordinated model to assist those who leave school early and/or those who are likely to leave school early. Implying that the Irish system of education contained a considerable

---

[113] See *Truancy/School Attendance Report*, (1994), Department of Education, p 4.
[114] O'Mahony, *Mountjoy Prisoners: A Sociological and Criminological Profile*, (1997), Gov Pubs.
[115] *European Social Fund Report*, p 180.
[116] *European Social Fund Report*.

degree of class bias, it concluded that increased relative levels of expenditure on the third level sector, post-Leaving Certificate Courses and the senior cycle of second level education has meant that the balance of labour market advantage is moving in favour of the relatively more advantaged in Irish society. The Report recommended a concentration of resources on this chronically marginalised group coupled with a radical restructuring of what is now "only a notional facilitatory framework that purportedly serves to advance them through the system."[117]

[5.84] Since 1996, the State has put in place a number of non-statutory initiatives which have improved the situation considerably. Only a co-ordinated nationwide cohesive plan, which ranges much wider than education, can begin to address these multi-faceted problems. The provisions of the Education (Welfare) Bill 1999 indicate that a serious attempt to redress the main deficits in the education system is finally being considered.

---

[117] *European Social Fund Report.*

Chapter 6

The Education Act 1998

Introduction

[6.01] Legislation in any social policy area is complex and this is particularly true of Irish education with its diffuse nature, denominational character and tradition of negotiated consensus. Public debate in the latter decades in Ireland shows a widespread desire to reassess educational provision and practice and to chart future directions. The scope, depth and intensity of that debate has seldom been equalled in the history of the State. The inclusion of some innovative features, which facilitated structured dialogue between the major parties in education prior to the enactment of legislation, has been a remarkable feature of that debate. The approach to educational change in Ireland is manifest in the negotiations with the parties in education which led up the enactment of the Education Act 1998 (the 1998 Act). As the schools are, in the main, constitutionally protected denominational schools, this was the only avenue open to the legislators.

[6.02] The 1998 Act is a singular landmark in Irish life as it formalises, for the first time in the history of the State, a national consensus in education distilled over a nine-year period of intense public debate, negotiation and compromise. While it is neither radical nor prescriptive legislation, its enactment represents a first step in the framing of a wider legislative base for first and second-level education. As such, it is a welcome and long overdue development. In the absence of any judicial consideration of any of the provisions of the Act, any analysis of its impact must necessarily be speculative. This chapter outlines the formulation of the agreement on which the Act rests; it summarises the main provisions; and speculates as to whether parents or students, affected by a breach of the Act, have a right of action under the statute.

[6.03] Other sections of the Act, which pertain to teacher employment and statutory rights to information, are contained in Chapters 10[1] and 12[2] and so there may be some unavoidable overlap between these chapters. This chapter does not purport to be a legal interpretation of the Education Act 1998 as such must necessarily await judicial interpretation and analysis.

---

[1]   Which deals with the establishment of student councils in post-primary schools.
[2]   See para **[12.77]** which deals with the requirement on a school to have an admissions policy.

Establishing a Legal Framework for Education

[6.04] The establishment of a legislative framework for education in Ireland is particularly challenging as the system of education had achieved over time a tradition of *ad hoc* growth with considerable flexibility and autonomy. A legislative framework seeks to provide a legal and administrative base for the system and strives to strike an appropriate balance between the interdependent rights and obligations of the child, parents, the teachers, the churches, the State and other agencies. In the context of creating a legal framework to support the provision of high quality education in South Africa, Beckmann articulates the necessity also for an equilibrium between the State and the civil community the legislation proposes to serve:

> "There should be a balance between the State and the civil community. Because the right to education belongs to the people and not to the state, the role of the State should be defined in legal terms which will prevent the state from establishing an educational dictatorship as if the right to education belongs to it."[3]

That such a framework should not be cast too rigidly or in too great detail is highly desirable lest it stifle school-based innovation and inhibit change. This is particularly true of the Irish setting which is legislating largely for denominational schools accustomed to considerable autonomy in the past.

[6.05] Legislation for education requires to be grounded in reality, taking cognisance of the religious, cultural and linguistic background of all the people and their educational traditions and history. It ought to graft on to what is best in the old stock, retaining its essential character, while nurturing a fresh, confident, growth. Above all, a legal framework for education ought to respect and balance the constitutional rights of all the parties in education in a fair and just manner.

[6.06] As education cannot be considered in isolation from the social and political realities of life, such legislation needs to be forward looking and must demonstrate its respect for the various traditions north and south of the border. Such a framework must necessarily be broadly based on democratic principles so as to cater for the diverse needs of all the people so as to facilitate reconciliation and rapprochement on this divided island.[4]

---

3   Beckman, 'Creating a Legal Framework to Support the Provision of High Quality Education in South Africa' *Education and the Law*, Bennett and Meredith, eds, (1997) No 2, pp 123, 126, p 126.

4   See 'Agreement Reached in the Multi-Party Negotiations', generally referred to as 'The Good Friday Agreement', p 1.

[6.07] As boards of management were in place in many Irish schools prior to the enactment of the 1998 Act, it is necessary to distinguish between these voluntary boards and the statutory boards of management established by the 1998 Act.

Voluntary Boards of Management

[6.08] Boards of management became a more common feature of Ireland's school system after 1975[5] when they were phased into primary schools being linked to increased capitation funding for schools. However, the passage of the boards into voluntary secondary schools was more dilatory and was attended by some controversy. When boards were established, powers were devolved voluntarily from the patrons[6] and trustees[7] to the boards. As these boards had no statutory origin, powers could be withdrawn from them at will and the patron or trustees could manage the school themselves, or appoint a single manager to do so. When comprehensive[8] and community schools were established, their Deeds of trust provided for boards of management *ab initio*. The Education Act 1998 provides for the establishment of statutory boards in all recognised schools, where practicable.[9]

Background to the Education Act 1998

Centralisation

[6.09] Both national and international[10] reports have been critical of the centralised structure of Ireland's system of education which is exceptional among OECD countries. The *OECD Reviews of National Education Policies: Ireland* (1991) identified the main constrains on change as:

    (a) the power of the teacher unions;

    (b) the power of the Vocational Education Committees (VEC); and

    (c) the power of the Catholic Church.

---

[5] Although they existed in some schools prior to that date, see *Trim Joint District School Board v Kelly* (1914) AC 667.

[6] In primary schools.

[7] In secondary schools.

[8] See the Schedule, Comprehensive Schools, ss 2-10; Draft Deed of Trust for Community Schools 1974, ss 2-7. Both sets of documents are included in O'Flaherty, *Management and Control in Irish Education,* (1992) Drumcondra Teachers' Centre, Appendices A and B.

[9] Section 14(1).

[10] See *Reviews of National Education Policies: Ireland* (1991); see also *OECD Economic Surveys: Ireland* (1995), pp 92-96.

Because of such constraints, it concluded that educational reform in Ireland is feasible only through "discreet negotiations and an unspoken search for consensus".[11]

[6.10] It is strongly arguable, however, that the chief constraint on change in Irish education is the Constitution itself as it enshrined the State's function in education as subsidiary. Because of this feature of constitutional law, prescriptive imposition of State educational policies through legislation is not generally available to the Irish State.[12] Hence, the approach to educational change must necessarily advance along the path of consultation, negotiation and agreement between the key agencies in education.

[6.11] Although the devolution of education to local bodies has been a recurrent proposition in the history of Irish education,[13] the establishment of local structures for education has been implemented solely for the vocational sector. Initiatives by the State, in the past three decades, to establish such structures have been unsuccessful. Since 1991, the search for agreement on appropriate structures has been articulated publicly in a manner unparalleled since the foundation of the State. The Education Act 1998 reflects the broad agreement of the partners in education which has emerged from this challenging and time-consuming consultative process.

Green Paper

[6.12] The Green Paper on Education[14] acknowledged the over-centralised character of education pointing out that the smallest administrative decisions were taken centrally by the Department.[15] Accordingly, it proposed two main structural changes:

(a) the reorganisation and radical devolution of the administration of education to local education authorities.[16]

(b) the establishment of statutory boards of management for all recognised schools with minimal intervention from owners or trustees and the Department,[17] the composition of such boards to be prescribed by law.[18]

---

[11] At p 38.

[12] *Cf* the Education Reform Act 1988 in England.

[13] McPherson's Bill 1919, *Programme for a Partnership Government*, January 1993; *Report of the National Education Convention*, Coolahan, ed, (1994), Gov Pubs, Ch 3; Education Act 1997, Pt 2.

[14] *Education for a Changing World*, (1992), Gov Pubs.

[15] Thereby distracting that body from its task of strategic policy-making, p 4.

[16] *Education for a Changing World*, (1992), p 27.

[17] *Education for a Changing World*, (1992), p 143.

[18] *Education for a Changing World*, (1992), p 144, *cf* Education Act 1998, s 14(1).

Approximately 900 submissions were received in response to the Green Paper which kindled a nationwide debate on education. However, it was the National Education Convention (the Convention) which distilled the essence of the debate on education in an unprecedented democratic manner.[19] Although the Convention was a forum and not a policy-making body, it influenced very significantly the substance and form of the ensuing White Paper on Education.[20]

National Education Convention

[6.13] From 11-21 October 1993, the Convention heard the views of 42 bodies involved in education and reported its findings. The *Report on the National Education Convention* (the Report) noted the high regard in which the people held the great contribution of religious orders in the provision and management of schools in the past.[21] At the same time, it identified a strong public desire for new forms of partnership which would reflect altered circumstances and attitudes. The Report observed the conscientious dilemmas facing non-believing parents who, while accepting the rights of the majority to denominational education, had no choice but to send their children to religiously-run schools.[22] Demands were made by some parents for a plurality of school type reflecting greater parental consciousness of their constitutional rights in this regard. The Report noted that the older model of patron, acting on behalf of parents, was coming under challenge.[23]

[6.14] The question of existing unused, or under-used church-owned school property was an issue of concern which was frequently related to the difficulties encountered by multi-denominational schools and gaelscoileanna in securing permanent accomodation.[24] The Report concluded that it would appear unacceptable for the State to have to buy back school buildings from the churches at current values in circumstances where the historical costs were largely originally paid for by the State. It appears that there was general agreement at the Convention that intermediate educational structures could play a valuable role in supporting the quality of educational provision within the system.[25] If the remaining concerns were satisfactorily addressed in the White

---

[19] The proceedings, which were conducted in public, received much media attention and a televised version of the proceedings was later deposited in the National Archives, becoming its first ever visual record.

[20] *Charting our Education Future* (1995), Gov Pubs.

[21] See *The Report of the National Education Convention*, Coolahan, ed, (1994) Gov Pubs.

[22] See the Report at p 32.

[23] See the Report at p 25.

[24] See the Report at, pp 31-32.

[25] See generally Ch 4.

Paper, the Report concluded, "it would seem that there could be widescale support for such structures within emerging new circumstances".[26]

Episcopal opposition to regional education boards

[6.15] The *Episcopal Commission on Education*[27] (the Commission) opposed the devolution of power from the church schools to any intermediate regional education body holding that:

(a) the philosophy of the denominational school cannot be laid down by the State;

(b) parents should have available to them schools which reflect their values and beliefs; and

(c) denominational schools are held in trust by the patron and trustees, who act as guarantors of the character of the school for successive generations of the Catholic community.[28] This character, the Commission posited, is identifiable by the provision of catechism and religious instruction, and by the presence of a religious ethos in the life of the school.

Furthermore, the Commission maintained that the two latter principles are recognised in the Constitution, which takes account of the historical and cultural heritage of denominational education and guarantees the right to establish and manage denominational schools without State penalty.

[6.16] For these reasons, the Commission submitted that educational legislation should acknowledge and reflect the Christian heritage which the education system seeks to preserve and transmit. The Commission further sought explicit legal protection for denominational schools in any future legislation.

Consensus on certain issues

[6.17] Agreement emerged at the Convention that future legislation:

(a) should build on a spirit of partnership between the key agencies in education,

(b) should not be too detailed,

(c) should be forward looking and remove existing anomalies, and

(d) should put in place principles linked to traditions of the past, reflective of current realities and enabling of future developments.

---

[26] See the Report at p 19.

[27] Representing the Roman Catholic representative body whose views were expressed by its representative Bishop Thomas Flynn.

[28] The Report, p 4.

While some movement appears to have taken place on the proposed establishment of intermediate education structures, the matter was not fully resolved to the satisfaction of the school authorities nor were their apprehensions relating to school governance been fully allayed.

Ministerial Position Papers

[6.18] The following year, the Minister for Education, Niamh Bhreathnach, published two Position Papers in order to clarify her Department's policy on the role of:

    (i) Intermediate education structures[29] (Regional Education Councils, or RECs),

    (ii) The governance of schools.[30]

(i) Position Paper on Regional Education Councils

[6.19] The Position Paper on the RECs made firm proposals for the functions, powers and duties of the proposed RECs and outlined their composition and geographical remit.[31] It envisaged that the RECs would:

    (a) provide support structures,[32]

    (b) empower local communities in the delivery of education locally, and

    (c) administer services such as teacher redeployment and substitute panels based on agreed national guidelines in consultation with individual schools.[33]

Significantly, it was conceded that the RECs would neither employ nor dismiss teachers nor would they become involved in the direct operation or management of schools as patrons or trustees. With regard to structural changes, the Minister pointed out that the Local Government Act 1991 provides for the devolution of functions from the central body to local authorities by provisional order, to be confirmed by an Act of the Oireachtas. Furthermore, the Minister for the Environment[34] passed an order in 1993 under this Act[35] establishing new regional authorities. It was proposed that all State aid towards the recurrent expenditure of schools would be allocated by block grant to the RECs.

---

[29] Minister for Education, Position Paper on Regional Education Councils, (1994), Department of Education.

[30] Minister for Education, Position Paper on the Governance of Schools, (1994), Department of Education.

[31] At pp 10-12.

[32] Position Paper on REC, p 17.

[33] Position Paper on REC, p 13.

[34] Michael Smith.

[35] Section 43.

[6.20] Predictably, it was the provision on future school ownership which was to prove the single most controversial issue. The paper envisaged that the RECs would own and lease new buildings to trustees and patrons according to the specified needs of the area with inbuilt periodic reviews of trustee and management arrangements. It was proposed that each REC would draw up an annual audit programme for all schools within its jurisdiction, which the Department would approve.[36] The Minister revised plans which would abolish at least eight of the country's 38 VECs and lead to the amalgamation of others.

(ii) Position Paper on the Governance of Schools

[6.21] The Paper on the Governance of Schools outlined a number of options for the structure, composition and functions of boards of management of primary and post-primary schools which took account of the proceedings of the National Education Convention. The Minister distinguished between the functions of patrons, trustees, governors and owners and those of boards of management. She assured the school authorities that, subject to the protection of individual rights and civil liberties, the exercise of their functions, in the promotion of ethos in the various schools, would not be affected by the paper's proposals.[37]

[6.22] The Minister was firmly of the view, however, that the composition of boards of management should reflect the increasing desire for partnership in the running of schools on the part of parents and teachers citing the family as "the primary and natural educator".[38] She maintained that the management structures of schools should reflect the reality that the State pays most of the capital and current costs of recognised schools. Accordingly, the Minister concluded that the Government and the Oireachtas have a legitimate concern that school administration should incorporate an appropriate degree of community involvement.[39]

[6.23] However, the Minister conceded the right of the churches to appoint voting majorities and the chairpersons of boards of management. Patrons would accordingly retain their right to nominate a majority of board members but they would be obliged to include a teacher and parent among their nominees. The Minister assured the churches that this right would be reflected and adapted in the new school structures. It was envisaged in the paper that a variety of board models would be put in place consistent with the above principles. The Minister invited the chief parties in education to round table conferences to further explore the unresolved difficulties.

---

[36] Position Paper on REC, p 14.
[37] 'The Governance of Schools', p 4.
[38] The 1937 Constitution, Article 42.1
[39] 'The Governance of Schools'.

Round Table Discussions

[6.24] Approximately 20 bodies were invited to round table discussions in September 1994 to respond to the Position Paper on the Governance of Schools. The Minister was hopeful that her proposals would strike an acceptable balance between the constitutional rights of school owners and those of parents and teachers. However, the Catholic Church representatives[40] made it clear that they found in the Minister's two Position Papers "the rubrics of a secularist agenda and a bid to control the schools to such an extent as to undermine the principle of subsidiarity".[41] They pointed out that legal and constitutional rights to the ownership of their schools severely limited the Minister's power to alter their powers and responsibilities except on a voluntary basis.

[6.25] Other Catholic, Protestant and secular representatives concurred with the views of the Catholic Church representative, threatening to litigate, if necessary, in order to protect their rights. Considerable retrenchment occurred. Nonetheless, the Minister pressed ahead with her plans for devolved education and in 1994 a White Paper was published which represented a considerable compromise in relation to aspects of the governance of schools.

White Paper

[6.26] The White Paper on Education asserted a valid role for the State in regulating school governance.[42] Legislation would be enacted, it stated, *inter alia*, for the governance of schools and its organisational structures and a phased transfer of functions to ten regional boards would follow. Such boards would own all new schools.[43] However, the Paper proposed to retain the existing variety of school types subject to curricular and financial constraints, and to leave undisturbed the ownership rights of schools *per se*. The denominational school authorities maintained that the Bill trespassed upon their constitutionally protected rights and threatened legal action. Nonetheless, the government pressed forward with its plan to draft a Bill which would make provision for devolved education.

The Education Bill 1997

[6.27] The Bill made provision in the interests of the common good, for a range of issues relating to first and second level education including, *inter alia*:

   (a) the establishment and maintenance of Education Boards, and

---

[40] Led by Bishop Thomas Flynn, Chairman of Episcopal Commission on Education.
[41] In his response to the Minister's proposal.
[42] The White Paper on Education (1994) at p 218.
[43] The White Paper at pp 166, 168.

(b) the management of schools through mandatory boards of management.[44]

Section 43 of the Bill provided:

> A school shall have a board of management to fulfil in respect of that school the functions assigned to that school by this Act, and each board shall be a body corporate with perpetual succession and power to sue and be sued in its corporate name.[45]

Considerable controversy surrounded the Bill and in quite an unprecedented manner, all the main denominational school authorities united in protest against what they perceived as statism in education or the advance of secularism. When the term of office of the 27th Dáil expired in 1997, a general election was called, prior to which educational issues became a pivotal element in public debate. If returned to power, the Fianna Fáil party promised that it would draft a new Education Bill which would omit devolution to regional authorities and build on the *status quo* in education.

[6.28] When the new coalition government took up office, it drafted a new Bill, the Education (No 2) Bill 1997, which, *inter alia*:

(a) omitted any plans for decentralisation;

(b) did not provide for mandatory boards of management;

(c) provided for the establishment of corporate bodies to make provision for support services for education; and,

(d) provided for the establishment of the National Council for Curriculum and Assessment.

This much amended Bill passed into law as the Education Act 1998 on 23 December 1998.

Provisions of the Education Act 1998

Part I

[6.29] The Education Act 1998 (the Act) makes provision for a range of issues relating to rights and duties in education, other than third level education, and it provides also for the structure and administration of the education system. The Act further provides, in the interest of the common good, for the education of every child in the State including any child with special educational needs by providing for:

---

[44] Cited in the Title to the Bill.
[45] *Cf* the Education Act 1998, s 14(1); see further s 5(2).

(a) primary and post-primary education;

(b) vocational education and training; and

(c) adult and continuing education.

In legislating for a complex system, which, for the most part, has not previously been subject to legislation, the Act seeks to respect the traditions and diversity of the school system while incorporating such contemporary concepts as partnership, transparency and accountability.

Commencement

[6.30] Section 1 provides that the short title of the Act is the Education Act 1998. It further provides that the Act is to be brought into force by ministerial order and that different parts of the Act may be brought into effect by different Ministerial orders and on different days. With regard to any purpose, function, provision or class of school for which the Minister has not made an order under s 1(2), these sections will be brought into effect two years from the date of its passing.

[6.31] As soon as practicable following the end of the first and second years following the date of enactment of the Act, the Minister is required to prepare a report on the implementation of the Act and to cause copies of such report to be laid before the Dáil and Seanad. The Intermediate Education (Ireland) Acts 1878[46]-1924 and this Act may be cited together as the the Education Acts 1878-1998 and shall be construed together as one.

Definition of Terms in the Education Act 1998

[6.32] Section 2 of the Act deals with interpretation and it defines the main terms used in the Act. Of particular significance are the following terms:

(i) Parent

[6.33] Among the most important definitions is that of "parent" which is broadly defined as follows:

> "parent" includes a foster parent, a guardian appointed under the Guardianship of Infants Acts 1964-1997 or other person acting *in loco parentis* who has a child in his or her care subject to any statutory power or order of a court, and in the case of a child who has been adopted under the Adoption Acts 1952-1998, or where the child has been adopted outside the State, means the adopter or adopters or the surviving adopter.

---

[46] Intermediate Education (Ireland) Act 1878, s 5(4) is amended by Education Act 1998, s 35, thereby deleting "provided that no examination shall be held in any subject of religious instruction, not any payment made in respect thereof."

(ii) Disability

[6.34] The term "disability" means:

(a) the total or partial loss of a person's bodily or mental functions, including the loss of a part of the person's body, or

(b) the presence in the body of organisms, causing or likely to cause, chronic disease or illness, or

(c) the malfunction, malformation, or disfigurement of a part of a person's body, or

(d) a condition or malfunction which results in a person learning differently from a person without the condition or malfunction, or

(e) a condition, illness or disease which affects a person's thought processes, perception of reality, emotions or judgment or which results in disturbed behaviour.

(iii) Characteristic Spirit

[6.35] This term means the characteristic spirit as referred to in s 15(2)(b) of the Act which refers to:

the characteristic spirit of the school as determined by the cultural, educational, moral, religious, social, linguistic and spiritual values and traditions which inform and are characteristic of the objectives and conduct of the school ...

[6.36] In common parlance, the characteristic spirit of the school is frequently referred to as the ethos of the school.

[6.37] Section 3 provides that any expenses which are incurred by the Minister in the administration of the Act shall be paid out of funds provided by the Oireachtas.

[6.38] Section 4 provides a vehicle for the services of notices, directions and other documents under the Act.

[6.39] Section 5 provides that every regulation and order, made pursuant to the Act, must be laid before each House of the Oireachtas and these will take effect unless they are annulled by either the Dáil or Seanad within the next 21 days on which that House has sat after the regulation or order is laid before it.

Aims and Objects of the Act

[6.40] The objects of the Act are set down in s 6. It provides that every individual concerned in the implementation of this Act shall have regard to the specified objects in pursuance of which the Oireachtas has enacted the Act. The objects may be summarised as follows:

(a) to give practical effect to the constitutional rights of children including children who have a disability or other special educational needs, as they relate to education;

(b) to provide that, as far as practicable, and within available resources, an appropriate level and quality of education is available to each person in the State;

(c) to promote equality of access to and participation in education and to promote the means whereby students may benefit from education;

(d) to promote opportunities for adults to avail of education through adult and continuing education;

(e) to promote the right of parents to send their children to a school of their choice having regard to the rights of patrons and the effective and efficient use of resources;

(f) to promote best practice in teaching methods;

(g) to promote effective liaison and consultation between schools, centres for education, the partners for education the local communities, local authorities, health boards and other persons or groups having a special interest in special educational needs and the Minister;

(h) to contribute to the realisation of national education policies and objectives;

(i) to contribute to the realisation of national education policies and objectives in regard to the extension of bi-lingualism in Irish society and in particular the achievement of a greater use of the Irish language at school and in the community;

(j) to contribute to the maintenance of Irish as the primary community language in Gaeltacht areas;

(k) to promote the language and cultural needs of students having regard to the choices of their parents; and

(l) to enhance accountability and transparency in the education system.

Ministerial Powers and Functions

[6.41] The main functions of the Minister for Education and Science (the Minister hereafter) are laid down in s 7 of the Act. They may be summarised as follows:

(a) to ensure, subject to the provisions of this Act, that there is available to each resident in the State, including those with a disability or special educational needs, support services together with a level and quality of education appropriate to meeting the needs of that person.

(b) to determine national education policy:

(c) to plan and co-ordinate -

　(i) the provision of education in recognised schools and centers for education, and

　(ii) support services.

[6.42] Further Ministerial functions, without prejudice to the generality of s 7(1) of the Act, are:

    (a) to provide funding to each recognised school and centre for education and to make provision for support services to the said institutions and to students, including those with a disability special educational needs, and their parents, as the Minister considers appropriate and in accordance with this Act;

    (b) to monitor and access the economy, efficiency and effectiveness of the education system provided in the State by recognised schools and centres of education ...;

    (c) to lease land or buildings to any person/body of persons for the purposes of setting up a school without prejudice to the establishment by patrons of schools which are established on land or in buildings not so leased, the extension and further development of such schools when established and the recognition of such schools when established in accordance with s 10 of the Act;

    (d) to provide support services through the medium of Irish to recognised schools which provide teaching through Irish and to any other recognised school which requests such provision;

    (e) to perform such other functions as are specifically provided for by this Act or any other enactment, and

    (f) to do all such acts and things as may be necessary to further the objects for which this Act is enacted.

With regard to the determination of national policy for education, the author believes that a more effective long-term policy would result if the Minister established a policy-making body of experts to advise him or her (under Part 1X of the Act). These persons could be drawn mainly from the partners in education. The National Education Policy Act 1996 of South Africa provides for:

    (a) the determination of national policy on education by the Minister;

    (b) prior consultation before such determination; and

    (c) the setting up of consultative bodies to facilitate such consultation.[47]

Restrictions on Ministerial Functions

[6.43] The Act provides that the Minister shall have all such powers as are necessary or expedient for the purpose of performing his or her functions.[48] However, s 7(4)(a) requires the Minister in carrying out such functions to have regard to:

    (i) the resources available;

---

[47] Section 2.
[48] Section 7(3).

(ii) the provision for education and training made by other agencies with funds provided by the Oireachtas;

(iii) the need to reflect the diversity of educational services provided in the State, and

(iv) the practices and traditions relating to schools or groups of schools existing at the commencement of this Part and the right of schools to manage their own affairs in accordance with this Act and any charters, deeds, articles of management or other such instruments relating to their establishment or operation.

Consultation with Partners in Education

[6.44] Section 7(4)(b) of the Act provides that, the Minister shall make all reasonable efforts to consult with the parties in education[49] and others who have a special interest in or knowledge of matters relating to education "as the Minister considers appropriate." Clearly consultation is envisaged by this section. However, the Minister may be free of the obligation to consult with the parties in education, it seems, where:

(a) he deems such consultation inappropriate; or

(b) he has made all reasonable efforts to consult.

Section 7(2)(c) represents a compromise between the interests of the Minister and those of existing school owners in regard to the ownership of schools. While the Minister will have the power to lease land or buildings for the purpose of establishing a school, patrons may still establish schools on lands or buildings which are not so leased. Furthermore, they may continue to establish and develop such schools when established and such schools will be recognised in accordance with s 10 of the Act.

[6.45] The Minister's recent press release on school buildings[50] indicates that the new schools, provided under the proposed new arrangements, will be in the ownership of the State and will be leased to the patrons under a lease or deed of trust.[51] There has been surprisingly little reaction by the denominational school authorities to this significant announcement. As the demand for new denominational schools since 1990 has been minimalist (only one such school, the Islamic school, has been established since then), the ownership of new schools will move gradually, it seems, to the State. However, the status quo will be retained in relation to existing schools and the churches still retain the right to establish schools as they have traditionally.

---

[49] Being the patrons, the national association of parents, recognised school management organisations, recognised trade unions and staff associations representing teachers.

[50] 10 January 1999.

[51] See Appendix E, Press Release, Minister for Education and Science, 'Historic Move in State Funding for School Buildings' 10 January 1999.

Part II: Schools

The Patron

[6.46] Section 8 not only defines the term "patron",[52] which is of ancient lineage,[53] it extends that term to embrace all recognised schools[54] and provides a procedure for identifying the person or body who is the patron of the school. Essentially, the Act recognises as patrons of a school for the purposes of the Act, those persons or bodies in control in all recognised schools at the date of commencement of Part II of the Act. Section 8(1) of the Act provides that the following shall be deemed to be the patron for the purposes of the Act and that patrons' names shall be entered by the Minister in a register:

(a) the person who, at the commencement of this section, is recognised by the Minister as the patron of a primary school, and

(b) the persons, who at the commencement of this section, stand appointed as trustees or as the board of governors of a post-primary school and, where there are no such trustees or such board, the owner of that school.

In cases other than those provided in s 8(1), the patron of a recognised school shall be the person who requested recognition of the school or his nominee.[55]

[6.47] In schools established and maintained by a VEC, the patron is the relevant vocational education committee.[56] Joint patrons may be registered where two or more persons exercise the functions of a patron.

[6.48] The Act provides that the patron of a school shall carry out the functions and exercise the powers conferred on him by any Act of the Oireachtas or instrument made thereunder, deed, charter, articles of management or other such instrument relating to the establishment or operation of the school.[57]

Identifying the Patron in Practice

[6.49] The Act confers statutory authority on those persons or bodies who already held the key positions in each sector. From the date of commencement of Part II of the Act, the following will be recognised as patrons of schools:

(a) Mainstream primary schools: the bishop of the diocese;

(b) Gaelscoileanna: the bishop of the diocese or *Foras Patrúnachta na Scoileanna Lán-Ghaeilge;*

---

[52] Sections 8 (1)(a) and 8(2).
[53] See Lord Stanley's Letter, Appendix F.
[54] Section 8 (1)(a) and s 8(1)(b).
[55] Section 8(2).
[56] Section 8(4).
[57] Section 8(6).

(c) Multi-denominational schools: the board of the company limited by guarantee which establishes the school;

(d) Model schools: the State;[58]

(e) Secondary schools: the trustee body,[59] the diocesan nominee[60] or the board of governors;[61]

(f) Comprehensive and community schools: the trustees as established under the schools' deeds of trust;

(g) VEC schools and colleges: the governing Vocational Education Committee;

(h) Privately owned schools: the owner of the school.

Functions of Schools

[6.50] The wide ranging and detailed functions of recognised schools are provided for in s 9 of the Act. Such schools shall provide education to students which is appropriate to their abilities and needs and without prejudice to the generality of the foregoing, it shall use its resources to:

(a) ensure that the educational needs of all students, including those with a disability or other special educational needs, are identified and provided for;

(b) ensure that the education provided by the school meets with the educational policy of the Minister, as determined from time to time, including curricular requirements in accordance with s 30 of the Act;

(c) ensure that students have access to appropriate guidance to assist them in their educational and career choices;

(d) promote the moral, spiritual, social and personal development of students and provide health education for them in consultation with their parents, having regard to the characteristic spirit of the school;

(e) promote equality of opportunity for male and female students and school staff;

(f) promote the development of the Irish language and traditions, Irish literature, the arts and other cultural matters;

(g) ensure that parents of a student, or in the case of a student who has reached 18 years, the student, have access in the prescribed manner to records retained by that school to the educational progress of the student;

(h) in the case of schools situated in a Gaeltacht area, contribute to the maintenance of Irish as the primary community language;

---

[58] See *Leyden v AG* [1926] IR 334.
[59] In voluntary secondary schools.
[60] In diocesan colleges.
[61] In Protestant schools.

(i) conduct its activities in compliance with any regulation made by the Minister under s 33;

(j) ensure that the need of staff involved in management functions and staff development needs generally in the school are identified and provided for;

(k) establish and maintain systems to access the efficiency and effectiveness of its operations including the quality and effectiveness of teaching in the school and the attainment levels and academic standards of students;

(l) to establish and maintain inter-school contacts and at other appropriate levels in the community served by the school;

(m) subject to this Act and in particular s 15(2)(d), establish and maintain an admissions policy which provides for maximum accessibility to the school.

Resource implications

[6.51] Clearly, the above section has massive resource and personnel implications. Much of the infrastructure to support certain provisions mentioned above have yet to be put in place. This cannot be done without the necessary personnel which further necessitates the training, education and securing of extra remedial teachers, career and guidance counsellors, special needs teachers, psychologists, speech therapists and curricular advisors. The effective implementation of this section will also require considerable in-service training for existing personnel in schools. As this section shall pass into law, at the very latest, two years from the date of the passing of the Act, ie on or after 23 December 2000,[62] there is much to be achieved.

Recognition of Schools

[6.52] Provisions relating to the recognition of schools for the purposes of the Act, the withdrawal of such recognition and the annual funding of schools are laid down in ss 10,[63] 11 and 12 of the Act. Section 10 provides for the recognition of schools which is a prerequisite to funding. Following a request being made, by the patron of a school or a proposed school, for the recognition of a school, the Minister may designate that school or proposed school to be a recognised school for the purposes of the Act provided certain criteria are complied with by the patron. Such criteria are set down in s 10 which provides:

(a) the number of students who are attending or are likely to attend the school is such or is likely to be such as to make the school viable,

(b) in the case of a proposed school ... the needs of students attending, or likely to attend the school cannot reasonably be met by existing schools,

---

[62] See Education Act 1998, s 1(3). The Act was signed into law by the Commission of the Executive Council on 23 December 1998 as the President was out of the country.

[63] In this regard see Ch 4.

(c) the patron undertakes that the school shall provide the curriculum in accordance with section 30,

(d) the patron agrees to permit and co-operate with regular inspection and evaluation by the Inspectorate,

(e) the school complies, or in the case of a proposed school, shall comply with health, safety and building standards as are determined by law and any further such standards as are determined from time to time by the Minister,[64]

(f) the patron undertakes that the school shall operate in accordance with such regulations and as may be made by the Minister form time to time under section 33 and with this Act and with any other terms and conditions as may reasonably be attached to recognition by the Minister.[65]

Subsection 3 is a statutory recognition of the *status quo*. A school, which on the commencement of this section, is in receipt of funds provided by the Oireachtas for education activities or for teachers' salaries, shall be deemed to be a recognised school.

Centres of Education

[6.53] Section 10(4) of the Act empowers the Minister to designate a place to be a centre for education, ie:

a place other than a school or a place providing university or other third level education, where adult or continuing education or vocational education or training, is provided and which is designated for that purpose under section 10(4).[66]

Withdrawal of Recognition

[6.54] Section 11 of the Act provides that where the Minister is satisfied that:

(a) the requirements under s 10(2) of the Act are not being met by a school, or

(b) the functions of a school are not being effectively discharged by a school, and

(c) when he or she is of the opinion that recognition should be withdrawn from that school,

he or she shall inform the following by notice in writing of that opinion and the reasons for that opinion; the board, the patron, the teachers, the student council where one exists and the parents of students.

[6.55] Section 11(2) provides:

---

[64] Note the absence of welfare from this section.
[65] See s 10 of the Act.
[66] Section 2(1).

If, after the expiration of three months from the date of the notice issued under subsection (1), and, after consideration of any representations made to the Minister by the board or the patron of the school, the teachers or the parents, or the student council where one exists, the Minister remains of the said opinion, the Minister may withdraw recognition from the school by notice in writing addressed to the board and the patron of the school, and such notice shall be effective on and from the last day of the school year following the school year in which the notice was addressed to the board or such later date as the Minister may determine.

[6.56] A period of three months, from the date of issue of the ministerial notice upon the school, is provided for this process of making representations to the Minister. If at the end of that period, a decision is taken to withdraw recognition, then this shall take effect from the end of the school year following the school year in which the decision was made or such later date as the Minister shall decide. In no case, however, will the notice period of withdrawal of recognition be less than twelve months.

[6.57] Clearly, in the light of the requirement of fair procedures, it is necessary that a reasonable time be allowed to such a school to improve its performance. However, this must be balanced against the rights of students attending the school to an adequate education during the period prior to school closure. However, there are circumstances[67] in which this period could conceivably run to a period of two to three years which is not an insubstantial period in a child's life. In view of the paramountcy of the rights of the child and its constitutional right to free primary education, a court could hold that the maximum period allowed to schools under s 11(2) was unduly generous as it conflicted with the right of the child to an adequate and appropriate education during this period.

[6.58] Furthermore, s 11(2) fails to provide for a shorter period of time for urgent cases of school closure thereby fettering the Minister's discretion in this regard. For these reasons, it may have been more prudent to leave the discretion as to time limits in s 11(2) with the Minister.[68] If this were the case, the last four lines of s 11(2) could read "and such notice shall be effective on:

(a) such period as may be prescribed, or

(b) if the Minister is of the opinion that the urgency of the case requires a shorter period, such period as the Minister may direct."

---

[67] If, for instance, a decision were taken on the last day of the school year to withdraw recognition from a school, the final date for withdrawal would be almost two years away and the Minister could further extend that period in certain circumstances.

[68] In the English context, it is notable that Education Act 1993, s 210(2) leaves the discretion as to time limits with the Secretary of State.

Section 11(3) of the Act imposes a duty on the Minister to make educational facilities available for those students who were enrolled in a school from which recognition has been withdrawn should the students require this.

Special Measures

[6.59] The Act seems to envisage that, when the functions of a school are not being effectively discharged or the requirements for recognition are not being met under s 11, that a range of quality assurance measures will be provided by regulation under s 33(a).

[6.60] Part V of the English Education Act 1993[69] makes provision for such measures. An inspector prepares a written statement of the action to be taken on foot of a report made following a statutory inspection. Where a school "is failing or likely to fail to give its pupils an acceptable standard of education,"[70] a range of "special measures"[71] may be taken including an order that overall control of a school be transferred to an Education Association.

Restoration of Recognition

[6.61] Under the Irish Education Act 1998, the Minister, if he is satisfied that the requirements of s 10 are being met and that the function of the school is being effectively discharged, may restore recognition to that school. However, that school has no entitlement to public funds in respect to the period during which recognition was withdrawn. A range of support and monitoring measures for such schools seems a pivotal requirement at this juncture and these hopefully will be included later under regulations.[72]

Funding of Schools

[6.62] Provision for the annual funding of schools is made under s 12 of the Education Act 1998. Section 12(1) provides that the Minister[73] shall determine and publish criteria by which recognised schools and centres for education are to

---

[69] See Part V of the Act, see s 204(3) and ss 214-218 incl.
[70] See s 204(3).
[71] The "special measures" under the Education Act include:
   (a) the appointment of extra governors by the LEA (s 214);
   (b) the suspension of the right to a delegated budget by the LEA (s 215);
   (c) a power to dissolve a grouping of schools and a prohibition on a school joining a group (s 216);
   (d) a prohibition on the balloting of parents as to whether grant-maintained status should be sought for a school (s 217);
   (e) that overall control of a school be transferred to an Education Association (s 218).
[72] See s 33(a).
[73] With the concurrence of the Minister for Finance.

be funded in the ensuing school year, which criteria may permit additional funding to recognised schools having regard to the level of educational disadvantage of students in these schools. Annually, on a date determined by him or her, the Minister shall make grants to recognised schools or centres for education except as otherwise provided in the Act in accordance with criteria determined by s 12(2). With regard to schools under the jurisdiction of VECs, grants will be paid to the relevant vocational education committee, which will then disburse these grants in accordance with the criteria. Section 12(4) and (5) provide the continuance of the existing practice, whereby certain schools are funded by way of block grant, eg Church of Ireland schools.

[6.63] Section 12 vests a wide discretion in the Minister, who may change every five years or less, to administer substantial amounts of public funds. This arrangement is unlikely to result in consistent, long-term policy for the funding of schools. The dispersal of public funds in education in an equitable and constitutional manner is an enormous responsibility for the Minister.

[6.64] It is highly desirable, therefore, that the Minister would establish a body corporate, under Part IX of the Act, as a funding agency or unit for the disbursal of public funds for education drawing on the expertise of the partners in education and other experts in the sphere. Such an approach would be likely to lead to a more structured, objective, democratic basis for the dispersal of public funds in education.

[6.65] This approach was adopted in England in the Education Act 1993 which established a funding agency for schools in England[74] and a funding authority for schools in Wales[75] appointed by the Secretary of State. These small bodies, which are constituted as bodies corporate, administer the funds and the Secretary of State is empowered to make grants to any funding authority of such amounts and subject to such terms and conditions as he may determine.

Part III: The Inspectorate

[6.66] Section 13 makes provision for the Inspectorate comprising the Chief Inspector and so many inspectors as the Minister considers appropriate[76] some of whom will be qualified psychologists or persons holding other expertise including expertise in the education of students with special educational needs.[77] This provision places the existing Inspectorate on a statutory basis for the first time and provides a statutory statement of its functions. As the powers in this

---

[74] See s 3 of the 1993 Act. This body comprises 10-15 persons.
[75] Section 4. This body comprises 8-12 persons.
[76] Subject to the provisions of s 13(11).
[77] Section 13(2).

section have traditionally been under the Minister's jurisdiction, there is, as one would expect, no reference to any consultation with the partners in education.

Functions of an Inspector

[6.67] Section 13(3) lays down the wide-ranging functions of an Inspector which include the obligation:

  (a) to support and advise recognised schools and centres for education and teachers in matters pertaining to the provision of education;[78]

  (b) to evaluate the quality and effectiveness of the provision of education in the State on a comparative basis and to report thereon to the Minister;

  (c) to conduct research into education and to provide support in policy formulation by the Minister;

  (d) to advise the Minister in matters pertaining to education policy and provision including curricular areas, assessment and teaching methods;

  (e) to perform such functions relating to the preparation and marking of the State school examinations as the Chief Inspector shall determine, together with the monitoring and evaluation of the contents and standards of such examinations and reporting thereon to the Minister.

  (f) to disseminate information regarding the performance by the Inspectorate of the functions provided for under s 13 and on successful initiatives in education implemented by schools and centres for education; and to

  (g) to promote excellence in the management of teaching and in the use of support services by schools and in and in the procedures for consultation and cooperation between schools and centres for education.

Inspectors who are Psychologists

[6.68] As well as the functions set out under s13(3), s 13(4) provides that without prejudice to the generality of sub-s (3), an Inspector to whom sub-s (2) applies shall have the following functions:

  (a) in consultation with parents, to access the psychological needs of students in recognised schools and to advise as appropriate those students, their parents and the schools in regard to the educational and psychological development of such students;

  (b) to advise recognised schools on policies and strategies for the education of children with special educational needs;

---

[78] For the details of this duty see s 13(3) of the Act.

(c) to advise the Minister on any matter relating to the psychological needs of students in recognised schools;

(d) in collaboration with parents and the Principal and teachers in recognised schools, to assist in the creation of a school environment which prevents or limits obstacles to learning which students may experience; and

(e) to advise the Minister on any matter relating to the linguistic needs of deaf students in recognised schools.

Secondment of Teachers to the Inspectorate

[6.69] When the teacher and the board consent, provision is made under s 13(6) for the secondment of teachers to the Inspectorate for such period as the Minister shall determine.

[6.70] Inspectors shall have all such powers as are necessary or expedient for the performance of their functions and shall be accorded every reasonable facility and co-operation by the board and the staff of a school or centre for education.[79] However, the procedures and criteria for such inspections may be determined by the Minister, from time to time, following consultation with the partners in education and others as the Minister considers appropriate and also by ministerial directions.[80]

[6.71] Section 13(8) provides that the Chief Inspector shall review any inspection carried out by an Inspector following a request for such review by a teacher or board of management.

[6.72] Section 13(10) is a carry-over provision which applies to those persons who immediately prior to the commencement of Part III of the Act held an office as "Chief Inspector, Inspector, Inspector of Guidance Service/ Psychologist and persons who were seconded to the Inspectorate". Section 13(10) provides that the Civil Service Commissions Act 1956 and the Civil Service Regulations Acts 1956-1958 shall apply to Inspectors.

Part IV: Boards of Management

[6.73] Section 14 of the Act provides that it is the duty of a patron to appoint, *where practicable*,[81] a board of management, the composition of which is agreed between the partners in education and the Minister.

[6.74] This provision is in sharp contrast with s 43(1) of the Education Bill 1997 which provided:

---

[79] Section 13(7).
[80] Section 13(8).
[81] Author's emphasis.

A school *shall have*[82] a board of management to fulfil in respect of that school the functions assigned to that school by this Act ...

Such a mandatory obligation on denominational schools to establish a board would appear to conflict with the school's constitutional right to manage its own affairs, to own, acquire and administer property and maintain institutions, for religious or charitable purposes.[83]

[6.75] The inclusion of the words "where practicable" in the Education Act 1998 permits some choice to the school authority although the failure to set up a board goes against the spirit of the Act which is to establish partnership in school management. Boards of management are conferred with body corporate status with perpetual succession and power to sue and be sued in their corporate name.[84]

[6.76] Section 14(3) provides that the *status quo* as to the management of schools shall continue until such time as the statutory boards of management are set up. Board members shall be appointed by the school patron except where Articles of Management provide otherwise. With the agreement of the patron and the partners in education, the Minister shall prescribe matters relating to the appointment of a board.[85]

[6.77] Section 13(7) provides that no action shall lie against a member of a board acting in good faith and in pursuance of the provisions of this Act or regulations made thereunder. This provision should allay the fears of board members, who in the past, were concerned that they might incur personal liability when acting as a member of a school board.

Functions of a Board of Management

[6.78] Section 15(1) provides:

It shall be the duty of a board to manage the school on behalf of the patron and for the benefit of the students and their parents and to provide or cause to be provided an appropriate education for each student at the school for which that board has responsibility.

In the performance of its functions, a board's duties may be summarised as follows, to:

    (a) act in accordance with the policies determined from time to time by the Minister;

---

[82] Author's emphasis.
[83] Article 44.2.6°.
[84] Section 14(2).
[85] Section 14(6).

(b) uphold the characteristic spirit of the school and be accountable to the patron for so doing;

(c) uphold and at all times and act in accordance with any Act of the Oireachtas or instrument made thereunder, deed, charter, articles of management or other such instrument relating to the establishment or operation of the school;

(d) consult with and keep the patron informed of the decisions and proposals of the board;

(e) publish, in such manner as the board with the agreement of the patron considers appropriate:

    (i) the school's admission policy;

    (ii) its policy in relation to participation in the school;

    (iii) its policy in relation to expulsion and suspension of students;

    (iv) its policy on admission to and participation by students with disability or who have other special educational needs and to ensure that the policy respects the principles of equality and that the right of parents to send their children to a school of their choice is respected and such directions as may be made from time to time by the Minister, having regard to the characteristic spirit of the school and that the constitutional rights of all persons, concerned are complied with.

(f) have regard to the principles and requirements of a democratic society and have respect and promote respect for the diversity of values, beliefs, traditions and ways of life in society;

(g) have regard to the efficient use of resources (and in particular the efficient use of grants provided under s 12), the public interest in the affairs of the school and accountability to students, their parents, the patron, staff and the community served by the school, and

(h) use the resources provided to the school from public monies in accordance with s 12, to make reasonable provision and accomodation for students with disability or other special educational needs, including, where necessary, alteration of buildings and provision of appropriate equipment.

Lest there be any doubt, s 15(3) elucidates that nothing in the Act shall confer or be deemed to confer on the board any right over or interest in the land and buildings of the school for which that board is responsible.

Dissolution of Boards by a Patron

[6.79] Subject to s 16, and to the consent of the Minister, the patron may:

(a) dissolve a board if he or she is satisfied that the functions of a board are not being effectively discharged; or may

(b) remove any board member provided he or she has given the board or board member one month's notice in writing explaining the reasons for the decision including the opinion of the patron and provided that any representations made have been considered.

The procedures for effecting such dissolution are set down in s 16(2), (3) and (4). A copy of every notice issued under this section together with any representations made to the patron shall be delivered to the Minister, as soon as may be after it is made.[86]

[6.80] Whenever a board is dissolved by the patron, he or she may, subject to the approval of the Minister, appoint any person or body of persons as the patron considers fit to perform the functions of the board.[87] Where a patron removes a board member, the resulting vacancy shall be filled in accordance with regulations made under s 14(6).

[6.81] Not later than six months following the dissolution of a board, or such longer period as the patron with the consent of the Minister considers appropriate, the patron shall provide in accordance with s 14 for the re-establishment of a new board. When the new board has been established, the functions of the dissolved board shall be re-vested in the new board and shall cease to be the functions of the person(s), if any appointed under sub-s (5).

Dissolution of Boards by a Patron at the Request of the Minister

[6.82] Section 17 provides that the Minister may require a patron to dissolve a board where:

(a) the Minister is satisfied that the functions of a board are not being effectively discharged, or

(b) a board wilfully neglects to comply with any order, direction or regulation of the Minister given or made under this Act, or

(c) a board fails to comply with any judgment or order of any court of competent jurisdiction,

The Minister must, by notice in writing, require the patron to dissolve the board for reasons which are stipulated in such notice and the patron shall dissolve the board accordingly as soon as may be following the date of such notice.

[6.83] Prior to serving a notice pursuant to sub-s 1, the Minister shall inform the board and the patron of his/her intention to do so and shall consider any representations made to him/her by or on behalf of the board or the patron within

---

[86] Section 16(4).
[87] Section 16(5).

one month of informing the board and the patron.[88] On the dissolution of a board, s 16(5) and s 16(7) shall apply.[89]

Accounts and Records by the Board

[6.84] Section 18 provides that a board[90] shall keep accounts of all receipts and expenditure and shall ensure that all such accounts are properly audited annually in accordance with best accounting practice. In so far as those accounts relate to moneys provided under s 12, accounts kept in pursuance of s 18 shall be made available by the relevant school for inspection by the Minister and by parents of students in the school.[91]

Report on Operation of Board

[6.85] Where the Minister or the patron is of the opinion that the functions of the board are not being effectively discharged, the Minister or the patron shall inform the board of that opinion and the reasons on which it is based.[92] Following consideration of any representations made by the board, the Minister or the patron, as the case may be, may authorise any person or persons deemed appropriate by the Minister, by the patron or by both[93] on any matter arising from or relating to the operation of that board. Special rights adhere to a person(s) appointed to prepare a report on the operation of the board. They are entitled at all reasonable times:

(a) to enter any premises occupied by the school concerned; and

(b) to be afforded every facility and co-operation by the board, the teachers and other school staff; and

(c) to be afforded access to all records in order that he or she can perform their functions under the Act.[94]

A principal or board is under a duty to supply the patron and the Minister with such information relating to the performance of the board's functions as the patron or the Minister, as the case may be, may require from time to time.[95] Where a patron proposes to exercise functions under this section he or she shall inform the Minister of the proposed course of action. Likewise, where the

---

[88] Section 17(2).
[89] Section 17(3).
[90] Except in the case of a school established or maintained by a VEC.
[91] Section 18(2).
[92] Section 19(1).
[93] Section 19(2).
[94] Section 19(3).
[95] Section 19(4).

Minister proposes to give effect to functions under this section, he shall inform the patron of his proposed actions.[96]

Reporting and Informing Parents

[6.86] A board is required to set up procedures for informing the parents of children in the school of issues relating to the operation and performance of the school. Such procedures *may* include the publication and circulation to parents, teachers and other staff and to a student council, where one has been established, of a report on the operation and performance of the school in any school year with particular reference to the achievement of objectives as set out in the school plan provided for under s 21.

The School Plan

[6.87] Section 21(1) provides that a board shall, as soon as may be following its appointment, make arrangements for the preparation of a plan, referred to in this section as "the school plan," and ensure that the plan is regularly reviewed and updated. The school plan shall set down the objectives of the school relating to equality of access to, and participation in the school by students with disabilities or those who have other special educational needs. It shall be prepared in accordance with such directions, including directions referring to consultation with the parents, the patron, the staff and students of the school, as may be given from time to time by the Minister in relation to school plans.[97] A board shall make arrangements for the circulation of copies of the plan to the patron, parents, teachers and other staff of the school.

Part V: The Principal and Teachers

Functions of the Principal and Teachers

[6.88] Section 22 provides that the principal and teachers of a recognised school are responsible for the instruction of students in the school and they must contribute to their education and personal development. Section 22(2) provides that without prejudice to sub-s (1), the principal and teachers shall:

(a) encourage and foster learning in students,

(b) regularly evaluate students and periodically report the results of the evaluation to the students and their parents,

(c) collectively promote co-operation between the school and the community which it serves, and

---

[96] Section 20.5.
[97] Section 21(3).

    (d) subject to the terms of any applicable collective agreement and their contract of employment, carry out those duties that -

        (i) in the case of teachers, are assigned to them by or at the direction of the Principal, and

        (ii) in the case of the Principal, are assigned to him or her by the board.

Section 22(d) takes into account the *status quo* in the profession thereby providing statutory protection, not only for the existing contracts of employment of teachers, but also for "any applicable collective agreement." This guarantee of teacher rights means that the employment conditions of existing teachers may not lawfully be altered unilaterally to their detriment.[98]

The Principal

[6.89] Section 23 provides that the board of management shall appoint the principal in accordance with procedures to be agreed between the partners in education subject to terms and conditions determined by the Minister with the consent of the Minister for Finance. Together with the functions of a principal already set down in s 22, he or she is further responsible for:

    (a) the day to day management of the school, including guidance and direction of the teachers and other school staff and be accountable to the board for that management;

    (b) providing leadership to the teachers and other staff and the students of the school;

    (c) creating an environment which promotes learning and fosters the professional development of the teachers;

    (d) setting and monitoring school objectives; and

    (e) encouraging parental participation.[99]

The principal shall have all such powers as are necessary to carry out his functions under the Act and he shall carry out such functions in accordance with such policies of the board of management and regulations made under s 33 of the Act.[100] Under sub-s (4), the principal is entitled to become a member of any and every committee appointed by a board.

[6.90] Where before the commencement of the Act, the employer of a post-primary principal is a body other than a board of management, that body shall, after the commencement of the Act, have the role outlined above, for the board of management in relation to the appointment of the principal.[101] Subsection (6)

---

[98] This right had already been judicially conceded by the Supreme Court in *McEneaney v Minister for Education* [1941] IR 430.

[99] Section 23(2).

[100] Section 23(3).

[101] Section 23(5).

provides that, wherever practicable, in carrying out his functions, a principal shall, in exercising his or her functions under s 23, consult with teachers and other school staff.

Provisions Relating to School Staff

[6.91] Section 24 applies to all recognised schools except schools which are established and maintained by a VEC. It provides that a board may appoint such and so many persons as teachers and other staff of a school as it, from time to time, considers necessary for the performance of its powers and functions under the Act. The following section makes it clear, however, that the numbers, qualifications and remuneration of staff paid out of moneys provided by the Oireachtas are subject to the Minister's approval, with the concurrence of the Minister for Finance.

[6.92] Subsection (3) provides that the board shall appoint teachers and other staff, who are to be paid out of public funds, and that the board may suspend or dismiss such teachers and staff in accordance with procedures agreed between the Minister and the partners in education or other staff as appropriate.

[6.93] Existing appointment, suspension and dismissal procedures of teachers or other staff, which were in operation immediately before the commencement of s 24 are to remain in place pending the agreement of procedures provided for in sub-s (3).

[6.94] Subsection (5) provides that the terms and conditions of employment of teachers and other staff of a school appointed by a board and who are to be paid from public moneys shall be determined by the Minister, with the concurrence of the Minister for Finance.

[6.95] Where all or a portion of the remuneration and superannuation of teachers and other school staff, is paid or is to be paid out of public funds, such remuneration or superannuation shall be determined from time to time by the Minister with the concurrence of the Minister for Finance.[102]

[6.96] Where at the commencement of s 24, the employer of the teachers or other staff in a post-primary school is a person or body of persons other than the board of management, that body shall, after the at the time of commencement and afterwards, have the role outlined above for the board of management in relation to staff. This means that the owner of a private school or the board of governors in a Church of Ireland school is substituted for the board in these subsections. This section is not applicable to staff of a vocational school who are covered by VEC legislation.

---

[102] Section 24(6).

Part VI: Miscellaneous

Duration of School Year, Week or Day

[6.97] Section 25 provides that the Minister may, from time to time, after consultation with the partners in education, prescribe:

    (a) the minimum number of days in a school year during which a school shall be open to receive students and provide them with instruction,

    (b) the minimum number of hours of instruction in a school day or in a school week, and

    (c) any matters related to the length of the school year, the school week or the school day and the organisation and structure of such year, week or day.

Section 25 contrasts sharply with the prescriptive character of s 53 of the Education Bill 1997 which provided that the Minister may, from time to time prescribe for (a), (b) and (c) as stated above. No provision was made for any consultation with the partners in education.

Parents' Association

[6.98] While parents' associations already existed in many schools prior to the coming into force of the Education Act 1998, these associations had no statutory origin or statutory powers. Section 26(1) of the Act provides that parents of students of a recognised school may establish from among their number a parents' association for that school.

[6.99] Subsection (2) provides:

> A parents' association shall promote the interests of the students in a school in co-operation with the board, Principal, teachers and students and for that purpose may -
>
> (a) advise the Principal or the board on any matter relating to the school and the Principal or board, as the case may be, shall have regard to any such advice, and
>
> (b) adopt a programme of activities which will promote the involvement of parents, in consultation with the Principal, in the operation of the school.

[6.100] In this regard, it is the board's duty to promote contact between the school, parents of students in the school and the community, to facilitate and give all reasonable assistance to parents who wish to set up such an association and to such an association when it is established.[103] A parents' association may make rules governing its meetings and the conduct and business of its affairs[104] and, where the association is affiliated to a national association of parents such rules shall be in accordance with guidelines issued by that body with the concurrence of the Minister.

---

[103] Section 26(3).
[104] Section 26(4).

Information to Students and Student Council

[6.101] A board is required to establish and maintain procedures for the purposes of informing students in a school of the school activities. Such procedures shall facilitate student involvement in the operation of the school, taking account of their age and experience in association with their parents and teachers.[105] This matter is dealt with in greater detail in Chapter 9 below.

Grievance Procedures

[6.102] The Minister with the agreement of the partners in education may, from time to time, prescribe procedures in accordance with which:

(a) the parent of a student, or in the case of a student who has reached the age of 18 years, the student, may appeal to the board against the decision of a teacher or other member of staff:

(b) grievances of students, or their parents, relating to the student's school (other than those which may be dealt with under paragraph (a) or s 29, shall be heard, and

(c) appropriate remedial action shall, where necessary, be taken as a consequence of an appeal in response to a grievance.[106]

The Minister, in prescribing procedures for the purpose of this section, shall have regard to the desirability of determining appeals and resolving grievances in the school concerned.[107]

[6.103] In their submission to the Green Paper (1993),[108] the National Parents' Council (NPC hereafter) sought the underpinning in law of a fair complaints procedure at school level and an independent appeals procedure for issues that are not resolved at school level. While the parents were desirous that such complaints would be generally resolved within the school, they envisaged cases of professional competence as being dealt with by the board in consultation with the Inspectorate and the Department. However, if complaints were not resolved within the school in a reasonable time (to be specified in regulations), the NPC sought recourse, as a legal right, to an independent appeals/tribunal committee. They submitted that it is a feature of any fair appeals system that it should be independent of the source of the original complaint.

[6.104] While s 28 of the Act provides for a complaints procedure within the school, this section does not fully accord with the wishes of some parents who

---

[105] Section 27.

[106] Section 28(1).

[107] Section 28(2).

[108] Green Paper Submission of NPC, (1993), pp 3-4; see also Addendum to Submission, "Parents as Partners in Education: Complaints Procedures/Appeals Procedures for Parents", Appendix 4. The author is grateful to the NPC for supplying this information.

sought an independent appeals procedure from the decision of a school. For this reason, it appears, we have not heard the last word on this issue.

Appeals to Secretary General

[6.105] Section 29 provides for appeals to the Secretary General of the Department of Education and Science in relation to permanent exclusions, certain suspensions and admissions. As this matter is discipline-related, this section is dealt with in Chapter 10.[109]

Curriculum

[6.106] Section 30 provides that, following such consultation with the parties in education which the Minister considers appropriate, the Minister may, from time to time, prescribe the curriculum for recognised schools, namely the subjects to be offered, the syllabus of each subject, the amount of instruction time to be allotted to each subject and the guidance and counselling provision to be offered in schools. Without prejudice to the generality of sub-s (1), the Minister:

    (a) shall have regard to the desirability of assisting schools to exercise their powers as provided for in subsection (4);

    (b) shall have regard to the characteristic spirit of a school or class of school in exercising his or her functions under this section,

    (c) may give directions to schools so as to ensure that the subjects and syllabuses followed are appropriate and relevant to the educational and vocational needs of the students in those schools,

    (d) shall ensure that the amount of instruction time to be alloted to subjects on the curriculum as determined by the Minister in each school day shall be such as to allow for such reasonable instruction time, as the board with the consent of the patron determines, for subjects relating to or arising from the characteristic spirit of the school, and

    (e) shall not require any student to attend instruction in any subject which is contrary to the conscience of the parent of the student or, in the case of a student who has reached the age of 18 years, the student.

The Minister may consult with the National Council for Curriculum and Assessment (NCCA) or with other persons or bodies he considers appropriate in regard to any curricular matter for recognised schools and may set up bodies to assist him in matters germane to this section.[110] Provided a school teaches the prescribed curriculum, it may provide other courses as the board considers appropriate.[111]

---

[109] School Discipline, below.
[110] Section 30(3).
[111] Section 30(4).

Teaching Through Irish

[6.107] Under s 31, the Minister is empowered to establish a body of persons:

(a) (i) to plan and co-ordinate the provision of text books and aids to learning and teaching through Irish,

(ii) to advise the Minister on policies relating to the provision and promotion of education through the medium of Irish,

(iii) to provide support services to such schools through the medium of Irish, and

(iv) to conduct research into any or all matters to which this section applies, and[112]

(b) to plan and co-ordinate the provision of textbooks and aids to the learning and teaching of Irish and to conduct research into and to advise the Minister on strategies which have as their objective the ehancement of the effectiveness in the teaching of Irish in recognised schools and centres for education.

The Minister may delegate to the body established in accordance with sub-s (1) any of his functions under s 31(1). While this body may advise the NCCA on matters germane to the Irish language which are stipulated in this section, the Minister retains ultimate control.

Educational Disadvantage

[6.108] In s 32 "educational disadvantage" means "the impediments to education arising from social or economic disadvantage which prevent students from deriving appropriate benefit from education in schools".[113] Under this section, the Minister shall by order, on foot of consultations with the partners in education or other persons at the Minister's discretion, establish a committee, to be known as the "Education Disadvantage Committee"(the Committee) to advise him or her on policies and strategies to be adopted to identify and correct educational disadvantage.

[6.109] An individual appointed by the Minister to the Committee will sit for a term not exceeding three years and such appointment may be renewed by the Minister. Up to half the membership of this Committee shall be appointed from voluntary bodies which have objects which the Minister considers germane to the work of the committee.

[6.110] The Committee may prepare and submit to the Minister a statement containing:

---

[112] Section 31(b) and ss 31(2)-31(7) inclusive.
[113] Section 32(9).

    (a) proposed policies and strategies for the identification and correction of educational disadvantage

    (b) the areas of activity to which the committee accords priority.[114]

In drawing up this statement the committee shall have regard to the resources available and the public interest in ensuring that the resources available are applied in an effective and efficient manner.[115]

The Making of Regulations

[6.111] Section 33 provides that the Minister, following consultation with the partners in education, may make regulations to give effect to this Act and, without prejudice to the generality of the foregoing, may make regulations relating to all or any of the following:

    (a) the recognition of schools and the withdrawal of recognition from schools;

    (b) the making of grants by the Minister to schools and centres for education;

    (c) the appointment and qualifications of persons who are to be employed as teachers in schools or centres for education;

    (d) the inspection of schools;

    (e) the building, maintenance and equipment of schools;

    (f) the length of the school year, school week and school day;

    (g) admission of students to school;

    (h) access to schools by school attendance officers and other persons;

    (i) access to schools and centres for education by students with disabilities or who have other special educational needs, including matters relating to reasonable accommodation and technical aid and equipment for such students;

    (j) procedures for the promotion of effective liaison and co-operation by schools and centres for education with local authorities (within the meaning of the Local Government Act 1941) and health boards (within the meaning of the Health Act 1970);

    (k) appeals; and

    (l) the curriculum of schools.

The obligation in this section requires the Minister to consult with the partners in education prior to making secondary legislation on any of the above matters. Clearly, the Minister is not bound by the result of any such consultation and, having consulted, may follow through with his own proposals.

---

[114] Section 32(5).
[115] Section 32(6).

Amendment of Intermediate Education Act 1878

[6.112] Section 35 repeals part of s 5 of the Intermediate Education Act 1878. The Act is the basis for the conduct of the Junior and Leaving Certificate examinations. This amendment will permit the State to introduce religious education as an examination subject in State examinations. Section 6 of the Intermediate Education Act 1878 is also amended by the repeal of subsection 4.

Amendment of Vocational Education Act 1930

[6.113] Section 36 amends the VEC Act 1930 as follows:

(a) in section 105(1) by the substitution of "a person" for an "officer of the Minister", and

(b) in sections 106 and 107 by the substitution of "a person" for "an officer" wherever it occurs.

Education Support Centres

[6.114] In s 37(1) "education support centre" means a place in which services are provided for schools, teachers, parents, boards and other relevant persons which support them in carrying out their functions in respect of the provision of education which is recognised for that purpose by the Minister in accordance with subs (2).

[6.115] The Minister may recognise a place as a support centre upon which occurrence, the name and address of such centre is entered in a register maintained by the Minister for that purpose which is accessible to the public during normal working hours.[116] An education support centre will be managed by a management committee which shall be a body corporate. No action shall lie against a member of such board in respect of anything done by such member in good faith and in pursuance of their functions as such members.[117] The Minister is empowered to withdraw recognition from a support centre[118] and he may make regulations governing such centres and their procedures.[119]

Part VII: National Council for Curriculum and Assessment

[6.116] Prior to the coming into force of the Education Act 1999, the National Council for Curriculum and Assessment (NCCA) was an unincorporated and non-statutory body of persons appointed by the Minister to assist the Minister with a range of duties including the drafting and implementation of a new curriculum for schools.

---

[116] Section 37(2).
[117] Section 37(4).
[118] Section 27(5).
[119] Section 37(6).

A New Statutory Body

[6.117] Section 38 of the Act provides that the Minister shall by order appoint a day to be the establishment day for the setting up of the NCCA to perform the functions assigned to it under the Act. The NCCA shall have the status of a body corporate. With the consent of the Minister, it shall also have power to acquire, hold and dispose of land or an interest in land and to acquire, hold and dispose of other property. Schedule 1 shall apply to the NCCA.[120]

[6.118] The composition of the NCCA shall be determined by order, made by the Minister following consultation with the partners in education and such other persons or bodies as the Minister deems appropriate.[121] Regarding the composition of the NCCA, the Minister shall ensure that it is representative of all levels of education, of the partners in education, of relevant business and industry, of Irish language organisations and of those with appropriate skills and experience. Members of the NCCA shall be appointed by the Minister in accordance with regulations made following consultation with the partners in education and such other persons deemed appropriate by the Minister.

Objects and Functions of the NCCA

[6.119] The object of the NCCA shall be to advise the Minister on matters relating to the curriculum for primary and post-primary schools and the assessment procedures employed in schools.[122]

[6.120] The functions of the NCCA are set down in s 40(2). It may advise the Minister on a range of issues, from time to time including:

(a) curriculum and syllabus review;

(b) effectiveness of education and early problem identification;

(c) strategies to assist inter-school student transfer;

(d) educational standards and related assessment mechanisms;

(e) review of in-service training of teachers;

(f) maintaining, managing, administering and investing all the money and assets of the Council;

(g) to accept gifts of money, land or other property upon trusts and conditions, if any, laid down by the donors and in accordance with this Act; and

---

[120] Section 39(3).
[121] Section 40(1).
[122] Section 41(1).

(h) to do all such acts and things as may be necessary to further the objects of the Council as the Minister may direct.

Staff

[6.121] The Minister is empowered to appoint a full-time chief executive officer to carry on, manage and control the administration of the NCCA.[123] Furthermore, the Minister may, with the consent of the Minister for Finance, appoint staff to assist the NCCA in the performance of its functions.[124] The NCCA will be grant-aided in each financial year by the Minister[125] from moneys provided by the Oireachtas[126] and is accountable to the Minister to keep all proper accounts and records of all monies received or expenditure incurred.[127] It shall provide the Minister with all such information relating to the performance of its functions as the Minister may, from time to time, require. The Council may establish committees and may delegate to such committees any of its functions that may be better or more conveniently performed by a committee. It is further required to report annually on its performance to the Minister.[128]

Part VIII: Examinations

[6.122] Part VIII of the Act which is currently in operation, provides for those examinations which are set out in Schedule 2. In addition it applies to any other examinations which the Minister in his discretion may prescribe. Under s 51, the Minister may make regulations as he considers appropriate for the effective conduct of examinations. He may also appoint a person(s) to advise him on any issue relating to examinations or on the conduct of examinations including appeals by candidates against the results of examinations.[129]

Offences

[6.123] It shall be an offence under s 52 of the Act for any person to do any of the following:

(a) to knowingly and without lawful authority publish an examination paper or part of an examination paper to another prior to the holding of the examination concerned,

(b) to have in his or her possession, without lawful authority, an examination paper or part thereof prior to the holding of the examination concerned,

---

123 Section 43(1).
124 Section 44.
125 With the concurrence of the Minister for Finance.
126 Section 45.
127 Section 46.
128 Section 48.
129 Section 51(2).

(c) to carry out any duties relating to the preparation of examination papers and knowingly and without lawful authority to provide a candidate or another with information relating to the material prepared by him with the intention of conferring an advantage upon a candidate over other candidates,

(d) to knowingly and wilfully credit a candidate with higher marks than the marks to which that candidate was entitled with the intention of conferring an advantage upon a candidate over other candidates,

(e) to knowingly and maliciously credit a candidate with lower marks than the marks to which he was entitled,

(f) to personate a candidate at an examination or knowingly allow or assist a person to do so at an examination,

(g) to knowingly and maliciously destroy or damage any material relating to an examination,

(h) to knowingly and maliciously obstruct any candidate or a person engaged in the conduct of an examination or otherwise interfere with the general conduct of an examination,

(i) to knowingly and without lawful authority alter any certificate or other record, including a record in a machine-readable form, containing the results of an examination.

(j) to knowingly issue or make use of any certificate or other document which purports to be a document issued by the person or body under whose authority the examination was conducted and to contain the results of an examination knowing that those results are false,

A person who knowingly aids, abets, counsels or procures another to commit any offence under sub-s (1) or conspires with another for the commission of any such offence, shall be guilty of such offence.

Fines

[6.124] A person who is guilty of an offence under s 50 shall be liable:

(a) on summary conviction, to a fine not exceeding £1,500 or (at the discretion of the court) to imprisonment for a term not exceeding 6 months, or to both such fine and imprisonment, or

(b) on conviction on indictment, to a fine not exceeding £5,000 or at the discretion of the court) to imprisonment for a term not exceeding 2 years, or to both such fine and imprisonment.[130]

Refusal of Access to Certain Information

[6.125] In view of the controversy surrounding the publication of league table examination results in England, s 53 of the Act is of particular interest. It empowers the Minister, notwithstanding any other enactment, such as the

---

[130] Section 52(3).

Freedom of Information Act 1997, to refuse access to any information which would enable the compilation of information (that is not otherwise available to the general public) in relation to the comparative performance of schools in relation to the academic achievement of students enrolled in them. The information to which the Minister may refuse access under this provision includes:[131]

(i)   the overall results in any year of students in a particular schools in an examination, or

(ii) the comparative overall results in any year of students in different schools in an examination.

Furthermore, the Minister may refuse access to information regarding the identity of examiners.[132]

[6.126] British style league tables[133] for primary or secondary schools have never found favour in Ireland, "where they are viewed across the political spectrum as a crude and insensitive measure of school performance".[134] While such tables do not appear to be the answer, this does not eliminate the need for a compromise system which would give some useful information to teachers, parents and students about the performance of their school.

[6.127] It is conceivable, that a parent,[135] adversely affected by the operation of s 53, may challenge that section as being unconstitutional. Such a parent could argue that, as the primary and natural educator of the child, the prohibition on access to information in s 53 of the Act militates against that right and against their parental rights of choice of school as guaranteed by Articles 42.2 of the Constitution. Accordingly, such a parent could argue that he or she is entitled to

---

[131] Without prejudice to the foregoing.

[132] Section 53(b).

[133] The Independent, 23 February 1999 carried a 36-page supplement which was referred to as a "guide to the best and the worst primary schools in England" while the Daily Telegraph of the same date included an 8-page guide on "primary performance".

[134] 'School Tables', Irish Times, editorial, 24 February 1999. A recent ERSI study (Dr Emer Smyth, 'Do Schools Differ?' ERSI, February 1999) supports the case against the compilation of such "league tables." It states that the variation in examination performance can frequently be largely explained by reference to the gender, social class and ability mix of pupils. This is also borne out by the English "league tables" which show that all the primary schools that came top of the local league tables acknowledged that, besides dedicated teachers, they had two factors in common:

(a)   a relatively affluent catchment area; and

(b)   parents who were very involved in their childrens' education, see "Professional parents and a dose of privilege make all the difference", Daily Telegraph, 24 February 1999, p 1 of the supplement on "league tables".

[135] Or student over the age of 18 years.

know the overall results of students in the school attended by his/her child and/or the comparative overall results in any year of students in different schools, so that he or she can exercise his/her constitutional right to choose the school with the best academic record.

[6.128] In its defence, the State could argue that the prohibition on such information was put in place by the State in its constitutional capacity as "guardian of the common good," and in response to widespread parental demands with a view to protecting the self-esteem of weaker children and those students who live in socio-economically deprived areas who generally perform less well in examinations. It appears that this debate will continue to run in Ireland for some time to come.

Part IX: Bodies Corporate

[6.129] Under Part IX of the Act the Minister, with the concurrence of the Government, may by order (to be known as an "establishment order") set up bodies corporate to provide support services relating to education. The performance of functions by such a body corporate is subject to the Minister's policy determinations. As has been seen, bodies corporate are not new to Irish education although earlier bodies corporate, supporting the national school system,[136] were non-statutory bodies established by Royal Charter.[137]

[6.130] The bodies corporate established under the 1998 Act have perpetual succession and a seal with power to hold land and to sue and be sued in their own corporate names. Persons appointed as principal officers of such bodies shall be accountable to the Minister for carrying out their functions under the Act. Prior to making an order under s 54 the Minister is required to consult with individuals directly affected by the proposed order or with trade unions or associations representing such persons. Moreover, prior to making an order under s 54, the Minister shall cause to be laid before the Dáil and the Seanad a draft of the proposed order and a resolution approving of the draft has been passed by both houses.

Establishment Orders

[6.131] Every establishment order shall contain such provisions as are considered appropriate by the Minister and the manner in which it shall perform its functions.[138] Such order shall also contain administrative provisions which the Minister considers appropriate[139] and shall be funded annually out of monies

---

[136] Ch 2, para **[2.25]**.
[137] Ch 2.
[138] Section 56.
[139] Section 57.

provided by the Oireachtas.[140] Power to revoke an establishment order rests with the Minister.[141]

[6.132] While the establishment of corporate bodies will, no doubt, ease the administrative burden which currently falls on the Department, these bodies remain under the Minister's authority. As such, they are no substitute for devolution of authority. Furthermore, they will most likely be established in the Dublin area and do little if anything to decentralise the powers of the Department of Education and Science.

Reliance on the Education Act 1998 by Parents or Students

[6.133] One question of particular interest is whether students or their parents, affected by a breach of the Education Act 1998, have a right of action under the Act. The matter has been considered in the English courts with regard to the Education Acts which may be of interest and relevance.

[6.134] In *X (Minors) v Bedfordshire County Council Appeals*,[142] the matter at issue was whether the careless performance by a school authority of its statutory duties, relating to the education and welfare of children, could ground an action for breach of statutory duty and for negligence by children adversely affected by the LEA's actions.

[6.135] The first set of appeals, which were concerned with child abuse cases, considered the question of whether children and parents, affected by a breach of statutory duty, have a statutory right[143] of action against school authorities (LEAs) if such breach arises from the authority's action or inaction. In the second set of appeals, which dealt with education matters, the action or inaction of three school authorities in regard to the provision of education for children with special educational needs was at issue.

The English Education Cases

Case 1

[6.136] In this case, the plaintiff claimed that the LEA had failed to ascertain that he suffered from a learning disorder requiring special educational provision and that the LEA had wrongly advised his parents in this regard. He also claimed that even when the LEA subsequently acknowledged his special educational needs, pursuant to the Education Act 1981, s 7(a), it wrongly

---

[140] Section 58.

[141] Section 59(1).

[142] *X (Minors) v Bedfordshire County Council; M (A Minor) v Newham LBC; E (A Minor) v Dorset County Council* [1995] 3 All ER 353 HL; [1994] ELR 67.

[143] In this case the Children and Young Persons Act 1969 and the Children Act 1989.

decided that the school the plaintiff was attending was appropriate to meet his needs. The plaintiff alleged breach of the LEA's statutory duties and common law duties claiming damages for the expense incurred by his parents who were required to place him at a special school in which his specific educational needs were finally assessed and his condition diagnosed and treated.

Case 2

[6.137] In the second case, the plaintiff alleged that the headmaster of his LEA maintained primary school had failed to refer him either to the LEA for formal assessment of his learning difficulties, which were consistent with dyslexia or to an educational psychologist for diagnosis. He also claimed that the teacher's advisory centre, to which he was subsequently referred, had also failed to identify his learning difficulties, and that such failure to assess his condition, (which would have improved with appropriate treatment) had severely limited his educational attainment and prospects of employment. The plaintiff claimed damages for negligence against the LEA.

Case 3

[6.138] The plaintiff in the third case alleged that, although he was of at least average ability, the LEA had placed him in special schools which were not appropriate for his educational needs and it had failed to provide any schooling for him at all. He claimed that such failure had resulted in his personal and intellectual development being impaired and he had been placed at a disadvantage in seeking employment. The plaintiff claimed damages against the LEA for breach of statutory duty under the Education Act 1944, the Education Act 1981 and the Education (Special Educational Needs) Regulations 1983.

[6.139] In each of the three above-mentioned cases, the plaintiff's statements of claim were struck out as disclosing no reasonable cause of action. On appeal, however, the Court of Appeal ruled that the claims alleging breach of statutory duty had been rightly struck out, but that the claims in negligence were neither unarguable or incontestably bad and should be permitted to proceed. The LEAs appealed to the House of Lords while the plaintiff in one of the cases cross-appealed.

House of Lords Decision

[6.140] The House of Lords held that private law claims against public authorities for damages could be classified into four categories as follows:

(a) actions for breach of statutory duty *simplicter* (ie irrespective of carelessness);

(b) actions based solely on the careless performance of a statutory duty in the absence of any other common law right of action;

(c) actions based on a common law duty of care arising either from the imposition of the statutory duty or from the performance of it; and

(d) misfeasance in public office, ie the failure to exercise, or the exercise of, statutory powers either with the intention to injure the plaintiff or in the knowledge that the conduct was unlawful.

In actions for breach of statutory duty *simpliciter*, the Court held that a breach of statutory duty was not by itself sufficient to give rise to any private law cause of action. A private law cause of action only arose, if it could be shown, as a matter of the construction of the statute, that the statutory duty was imposed for the protection of a limited class of the public and that Parliament intended to confer on members of that specific class a private right of action for breach of the duty.[144]

[6.141] The mere assertion of the careless exercise of a statutory power or duty was not sufficient in itself to give rise to a private law cause of action. The plaintiff also had to establish that the circumstances were such as to raise a duty of care at common law. Furthermore, there was no common law duty of care in relation to the taking of decisions involving policy matters, since the courts could not adjudicate on such policy matters.

[6.142] Accordingly, a claim alleging negligence in the exercise of a statutory discretion, involving policy considerations, would *pro tanto* fail as being non-justiciable. The fact that breaches of duty under the Education Acts might give rise to successful public law claims for a declaration or an injunction did not show that there was a corresponding private law right to damages for breach of statutory duty.

[6.143] In the case of children with special educational needs, although they were members of a limited class for whose protection the statutory provisions were enacted, there was nothing in either the 1944 Act or the 1981 Act which demonstrated an intention on the part of Parliament to confer on that class an action for damages. The involvement of parents at every stage of the decision-making process under the 1981 Act and their rights of appeal against the authority's decision, demonstrated that Parliament did not intend, in addition, to confer a right to sue for damages. Administrative failure was best dealt with by the statutory appeals procedure rather than by litigation and courts should be extremely reluctant to impose a common law duty of care in the exercise of

---

[144] Applying *Cutler v Wandsworth Ltd* [1949] 1 All ER 544 and *Lonrho Ltd v Shell Petroleum Co Ltd (No 2)* [1981] 2 All ER 456.

discretionary powers or duties conferred by Parliament for social welfare purposes.

[6.144] Applying these principles to the above mentioned sex abuse and education cases, the court held that the claims based on statutory duty in the Welfare and Education Acts had been rightly struck out. The negligence dimension of these cases, however, is dealt with in Chapter 9.

[6.145] While the above cases are not binding on an Irish court, they are likely to be persuasive. Hence, it appears that the Irish courts would be unlikely to hold that the Oireachtas intended to confer a right on parents to sue for breach of statutory duty under the Education Act 1998.

Chapter 7

European Community Competence in Education

Introduction

[7.01] The Treaty of Rome contains no express legal basis for Community involvement in general education. It seems that the Community's founding fathers did not view general education as directly pertinent to the objectives of the Treaty of Rome as Jean Monnet's celebrated statement indicates: "If I could do it all again, I would start with education".[1] This chapter will trace the evolution in European Community law (EC law) of the law on education,[2] with a view to assessing its impact on education in Ireland. It will show that the current status of EC law and policy on education, evolved from an extremely limited jurisdictional base. Mainly through judicial activism in the Court of Justice (the ECJ hereafter), Community competence in educational policy has developed so that, in certain instances, it appears to have trespassed on education policy in the Member States. The legal basis for Community policy on education will be considered in two parts.

[7.02] Part 1 deals with the period prior to the Treaty on European Union[3] (1992) (TEU) during which the scope of EC policy in education was uncertain but evolving. Community policy in education is traced from the Treaty of Rome (1957) to the implementation of the TEU. The freedom of movement principle is examined from the viewpoint of teachers and students as well as the growth of the common vocational training policy. A consideration of the rights of migrant workers and their families in other Member States is a central part of this section. Teacher qualifications are also discussed in the light of Community law. This section then concerns itself with the application of Community law by the national courts.

[7.03] Part 2 of this chapter looks at the period following the TEU when specific competence in education, as distinct from vocational training, was conferred on the Community for the first time. It also includes the education-related provisions of the Treaty of Amsterdam (1997).[4]

---

[1] Cited in European Parliament, Session Documents 1988/89, Document A 2-0285/88, Series A, Explanatory Statement, p 11.
[2] See generally McMahon and Murphy, *European Community Law in Ireland*, (1989), Butterworths.
[3] (1995) OJ C191 29.7.92, p 1.
[4] (1997) OJ C340 10.11.97, p 1.

Member State Sensitivity to Community Intervention in Education

[7.04] Education is deeply rooted in the local, regional and national culture[5] of each Member State being the outcome of unique histories, cherished values and distinctive aspirations.[6] It is scarcely surprising, therefore, that educational policy is one of the most sensitive spheres of Community policy-making.[7] Speaking extra-judicially Lenaerts J, of the Court of First Instance of the EC, believes that this is undoubtedly the reason why some Member States have devolved to their regional authorities the power to deal with educational issues,[8] a precaution largely eshewed by Ireland. Apparently, certain Member States perceive devolution of education to local or regional bodies as a measure of protection against Community intrusion in education. Member State sensitivity to Community intervention in education was particularly evident at the launch of the *Lingua* project, (an EC language schools programme)[9] when Germany and Britain limited the programme to the sphere of post compulsory school education. Both countries stressed that they had not transferred to Brussels part of their sovereignty by acquiescing in Community intervention in their school curricula.

PART I: THE LEGAL BASIS FOR COMMUNITY INTERVENTION IN EDUCATION IN THE MEMBER STATES PRIOR TO THE TEU

Education and the Treaty of Rome[10]

[7.05] Following the Treaty of Rome (1957), the Member States retained jurisdiction over general education subject only to the application of certain Community principles which became the main mechanisms by which the

---

[5] See McMahon, *Education and Culture in European Community Law*, European Community Law Series, No 8, (1995), Athlone Press, London, Part 1.

[6] On this point see Martin in 'Debates on European Parliament', 24 October 1986, OJ Annex No 2 344/275 at 282.

[7] See further Verbruggen, 'European Community Educational Law A Short Overview' in *Subsidiarity and Education: Aspects of Comparative Educational Law*, de Groof, ed, (1994), Acco, Leuven, p 47; Neave, *The EEC and Education*, (1984), Stoke-on-Trent; Lonbay, 'Education and Law: the Community Context', 14 ELR (1989), 363-388; Hennis, 'Access to Education in the European Communities', 3 Leiden Journal of International Law (1990), 35-44.

[8] Lenaerts, 'Subsidiarity and Community Competence in the Field of Educations' in de Groof, *Subsidiarity and Education: Aspects of Comparative Educational Law*, p 118 citing the example of the Belgian "Communities", the German "Lander" or the Spanish "Communidades Autonomas."

[9] Promoting the fostering of foreign language teaching arising from Decision 89/489, [1989], OJ L239.

[10] Note: The Treaty of Amsterdam which came into force on 1 May 1999 renumbered the Articles of the EC Treaty. The new Article numbers are given with the previous numbers in brackets.

Community influenced the education systems of the Member States prior to the coming into effect of the TEU. These principles may be stated as follows:

(a) freedom of movement;[11]

(b) freedom of establishment;[12]

(c) freedom to provide services;[13]

(d) the non-discrimination principle;[14] and

(e) the common vocational training policy.[15]

Freedom of Movement for Workers

[7.06] Those persons classified as "workers" in Community law are entitled to a wide body of social rights in other Member States. Individuals who are not classified as workers are, of course, entitled to rights of establishment and rights to provide services in other member States.

[7.07] Article 39(2) (ex Article 48(2)) of the EC Treaty provides for the "abolition of any discrimination based on nationality between workers of the Member States as regards employment, remuneration and other conditions of work and employment." This provision expands on the basic Community tenet, enshrined in Article 12 (ex Article 6) of non-discrimination within the jurisdiction of the EC Treaty.[16] Article 39(3) (ex Article 48(3)) further amplifies the scope of these rights. It provides that workers are entitled to the right, subject to some exceptions:

(a) to accept offers of employment made to them;

(b) to move freely throughout the Member States for such purpose;

(c) to stay in a Member State for the purpose of employment, subject to the same provisions governing the employment of nationals of that Member State;

(d) to remain in a Member State, having been employed there, subject to certain conditions.

---

[11] Article 48 EEC (now Article 39 EC).

[12] Article 52-58 EEC (now Articles 43-48 EC).

[13] Articles 59-66 EEC (now Articles 49-55 EC).

[14] Article 7 EEC (now Article 12 EC).

[15] Article 127 EEC (now Article 150 EC), see further McMahon and Murphy, *European Community Law in Ireland* (1989), Butterworths, Ch 18.

[16] A worker who is a national of a member State may not, in the territory of another Member State, be treated differently from national workers by reason of his nationality in respect of any conditions of employment and work, in particular as regards remuneration, dismissal, and should he become unemployed, reinstatement or reemployment.

It is notable that none of the above-mentioned rights expressly include a right on the part of the worker to education rights in the host Member State.

The public service

[7.08] Exemption from the freedom of movement principle has been granted, *inter alia,*[17] to the public service[18] and for the exercise of official authority under Article 45 (ex Article 55). Because of the protection afforded by Article 39(4) (ex Article 48(4)), Member States can lawfully exclude nationals from other Member States from the following services:

(a) their public service;

(b) the armed forces;

(c) the judiciary;

(d) the police;

(e) the tax authorities; and

(f) the diplomatic corps.[19]

Central to all of this was the question of whether the institutions in which public education is given, such as schools, constitute part of the "public service" to which this exemption applies.[20]

[7.09] In *Commission v Belgium,*[21] the Commission considered that Belgium had exceeded its jurisdiction by excluding foreign nationals from certain public service positions. In that case, the ECJ applied a narrow, functional test by assessing the duties required by the posts in the light of Article 48(4) EEC. It ruled that the exception extended solely to "posts which involve direct or indirect participation in the exercise of powers conferred by public law and duties designed to safeguard the general interests of the State or other public authorities".[22]

[7.10] Whether these strictures applied to private schools was another issue to be resolved by the ECJ. Greek legislation regulated private schools and private lessons at home in such a manner that non-Greek persons were excluded from authorisation. When this legislation was first challenged by the Commission, the

---

[17] See Article 39(4) (ex Article 48(4)) and Article 46 (ex Article 56) and Directive 64/221.

[18] Article 39(4) (ex Article 48(4)).

[19] Member States may derogate from the free movement obligations in regard to workers on the basis of public policy, public security and public health (Article 39 (ex Article 48); McMahon and Murphy, *European Community Law in Ireland,* (1989), Butterworth, p 359.

[20] Article 39(4) (ex Article 48(4)). See further O'Keefe, 'Judicial Interpretation of the Public Service Exception to the Free Movement of Workers' in *Constitutional Adjudication in European Community and National Law,* (1992) Curtain and O'Keefe, eds, Butterworths, p 89.

[21] Case 149/79 [1980] ECR 3881 and later [1982] ECR 1845.

[22] Case 149/79 [1980] ECR 3881 and later [1982] ECR 1845.

ECJ held that to establish a private school or teach in one, or to give private lessons at home was unconnected with the exercise of official authority under Article 45 (ex Article 55) as the Greek government had pleaded.[23]

[7.11] Accordingly, the ECJ ruled that by prohibiting non-nationals from setting up *frontistiria* (coaching establishments)[24] and from giving private lessons at home, the Greece had breached Articles 52 EEC and 59 EEC (now Article 43 and 49 EC). The ECJ further held that by prohibiting or restricting access for nationals of other Member States working in Greece, and their families, to the posts of director or teacher in *frontistiria* and in private music and dancing schools, Greece had failed to fulfil its Treaty obligations under Article 48 EEC. When no legislative steps were taken to comply with this judgment, Greece was once again before the ECJ which confirmed its earlier decision.[25]

[7.12] Inevitably these issues led to a consideration of whether schoolteachers fell into the category of "worker" under Article 48(4) EEC (now Article 39(4) EC) entitling them to benefit from the freedom of movement principle throughout the Community. The rights of teachers and students to pursue an education in Member States other than their own has gradually evolved, *inter alia,* from the case law of the ECJ over the past 13 years.

Freedom of movement for teachers

[7.13] The term "worker" is not defined in the EEC Treaty. However, the ECJ has interpreted it very broadly to include the following:

(a) part-time workers;[26]

(b) a part-time music teacher in receipt of supplementary State benefits;[27]

(c) a salaried student teacher;[28]

(d) a secondary teacher;[29] and

(e) foreign-language assistant teachers.[30]

---

[23] Case 147/86 *EC Commission v Greece* [1988] ECR 1637.

[24] These institutions supplement the normal curricula at the three levels of education.

[25] Case C-328/90 *Commission v Greece* [1992] ECR 1-425.

[26] Case 53/81 *Levin v Staatssecretaris van Justitie* [1982] ECR 1035.

[27] Case 139/85 *Kempf v Staatssecretaris van Justitie* [1986] ECR 1741.

[28] Case 66/85 *Lawrie-Blum v Land Baden Wurttemberg* [1986] ECR 2121 in which a British national was refused access to the *Referendar* (a practical course for student teachers) in Germany.

[29] Case C-4/91 *Bleis v Ministere de l'Education Nationale* [1991] ECR 1-5627, reference for a preliminary hearing.

[30] Case 33/88 *Allué and Coonan v Universita delgi Studi di Venezia* [1989] ECR 1591, reference for a preliminary ruling: [1993] ECR 1-4309, see also Case C 272/92 *Spotti v Freistaat Bayern* judgment of the Court of 20 October 1993 extracted from a JUSTIS database.

In all of these cases, the ECJ held that the public service exception in Article 48(4) EEC (now Article 39(4)) did not apply to any of these teachers. While teachers generally stand to benefit from the guaranteed mobility which Article 48 EEC (now Article 39 EC) establishes, Curall posits the view that such protection may not apply to head teachers who appear to have a special relationship of allegiance to the State by virtue of their being accountable for the proper use of public money and public property.[31] Whether the ECJ would accept this line of argument remains to be seen.

[7.14] In *Lawrie-Blum*,[32] the ECJ found a trainee-teacher, who gave lessons for a few hours weekly, to be a worker if her teaching activities were "effective and genuine". It stated that:

> "The essential feature of an employment relationship ... is that for a certain period of time a person performs services for and under the direction of another person in return for which he receives remuneration."[33]

[7.15] Particular difficulties have arisen in some countries regarding the employment rights of foreign language assistant teachers in the host countries. This category of teachers have consistently claimed covert discrimination by the host countries and clearly this is an on-going problem that has yet to be resolved.

Principle of Equal Treatment

Foreign language assistants

[7.16] The principle of equal treatment, of which Article 39(2) (ex Article 48(2)) of the EC Treaty is one embodiment, prohibits not only overt discrimination based on nationality but also all covert forms of discrimination which, by the application of other distinguishing criteria, in practice, achieve the same result.[34] The equal treatment principle precludes the legislation of a Member State from limiting the employment contracts of foreign language assistants in universities to one year, with the possibility of renewal, where in principle no such limit exists with regard to other teachers.[35]

[7.17] Community law does not prohibit the conclusion of contracts of employment of foreign language assistants for a limited period if it seems, at the

---

[31] Currall, 'Education Rights under the EC Treaty' in *Mobility of People in the European Community*, (1989), Dublin, ICEL, p 13 at pp 20-21.

[32] Case 66/85 [1986] ECR 2121.

[33] Case 66/85 [1986] ECR 2121, para 17 of the judgement.

[34] See in particular Case 41/84 *Pinna di Caisse d'Allocations Familiales de la Savoie* [1986] ECR 1.

[35] Joined cases C 259/91, C 331/91 and C 332/91 *Allué and Coonan v Universita delgi Studi di Venezia and Universita degli studi di Parma*, Case 33/88; [1989] ECR 1591.

time of the appointment, that the teaching requirement will not exceed that period. Contracts which are intended to meet continuous needs for teaching, however, must be concluded for an indeterminate period in the same manner as the employment relationship of other teachers fulfilling such needs.[36] Since the vast majority of foreign language assistants are foreign nationals, such a difference of treatment would clearly place them at a considerable disadvantage by contrast with nationals of the host country and therefore this constitutes discrimination under Article 39(2) (ex Article 48(2)) unless it is justified by objective reasons, which do not include the need to ensure up-to- date instruction.[37]

[7.18] The applicant in *Bleis*[38] was a German national, with a degree from a French university, who sought registration from the French Ministry of Education for the external competition for the Certificate of Aptitude as a secondary teacher. By contrast with Irish teachers, French teachers are civil servants and French law provided that "No-one may be appointed to the civil service: (1) if he does not have French nationality".[39] Thus, the Ministry refused the applicant's request on the grounds of nationality. Bleis then applied to the Administrative Court (Paris) alleging that the relevant French legislation operated a discrimination on the grounds of nationality with regard to access to second level teaching. The Court stayed its judgment and referred the matter for a preliminary ruling to the ECJ.

[7.19] The ECJ held that it is common ground that teachers, like other civil servants, are "workers" within the meaning of Article 48 EEC (now Article 39 EC) and are consequently beneficiaries of the freedom of movement right. The ECJ seized the opportunity to further clarify the limitations of the term "public service". It considered that this term refers to:

> "a series of posts which ... presume on the part of those occupying them the existence of a special relationship of allegiance to the State and reciprocity of rights and duties which form the foundation of the bond of nationality."[40]

It concluded that the activity of teaching *per se* did not involve a direct or indirect exercise of State duties or manifest a special relationship of allegiance to the State.[41] In principle, under Community law, teaching positions must be

---

[36] Joined cases C 259/91, C 331/91 and C 332/91.

[37] Case C 272/92 *Spotti v Freistaat Bayern*, [1994] 3 CMLR 629.

[38] Case C-4/91 *Bleis v Ministere de l'Education Nationale* [1991] ECR 1-5627.

[39] Article 5 of the French Law, No 83-634 of 13 July 1983, Journal Officiel de la Republique Francaise, 14 July, 1983, p 2174.

[40] Case C-4/91 *Bleis v Ministère de l'Education Nationale*, [1991] ECR 1-5627; see also Case 149/79 *Commission v Belgium* [1980] ECR 3881.

[41] Citing Case 66/85 *Lawrie-Blum v Land Baden-Wurttemberg* [1986] ECR 2121, 2135; [1987], 3 CMLR 389, para 20.

open to nationals of other Member States without any restrictions on the grounds of nationality. The reality, however, frequently falls well short of the ideal.

Member State reluctance to accept teachers from other Member States

[7.20] It seems that some Member States, particularly those in which teachers have achieved the status of civil servants, still apply a condition of nationality in regard to teaching and other posts in State schools. The Commission threatens to bring cases against these countries. Recently, the Commission took a case against the Grand Duchy of Luxembourg for failing to fulfil its obligations under Community law in this respect. As regards posts in public sectors such as research, education, health, inland transport, water, gas, electricity and posts and telecommunications, Luxembourg submitted that only nationals can be depended on to show the special degree of integrity and trustworthiness which must be capable of being required of civil servants and public employees.

[7.21] With reference to the sphere of education, the Luxembourg government submitted that teachers must be Luxembourg nationals in order to transmit traditional values and that, in view of the size of the country and its specific demographic situation, the nationality requirement was an essential condition for preserving Luxembourg's national identity. Its identity could not be preserved, it argued, if the majority of teachers were from other Member States of the Community. With regard to primary and secondary school teachers, it pointed out that these teachers perform non-commercial functions which actually entail safeguarding the general interests of the State.

[7.22] By way of response, the ECJ pointed out that, in a sector such as education, the exclusion of nationals from all the posts in this sector cannot be justified by considerations referring to the preservation of national identity. This legitimate interest,[42] the ECJ observed, could still be effectively safeguarded otherwise than by a general exclusion and furthermore, it reminded Luxembourg that nationals of other Member States in common with nationals of the host Member State, must fulfil all the conditions for recruitment, training, experience and language knowledge in common with its nationals.

[7.23] The ECJ referred to the well settled law in this sphere[43] which held that the concept of public service within the meaning of Article 48(4) EEC (now Article 39(4) EC) requires uniform interpretation and application throughout the Community. These findings, the ECJ stated, cannot be shaken by considerations

---

[42] Recognised by Article F(1) of the TEU.
[43] Case 152/73 *Sotgiu v Deutsche Bundespost* [1974] ECR 153; Case 149/79 *Commission v Belgium* [1980] ECR 3881.

relating to the preservation of national identity in a demographic situation such as that prevailing in Luxembourg. The ECJ gave a declaration that Luxembourg, by maintaining a nationality requirement in relation to workers who are nationals of other Member States, as regard access to civil servant or public employee posts, such as, *inter alia*, teaching posts, had failed to fulfil its obligations under Article 48 EEC (now Article 39) and Articles 1 and 7 of Council Regulation (EEC) No 1612/68 on freedom of movement for workers within the Community.

[7.24] In Ireland, the position pertaining to the freedom of movement principle must be read in the light of:

    (a) Irish language requirements;

    (b) the *Gröener v Minister for Education*[44] judgment; and

    (c) subsequent secondary legislation.

Equal treatment for men and women: transsexuality

P v S and Cornwall County Council

[7.25] Equal treatment and the relevance of Directive 76/207 EEC[45] (Equal Treatment Directive) for the dismissal of a transsexual employee of a public employer, arising out of an employee's gender reassignment, was at issue in *P v S and Cornwall County Council*.[46] In April 1991, P was employed as a manager at an educational establishment operated by Cornwall County Council. One year later P informed S, the principal and chief executive of that establishment, that she[47] intended to undergo a gender reassignment operation and would be returning to work dressed as a woman.

[7.26] Initially, S seemed supportive, but later, essentially due to the opposition of the board of governors, had a change of mind. In 1992, when P underwent initial surgical treatment, the governors decided to dismiss her and gave her three months' notice. The following year, P took her case to the Industrial Tribunal which found that she had been dismissed for undergoing a gender

---

[44] Case 379/87, ECR [1989] 3967.

[45] Council Directive 76/207 EEC on the implementation of the principle of equal treatment for men and women as regards access to employment, vocational training and working conditions.

[46] Case C-13/94, 1-2145; 1-2159, reference for a preliminary ruling from the Industrial Tribunal, Truro, Opinion of Advocate General Tesauro, delivered 14 December 1995; judgment of the ECJ, 30 April 1996; see also *Grant v South West Trains Ltd* [1998] IRLR 188 in which it was held that the plaintiff employee was not entitled under her contract of employment to require the defendants to extend travel concessions to the woman with whom she lived, in circumstances in which the contractual conditions specified that the concession would only be granted in respect of a partner of the opposite sex.

[47] As the Industrial Tribunal, Advocate General Tesauro and the ECJ (mainly but not entirely) referred to P throughout as female, the author follows the same convention.

reassignment operation and not for redundancy as claimed. Being uncertain whether the discrimination fell within the scope of the Equal Treatment Directive, the tribunal referred a number of questions to the ECJ.

Judgment of European Court of Justice

[7.27] The ECJ considered whether the dismissal of a transsexual employee by a public employer breached Community law and in particular, the Equal Treatment Directive. The ECJ, adopting Advocate General Tesauro's recommendations given in his Opinion,[48] found that such discrimination violated Community law as Article 5(1) of the Directive precludes the dismissal of a transsexual for a reason related to a gender reassignment. It considered that the ambit of the Directive cannot be confined simply to discrimination based on the fact that a person is of one or other sex. In view of the purpose of the Directive, and the nature of the rights which it seeks to safeguard, the ECJ held that its scope is also such as to apply to discrimination arising from gender reassignment of the person concerned.

Relevance for Irish schools

[7.28] While the *Cornwall* judgment has significant implications generally for employment law in the Member States and accordingly for Ireland, it has a lesser application for Irish schools by virtue of the fact that the majority of such schools are not public institutions. In the voluntary secondary school sector, clearly it would have no application as the schools are privately owned. Neither would it be applicable, it appears, in State-aided, church-owned schools such as national schools. It is conceivable, however, that it could apply in public sector schools and colleges such as those under the jurisdiction of the vocational education committees. It may be concluded that, while the *Cornwall* judgment has greatly improved the legal status of transsexuals in employment law, its application in the school context is a highly sensitive one which is not without its problems.

The Freedom of Establishment

[7.29] Essentially, the right of establishment permits nationals and companies in the Member States to set up farming or business enterprises, such as schools or colleges or branches, agencies or subsidiaries thereof, in any Member State provided these activities do not discriminate on the grounds of nationality.[49]

---

[48] Which are of particular interest, see further Carolan, "*P v S and Cornwall County Council*: The European Court of Justice, The Equal Treatment Directive, and Transsexuality," 1998, European Law, Irish Law Times, No 9, 136-139.

[49] See further McMahon and Murphy, *European Community Law in Ireland*, p 363 *et seq*; McMahon, 'Ireland and the Right of Establishment in the Treaty of Rome', VI (1971) Ir Jur (ns), 271-292.

The Freedom to Supply Services

[7.30] The supply of services, on the other hand, deals with the provision of non-wage earning skills or activities on a once-off, occasional or temporary basis between the Member States.[50] In the education context, this could mean:

(a) an assessment made by a psychologist, psychiatrist, counsellor, or analyst on an Irish child in another Member State; or

(b) the provider of such a service travelling to Ireland to provide such a service; or

(c) the provision of the service to the child by other means of communication eg by letter, telephone, tape, diskette or e-mail.[51]

The former Article 128 EEC (now Article 150 EC) permitted the Council to lay down the general principles of a common vocational training policy for the Member States while Article 57 EEC (now Article 47), provided for measures to implement mutual recognition of diplomas throughout the Member States.

Education in the Member States

[7.31] In the Community, education is generally provided in mainstream schools in which teachers are employed either under contracts of employment with a private or public institution or having the status of civil servants ie employed by the State. In this situation, the principle of freedom of movement of workers applies rather than those of freedom of establishment and freedom to provide services.

[7.32] Education may also be provided by self-employed individuals or by bodies who desire to establish a private school or to set up services, (eg distance learning, language teaching or the teaching of technology skills), between the Member States. In this context, the providers of such education may not be discriminated against in any Member State as the freedom of establishment principle and freedom to supply services respectively apply.

[7.33] The scope of Community competence in education was clarified in 1985 in *Gravier v City of Liège*[52] in which the ECJ held that the Community had no jurisdiction to harmonise the education laws of the Member States as "... educational organisation and policy is not as such included in the spheres which the Treaty has entrusted to the Community institutions".[53] Of course, this

---

[50] McMahon and Murphy, p 372 *et seq.*
[51] McMahon and Murphy, p 372.
[52] Case 293/83, [1985] ECR 595.
[53] Case 293/83 [1985] ECR 595, ground 19; see also Case 127/86, *Commission v Greece* ECR [1988], 1648, the Greek government argued that, "not being part of economic life, but being closely linked with the traditional and cultural life of a Member State, education was deliberately excluded [from the EEC Treaty]".

statement must now be read in the light of the TEU which has conferred some specific competence in education on the Community. As will be seen, the Community's competence in education evolved tentatively over many decades.

Tentative Growth of a Community Education Policy

[7.34] Prior to the TEU, Community education policy did not fully accord with Community law[54] as the EEC provided no express legal basis for education. Initially education policy was confined to non-binding decisions, resolutions and agreements made under international public law.[55] While some binding Community law existed, it resulted from other initiatives that were taken to set up the common market which gradually influenced education policy in the Member States. The circuituous route by which Community law on education emerged resulted in a piece-meal, complex *corpus* of rules relating to education.

[7.35] It became clear in time that mobility of workers in the host Member State would not materialise unless the rights of migrant workers and their families to integration and broadly based social and cultural rights were vindicated. Article 40 (ex Article49 EEC) envisages that further measures would facilitate the freedom of movement of workers "by progressive stages". Thus Article 40 (ex Article 49 EEC) became the operative provision under which most of the secondary legislation, giving effect to the freedom of movement of workers under Article 39 (ex Article 48 EEC) was effected. Among these are a number of important regulations, directives and decisions of the ECJ including Council Regulation 1612/68[56] which further facilitated the free movement of migrant workers within the Community.

Council Regulation 1612/68

[7.36] By contrast with Article 7(3) EEC (now repealed), Council Regulation 1612/68 EEC (the Regulation) extends not only to rights referring to entry and employment but also to provisions relating to "other working conditions". It safeguards both the migrant worker and his family from discrimination and refers to all categories of education. However, the Regulation does not make any express provision for those who travel to another Member State exclusively for study purposes. The regulation is divided into three Titles which are concerned with:

---

[54] De Witte, 'Introduction' in *European Community Law of Education*, de Witte, ed, (1989), Baden-Baden, Nomos, pp 9-10.

[55] Verbruggen, 'European Community Education Law, a Short Overview', in *Subsidiarity and Education: Aspects of Comparative Educational Law*, de Groof, ed, (1994), Acco, Leuven, p 48; de Witte, *European Community Law of Education* (1989), Baden-Baden, Noma, p 204.

[56] Of 15 October 1968 on freedom of movement for workers within the Community, OJ L257/2, 19 October, 1968.

(i)   Eligibility for Employment (Arts 1-6);

(ii) Employment and Equality of Treatment (Arts 7-9);

(iii) Worker's Families (Arts 10-12).

Article 12 of the Regulation deals specifically with education and guarantees to the children of migrant workers in the host country equal access to its educational institutions on the same grounds as nationals provided they are residents. Article 12 at paragraph 1 provides:

> the children of a national of a Member State shall be admitted to the state's general educational, apprenticeship and vocational training courses under the same circumstances as the nationals of that state, if such children are residing in its territory.

Migrant Worker: Education Rights under Article 7

[7.37] The first to benefit from the protection of the Regulation was the migrant worker himself, provided he or she was a Community national. Article 7(3) of the Regulation provided that workers who are non-nationals shall, under the same conditions as nationals, have access to training in vocational schools and retraining centres. Article 7(2) of the Regulation provided that the migrant worker should receive "the same social and fiscal advantages" as nationals.[57] The ambit of Article 12 of the Regulation was further expanded by a number of decisions which indicate that there may be a distinction between the entitlement of different categories of worker under Article39 (ex Article 48 EEC).[58] Categorising a person as a worker is the initial step in the assessment of his entitlements to educational rights as the following cases illustrate.

[7.38] The decision in *Lair v Universität Hannover*[59] established that migrant workers can claim equal treatment with nationals with regard to access to a maintenance grant, if such is provided, constituting a "social advantage" under Article 7(2) of the Regulation.[60] Lair was a French national who had been a bank employee for 18 months in Germany. Having left that post she worked intermittently in a number of posts in the host State. Lair's application for a training grant to study languages at university was refused on grounds, applicable to foreigners only, that she failed to meet the criteria of having been involved in regular professional activity for five years preceding the starting date of the training course. The ECJ considered that assistance given for a student's

---

[57] See Case 249/83 *Hoeckx v Openbar Centrum voor Maatschappelijk Welzijn Kalmthout*, [1985] ECR 973.

[58] See Weatherill and Beaumont, *European Community Law* (1994), Penguin, p 501, p 501 *et seq*: Verbruggen, 'European Community Education Law, a Short Overview', pp 49-51.

[59] Case 39/86 [1988] ECR 3161.

[60] *Cf* the position of students as a result of *Gravier v City of Liege* [1985] ECR 595.

maintenance and training is likely to improve the student's professional qualifications and promote social advancement and that the grants and benefits accruing to the student are means related in national law and are thus dependent on social criteria. The totality of these factors, the ECJ concluded, amounted to a social advantage within the context of Article 7(2) of the Regulation. The court made it clear that the worker is entitled to claim the maintenance grant only where there is continuity between the prior work undertaken and the purpose of study, except where the claimant is involuntarily unemployed and has been obliged to retrain.

[7.39] In *Brown v Secretary of State for Scotland,*[61] the ECJ ruled that the term "worker," for the purposes of education grants falling within Article 7(2) or Article 7(3) of Regulation 1612/68, does not include a person who enters a Member State and works there for eight months prior to commencing a university course, for which he had already been accepted, before entering that State. Brown, who was born and educated in France, held dual French and British nationality. He entered and was employed in Scotland as a full-time salaried trainee engineer for eight months prior to taking up a place in the engineering faculty at Cambridge university. Whilst Brown was entitled to non-discriminatory access to education in the host State, the ECJ held he could not rely on the term "worker", for the purposes of education grants to claim a maintenance grant, as distinct from a grant for fees, to cover the duration of study on the same terms as a national of the host State. Brown's parents had ceased to work and live in the United Kingdom and had become resident in France before the plaintiff was born. While it was accepted that Brown was a worker and that the grant amounted to a social advantage within Article 7(2) of the Regulation, the ECJ considered his status as a worker rested solely on admission to university for the purpose of undertaking studies.

[7.40] Clearly the ECJ was distinguishing between the status of certain categories of worker and the results that may accrue from that distinction.[62]

Residence Requirements in the Host Member State

[7.41] An important constraint was placed on the scope of Article 7(2) of the Regulation in the context of social and tax benefits in *Centre Public de l'Aide Sociale de Courcelles v Lebon.*[63] For the first time, the ECJ distinguished between migrant workers who are lawfully resident, as a result of obtaining a position in the host Member State, and those who have been granted temporary

---

[61] Case 197/86 [1988] ECR 3205.
[62] See Lonbay, 'Education and the Law: The Community context' 14 ELR, (1989), 375-380, 375-380; see further Weatherill and Beaumont, *European Community Law* (1994), Penguin, p 502.
[63] Case 316/85, [1987] ECR 2811.

rights of residence in pursuit of work, in that only the former may be beneficiaries of that Article.

[7.42] Access to education in the Member States[64] was raised again in 1989 in the joined cases *Echternacht and Moritz v Netherlands Minister for Education and Science.*[65] These cases involved German students who had been educated in the Netherlands where their parents were employed. When their parents returned to Germany, the children wished to remain in the Netherlands to attend college as their qualifications acquired there were not recognised in Germany. Accordingly, they sought grants from the Netherlands Ministry of Education although they did not possess the residence permits required by the Netherlands law on aliens. The ECJ held that "vocational training" courses extend to university studies in economics in the context of the free movement of workers and within the meaning of Article 12 of the Regulation. Under this Article, equal treatment for the children of Community workers extends to any form of education, whether it is vocational or part of general education.[66]

[7.43] The case of *Matteucci v Communaute Francaise De Belgique,*[67] established that Article 7 of the Regulation must be read so as to ensure that a Member State which has mutually agreed bilaterally with another Member State to grant educational scholarships to the latter's nationals must accept in the definition of such nationals those Community citizens from other Member States even when the inter-State agreement pre-dates the EEC Treaty.

Spouse of Migrant Worker: Education Rights

[7.44] Article 7 did not provide for spouses of migrant workers in the matter of educational rights. It appears that the ECJ compensated for this omission in the *Forscheri v Belgium*[68] decision. The applicant and her husband were both Italians, resident in Belgium where the husband was employed. Mrs Forcheri wished to attend a course in training for social workers at a non-university college. The question at issue was whether Forcheri could be lawfully required to pay a fee (*minerval*), when Belgian nationals were exempted from such fee? The ECJ ruled that although educational policy is primarily a matter for the Member States, access to education is within the ambit of the EEC Treaty. For the first time, the ECJ grounded a right to equal treatment with nationals in respect of vocational training on Article 7 EEC (now repealed), read in conjunction with Article 128 EEC (now Article 150 EC), rather than on the

---

64 Gould, 'Equality of Access to Education', (1989) 52 MLR, 540; Lonbay, 363.
65 Cases 389/87 and 390/87, [1989] ECR 723.
66 Cases 389/87 and 390/87, [1989] ECR 723.
67 Case 235/87, [1988] ECR 5589.
68 Case 152/82, [1983] ECR 2323, [1984] 1 CMLR 334.

provisions pertaining to workers. As will be seen, this case laid the foundation for the subsequent expansion of the term "vocational training" and the evolution of the Community's common vocational training policy.

Family of Migrant Worker: Education Rights

[7.45] It is now proposed to consider the scope of Article 12 of Regulation 1612/68 in regard to the education of the family of migrant workers. In *Casagrande v Landeshauptstadt Munchen*,[69] the plaintiff, of Italian parentage, was resident since birth in Munich. He was refused an educational award on the grounds that he did not possess the necessary criteria. This award, pursuant to the Bavarian Promotion of Education Act, had been restricted to German nationals, persons entitled to political asylum and stateless aliens. When the plaintiff initiated proceedings to achieve the award, the administrative court referred the question of whether the criteria for eligibility conflicted with Article 12 of Regulation 1612/68.

[7.46] The ECJ affirmed the Community's competence[70] to ensure that the children of a national of a Member State, who are or have been employed in the sovereign territory of another Member State, have a right, to all the same educational advantages, including grants, as are afforded the nationals of that State in that part of its territory, if such children are residing in the territory of the latter State. The wider issue of whether and to what degree the Community could lawfully interfere with the education of the Member States was answered in the circumstances of this case as follows:

> Although education and training policy is not as such included in the spheres which the Treaty has entrusted to the Community institutions, it does not follow that the exercise of powers transferred to the Community is in some way limited if it is of such a nature as to affect the measures taken in the execution of a policy such as that of education and training.[71]

The ECJ wished to ensure that problems encountered by the worker and his family did not militate against the exercise of their Community rights pursuant to the Treaty and secondary legislation. Accordingly, it interpreted Article 12 in the light of the regulation's objective, so that it extended to general measures intended to facilitate educational attendance and thus included, in the case of *Casagrande*, a study grant. This was the first of the *corpus* of cases concerning the free movement of workers and education. The decision in *Casagrande* was affirmed one year later in *Alaimo v Prefet du Rhone*[72] when the ECJ confirmed

---

[69] Case 9/74, [1974] ECR 1, 779.
[70] Under Article 12 of Regulation 1612/68, para 1.
[71] Article 12 of Regulation 1612/68, para 12.
[72] Case 68/74; [1975] ECR 109.

that Article 12 of Regulation 1612/68 was required to be interpreted so as to ensure that children of migrant workers achieved an equal position in respect to all rights arising from admission to educational courses.

[7.47] Council Directive 77/486/EEC[73] was adopted on the education of migrant workers' children in 1977.[74] This Directive, which gives rise to the first binding Community policy obligation in education is an important step in the emergence of a Community policy in education. The Directive makes provision for special educational support for the children of migrant workers. On transfer to the host Member State, such children are given a right to additional teaching to assist them in acquiring the language of the host country. For its part, the host country, in accordance with its national circumstances and legal system, must adopt suitable measures to promote the teaching to such children of the language and culture of their State of origin.[75] In addition, this Directive makes express provision for a variety of schemes which have made an important contribution to educational initiatives and to student and teacher mobility throughout the Community such as the *Socrates* and *Leonardo Da Vinci* programmes. Furthermore, case law has clarified that dependant children of migrant workers now have a right to benefit from the educational provision of the host State on equal terms with dependant children of nationals.[76]

[7.48] While the rights of family members derive from the migrant worker, it is clear that the concept of social integration, explicit in *Echternacht and Moritz v Netherlands Minister for Education and Science*,[77] does not necessarily require that the relationship from which the rights flow amounts to permanent cohabitation.[78] Thus, a member of the migrant worker's family, who is not a national of a Member State, has the derivative right to remain in and to move independently throughout the host State even when not residing permanently with the migrant worker.[79]

Recognition of Qualifications

[7.49] Realistically, there could be little advancement towards the goal of a common market in Europe without an appropriate and efficient system of

---

73 OJ 1977 L166/20.
74 Of the 25 July 1977 on the education of children of migrant workers.
75 See de Witte, 'Educational Equality for Community Workers and their Families' in *European Community Law of Education* de Witte, ed, (1989), Baden-Baden, Nomos, p 75.
76 Case 9/74 *Casagrande v Landeshauptstadt Munchen* [1974] ECR 773; 68/74 *Alaimo v Prefet du Rhone* [1975] ECR 109; Case 293/85 *EC Commission v Belgium* OJ C 60, 4.3.88, at 5.
77 Cases 389/87 and 390/87 [1989] ECR 723.
78 See also Case 237/83 *Diatta v Land Berlin* [1985] ECR 567.
79 See Article 11 of the Regulation; also Case 131/85 *Gul v Dusseldorf* [1986] ECR 1573.

recognition of qualifications which was necessitated by the diversity of the education systems of the Member States.[80] If a worker acquired a qualification in Ireland (the "home Member State") but could not use that qualification in another Member State ("the host Member State"), they would be most reluctant to move to that country, even if permitted to reside and work there.[81]

[7.50] At first, the approach of the Commission was to harmonise qualifications in individual sectors of employment such as, *inter alia*, the profession of pharmacists, general practitioners, nurses and veterinary surgeons. The less than encouraging results of the sectoral directives,[82] which had automatic effect, led the Community to adopt a general system of professional recognition in the 1989 Directive, as amended by Directive 92/51/EEC, which applies to all regulated professions requiring university training not already regulated under other directives. The 1989 Directive complements a variety of sectoral directives which were already in place.[83] By contrast with the sectoral systems, however, it did not create automatic effect.[84]

Recognition of Teacher Qualifications

[7.51] It has been established that teaching cannot be regarded as employment in the public service within the meaning of the exception contained in Article 39(4) (ex Article 48(4)). In principle, therefore, teaching posts must be open to nationals of other Member States without any restriction on the grounds of nationality. The professional qualifications which a teacher must possess in order to work in another Member State are governed either by Council Directive 89/48/EEC[85] (the Mutual Recognition of Diplomas Directive, hereafter the 1989 Directive), or by Article 39 EC (ex Article 48)[86] interpreted by the case law of the ECJ.

---

[80] See further Hyland, "Recognition of Qualifications of Migrant Workers - The Irish Situation" in *Free Movement of Workers in Ireland*, (forthcoming), Irish Centre for European Law, Trinity College, Dublin.

[81] See Hyland, p 29.

[82] See Perteck, 'Free Movement of Professionals and Recognition of Higher Diplomas' in *Yearbook of European Law*, Bard and Wyatt, eds, 1992, Oxford University Press, 1993, p 293: Verbruggen, 'European Community Educational Law: A Short Overview', *Subsidiarity and Education: Aspects of Comarative educational Law*, de Groof, ed (1994), Acco, Leuven, pp 64-65, n 84.

[83] See Perteck, p 295.

[84] See Perteck, p 276.

[85] Of 21 December 1988 on a general system for the recognition of higher-education diplomas awarded on completion of professional education and training of at least three years duration, OJ 1989 L 19/16.

[86] Article 39 of the *Treaty of Amsterdam*.

[7.52] Directive 92/51/EEC[87] (recognition of vocational training), which was adopted on 18 June 1992, modifies in part the operation of the 1989 Directive and establishes a second general system which covers diplomas awarded for studies of at least one year. While these arrangements reinforce the right of teachers throughout the Community to use professional skills in any Member State, in practice major obstacles to integration continue to exist.

Mutual Recognition of Professional Qualifications

[7.53] The 1989 Directive did not envisage the harmonisation of the training/ education periods leading up to qualification in the Member States. Rather it was grounded in mutual agreement between the Member States that a national of a Member State, who acquired therein a qualification of at least three years of higher education, was, in principle, qualified to practice his or her profession in another Member State. In the event of disparities arising between the professional requirements in the Member States, the 1989 Directive provided for certain compensatory measures. The recognition accorded need not be automatic as the host Member State may impose:

(a) an adaptation period not exceeding three years[88] or,

(b) an aptitude test.[89]

However, in total the professional experience required may not exceed four years. The applicant, with some exceptions, must be given the right to choose between the adaptation period and the aptitude test. That this could prove a crucial right for the applicant is clear, for if the aptitude test is raised so high as to exclude recognition, the adaptation period becomes a more realistic alternative. Documentary proof may also be sought, by the host Member State, of persons wishing to take up a "regulated profession"[90] to establish that the applicant is of good character or repute, that he or she is not bankrupt or suspended from the relevant profession for serious professional misconduct or for a criminal offence.[91] Such documents may be replaced by a declaration on oath or, in States where there is no provision for declaration on oath, by a solemn declaration.[92]

---

[87] Directive 92/51/EEC of 18 June 1992 on a second general system for the recognition of professional education and training to supplement Directive 89/48/EEC, OJ 1992 L209/25.

[88] Council Directive 89/48/EEC, (f) and Article 4(b) ie a "period of supervised practice" which shall be the subject of an assessment.

[89] Council Directive 89/48/EEC, (g).

[90] This means "the regulated professional activity or range of activities which constitute this profession in a Member State," Article 1(c). See Pertek, 'Free Movement of Professionals and Recognition of Higher Diplomas' in *Yearbook of European Law*, Bard and Wyatt, eds, (1992), Oxford University Press, 1993, p 298.

[91] Council Directive 89/48/EEC, Article 6.

[92] Council Directive 89/48/EEC.

[7.54] Academic recognition in the Member States, which is closely related to the content of education, has to date been the preserve of the Member States and Community law has acknowledged this exclusive jurisdiction.[93] Furthermore, the Member States retain the competency to lay down the procedures and criteria governing the use of a post-graduate academic title in their own jurisdiction.[94]

Implementation in Ireland

[7.55] The designated authority for the assessment of prospective secondary teachers who desire to teach in Ireland is the Registration Council for Secondary Teachers.

[7.56] The 1989 Directive was implemented in Ireland by the European Communities (General System for the Recognition of Higher Education Diplomas) Regulations 1991 which came into effect from 4 January 1991.[95] The new provisions governing the recognition in national schools of European Union qualified teachers other than those trained within the State are contained in Department of Education, Circular 19/96. As a rule questions will not arise about competence in the English language of teachers who hold their teacher recognition from a Member State where English is the mother tongue. In order to satisfy the Irish language requirements, in mainstream schools, generally applicants must:

    (a) have obtained a pass in *Scrúdú le haghaidh Cáilíochta sa Ghaeilge* (SCG); those candidates who hold third level qualifications in Irish may be exempted from part of the SCG; and

    (b) provide evidence that they have attended an approved language course in the Gaeltacht.

[7.57] Quotas have been imposed at university level on teacher undergraduates, and teacher training colleges, in an attempt to restrict the number of posts available to the numbers qualifying for those posts. However, to avoid this difficulty, many students take the more circuituous route into the teaching profession, by qualifying in the United Kingdom, and then seeking access to the home employment market. Hence, most of those invoking the recognition rules are persons of Irish nationality seeking to return to Ireland. As Hyland points out, the use of 1989 Directive in Ireland has created the extraordinary situation that approximately 30% of secondary school teachers seeking assessment of their qualifications are Irish nationals presenting non-Irish qualifications.[96]

---

[93] Case 293/83 *Gravier v City of Liege* [1985] ECR 595.
[94] Case 19/92 *Kraus v Land Baden-Wurttemburg* discussed in JUS letter 16-93.
[95] SI 1/1991.
[96] Hyland, 'Recognition of Qualifications of Migrant Workers-the Irish Situation' in *Free Movement of Workers in Ireland*, forthcoming, ICEL, pp 29-51 at 40-41.

[7.58] In 1997, in *McCann v Minister for Education*[97] Costello P ruled that Article 52 (now Article 43 EC) did not apply to an Irish teacher who had acquired her qualification abroad, and had returned to teach in Ireland. Between 1970-1973, the applicant in the *McCann* case undertook a general course in teacher training at an English college. The chief portion of this course related to art and design. The applicant had acquired a certificate in education from Leicester University and had completed the required probationary period in England in 1973/1974. On her return to Ireland in 1974, the applicant took up a post as teacher of art and design in County Kildare. Her application for registration as a secondary teacher to the Registration Council, in 1986, was refused as her qualifications were not considered to be the equivalent of those prescribed in Ireland.

[7.59] However, the applicant was employed on a non-incremental basis until she acquired a diploma from the Irish National College of Art and Design in 1991. In 1992 the applicant was appointed as a fully qualified registered teacher on an incremental basis. She then applied to the Department to have her previous teaching experience, comprising eighteen years in Ireland, taken into account for incremental purposes and later sought incremental credit for her year's teaching service in England. Both requests were refused by the Registration Council on the grounds that neither of these periods constituted "approved teaching service in Ireland" and hence they did not constitute registrable service for the incremental scale. The applicant instituted judicial review proceedings in the Irish High Court seeking to quash decisions of the Department of Education concerning a non-statutory scheme for payment of incremental salaries to secondary teachers. The applicant argued, *inter alia*, that:

   (a) the right of freedom of establishment in Article 52 EEC (now Article 43 EC) required Member States to give recognition to equivalent foreign qualifications;

   (b) that her qualifications would have been acceptable to the education authorities in England;

   (c) that accordingly the Department's refusal to recognise her qualifications was invalid;

   (d) that the Departmental rules favoured individuals qualified in Ireland and were accordingly in breach of Article 6 EEC (now repealed).

[7.60] Costello P held that the right of freedom of establishment in Article 52 EEC is conferred on the nationals of Member States in the territory of another Member State and as the applicant was an Irish citizen working in Ireland, no

---

[97] [1997] ILRM 1.

breach of Article 52 EEC could arise in this case. Likewise, he held that as Article 6 EEC prohibited discrimination on the basis of nationality there could be no breach of that Article either because of the applicant's Irish nationality. Neither, Costello P held, could the applicant establish indirect discrimination under Article 3 of Regulation 1612/68 because of her Irish nationality.

[7.61] In *Land Nordrhein-Westfalen v Karl Uecker* and *Vera Jacquet v Land Nordrhein-Westfalen*[98] the ECJ held, *inter alia*,[99] that:

> "Any discrimination which nationals of a Member State may suffer under the law of that State falls within the scope of that law and must therefore be dealt with within the framework of the internal legal system of that State."

Hence, it is beyond doubt that Community law does not apply to situations which are entirely internal to a Member State. However, in the case of *McCann,* there are distinguishing features as the applicant in that case had lived, worked and acquired her qualifications in another Member State.

[7.62] In *R v Singh,*[100] the Court held that a national of a Member State who has gone to another Member State, in order to exercise his right to work there in accordance with Article 48 EEC (now Article 39 EC), and subsequently returns to establish himself as self-employed in the home Member State, was entitled under Article 52 EEC (now Article 43 EC) to have his spouse accompany him on similar conditions as those established under Community law. The rationale underpinning this decision was to ensure that a national of a Member State would, if he left his home Member State to become employed or self-employed in another Member State, on his return be entitled to equivalence of conditions of entry and residence to those which he would enjoy in another Member State. Otherwise, the worker would be deterred from leaving his country of origin to work in another Member State as envisaged by the Treaty of Rome.

[7.63] Likewise in *Scholz v Opera Universitaria di Cagliari,*[101] the ECJ permitted an Italian national to rely on the principle of free movement in Italy. It held that any Community national who, regardless of his place of residence and nationality, has exercised the right to freedom of movement for workers and who

---

[98] Joined cases C 64/96 and C 65/96 ECR [1997] ECR, judgment of the Court (Third Chamber) of 5 June 1997, extracted from a JUSTIS database.

[99] The court also held that a national of a non-member country married to a worker having the nationality of a Member State cannot rely on the right conferred by Article 11 of Regulation 1612/68 when that worker has never exercised the right to freedom of movement within the Community.

[100] Case C-370/90, [1992] ECR 1-4265.

[101] Case C-419/92, [1994] ECR I-505. The facts are set out at para **[7.77]** below.

has been employed in another Member State, falls within the scope of the aforesaid provisions.

[7.64] These latter two cases imply that it is arguable in Community law that individuals who have left their country of origin to exercise their right to free movement and their right to work and subsequently return to their home Member State may rely on the freedom of movement principles of Community law. The issue in the *McCann* case, however, was complicated by another factor, that the qualification at issue was not considered to be the equivalent of those prescribed in Ireland.

Teacher Mobility: Difficulties Encountered

[7.65] Teacher training and education is closely linked to culture, language and nationalism and many countries prefer to choose their cohort of teachers from the ranks of their nationals. To this end, Member States can impose linguistic requirements in their own language which may only be achieved by a teacher with a high degree of fluency in that language. There is also the matter of external examinations in some countries. In Germany, for instance where a secondary teacher must be capable of teaching two subjects, an extra examination is required of a teacher from another Member State, thus constituting a further obstacle. Further difficulties arise from the fact that teacher training and education in the Member States varies widely as regards duration (two to five years), organisation, content, teaching theory and practical training. Not surprisingly, Member States which have a five year programme of teacher studies, are reluctant to confer equal status on those from other Member States with a two-year qualification. Some Member States still provide teacher training in institutions other than universities while in others student teachers must attend university. It is feared that the Member States, because of the sensitivty of this sphere, may utilise the variations arising between the duration and content of education and training to discourage individuals from application and thus exclude people from the system of recognition.[102]

Recognition of Academic Titles in Member States

[7.66] German law requires that German nationals, who have acquired an academic title in a foreign institution of higher education, must apply for authorisation from the competent ministry in the relevant land, in order to use that title in Germany. The applicant, in *Kraus v Land Baden-Wurttemberg*,[103] was a German national, who had passed the first State examination in law in Germany in 1986. He obtained the LLM[104] degree from Edinburgh University in

---

[102] Pertek, p 314.
[103] Case C-19/92, discussed in JUS letter 16-93.
[104] Master of Laws.

1988 but refused to make the necessary formal application for permission to use his title in Germany alleging that this procedure was discriminatory and constituted a breach of free movement of persons. When his request to use his title without authorisation was refused, the applicant took his case to the *Verwaltungsgericht* in Stuttgart which referred the matter to the ECJ for a preliminary ruling.

[7.67] The ECJ observed that the situation of a Community national, holding an academic title acquired through postgraduate studies awarded in another Member State, which facilitates the access to a profession, is governed by Community law even with regard to his relations with the Member State of which he is a national. However, 1989 Directive did not cover a course of academic study of only one year, such as that of the applicant, while Directive 92/51/EEC was adopted after the period of the dispute and the period for transposing it had not then expired (18 June 1994). Under these conditions (absence of harmonisation of national legislation), the ECJ held that the Member States were still competent to set down the procedures governing the use of an academic title within their territory.

[7.68] The ECJ considered that the fact that a Member State implements a procedure for issuing administrative authorisations prior to the use of postgraduate titles acquired in another Member State and provides for penal sanctions in the event of non-compliance, is not *per se* incompatible with the requirements of Community law. It considered that the necessity to safeguard the public against the abusive use of an academic title, which does not comply with the standards laid down in the country where the holder of the diploma intends to use it, amounts to a legitimate interest which can justify restrictions on the fundamental freedoms established by the EEC Treaty. Accordingly, the ECJ replied to the German court as follows:

> "that Articles 48 and 52 of the EEC Treaty[105] must be interpreted as meaning that they do not preclude a Member State from prohibiting one of its nationals, who holds an academic title acquired through postgraduate studies and awarded in another Member State, from using that title in its territory without obtaining administrative authorisation for the purpose provided that:
>
> (a) the authorisation procedure is solely intended to verify whether the academic title acquired through postgraduate studies was duly awarded;
>
> (b) the procedure is easily accessible and is not subject to the payment of excessive administrative charges;
>
> (c) any decision of refusal is open to judicial review;

---

[105] Now Articles 39 and 43 EC.

(d) the person concerned may ascertain the grounds for that decision;

(e) the penalties prescribed for non-observance of the authorisation procedure are not disproportionate to the seriousness of the offence."

Linguistic Requirements for Irish Teachers

[7.69] Linguistic requirements attached to teaching positions are lawful when they are concerned with the necessity to master the language of instruction in the Member State.[106] Article 3 of Regulation 1612/68 prohibits *indirect discrimination* ie measures, including linguistic requirements, which have as their sole or main aim or outcome to preclude other Community nationals from participating in the employment offered. This statement, however, does not apply to "conditions relating to linguistic knowledge required by reason of the nature of the post to be filled".

[7.70] The legal position obtaining when there is included a requirement to have a knowledge of a language other than the vernacular seems to depend on the status of that language.

[7.71] Permanent teachers in Irish vocational colleges, in which the language of instruction is usually English, have traditionally been required to have a competency, but not necessarily fluency, in the Irish language (the *Ceard Teastas* requirement applies). In *Groëner v The Minister for Education*,[107] the ECJ attempted to balance Ireland's politically sensitive "special linguistic situation" with the Community's aim of freedom of movement for workers. The plaintiff, a national of the Netherlands, who had been a part-time teacher of art for two years at a VEC College of Marketing and Design in Dublin, applied for a permanent post in 1984. While successful in the competition, the plaintiff failed the proficiency test in oral Irish (the *Ceard Teastas*). On a referral from the Irish High Court, the ECJ held that:

> "The EEC Treaty does not prohibit the adoption of a policy for the protection and promotion of a language of a Member State which is both the national language and the first official language. However, the implementation of such a policy must not encroach upon a fundamental freedom such as the free movement of workers. Therefore, the requirements deriving from measures intended to implement such a policy must not in any circumstances be disproportionate in relation to the aim pursued and the manner in which they are applied must not bring about discrimination against nationals of other Member States."

---

[106] Council Regulation 1612/68, Article 3.3; see generally Glendenning and Whelan, 'Irish Educational Structures' in *The Legal Status of Teachers in Europe: Mobility and Education*, de Groof, ed, (1995), Ultgeveri Acco, Belgium, p 207.

[107] Case 379/87 [1989] ECR 3967, p 9.

[7.72] The ECJ noted the Irish State's long-standing policy for promoting the Irish language in particular through education as a means of expressing national identity and culture. In particular, it considered its constitutional status as the first official and national language.[108] It interpreted the phrase "conditions relating to linguistic knowledge required by reason of the nature of the post to be filled" in Article 3 of Regulation 1612/68 in a manner sympathetic to Ireland's cultural and national values and concluded that the nature of the post justified a linguistic requirement:

> "The importance of education for the implementation of such a policy must be recognised. Teachers have an essential role to play, not only through the teaching which they provide but also by their participation in the daily life of the school and the privileged relationship which they have with their pupils. In those circumstances it is not unreasonable to require them to have some knowledge of the first national language."[109]

[7.73] While this judgment seems ideal from a national standpoint, it is scarcely satisfactory from a Community perspective. In allowing the exemption for the protection of the Irish language, the *Groëner* judgment appears to have doubly advantaged Irish teachers who can avail of teacher mobility in all other Member States without, it seems, the full duty of reciprocation. Yet, the ECJ carefully qualified the scope of its decision stating that the level of linguistic knowledge required of the candidate must not be disproportionate in relation to the objective pursued within the meaning of the final paragraph of Article 3(1) of Regulation 1612/68. It further required that nationals of other Member States, where they have failed the oral examination, should have an opportunity to re-take such examination when re-applying for a post.[110] These concessions, afforded a constitutionally protected national and first official language of a Member State, are highly unlikely to apply in the case of minority languages or dialects.

Limited Waiver of Irish Language Requirements for Certain Teachers

[7.74] Recently, the Irish language requirement has been waived by Ireland in certain instances eg for teachers employed in "special schools"[111] and in "special classes"[112] in mainstream national schools. In such instances, primary teachers

---

[108] Under Article 8 of the Constitution.

[109] *Groëner v The Minister for Education* [1989] ECR 3967.

[110] *Groëner v The Minister for Education* [1989] ECR 3967 at 9, para 23; this requirement has been taken into account in *Circular 19/96* governing arrangements for nationals of other Member States who wish to take the Irish qualifying examination.

[111] Schools for the handicapped and other categories of pupil.

[112] Those classes in ordinary national schools in which children with learning difficulties and other disabilities are taught.

trained outside Ireland may receive recognition and sanction by the Minister without the Irish language requirement. With reference to such exemptions the *Groener* case stated:

> "It must also be pointed out that where the national provisions provide for the possibility of exemption from that linguistic requirement, where no other fully qualified candidate has applied for the post to be filled, community law requires that power to grant exemptions to be exercised by the Minister in a non-discretionary manner."[113]

Clearly, the above statement applies only "where no other fully qualified candidate has applied for the post". If no such candidate applies, then Community law requires that Ireland does not discriminate between teachers who are Irish nationals and teachers who are other Community nationals applying. Previously, it was required by the Irish State that the requisite linguistic knowledge of the Irish language must be acquired within the national territory. The *Groener* judgment stated: "... the principle of non-discrimination precludes the imposition of any requirement that the linguistic knowledge in question must have been acquired within the national territory."[114] Ireland has since altered its language policy in this regard to comply with Community law.

[7.75] In the years 1993-1994 Irish teachers were among the largest beneficiaries of EC rules guaranteeing mutual recognition of professional qualifications. Britain received 55% of all EC applications during the period 1993-1994.[115] A recent EC Commission report has revealed that of the 2,904 foreign teaching qualifications recognised in Britain in 1993-1994, 1,277 of these were Irish qualified.[116]

[7.76] During the same period (1993-1994), Ireland reciprocated by recognising some 899 foreign qualifications including those of 85 lecturers in Regional Technical Colleges and 42 secondary school teachers.[117] Linguistic requirements in other Member States constitute an invisible obstacle to teacher mobility from Ireland. Judicial activism in the ECJ has meant that the previous Article 128 EEC (vocational training) became one of the key provisions of the Treaty facilitating mobility of workers generally and inevitably the mobility of teachers.

---

[113] *Groëner v The Minister for Education* [1989] ECR 3967, para 22.
[114] *Groëner v The Minister for Education* [1989] ECR 3967, para 23.
[115] Smith, 'Irish-qualified teachers benefit from EU directive on professions', Irish Times, 22 February, 1996, 2.
[116] Smith.
[117] Smith.

Other Types of Indirect Discrimination

[7.77] As de Witte points out, particular features of a selection method for employment may be held to be indirect discrimination.[118] This is well illustrated by the decision in *Scholz v Opera Universitaria di Cagliari and Cinzia Porcedda*,[119] a non-educational case which has application for the teaching profession. The applicant who had travelled from Germany to Sardinia had become an Italian national as a result of her marriage. She applied for the post of canteen assistant in the university of Cagliari. A system of points rating was operated whereby candidates in the Italian public service were granted points for previous service. By contrast, the applicant was allocated no points for her previous work experience in the German postal service and so was not offered a post. The Court ruled that the failure to grant the applicant points for her previous experience in another Member State amounted to unjustified indirect discrimination. This decision, if correctly applied throughout the Community, has important implications for teachers with some work experience which may no longer be overlooked in the host State in respect of access, promotion and remuneration.

The Evolution of a Common Vocational Training Policy

Vocational Training

[7.78] By contrast with general education, vocational training was an issue of Community concern *ab initio*[120] as it was employment related and had the potential to advance the prosperity of the Member States and the development of the Common Market.[121] The early definition of "vocational training" was a narrow one meaning training for a specific job, in particular manual or basic skills.[122] The legal basis for Community involvement in vocational training policy is the former Article 128 EEC (now Article 150 EC): "The Council shall ... lay down general principles for implementing a common vocational training policy capable of contributing to the harmonious development both of national economies and of the common market". Article 118 EEC made the Commission responsible for fostering close co-operation between the Member States concerning elementary and advanced vocational training.

---

[118] De Witte, *European Community Law of Education* (1989), Baden-Baden, Nomos, pp 45-46.
[119] [1994] ECR 505.
[120] See the former Article 128 EEC; Article 7(3) EEC.
[121] See further Green, Hartley and Usher, *The Legal Foundations of the Single European Market*, (1991), Oxford University Press, p 175; Flynn, 'Vocational Training in Community law and Practice', *Yearbook of European Law*, 1988, pp 59-85.
[122] Article 128 EEC; Article 7(3).

Equal Access to Vocational Training: an Evolving Right

[7.79] The decision in *Gravier v City of Liège*[123] established that, where the course constitutes vocational training, Article 7 EEC prohibits discrimination on the grounds of nationality between nationals of the host Member State and nationals of other Member States in respect of the payment of tuition fees but not of maintenance fees. The ECJ further expanded the concept of vocational training[124] to include any form of instruction which led to qualifications for a profession, trade or specific employment or conferred special ability to practice that profession, trade or employment whatever the age and educational background of the student and even if the programme of instruction included general education. Accordingly, this broad definition of "vocational training," which included instruction in the art of strip cartoons, in the circumstances of this case, enabled the ECJ to apply the principle of non-discrimination to access to education.

[7.80] The Belgian Education Act 1985, by implementing a differential fee for nationals of other Member States, failed to take account of the *Gravier* decision. Following a successful challenge by the Commission, the Belgian legislation was redrafted in line with Community law.[125] The question of whether the term "vocational training" included university education for the purposes of Article 128 EEC was considered in *Blaizot v City of Liège*.[126] Certain Belgian universities had refused to refund the supplementary enrolment fees to 17 veterinary students, all French nationals, who paid their fees on 13 February 1985, the day on which the *Gravier* judgment was delivered. Subsequently, the national court submitted the matter to the Commission which held the fees were improperly charged as they were discriminatory contrary to Article 7 EEC.[127] Although the Member States generally appeared to view "vocational training" as specific skills learned by craftspersons and tradespersons,[128] this landmark decision ruled that university studies prepare for a trade qualification or provide the necessary training therefor, the only exceptions being certain courses of study which are intended for those wishing to approve their general knowledge rather than prepare themselves for an occupation.[129] Urgent matters including

---

[123] Case 293/83 [1985] ECR 593.
[124] Following the general guidelines drawn up by the Council in 1981.
[125] Case 293/85 *Commission v Belgium* [1985] ECR 3521.
[126] Case 24/86 *Blaizot v University of Liege* [1988] ECR 379.
[127] The direct effect of Article 7 EEC did not protect those students who paid fees prior to 13 February 1985, except in the case of those who had initiated claims or legal proceedings prior to that date.
[128] See Flynn in 'Gravier: Suite du Feuilleton' in *European Community Law of Education*, de Witte, ed, (1989), Baden-Baden, Nomos, p 99.
[129] Case 24/86 *Blaizot v University of Liege* [1988] ECR 379 at 404.

legal uncertainty led the ECJ to move to set boundaries to the effects of its decision retrospectively. Any re-consideration of earlier legal relationships would be likely to impact most adversely on the administration and financing of universities.[130]

[7.81] The Belgian State,[131] in the *State (Belgium) v Humbel*,[132] sought to recover from a Frenchman living in Luxembourg, a *minerval* in regard to his son's education at a Belgian secondary school. In this instance, it was not from the host Member State (Luxembourg) but from another Member State (Belgium), that an equal treatment of the migrant worker's child was sought. The ECJ concluded that Article 12 of Council Regulation 1612/68 did not give rise to such an obligation. The ECJ also ruled that a one year course of study, which is part of a programme of instruction constituting education which prepares for a qualification for a particular profession, trade, or employment, is vocational training for the purposes of Community law.

[7.82] In *Lair v Universität Hannover*[133] and *Brown v Secretary of State for Scotland*,[134] the ECJ held that a vocational school, is not merely a school which wholly or in part provides vocational training. This term "has a narrower meaning and refers solely to establishments which provide only instruction sandwiched between periods of employment or else closely connected with employment, particularly during apprenticeship".[135]

National Courts applying EC Rules

Covert Discrimination

[7.83] The case of *McMahon v Department of Education and Science*[136] provides an example of covert discrimination. This case was taken in the English courts by an Irish-born primary teacher who applied for and was refused a grant and reduced fees, on the same basis as British nationals. He argued that that:

(a) he was a "worker" within the meaning of Article 7 EEC;

(b) that his course in teacher training was "vocational training" within the meaning of the former Article 128 EEC;

(c) that he was discriminated against under Community law.

---

[130] Case 24/86 *Blaizot v University of Liege* [1988] ECR 379.

[131] Under Article 117 EEC.

[132] Case 263/86 [1988] ECR 5365.

[133] Case 39/86, *Lair v Universitat Hannover* [1988] ECR 3161, para 26.

[134] Case 197/86 [1988] ECR 3205, para 12.

[135] Cited in Case 235/87 *Matteucci v Communaute Francaise De Belgique* [1989] 1 CMLR 357 at 364.

[136] [1982] 3 WLR 1129; [1982] 3 CMLR 91.

As he was denied a grant and reduced fees on the same basis as British nationals, the Court held McMahon had been covertly discriminated against under Community law.[137] Since the English courts did not refer the matter to the ECJ, no authoritative decision emanated from the latter court until *Brown v Secretary of State for Scotland*[138] and *Lair v University of Hanover*.[139] The opinion of Advocate General Sir Gordon Slynn in *Commission v Belgium*[140] confirmed the earlier finding in *McMahon*,[141] that a course on teaching skills, (a teachers' training course), was vocational in nature.[142]

General Qualifications Required for Teaching in Second Level Schools in Ireland

[7.84] There are four types of second-level school in this State: secondary, vocational, community and comprehensive. The conditions and qualifications relaying to registration as a secondary teacher are prescribed by the Registration Council. The Council is statutorily constituted body which includes representatives of the universities, school management, teacher organisations and the Minister for Education in its membership. The Council prescribes that each applicant for registration as a secondary teacher must among other things hold a Degree teaching qualification acceptable to the Council and to hold an acceptable specialist qualification in one of the following subjects: Art, Home Economics, Physical Education, Music, Religious Education, Woodwork or Metalwork. He or she must also pass a test of competency in oral Irish. All teaching appointments in vocational schools are made by the Vocational Education Committee. In general, the qualifications required for appointment as a vocational teacher are a relevant primary degree and An Ceard Teatas Gaelige or equivalent qualification. An Ceard Teastas Gaelige is a certificate of a person's competency to teach through Irish. To teach in a Community or Comprehensive school an applicant must hold a relevant primary degree and the Higher Diploma in Education of an Irish University or an approved equivalent qualification with an acceptable qualification in Irish.

[7.85] In order to qualify for payment of incremental salary from this Department, a secondary teacher holding qualifications not previously given general recognition by the Registration Council must have them assessed by the Council.

---

[137] McMahon relied mainly on Article 7 EEC and Council Regulation 1612/68 EEC, paras 2 and 3.

[138] [1988] 2 CMLR 836.

[139] Case 39/86 *Lair v Universitat Hannover* [1988] ECR 3161.

[140] Case No 293/85, [1988] ECR 305, a case held inadmissible on procedural grounds.

[141] [1982] 3 CMLR 91.

[142] *Cf R v Inner London Education Authority ex parte Hinde* [1985] 1 CMLR 716, in which a university LLB course was held not to constitute vocational training.

In the case of vocational, community and comprehensive teaching, the assessment procedure is carried out by the relevant section of this Department. The criteria for evaluating qualifications are basically the same in each case and assessments are carried out on an individual basis.

Teacher Redundancy: Redeployment and EC Rules

[7.86] Redundancy and redeployment panels for schools were discussed in Chapter 3 and the issue of their legality in Community law arises in this chapter. From a Community law perspective, these schemes operate a "closed shop" type of arrangement which is beneficial to the incumbents of teaching posts in Ireland (largely nationals). On closer scrutiny, however, the panels block access to the teaching profession both to nationals and non-nationals. While these schemes block access to the profession to a notional group of non-nationals who are suitably qualified to teach in Irish schools, they do not appear to arbitrarily discriminate between nationals and non-nationals. The principle of equality is a basic tenet of Community law which indicates that equals must be treated equally.[143] However, the principle of equality does not make all forms of discrimination unlawful but only such discrimination which amounts to "arbitrary discrimination".[144] In establishing whether these redundancy schemes are arbitrarily discriminatory, the ECJ would most likely consider the *raison d'être* of existing schemes which is primarily to ensure continuity of service for teachers already in employment. The ECJ has made it clear, however, in *Wilhelm v Bundeskartellamt*,[145] that it will not permit Member States to introduce or retain measures capable of prejudging the practical effectiveness of the Treaty.

[7.87] Article 7 of the EEC Treaty (now Article 12 EC) which prohibited each Member State from applying its law differently on the ground of the nationality of the parties concerned is not concerned with the disparities in treatment or the distortions which may result, for persons and undertakings subject to the jurisdiction of the Community, from divergencies existing between the laws of the Member States, provided that these affect all persons subject to them in accordance with objective criteria and without regard to their nationality.

[7.88] It appears to the author that the above-mentioned schemes, although they may become increasingly difficult to operate in a modern context, are unlikely to constitute indirect discrimination in Community law as they do not seem to prejudice the practical effectiveness of the EC Treaty itself. It will be recalled

---

[143] McMahon and Murphy, *European Community Law in Ireland*, (1989), Butterworths, pp 137-138.

[144] Case 88/78, *Kendermann* [1978] ECR 2477.

[145] Case 14/68 [1969] ECR 1.

that the secondary school redeployment scheme has survived a constitutional challenge in *Greally v The Minister for Education, The AG and the ASTI*.[146]

Transfer of Undertakings

[7.89] In the past, employees had no rights whatever when the business for which they worked was transferred to another. The transfer of undertakings was dealt with by Council Directive 77/187 EEC[147] which was transposed into Irish law by European Communities (Safeguarding of Employees Rights on Transfer of Undertaking) Regulations 1980.[148] The purpose of the Directive and the Regulations is to safeguard the rights of employees arising from a contract of employment or a relationship in the event of a transfer of a business, in which they are employed which involves a change of employer. The Directive applies to the transfer of an undertaking, business or part of a business to another employer effected by contract or by some other disposition or operation of law, judicial decision or administrative measure.[149]

The Scope of the Directive

[7.90] While some doubts initially surrounded the ambit of the application of the Directive, the ECJ has consistently given a very broad interpretation as to whether or not a transfer of undertakings has taken place. It is now clear that for an economic activity to amount to an undertaking, it does not have to be a profit-making activity.[150] Clearly, the Directive now applies to public and private undertakings engaged in economic activities whether or not they are operating for gain.[151] As Byrne points out,[152] this definition has the effect of allowing within the scope of the Directive/Regulations, *inter alia*:

    (a) local authorities;

    (b) State and semi-State bodies;

    (c) schools, colleges and other educational establishments; and

    (d) trade unions and associations.

---

[146] High Court, unrep, 29 January 1999 *per* Geoghegan J.

[147] OJ 1977 L61, 5.3, p 26 which was grounded in Articles 100 and 117 of the Treaty of Rome. See also Directive 98/50/EC of 29 June 1988 which amends Directive 77/187/EEC.

[148] SI 306/1980.

[149] Case 135/83, *Abels* ECR [1995] 469.

[150] *Dr Sophie Redmond Stichting v Bartol* [1992] IRLR 366.

[151] Council Directive 98/50/EC amends Council Directive 77/187/EEC, Article 1.1 (C).

[152] Byrne, *Transfer of Undertakings*, (1999), Blackhall Publications, p 57 and generally see also McMahon and Murphy, *European Community Law in Ireland*, (1989), Butterworths, p 511 *et seq*; *The Acquired Rights Directive*, Kerr, ed, (1996), Irish Centre for European Law, Trinity College; O'Donnell, 'Transfer of Undertakings: The Acquired Rights Directive', lecture delivered 21 March 1996 to Bar Council, Continuing Legal Education Programme.

[7.91] In the education sector, it seems that the Directive may apply, *inter alia*, to the transfer of a school or part thereof to another employer and to the amalgamation of two or more schools into one new unit with a new employer. This latter situation could arise where, for example, a voluntary secondary school merges with a vocational school so as to form a new entity such as a community school. The new employer, in this instance would be the trustees of the community school.

Application of Certain Criteria

[7.92] The ECJ, however, has ruled that certain criteria must be applied to a situation in order to determine whether it constitutes a transfer, the most pivotal of these being whether the economic unit retains its identity,[153] (in the education context as a school or college). The assessments which are necessary in order to determine whether there is a transfer for the purposes of the Directive are a matter for the national courts. A number of factors are normally taken into account which in the school context would apply as follows:

    (a) the nature of the undertaking or business, eg public school or private school or a merging of both strands;

    (b) whether or not the students are transferred to the new entity;

    (c) the degree of similarity carried on prior to and after the transfer;

    (d) the duration, if any during which those activities were suspended;

    (e) whether or not the majority of teachers are taken over by the new employer;

    (f) whether capital assets and other tangible assets are transferred; and

    (g) the value of all intangible assets at the time of transfer.

The above factors or criteria are single elements in the total assessment which must be applied but which may not stand alone.[154]

Obligations falling on Employers

[7.93] The Directive obliges employers, both as transferors and transferees, to inform employees' representative bodies and unions of the transfer in good time and prior to the transfer of the following:

    (a) the date or proposed date of the transfer;

    (b) the reasons for such transfer;

    (c) the legal, economic and social implications for employees; and

    (d) any measures envisaged in relation to employees.[155]

---

[153] Case C-392/92, *Schmidt*, [1994] ECJ, judgment delivered 14 April 1994.
[154] See Case 24/85, *Spijkers*, [1986] ECR 1119.
[155] Section 111, Article 6(1).

If the transferor or the transferee envisage measures in relation to their employees, they are obliged to consult with the representatives of the employees (the trade unions or professional body) in good time on such measures with a view to reaching agreement.[156]

[7.94] With regard to dismissals, the Directive provides protection of the employees concerned against dismissal by the transferor or the transferee but "does not stand in the way of dismissals that may take place for economic, technical or organisational reasons entailing changes in the workforce."[157]

[7.95] The net issue before the English court in *National Union of Teachers v The Governing Body of Saint Mary's Church of England (aided) Junior School*[158] was whether or not a Community Directive[159] could be invoked by an individual in national law[160] as against a voluntary school.

[7.96] The applicants were employed as teachers in the respondent infant school which was closed by the Local Education Authority (LEA). The Diocesan Board suggested the establishment of a new voluntary aided school, whose governing body was set up under the Education (No 2) Act 1986, which would provide for 4 to 11 year-olds. These proposals were sanctioned by the Secretary of State for Education. Following their unsuccessful application for posts in the new school, the applicants were made redundant. They alleged unfair dismissal against the governors on the grounds that they were not really redundant in fact and so the Transfer of Undertakings (Protection of Employment) Regulations and the Business Transfer Directive which the Regulations implemented, applied. The English Regulations defined an undertaking as a "commercial venture," and so the Tribunal held that the Regulations did not apply to the school in question. As the Directive did not expressly confine its powers to a "commercial venture", the applicants then sought to rely on the Directive for the purpose of direct effect.[161]

---

[156] Article 6(2).

[157] Memorandum from the Commission on acquired rights of workers in cases of transfers of undertakings, Guideline on the Application of Council Directive 77/187/EEC based on the case law of the Court of Justice of the European Community.

[158] [1995] 3 CMLR 638; [1995] ICR 317; for an interesting commentary on this issue, see Marston and Thompson, 'Voluntary -aided schools and the direct effectiveness of EC Directives' in *Education and the Law,* (1996), Vol 8, No 2 153.

[159] Directives are binding on all Member States as to the results to be achieved; see further McMahon and Murphy, *European Community Law in Ireland,* (1989), Butterworths, pp 156-157, also Article 189 EEC.

[160] Be directly effective, see Case 26/62 *Van Gend en Loos v Nederlandse Belastingadministratie* [1963] ECR 1; [1963] CMLR 105.

[161] When dealing with Directives, which are binding on all Member States as to the result to be achieved, Community law distinguishes between (a) vertical direct effect (where an individual can enforce rights against the State), and (b) horizontal direct effect, where an individual can enforce rights against another individual, see further McMahon and Murphy, *European Community Law in Ireland,* (1989), Butterworths, 9.11. The ECJ has clarified that, in the case of Community Directives, there can only be vertical direct effect.

When the requirements for direct effectiveness are met, there can only be direct effect as against an institution which is regarded as "an emanation of the State". The court concluded that, although the school provided a public service, it was not "an emanation of the State" for the purpose of direct effect and so the directive could not be directly effective in the case of this voluntary school.

[7.97] The Irish (Safeguarding of Employees Rights on Transfer of Undertaking) Regulations 1980[162] do not define an undertaking as a "commercial venture" and so it is conceivable that voluntary schools would come within the scope of the Irish regulations for the purposes of acquired rights.

PART II: THE LEGAL BASIS FOR COMMUNITY LEGISLATION ON EDUCATION FOLLOWING THE TREATY ON EUROPEAN UNION

The Treaty on European Union

[7.98] The Treaty on European Union (1992) (TEU) established a new entity termed the European Union which is grounded in the three founding Communities and is reinforced by the policies and initiatives of the TEU. Much of the TEU with amendments to the EC Treaty. The word "economic" is omitted from the name of the Community emphasising the fact that the Community is no longer merely an economic body.[163]

[7.99] Article 8 EC (now Article 17 EC) establishes European Union citizenship which is held by every person holding the nationality of a Member State. The complete text of some Articles is new while others contain only minor drafting changes. Article 6 EEC[164] was repealed. Articles 7 EEC and Article 8 EEC become Articles 6 EC (now Article 12 EC) and 7 EC (now repealed) respectively while Articles 126 EEC, 127 EEC and 128 EEC were repealed.

Educational Framework

[7.100] The TEU provides, *inter alia*:

(a) a closer framework for a European Union; and

(b) a basis for reinforced cooperation in education and training, complementing the measures employed by the Member States.[165]

---

[162] SI 306/1980.

[163] Article 3 EC extends to 20 diverse spheres of Community interest.

[164] On economic policy coordination.

[165] See 'Twin-Track Europe' *Legal Issues of the Maastricht Treaty*, O'Keefe and Toomey, eds, (1994), London; Chancery Law; Shaw, 'Education and the Law in the European Community', Journal of Law and Education (1992), 21 415.

Article 3(p) envisaged that the activities of the Community, "as provided in this Treaty," would include "a contribution to education and training of quality and to the flowering of the cultures of the Member States."[166]

[7.101] Articles 126 EC (now Article 149) (education) and 127 EC (now Article 150) (vocational training) jointly comprised a "Chapter" in the Title of the EC Treaty on "Social Policy, Education, Vocational Training and Youth." While initially, these seem to be new Community competences, with the exception of vocational training, Articles 126 EC and 127 EC (now Articles 149 and 150) did not expand the ambit of Community jurisdiction to totally new areas. Rather, these Articles assimilated and institutionalised the jurisprudence[167] of the ECJ based on the former Article 128 EEC, (repealed by the TEU) and other relevant Articles and secondary legislation.[168] It is notable that the TEU introduces separate policy objectives for education and vocational training each having distinct decision-making procedures.[169]

[7.102] By inserting an article on education, (Article 126 EC (now Article 149)), into the EEC Treaty,[170] the TEU conferred a certain express competence in education on the Community for the first time.[171] Significantly, all types of education, not previously considered to be vocational training under the former Article 128 EEC, fell within the scope of Article 126 EC (now Article 149).[172] This means that Community competence in education extends to pre-school education, primary education, general secondary education and courses of study in university which "because of their particular nature, are intended for persons wishing to improve their general knowledge rather than prepare themselves for an occupation".[173] Because Article 126 EC (now Article 149) has now provided a legal basis for education in the Treaty, it will no longer be necessary to take the

---

[166] See Title X, Article 128 EC (Culture).

[167] See the concept of *"acquis communautaire"* in Lenaerts, 'Subsidiarity and Community Competence in the Field of Education' in de Groof, *Subsidiarity and Education: Aspects of Comparative Educational Law*, pp 120-123.

[168] Lenaerts, p 118.

[169] Article 189b (now Article 251) of the EC Treaty ("the co-decision procedure") applies to education while Article 189c (now Article 252) of the EC Treaty ("the cooperation procedure") applies to vocational training.

[170] For the full text of the EC Treaty consequent on the entry into force of Title II of the TEU, see OJ 1992, C 224.

[171] See Beaumont and Moir, *The European Communities (Amendment) Act 1993 with the Treaty of Rome (as amended): Text and Commentary*, (1994), London, Sweet and Maxwell, 32-138, 32-141.

[172] See further Lenaerts, p 125.

[173] Case 24/86, *Blaizot v University of Liege* [1989] 1 CMLR 57.

circuitous route, formerly provided by "vocational education",[174] in order to permit the Community to establish an education policy.

Subsidiarity

[7.103] While Article 126 EC (now Article 149) confers on the Community a more assured role and an outline competence in education, the phrase "fully respecting the responsibility of the Member States for the content of teaching and the organisation of education systems and their cultural and educational diversity" qualifies its outcome. The overarching concept of subsidiarity[175] and the principle of proportionality,[176] which are included in the TEU Preamble and enacted by Article 3b EC (now Article 5) may act as restraints in areas which do not fall within the Community's exclusive competence such as education and vocational training. Nonetheless, the Community can now rely on a more assured constitutional basis in education than that formerly provided by the Treaty of Rome.

[7.104] Furthermore, Article 126(4) (now Article 149(4) EC specifically excludes harmonisation of the laws of the Member States in education; yet one of the objectives in fostering co-operation between the Member States is "voluntary" harmonisation of national education policies and this objective is backed by Community financial support proportionate to the degree of co-operation forthcoming from the Member State.

[7.105] Although the Community's action in education is expressly constrained by Article 126(2) (now Article 149(2)) EC and by Article 3b (now Article 5) EC, paragraph 3,[177] it may still exert considerable influence on education in the Member States by virtue of its financial support, particularly in the less well-resourced countries. The European Social Fund has provided £184 million for the training of Irish apprentices since 1990,[178] which constitutes 60% of total

---

[174] Under Article 128 EEC (now repealed).

[175] The principle of subsidiarity, one of the fundamental concepts of the EC legal system, permits the Community, in spheres not falling within its express competence, to act only where what requires to be done cannot be adequately achieved by the Member States, but can be better accomplished by the Community because of its scale or effects. See Emilou (1992), "Subsidiarity: an effective barrier against the enterprises of ambition?", 17 ELR, p 383; Lord Mackenzie-Stewart 'Subsidiarity - A Busted Flush?', *Constitutional Adjudication in European Community and National Law*, p 19; Rudden and Wyatt, *Basic Community Laws*, (1993), Oxford University Press.

[176] "Any action by the Community shall not go beyond what is necessary to achieve the objectives of this Treaty."

[177] "Any action of the Community shall not go beyond what is necessary to achieve the objectives of this Treaty."

[178] See Pollack, Education Correspondent, 'FÁS gets a mixed Euro-fund report' in Education and Living, Irish Times, 2 February 1999, p 2.

expenditure, while one third of all government expenditure on higher education is funded by the EU.[179] The Social Fund Reports also impact significantly on the governments of the Member States.

[7.106] Article 126 EC (now Article 149) seems to envisage that a balance be found between the extent of the Community's action in education and the core powers reserved to the Member States in education. For their part, the Member States may not take refuge from their "responsibility" set out in Article 126(1) (now Article 149(1)) EC but rather they must eliminate all obstacles in national law which obstruct the required co-operation.[180]

[7.107] While it is arguable that the powers vested in the Community by Article 126 (now Article 149) EC are limited, they lay down Community aims in education while re-emphasising that these areas essentially continue to be the responsibility of the Member States. Because of the importance of education to the evolution of the common market and to European integration generally, Community law is likely to exert a more significant influence on the evolution of educational policy in years to come.[181]

Vocational Training

[7.108] Article 126 EC (now Article 149) provides for "incentive measures" in education. By contrast, Article 127 (Article 150) EC, dealing with vocational training, provides for a "policy" which the Community will implement in that sphere. However, it adds similar exclusions of competence as are found in the Article on education ("fully respecting the responsibilities of the Member States for the content and organisation of vocational training" and "excluding any harmonisation of the laws and regulations of the Member States". Likewise the "policy" envisaged by Article 127 (now Article 150) EC is grounded in fostering co-operation between the Community and the Member States as is apparent from Article 127(2) (now Article 150(2)) which lays down the aims of Community action in the field of vocational training.

Human Rights in the TEU

[7.109] The European Convention on Human Rights has been expressly recognised as part of the EU Treaties by virtue of the TEU.[182] This is the first time a specific provision on human rights is included in a Community Treaty and so the emerging interface between Community law and human rights issues has enormous potential which may to impact on educational-religious issues in

---

[179] *OECD Economic Surveys: Ireland*, (1995), p 110, n 31.
[180] See Article 5 (now Article 10) EC.
[181] See further Shaw, *European Community Law*, (1993), London, Macmillan, p 331.
[182] In Article F(2).

the Member States. This is another possible route by which Community law may influence education in the Member States.[183] It has already been held that the Community and its institutions can infringe the right of an individual to practice his religion and so constitute religious discrimination.[184]

The Treaty of Amsterdam

The Treaty of Amsterdam amending the Treaty on European Union, the Treaties establishing the European Communities and Certain Related Acts came into force on 1 May 1999.

Article 149: Education

[7.110] As amended by the Treaty of Amsterdam, the EC Treaty contains a Chapter 3 Title XI, which is headed "Education, vocational training and youth," and includes Article 149 (ex Article 126) on education and Article 150 (ex Article 127) on vocational training.

[7.111] Article 149 (ex Article 120) reiterates the Community's commitment to the development of quality education by means of encouragement, cooperation and support "while fully respecting the responsibility of the Member States for the content of teaching and the organisation of education systems and their cultural and linguistic diversity." It states that Community action shall be aimed at developing the European dimension in education, encouraging student and teacher mobility, promoting cooperation between educational establishments and developing exchanges of information and experience on issues common to the education systems of the Member States. It further states that Community action shall encourage the growth of distance education and youth exchanges and together with the Member States, it shall foster co-operation with third countries and competent international organisations in the field of education.

[7.112] In order to contribute to the achievement of these objectives, the Council, acting in accordance with the procedure in Article 251 (ex Article 1896), following consultation with the Economic and Social Committee and the Committee of the Regions, shall "adopt incentive measures, excluding any harmonisation of the laws and regulations of the Member States." It shall adopt recommendations acting by a qualified majority on a proposal from the Commission.

---

[183] See further Power, 'Human Rights and the EEC' in Heffernan with Kingston, *Human Rights: a European Perspective*, (1994), Round Hall Press in association with Irish Centre for European Law, p 81.

[184] *Prais v Council* [1976] ECR 1589.

Article 150: Vocational Training

[7.113] Article 150 (ex Article 127) states:

> The Community shall implement a vocational training policy which shall support and supplement the action of the Member States, while fully respecting the responsibility of the Member States for the content and organisation of vocational training.

[7.114] It states that Community action shall aim to facilitate adaption to industrial changes, especially through vocational training, to improve initial and continuing vocational training and to facilitate access to and mobility within vocational training. It shall also aim to stimulate cooperation on training between educational or training establishments or firms and develop exchanges of information and experience on issues common to the training systems of the Member States. Together with the Member States, the Community shall foster co-operation with third countries and competent international organisations in the sphere of vocational training.

[7.115] With reference to the position of the Irish language, while Irish is not recognised as an official language or a working language of the Community, it is one of the dozen languages listed in Article 314 EC (ex Article 248). Accordingly, each successive Treaty is published, *inter alia*, in Irish and such texts are of equal status and authenticity as those in the eleven other languages. Article 314 EC establishes a right for any citizen to correspond with the Community institutions in Irish.

Conclusion

[7.116] Community policy in education is likely to remain an issue of sensitivity. No doubt it will still be difficult for the Community to strike an acceptable balance between its legitimate interests in education and vocational training and the substance of education, which remains largely a matter for the Member States. While it is clear that any incentive measures must stop short of harmonisation of Member State laws or regulations, there is much that can be mutually accomplished.

[7.117] Because of the inherent dissonance between Ireland's largely denominational system of education and the secular system common to most of the Community, tensions are likely to arise in sensitive areas of education law. Such areas may include issues related to the religious and philosophical beliefs of parents, the rights of the child and employment rights of teachers which conflict with the characteristic spirit of the school. On the other hand, education in Ireland seems more open to Community influence than most other Member

States because of the highly centralised nature of the system and because of the massive EU investment in that system.

[7.118] While making a worthwhile contribution to the European Union, it is critical that Ireland retains its essential character and cultural, linguistic and educational heritage. Some Community measures may be passed without democratic legitimacy, may override national sensitivities and consensus, or may intrude too deeply into the substance and character of education and these measures must be resisted. In weaving the tapestry of an integrated Europe, diversity ought to be cherished and a balance achieved. It behoves the Member States, therefore, to remain continuously vigilant in striving to retain a healthy equilibrium in Community educational affairs.

Chapter 8

Human Rights and Education

Introduction

[8.01] It has been internationally recognised in developed countries for many decades that there are "some frontiers of freedom which nobody should be permitted to cross".[1] As Berlin points out, the rules which determine these frontiers may be called natural rights, the word of God, natural law, the demand of utility or the permanent interest of man. These norms, which derive from nineteenth century concepts of liberty,[2] have in time given rise to established international standards and judicial machinery which require compliance from the individual States who have signed and ratified the various Conventions. These latter instruments aim to lay down certain international standards to be observed by the contracting States in their relations with individuals under their jurisdiction. A wide disparity still exists, however, between the ideals in human rights instruments and the situation pertaining in the various contracting States.[3]

[8.02] This chapter will focus on that most significant human right, the right to education, in the absence of which many other human rights are likely to be beyond reach. Initially the background and rationale of human rights law is outlined. Next, the right to education in human rights law is considered and the institutional structure is abstracted. For convenience, an examination of the education-related case law, based on Protocol 1(2) of the European Convention on Human Rights follows the main themes addressed in the case law:

(a) linguistic choice;

(b) integrated sex education;

(c) corporal punishment; and

(d) religion.

Finally, an analysis of relevant aspects of Irish education follows in the light of the case law.

---

[1]   See Dorr, 'An Introduction to Human Rights Developments since 1945', *Human Rights: A European Perspective*, Heffernan, ed, (1994) Round Hall Press in association for Irish Centre for European Law, p 1 citing Berlin, *Four Essays on Liberty*, (1969), Oxford.

[2]   Berlin, *Four Essays on Liberty*, (1969), Oxford, p 165.

[3]   See O' Malley, 'The Developments of International Human Rights Law: a Look to The Future' in Heffernan, *Human Rights*, p 20.

The Right to Education in Human Rights Law

[8.03] Human rights instruments[4] derive mainly from the work of the United Nations (UN) and the Council of Europe.[5] The latter body advanced the concept of "permanent education"[6] and it is now accepted in most developed countries that education is a continuous, lifelong pursuit. While acknowledging the broad application of the term "education", international instruments usually focus on the narrower view of education, ie as scholastic instruction given in educational institutions.[7] The European Court of Human Rights specifically acknowledged this distinction in *Campbell and Cosans v UK* when it stated:

> "The court would point out that the education of children is the whole process whereby, in any society, adults endeavour to transmit their beliefs, culture and other values to the young, whereas teaching or instruction refers in particular to the transmission of knowledge and to intellectual development."[8]

[8.04] In international law, as in Irish law, the child is generally perceived as subject to the authority of its parents or legal guardians.[9] Although this approach is now showing signs of change, the right of the child to education has been slow to emerge. Human rights law has traditionally focused largely on the rights of parents to discharge a degree of control over the State in respect of their children's education rather than on the rights of the child *per se* to education.[10]

[8.05] Most international human rights instruments do not place any obligation on States to provide any pre-school education which is regrettable in view of the fundamental importance of such education.[11]

Institutional Framework for Education Rights

[8.06] Regrettably, the Declaration on the Rights of the Child (1924) did not specifically refer to the rights of the child to education *per se*. Neither did the

---

4   See *Basic Documents on Human Rights*, Brownlie, ed, (3rd ed, 1992), Oxford, Clarendon Press; *International Documents on Children,* Van Bueren, ed, (1993) Dordrecht.
5   A body established in 1949 as a kind of social and philosophical complement to the military aspects of European cooperation represented in the North Atlantic Treaty Organisation.
6   See Jacobs, *The European Convention on Human Rights* (1975), Oxford, Clarendon Press, p 172.
7   Van Bueren, 'Education: Whose Right is it Anyway?' in Heffernan, *Human Rights*, pp 339-349. See further Szabo, *Cultural Rights*, (1974) Leiden.
8   (1892) 4 EHRR 293 at 303.
9   See further Beddard, *Human Rights and Europe*, (3rd ed, 1993), Cambridge, Grotius Publications, pp 78-83.
10 See 'Access to German Minority Schools in Upper Silesia' [1931] PCIJ Report Series A, No 40, 8.
11 See further Van Bueren, 'Education: Whose Right is it Anyway?', in Heffernan, *Human Rights*, p 340.

Universal Declaration of Human Rights (1948) include any express reference to the right of a child to education.[12] It was not until 1959 and the Declaration on the Rights of the Child that the first worldwide reference to the specific right of the child to education was given formal expression in human rights law. Principle 7 provides that "[t]he child is entitled to receive education ...". Although the terms of the 1959 Declaration were not legally binding, Principle 7 voiced principles of law which would have a profound impact on human rights law globally as they would be acted upon by the Member States of the UN, ratified by the General Assembly of the UN and subsequently assimilated into national constitutions.[13]

The European Convention on Human Rights and Individual Freedoms

[8.07] The international treaty most germane to education is possibly the European Convention on Human Rights (ECHR) and the enormous challenge of formulating an acceptable cross-frontier right to education is clear from its protracted drafting process, the extent and complexity of the preparatory documents (*travaux preparatoires*),[14] the reservations expressed in regard to Protocol 1(2) by some of the contracting States (including Ireland)[15] and the postponement of the inclusion of a right to education to the First Protocol of the Convention.

[8.08] The Council of Europe wished to protect or regulate the right to education as it considered that the educational indoctrination of children was one of the most insidious methods utilised by totalitarian movements, parties or Governments in Europe "to subjugate a people".[16] The ECHR was signed in Rome on 4 November 1950 and entered into force on 3 September 1953. It did not contain an article on education although such an article was planned for inclusion. A related article, Article 9, on freedom of thought was included, however, which was sanctioned earlier by the Council of Europe: "Everyone has the right to freedom of thought, conscience and religion ...".[17] While Article 9 is relevant to educational matters, it appears extremely difficult to sustain a successful application grounded in that Article alone.[18]

---

[12] See *Universal Declaration of Human Rights* (1948) cited in *Human Rights, Problems, Perspectives and Texts*, Dowrick, ed, (1979) London, Saxon House.

[13] Lauterpacht, 'The UN Declaration of Human Rights' in British Yearbook of International Law, 25 (1948) 354.

[14] Teigten, *Collected Edition of the Travaux Preparatoires of the European Convention on Human Rights*, Council of Europe, 1985. This preparatory material comprises eight volumes and casts light on the many difficulties that arose in drafting the right to education.

[15] And also Sweden and the United Kingdom.

[16] *Travaux Preparatoires*, Meeting of the Committee of Experts, Vol III, p 262.

[17] Article 9 in accordance with Article 18 of the UN Declaration.

[18] See *Arrowsmith v UK* ECHR Decisions and Reports, Vol 19 (October 1980) 5.

[8.09] The drafting of the education article, which emerged as Protocol 1(2) took almost three years to accomplish. As a result Protocol 1(2) did not enter into force until 18 May 1954. Disagreement arose between the international drafters on many complex and sensitive issues:

(a) whether the right to education was sourced in positive or fundamental law;[19]

(b) whether this right is vested in the child or in parents;

(c) as to the methods States should employ to protect this right in their internal legislation;

(d) as to the question of "how, and to what degree, are the rights of parents to be safeguarded when the State is necessarily assuming major responsibility for education?"[20]

(e) whether the right of every person to education imposed a corresponding obligation on the State to ensure that everyone is educated;

(f) whether the contracting States were to accept that children could be raised as atheists or agnostics.[21]

[8.10] Article 2 of Protocol 1, which became one of the most contentious Articles in the Convention, finally read:

> No person shall be denied the right to education. In the exercise of any functions which it assumes in relation to education and to teaching, the State shall respect the right of parents to ensure such education and teaching in conformity with their own religious and philosophical convictions.

Disagreement arose as to whether the term "function"[22] was to be plural or singular. The French text is the authentic one and it always uses the plural. Furthermore, the European Court of Human Rights has accepted the plural (functions) as being correct.[23] In cases which have given rise to disagreement, the Strasbourg Court has used the *travaux preparatoires* (the *travaux* hereafter)

---

[19] ECHR Decisions and Reports, Vol 2, 100. At the first session of the Consultative Assembly Monsieur de la Vallee-Poussin (Belgium) considered the prior parental right in education to be "... a social right, which is fundamentally a natural right" and the Italian delegate, Boggiano-Pico agreed that "These rights come from a natural and eternal law to which we are subject .... Thus ... neither the State nor even the Church, has the right to intervene between parents and their children."

[20] Lord Layton (UK), ECHR Decisions and Reports, Vol 11, 54.

[21] See Roberston, *Human Rights in Europe*, (2nd ed, 1977) Manchester University Press, p 124 *et seq*.

[22] See *Travaux*, Vol VI, pp 10-11. In later debates and amendments the term "function" is used in the singular (Vols V, p 68, V1, p 248, VIII, p 128) but later still in the plural (Vols VI, pp 44-5, VII, p 142).

[23] *Kjelsden v Denmark* 1 EHRR 711 at 728.

as a supplementary means of interpretation.[24] Three interconnected components of the right to education fall under Protocol 1(2).

[8.11] Article 2 provides, in its initial sentence, that the State shall not deny any person the right to education. The State may not interfere, therefore, with an individual's exercise of the right to education eg by excluding him or her from the benefit of State-provided educational opportunities.[25] If challenged, this places the State in a stronger position than if the duty were affirmatively stated, as an aggrieved person has the burden of establishing that the State has actually denied the individual the right to education. This burden has been met, to date, in one case only, *Campbell and Cosans v UK* which is discussed below.[26]

[8.12] The second sentence of Article 2 gives discretion to the State to ascertain the nature and ambit of its commitment to education and teaching. Generally, this indicates that the State is not obligated to establish certain types of educational opportunities or to ensure that each person achieves the education he or she desires. In addition, sentence two pledges the right of parents in regard to their children's education, to have their religious and philosophical convictions respected by the State. The Commission and the Court of Human Rights (the Court hereafter) have generally had to consider all three components of Protocol 1(2) read together.

United Nations: Human Rights Instruments

[8.13] Distinct aspects of the right to education were included in the UN International Covenant on Economic, Social and Cultural Rights 1966[27] (ICESCR) and in the UN International Covenant on Civil and Political Rights 1966 (ICCPR).[28] Clearly, the rights protected in these Covenants and in the ECHR spring largely from the Charter of the United Nations and the UN Universal Declaration of Human Rights 1948.[29] Article 26 of the latter Declaration is wide ranging and the ICESCR has followed its recommendations on education closely.

International Covenant on Economic, Social and Cultural Rights 1966

[8.14] Article 13.2 of the ICESCR provides as follows:

---

[24] *Belgian Linguistic Cases*, Series A, No 6 (1979) 1 EHRR 252; Series B (1967) 1 EHRR 241; *James et al v UK* 8 EHRR 123; see Merrills, *The Development of International Law by the European Court of Human Rights*, (1993), Manchester University Press, p 90.

[25] See *Short Guide to the Convention on Human Rights* (1991) Council of Europe, p 100-101.

[26] See para **[8.44]** below.

[27] Article 13, see Brownlie, *Basic Documents on Human Rights* (3rd ed, 1992) Oxford, pp 118-119.

[28] ICCPR, Articles 1, 18, 19, 27, pp 125-143.

[29] UN Universal Declaration of Human Rights, Part III, p 21.

The States Parties to the present Covenant recognize that, with a view to achieving the full realisation of this right:

(a) Primary education shall be compulsory and available free to all;

(b) Secondary education in its different forms, including technical and vocational secondary education, shall be made generally available and accessible to all by every appropriate means, and in particular by the progressive introduction of free education;

(c) Higher education shall be made equally accessible to all on the basis of capacity, by every appropriate means, and in particular by the progressive introduction of free education;

(d) Fundamental education shall be encouraged or intensified as far as possible for those persons who have not received or completed the whole period of their primary education.[30]

From the above Article, it is clear that the ICESCR puts in place a hierarchy of State educational obligation which is analogous to the provisions of Article 42.4 of the Irish Constitution, with the heaviest burden resting at first level. Furthermore, the ICESCR underscores the buttressing of fundamental education for early school leavers from primary education. In the Irish context, these children have been identified as those 1,000 or so pupils who leave annually, many of whom are children of Travellers.[31]

[8.15] Arguably, a similar intent is envisaged by Article 42.5 of the Irish Constitution.

The Convention on the Rights of the Child 1989

[8.16] It was not until 1989 that the Convention on the Rights of the Child (CRC) achieved the status of a UN human rights treaty which was adopted by the UN General Assembly in November 1989. With the arrival of the child into the previously bipartite State-parent relationship, a new approach is apparent in international law. This Convention sets out for the first time in the form of a treaty an extensive inventory of children's rights which stretch far beyond those previously protected in human rights agreements. This very significant treaty was ratified by Ireland in 1992[32] indicating a courageous step for the Irish State.

[8.17] As a result of this Convention, the child is not only entitled to education but to specific rights when in educational institutions.[33] In addition, Article 20

---

[30] ICESCR, Article 13.2.

[31] See Ch 5.

[32] See 'Move on rights of children', Irish Times, 29 September 1992, 3; *Human Rights: The Rights of the Child*, Fact Sheet, No 10, Geneva, UN, 1991; The Convention is included in *The Rights of the Child: Irish Perspectives on the UN Convention*, Dublin, Council for Social Welfare-a Committee of The Catholic Bishops' Conference, 1991.

[33] Van Bueren, 'Education: Whose Right is it anyway?', in Heffernan, *Human Rights*, p 339.

provides that if a child is deprived of his family environment either temporarily or permanently or his own best interests indicate that he cannot be allowed to remain in that environment, then that child is entitled to special protection and assistance provided by the State including nutrition, clothing and housing.

[8.18] Article 37 provides that children deprived of liberty shall be treated with humanity and respect, that they be separated from adults unless it is considered in the child's best interest not to do so. They are further entitled to maintain contact with family, save in exceptional circumstances and have the right to prompt access to legal and other assistance. Finally, these children have the right to challenge the deprivation of their liberty before a court or other competent, independent or impartial authority and they are entitled to a prompt decision of such action.

[8.19] Recent constitutional case law indicates that, although Ireland has ratified the CRC, provision for needy children and young offenders is manifestly inadequate.[34] With reference to provision of facilities for youth in Ireland, the US State Department, in its 1995 report on human rights worldwide, observed in Ireland "a lack of separate areas for young people [which] results in fourteen and fifteen year-olds being mixed in with adult prisoners,"[35] a practice which breaches Article 37(c) of the CRC.[36]

Education in the CRC

[8.20] The CRC contains singularly important provisions relating to education and its function, including recognition of the child's right to education, to access to education and to educational and vocational information and guidance.

[8.21] It requires State parties to take measures to encourage regular attendance at schools and to reduce the drop-out rate from schools. As in the ICESCR,[37] the primacy of first level education is underscored in the CRC.[38] Hence, in international law, first level education is seen *as an absolute minimum of education* which the State parties must provide free of charge. It can be strongly

---

[34] See Chs 4 and 5 of this book; *Crime and Poverty in Ireland*, Bacik and O'Connell eds, (1988), Round Hall Sweet and Maxwell; *Focus on Residential child Care in ireland: 25 years since the Kennedy Report*, (1996), research carried out by McCarthy, Kennedy and Matthews, Dublin, Focus Ireland.

[35] O'Cleary, 'Sex abuse, rape "are common" in Republic, says US State Department' Irish Times, 3 February 1995, p 5.

[36] "In particular, every child deprived of liberty shall be separated from adults unless it is considered in the child's best interest not to do so ..."

[37] ICESCR, Article 13.2(a).

[38] CRC, Article 28.

argued, therefore, that this requirement implies the buttressing of first level education by the provision of

    (a) early support services for needy and problematic children;

    (b) continuous State supervision in respect of school attendance;

    (c) the collection of a nationwide data bank on exclusions from school;

    (d) compensatory measures for early school leavers including those with drug-related problems.[39]

School discipline

[8.22] With reference to school discipline, the CRC provides that State parties take all suitable measures to ensure that school discipline is administered in a manner consistent with the human dignity of the child and in conformity with the Convention.

Educational objectives

[8.23] Article 29 states that education should include among its objectives:

    (a) the development of the child's personality and talents;

    (b) respect for fundamental freedoms and values;

    (c) respect for the child's own cultural identity and that of others; and

    (d) respect for the natural environment.

Sex abuse and exploitation

[8.24] In addition the CRC aims to protect children from abuse and exploitation including sexual abuse.[40] It specifically requires State parties to take all appropriate national, bilateral and multilateral measures to prevent, the inducement or coercion of a child to engage in any unlawful sexual activity, the exploitation of children in prostitution and other unlawful sexual practices, and the exploitation of children in pornographic performances and materials.

Judicial Interpretation of Protocol 1(2) of the ECHR

[8.25] The ECHR and Protocol 1(2) relate to matters normally falling within the domestic legal order of the contracting States. Although the right to education is stated in absolute terms in Protocol 1(2), this does not mean that such rights can be considered as unqualified. Neither is the right to education confined to children but it is in this context chiefly that it has led to litigation in the European Court of Human Rights (the Court).

---

[39] CRC, Article 28.

[40] CRC, Article 34.

Linguistic Preferences of Parents

[8.26] In the *Belgian Linguistic* cases[41] (1968) parents contended that the phrase "philosophical convictions" in Protocol 1(2) extended to their cultural and linguistic preferences. Consequently, they argued, that parents had the right to choose the language of education for their children. In Belgium, French-speaking parents, resident in areas specified under Belgian linguistic laws as Dutch-speaking, were precluded from sending their children to French-speaking schools. The penalties for failing to comply with the laws, eg, by operating a French language school in a Dutch unilingual region, included the denial of public support for and official recognition of such schools by the Belgian State.

[8.27] Six groups of aggrieved parents contended before the Commission that the Belgian linguistic laws were incompatible with the ECHR (Article 2.8 and Article 14) and Protocol 1(2) as they did not conform to their philosophical convictions. Furthermore, these arrangements, they argued, interfered with their family life as their children were obliged to speak a language, other than the home language, at school. The Commission referred the matter to the Court which was concerned chiefly with Article 2 of Protocol 1. It held that this Article enshrined a "right"[42] to education as confirmed by the *travaux*. Its negative formulation, the court considered, indicated that the contracting States did not recognise that such a right would require them to establish, at their own expense, or to subsidise education of any particular type or any specific level.[43] Rather, the application of the right denoted the existence and the maintenance of a minimum education provided by the State. Otherwise, the Court reasoned, the protected right would be non-existent especially for those who could not afford it.

[8.28] The Court found that Article 2 is primarily, but not exclusively, involved with the right of access to elementary education.[44] It recognised the need for implied limitations to the right to education and ruled that its scope must necessarily be qualified by national regulation so that it may differ from State to State and may evolve over time. In future years, therefore, Article 2 of Protocol 1 may be relied upon to guarantee access to new educational developments in the contracting States to beneficiaries who comply with the objective conditions of entry, eg pre-school education or free university education. In order that the right to education can be effective, however, Article 2 requires the contracting States to supply students with official recognition or certification of the studies they

---

[41] *Belgian Linguistic Case (No 1)* 1 EHRR 241; *Belgian Linguistic Case (No 2)* 1 EHRR 252.
[42] Which was later recognised as a fundamental right, *Kjelsden v Denmark*, 1 EHRR 711 at 729.
[43] *Belgian Linguistic Case* 1 EHRR 252 at 253.
[44] *X v UK* D & R 2 (1975), p 500.

have completed. Ireland has complied with this requirement by establishing the National Education and Training Certification Board (NETCB).[45]

[8.29] By placing no obligation on the contracting States to respect parents' linguistic preferences but only their "religious and philosophical convictions," the Court limited the meaning of the second sentence of Protocol 1(2). In determining what constituted such convictions, both the Commission and the Court referred to the *travaux* as an aid to establish the intentions of the contracting States. They concluded that the drafters of Protocol 1(2) did not intend to protect the linguistic choice of parents and were guided by this principle.

[8.30] Because the right to receive education in the language of one's choice was beyond the protection of Protocol 1(2), the Belgian Government was entitled to withdraw public support and official recognition from French language schools which did not comply with its laws. Thus, the right to education guaranteed the right of access to educational establishments existing at a given time but it imported no linguistic requirements. A difference in treatment by the State was held to be not *per se* discriminatory, provided it could be objectively and reasonably justified.

[8.31] The Court held against Belgium on one point only;[46] that the legislative provision which prevented French-speaking schools in the "special status" communes in the Brussels suburbs from accepting pupils outside the area, but allowed Dutch-speaking schools to accept such pupils, was discriminatory treatment based on language.[47] This provision discriminated solely on the basis of parental residence and was not uniformly applied to families of both national languages. Neither, the Court held, did it respect "a reasonable relationship of proportionality between the means employed and the aims sought".[48] Consequently, new educational legislation had to be enacted in Belgium.

[8.32] In this case, the Court made one exception, which has special relevance for the Irish language. Where the language of one's choice is also the national language or one of the national languages, it held that even in the absence of any express provision in Article 2, the right to education necessarily implied that its beneficiaries be afforded the right to be educated in the national or in one of the national languages.[49] This indicates that an Irish person has an implied human right to be educated in Irish-language schools. However, the right to education in Article 2 would be unlikely to extend to the special status treatment founded on

---

[45] Cullen, 'New certification body will be set up', Irish Times, 13 January 1995, p 4.
[46] By an 8:7 vote.
[47] As prohibited by Article 14 read together with the first sentence of Article 2.
[48] *Belgian Linguistic Case* 1 EHRR 252 at 253.
[49] *Belgian Linguistic Case* 1 EHRR 252.

language, such as the more favourable treatment and funding of gaelscoileanna. Such treatment would most likely fall foul of the ECHR[50] as being discriminatory treatment founded on language in that it was not applied uniformly to families of both official languages (Irish and English), and that it did not respect a reasonable relationship of proportionality between the means employed or the aims sought.

[8.33] The *Groëner v Minister for Education* case,[51] which is discussed more fully in the previous chapter,[52] represents a delicate balancing of language, culture and human rights issues. Essentially it dealt with that most sensitive of matters; the power of the Irish State to protect and promote the use of a national language in regard to Irish language requirements for teachers. While the ECJ finally upheld the right of the Irish State to foster and safeguard the Irish language in the particular circumstance of this case, it held that the requirements deriving from measures intended to implement such a policy must not in any circumstances be disproportionate in relation to the aim pursued.

[8.34] The question of sex education programmes for schools, which has been controversial in Ireland, has been considered by the Court in *Kjelsden v Denmark*.[53]

Compulsory Sex Education in Schools

[8.35] Parental rights relating to the introduction of a mandatory sex education programme in Danish State schools were at issue in *Kjelsden v Denmark*.[54] The Court considered the scope of the State's duty in the drafting and implementation of a sex education programme for State schools and further established the boundaries of the right to education.

[8.36] Prior to 1970, sex education in Danish elementary schools was a separate, optional subject. Integrated, and hence compulsory, sex education was introduced into these schools in 1970 by The State Schools Act 1970. State subsidised private schools, however, were exempt from this requirement and were merely obliged to impart factual biological information. A group of parents of children of school age alleged that compulsory sex education conflicted with their Christian parental convictions and thus breached Protocol 1(2). They referred the matter to the Commission which found no breach of Protocol 1(2) and no breach of Articles 8 and 9 or of Article 14. The Commission referred the case to the Court.

---

[50] Article 14 read in conjunction with the first sentence of Article 2 of Protocol 1.
[51] Case 379/87 [1989] ECR 3967; see further McMahon (1990) 27 CML Rev 129.
[52] Ch 7, para **[7.71]-[7.74]**.
[53] 1 EHRR (1976) 711.
[54] 1 EHRR (1976) 711.

[8.37] The Court found that the second sentence of Protocol 1(2), which is an adjunct of the first, makes parents primarily responsible for the "education and teaching" of their children. It indicated that the duty falling on the State in the second sentence of Article 2 "bound States in the exercise of each and every function that they undertook in the sphere of education and teaching, including the organisation and financing of public education".[55] It held that the parental right to respect for their religious and philosophical convictions is grafted on to the fundamental right to education in the first sentence and so must be read harmoniously in the context of the whole Convention, particularly Articles 8, 9 and 10. As a result, Article 2 pertained to each of the State's functions and enjoined the State to respect parents' religious or philosophical convictions throughout the entire State education programme, both religious and secular.

[8.38] The Court maintained that the second sentence of Article 2 implies that the setting and planning of the curriculum fall in principle within the competence of the contracting States while acknowledging their diversity:

> "It follows in the first place ... that the setting and planning of the curriculum fall in principle within the competence of the Contracting States. This mainly involves questions of expediency on which it is not for the Court to rule and whose solution may legitimately vary according to the country and to the era. In particular, the second sentence of Article 2 of the Protocol does not prevent States from imparting through teaching or education information or knowledge of a directly or indirectly religious or philosophical kind. It does not even permit parents to object to the integration of such teaching or education in the school curriculum for otherwise all institutionalised teaching would run the risk of proving impracticable."[56]

[8.39] However, the Court proceeded to set some boundaries to the State's role in this regard. It held that the State must take care that information or knowledge contained in the curriculum is conveyed in an:

> "... objective, critical and pluralistic manner. The State was forbidden to pursue an aim of indoctrination that might be considered as not respecting parent's religious and philosophical convictions, that is the limit that must not be exceeded."[57]

There is some tension between these two latter statements which has relevance for the problems associated with the integrated curriculum in Ireland.

[8.40] The Court made it clear that there are limits beyond which the State may not go in that it may not enjoin a certain ethical or moral view of life and it may

---

[55] *Kjelsden v Denmark* 1 ECHR (1976) 711.
[56] See *Kjelsden v Denmark* 1 ECHR (1976) 711 at 730.
[57] See *Kjelsden v Denmark* 1 ECHR (1976) 711, at 712.

not pursue "an aim of indoctrination." However, is it possible for the State to permit integration of information or knowledge of a religious or philosophical nature into the curriculum and at the same time endeavour to foster a non-partisan and pluralistic approach? *Kjelsden* seems to imply that under international law, the State may avert its gaze from integration in the school curriculum so long as it does not follow an aim of indoctrination and that, moreover, parents may not object to such integration.

[8.41] Even though the challenged sex education programme in *Kjelsden* involved considerations of a moral order, the Court found that these, being very general in character, did not overstep the bounds of what a democratic State might have regarded as the public interest. The aim of the programme was "clearly not to impose upon the children a certain ethical or moral view of life". Thus, the Court concluded that nothing in the challenged statute indicated that the sex education provided would indoctrinate the children in any manner. It further observed that the Danish State, like the Irish State, had preserved options for parents who wished to avoid integrated sex education for their children in that it heavily subsidised private schools which were less strictly bound in this regard and that it permitted home education.[58] The Court held by 6:1 votes that there was no breach of Protocol 1(2), taken alone, or in conjunction with Article 14, and unanimously that there was no breach of Articles 8 and 9 read together with Protocol 1(2).

[8.42] It reached this decision in the light of the first sentence of Protocol 1(2) and in the context of the entire Convention particularly Articles 8, 9 and 14. The disputed legislation was found not to offend the applicants' religious and philosophical beliefs to the extent prohibited by the second sentence of Protocol 1(2) as it was not "an attempt at indoctrination aimed at advocating a specific kind of sexual behaviour." Neither, the court considered, did it affect the right of parents to enlighten, advise or guide their children in accordance with their own religious and philosophical convictions.

[8.43] Sex education continues to be an integral and obligatory part of instruction in Danish elementary State schools. A teacher cannot, however, be compelled against his or her will to give the more explicit kind of sex instruction referred to in the Danish Executive Order of 1972.[59] Private schools, on the other hand, remain free to decide to what degree they wish to align their teaching, in this sphere, with the rules that apply to State schools.

---

[58] See *Kjelsden v Denmark* 1 ECHR (1976) 711.
[59] No 313 of 15 June 1972, s 1(3).

Corporal Punishment as a School Sanction

[8.44] Scholastic corporal punishment was at issue in *Campbell and Cosans v UK*[60] in which the meaning of the second sentence of Article 2 was further elucidated. In this case two parents, as joint applicants, challenged the use of the leather strap[61] as a disciplinary sanction in Scottish State schools. Mrs Campbell objected to this type of punishment although her son was not punished corporally. Because Jane Cosans's son refused to yield to such punishment, he was suspended from school. Further, his parents refused to accept the school's right to administer the sanction of corporal punishment so Mrs Cosan's son was refused readmission to school.

[8.45] Both parents alleged that the school's system of corporal punishment violated Article 3 of the ECHR and Protocol 1(2). They claimed, *inter alia,* that their sons had been denied the right to education as their school had refused to guarantee that the sanction of corporal punishment would not be used. Mrs Cosans further argued that the suspension of her son from school breached Protocol 1(2). The Commission referred the case to the Court which distinguished between education and teaching.[62]

[8.46] It considered that the function assumed by the State in formulating general policy *in State schools* must be taken to extend to questions of discipline in general as the State's disciplinary role was an integral part of any educational system.[63] Accordingly, the Court held that a school's disciplinary system fell within the right to education in Protocol 1(2).[64] It accepted that corporal punishment was a matter of "philosophical conviction" as the applicants' views related "to a weighty and substantial aspect of human life and behaviour". Having appraised the case in its own context and in the light of the entire ECHR, the Court considered "philosophical convictions" to be such convictions as are worthy of respect in a democratic society,[65] which are not incompatible with

---

[60] [1982] 4 EHRR 293.

[61] Note the sustained attack mounted on Rule 96 of the 1932 edition of the Rules for National Schools, which governed the use of corporal punishment in Ireland, when the Minister, Jack Lynch, sought to regularise the use of Christian Brother's leather strap instead of "a light cane", see Circulars 17/56, September 1956 and 21/56 December 1956; see further O'Connor, op cit, pp 37-8.

[62] *Campbell and Cosans v UK* [1982] 4 EHRR 293 at 303.

[63] See *Campbell and Cosans v UK* [1982] 4 EHRR 293 at 294.

[64] A right also recognised in Article 28 of the CRC. Article 8 of the ECHR may also be relevant as a child, while in school, is in the public domain where he has to learn to respect the privacy of others. In turn he is entitled to have his own private life respected and be treated with dignity see *Costello-Roberts v UK*, 25 March 1991, Case No 89/1991, The Times, Law Report, 26 March 1993, p 38. This right is also protected by Article 16 of the CRC.

[65] *Campbell and Cosans v UK* [1982] 4 EHRR 293 at 294; see *Young and Webster v UK* (1981) 4 EHRR 38, para 63.

human dignity, and that do not conflict with the fundamental right of the child to education.[66]

[8.47] Further, the Court held that the scope of the obligation to respect parental religious and philosophical convictions under Protocol 1(2) is not limited to the content of educational instruction or the method of conveying information and knowledge but includes the organisation and financing of public education, the supervision of the educational system in general, and matters of discipline.

[8.48] While the *Campbell and Cosans* case centred on the rights of children and parents *vis-à-vis* the State rather than on parent-teacher rights, the Court recognised the *in loco parentis* basis of the teacher's authority in common law countries which is grounded in the Roman law concept of *patria potestas*.[67] It noted the right to use corporal punishment in common law countries, at that time (1982), was "vested in teachers by the common law and is not delegated by the State". The Court observed that this right was subject to the limitation imposed by the common law, that it should be "moderate and reasonable", and to any conditions incorporated into a teacher's contract and that it could be changed only by Act of Parliament.[68]

[8.49] The Court decided unanimously that no violation of Article 3 had been established but that there had been violations of the first and second parts of Protocol 1(2). As a result the UK was obliged to pay almost £13,000 in compensation and legal costs to the Campbell and Cosans families as it had failed to guarantee parents that their children would not be exposed to corporal punishment in State schools in the face of conscientiously held parental philosophical convictions.

[8.50] A number of similar complaints from schools in the UK followed which were declared admissible but were subsequently settled amicably. The decision to change the law relating to corporal punishment as a school sanction in the UK was made by the slimmest of margins in both Houses of Parliament.[69] Finally, provision for the abolition of corporal punishment in all State-supported

---

[66] *Campbell and Cosans v UK* [1982] 4 EHRR 293 at 305.

[67] See *Black's Law Dictionary*, (5th ed, 1979), p 1014.

[68] Ireland did not comply with this requirement until 1997, see Non-Fatal Offences Against the Person Act 1997, s 24. It seems the Irish government was well advised of the likely outcome of the *Campbell and Cosans* case as the Minister for Education, John Boland TD, prohibited corporal punishment in all Irish schools by Department Circular 9/82 on 1 February 1982.

[69] In the House of Lords the amendment to abolish corporal punishment succeeded by 94 votes to 92, 22 July 1986 while the vote in the House of Commons succeeded by 231 votes to 230. See further Newell, 'The beaters beaten', Times Educational Supplement, 14 August 1987, pp 14-15.

English, Scottish and Northern Irish schools was included in The Education (No 2) Act 1986.[70]

[8.51] The fact that the independent schools, whose fees are fully met by the parents, were excluded from this legislation led to a further challenge. Unsuccessful efforts were made, in the case of *Y v UK*[71] and in *Costello-Roberts v UK*[72] to extend the ban to private schools. In the latter case seven year-old Jeremy Costello-Roberts, a pupil in a private boarding school, was slippered in private three times on his buttocks, through his shorts, with a rubber-soled gym shoe by the headmaster. The Court held, by a slim majority, that the punishment inflicted on this boy did not constitute "degrading punishment" under Article 3 as it did not reach the required threshold of severity.[73]

[8.52] In Ireland, the Law Reform Commission's recommendation was finally implemented by the Non-Fatal Offences Against the Person Act 1997, s 24 came into force in August 1997, thereby bringing Ireland into line with all other European countries. The abolition of criminal immunity for teachers, however, in no way affects the use of force which is otherwise available under the law. Reasonable physical force may still be used by teachers to avert immediate danger of personal injury to any person including the pupil or the teacher concerned or to avert immediate danger to the property of any person including that of the pupil or teacher concerned.[74] This issue is discussed in greater detail in Chapter 9.

Religious Instruction/Religious Education in Schools

[8.53] There has been a long history of controversy in Europe concerning the place of religion in schools. The right to participate in religious teaching is protected by Article 9 of the ECHR. A study of the *travaux* reveals that the protection of Protocol 1(2) was conceived initially as a shield for religious beliefs against totalitarian indoctrination of children by States in schooling and education functions. The term "philosophical" was added, it seems, to include protection for the parental convictions of non-believing or agnostic parents.[75] It

---

[70] Sections 47, 48; Important provisions relating to school discipline are also included in the Education Act 1997, ss 2-12.

[71] The Commission was of the opinion that there had been a violation but the Court approved an amicable settlement in November 1992. Without admitting liability the UK made an *ex gratia* payment of £8,000 plus costs to the applicants, see further Beddard, *Human Rights and Europe*, (3rd ed, 1993) Cambridge, Grotius, p 86.

[72] (1995) 19 EHRR 112.

[73] "Private school slippering was not degrading punishment," *Costello-Roberts v UK*, (1995) 19 EHRR 112, The Times, Law Report, 26 March, 1993, p 38. Corporal punsihment is now abolished by law in all English schools.

[74] See Non-Fatal Offences Against the Person Act 1997, s 18.

[75] *Belgian Linguistic Case*, Opinion of the Commission, 'Publications of the Court', Ser B, par 379 at 282.

may be deduced from Protocol 1(2), that where compulsory religious instruction is provided in State schools, parents must be permitted, if they so desire, to make alternative arrangements, a provision which is also part of Irish constitutional law.[76]

The Swedish Reservation

[8.54] When signing Protocol 1(2), Sweden faced a dilemma which either required it to change its domestic legislation or to express a reservation to the Protocol. It chose the latter option and added the reservation:

"Sweden could not grant to parents the right to obtain, by reason of their philosophical convictions, dispensation for their children from the obligation of taking part in certain parts of the education in the public schools, and also ... the dispensation from the obligation of taking part in the teaching of Christianity in these schools could only be granted for children of another faith than the Swedish Church, in respect of whom a satisfactory religious instruction had been arranged."[77]

[8.55] Sweden's reservation has been unsuccessfully challenged on two occasions. In *Karnell and Hardt v Sweden*[78] the applicants, being members of a minority church in Sweden,[79] petitioned the Commission, on the grounds of Protocol 1(2), as their request to have their children exempted from the State religion in school had been refused by the Swedish State. They also alleged that the Evangelical-Lutheran Church had been refused permission to provide alternative religious instruction for the children. Initially, the application was brought by the Church itself but four individual parents were joined later.

[8.56] The Commission pointed out that the second sentence of Article 2 applies only to parental rights and so the application, in so far as it was brought by a Church, was inadmissible. It held that a Church, being a corporation and not a natural person, was incapable of exercising the rights vested in Article 2. To the extent that the application was made by four individual applicants, however, it was held admissible. Prior to the Commission's decision, the Swedish King ordered that the parents' request be complied with and that the religious instruction in question be separated from other curricular subjects in order to facilitate the exemption.[80] On the withdrawal of their application, the applicants were given assurances that:

---

[76] Article 44.2.4°.

[77] *Cf McCallum v Board of Education* [1948] 333 US 203 in which the USA Supreme Court held that no person may be required to attend religious instruction in a State-recognised or State-aided institution.

[78] (No 4733/71), Yearbook of the European Convention on Human Rights 1971.

[79] The Evangelical-Lutheran Church.

[80] *Karnell and Hardt v Sweden*, (No 4733/71), Yearbookof the European Convention on Human Rights, 1971; ECHR, Collection of Decisions, 39 (1972), 75; see Clarke, 'Freedom of Thought in Schools: A Comparative Study', 35 (1986) ICLQ 271; Kiss, 'La Protection internationale du droit de l'enfant a l'education', *Droits de l'Homme*, (1973), pp 467-87.

(a) pupils affiliated to their Church would, if their parents so requested, be exempted from compulsory religious instruction;

(b) such religious instruction would be separate from instruction in other subjects in classes in which exempted pupils participated; and

(c) any exempted pupil would not be disadvantaged by reason of not having religious instruction at school.

[8.57] In 1988 another challenge to this provision was taken in *Angellini v Sweden*.[81] A Swedish mother and her daughter, both atheists, applied unsuccessfully to the school, the school board and the National School Board to have her daughter exempted from participation in the teaching of religious knowledge. It was clear that the daughter, being an atheist, would not be receiving any "other religious instruction" as required by the 1971 Decree. The applicants applied to the Commission alleging that the second applicant was required to participate in the teaching of religious knowledge in breach of Articles 9, 14 and 17 of the ECHR. They submitted that when a child, who is an atheist, is obliged to adopt a Christian way of thinking, freedom of thought guaranteed under Article 9, was violated together with parental freedom of conscience as the parent, holding values other than Christian ones, is not guaranteed the right to bring up his/her children in an atheistic manner. The applicants also referred to Protocol 1(2) and the reservation made by Sweden in respect of that Article.

[8.58] The Commission confined itself to the facts of the individual case and did not make a general review of instruction in religious knowledge in Swedish schools. It found no indication that Sweden's reservation was contrary to Article 64 of the ECHR and so regarded it as valid.[82]

[8.59] The Commission had already examined this reservation in *Kjelsden* and it concluded that "the reservation gives almost complete freedom to the Swedish government to organise child education regardless of the religious and philosophical convictions of parents".[83] Consequently the Commission held that the exemption could only be granted in cases of children belonging to a religious faith other than the Swedish Church for whom satisfactory alternative religious education could be arranged and children of parents holding particular philosophical convictions could not be granted exemptions. The Commission found that in this case there had not been a breach of the ECHR or Protocol 1(2) by Sweden.

---

[81] (1988) 10 EHRR 123.

[82] *Angellini v Sweden* (1988) 10 EHRR 123 at 126.

[83] *Angellini v Sweden* (1988) 10 EHRR 123 at 126 citing *Kjelsden v Denmark* (1979) 1 EHRR 711.

[8.60] Sweden's reservation sits uneasily in the context of the ECHR as a whole which views the second sentence of Article 2 as safeguarding the possibility of pluralism in education, as an essential element for the preservation of the "democratic society" as promoted by the ECHR.[84] The Strasbourg Court itself has held that the ECHR is to be read as a whole and especially in the light of Articles 8, 9 and 10.[85] It is worth noting that specific protection for persons such as the Angellinis is provided in the UN Convention against Discrimination in Education[86] which states "that no person or group of persons should be compelled to receive religious instructions inconsistent with his or their convictions".[87] While Sweden's reservation to Protocol 1(2) has not been withdrawn, the 1985 Swedish School Law[88] now makes provision for exemption of pupils from religious instruction.

Religious Discrimination

[8.61] It has been held that the European Community and its institutions can infringe the right of an individual to practice his or her religion and so constitute religious discrimination.[89] Religious discrimination, as opposed to racial discrimination, is allowed in certain English schools so that they may retain the character of a school instituted to provide a specific type of education. In *Choudhury v Governors of Bishop Challoner Roman Catholic Comprehensive School*,[90] a voluntary aided school, established to provide education on Christian and specifically Roman Catholic principles, was held to be entitled to discriminate in favour of Christians and especially Roman Catholics in its admission policy if the number of parental preferences for application exceeded the number of places available. Such a policy was considered reasonable in view of the fact that the school was established to foster and maintain a Roman Catholic ethos. Hence it was not unlawful to have it in mind as a reason for refusing to facilitate the parental preferences of Muslim and Hindu parents under the Education Act 1980, s 6.

---

[84] *Kjelsden v Denmark* (1979) 1 EHRR 711 at 729.
[85] *Kjelsden v Denmark* (1979) 1 EHRR 711 at 729-30; *Belgian Linguistic Case* (1979) 1 EHRR at 280.
[86] Article 5(b);
[87] Article 12(1) of the UN Convention on the Rights of the Child merely provides for the general right of the child to freedom of expression.
[88] The School Law 1985, Ch 3, s 12; 1100, paras 1, 2 and 3 effected in *Government Decree of 1991*, (1991), SKOLFS: 13.
[89] *Prais v Council* [1976] ECR 1589.
[90] [1992] 3 All ER 277.

The Religious Ethos of Catholic Schools and the ECHR

[8.62] The problem of integrated religious instruction is more complex in voluntary secondary schools (more than 60% of Irish secondary schools) whose special doctrinal nature has been recognised in Canadian,[91] New Zealand[92] English[93] and Irish law.[94] As already noted, these schools strive, as part of their educational mission to convey a specific religious ethos to their pupils. However, the Strasbourg Court has held that compulsory education in one religion would violate Article 2.[95] In order to comply with the ECHR if these schools accept children of other faiths or none, they must implement a "conscience clause" allowing their withdrawal from religious instruction as is also required by Article 44.2.4° of the Constitution. However, the *Kjelsden* decision recognised the impossibility of a perfect separation of religious and philosophical and secular subjects:

"In fact, it seems very difficult for many subjects taught at school not to have, to a greater or lesser extent, some philosophical complexion or implications. The same is true of religious affinities if one remembers the existence of religions forming a very broad dogmatic and moral entity which has or may have answers to every question of a philosophical, cosmological or moral nature."[96]

What the ECHR and Protocol 1(2) appear to prohibit is:

(a) the integration of religious and philosophical concepts in the secular curriculum to the extent that it amounts to an "aim of indoctrination"; and

(b) that teachers must also refrain from "indoctrination" while teaching secular subjects.

This seems to prohibit *formal* religious instruction during the secular curriculum but would not preclude some *informal* religious or philosophical concepts from impinging on secular education.

---

[91] *Caldwell v Stuart*, SC, Vol 2 1984, 603.
[92] *Rich v Christchurch Girls' School Board of Governors* [1974] (No 1) 1 NZLR CA *per* White J in which it was held that "the secular clause" in the Education Act 1964 did not apply to a voluntary secondary school and so the Board of Governors were entitled to include or approve a form of religious observance during the daily school assembly.
[93] *Choudhury v Governors of Bishop Challoner Roman Catholic Comprehensive School* [1992] 3 All ER 277.
[94] *Flynn v Power* [1985] IR 648.
[95] *Belgian Linguistic Case* (1979) 1 EHRR 252.
[96] At p 730 of the judgment, para 53.

[8.63] It would also prohibit the State from setting down aims of indoctrination in the school curriculum such as those already referred to in the 1971 curriculum.[97]

[8.64] Read in conjunction with the constitutional guarantee given in Article 44.2.4° it seems that a return to the separation of the teaching of formal religious and secular subjects in Irish primary schools is the only viable way forward. School organisation could facilitate parents, who wish to withdraw their children from formal religion instruction by time-tabling such classes in order to ensure that the rights of children of other faiths or none are respected.[98]

Irish Education and Protocol 1(2) of the ECHR

[8.65] When signing Protocol 1(2), Ireland also entered a reservation, which indicates a paternalistic approach to education which is reflected in its constitutional background.[99] It contended that the right to education in Protocol 1(2) was not sufficiently explicit in ensuring to parents the right to provide education for their children in their homes or in schools of the parents' own choice, whether or not such schools were private schools or schools recognised or established by the State.[100] In the light of increasing marital breakdown, growing parental failure in care and education and a greater emphasis on childrens' rights, this reservation now seems somewhat outdated.

[8.66] Quite apart from the above reservation, a fundamental tension appears to exist between the aims of Protocol 1(2) and those of Ireland's largely denominational education system. Essentially, the Protocol strives to safeguard the possibility of pluralism in education[101] while Irish denominational school authorities aim to pass on the faith of one specific denomination in a religious atmosphere as an integral part of their educational mission. As has been seen, the Catholic Church in particular envisages the place of integrated religious instruction as central to that aim.

[8.67] Clarke believes that current Irish educational policy is incompatible with the ECHR.[102] Children, he argues, have a right to attend State-funded schools

---

[97] *Curraculum na Bunscoile*, Teachers' handbook, 1971, Part 1, Department of Education, pp 19 and 23.

[98] Clarke advances two educational policies which he considers might meet parent's expectations and be compatible with Protocol 1(2), 'Freedom of Thought and Educational rights in the European Convention', Ir Jur 1987, pp 53-54.

[99] See Ch 3.

[100] [1954] Ir TS, No 3.

[101] *Kjelsden v Denmark* (1979) 1 EHRR 711.

[102] Clarke, 'Freedom of Thought and Educational Rights in the European Convention', Ir Jur 1987, 50-54; see also Clarke, 'Freedom of Thought in Schools: A Comparative Study', in Simmonds and Hampton, eds, International and Comparative Law Quarterly, 35 (1986), 271-301.

while possessing at the same time a right not to be instructed in a denominational manner. This, Clarke asserts, is impossible in virtually all existing national schools and in the majority of secondary schools. The alleged widespread failure to implement the constitutionally guaranteed withdrawal right from denominational religious instruction[103] and the official recognition given to the integration of religious studies in the curriculum, he asserts, combine to privilege the majority religious denominations while ignoring the rights of the minority or non-religious parents.[104]

[8.68] However, Clarke takes the matter to extremes when he contends that State-funded schools must give priority to non-discriminatory admission policies in preference to the claim of religious parents to have their children educated, at public expense, in a religious *milieu* which corresponds to their own religious or philosophical convictions.[105] If this proposal were widely implemented, it could conceivably dilute the ethos of all denominational schools and militate against the very existence of minority denominational schools.[106]

[8.69] Thus, by advancing the case of the minority too far, the right of the majority could be dissipated. While denominational schools are undoubtedly entitled to protect their capability to deliver the type of religious and moral education which forms part of their *raison d'être*, the State also has an obligation to provide alternative school types to facilitate parental choice of school.

[8.70] Protocol 1(2) guarantees the right of non-discriminatory access to publicly-funded schools, however. Yet, a difference in treatment was held not *per se* discriminatory in the *Belgian Linguistic (No 2)* case,[107] provided an objective and reasonable justification could be given which showed a reasonable balance between the aim sought and the means employed. Clearly, the admission of some children of different faiths to a denominational school is envisaged by Protocol 1(2), but this does not equate to open access to all pupils which could undermine the ethos of the denominational school. Open access to all creeds in the Irish denominational schools could also override the State's obligation to respect the "religious and philosophical convictions" of the majority of parents who have an implied constitutional right to choose a denominational education for their children.

---

[103] Article 44.2.4° of the Constitution; see generally, Alvey, *Irish Education: The Case for Secular Reform.*

[104] Clarke, 'Freedom of Thought and Educational rights in the European Convention', Ir Jur 1987, 51.

[105] Clarke, at 53.

[106] Eg Church of Ireland schools.

[107] (1979) 1 EHRR 241.

[8.71] It should be noted that when s 30 of the Education Act 1998 comes into force, s 2(e) of that Article requires that, without prejudice to the generality of sub-s (1), the Minister:

> shall not require any student to attend instruction in any subject which is contrary to the conscience of the parent of the student or in the case of a student who has reached the age of 18 years, the student.

[8.72] In summary, Protocol 1(2) of the ECHR can be viewed to a degree as a shield for, *inter alia,* educational rights which the majority of European countries perceive as a fundamental right vested primarily in parents. It guarantees that certain parental rights will not be overridden even though the State assumes the major responsibility in education. Yet, remarkably, the *Campbell and Cosans* case remains the sole case in which the Court has established a breach of the right to education under the first sentence of Protocol 1(2). It must be concluded, therefore, that the Court is reluctant to interfere in a Contracting State's educational system unless there is a blatant breach of human rights.

Sex Education

[8.73] In the light of the *Kjelsden* judgment, has the Irish State the authority to draft and implement an appropriate sex education programme for Ireland's mainly denominational State-aided schools? From the perspective of international law, the following areas of education are within the jurisdiction of the State in State schools:

(a) the general organisation and financing of education;

(b) the setting and planning of the curriculum;

(c) disciplinary matters; and

(d) basic sex education.

From the human rights point of view, it is clear from Article 19 of the CRC that the Irish State retains an overarching human rights responsibility to protect the child from, *inter alia*, child abuse while in the care of parent(s), legal guardians or any other person who has care of the child.

These responsibilities include legislative, administrative, social and educational measures which extend to and include a basic sex education programme based on factual biological information. Article 34 of the CRC reiterates that State parties undertake to safeguard the child from all forms of sexual exploitation and sexual abuse including national, bilateral and multilateral measures to prevent:

(a) the inducement or coercion of a child to engage in any unlawful sexual activity;

    (b) the exploitative use of children in prostitution or other unlawful sexual practices;

    (c) the exploitative use of children in pornographic performance and materials.

It follows that, if the State is to discharge its duties in respect of the above provisions, it must draft and implement a programme of basic sex education in schools. However, this programme may not pursue an "aim of indoctrination" or promote a certain ethical or moral view of life.[108] This implies that a basic sex education programme drawn up by the State for schools must be ideologically neutral as it may not present or promote a programme with a religious slant or bias.

[8.74] Once the State has devised and presented this programme to the schools, however, the denominational school authorities have a right to adjust that programme so that it reflects the ethos of their schools. The Minister has begun to phase in a sex education programme in Irish schools but has left a high degree of autonomy in this matter to individual boards of management. The controversy surrounding this sphere of Irish life, however, is unlikely to disappear.

Incorporation of the ECHR in Ireland?

[8.75] The ECHR established what has proved to be one of the most fruitful mechanisms in international law for regulating certain issues which also fall within the ambit of domestic law.[109] From 1 November 1998, there will be a direct right of access to the European Court of Human Rights. The UK has enacted the Human Rights Act 1998 incorporating the ECHR into its domestic law and Northern Ireland is also preparing to follow its example. Ireland will shortly be the only member of the EU who has not incorporated the ECHR into its domestic law. This will leave Ireland out of step with its European neighbours[110] and Northern Ireland at a crucial time in its history when nationwide peace initiatives are finally being implemented.

[8.76] Thus, persons living here, who contend that their rights under the ECHR have been breached, are unable to plead their case in the Irish courts as the ECHR is not part of Irish law. If such persons wish to proceed to the European Court of Human Rights, they must first exhaust all domestic remedies under the Irish courts, a cumbersome and expensive process. As the Irish courts are not bound by the decision of the European Court of Human Rights on an analogous

---

[108] *Kjelsden v Denmark* 1 EHRR (1976) 711.

[109] See further Warbrick, 'Rights, the European Convention on Human Rights and English Law' in ELR, Vol 19, (1994), 34.

[110] See Farrell, 'Ireland out of step on European rights', Irish Times, 29 December 1997, 2.

case, it is necessary for the Irish litigant to take a further case to the European Court of Human Rights in order to secure a similar decision against the Irish authorities.

[8.77] The case of *Norris v AG*[111] illustrates the difficulty encountered in vindicating homosexual rights in Ireland even though the European Court of Human Rights had already decided the issue in Northern Ireland in *Dudgeon v UK*[112] two years earlier. Apart from this expensive, cumbersome and time-consuming process, there are further difficulties with implementation of decisions. While the Court may award damages and costs to the successful applicant, its decisions are binding on the respondent State solely as a matter of international law. So, in the absence of incorporation or a newly ratified international agreement giving sanction, these decisions cannot be enforced in domestic courts.[113] There is an urgency for Ireland to incorporate the ECHR into domestic law lest it become the human rights Cinderella of Europe.

Human Rights and the Irish System of Education

[8.78] In Ireland, remarkable progress has been made throughout the entire general education system in the past three decades. Primary education has altered radically in its teaching methods and ideology while post-primary provision has expanded, diversified and become more accessible to the less able student. The provision of free second level education has raised participation rates to a level slightly above the OECD average while the expansion in higher education has left Ireland second only to Japan in the percentage of young workers with a scientific or engineering degree.

[8.79] Latterly, many innovative non-statutory schemes have focused on the identified deficiencies in the system of provision and the financing of these schemes has been greatly assisted by the European Social Fund.

[8.80] Despite this general progress, Ireland's human rights record, in regard to education, falls well short of international standards in some respects which include:

   (a) the grossly inadequate provision made for deviant young persons and young offenders;

   (b) the rights of those persons with disabilities, in particular those with severe and profound disabilities;

---

[111] [1984] IR 36.

[112] (1982) 4 EHRR 149.

[113] See further Dillon-Malone, 'Individual Remedies and the Strasbourg System in an Irish Context', in Heffernan, *Human Rights: A European Perspective*, 48.

(c) the treatment and education of Traveller children;

(d) the treatment and follow-up of early school leavers;

(e) inadequate State supervision of school attendance;

(f) compensatory measures for the disadvantaged, although the Minister's recent provision for this category is most welcome;[114]

(g) the apparently uneven distribution of resources for the various levels of education in particular first level education and the failure to provide support services for less able pupils.

[8.81] The growing pluralism of Irish society is making new demands on our schools. Children of other races, and other faiths or none, must be accorded respect and sensivity. The submission of the CPSMA to the Commission on School Accommodation stated:

"Catholic Primary Schools all over the country welcome children of all faiths and of none. We are committed to respecting and celebrating differences of belief, traditions and cultures."[115]

[8.82] In order to support and explore the practical applications of this commitment, the *Report of the Technical Working Group of the Commission on School Accommodation* calls for the establishment of a working party to formulate "good practice" guidelines on inclusivity in primary schools.[116] It is submitted that this is a very worthwhile proposal which, if handled correctly, could assist greatly in pointing the way forward.

[8.83] It will be noted that the deficits in this chapter on human rights correspond broadly with those earlier identified in the constitutional chapters. As the European Court of Human Rights has frequently emphasised, the machinery instituted by the ECHR is of a secondary nature and the onus falls primarily on the national courts to safeguard the fundamental rights and freedoms of the individual. Nonetheless, it is submitted that if the CRC were complied with in Ireland, this would go a long way to solving contemporary problems in this sphere. Finally, the Amsterdam Treaty requires the EU to respect the rights safeguarded by the ECHR as "general principles of Community law". Our EU partners have in recent years increasingly tended to incorporate the ECHR into their domestic law and if this measure were adopted in Ireland, it would bring a much greater degree of equity into Irish life generally and specifically into Irish education. A further reason for incorporation is the fact that shortly citizens of Northern Ireland will be able to plead the ECHR

---

[114] Press Release, 5 November 1998.

[115] *Report of the Technical Working Group*, p 82.

[116] *Report of the Technical Working Group*, p 82.

through their local courts leaving a much less effective mechanism available to their counterparts south of the border. This is unlikely to be an incentive to the current peace initiatives in a divided country.

A New Human Rights Commission in Ireland

[8.84] Legislative proposals for an independent human rights commission were circulated on 10 February 1999 as part of the Good Friday Agreement. It appears that there will be Human Rights Commissions both north and south of the border with a joint committee to consider human issues in the island of Ireland. Concerns have been expressed regarding the narrow remit of the northern body and over the lack of public debate in regard to the southern body. The UN High Commissioner for Human Rights, Mrs Mary Robinson, has recently voiced her concern publicly that both commissions should have a sufficiently wide remit and should comply with the UN's Paris Principles for national human rights institutions. The president of this commission, who will hold the position for a maximum of five years, will be either a High Court or Supreme Court judge. In carrying out inquiries, the commission will have similar powers as the ombudsman to obtain information and documents. This body will have a wide brief to examine matters ranging from allegations of torture or ill treatment to discrimination against the disabled. The commission will also be required:

    (a) to review current legislation on the protection of human rights;

    (b) to consult with international bodies;

    (c) to examine requests from the government; and

    (d) to promote understanding and awareness of human rights in Ireland.[117]

This could become a most exciting and worthwhile development with the obvious potential of reaching out into both communities as an initial step into the future.

---

[117] *Irish Independent,* 11 February 1999, 14.

Chapter 9

The Teacher's Duty of Care: Negligence

Introduction[1]

[9.01] This chapter is concerned with negligence as a breach of duty of care. It attempts to extract the legal principles underpinning decided cases on negligence in schools bearing in mind that the law in this area is uncertain, evolving and in no way definitive. Some of the older cases cited, although perhaps admirable in their reasoning, may be somewhat out of step with modern thinking. Others have been decided in the context of small rural schools in less litigious times when the schoolmaster was perceived as the coadjutor of the priest. Case law emanating from such settings may have little relevance for large urban schools where hundreds of pupils are milling about. Cases from other common law jurisdictions are cited with an awareness that these cases are not binding on an Irish court but may be of persuasive influence.

[9.02] Duty and negligence are co-related and an action for negligence is grounded on the breach of a duty to exercise reasonable care in the circumstances of a specific case.[2] The pedagogical duties of care and protection, on the one hand, and control and discipline, on the other, are dual facets of a single duty; the teacher's legal duty of care. Teachers discharge this legal duty through the exercise of care and supervision of their pupils. Although negligence and school discipline are closely linked, they are considered separately in this book.

A Branch of General Law of Negligence

[9.03] In the past, the term "negligence" was used in a variety of senses usually indicating inadvertence on the part of the defendant.[3] While in the nineteenth century, negligence began to develop as a separate ground for liability, it was only in the twentieth century that the conceptual dimensions of the tort were fully formulated.[4] Negligence has been defined as:

---

[1]   An earlier version of this chapter appeared in an article in the Bar Review, April 1997, p 241.

[2]   *Gilmour v Belfast Harbour Commissioners* [1933] NI 114 at 148 *per* Megaw J, 1932.

[3]   McMahon and Binchy, *Irish Law of Torts*, (2nd ed, 1990), Butterworths, p 85 and generally Ch 5; *Charlesworth and Percy on Negligence*, (1997), Sweet and Maxwell, in Ch 1, (1) negligence as a state of mind; (2) negligence as careless conduct; and (3) negligence as a duty to take care.

[4]   McMahon and Binchy, p 85.

"the omission to do something which a reasonable man, guided upon those considerations which ordinarily regulate the conduct of human affairs, would do, or doing something which a prudent and reasonable man would not do"[5]

[9.04] Negligence is a tort, which involves a person's breach of a duty, imposed upon him by law, to take care, which results in damage to the complainant.[6] Negligence as it relates to teachers and schools is a branch of the general law of negligence.[7] Any attempt, therefore, to describe the law relating to schools[8] must necessarily consider the upholding legal principles from the general law. The tort of negligence may arise from a positive act or omission and in general must comprise three necessary components:

1. The existence of a duty to take care which is owed to the plaintiff;

2. The failure to reach the standard of care prescribed by law with the consequent breach of such duty; and

3. Resultant damage occasioned to the plaintiff which is causally connected to the breach of duty.[9]

There is still no overall measure of agreement on the boundaries of the above three components; duty, causation and remoteness, which, as is apparent from the case law, run continually into one another.[10]

[9.05] As the scope of negligence is as wide as human errancy and the categories of negligence are never closed,[11] the circumstances in which negligence may arise are manifold and varied. This is particularly true of the school setting where the propensity of pupils for mischief adds a further degree of complexity to the situation, which can never be discounted. While the principles on which liability rests are identifiable, it is impossible to state whether any one set of circumstances could ground liability. Pupils may be injured in a school in a very wide variety of situations which may include the following:

---

[5] *Blyth v Birmingham Waterworks Co* (1856) 11 Exch, 781 at 784 *per* Alderson B.

[6] See Percy and Walton, *Charlesworth and Percy on Negligence*, (1997), Sweet and Maxwell, Ch 1.

[7] Heuston and Buckley, *Salmond and Heuston on the Law of Torts*, (21st ed, 1996), pp 233-234; *Charlesworth and Percy*, Chs 13, 8-128 to 8-151.

[8] McMahon and Binchy, Ch 16; Linehan, 'The Schoolteacher and the Law of Negligence' (1965) 31 Ir Jur 38; Delaney, 'Injuries to School Children; The Principles of Liability', (1962-1963) 28-29 Ir Jur 15; Binchy, 'Schools Liability in Negligence', 78 Incorporated Law Society of Ireland Gazette (1984) 153 at 185; 15 *Halsbury's Laws*, (4th ed, 1990), Butterworths.

[9] *Charlesworth and Percy*, pp 15-17, para 1-25; McMahon and Binchy, p 149.

[10] See *Roe v Minister for Health* [1954] 2 QB 66 at 85 *per* Denning J; *Lamb v Camden LBC* [1981] QB 625, 634 *per* Denning J.

[11] *Donoghue v Stevenson* [1932] CA 562.

(a) by dangerous articles which have been left lying about in places to which children have access;[12]

(b) by paper darts made and thrown by the pupils themselves;

(c) by being sent on errands which are beyond their capacity;

(d) by a wandering dog in the school yard;[13]

(e) by the careless acts or omissions of teachers and psychologists for formal assessment of educational needs; or

(f) in any other circumstance where foreseeable dangers may arise.

The difficulty lies in applying the law correctly to the facts of any particular case arising out of a wide variety of circumstances. As Stephenson LJ observed in *Porter v City of Bradford MBC*[14] "It is quite clear what the duty of an education authority and of its teachers is; the difficulty is to apply the law correctly to the facts of any particular case". It is for the courts to decide whether there has been negligence in each individual case coming before them.

The Standard or Measure of Care

Judicial Approaches

[9.06] If a pupil is injured in school as a result of negligence and an action follows, the courts seek to establish whether or not there was adequate supervision at the time of the accident and whether suitable precautions were taken to prevent the foreseeable accident. From an examination of the case law, three judicial approaches to negligence in schools are apparent:

1. The traditional *"in loco parentis"* doctrine is frequently applied to the school context which is considered below;

---

[12] See injury resulting from a piece of phosphorus left lying about in a conservatory in *Williams v Eady* (1893) 10 TLR 41 CA; In *Beaumont v Surrey County Council* (1968) 66 LGR 580, heavy discarded trampette elastic was placed by a PE teacher in a litter bin in an area to which second level students had access. Some boys found the elastic and used it in "horseplay" thereby seriously injuring one boy's eye. Although the school had structured a good system of supervision, it had not been implemented in the schoolyard during the first ten minutes when the accident occurred. The court found for the plaintiff holding that the elastic was attractive to students, that the "horseplay" was foreseeable, as was the injury, and that the system of supervision was operating inadequately on the day in question.

[13] See *Helly v Gilhooley*, High Court, unrep, November 1994, in which the plaintiff was injured while walking along the footpath towards the school premises when he was knocked down by two dogs. Costello P stated "The School Authorities, I don't think, can be held liable if dogs get into the premises and it is my view that the Plaintiff is putting too high a duty of care in urging that such a duty exists".

[14] Court of Appeal, unrep, 14 January 1985, p 1.

2. Some judges prefer the ordinary language of the law of negligence and they apply the test of reasonable care and reasonable foreseeability to the school situation;[15]

3. Alternatively, the courts may apply the "reasonable professional standard" in that they expect a professional person such as a teacher, guidance counsellor or psychologist, to apply "the average amount of competence associated with the proper discharge of the duties of that profession".[16] This latter approach has been applied in a number of recent English cases which are discussed later in this chapter.[17]

In Loco Parentis

[9.07] More than 100 years have passed since Lord Esher cited, with approval, Cave J's *dictum* in *Williams v Eady*.[18] In that case a successful action for damages was brought against the school for leaving a piece of phosphorous lying about in a conservatory which later injured a pupil. The boy had taken the phosphorous so that he could rub it on hockey balls to make them luminous at night. Affirming the lower court's finding, Lord Esher, then Master of the Rolls, ruled that the law in this context was correctly laid down by the trial judge:

> "that the schoolmaster was bound to take such care of his boys as a careful father would take of his boys, and that there could not be a better definition of a schoolmaster. Then he was bound to take notice of the ordinary nature of young boys, their tendency to do mischievous acts, and their propensity to meddle with anything that came in their way."[19]

[9.08] This maxim has been modified, extended and applied in such a wide range of cases for more than a century so that it may be taken as well settled law that teachers are under a legal duty of care to take reasonable care that their pupils meet with no foreseeable injury while under their control.[20] It is well settled law that a schoolteacher or school authority owes a duty of care to pupils

---

[15] *Ryan v Madden* [1944] IR 154; *O'Gorman v Crotty and O'Connor* [1946] Ir Jur 34; *Beaumont v Surrey County Council* (1968) 66 LRG 580; *Richard v Victoria* [1969] VR 138-9; *Mapp v Gilhooley* [1991] 2 ILRM 695.

[16] *Sim v Rotherham BDC* [1986] 3 All ER 405.

[17] Cited as the *Dorset, Hampshire and Bromley* appeals ("the education appeals") to the House of Lords (cited as *X (Minors) v Bedfordshire County Council Appeals*); these included the following cases; *X (Minors) v Bedfordshire County Council*; *M (a Minor) v Newham LBC*; *E (a Minor) v Dorset County Council*; *Christmas v Hampshire County Council*; *Keating v Mayor and Burgesess of the London Borough of Bromley* [1995] ELR 404, HL.

[18] (1893) 10 TLR 41 CA.

[19] (1893) 10 TLR 41 CA.

[20] See *O'Gorman v Crotty and O'Connor* [1946] Ir Jur 34 (HC, O'Byrne J); *Ralph v LCC* (1947) 63 TLR 546 where a 14 year old plaintiff playing a game of "touch" put his hand through a glass panel in the hall, liability was imposed on the school on the grounds that a reasonable and prudent parent would have foreseen the possibility of an accident. The Court of Appeal affirmed the decision.

which arises from the fact that parents have entrusted their children to the care and control of the school.[21] However, there has been criticism of the *in loco parentis* principle as being somewhat unrealistic in large schools[22] and Salmond and Heuston state that it is simpler to say, in such instances, that the duty of a schoolteacher is to take such care as is reasonable in the circumstances.[23] In countries where the State employs the teacher, it has been argued that teachers have a separate professional authority.

Pupil-Teacher Relationship

[9.09] The duty of care derives from the teacher-pupil relationship and its temporal ambit will be determined by the circumstances of the relationship at the material time.[24] Perhaps Boreham J's statement in *Van Oppen v Trustees of the Bedford Charity*[25] summarises the diffuse role of the school:

> "It is fundamental to the relationship between school and pupil that the school undertakes to educate him in as wide a sense as it reasonably can. This involves the school having the pupils in its care and it involves the pupils in various activities in the classroom, in the chapel, in the gymnasium, on the sports field and so on. There are risks of injury inherent in many human activities, even of serious injury in some. Because of this, the school, having the pupils in its care, is under a duty to exercise reasonable care for their health and safety. Provided due care is exercised in this sphere, it seems to me that the school's duty is fulfilled. The law expects no more, nor, I venture to think, do reasonably prudent parents."[26]

[9.10] While the law does not require the continuous supervision of pupils at every moment of the day,[27] in discharging the duty of care, it is essential to have an efficient system of supervision in operation in the school. In ascertaining the liability of the school it has been held that the test applied by the courts is one of reasonableness and not of perfection.[28] Davies J in *Lyes v Middlesex County*

---

[21] *Williams v Eady* (1893) 10 TLR 41 CA; *Murtagh v Board of Management of St Emer's National School*, 2 [1991] ILRM 549.

[22] See *dictum* of Geoffrey Lane J in *Beaumont v Surrey County Council* (1968) 66 LGR 580; Brazier and Murphy, *Street on Tort* (10th ed, 1999) Butterworths.

[23] Heuston and Buckely *Salmond and Heuston on the Law of Torts*, (21st ed, 1996), p 233.

[24] *Geyer v Downs* [1977] 138 CLR 91 at 95; *Mapp v Gilhooley* [1991] 2 ILRM 695 HC.

[25] [1989] 1 All ER 273; [1989] 3 All ER 389 CA. Borehan J gave reserved judgment dismissing bith the rugby and insurance claims. The claim in the Appeal Court was in respect of the insurance claim alone.

[26] See *Van Oppen v Trustees of the Bedford Charity* [1989] 3 All ER 389 CA at 291.

[27] *Courtney v Masterson* [1949] Ir Jur 6 at 7.

[28] *Healy v Dodd* [1951] Ir Jur 22; *Lennon v McCarthy*, Supreme Court, unrep, 13 July 1966, O'Dalaigh CJ; *Mapp v Gilhooley* [1991] 2 ILRM 695.

Council[29] prudently adjusted Cave J's *dictum* in *Williams v Eady*[30] when he held that the standard of care required of a teacher is:

> "that of a reasonably prudent parent judged not in the context of his own home but in that of a school, in other words a person exhibiting the responsible, mental qualities of a prudent parent in the circumstances of school life."

This doctrine, generally referred to as "the careful parent test," is well settled in English case law and appears to have been adopted into Irish law by the following cases: *Lennon v McCarthy*,[31] *O'Gorman v Crotty and O'Connor*[32] and *Murtagh v Board of Management of Saint Emer's National School.*[33]

Second Level Teachers

[9.11] The legal obligation falling on second level teachers to supervise pupils outside of specified classroom teaching duties is somewhat unclear as there is a dearth of Irish case law in this sphere.[34] However, in *Sim v Rotherham Borough Council*,[35] an English court held that the professional obligations of a secondary teacher cannot be confined to the imparting of academic knowledge. Lord Wilberforce stated that the relationship of teacher and pupil goes further and includes duties of care and discipline. He concluded that such teachers are under a contractual obligation, *inter alia*, to "cover" for absent colleagues and the failure of some teachers to do so was a breach of contract.

When the Duty of Care Arises: at Work and at Play

[9.12] It seems that schoolteachers are under a duty of care towards their pupils while they are on the school premises, whether in the schoolroom or in the playground.[36] However, it has been held that no teacher can be expected to keep a continuous vigilant watch on every pupil[37] unless there is some reason for the teacher to be put on alert or to have their suspicion aroused.[38] In 1951, an allegation of failure to implement adequate disciplinary control and supervision was made against a County Mayo school when a handcuffed pupil was injured when climbing a school wall during a game of "still". One group of children

---

[29] (1962) 61 LGR 443.
[30] (1893) 10 TLR 41 CA.
[31] Supreme Court, unrep, 13 July 1966.
[32] [1946] Ir Jur 34.
[33] [1991] 2 ILRM 533 at 549.
[34] At the time of writing Part V of the Education 1998 had not been in operation.
[35] [1986] 3 All ER 405.
[36] United Kingdom, Laws, Statutes etc, 15 *Halsbury's Laws,* (4th ed), London, Butterworth, p 563; *Sim v Rotherham Borough Council* [1986] 3 All ER 405.
[37] *Good v INLEA* (1980) 10 Fam Law 213 CA.
[38] *Moore v Hampshire County Council* (1982) 80 LGR 481 CA.

were acting as "poteen makers" while others played the role of "police men" effecting arrests. The handcuffs, previously confiscated by the principal, had been secretly returned to the school by his son at a later date. At the time of the accident, a teacher was supervising and there was nothing to "arouse his suspicion" that the handcuffs had been returned to the school. In finding for the school managers, the judge stated, they were not guilty of any breach of duty:

"Children and parents of children must realise that teachers are not insurers and that the teachers are not responsible for every accident during school hours ... I have great difficulty in seeing how such an accident could have been prevented by the most vigorous control and supervision."[39]

[9.13] Neither is it part of a teacher's duty to foresee every act of stupidity that may occur in the course of the school day. However, it is necessary to strike a balance between too rigid supervision and the commendable aim of promoting sturdy independence in pupils as they grow towards maturity.[40] As the Court of Appeal stated in *Simkiss v Rhondda Borough Council*,[41] one was obliged to balance the robustness which would make children take the world as they found it and the tenderness which would give them nurseries wherever they went. When confronted with a plaintiff who had sustained injury by falling on a floor with no matting in 1932, the judge sought to avoid the latter extreme when he stated:

"If there had been matting it would have been said that there ought to have been a mattress; and if there had been a mattress it would have been said that there ought to be a feather-bed, and if there had been a feather-bed, that the boys ought to have been wrapped up in cotton wool or rubber."[42]

[9.14] Perhaps this case reflects the robustness of life in the 1930s and, accordingly, it does not lay down proper guideline for contemporary schools.

Boundaries of the School Day

[9.15] Difficulties sometimes arise because of the imprecise nature of boundaries or limits of the school day. Case law indicates that the teacher's duty of care normally ceases when the pupils are properly dismissed from the school premises and the pupil-teacher relationship is severed.[43] On the other hand, there

---

[39] *Healy v Dodd* [1951] Ir Jur 22 HC.
[40] *Schade v School District of Winnipeg (No 1)* 19 DLR (2nd) 199 at 305.
[41] (1983) 1 LGR 460 CA.
[42] *Jones v LCC* 48 TLR 368, (KBD 1932).
[43] *Dolan v Keohane and Cunningham,* High Court, unrep, 14 February 1992, Keane J; *Good v INLEA* (1980) 10 Fam Law 213, in which the court held that the teacher's duty of care ended when the pupils left the school premises either to be collected by parents or to attend an adjacent play centre.

is no case which lays down that there is no duty of supervision prior to official "school hours" however that expression may be understood.[44] The question, it seems, must depend upon the nature of the general duty to take reasonable care in all the circumstances.[45]

[9.16] The English and Irish courts seem reluctant to impose a duty on schools outside of their normal routine. In *Dolan v Keohane and Cunningham*,[46] the court held that a school's duty to supervise does not extend to pupils waiting for a bus, some distance outside the school grounds after school hours.

English case law

[9.17] In *Ward v Hertfordshire County Council*,[47] primary school pupils were permitted to assemble in the playground, which was surrounded by a unrendered flint wall, prior to the commencement of the school routine. Here they played in an unsupervised manner from 8.15 am until 8.55 am when they entered their classrooms. One morning an eight-year-old, who was racing about, collided with the school wall and was seriously injured. In the lower court, the plaintiff was awarded £950 damages as the wall was considered by the court to be inherently dangerous. The court found that the school authority was in breach of its statutory[48] and common law duty to take reasonable care for the safety of its pupils.

[9.18] The Court of Appeal took a different view, however, and unanimously reversed this decision. Lord Denning MR noted that one third of the village walls were of unrendered flint and he was of the view that they were not dangerous. Moreover, the headmaster stated that, even if he were in the playground, he would not have prevented the pupils playing and running about. Salmon LJ, concurring, stated that even if there had been a teacher present, he could see no reason why he should have prevented the pupils chasing or playing. Thus, the Court of Appeal found the supervision factor irrelevant in this instance. He emphasised, however, that if the pupils had been engaged in fighting or some dangerous game, which a teacher should have stopped if he had been present, the fact that there was no supervision at that time might have afforded any pupil who was injured a good cause of action.[49]

---

[44] On this point, see *Geyer v Downs* (1977) 138 CLR 91-105, 103-4.

[45] *Geyer v Down* (1977) 138 CLR 91-105.

[46] High Court, unrep, 14 February 1992, Keane J.

[47] (1969) 67 LGR 418; (1970) 68 LGR 151 CA.

[48] Occupiers Liability Act 1957.

[49] (1970) 68 LGR 151.

[9.19] In *Mays v Essex County Council*,[50] the plaintiff pupil, who was injured while playing on ice a few minutes before the school routine began at 9 am, also failed in an action for negligence. The judge stated he did not believe that parents had any right to impose responsibility on teachers outside school hours:

> "life is full of physical dangers which children must learn to recognise and develop the ability to avoid. The playground is one of the places to learn."[51]

[9.20] A pivotal element in the latter case was that the school principal had written to parents asking them not to send their children in too early.[52] Furthermore, although the school authority had issued a circular stating that the school yard should be supervised for 15 minutes prior to opening time and after closing time, this circular had not been issued to the school in question or to neighbouring schools.

[9.21] It is conceivable, however, that if the pupil-teacher relationship is habitually allowed to arise prior to official opening time or habitually permitted to extend beyond the official closing time, that a school's liability could be extended.[53] In such circumstances, a court could find that:

(a) the school had acquiesced in the presence of such pupils;[54] or

(b) that it had assumed responsibility for its pupils beyond the limits of the school day; or

(c) that the school had given rise to an expectation that the pupils would be supervised outside of the normal school routine.

[9.22] Liability for accidents to pupils arising before the official school routine commenced was imposed on two Australian schools in *Geyer v Downs*[55] and *Commonwealth of Australia v Introvigne*[56] which will now be considered.

Australian case law

[9.23] In *Geyer v Downs*,[57] the High Court of Australia ruled that a headmaster owed a duty of care to an eight year old pupil who was playing in the schoolyard before the daily routine began. The playground was not supervised at the time of the injury. On the head master's instructions, the school gates were generally

---

[50] The Times, 11 October 1975.
[51] *Cf Commonwealth of Australia v Introvigne* [1981-1982] 150 CLR 285.
[52] For a sample letter in this regard see Oliver Mahon, *Negligence and the Teacher*, (1995), Ennis Teachers' Centre, p 92.
[53] 15 *Halsbury's Laws*, p 566 at para 9.74.
[54] 15 *Halsbury's Laws*, p 566 at para 9.74.
[55] (1977) 138 CLR 91-105.
[56] (1981-1982) 150 CLR 285.
[57] (1977) 138 CLR 91-105.

opened between 8 am and 8.15 am. The plaintiff arrived at approximately 8.45 am. Official supervision of pupils commenced at 9 am. The headmaster knew that 100-150 girls were in the playground by 8.30 am each morning. In evidence, the headmaster stated that he regarded it as a community service to let the children into the school yard because it was a working district with many working mothers.[58] In addition, he stated, that he had orally prohibited games in the playground prior to 9 am. Furthermore, the headmaster confirmed that "the rule" was drawn to the attention of parents at parents' meetings although he acknowledged that no written advice had been sent to parents informing them that there would be no supervision provided by the school prior to 9 am and no effort was made to communicate with those parents who did not attend such meetings. However, two members of the school staff stated in evidence that they had never heard of "the rule". The jury found that the headmaster had created a factual situation in which he was under a duty to ensure that there was adequate disciplinary control of his pupils prior to 9 am. If he was unable to perform his duty at this time, then he should not have assumed the relationship of master towards pupils at an earlier hour as the jury found he did.

[9.24] In *Commonwealth of Australia v Introvigne*[59] a pupil was injured shortly before school instruction commenced when part of a flagpole, on the halyard[60] of which boys had been swinging, fell on him. At the time of the incident, the playground, in which approximately 900 pupils had assembled, was supervised by only one teacher, the others being at a staff meeting which had been called to inform the staff of the death of the principal. Brennan J emphasised that this was not a case of a school authority's vicarious liability for the negligent acts of a teacher. Rather it was a case of negligent omission by a school authority to take reasonable steps to protect a pupil. In this case, there was a failure to exercise proper supervision of the playground, and a failure to padlock the halyard.

[9.25] The High Court held that the calling of the staff meeting did not preclude the discharge of the duty of care and so the necessary steps to discharge the duty were not taken:

> "It was foreseeable that in the unsupervised clamour of boys around the flagpole, some would enjoy the opportunity to swing upon the halyard and risk bringing down the truck. The foreseeable folly of youthful exuberance made supervision or the padlocking of the halyard necessary if the boys were to be safeguarded from the risk of injury."[61]

---

[58] (1977) 138 CLR 91 at p 99.
[59] (1981-1982) 150 CLR 285.
[60] Being a rope or tackle for hoisting or lowering flags, sails or yards.
[61] *Cf Ramsey v Larsen* (1964) 111 CLR 30.

By establishing a school which was maintained on its behalf, the court ruled that the Commonwealth fell under a duty of care to children attending the school, and that the Commonwealth was in breach of duty in failing to provide adequate supervision of the pupils in the period preceding the commencement of instruction and in failing to ensure the halyard was padlocked to the pole. The English case *Carmarthenshire County Council v Lewis*[62] was applied by the court.

A Safe System of Supervision

[9.26] It is for the principal to ensure that an adequate system of supervision is in operation in the school[63] and parents should receive adequate notice of any change in the operation of that system. This is particularly important in the case of younger pupils who may be met by parents at the school. The facts in *Barnes v Hampshire County Council*[64] concerned a five year-old pupil who had been dismissed from school five minutes before parents were advised to meet their children. The pupil wandered off alone and was injured on a busy road. In the House of Lords, liability was imposed on the school for failing to take adequate precautions against this occurrence. It considered that five minutes was not a negligible period and that the release of the pupils prior to official closing time was an indication of negligence on the part of the school.

[9.27] When school activities extend beyond the normal school routine as when a school tour takes place, during a football match or other extra-curricular activity, the school's duty of care continues to apply. In such circumstances, the system of supervision should devolve responsibility for the proper dismissal of the pupils on the teachers in charge on the day in question. Part of the discharge of that duty entails checking that all the pupils have left the school premises.[65] If parents are involved in supervision on schools tours, they should be advised as to what is expected of them and be under the general supervision of a teacher. Accidents may also occur when students are on work experience.

[9.28] In *Byrne v County Dublin Vocational Education Committee (VEC)*,[66] the plaintiff alleged that he suffered a serious back injury when assisting the garage proprietor, with whom he was engaged on a work experience programme, to remove a gear box from a car. The plaintiff had failed to report the matter to proprietor at the time and the first knowledge the VEC had received of the

---

[62] [1955] AC 549.

[63] *O'Gorman v Crotty and O'Connor*, 34 Ir Jur (1946) 6.

[64] [1969] 3 All ER 746.

[65] See *Baxter v Barker*, The Times, 24 April 1903, cited in Barrell and Partington, *Teachers and the Law*, (1985) p 409.

[66] High Court, unrep, 8 November 1991, Lynch J.

matter was well over one year after the occurrence of the accident. Nonetheless, Lynch J held that the accident had happened and that it arose from a breach of the Factories Regulations and so liability attached to the defendants. However, the judge was satisfied that the plaintiff's injury had been relatively trivial and he awarded £6,000 plus costs.

The Degree of Care

[9.29] The law has never required teachers to keep a vigilant watch on every pupil every minute of the school day,[67] unless there is some reason to be put on the alert or to arouse suspicion.[68] Nonetheless, in the discharge of the duty of care, it is essential to establish that there was an effective system of supervision in place and that it was being implemented at the material time. The degree of care required, which is expressed through supervision, alters with the circumstances of the case and may be stated to depend on:

(a) the age of the pupils;

(b) the mental maturity of the pupils;

(c) the nature of the activity in hand;

(d) the degree of supervision required; and

(e) the opportunity the teachers had (if any) to prevent or minimise the mischief complained of.

As Barr J stated in *Mapp v Gilhooley*[69] "in the absence of a regime of draconian servitude, it is impossible to keep very young children under complete control while at play".

[9.30] It appears, therefore, that the degree of supervision required by the courts when children are at play is less rigorous than that required in the academic class. Possibly, acknowledging the fact that some degree of disciplined behaviour is necessary if pupils are to be educated, the courts usually require a higher degree of supervision when pupils are under instruction than when they are in the playground.[70] In practical classes, the risk of injury is likely to be

---

[67] *Rawsthorne v Ottley* (1937) 3 All ER 902; *Courtney v Masterson* [1949] Ir Jur 6 at 7, HC, Black J; *Lennon v McCarthy*, Supreme Court, unrep, 13 July 1966; *Good v Inner London Authority* (1980) 10 Fam Law 213.

[68] *Healy v Dodd*, (1951) Ir Jur 22 at 23; *Moore v Hampshire County Council* (1982) 80 LGR at 481 CA; *Mapp v Gilhooley* [1992] 2 IR 253.

[69] [1992] 2 IR 253; (1991) 2 ILRM 695. This case was appealed to the Supreme Court where, because of the admission of the unsworn testimony of an eight year old child, is was held to be a mistrial. The case was then returned to the Circuit Court in Sligo for a retrial. The Court found for the school. The plaintiff then appealed to the High Court which upheld the decision of the Circuit Court.

[70] 15 *Halsbury's Laws*, citing *Crouch v Essex County Council* (1966) 64 LGR at 240.

higher than in the academic class and so the degree of care required by a court may be higher than that required in the academic class.

Good Standard and Approved Practice

[9.31] In deciding whether or not the duty of care was discharged by a teacher, a court may seek to establish whether a teacher had followed "good standard and approved practice" with no inherent defects,[71] in the conduct of his class.[72] Accordingly, if a teacher is doing something unorthodox, it will be much more difficult to establish that he had discharged the duty of care required. In the conduct of a practical class, the teacher ought to be able to demonstrate the steps taken by him to prevent the foreseeable accident.[73]

[9.32] When pupils are involved in specialist classes, the kind of supervision ought to be tailored to the activity in hand. If particular hazards are involved, clear instructions and warnings ought to be given and a teacher should be present throughout the full class. That the age and mental maturity of pupils are pivotal factors is well demonstrated by the following cases. In *Butt v Cambridgeshire*,[74] an experienced teacher gave pointed scissors to nine and ten year old girls to cut out illustrations during geography class. While the teacher was present, another pupil waived her scissors about thereby seriously injuring the plaintiff's eye. The Court of Appeal reversed the decision of the lower court ruling that the teacher had conducted the class in an efficient manner and that on the evidence of experienced teachers, there was no fault in the system of supervision.

[9.33] A somewhat similar case had a different sequel in *Black v Kent County Council*.[75] In that case, a seven year old pupil was given the choice of round ended scissors or pointed scissors and choose the latter which resulted in injury to him when his chair was jogged. The Court of Appeal held that the teachers were guilty of an error of judgment as it was prudent to provide blunt ended scissors for pupils of up to eight or nine years. It is worth noting that the Court accepted as guidance the Department of Education and Science booklet *Safety at School* which recommended the use of round ended scissors for children of the plaintiff's age.

---

[71] *Roche v Peilow* (1986) ILRM in regard to a solicitor's duty of care; *Wright v Cheshire County Council* [1952] All ER 565; *Cf Gibbs v Barking Corporation* [1936] 1 All ER 115.

[72] *Wright v Cheshire County Council* [1952] 2 All ER 789.

[73] See *Smith v Jolly,* Irish Times, 18-19 May 1984, O'Hanlon J; *Mulligan v Doherty,* Supreme Court, unrep, 17 May 1966; *Wright v Cheshire County Council* [1952] 2 All ER 565 in which the teacher established that she had followed a recognised form of instruction in the conduct of a physical education class in which a 12 year old boy was injured.

[74] (1970) 68 LGR 81; see further 15 *Halsbury's Laws*, p 563.

[75] The Times, 23 May 1983.

Student Maturity

[9.34] In the case of students approaching maturity, the degree of care required is generally less stringent than that required in the case of younger pupils[76] as the courts take into account the maturity of the student. This point was illustrated recently in *Donoghue v Westmeath VEC*[77] in which the 14 year old plaintiff injured his left index finger while using a bandsaw during a metal work class. It was alleged that the plaintiff had used the bandsaw only once before and at the material time the guard was absent. However, the class teacher gave evidence that this particular class had used the bandsaw over a five year period and that the guard was in place at the material time. The teacher also stated that he always set the saw at the correct setting whenever he used the bandsaw. Finding for the school, Budd J stated that if a student was not following the instructions given such an accident could occur. If the teacher had failed to use the guard, clearly the result would most likely have been different despite the maturity of the student.

[9.35] That student maturity may not always be a shield against negligence is also clear from the Canadian case *James v River East School Division*[78] in which the plaintiff, an 18 year old "above average student," suffered injury when attempting to heat nitric acid in her school laboratory. The court found that instructions for the experiment had failed to refer to the requirement to wear goggles which were provided for the safety of the students. Finding for the student, the judge emphasised that students must be told when necessary to "wear goggles".

[9.36] A 16 year old student successfully alleged negligence against a school principal, a nominal defendant, for £2,500 and costs for personal injuries sustained during a hurling match, as the school had failed to provide him with a protective helmets during the match.[79] If goggles or other protective clothing, appliance, convenience, equipment or other means, are supplied by the board for the safety of pupils and teachers, there is a statutory duty on the teacher under

---

[76] *Mulligan v Doherty*, Supreme Court, unrep, 17 May 1966; *Smith v Jolly*, High Court, unrep, 17-18 May 1984, Irish Times, 18 May, 1984, p 8 and 19 May 1984 p 18; *Walsh v Bourke*, 25-26 January 1985.

[77] High Court, unrep, March 1995, Budd J, see also *Hennessy v City of Waterford VEC*, Circuit Court, 12 December 1990 in which the court held the VEC was not legally liable when pupils aged 13-16 injured another boy when they placed a hurley between his legs and raised him off the ground causing him to fall. Dismissing the case, Judge Moriarty stated that if he had a son of that age group, he would permit him to play unsupervised and that the school were not insurers of their pupils.

[78] 58 DLR (3d) 311 Manitoba QB 1975.

[79] "Hurt school hurler's £2,500," Sunday Independent, 5 November 1989, p 2.

the Safety, Health and Welfare at Work Act 1989 to ensure that any such article is worn or used.[80]

Pupils of Tender Years

[9.37] From the case law, it seems that the obligation cast by the common law upon teachers of very young pupils is greater than that required in the case of older pupils. In *Ryan v Madden*,[81] a teacher of an infant class was held to be negligent in failing to exercise supervision as her pupils emerged from an upstairs classroom at the end of the school day. While the teacher remained in her classroom, her five year old pupil suffered injury as a result of sliding down a stair banister. In this important precedent, it was established that the school manager was legally liable, by virtue of vicarious liability, for the negligence of his employee (the teacher) during the course of her employment.

Contributory Negligence and Children

[9.38] While the law holds that children of tender years are incapable of contributory negligence, children of ten or eleven years have been considered capable of contributory negligence.[82] In the case of a child, the authoritative statement of the legal principles relating to contributory negligence was aptly summarised by Byrne J in *Fleming v Kerry County Council:*[83]

> "In the case of a child, the standard is what may be reasonably expected, having regard to the age and mental development of the child and the other circumstances of the case."

Where both the plaintiff and defendant are negligent, it is a matter for the court to decide the degree of fault of both parties and to apportion damages accordingly.[84]

Bus-Related Duties

[9.39] Supervisory duties may arise in respect of the control and discipline of pupils awaiting buses at the end of the school day. The discharge of the duty of care in this regard seems to depend largely on the point of assembly of the pupils. In *Good v ILEA*,[85] the court held that the teacher's duty ended when the

---

[80] Section 9(1)(a) and (c).

[81] [1944] IR 154.

[82] *O'Gorman v Crotty*, HC [1946] Ir Jur, 34, the Court did not actually find this boy guilty of contributory negligence but only capable of being guilty of contributory negligence; see further *Hosty v McDonagh*, Supreme Court, unrep, 29 May 1973.

[83] [1955-1956] Ir Jur 71 at 72.

[84] Civil Liability Act 1961 ss 34 and 40; *Hosty v McDonagh*, Supreme Court, unrep, 29 May 1973.

[85] (1980) 10 Fam Law 213 CA.

pupils left the school premises either to be collected by parents or to attend an adjacent play centre. It might be otherwise, however, if the bus was parked on the school premises as then the court might consider that the pupil-teacher relationship had not been severed. If the bus comes onto the school premises to pick up pupils, the discharge of duty would appear to require reasonable supervision and the orderly conduct of pupils while entering buses. In such instances, some form of discipline would most likely be required as it would be reasonably foreseeable that in the absence of any supervision, that a pupil could be injured as a result of youthful "high spirits" at the end of the school day. Some teachers voluntarily undertake the supervision of pupils awaiting buses outside the school premises. If this is the case, they ought to exercise the same standard of care as they would apply when discharging their contractual duties.

[9.40] Case law suggests that if a pupil on his other way to and from school behaves in a manner detrimental to school discipline, the school may impose a sanction.[86] A school, it seems, may implement a sanction against pupils who misbehave on their way to and from school and this includes those travelling on buses to school.

Duties of a Bus Driver

[9.41] A bus driver's duty of care to his child passengers was at issue in *Mulcahy v Lynch and Butler.*[87] In this case, Keane J, applying *McDonald v CIE,*[88] ruled that there is a heavy responsibility on a driver of a vehicle approaching a school bus when the bus has stopped to allow children to dismount. This duty, he stated, can only be discharged by the approaching driver by driving slowly, by keeping a lookout and, by blowing the horn in circumstances where the approaching car is obscured from view by the presence of the bus.

[9.42] This finding has obvious implications for all drivers approaching a stationary school bus from which children are dismounting. It is particularly relevant for parents and teachers who drive habitually in such circumstances.

The "Pure Accident"

[9.43] The law knows no remedy for the "pure accident" as in such circumstances no legal liability arises.[89] As Byrne J stated in the High Court in *Healy v Dodd*:

---

[86] *Cleary v Booth* (1893) 1 KB 465; *R v Newport (Shropshire) Justices ex p Wright* [1929] 2 KB 416; *Spiers v Warrington Corporation* [1954] 1 QB 61; *The State (Smullen) v Duffy* [1980] ILRM 46.

[87] Supreme Court, unrep, 25 March 1993, Law Report, Irish Times, 12 July, 1993, p 14.

[88] (1971) 105 ILTR 13, Budd J.

[89] *Webb v Essex County Council*, Times Educational Supplement, 12 November 1954; *Clarke v Bethnal Green Borough Council* (1939) 55 TLR 519 which involved an accident to a child swimmer.

"Children and parents of children must realise that teachers are not insurers and that the teachers are not responsible for every accident in school hours. That would be an intolerable burden for the teacher."[90]

[9.44] This point was well illustrated in the High Court in *Smith v Jolly*[91] in which the 17 year old plaintiff failed in her action based on inadequate instruction in regard to a new physical education exercise at her second level school. The teacher had demonstrated the putting of the four kilo shot and had moved along the "field". Despite expert evidence that the shot was "a lethal weapon" and that the teacher should never leave the area in which a putting competition was taking place, the jury[92] held the school had not been negligent in failing to provide a safe system for the conduct of the class. While the plaintiff clearly had a right to have her person protected from the careless acts or omissions of a teacher, for whom the school authorities were vicariously liable, she had no right to protection from purely accidental injury or from the outcome of such injury.

[9.45] In *Gow v Glasgow Education Authority*[93] a seven year old blind boy was injured by another boy jumping on his back. However, the court considered this incident as an "unforeseeable misfortune" that was unlikely to be averted even by adult supervision. These latter cases underscore the fact that where injuries are sustained by pupils in schools as a result of the "pure accident," then no legal liability arises on the part of the school. A 15 year old student, in *O'Regan v Co Limerick VEC*,[94] sustained a hip injury when her chair was pulled from under her by a fellow pupil during an interval between two classes. Dismissing the case, the judge stated that this case should never have been brought before a court in the first instance.

[9.46] A 1954 case was the sequel to an accident involving a five year old pupil who injured himself while jumping from an agility stool almost half his height during a physical education class. The headmistress argued that the object of the exercise was to nurture confidence. The court held there was no negligence in this instance as there was nothing to show it was other than an accident.[95]

[9.47] The courts recognise that risks of injury arise in this sphere and accidents cannot be eliminated. This is well illustrated by the recent Supreme Court decision in *Flynn v O'Reilly*.[96] This case arose from a school sports day which

[90] [1951] Ir Jur 22; this point was also emphasised by Boreham J in *Van Oppen v Trustees of the Bedford Charity* [1989] 1 All ER 273 CA at p 291.
[91] Irish Times, 18-19 May 1984, pp 8 and 18 respectively.
[92] Juries have since been abolished in personal inuries cases.
[93] [1922] SC 260.
[94] Limerick Circuit Court, unrep, 24 January 1991, O Higgins J.
[95] *Webb v Essex County Council*, Times Educational Supplement, 12 November 1954.
[96] Judgment, ex tempore delivered on 11 January 1999, O'Flaherty J (SC).

took place in a very small field[97] which was generally used for hurling and camogie.

[9.48] On the day in question between 90-100 pupils were participating in various races including sprints, egg and spoon races etc. Then, along came a rather unusual type of race, a running backwards race, in which 15-20 boys and girls took part. One eleven year old pupil, while running backwards, stated that she caught her foot in some kind of hole or depression in the ground and fell fracturing her left wrist. The plaintiff submitted that the field was somewhat rough, uneven and unsuitable for a backward running race. Smyth J in the High Court, having visited the *locus* of the accident and having performed an experiment on it, which was not included in evidence, held that there was no negligence on the part of the school teachers:

> "I find as a fact that and as a matter of probability that the plaintiff was not as far off the centre of the pitch as she thinks and was not on, at or near the periphery of the field, though she was towards it, away from the centre, but not in the position in which she thinks or near the sidewall. Had she been so Mrs Ryan should and would, for she struck me as a very alert teacher, have seen her fall. The plaintiff says she tripped over something, it was a hole covered with grass of about two inches deep. And that immediately after she fell or before being taken into the school she noticed this."

[9.49] On appeal to the Supreme Court, O'Flaherty J, delivering the *ex tempore* judgment of the Court,[98] stated "There must be some risk attached to all forms of sports day. In a hard surfaced playground people will come to grief from time to time". He approved and applied O'Dálaigh CJ's decision in *Lennon v McCarthy*[99] drawing an analogy between the two cases.

[9.50] In the *Lennon* case, a pupil of much the same age as the plaintiff in *Flynn*, was involved in a game of "tig" with fellow pupils in a hollow below the school yard. As they ran, one boy pushed the branch of some hawthorn bushes out of his way and the pursuing boy was struck in the eye by the rebounding branch. The injured boy sued the manager and school principal for negligence. O'Dálaigh CJ, for the Court, held that the duty of the schoolmaster is to take such care of his pupil as a careful parent would do for his children and that when normal healthy children are in the playground, it is not necessary that they be under constant supervision. What happened in this case, O'Dálaigh CJ stated, was "an accident such as is inseparable from life and action and no

---

[97] 64 yards by 33 yards.

[98] In this three judge decision, the other judges being Keane and Murphy JJ.

[99] Supreme Court, unrep, 13 July 1996 *per* O'Dalaigh CJ; see McMahon and Binchy, *A Case Book on the Irish Law of Torts* (2nd ed, 1990), p 182.

circumstances exist which would warrant placing responsibility for it on the plaintiff's school teacher".

[9.51] O'Flaherty J considered that the *Flynn* case arose from much the same situation. While there was a consensus that the field in question was not Wimbledon, Landsdowne Road or Wembley or some such place, he stated, it was for rather simple games and, to adopt O'Dalaigh CJ's words, it would be unreal to say that a parent would regard this field as dangerous. Indeed the history of the field did not indicate that any person had suffered injury there before this accident. O'Flaherty J, having considered the very careful judgment of the trial judge, stated:

> "... even accepting that there was some indentation or some unevenness and accepting that there is some risk attached to people running backwards as opposed to running forwards and that that is more hazardous, nonetheless, do we lay down that that should be forbidden in a way that would prevent children having due freedom to play and engage in sports? We think that would be too strict a rule. It would be to do what the law commands us in assessing negligence not to do, which is to impose standards which are unreasonable having regard to all the circumstances. It would really be to attempt to introduce a rule of absolute liability which would be to go too far."

[9.52] The Supreme Court dismissed the appeal. Finally, referring to the very general grounds of appeal in the instant case, O'Flaherty J stated that, in future, it would be important to try to be as explicit as possible in setting forth the grounds of appeal.

Critical Comment

[9.53] The *Flynn* case is a very significant one for schools and school authorities. In establishing that the school was not legally liable in the circumstances of this case, the Supreme Court set down a boundary line beyond which it is unlikely to go. Essentially, it will not prevent children having the freedom to play and engage in sports even though there is a degree of risk of injury involved in these activities. It will not hold school authorities and teachers liable for every accident that may occur in a school and it accepts that some accidents will happen despite the implementation of supervision by teachers. If the Supreme Court held otherwise in the *Flynn* case, it is conceivable that schools would become more litigious, and accordingly more reluctant to engage in sporting activities and games, or to hold sports days, which are frequently the most memorable days in a child's life. Furthermore, a finding of absolute liability for the welfare of pupils or a general movement in that direction, in the opinion of the author, could lead to a formal rigidity in school life and to a narrowing of the scope and focus of the activities available to children while in school, thereby militating against the welfare and interest of the children themselves.

Insurance

[9.54] Parents are under no duty to insure their children. However, they frequently take out personal accident insurance fearing that their children may be injured in school in circumstances where the school is not legally liable (eg in the case of a "pure accident"). As there is no duty on parents to insure, neither is there a general legal duty on those in *loco parentis* (eg schools) to insure even against negligence. As Boreham J stated in *Van Oppen*,[100] "No doubt it is prudent for a school to insure against negligence but that is in its own interests; it is under no duty to the pupils to do so". This case also indicates that there is no legal obligation on the school to inform parents of the need to take out personal accident insurance. However, the majority of schools insure their legal liability and schools may be required to do so by departmental rules or regulations.

[9.55] Community[101] schools have distinctive arrangements in that their Deeds of trust include an indemnity which indicates that the State carries its own insurance against fire damage to the school buildings and against occupier's liability. Furthermore, in these schools, the State indemnifies the board and the staff in respect of actions taken against them arising out of the discharge of their duties whether in respect of pupils or otherwise. The State carries its own insurance in respect of visitors, parents and others lawfully on the school premises and it indemnifies the board and the staff against claims by visitors, parents and others who are on the school premises without permission where such claims do not disclose a wrongful act of the part of the board or staff.

The Liability of the School Authority

[9.56] The concept that a school is in *"loco parentis"* does not fully state the legal responsibility of the school. Murphy J, in *Commonwealth of Australia v Introvigne*,[102] stated that "a school authority owes to its pupils a duty to ensure that reasonable care is taken of them whilst they are on the school premises during the hours when the school is open for attendance". This, he considered,

---

[100] [1989] 1 All ER 273 at 287, 291.

[101] See *Articles of Management in Model Agreement*, 'Community Schools Community Colleges in the Archdioces of Dublin', 1982, Education Secretariat, Archbishop's House, Dublin, pp 24-25 for Community Schools and 36-37 for Community Colleges.

[102] (1984) 150 CLR 258 at 275.

was a duty akin to that duty owed by a hospital to a patient,[103] the performance of which cannot be delegated to others.[104]

[9.57] The liability of a school authority for injury sustained by a pupil attending the school, while it includes vicarious liability is wider than vicarious liability[105] and includes statutory liability which is discussed below.[106] While the school's duty relates only to matters over which the school has control,[107] in some respects this duty may go beyond parental duty as a school may have special knowledge about some matters that the parent does not have.[108] Such knowledge does not enlarge the ambit of the school's duty, however, it brings into account an important and sometimes essential consideration in deciding whether or not a schoolteacher has discharged that duty. Although the school is not responsible for the pupil's economic loss or welfare, it has a duty to ensure that, *inter alia*, its activities are reasonably safe and well organised.[109]

Vicarious Liability

[9.58] It is well settled that the board of management (previously the manager) is vicariously liable for the negligence of its teachers while they are acting in the course of their employment.[110] It appears that the board may not be legally liable if it can establish that the teacher or other employee was acting outside the scope of his authority[111] or was on a "frolic" of his own.[112] Vicarious liability can arise, at least potentially, for the actions of a principal who gave negligent advice regarding the educational needs of a pupil as Lord Browne-Wilkinson indicated in *X (Minors) v Bedfordshire County Council* "a school which accepts a pupil assumes responsibility not only for his physical well-being but also for his educational needs." In giving such advice, the standard of care applying would

---

[103] *Commonwealth of Australia v Introvigne* (1984) 150 CLR 258 at 271 citing *Ramsey v Larsen* (1964) 111 CLR at 28 and *Gold v Essex County Council* [1942] 2 KB 293 at 304.

[104] *Commonwealth of Australia v Introvigne* (1984) 150 CLR 258 citing *Cassidy v Minister for Health* [1951] 2 KB 343 at 363, Denning J.

[105] *Van Oppen v Trustees of the Bedford Charity* [1989] 1 All ER 273 at 287.

[106] See below para **[9.62]** *et seq.*

[107] *Van Oppen v Trustees of the Bedford Charity* [1989] 1 All ER 273 at 291; *Commonwealth of Australia v Introvigne* (1981-2) 150 CLR 258 at 269.

[108] *Van Oppen v Trustees of the Bedford Charity* [1989] 1 All ER 273, *per* Boreham J.

[109] *Van Oppen v Trustees of the Bedford Charity* [1989] 1 All ER 273 at 290.

[110] *Ryan v Madden* [1944] IR 157; *McKeown v Flynn* (1935) ILTR Vol 61; *Hosty v McDonagh*, Supreme Court, unrep, 29 May 1973.

[111] Libel, slander and assault are frequently excluded in insurance policies.

[112] *McCann v Mannion* LXVI ILTR 1930 161; *McGee v Cunnane* LXVI 1932 147; *O'Callaghan v Collins*, Irish Independent 1 December, 1990, p 1. All of these case deal with the administration of scholastic corporal punishment; see Non-Fatal Offences Against the Person Act 1997, s 24 which abolished the common law rule in respect of immunity of teachers from criminal liability for physical chastisement of pupils.

be that of the reasonable principal and not that of another professional such as an educational psychologist.[113]

[9.59] In a negligence action, the plaintiff may sue either the teacher or the board, or both, although it is unusual for the teacher alone to be sued,[114] the board of management being the body of substance. When damages have been awarded against a board as a result of the serious or gross personal negligence of a teacher, the board retains the right in law to seek from the teacher as joint tortfeasor an indemnity or contribution. As Osborough points out, this traditional tenet, which confers on an employer answerable under vicarious liability the right to seek an indemnity or contribution from the primary tortfeasor, underscores the necessity for the teacher to be insured.[115] Two cases illustrate the operation and the significance of this legal principle.

Contribution and Indemnity from the Teacher

[9.60] In *Ryan v Fildes*[116] an English manager exercised his right to full indemnity from a teacher who had boxed a pupil on the ear who subsequently became deaf in that ear. In *Hosty v McDonagh*,[117] an Irish manager exercised his legal right to contribution from a teacher employee in a negligence action against him as manager of the school. This case concerned the escape of a ten year-old pupil from the school onto the roadway at 12.30 pm where she was seriously injured by a passing car. The plaintiff sued the car driver and the school manager alleging negligence and the latter joined the school principal as a third party to the proceedings. In the High Court, the plaintiff was awarded damages of £3,010 which was apportioned as follows:

  (a) 65% to the car driver;

  (b) 25% to the school manager; and

  (c) 10% to the plaintiff (for contributory negligence).

[9.61] An order was made, however, requiring the principal to indemnify the manager to the full extent of his damages. The car driver and the principal appealed this decision, the former against his apportionment of the damages and the latter against the order made against him. The Supreme Court could have ordered a re-trial but, to avoid extra costs, exercised its jurisdiction to deal with

---

[113] *X (Minors) v Bedfordshire County Council* [1995] 2 AC 663 at 763.

[114] *X (Minors) v Bedfordshire County Council* [1995] 2 AC 663.

[115] Osborough, 'Irish Law and the Rights of the National Schoolteacher I', 14 (1979) Ir Jur, (ns), Pt 1, Vol 14, pp 36-50 at p 40, fn 16; on this point see allegations made by the second defendant in *Cotter v Ahern* High Court, unrep, 25 February 1977.

[116] [1938] 3 All ER 517.

[117] Supreme Court, unrep, 29 May 1973.

the matter at that point. The Court set aside the jury's award of £3,010 in the High Court and awarded damages of £1,510 to be apportioned as follows:

(a) 45% to the car driver;

(b) 25% to the manager (as he had not appealed his apportionment); and

(c) 30% to the plaintiff.

The court held that the school manager was entitled to recover, by way of contribution, one third of his damages from the school principal.

Statutory Duties

[9.62] The Fire Services Act 1981 requires, *inter alia*, those in control of schools to guard against the outbreak of fire on the school premises and to ensure as far as reasonably practicable the safety of persons on the premises in the event of an outbreak of fire.[118] Accordingly, a range of obligations fall on school authorities in regard to fire prevention.[119] This Act also makes provision for the service of "Fire Safety Notices" by a Fire Authority on the owner or occupier of any building which appears to the Authority to be "a potentially dangerous building" which is defined in s 19 of the Act.

Safety, Health and Welfare

[9.63] While the duties under the Safety, Health and Welfare at Work Act 1989 and secondary legislation made thereunder,[120] are directed primarily at employee protection, discussed elsewhere in this book,[121] duties also fall on the employer in ss 6-8 of the Act requiring him or her among other duties:

> to conduct his undertaking in such a way as to ensure, so far as is reasonably practicable, that persons not in his employment who may be affected thereby are not exposed to risks to their safety and health.

[9.64] The employer is under a further duty deriving from the Safety, Health and Welfare at Work Act 1989 (General Application) Regulations 1993 to report certain accidents to the Health and Safety Authority[122] where an accident occurs at a place of work as a result of which an employee dies or is prevented from performing his normal work for more than three consecutive days excluding the

---

[118] Section 18(2) of the Fire Services Act 1981.

[119] See further Code of Practice for the Management of Fire Safety in Places of Assembly, 1989, Department of Environment, which applies to non-residential colleges or schools.

[120] See particularly Safety, Health and Welfare at Work Act 1989 (Control of Specific Substances and Activities) Regulations 1991 (SI 285/1991); Safety, Health and Welfare at Work Act, 1989 (General Application) Regulations 1993 (SI 44/1993); Safety, Health and Welfare at Work Act 1989 (Carcinogens) Regulations 1993 (SI 80/1993).

[121] See Ch 11.

[122] See Part X of the General Application Regulations 1993 and in particular regulation 59.

day of the accident but including any days which would not have been working days. The duty also applies in the case of any person who is not at work but who as a result of an accident related to a place of work or a work activity dies or suffers any injury or condition as a result of an accident which results in the person requiring treatment from a registered medical practitioner or treatment in a hospital as an in-patient or an out-patient, or there is a dangerous occurrence. In such circumstances the responsible person shall:

(a) in the case of a death, supply the Authority by the quickest practicable means with the names of the deceased, particulars and the location of the accident, and

(b) as soon as practicable send a written report in the approved form to the Authority of the death, injury, condition, accident or dangerous occurrence.[123]

The responsible person (usually the principal acting on behalf of the board), must keep written records of any accident or dangerous occurrence which is required to be reported under Regulation 59, for a period of ten years from the date of the accident or dangerous occurrence.

[9.65] The Schools Occupational Accidents and Illnesses Survey 1994, which was included in the *Report of the Advisory Committee on Occupational Safety and Health at First and Second Levels in the Education Sector to the Health and Safety Authority (1995)*,[124] stated that the education sector is not particularly high-risk in terms of accidents to employees. However, it observed indications of serious under-reporting of accidents in schools generally. The survey found that pupils and visitors to schools suffered 4,734 reportable accidents, although few, if any, were reported to the Health and Safety Authority.[125] This underscores the necessity for training for school management and teachers in regard to health and safety legislation and civil liability matters together with the need to focus on the maintenance of school premises and play areas.

Structural Defects

[9.66] When accidents arise as a result of structural defects on the school premises, liability rests with the occupier of the premises who is generally the board of management. Under the Occupiers Liability Act 1995 the pupils are regarded as visitors on the school premises. Equipment ought to be in good order and should be regularly checked. As McMahon and Binchy observe,[126] the

---

[123] See further ss 58-63 inclusive of the General Applications Regulations 1993.

[124] Health and Safety Authority, 1995, p 3. The survey had a response rate of 57%.

[125] Advisory Committee Report, Health and Safety Authority, 1995, p 7.

[126] McMahon and Binchy, *Irish Law of Torts*, (2nd ed, 1990), p 304.

language of occupier's liability is apparent in some of the earlier cases such as *Courtney v Masterson*[127] and *Lennon v McCarthy*.[128]

School Authority's Liability to Third Parties

[9.67] In *Mapp v Gilhooley*,[129] Barr J held that the duty of care owed by a school authority to pupils while on its premises in the course of normal school activities is to protect them from foreseeable risks of personal injury or harm. That a school's responsibility may include a duty to third parties, who are injured as a consequence of a pupil's escape from the school on to a street, is clear from *Carmarthenshire County Council v Lewis*.[130] In that case, the plaintiff's husband was killed when trying to avoid a four year-old pupil who had strayed on to the road from the adjacent school. In the House of Lords, it was held that the supervising teacher was not negligent. However, the Court considered that the escape of the child was a foreseeable event so the school authority was held liable for failing to take sufficient precautions to prevent this escape, eg by locking the gates or by making them sufficiently difficult to open so as to ensure that they could not be opened by a child so young that it could not be trusted alone on the street.[131] The case of *Hosty v McDonagh*[132] indicates that this was the law in Ireland also.

[9.68] However, the recent case of *Nwabudike v Southwark London Borough Council*,[133] had a different outcome. In this instance the plaintiff pupil was injured when he ran out of his primary school during the lunch break into the path of a car, the court found the school had not breached its duty of care to the pupil. Zucker J stated that it was the duty of the school to take all reasonable and adequate steps to prevent a child leaving the premises at a time when he should have been in school but that no school could ever ensure that accidents would never occur, particularly when a child was determined to break the rules designed to protect him. The judge accepted the fact that only one similar incident had occurred in the previous six years in that school as evidence that all proper and reasonable steps to ensure the safety of the children had been taken by the school.

---

[127] [1949] Ir Jur 6.
[128] Supreme Court, unrep, 13 July 1966.
[129] *Mapp v Gilhooley* [1991] 2 ILRM 695.
[130] [1955] AC 549 reversing the decision of the lower court.
[131] [1955] AC 549 at 563.
[132] Supreme Court, unrep, 29 May 1973.
[133] The Times Law Reports, 28 June 1996.

School Tours

[9.69] Teachers responsible for school tours and educational visits continue to be *in loco parentis* during the school tour or educational visit although courts have recognised that supervision is more difficult in these circumstances.[134] While accidents may occur during the best organised and supervised tours, careful planning and reasonable supervision is essential so as to avoid foreseeable injury to pupils. Clearly, the risk of injury is greater when pupils are mountaineering,[135] canoeing, sailing or skiing[136] so it is prudent to increase the number of supervisors accordingly. If parents or others agree to act as supervisors, they ought to be advised of what is expected of them and be placed under the overall, general supervision of an experienced teacher. All reasonable steps ought to be taken by the school as its obligations extend throughout the whole course of the tour and may continue beyond the normal school day times. If the class includes pupils with disabilities, it is prudent to increase the number of supervisors.

[9.70] It is also prudent to have written parental consent and board of management approval for school tours and to ensure that parents give their written consent to any medical treatment which may be necessitated for those pupils under sixteen years. Parental consent or the signing of an indemnity will not, of course, prevent a parent instituting negligence proceedings against the school. Section 21 of the Non-Fatal Offences Against the Person Act 1997 provides that a minor who has attained the age of sixteen years may personally consent to any surgical, medical or dental treatment and that it shall not be necessary to obtain any parental consent in such instance. However, it may be wiser to seek written consent for any medical treatment from all parents.

[9.71] Schools frequently devise policies on school tours and this practice is to be recommended. Pupils and parents ought to know in advance what the policy states regarding smoking, drug-related offences, alcohol consumption and other contentious areas. However, no school policy can cover every eventuality that may arise and this document should state that the board of management retains an overall discretion in the event of the unexpected occurrence arising.

[9.72] Some English school tours illustrate how inadequately supervised school tours can lead to disaster as was the case in *Porter v City of Bradford MBC*.[137]

---

[134] *Jacques v Oxford County Council* (1968) 66 LGR 440.

[135] In 1972-1973, three fatal accidents occurred during English school tours, one in the Cairngorms, one in Snowdonia and one in the Lake District, see Barrell and Partington, pp 493-495.

[136] In 1988 four teenage pupils, who were left unsupervised for approximately 50 minutes while skiing, fell 300 feet to their deaths, The Times, 27 January 1989; see similar cases in Harris, *The Law Relating to Schools*, (1990) Fourmat Publications, p 261.

[137] Court of Appeal, unrep, 14 January 1985.

This case arose out of a field trip organised by a geology teacher for his 12 to 15-16 year old students to Shipley Glen. One of the group, "P", had been rolling large stones down an incline at the base of which were five of the other students when the teacher remonstrated with him. The teacher continued up the glen with a group of more serious-minded students of geology. When the teacher was out of sight and sound of the earlier mischief-maker and his friends, P commenced throwing stones from a bridge over a 15 minute period during which period he dropped a stone on a pupil's head fracturing her skull. Bennett J, in the High Court, held the teacher was negligent as, in the light of the earlier occurrence, he was put on notice of P's mischievous propensities. This was a foreseeable danger and the teacher, the judge stated, should have used his best efforts to keep the party together. On appeal, Stephenson LJ upheld the decision. While he did not wish to impose on teachers a duty of supervision which went beyond that of a reasonable parent, he stated, this teacher had failed in his duty to supervise this particular set of pupils.

[9.73] In *Last v Tipperary (NR) VEC*,[138] a tour to the Clare Glens for a group of first year Community College students had a different outcome. Two teachers were in charge of 30 students. Having dismounted the bus, one group of students followed one of the teachers while another group mounted a higher path. The plaintiff stated that when the teacher told them to come down to the lower level, he began to walk down but it was too steep and he collided with a tree injuring himself. His knee, he stated, was affected by the cold and was sore when he cycled for two or three miles. Dismissing the case, the judge concluded that the plaintiff himself had not exercised reasonable care.

Volunteers

[9.74] Parents frequently volunteer or are requested to assist in such activities. The teacher in charge ought to brief supervising parents on the nature of the school tour (or other activity) and on what is required to be done or avoided in the course of the day. Furthermore, key areas of supervision, such as road crossing, should be retained by the supervising teachers. If volunteers are permitted to supervise games, they ought to be well acquainted with the rules of the game, be capable of enforcing the rules of the game, and they should penalise any rough play.

[9.75] If a game shows signs of getting out of control, it should be abandoned immediately. While the assistance of parental or other supervisors (eg student-teachers or senior pupils) may be invaluable in schools, there are occasions when

---

[138] Circuit Court, 20 January 1997.

such persons should not be left to supervise alone as they may have insufficient skill or experience in handling a crisis or a potentially dangerous situation.

Road Crossing

[9.76] When pupils are being taken through the streets as part of the school activities, the teacher's duty to take reasonable care for the welfare of his or her pupils continues. In *Toole v Sherbourne Pouffes Ltd*,[139] the then six year old pupil plaintiff was seriously injured by a van at a patrolled road crossing. The plaintiff and his class had left the school with his teacher who walked at the head of the "crocodile" of pupils as they approached the school crossing on the main roadway. When close to the road crossing, the plaintiff appears to have darted out suddenly on to the crossing where he was struck by a passing van.[140] The trial judge exonerated the van driver but imposed liability on the local authority who employed the patroller and on the teacher who had used a defective system of crossing the road. On appeal, Lord Denning scrutinised, *inter alia,* the sytem of road crossing employed by the teacher at the material time and concluded:

> "On the material before us, the fault was the fault of the man on the pedestrian crossing; and I would not blame anybody else, neither the system nor the teacher."[141]

[9.77] Teachers do not have control over traffic and unpatrolled road crossings. If such a duty is assumed, however, the teacher must discharge it reasonably and to the best of his ability. However, a teacher who undertakes assumed duties on an habitual basis may give rise to an expectation that he will continue to discharge that duty and failure to do so may result in a finding of negligence.[142]

Physical Education and Sporting Activities

[9.78] The courts recognise that an holistic education should include physical education (PE hereafter) and that accidents will happen. Teachers are not required by legislation to have a specific qualification for teaching PE or games. Yet, in order that they can discharge their common law and statutory duties,[143] employers must ensure, where inherent dangers and risks exist, that they are qualified and experienced to handle those risks. Equipment and sporting activities should be within the range of the pupils' capabilities and within the

---

[139] [1971] RTR 479.

[140] I am indebted to Oliver Mahon BL for drawing my attention to this case, see Mahon, *Negligence and the Teacher*, (1995) Ennis Teachers' Centre, p 46.

[141] [1971] RTR 479 at 483.

[142] See generally Barrell and Partington, *Teachers and the Law* (1985), Methuen, pp 418-420.

[143] Under the Safety, Health and Welfare at Work Act 1989 and (General Application) Regulations 1993 (SI 44/1993).

competence of teachers. High-rebound equipment such as trampettes can give rise to serious spinal injuries so a court would be likely to require that a teacher using such apparatus would possess a third level PE qualification in order to discharge his duty of care.[144] In 1968 the English Department of Education and Science (England) warned of the dangers attached to apparatus giving a high rebound and to the "Fosbury flop" method of high jumping[145] ie jumping backwards and landing on the back.

[9.79] In *Kershaw v Hampshire County Council*[146] a twelve year-old girl suffered injury as a result of vaulting and somersaulting over a box having bounced on the trampette when the teacher was absent from the gymnasium. The judge held that the use of a trampette was somewhat more dangerous than the usual springboard and that the trampette's use had a greater tendency to lead to an accident. He ruled that the teacher's presence was necessary in order to provide the necessary support and supervision required during this particular exercise. If the teacher had to attend another group in the gymnasium, or absent herself entirely, she should have stopped the activity until her return. While trained and experienced teachers of PE will know how to deal with advanced exercises, this may not be the case with teachers who have not received adequate training in the use of equipment of this kind.

Pupils with Disability

[9.80] Good communication between home and school is necessary concerning a pupil's health and fitness for PE activities and sport. While no negligence was held to exist where a slow learner sustained injury when vaulting over a "horse,"[147] it may have been otherwise if that pupil was under a disability. The case of *Moore v Hampshire County Council*[148] indicates that if a pupil is suffering from a known or suspected disability, more vigilant supervision and more positive instruction than normal may be required. The plaintiff, who suffered from a congenital hip defect, injured her ankle during a PE class. The pupil's mother had written to the school prohibiting her daughter's participation in any form of PE or games. It seems the pupil persuaded her teacher to allow her to participate in a PE activity during which she was injured.

---

[144] See 'Safety in Physical Education', 1980, Department of Education and Science (HMSO), p 15.

[145] See Administrative Memorandum, No 2/68; 'Physical Education Apparatus in Schools and Colleges' cited in Barrell and *Teachers and the Law,* (1985), Methuen, p 399.

[146] Unreported, 1982 case cited in *The Head's Legal Guide*, 3-104.

[147] "£15,000 claim by schoolboy is dismissed," Evening Press, 12 November 1985, Martin J.

[148] (1982) 80 LGR 481.

[9.81] On appeal from the lower court, which held for the school, Lord Denning stated that the standard required of a teacher was reasonably high and in this case that standard had not been discharged. He was of the view that the teacher, who was already on notice of the pupil's deficiency, should have checked the situation with the mother before allowing the pupil to participate in the class. Further, the judge continued, the teacher should have given the girl more positive instructions and closer supervision. In the judge's opinion, this was a case without a defence. Lord Watkins emphasised that where a school's attention is drawn to a child's medical condition and a prohibition is put on any form of physical activity, the school is under a special duty to follow that instruction until there is a relaxation of the prohition from the quarter in which it is given.[149]

[9.82] In *Morrell v Owen*,[150] it was held that the duty of care owed by coaches and organisers of a sporting event for persons with disabilities is more onerous than that owed to able-bodied participants. This case involved a training session organised under the control of a British Sports Association for such persons during which a paraplegic amateur archer was injured. A training session was taking place concurrently with a discus-throwing session in a hall which was divided by a fishnet-curtain when one discus went off course and struck the archer on the head causing him permanent brain damage. As the accident was reasonably foreseeable, the judge found for the injured archer. He stated that the duties of those who coach disabled athletes included instruction in safe practice and procedure, provision of a safe entrance and exit to practice areas, and provision of some person to keep watch over the movement of the disabled athletes. It may be concluded, therefore, that when a school is dealing with disabled pupils, more vigilant supervision and more positive instruction is generally required in order to discharge the duty of care.

Suitable Apparel

[9.83] Schools ought to ensure that both pupils and parents are familiar with its rules and that such rules are consistently applied. This is particularly true with safety-related rules. Pupils ought to be properly attired for PE and games and school rules should state what the appropriate clothing comprises.[151] It is usual to prohibit, in the interest of the pupils' safety, the wearing of jewellery during such classes.[152]

---

[149] (1982) 80 LGR 481.

[150] The Times, 14 December 1993.

[151] Barrell and Partington, p 401, mention an unreported case in which a child slipped and injured himself while doing gymnastics in stockings.

[152] See generally *The Head's Legal Guide*, Bulletin, Issue 9, March 1994, School Sports, p 13.

Extra Precautions

[9.84] Accidents may occur when pupils are vaulting over a piece of equipment and *Gibbs v Barking Corporation*[153] underscores the importance of providing some form of "stand-by" assistance when pupils are landing. The judge, in the Court of Appeal, stated "the games master does not seem to have acted with the promptitude which the law requires". On the other hand, when four classes were in the gymnasium and one boy was injured while vaulting over "a buck," when the teacher was engaged with another class, it was held that the supervision accorded with standard practice as the exercise had been safely performed for years.[154] By contrast, in a Canadian case liability was imposed on the school when an overweight thirteen year-old student, who had shown anxiety over the performance of the exercise, was required by the teacher to take a jump from a height of seven feet.[155]

Games Generally

[9.85] In sporting events generally, the law of the land plays an important role[156] in that no individual can licence another to commit a crime. This is an evolving area of tort both here and in England.[157] The case of *R v Billinghurst*[158] was a prosecution for criminal violence on an English rugby field for a field assault. The law further evolved in *Condon v Bassi*[159] when an award of £4,000 damages to a soccer player, who sustained a broken leg in an illegal tackle, was upheld by the Court of Appeal.

[9.86] In 1996, it was held in *Smolden v Whitworth*[160] that a referee can be held liable in negligence for injury suffered by a player during a Rugby Union match. The 17-year-old plaintiff was injured when a scrum collapsed and his neck was broken. A significant element in this finding was that it was a Colt's game (for those under 19 years) to which special rules and regulations applied.

[9.87] The judge at first instance accepted expert evidence that approximately six collapsed scrummages would not be abnormal for such a game, that about

---

[153] [1936] 1 All ER 115.

[154] *Wright v Cheshire County Council* [1952] 2 All ER 789.

[155] *Boese v Board of Education of Saint Paul's Roman Catholic Separate School District*, No 20, 97 TLR (3d) 643, Sirois J.

[156] See *R v Bradshaw* (1878) 14 Cox cc 83; *R v Donovan* (1934) 2 KB 498.

[157] See further Edward Grayson, 'Breaking new ground in schools', NLJ, 29 July 1988, p 532; See generally Grayson, *Sport and The Law*, (1995), Butterworths, pp 121-2.

[158] [1978] Crim LR 553.

[159] [1985] 2 All ER 453.

[160] TLR, 19 April 1996; see further Robinson, "Damages for academic under-performance; pupils as plaintiffs in Bennet and Meredith, eds, *Education and the Law* 9 (1997), 93 at 95-6; see also *Education and the Law* 8 (1996) 174.

three or four times that number had occurred during the game in question, and the referee had fallen below the standard of a reasonably competent referee in dealing with the scrummages during the game resulting in the plaintiff's neck injury.

[9.88] Moreover, there was clear evidence that the referee had neglected to enforce the "crouch-touch-pause-engage tactic" designed to alleviate the dangers caused by the forceful coming together of the scrums.

[9.89] In the light of the totality of the evidence, the judge found that the second defendant was liable to the plaintiff for his acts and omissions during the game. He rejected the referee's defence of *volenti non fit injuria* stating that although the plaintiff had consented to the risk of injury in this game, he could not by inference be held to have consented to the referee's breach of duty. In upholding the trial judge's decision[161] the Court of Appeal ruled that:

    (a) the degree of care required of a referee was that which was appropriate in all the circumstances of the case;

    (b) full account required to be taken of the factual context in which a referee exercised his powers and functions;

    (c) the referee could not properly be held liable for errors of judgment, oversights or lapses of which any referee could be guilty in the setting of a fast-moving and vigorous game; and

    (d) the threshold of liability was high and would not be easily crossed.

Even though there was no precedent for this decision, the Court held the imposition of liability on the referee in these circumstances was just and reasonable and was not contrary to public policy.

School Games and Sports

[9.90] Turning to the school context, in body contact sports such as football and rugby, an adequate standard of instruction, coaching and refereeing must be provided by the school to ensure that certain techniques are performed so as to avoid serious injury to participants. When teachers are in charge of school games, their primary responsibility is to supervise and control the game, and to penalise rough play. It seems that a defence of "general and approved practice" may only succeed when a teacher implements strict supervision of games.

[9.91] Games should be played only in suitable areas and when pupils are familiar with the rules of the game. It has been held that if the teacher knows, or ought to have known, that a game is being played in a dangerous manner or in an unsuitable place and therefore likely to make it dangerous, he is negligent if he

---

[161] [1997] ELR 249 CA.

does not take proper steps to prevent danger.[162] The school may be judged liable if the game is of such a nature or is played in such a manner as would be likely to cause an accident, but apparently not otherwise.[163]

[9.92] However, the courts recognise that risks of injury arise in this sphere and accidents cannot be eliminated. In *IRC v McMullen*[164] the House of Lords affirmed earlier decisions that school sport is classified as "purely educational". The widely-publicised *Van Oppen*[165] decision dealt with a number of legal, sporting and insurance issues. In that case, the 16-year-old plaintiff suffered very severe injury to his cervical spine when making a tackle in a rugby game. He later sued his school for alleged inadequate rugby coaching or instruction, failing to advise his father of the risk of serious injury in rugby football, failing to advise his father of the need to take out personal injury insurance, and for omitting to arrange such insurance.

[9.93] This case does not deviate from previous precedents governing liability for personal injuries sustained during games or sport. However, it attempts to extend the parameters in respect of the insurance claim. The previous year the school had received a report from the Medical Officers of Schools' Association (MOSA) recommending that personal accident insurance be taken out to cover rugby injuries. At the time of the accident the school had not effected such insurance cover although it insured later in 1981. The duty of care in respect of sport and games was laid down by Boreham J in *Van Oppen* as a duty:

(a) not to require the pupils to participate in any activity which a reasonable parent would consider carried an unacceptable risk of injury (rugby football was not within this category);

(b) to take reasonable care to ensure that the game was properly organised and supervised; and

(c) to take reasonable care to ensure that the pupils were taught and applied the basic skills and proper techniques so that they could play the game with reasonable safety.

---

[162] 15 *Halsbury's Laws*, 564 citing *Gilmore v West Hampshire Corporation* (1937) 81 SJ 630; note the statutory duty under s 9(1)(d) of the Safety, Health and Welfare at Work Act 1989 which requires an employee to report to his employer or his immediate supervisor, without unreasonable delay, any defects in plant, equipment, place of work or system of work, which might endanger safety, health or welfare, of which he becomes aware.

[163] 15 *Halsbury's Laws*, 564 citing *Gillmore v LCC* [1938] 4 All ER 331, *Dziwenka v The Queen in the Right of Alberta* (1971) WLR 356; *Cf Jones v LCC* (1932) 48 TLR 577 and *Ward v Hertfordshire County Council* (1970) 1 WLR 356; [1970] 1 All ER 535.

[164] [1981] AC 1.

[165] *Van Oppen v Trustees of the Bedford Charity* [1989] 1 All ER 273, [1989] 3 All ER 389.

[9.94] These basic principles are broadly applicable to all games. The Court affirmed that the school's duty of reasonable care extended to foreseeable injury to a pupil's person and property both in school and on the playing fields. It ruled, however, that the school in the instant case was not negligent in the conduct of the game and that there was no general duty to insure even against negligence.[166]

Teacher Participation in Games

[9.95] On some occasions, teachers participate with students in games and sports. In *Affutu-Nartoy v Clarke and INLA*[167] "a wholly admirable teacher" and his employer were held liable for damages for unlawfully tackling a 15- year-old boy, smaller than himself, during a rugby game. While participating in the game, the teacher momentarily forgot he was playing with young boys and used his adult strength in a high tackle allowed by the rules of the game. The court held that the teacher owed the traditional duty of care to the plaintiff, which was forseeably breached because of the age and size differences of the players. It considered that, while it was wrong for the teacher to have any physical contact with a boy in these circumstances, it was not wrong for him to have positioned himself on one of the teams so as to demonstrate the normal contact skills of the game such as catching, passing and kicking.

[9.96] By analogy, the above legal principles also apply to other contact sports such as hurling, camogie, hockey, football and cricket when a teacher can foresee the possible outcome of active participation by an adult. In *Martin v The Downs School*,[168] a 13-year-old pupil was hit by a cricket ball bowled by the schoolteacher in charge. It was alleged that the teacher bowled too high and at too fast a speed and had also failed to provide protective head gear for the pupil. This matter was settled out of court and the court approved the settlement.

Swimming

[9.97] The degree of care required when pupils are involved in swimming is likely to be higher than in an academic class as the risk of injury is higher at this time. Strict supervision of pupils is necessary at the swimming pool and on the way to and from the pool. The courts, however, recognise that children can meet with accidents even when they are under supervision as *Clarke v Bethnal Green Borough Council*[169] indicates. In this case the plaintiff was injured when standing on a springboard prior to diving. Another child clung to the board from underneath and when he let go of the springboard, it shot upwards pitching the

---

[166] *Van Oppen v Trustees of the Bedford Charity* [1989] 1 All ER 273 at 287, 291, [1989] 3 All ER 389.

[167] The Times, 9 February 1984.

[168] (1991) *Halsbury's Laws*, MR 91/1653.

[169] (1939) 55 TLR 519.

plaintiff off-course and on to the edge of the baths. The court held that this was an unprecedented, unforeseeable accident and so the swimming pool attendant could not reasonably be expected to guard against it.

[9.98] In the English context, the *Head's Legal Guide*[170] points out that where a school uses a public pool, it must comply with the supervision and life guarding policy operating at that pool. Regardless of where the swimming is taking place, the Guide makes a number of recommendations which may be of assistance to schools in organising their swimming policies.[171] As to the size of the group of swimmers, that will depend on the age and mental maturity of the pupils, the proportions and facilities of the pool and the number of teachers and instructors on duty. The amount of supervision required will depend on a number of factors including:

    (a) the degree of the disability,[172] if any, of the pupils involved;

    (b) the age and mental maturity of the pupils;

    (c) the type of swimming pool and its facilities; and

    (d) the skill of the instructor.[173]

The decision in *Morrell v Owen*[174] indicates that where pupils with disability are involved the degree of supervision required by a court may be higher than that normally expected so it is prudent to increase the number of supervisors of swimming classes accordingly.

Educational Malpractice

[9.99] In Ireland, the past decade has shown a remarkable growth of public interest in education and an unprecedented analysis of the legal context within which teachers operate. Revised marking schemes, promotional posts, appeals, lost examination papers, fair procedures, misdescribed courses, negligent advice in the filling of Central Application Office forms all provide potential grounds for complaint.[175] From the case law on educational malpractice in the USA and elsewhere, it is likely that the Irish courts in the future will litigate the issue of whether a poorly-educated pupil would have a case in negligence against the school on the grounds of the school's poor performance.[176]

---

[170] *Croner's Head's Legal Guide*, (1994), Kingston, Surrey, 3-112 to 3-114, which is updated annually; see also booklet entitled "Swimming Pools" published by the then Department of Education and Science in 1993 available from HMSO.

[171] See *Croner's Head Teacher's Bulletin*, Issue 9, March 1994 on School Sports, pp 14-15.

[172] *Head's Legal Guide*, see 'Swimming Regulations in Special Schools', 3-113 to 3-114.

[173] *Head's Legal Guide*, Swimming Regulations in Special Schools.

[174] The Times, 14 December 1993.

[175] In the English setting, see Times Higher Education Supplement, 12 July 1996, p 9.

[176] See McMahon and Binchy, Ch 16 at p 303.

[9.100] In England, the question of "failing schools" has been the subject of much public debate. The closure of Hackney Downs school,[177] under the Education Act 1993 for failing to provide its pupils with an acceptable standard of education[178] brings to the fore the question of the possible liability of a school to its pupils and their parents for incompetent teaching, an issue which the Irish courts have not yet been called upon to address.

Educational Malpractice in the USA

[9.101] Educational malpractice cases in the USA fall mainly into two main groups:

   (a) alleged failure to educate in rudimentary skills; and

   (b) alleged incorrect placement in a programme of special education.[179]

The outcome of these cases suggest a reluctance to open the floodgates to educational malpractice suits[180] on the grounds of public policy even when plaintiffs suffer loss, damage or injury as the case of *Snow v State*[181] illustrates. In that case the three year old plaintiff was administered an intelligence quotient (IQ) test on foot of which he was sent to a special State school for mentally retarded children. Subsequently, it was discovered that the boy was merely suffering from deafness which was not diagnosed because the IQ test administered was inappropriate for deaf children. The trial judge found for the plaintiff and the New York Appellate Division upheld his decision stating, however, that the cause of action was grounded in medical negligence rather than in educational negligence.

Academic Underperformance in England

[9.102] Recent Court of Appeal cases[182] in England recognised the possibility of legal action against a Local Education Authority (LEA) if those whom the

---

[177] And the William Tyndale school in the 1970s.

[178] See Harris, (1996) 'Too bad? The closure of Hackney Downs School under Section 225 of the Education Act 1993' in *Education and the Law*, 8, 109-125, 109; see further, Harris (1994), 'Poor educational standards and Part V of the Education Act 1993', *Education and the Law* 6, 63-73, 70.

[179] See further McGlade-Cooney, 'Educational Malpractice Suits - Another American Import?' The Irish Student Law Review, (1991) 1, 4-13.

[180] See *Peter W v San Francisco United School District* 60 Cal App 3d 814; Cal Rptr 854 (1976); *Donoghue v Copiague Union Free School District* 64 AC 2d 29; 407 NYS 2d 874 (1978); affd, 47 NY 2d 440 391 NE 2d 1352; 418 NYS 2d 375 (1979); *Hoffman v Board of Education* 64 AD 2d 369; 410 NYS 2d 99 (1978); reversed, 49 NY 2d 121 400 NE 2d 317,424 NYS 2d 376 (1979).

[181] 98 AD 2d 442; 469 NYS 2d 959 (1983); affd, 64 NY 2d 745 NE 2d 454; 485 NYS 2d 1987 (1984).

[182] Cited as the *Dorset, Hampshire and Bromley* appeals ("the education appeals") to the House of Lords (cited as *X (Minors) v Bedfordshire County Council Appeals* [1995] 2 AC 633 HL; these included the following cases; *X (Minors v Bedfordshire County Council; M (a Minor) v Newham LBC; E (a Minor) v Dorset County Council; Christmas v Hampshire County Council; Keating v Mayor and Burgesess of the London Borough of Bromley* [1995] ELR 404, HL.

authority employs to cater to the needs of a child with special educational needs, such as educational psychologists, teachers and counsellors, negligently fail to access and make provision for such needs thereby affecting prejudicially the child's attainment and employment prospects.

[9.103] The cases of three children with similar problems were heard together. One child was suffering from dyslexia, another had learning difficulties while the third alleged that the LEA failed to place him in a reasonably appropriate school and had failed to properly enquire into his educational capacity. They claimed that the LEAs were in breach of their duty of care by failing to provide for their special needs and claimed damages for personal and intellectual impairment and lack of development which they allegedly suffered as a result of the breach of duty.

[9.104] The Court of Appeal held that the above-mentioned employees of the LEA would be in a position to foresee injury to the pupils if they acted carelessly towards them as all of those positions created a sufficiently proximate relationship to give rise to a duty of care:

(a) a teacher would create such a relationship when advising on learning capacity;

(b) an educational psychologist would create such a relationship when presenting a professional opinion on a pupil's learning capacity; and

(c) a council official would create such a relationship when advising or acting on foot of that report as to what ought to be done.

[9.105] In the *Dorset, Hampshire and Bromley*[183] appeals ("the education appeals") to the House of Lords the Court held that individuals and school authorities, vicariously as employers, could be held liable to pay common law damages for failure to discharge the standard of care of a reasonable professional. In these appeals the standard of care laid down in *Bolam v Friern Hospital Management Committee*[184] was applied while the test in *Dunne v National Maternity Hospital*[185] would most likely be followed in Ireland.

[9.106] The Court held that a local authority was not vicariously liable for the actions of social workers and psychiatrists instructed by it to report on children who were suspected of being sexually abused because it would not be just and reasonable to impose a duty of care on the local authority or (*per* Lord Nolan) it would be contrary to public policy to do so. The duty of the social workers and psychiatrists was to advise the local authority in regard to the welfare of the

---

[183] [1995] 2 AC 633 HL.
[184] [1957] 1 WLR 582.
[185] [1989] ILRM 735.

plaintiffs but not to advise or treat the plaintiffs. This decision contrasts sharply with the outcome in "the education cases" where the LEA was held to be holding itself out to provide services to members of the public.

The Education Cases

[9.107] In *E (a Minor) v Dorset County Council*[186] the claim was grounded on the fact that the LEA was holding itself out as offering psychological services and advice to the public. The court held that a statutory body offering such a service was generally in a similar position to any private person or organisation offering such a service, ie it was under a duty of care to persons using the service to exercise care in its conduct.

[9.108] In holding the LEA vicariously liable for the actions of its employees, the psychologists, the court found no potential conflict between the psychologists' duty to the plaintiff and his duty to the LEA. If the claim was justiciable, then the ordinary principles of negligence applied whether the damage to the plaintiff was reasonably foreseeable, whether there was proximity of relationship between the parties; and whether it was fair, just and reasonable to impose such a duty of care.

[9.109] In particular, the requirement that it had to be just and reasonable to impose a common law duty of care in all the circumstances before liability in negligence would be imposed, applied not only where the plaintiff's claim was for pure economic loss, but also where the claim was for physical damage.[187]

[9.110] In *Christmas v Hampshire County Council*,[188] the plaintiff, who had special educational needs, alleged that his head teacher in a primary school had failed to refer him for formal assessment or to an educational psychologist. He further alleged that the county advisory service had failed to identify, diagnose and assess his dyslexia or to refer him to an educational psychologist. As a result of these failures, the plaintiff claimed he had been placed at a considerable disadvantage in achieving his potential and that his job opportunities and prospects had been greatly diminished. The court ruled that the LEA was vicariously liable for the negligence of the headmaster in failing to refer the plaintiff for formal assessment and to an educational psychologist, and the negligence of the county advisory service who failed to identify, diagnose and

---

[186] *X (Minors) v Bedfordshire County Council* [1995] 2 AC 633 HL; *M (a Minor) v Newham LBC; E (a Minor) v Dorset County Council; Christmas v Hampshire County Council; Keating v Mayor and Burgesess of the London Borough of Bromley* [1995] ELR 404, HL.

[187] *Geddis v Properties of Bann Reservoir* (1878) 3 App Cas 430; *Anns v Merton London Borough* [1977] 2 All ER 492 and *Home Office v Dorset Yacht Co Ltd* [1970] 2 All ER 294 considered.

[188] [1995] ELR 404 HL.

assess the plaintiff's dyslexia or (i) to refer or (ii) to advise referral to an educational psychologist.

[9.111] Thus, educational psychologists and other members of the staff of an education authority, including teachers, were held to owe a duty to use reasonable professional skill and care in the assessment and determination of a child's educational needs and the authority was vicariously liable for any breach of such duties by its employees.[189]

[9.112] It is submitted that issues related to the alleged incorrect marking of examination papers, and alleged incorrect or negligent careers advice are two areas which could conceivably ground an action in the Irish courts in the future. One Australian case is relevant to this context.[190] In New South Wales, the plaintiff who was sitting for the Higher School Certificate examination, was wrongly marked in one subject with the resultant loss of his place at his chosen third level institution. This apparently clear case of educational negligence, however, was settled out of court.

New Developments in Tort

Violent Pupils

[9.113] There have been a number of assaults on teachers, both here and in Britain,[191] by violent pupils in recent years and the Philip Lawrence murder in particular has focused public attention on this serious problem. Although an action will not normally lie against the parent or guardian of a pupil who has injured or damaged the person or property of another, a parent may be liable in certain instances. McMahon and Binchy have summarised the circumstances relating to a broad range of conduct in which negligence may arise as a result of:

    (a) dangerous articles;

    (b) the child's dangerous propensities; and

    (c) failure to control the child properly.[192]

[9.114] Thus, a parent may be liable if he or she negligently entrusts a dangerous article to a child in circumstances where injury to the child or another person is foreseeable.[193] So if a parent gives his son a weapon as he boards the school bus

---

[189] See further *X (Minors) v Bedfordshire County Council; M (A Minor) v Newham LBC; E (A Minor) v Dorset County Council;* [1995] 3 All ER 353 HL.

[190] Cited in Ramsey, 'Educational Negligence and the Legislation of Education' (1988), University of New South Wales Law Journal, 2, 194-219.

[191] See *R v Higgitt,* The Times, 17 March 1972; Daily Mail, 16 March 1972; see further Barrell and Partington, *Teachers and the Law* (1985), Methuen, pp 464-467.

[192] McMahon and Binchy, p 295 and generally Ch 16.

[193] *Newton v Edgerley* [1959] 1 WLR 1031 at 1032.

and a child or a teacher is subsequently injured in school, the parent may be liable. However, each case depends on its own facts. Likewise, if a parent knows that his child has attacked others and has taken no initiative to protect others from such foreseeable harm, then he may also be answerable in negligence.

Duty of School Authority

[9.115] The extent to which school authorities owe a duty of care to a teacher, to other employees and to their pupils, for personal injuries sustained as a result of an assault by a pupil known to the school to be of a violent disposition and propensity has not been addressed by the Irish courts. However, the following three cases suggest that such criteria could ground an action against the school.

[9.116] The case of *Trim Joint District School Board v Kelly*[194] arose out of yard supervision in Trim Industrial School on 12 February 1912. John Kelly, an assistant master in the school was supervising boys in the playground as part of his duties, when he was assaulted by a number of them and struck on the head with heavy wooden mallets. As a result of his injuries, the teacher died. In an action brought by his next-of-kin, damages of £100 were awarded by the County Court judge under the Workmen's Compensation Act 1906 (the 1906 Act). The school appealed to the House of Lords arguing that the teacher's death did not arise out of the course of employment. At issue was the meaning of the expression "accident arising out of and in the course of employment" within the meaning of the 1906 Act. In affirming the decision of the lower court, the House of Lords stated that the character of the school and the class of boy must be taken into account. The boys, it observed, came from the workhouses and many of them were "turbulent and unruly". The Court held that the teacher's death was caused by accident which arose out of employment within the meaning of the 1906 Act. Earl Loreburn stated:

> "This unfortunate man was killed because it was his duty to maintain discipline in a school and while he was actually doing his duty there. There had been a conspiracy among the boys to assault and wound him because he did his duty and in pursuance of the conspiracy two of the boys struck him a fatal blow."[195]

The appeal was dismissed and the boys, who were tried for murder, were convicted of manslaughter. Damages of £200 were awarded to John Kelly's next-of-kin.

[9.117] The more recent English decision in *Campbell v Tameside MBC*[196] gives weight to the view that a teacher injured by a violent pupil, known to the board

---

[194] [1914] AC 667.
[195] [1914] AC 667.
[196] [1982] 2 All ER 791.

to be of a dangerous propensity, could succeed in a negligence action against the school board. The teacher plaintiff in this case suffered severe personal injuries as a result of an attack in class by a violent eleven year old pupil and as a result had to take early retirement. She subsequently sought to bring an action against the Local Education Authority (LEA) arguing that it was negligent in permitting a child of such violent disposition to attend an ordinary school. The LEA refused to disclose the relevant documents, which, it was contended, would show that it had knowledge of the pupil's violent nature. Holding for the teacher, in the Court of Appeal, Ackner LJ stated that "the private promise of confidentiality must yield to the public interest ...". Accordingly, he upheld the decision of the lower court that the documents be disclosed in the light of public interest. Access to information under the Data Protection Act 1988, the Freedom of Information Act 1997 and the Education Act 1998, is the subject matter of Chapter 12 below.

Team Negligence

[9.118] The issue of "team" negligence arose in an English hospital case, *Wilsher v Essex Area Health Authority,*[197] which is analogous to the school situation. The proposition was advanced in this case, by counsel for the plaintiff, of setting a "team" standard of care, whereby each of the persons who constituted the staff of the unit, held themselves out as capable of undertaking the specialised procedures which the unit set out to perform. This concept of "team" negligence sought to attribute to each individual member of the team a duty to live up to the standards of the unit as a whole. While this concept was not established, the court held there was no reason why, in certain circumstances, a health authority could not be directly liable to a plaintiff if it failed to provide sufficient or properly qualified or competent medical staff for the unit.

[9.119] Relating the findings of this case to the school situation, it appears that the onus lies with the school authority and also with the Department to provide properly qualified and competent staff for schools. Such competence obviously includes the ability to maintain the degree of order or discipline necessary to permit the educative process to take place. Clearly, it would also include the professional degree of competence required to teach all the subjects of the new curriculum and syllabus.

---

[197] [1986] 2 All ER 801 (CA).

Chapter 10

The Teacher's Duty of Care: School Discipline

Introduction

[10.01] It is generally accepted that a certain degree of order or discipline is
necessary if the educative process is to take place. Hence, the advice given to the
young teacher in Laurence's novel, *The Rainbow* is equally pertinent today: "you
have to keep order if you wish to teach".[1] How the requisite degree of order is to
be achieved, however, is a perennial problem, not just in Ireland but globally. As
has been seen in Chapter 8, the administration of school discipline is also a
human rights issue.[2] Article 28.1(e) of The Convention on the Rights of the
Child[3] requires State parties to take all appropriate steps to ensure that school
discipline is administered in a manner consistent with the child's human dignity
and in conformity with the Convention. This chapter aims to extract the legal
principles which underpin school discipline in contemporary schools.

A Tradition of Informality

[10.02] The distinctive non-State character of Irish schools has led to a tradition
of informal disciplinary procedures[4] governed almost entirely by rules,
regulations and circulars issued by the Department of Education.[5] In the past the
disciplinary authority of teachers went largely unchallenged. Although school
discipline was subject to the application of basic legal principles, the law seldom
intruded on this sphere of school life as few school discipline cases were
litigated in the Irish courts.[6] Little conflict was perceived to exist between the
disciplinary role of the teacher and the obligations of church and State in

---

[1] (1949), Penguin, p 25.
[2] See para **[8.22]** above.
[3] Which Ireland has signed and ratified.
[4] *Cf* the position in Europe, see *The Legal Status of Pupils in Europe*, de Groof and Penneman,
eds, (1998) Kluwer Law International.
[5] See Department of Education Circulars 8/82; 20/90; Circular M 33/91, Guidelines towards a
Positive Policy for School Behaviour and Discipline: A Suggested Code of Behaviour and
Discipline for Post-Primary Schools. For judicial criticism of informal administrative methods
see *O'Callaghan v Meath VEC*, High Court, unrep, 30 November 1990, Costello P, p 1;
McCann v Minister for Education [1997] ILRM 1.
[6] See however, *McCann v Mannion* (1932) ILTR 161; *McGee v Cunnane* (1932) ILTR 147; *State
(Smullen) v Duffy* [1980] ILRM 46; *O'Callaghan v Collins*, Irish Independent 1 December,
1990, 1; *Murtagh v Board of Management of St Emer's National School* [1991] 2 ILRM 549.

education. Consequently, the teacher's role in school discipline remained, until recently, unregulated by statute being subject mainly to non-statutory rules and regulations. Hence, it is necessary to seek guidance from earlier cases or from decisions emanating from other common law jurisdictions which may be of persuasive influence only in the Irish courts.

Changing Social and Legal Context

[10.03] That approaches to school discipline have changed radically is clear from a perusal of Joyce's *A Handbook of School Management*[7] in which he describes a rigid code of conduct where each pupil "toed the line" ie they stood around "in drafts" with their toes touching a line in the form of an arc adopting the methods of Joseph Lancaster for the education of the masses.[8]

[10.04] The Irish Law Times and Solicitors' Journal of September 1893 states that it is clear law and has always commended itself to the common sense of mankind that the relation of master and pupil carries with it the right of reasonable punishment. It also draws attention to the complaints of excessive punishment in Irish schools of that time which is endorsed by National Archive material.[9] The belief that corporal punishment of pupils served important educational interests is firmly rooted in both Jewish[10] and Christian[11] traditions. This belief was supported by the common law which, subject to any statutory constraints, upheld the parents' right to discipline their child whether by use of a cane or by other means.[12] Thus, the common law upheld the right of the teacher, until recently,[13] to use moderate reasonable corporal punishment on pupils in his or her role as parental substitute during the school day.[14] What constituted reasonable punishment would depend on the facts of the case, the age of the

---

[7] Joyce, *A Handbook of School Managment* (4th ed, 1872), McGlashan and Gill.

[8] The rod or ruler seem to have figured centrally in a number of indigenous hedge-schools. Carleton spoke of the use of a large broad ruler as "the emblem of his power, the woeful instrument of executive justice and the signal of terror to all within his jurisdiction." See *Traits and Stories of the Irish Peasantry*, (1843/44), Dublin, Curry, pp 293-302; Porter, *The Life and Times of Henry Cooke,* DD, LLD, President of Assembly's College, (1871), Belfast, London, Murray, pp 3-4; Little, *Malachi Horan Remembers*, (1976), Mercier, p 52; Walters, *The Story of a Hedge School Master*, (1974), Mercier, p 33.

[9] In National Archive Office, Bishop Street, Education File (ED) File 998, 603, 709, 1933, 2004, 2063, 2200, 2271; ED file 9 4414 details a case heard at Union Hall Petty Sessions in which it was alleged that a pupil received 16 slaps of a holly stick 16 times in one day for failure at lessons; see further *Ballinrobe Chronicle*, 21 June 1884.

[10] *The Babylonian Talmud*, Epstein, ed, (1935), London, Soncino Press, p 106.

[11] *Good News Bible*, Proverbs, (1976), Fontana, paras 12.13, 13.24, 15.17, and 19.18.

[12] *Mansell v Griffin* [1908] 1 KB 166-7.

[13] See Non-Fatal Offences Against the Person Act 1997, s 24.

[14] *Street on Torts* (10 ed, 1999) Brazier & Murray eds, Butterworths

pupil, the severity of the punishment, and the alleged offence. If the punishment was found not to be moderate and reasonable, then the teacher could be rendered liable to civil[15] or criminal proceedings.[16] Case law reflects changing social norms as O'Halloran J reminds us in *Crewe v Star Publishing Co Ltd*.[17] Legal precedents, he stated, cannot be regarded as inflexible yardsticks but rather as convenient sensitive instruments fashioned and refashioned in the judicial process in order to record and harmonise the relationship between the law and changing social and business outlooks.

[10.05] Scholastic corporal punishment has been abolished by law[18] and any use of this sanction, by a teacher on a student, is a crime.

Abolition of Physical Chastisement of Pupils

[10.06] That statute law also mirrors societal values and attitudes is clear from s 24 of the Non-Fatal Offences Against the Person Act 1997 (the 1997 Act) which provides: "The rule of law under which teachers are immune from criminal liability in respect of physical chastisement of pupils is hereby abolished." Consequently, any physical chastisement of a pupil by a teacher would now leave the teacher open to criminal and civil proceedings. This was demonstrated recently in Abbeyfeale District Court where a school principal pleaded guilty to assaulting a pupil in March 1998 and was fined £50. Civil proceedings may follow.

Justifiable Use of Force

[10.07] However, the 1997 Act provides for the justifiable use of force in certain circumstances. Section 18(1) provides:

> (1) The use of force by a person for any of the following purposes, if only such as is reasonable in the circumstances as he or she believes them to be, does not constitute an offence -
>
> (a) to protect himself or herself or a member of the family of that person or another from injury, assault or detention caused by a criminal act; or
>
> (b) to protect himself or herself or (with the authority of that other) another from trespass to the person; or
>
> (c) to protect his or her property from appropriation, destruction or damage caused by a criminal act or from trespass or infringement; or

---

15 *O'Callaghan v Collins*, High Court, unrep, 23 November 1990.
16 See *R v Hopley* (1860) 2 F and F 202; *McCann v Mannion* (1932) ILTR 161 and *McGee v Cunnane* (1932) ILTR 147.
17 (1942) 58 BCCR 103.
18 Non-Fatal Offences Against the Person Act 1997, s 24.

(d) to protect property belonging to another from appropriation, destruction or damage caused by a criminal act or (with the authority of that other) from trespass or infringement; or

(e) to prevent crime or a breach of the peace.

(2) "use of force" in subsection (1) is defined and extended by section 20.[19]

It is only as cases come before the courts that a proper understanding of the concept of reasonable force in Irish schools will emerge. At this juncture, it may be helpful to examine some American cases in which the concept of reasonable force has been judicially considered bearing in mind the very distinctive disciplinary contexts in the two countries.

USA case law: the concept of reasonable force

[10.08] A liberal approach to student behaviour is apparent in some earlier American Supreme cases which deal with the public schools. In *Tinker v Des Moines Community School District*,[20] difficulties arose when public school students were prohibited from wearing black armbands during school hours in order to publicise parental objections to the Vietnam war. The Supreme Court held that such a prohibition violated the students' constitutional "right to free speech" under the First Amendment as students do not leave their "due process" rights at the door of the school but that they follow them into school and should pervade every aspect of schooling.

[10.09] The court stated that the nation had repudiated the aim of conducting its schools so as to foster a homogenous society. Rather the American classroom, it observed, was the market-place of ideas. Students were required to live out their lives in "a relatively disputatious society" and had to undertake "the risk of hazardous freedom". Hence, the Court considered that the future of the nation relied upon leaders trained through the robust exchange of ideas and opinion. Accordingly, it held, that State-operated schools might not be "the enclaves of totalitarianism" and school authorities did not have absolute authority over their pupils. The Court stated that the vigilant protection of constitutional freedoms was nowhere more important, than in the community of American schools.[21] In his dissenting judgment, Black J stated that he deemed the Court's decision ushered in an entirely new era in which the power to control public school students would be transferred from teachers to the Supreme Court.[22]

---

[19] Non-Fatal Offences Against the Person Act 1997, s 18.

[20] (1968) 393 US 503, 21 L ED 2d 732, 89 SC 733.

[21] (1968) 393 US 503, 21 L ED 2d 732, 89 SC 733 at 734-735, 739.

[22] (1976) 419 US 565, 43 L Ed 2d 725, 95 S Ct 729; see Clegg, Discipline in the Classroom, Free Congress Research and Education Foundation, USA, ERIC Document Reproduction Service, No ED 250769, p 8; Goldsmith, Student Discipline Codes: Developments, Dimensions, Directions: a Legal Memorandum, ERIC Doc ED 202108 1981.

[10.10] The case of *Goss v Lopez*[23] arose out of a riot in a school lunchroom. In that case, the United States Supreme Court held that even though there may have been an immediate need to send home everyone in the lunchroom so as to preserve school order and property, this did not justify a unilateral suspension of pupils. It was still necessary to gather facts, confront the students with them and give them an opportunity to explain their behaviour. Essentially, the court held that school students do not leave their natural justice or due process at the school door but rather such justice pervades every aspect of schooling.

[10.11] Some 20 years later, a sea-change is evident in judicial interpretation of some modern case law brought about by the level of violence in some contemporary American classrooms and the litigious outlook pervading society generally. Public school personnel now require to have a conceptual understanding of the concept of reasonable force in the maintenance of student discipline.[24]

[10.12] In *Wallace v Batavia School District*,[25] an Illinois high school teacher intervened in a classroom fight involving two sixteen year olds who were screaming obscenities at one another. The teacher ordered the students to sit down and be quiet. When they continued to fight, he stepped between them and asked the real trouble-maker to leave the classroom. As she reluctantly moved, the teacher grabbed her by the elbow and wrist, to hasten her exit, but the student complained of pain and the teacher loosened his hold. The student alleged that the teacher caused injury to her elbow and sued the school district and the teacher for breach of her rights under the Fourth and Fourteenth Amendments.

[10.13] The seventh Circuit Court of Appeal affirmed the decision of a lower court which found for the teacher and the district, applying a test of reasonableness, which compelled the teacher to use immediate, effective action. This approach seems balanced and eminently sensible. Given the context of the school environment if which students do not enjoy the same liberty as a private citizen, and because classroom order and effective discipline are crucial to education, the court ruled that the teacher's actions in using physical force to restrain and control students, were reasonable when there is a threat of injury or damage to property.

[10.14] A different line of reasoning is manifested in *Caldwell v Griffen Spalding Board of Education*[26] which involved a freshman in the high school

---

[23] (1975) 419 US 565.

[24] On this issue, see Frisby and Beckham, 'Developing School Policies on the Application of Reasonable Force', 122 Ed Law Rep 27 (January 8 1998).

[25] 1995 68 F 3d 1010 reported in 104 Ed Law Rep 132.

[26] (1998) 503 SE 2 d 43 reported in Education Law Reports 904 and in The University of Oklahoma, School Law Reporter, Rossow, ed, 40 (1998) 12 at 121.

football team who was attacked and beaten by a fellow team member during an "initation ritual" at summer camp. The student's parent sued, alleging that the school officials were negligent in failing to protect his son from attack by his peers. The trial judge found for the school board on the grounds of sovereign immunity and for the official coach and school principal on the grounds of official immunity. On appeal, the Court of Appeals of Georgia affirmed the decision holding that the supervision of student safety is a discretionary function and that under Georgia law no liability exists without a showing of actual malice or actual intent to cause injury and actual malice excludes any concept of implied malice or "reckless disregard". One concurring opinion put forward a suggestion that the appellate courts and the legislature should reconsider whether the supervision of students should be considered a discretionary function and whether Florida's stance that "the duty to supervise high school students is generally ministerial in nature."

[10.15] This rather extreme approach is also apparent in *Daniels v Gordon*[27] in which a middle school student alleged that he was injured when he was choked and restrained by his teacher during a class. The teacher argued that the student was a discipline problem and that when she requested him to look at her and he refused, she then grasped his face and turned it towards her. The student sued alleging that the teacher had breached Georgia law governing corporeal punishment and that the principal had failed to enforce school policy in regard to discipline by omitting to take action against the teacher.

[10.16] In the lower court, summary judgment was given for the school. The Court of Appeals for Georgia affirmed that decision holding that both the teacher's actions and principal's actions were discretionary in nature entitling them to official immunity. The judiciary, it appears, appreciate that in certain fraught situations, a teacher of normal prudence may act with less restraint than is usual. Hence, the use of reasonable bodily restraint on a student is generally permitted with greater justification arising for speedy and precise reaction as the danger increases.[28] By holding that the supervision of second level students is a discretionary function, or by conferring official or ministerial immunity on teachers, the courts in the latter two cases absolved the school and teachers from all responsibility, a solution which may not always lead to an equitable outcome.[29]

---

27 (1998) 503 S E 2d 72 reported in 128 Ed Law Rep 909 and in Rossow, at 121.

28 Frisby and Beckham, pp 3-4.

29 The concept of official or ministerial authority (deriving from a legal mandate) has resonances of the concept of magisterial authority (inherent authority deriving from the *in loco parentis* principle or from statute) referred to in *Glynn v Keele University* [1971] 1 WLR 487 and *State (Smullen) v Duffy* [1980] ILRM 46 at 53.

[10.17] Where unreasonable restraint is used on students, however, such as locking a child with a mental and physical disability in a school rest-room,[30] or tying a child to a chair for more than a day,[31] this would most likely lead to legal liability on the part of the school authority which is vicariously liable for the civil wrongs of the teacher in the course of employment.

Appeals under the 1998 Act

[10.18] Section 28 of the Education Act 1998 provides that the Minister, following consultation with the parties in education, may prescribe for grievance and other procedures as already indicated in Chapter 6.[32] With regard to parent-teacher or student-teacher appeals, these are envisaged as internal appeals only ie to the school board. Prior to considering the application of s 29 of the Education Act 1998, a distinction will be made relating to the categories of school discipline.

Categories of School Discipline

[10.19] From an analysis of the case law relating to school discipline issues, it appears that there are two main categories of discipline; (a) internal or domestic school discipline and (b) disciplinary decisions of a quasi-judicial nature. Pennycuick VC in *Glynn v Keele University*[33] pointed out that the setting of school life is distinctive from ordinary life because it involves a special element, the relationship of teacher and pupil. In school, the teacher is charged with the supervision of the pupil. Where this relationship exists, it seems, there is a wide range of circumstances in which the school may impose sanctions by way of internal discipline. Here, the school is acting within the scope of its inherent authority conferred on it by society. It is acting in a magisterial[34] capacity and it has a moral duty to act fairly. In the Irish context, Finlay P also referred to the magisterial responsibility of the school in *The State (Smullen) v Duffy*.[35]

[10.20] Any school disciplinary issues or decisions which emanate from the inherent authority of the school appear to be within the jurisdiction of the school itself. The Supreme Court did not expressly refer to the magisterial authority of the school in *Murtagh v Board of Management of St Emer's National School*[36]

---

30 *Gerks v Deathe* (1993) 832 F Supp 1450 W D Okla reported in 86 Ed Law Rep 780.
31 *Jefferson v Ysleta Ind School Dist* 817 F 2 d 303 (5th Circuit, 1987) reported in 39 Ed Law Rep 17.
32 See para **[6.102]**.
33 [1971] 1 WLR 487.
34 From the Latin *magistralis, register* meaning pertaining to or befitting a master or magistrate, Hayward and Sparkes, *Cassell's English Dictionary,* London, Cassell, p 701.
35 [1980] ILRM 46 at 53.
36 [1991] 2 ILRM 549, this case has echoes of Pennycuick VC's judgment in *Glynn v Keele University* [1971] 1 WLR 487.

when it reviewed the procedures relating to the three day suspension of a child from a Longford national school[37] for insulting a teacher during a supervision period. However, the Court implied that this was the case when it pointed out that this sanction was part of the "ordinary disciplinary procedures inherent in the school authorities and granted to them by the parents who have entrusted the pupil to the school".[38] As the law stood at that time, McCarthy J put the matter beyond doubt when he stated:

> "The enforcement of discipline in a National School is a matter for the teachers, the principal teacher, the Chairperson of the board of management and the board itself; it is not a matter for the Courts, whose function, at most, is to ensure that the disciplinary complaint was dealt with fairly."[39]

[10.21] Hederman J went on to enumerate a number of disciplinary sanctions which would not be reviewable by the High Court as, he stated, they emanated from the ordinary disciplinary powers vested in the school authorities who are *in loco parentis*. Such matters, he indicated would include a three-day suspension of a child from school and the ordering of a pupil by a sanction to stay in school for an extra half hour to write out lines,[40] or the ordering of a pupil to write out lines while he is at home.

[10.22] While it may be argued that Hederman J's comments on detention and homework are merely *obiter,* they, nonetheless, give some judicial support to these sanctions. It appears that in matters relating to the internal discipline of the school, the courts will not interfere with the discretion of the school authority.

Quasi-Judicial Decisions

[10.23] Other school decisions have a greater impact on the lives of students, for instance, when a school permanently excludes a student, or suspends a student for a long period or refuses to enroll a student.[41] In such circumstances, a school

---

[37] Departmental Circular had also affirmed that the three day suspension of a child from school was within the principal's authority without further reference, Department of Education, Circular 7/88, "To the Boards of Management and Principal Teachers of National Schools: Discipline in National Schools." Circular 20/90 and its appendices replaces Circular 7/88 and amends Rule 130 by the addition of parts (v) and (vi).

[38] Hederman J.

[39] *Murtagh v Board of Management of St Emer's National School* [1991] 2 ILRM 549 *per* McCarthy J.

[40] Difficulties, however, may arise with this sanction when a parent withdraws in writing previously existing authority from the school to detain his or her child, see *Terrington v Lanchashire County Council,* Blackpool County Court, unrep cited in Liell and Saunders, eds, *The Law of Education,* (9th ed, 1987) Butterworths, the law in England has been changed in this regard as the Education Act 1997 s 5 makes the detention of pupils after school hours lawful despite the absence of parental consent.

[41] The term "student" for the purposes of subs 1(c) means a person who applies for enrolment at a school and that person or his parents may appeal against a refusal to enrol him or her in the same manner as a student or his or her parents may appeal a decision under this section.

may be perceived by a court to be acting in a quasi-judicial capacity[42] because it is making decisions of a serious nature which influence the rights and liabilities of students. In these instances, there is a legal obligation to act fairly and to implement fair procedures. Accordingly, parents, or the student who has reached his or her eighteenth birthday, may seek the leave of the High Court to have school decisions of a quasi-judicial nature reviewed by the High Court on procedural grounds only ie on the grounds of fairness. When s 29 of the Education Act 1998 comes into operation, it will provide a mechanism or procedure under which "parents," or the student if he/she has reached the age of eighteen years, may appeal the decision to an independent body established under the Act.

Appeals to the Secretary General of the Department of Education and Science

The Impact of Section 29

[10.24] Section 29 of the 1998 Act provides that the decisions of a board of management may be appealed when it:

    (a) permanently excludes a student from a school,

    (b) suspends a student from attendance at a school for a period to be prescribed for the purpose of this paragraph, or

    (c) refuses to unroll a student[43] in a school, or

    (d) makes a decision of a class which the Minister following consultation with patrons, national associations of parents, recognised school management organisations, recognised trade unions and staff associations representing teachers, may from time to time determine may be appealed in accordance with this section.

[10.25] This section of the 1998 Act will channel appeals from the type of school decisions mentioned above to appeal committees which will be established by the Minister under this section. A person making an appeal will be required to use the following procedure:

    (a) exhaust or conclude any appeals procedure provided by the school or patron under s 28 ie the grievance procedure which will, most likely, be an internal appeal within the school which stops at board level;

---

[42] Having a character which is partly judicial eg where there is an exercise of discretion following the hearing of evidence, as in the case of proceedings before an arbitrator, Murdoch, *A Dictionary of Irish Law* (1988), Topaz, p 414.

[43] The term "student" for the purposes of subs 1(c) means a person who applies for enrolment at a school and that person or his parents may appeal against a refusal to enrol him or her in the same manner as a student or his or her parents may appeal a decision under this section.

(b) utilise and exhaust the appeals procedure under s 29 (which is an independent appeal procedure established by law which generally stops at Ministerial level);

(c) If the appellant has exhausted procedures (1) and (2) above and is still dissatisfied with the outcome, he or she may then seek leave of the High Court to have the matter reviewed by the court, on procedural grounds only.[44]

Who may appeal?

[10.26] Those persons entitled to appeal under s 29 are the parent of the student, or in the case of a student who has reached the age of eighteen years, the student. Other categories, however, also fall under the term "parent" such as a foster parent, a guardian appointed under the Guardianship of Infants Act 1964, other persons acting *in loco parentis* who have a child in their care subject to any statutory power or order of a court eg a Health Board, adoptive parents living in Ireland in the case of a child who has been adopted under the Adoption Acts 1952-1998 or the adopter or adopters or the surviving adopter where the child has been adopted outside the State.

[10.27] Such persons, within a reasonable time from the date on which the parent or student was informed of the decision and following the conclusion of any appeal procedures provided by the school or the patron under s 28, may appeal that decision to the Secretary General of the Department of Education and Science and that appeal shall be heard by a committee appointed under sub-s (2).

Appeal committees

[10.28] Section 29(2) provides for the appointment of one committee or more by the Minister for the purpose of hearing and determining an appeal under this section to be termed an "appeal committee", each of which shall include as a member an inspector, and such other persons as the Minister considers appropriate. The Education (No 2) Bill 1997 included a practising barrister or solicitor, of not less than ten years standing, on the appeal committee.[45] This provision was amended so as to exclude this category. However, the Minister still has the discretion to include this category under "such other persons as the Minister considers appropriate". In view of the fact that such appeals frequently involve complex legal and constitutional principles, it would seem imprudent to exclude such expertise from the appeal committees.

---

[44] Seeking the remedy of Judicial Review which is a discretionary remedy.
[45] Section 29(2).

[10.29] The chairperson of such committee, who will be an appointee of the Minister, will, in the case of an equal division of votes, have a second or casting vote.[46]

Procedures for appeals

[10.30] Procedures in regard to the appeals committees may be determined from time to time by the Minister following consultations with the partners in education and he shall ensure that:

    (a) the parties to the appeal are assisted to reach agreement on the issues the subject of the appeal where the appeals committee is of the view that such agreement is practicable,

    (b) hearings are conducted with the minimum of formality consistent with giving to all parties a fair hearing , and

    (c) appeals are dealt with in a period of 30 days from the date of the receipt of the appeal by the Secretary General, except where the, on the application in writing of appeals committee stating the reasons for a delay in determining the appeal, the Secretary General consents in writing to extent the period by not more than 14 days.[47]

Having determined an appeal under this section, the appeals committee shall send written notice of its determination, and the reasons therefor, to the Secretary General.[48]

[10.31] Where an appeals committee upholds a complaint made to it either wholly or partially, and it appears to it that any matter, being the subject of the complaint (so far as upheld), should be remedied, it shall make recommendations to the Secretary General as to the action to be taken.[49] "As soon as practicable" following the receipt of the notice referred to in sub-s (5), the Secretary General -

    (a) shall by notice in writing, inform the person who made the appeal and the board of the determination of the appeals committee and the reasons therefor, and

    (b) in a case to which subsection (6) applies, may in such notice give directions to the board as appear to the Secretary General (having regard to any recommendations made to the appeals committee) to be expedient for the purposes of remedying the matter which was the subject of the appeal and the board shall in accordance with such directions.[50]

---

[46] Section 29(3).
[47] Section 29(4).
[48] Section 29(5).
[49] Section 29(6).
[50] Section 29(7).

In view of the fact that those pupils, on whose behalf the appeals are made, may be out of school for 44 days, when the Secretary General receives the appeal committee's decision, the author is of the view that the phrase "as soon as practicable" in s 29(7) is too vague. A specified period of three weeks should be more than adequate in these circumstances.

[10.32] Provision is made, from time to time, for the review of ss 28 and 29 by the Minister in consultation with the partners in education and the first review shall take place not more than two years from the commencement of this section.[51]

Appeals in VEC schools

[10.33] Where a school is established or maintained by a VEC, an appeal against the decision of a board in such school shall lie, in the first instance to the VEC and afterwards to the Secretary General in compliance with sub-s (1).[52] The Minister may, from time to time, after consultation with the VECs, national associations of parents, recognised trade unions and staff associations representing teachers, prescribe -

   (a) the procedures for appeals under this section to Vocational Education Committees, and

   (b) which appeals shall enquire into whether the procedure adopted by a board in reaching a decision or conducting an appeal was fair and reasonable and which appeals shall be by way of a full re-hearing.[53]

The Secretary General has power to assign the responsibility for the performance of his functions in this section[54] to another officer of the Department of Education and Science.[55]

Comment on sections 28 and 29

[10.34] The effective operation of s 29 of the 1998 Act will be heavily dependent firstly on the provision of adequate and appropriate support services within the original school such as remedial teaching, speech therapists, teacher aides and psychological services. The success of these sections will also be closely linked to the establishment of appropriate alternative provision for certain highly disruptive pupils who constitute a danger to their peers and/or to teachers in the original school. These pupils who cannot be accommodated in mainstream schools still have a constitutional right to be educated and resources must be found to accommodate their needs including the provision of an alternative and

---

[51] Section 29(8).
[52] Section 29(9).
[53] Section 29(10).
[54] Under the Public Service Management Act 1997, s 4(1)(i) and s 9.
[55] Section 29(11).

innovative curriculum. Clearly, s 29 is one of the most important provisions in the 1998 Act. As well as adequate resources, its successful operation will require determination, patience and goodwill on the part of all concerned.

[10.35] Parental concerns were voiced when the Education (No 2) Bill was passing through the Oireachtas regarding the appeals sections of the bill. the national parents' council (primary) alleged that the appeals mechanism in s 28 was unfair in that it failed to include bad teacher conduct towards pupils, and it petitioned its members to demand that the Bill be amended accordingly. Parents argued that there were no good child-centred reasons for restricting the appeal machinery, and that administrative inconvenience or the resistance of those whose decisions would be questioned were not sufficient reasons for doing so.[56]

[10.36] In this sphere, where the intersecting rights of the child, parents, teachers and denominational school authorities coalesce, parents were of the view that ss 28 and 29 did not achieve fairness between the parties. Of course, the State could only negotiate s 28 with the denominational school authorities, it could not mandate it or go beyond board level except with their agreement. Because of the inherent tensions between the wishes of parents and the denominational school authorities, s 28 of the Act has the potential for future difficulties.

The Disciplinary Responsibility of the School

[10.37] Apart from the provisions of the 1998 Act,[57] responsibility for the substance of school discipline remains with the individual school authority provided basically fair procedures[58] are followed in quasi-judicial decisions. The division of responsibility for disciplinary issues is normally set down in the schools' articles of management or governing rules or regulations. Further details of school discipline are generally left to the individual school subject to the board's and patron's authority. Such matters may include:

    (a) the standard of behaviour or conduct required by the school of its students;

    (b) the norms and standards of behaviour relating to school climate or ethos;

    (c) the drafting and implementation of:

        (i) School rules;

        (ii) Codes of discipline and sanctions to be used;

        (iii) Anti-bullying policies;

---

[56] National Parents Council (Ms Kilfeather).
[57] Sections 22, 23, 24, 28, 29.
[58] Article 40.3.1°.

(iv) Policies relating to school tours;

(v) Policies relating to outdoor pursuits and sporting activities, and

(vi) Other discipline-related policies.

[10.38] The Department has issued Circulars which have set down procedures which will ensure that the principles of natural justice and fair procedures are implemented in these circumstances. These Circulars stress:

(a) that parents should be informed of their right to come to the school to discuss their child's misbehaviour with the principal and/or the class teacher particularly when a suspension of a pupil is contemplated;

(b) that students should be informed when instances of serious misbehaviour on their part are being recorded;

(c) that a teacher should report repeated incidents of misbehaviour to the principal while keeping a record of all such incidents; this record should indicate the warnings and/or advice given to the child on the misbehaviour and the consequences of its repetition; and

(d) that schools' policy on behavioural matters should be communicated clearly and fully to parents.

[10.39] It is also important that any decision-making body established by the school relating to the implementation of serious sanctions be free from bias in its composition and in its decision-making process. For this reason, the decision-making body should not include as a member the teacher of the student whose misbehaviour is at issue.

[10.40] Clearly, school disciplinary issues are moving towards greater formality as s 23 of the Education (Welfare) Bill 1999 indicates. Section 23(1) provides that the board of management of a recognised school shall, following consultation with the principal, teachers, parents and the welfare officer for the area prepare in accordance with sub-s (2) a code of behaviour in respect of the students registered at the school (to be known as a code of discipline). Such a code shall specify:

(a) the types of behaviour on the part of a student that may require disciplinary measures to be taken in relation to him or her;

(b) the nature of the measures referred to in paragraph (a);

(c) the procedures to be followed before a student may be suspended or expelled from the school concerned;

(d) the grounds for removing a suspension imposed in relation to a student; and

(e) the steps that will be taken to ensure that a student who is expelled will receive a prescribed minimum education.

[10.41] In the preparation and implementation of the code of discipline, the board of management shall have regard to such guidelines as may be issued by the National Educational Welfare Board.[59] In registering a child at the school, as is required by s 20, the principal of a recognised school shall provide the parents of such child with a copy of the code of discipline in respect of the school concerned.[60] On a request being made either by a registered student or a parent of such student at the school, the principal shall provide the student or parent with a copy of the code of discipline in regard to the school concerned.[61]

Intervention of the Criminal Law

Police Visits and Investigations

[10.42] On occasion, police officers visit schools in order to investigate alleged offences. While principals and other teachers have obligations to students and their parents, they may not obstruct a police officer in the course of his or her duties. As the school stands *in loco parentis* to the student, the student's parents should be contacted immediately. However, if the police are acting under statutory powers to bring a child requiring care or control before a juvenile court, then they may not be lawfully obstructed. Neither may they be lawfully obstructed if they are in possession of a warrant.[62]

The Judges' Rules

[10.43] As O'Higgins CJ pointed out in *The People v Farrell*,[63] the Judges' Rules are not rules of law but are rather rules for the guidance of persons taking statements. Any interrogations conducted by the police ought to be in accordance with the Judges' Rules which are concerned with the taking of statements and the administration of cautions and with seeking to ensure that any evidence resulting from an investigation is admissible in court.[64] Currently, the Judges' Rules[65] applicable in the Irish courts are those laid down by Walsh J in *People v Cummins*[66] and these derive from the old Judges' Rules of 1918 since replaced, in England only, by the 1964 Rules.[67]

---

[59] Section 23(3).
[60] Section 23(4).
[61] Section 23(5).
[62] See generally, Barrell and Partington, *Teachers and the Law* (1985), Methuen, p 630.
[63] [1978] IR 13 SC.
[64] See Ryan and Magee, *The Irish Criminal Process*, p 114 *et seq.*
[65] See Ryan and Magee, pp 114-5.
[66] [1972] IR 312, 317-318 SC.
[67] See [1964] 1 All ER 237.

[10.44] In the event of the police wishing to interview a specific student, the principal or senior teacher should ask them to await the arrival of a parent so that any investigation may be conducted in the parents' presence. If this request is refused, the principal ought to insist on being present during the interview. If the principal is male, and a female student is being interrogated, a female teacher should also be present. Similarly, if the student being interrogated is male and the principal is female, then a male teacher should be present. If a pupil is to be searched, the principal should request that this be done when parents are present. In the event of a student being removed from the school, or the holding of an identity parade on the school premises, a principal should immediately seek the advice of his board of management and, if necessary, professional advice.[68] In *Travers v Ryan*[69] Finlay P stated that in regard to a person under 14 years of age it is most desirable in the interest of justice that, unless there are practical impossibilities, if they are suspected of crime they should not be questioned except in the presence of a parent or some other person "of an adult kind" in the position of guardian.

Persons in Authority

[10.45] Teachers should not use threats or inducements in order to secure a confession of guilt from students. In instances where threats or inducements have been used so as to secure a confession, that confession will be inadmissible in evidence only if it issued from "a person in authority." In the school setting, a headmistress has been held to be "a person in authority" in relation to pupils in her school. In *R v McLintock*,[70] M a pupil at a boarding school was convicted of larceny and was given probation. It was alleged she had stolen money belonging to G who had a flat at the school.

[10.46] The sole evidence against M was four admissions, three of which had been made to O, the headmistress. M was questioned by O in the presence of G when O repeated three times "You had better admit it ... you had better own up", and then referred to the police. M then admitted guilt. Later that day, O again questioned M who made fresh admissions.

[10.47] At the pupil's trial the prosecution conceded that the first three confessions to O were inadmissible because they were induced by a threat. However, a later confession made voluntarily to F, another pupil stating "I am not going to deny it because I did", was admissible. On appeal, the court held that the trial judge had applied the proper test, ie that the prosecution proved

---

[68] In the English setting, see Barrell and Partington, pp 630 *et seq*.
[69] [1985] ILRM 163.
[70] [1962] Crim L R 549.

beyond reasonable doubt that at the time on the admission to F, the inducement or threat made earlier in the day was still not operating on M's mind.

Proposed Decentralisation: Democratic School Structures

[10.48] Recent attempts to introduce greater democracy into Irish educational structures, through the establishment of Regional Education Councils (RECs hereafter), were abandoned after the demise of the Education Bill 1997. If that Bill had passed into law, it is likely that both the RECs and the schools would have become part of public law for the first time.[71] Had this occurred, the English experience indicates that educational issues in Ireland would have become a fertile source of applications for judicial review.[72] In future, judicial review of school decisions in Ireland will be available but on narrower grounds.

Source of School's Disciplinary Authority

[10.49] Traditionally the teacher's power to assert a disciplinary authority over pupils was held to derive from the *in loco parentis* doctrine through parental delegation. Where State systems of education exist, as in England, there appears to be a movement away from the concept of parental delegation towards an acceptance of the fact that teachers' disciplinary powers derive from their independent professional status as teachers.[73] The Elton Report[74] recommended that such powers be incorporated into statute law and this recommendation has to some degree been implemented. This, of course does not apply to corporal punishment which was abolished in the majority of English schools by the Education (No 2) Act 1986. [75]

Source of the Schoolteacher's Authority

[10.50] The traditional approach, that the schoolteacher is delegated certain parental rights during the course of the school day, is apparent in the early case law.[76] In *Fitzgerald v Northcote* (1865),[77] which involved the expulsion of an

---

[71] On this point, see Hogan, 'Constitutional Issues Raised in the Educational Bill, 1997', The Bar Review, Vol 2, April 1997, p 215 at 216, 218 (n 9).

[72] See Meredith, 'Recent Educational Disputes and the Courts', *ACE Bulletin*, 26 November/ December 1988, p 4.

[73] Professor Neville Harris, 'The Autonomy of the Teacher: Education Law and Education Standards in England and Wales', Paper delivered to Education Law Association, Salzburg, 19 December 1998; see also the United States cases cited above which refer to official and ministerial immunity on the part of the teacher, para **[10.08]** above *et seq.*

[74] Elton Report, Discipline in Schools, (1989), London, HMSO,.

[75] See School Standards and Framework Act 1998, s 131.

[76] *R v Hopley* (1860) 2 F & F 202; *Fitzgerald v Northcote* (1865) 4 F & F 656 at 664; *Williams v Eady* (1893) 10 TLR 41 CA; see also Yearbook 7, Edward 1V.

[77] (1865) 4 F & F 656 at 664.

Irish judge's son from an English public school, the judicial analysis of the schoolteacher's authority is particularly instructive. The plaintiff had been sent to a Roman Catholic College at Oscott for his education. Following the youth's expulsion from the school, for his involvement in an allegedly subversive conspiracy, Fitzgerald J sued the two head teachers, (both clerics) for assault and false imprisonment of his son.

[10.51] The court held that the authority of the schoolteacher was, while it existed, the same as that of the parent(s) and this delegated authority included the imposition of reasonable restraint upon the child by way of prevention or punishment of disorderly conduct.[78] However, it considered that the schoolteacher's authority did not confer a discretionary power of expulsion but only for reasonable cause. The jury found in favour of the Irish student who was awarded damages of one farthing.

[10.52] In *Price v Wilkins*,[79] which dealt with a breach of contract to pay school fees, the judge described the relationship between the schoolmaster and the parents of his pupil as follows:

> "The parent surrenders for the time being a part of his otherwise exclusive right to direct and control the child, and certainly undertakes that the master shall, so far as he and his action are concerned, be at liberty to enforce with regard to his son the rules of the school, or, to put it at the very lowest, at all events such rules as are known to him and assented to by him."

Nonetheless, the judge considered that in cases of conflict, parental authority must prevail.[80] This case points up the importance of ensuring that parents are fully aware of the school rules and disciplinary policy. In practice, many schools adopt the prudent practice of requiring parents to read and sign such rules. If s 23 of the Education (Welfare) Bill 1999 passes into law teachers will have statutory duties in relation to certain aspects of school discipline.

General Principles of Liability

[10.53] Phillimore J was one of the first to lay down the general principles by which school discipline is governed. In *Mansell v Griffin*[81] he indicated that the ordinary authority, in regard to classroom discipline, extends to the class teacher.

---

[78] *Fitzgerald v Northcote* (1865) 4 F & F 656; *Williams v Eady* (1893) 10 TLR 41 CA; *Geyer v Downs* (1977) 38 CLR 93; *Commonwealth of Australia v Introvigne* (1981/82), 150 CLR at 563; see generally United Kingdom, Laws and Statutes, 15 *Halsbury's Laws of England*, (4th ed, 1977), Butterworths.

[79] (1880) 58 LT 680.

[80] (1880) 58 LT 680 at 681.

[81] [1908] 1 KB 160 at 168.

With respect to punishment and sanctions generally, he considered it sufficient for the teacher to be able to say:

> "The punishment which I administered was moderate; it was not dictated by any bad motive, and it was such as is usual in the school and such as the parent of the child might expect that the child would receive if it did wrong."

It would be difficult to improve on this brief statement as a general guiding principle underpinning all school sanctions.

[10.54] The case of *R v Hopley*[82] is authority for the principle that the teacher's disciplinary powers must at all times be exercised in a reasonable manner even if parental permission to exceed moderate limits is given. In that singular case, a schoolmaster, following a boy's return to an English boarding school, wrote to his father proposing to beat him severely "to subdue his alleged obstinacy". On receiving the father's assent in writing, the schoolmaster, who beat the boy secretly in the night so that he later died of his injuries, was found guilty of manslaughter.

[10.55] As already observed, case law also indicates that the authority of the teacher to discipline the pupil is not confined to offences committed by the pupil on the school premises but extends to acts done by such pupil on his way to and from school.[83] Thus, it seems a school may lawfully impose a sanction on its pupils for misbehaviour on buses on the way to and on the way home from school without extending its liability.

Acting within the Scope of Employment

[10.56] If the teacher is acting within the scope of his employment when disciplining his pupils, then the board is generally vicariously liable for the teacher's civil wrongs[84] as the decision in *Trim Joint District School Board v Kelly*[85] indicates.[86]

[10.57] If the teacher exceeds the limits of his authority, or refuses to comply with the directions of the board, then the board may not be legally liable for such wrongs. This latter point was well illustrated in *O'Callaghan v Collins*[87] which was defended by the INTO on behalf of the teacher in 1990. In this case, a teacher who admitted that she gave her pupil "a tiny tap" with a ruler, was

---

[82] (1860) 2 F & F 202.

[83] *Cleary v Booth* (1893), 57 JP at 375; *R v Newport (Shropshire) Justices ex p Wright* (1929) 2 KB 416; *The State (Smullen) v Duffy* (1980) ILRM 46.

[84] *Ryan v Madden* [1944] IR 157.

[85] [1914] AC 667.

[86] See para **[9.116]** above.

[87] High Court, unrep, 23 November 1990.

cleared by a jury[88] of assaulting her pupil. At the time of the administration of this sanction, corporal punishment had been prohibited by Circular,[89] but it had not been abolished by law.

[10.58] Consequently, teachers retained the common law right to administer moderate and reasonable corporal punishment to a pupil until the coming into force of the Non-Fatal Offences Against the Person Act 1997 in August 1997.

Second Level Teachers

[10.59] There has been little judicial interpretation, if any, of the disciplinary role of second level teachers and in particular those employed in voluntary secondary schools in Ireland. However, the English case of *Sim and Rotherham Borough Council*,[90] which was decided prior to the recent English statutes regulating school discipline,[91] may cast some light on the matter. In that case, Lord Wilberforce concluded that teachers were professionals. As such, he held that the professional obligations of a secondary teacher cannot be confined to the imparting of academic knowledge. The relationship of teacher and pupil, he continued, goes further and includes duties of care and discipline:

> "A teacher who found two pupils fighting in a school corridor would be expected to try to deal with it. The teacher would, in my view, be under a professional obligation to deal with it, although what could or should in practice be done, would obviously depend on the circumstances."

This statement indicates that the secondary schoolteacher has duties of supervision which extend beyond the ambit of classroom teaching and supervisory duties which depend upon the particular circumstances at the material time.[92]

School Sanctions

(1) Detention

[10.60] Normally, when pupils are properly dismissed at the end of the school day, the pupil-teacher relationship is severed[93] and pupils return to the care and

---

88 Juries have since been abolished in such cases.
89 Department of Education, Circulars 9/82 and 7/88 which had amended Rule 130 of the Rules for National Schools.
90 [1986] 3 All ER 405, see Ch 8, p .
91 See above paras **[0.00]**.
92 *Smith v Jolly*, Irish Times, unrep, 18 May 1984, p 8; Irish Times, 19 May 1984, p 18; *Mulligan v Doherty*, Supreme Court, unrep, 17 May 1966.
93 On the relationship between schoolmaster and pupils and on the voluntary assumption of this relationship before the official school day commenced, see *Geyer v Downs* [1976-1977] CLR 91 at 94; see also *Fitzgerald v Northcote* (1865) QB 656 at 663-668.

control of their parents or guardians. Detention after school hours, it seems, is seldom used in primary schools but is commonly employed as a disciplinary measure in second level schools. In law, no person may restrict the liberty of another without lawful excuse. The question to be addressed here is what is the legal basis of the schoolteacher's authority to detain the person of his pupil after school hours?

[10.61] As noted in *Fitzgerald v Northcote*,[94] there is a paucity of authority on the schoolteacher's right to retain the person of his scholar. Moreover, existing authorities are largely ancient practice to be deduced by analogy. The position of the schoolteacher seems to be that of a temporary guardian of the pupil.[95] Cockburn J's decision in the *Fitzgerald* case indicates some support for detention:

> "While the relation of master and scholar exists, therefore, it seems that ... reasonable restraint of the person - either to prevent running away, or to punish breaches of discipline - may be justified."[96]

[10.62] While Philimore J in *Mansell v Griffin*[97] indicated that the in-school detention of a pupil during play intervals was reasonable, other considerations had to be borne in mind, he stated, if the detention is at the end of the school day. As post-school detention occurs at a time when control of the pupil has returned to the parent, the importance of express or implied parental consent in the Irish context[98] appears pivotal.

[10.63] As already observed, Hederman J in *Murtagh v Board of Management of St Emer's National School*,[99] gave some judicial support to detention after school hours when he included it among a list of sanctions which would not be subject to judicial review.[100] That unreasonable detention may be unlawful, however, is clear from the case of a teacher who left his 12-year-old pupil locked in a schoolroom. The court held that the pupil had been falsely imprisoned and a decree of £50 was given against the teacher.[101] Reasonable detention, on the other hand, is likely to receive the support of the court unless parental consent for such detention has been withdrawn in writing from the school.

---

[94] (1865) QB 656 at 663 *et seq.*
[95] Yearbook 7, Edward 1V; Yearbook 2, Edward 1V.
[96] (1865) QB 656 at 738.
[97] [1908] 1 KB 160 at 168.
[98] Section 5 of the English Education Act 1997 makes detention outside school hours lawful despite the absence of parental consent.
[99] [1991] 2 ILRM 549.
[100] See above paras **[10.21]**.
[101] Reported in 'News of the Week', (1934), 68 ILTS, 107.

[10.64] The legal position in England is well illustrated in *Terrington v Lancashire County Council*[102] in which a teacher who held a class in detention for ten minutes after school hours, in order to establish sound discipline at the beginning of the school year, was alleged to have falsely imprisoned his pupil. In the lower court, the judge found that, although there was a false imprisonment, the school authority had discharged the burden of proof and so the imprisonment was justified.

[10.65] On appeal to the County Court, the plaintiff's father stated that, both orally and in writing, he had withdrawn previously existing authority from the school to detain his son for minor indiscipline. He contended that the blanket detention imposed by the school was unreasonable as his son was not involved in the indiscipline on the day in question. Dismissing the claim, the judge stated that while blanket detention should only be used as a last resort and punishment should not be indiscriminate, in some instances the whole class could be responsible for indiscipline. He made it clear, however, that if the pupil's father had withdrawn his authority from the school to administer detention for minor indiscipline then the claim for false imprisonment would succeed. The judge was of the view that the father's letters did not go this far and were only a protest against this form of punishment.

[10.66] Concerns expressed by teachers bodies led in time to a change in the law in England in this sphere. Section 5 of the Education Act 1997 made provision for lawful detention outside school hours despite absence of parental consent. However, the law in Ireland has not been changed, so parental consent to post-school detention, either express or implied, is still centrally important here. Because of this, post-school detention is a sanction which needs to be structured, administered and supervised with reasonable care. Arguably, any attempt to change the law in Ireland so as to make post-school detention lawful would, in the absence of parental consent, be constitutionally vulnerable in the light of parental priorities in Article 42. Any such changes would have to be negotiated with the school authorities, parents and teachers unions and professional bodies.

[10.67] The case of *Hunter v Johnson*[103] concerned the detention of a pupil for 45 minutes after school in order to do homework. This sanction was imposed even though the pupil's mother had prohibited homework in a letter to the school which was constituted under the Elementary Education Acts 1870-1876. On appeal from the lower court, where the case was dismissed, the judge held that post-school detention for failure to do homework, which a parent had forbidden,

---

[102] *Terrington v Lanchashire County Council*, Blackpool County Court, unrep, cited in Liell and *The Law of Education*, Saunders, eds, (9th ed, 1987) Butterworths.
[103] (1884) 13 QBD 225 at 635.

was unlawful as there was neither express nor clearly implied authority for the headmaster to exercise such a power. Accordingly, he ruled that the schoolteacher, in the face of that finding, had no authority to detain the pupil.

[10.68] Older cases, however, may not lay down accurate guidelines for contemporary school life. Homework is now an established practice in most schools and Hederman J's *dictum* in the *Murtagh* case suggests that it is judicially acceptable in Ireland.

[10.69] A stronger case can be made out for school detention where parents have read and signed school rules or codes of discipline which state clearly that detention is a usual sanction in the school, the reasons for which it will be employed,[104] when it will be implemented[105] and the period of detention (which should be moderate and reasonable).

[10.70] Any changes in these arrangements should be brought to the attention of parents. The National Association of Headteachers (England) advised their members that cognizance should be taken of any special factors which might make this disciplinary measure unsuitable or unwise. These might include:

(a) the age of the child;

(b) the distance between home and school;

(c) travel facilities;

(e) individual handicaps; and

(f) risk of molestation on the way home from school.[106]

(2) Exclusion

[10.71] Traditionally, exclusion meant debarment from school on medical grounds.[107] National Archive files indicate that this sanction was used in the nineteenth century for a variety of purposes such as failure to bring turf to school, failure to pay fees,[108] and the debarment from schools of persons of religions other than the denomination of the school.[109]

---

[104] Such a list should not be exhaustive but should include a phrase which allows discretion to the board of management to detain for other reasons.

[105] This point has been taken into account in Department Circular 20/90, p 1.

[106] *Council Memo on Discipline in Schools*, para 64.

[107] *Walker v Cummings* (1912) 107 LT 304 in which the court upheld the exclusion of a child with a verminous head from school.

[108] School fees in primary schools were abolished by the Irish Education Act 1892.

[109] Ireland, National Archives, Bishop Street, Dublin, Education Files, File 9, 559, 642, 2604. The latter file illustrates that the Commissioners for National Education clearly understood the distinction between exclusion and suspension.

[10.72] The common contemporary usage of the term "exclusion" has broadened to include disciplinary measures. While the term "exclusion" is used in the Education Act 1998, it is not defined in that Act. In England, the Education (No 2) Act 1986 made provision for fixed exclusion, indefinite exclusion and permanent exclusion.[110]

[10.73] In practice, exclusion is a sanction by which a pupil prevents himself by his behaviour, from being admitted to school.[111] Generally, exclusion means debarment from school for a specified period during which the compliance of the pupil or parents with a requirement of the school is sought, eg the maintenance of standards of behaviour, dress, or hygiene. In the case of a pupil who is excluded for disruptive behaviour, the condition is that he undertakes to comply with the school rules or code of discipline on his return. Once the condition is fulfilled by the pupil, he must be allowed back into the school. By the reasonable use of exclusion, time is made available for negotiating with parents and students and in seeking their co-operation prior to the use of the more serious sanction of suspension.[112]

[10.74] In latter years, the distinction between the terms exclusion, suspension and expulsion has been blurred by the usage of such terms as "indefinite exclusion" which may in effect become suspension and "permanent exclusion" which is effectively expulsion.

[10.75] The blurring of these terms seems to have arisen as a result of Goddard CJ's decision in *Spiers v Warringtom Corporation*[113] in which he distinguished between exclusion and suspension although he studiously avoided using the term "exclusion" lest perhaps it would be abused by schools. Eva Spiers, a pupil, frequently came to school wearing blue jeans and thus failed to comply with a school rule relating to dress. On each occasion, she was sent home and requested to change into a dress but refused, for alleged but unsubstantiated medical reasons. Following her absence over a period, Eva's father was prosecuted for his daughter's non-attendance at school.

[10.76] Goddard CJ made it clear that as this was a county secondary school under the provisions of the Education Act 1944, he was dealing with a point of law and not a social point. He considered that a head teacher must be responsible for the discipline of the school and the articles of management affirmed this point. The headmistress, he stated:

---

[110] Sections 22-28.
[111] See Department of Education Circular, 20/90, p 10.
[112] Adams, *Law and Teachers Today*, (2nd ed, 1984) Hutchinson, p 162.
[113] (1954) I QB 61.

"... did not suspend this child at all. She was always perfectly willing to take her in; all that she wanted was that she should be properly dressed. Suspending is refusing to admit to the school; in this case the headmistress was perfectly willing to admit the girl but was insisting that she be properly dressed."[114]

Reversing the finding of the lower court, the judge ruled that not only was the headmistress within her rights, but that she was complying with her duty in implementing this sanction. Moreover, he held that the parent, knowing that the girl would not be admitted and insisting on her being dressed in such a manner, had committed an offence. This case, which was decided 45 years ago, may not reflect contemporary standards and norms of dress which have become more liberal.

[10.77] In some instances, cases concerning school dress may have political overtones as one Northern Ireland case illustrates. A Comber High school student was refused entry to school because she refused to remove a Red Hand of Ulster badge on her uniform, and consequently failed to attend school over a period.[115] Subsequently the student's father was fined £25 at Ards Juvenile Court for failing to ensure his daughter's attendance at school. This case is reminiscent of *Tinker v Des Moines Community School District*[116] which is discussed above.[117]

(3) Suspension

[10.78] The term "suspension" is used in the 1998 Act but it is not defined in that Act. With regard to suspension in practice, there is a clear intention to bar pupils from attendance at school for a specific period of time. Schools ought to take account of any provisions in their articles of management and Departmental Circulars in regard to this sanction. Schools frequently include such procedures in their codes of discipline or behaviour. If long-term suspension is used by a school, it is important that the rules of natural justice are applied as the school would be likely to be acting quasi-judicially and such a decision may be subject of an appeal under s 29 of the Education Act 1998.[118]

[10.79] However, the case of *The State (Smullen) v Duffy*[119] indicates that there are exceptional circumstances in which a school may lawfully impose immediate long-term suspension without notice or procedures, eg where there is danger to life and property. In that case, the fairness and validity of a school's suspension

---

[114] (1954) I QB 61 at 66.
[115] 'Father fined over School Incident', Irish Times, 23 January 1987.
[116] (1968) 393 US 503, 21 L ED 2d 732, 89 SC 733.
[117] See para **[10.08]**.
[118] See Kelly, *Fundamental Rights in the Irish Constitution*, p 305.
[119] [1980] ILRM 46.

procedures were challenged by two students in a Dublin Community school who had become involved in a gang fight with a number of other students of the school, outside the school gates. During the fight, two students were stabbed. On the following day, the principal investigated the incident and interviewed a number of boys who were involved in the fight but failed to interview the second-named prosecutor who was then hospitalised.

[10.80] Following an investigation, the principal suspended 8 students the next day, among them the two prosecutors, aged 14 and 15 years. He then wrote to their mother informing her of the suspension stating that he would be requesting the school board to expel the boys at the next board meeting. He further informed her that she could make representations, by way of appeal, to the board at its next meeting. However, the right of appeal was not exercised by the mother or the boys when the matter was fully investigated by the board which decided to suspend the two prosecutors until the end of the school year, with a view to their finding another school. Effectively, this was expulsion.

[10.81] The two prosecutors then applied to the High Court for an order to quash the school's decision to suspend them on the grounds that:

(a) the draft articles of management[120] and the procedures followed by the school were not in accordance with natural justice;

(b) the failure of the board to permit the prosecutors to be legally represented at its meeting which considered their fate, was a denial of natural justice in regard to the making of a decision of considerable importance to them;

(c) the procedures implemented by the board, which denied them a right of audience at their meetings, was wanting in natural justice; and

(d) the failure of the principal to interview the hospitalised boy before deciding to suspend him was reached by a method otherwise than in accordance with natural justice.

It was submitted on behalf of the respondents that there is no legal obligation on a school to afford the parents of a pupil or the pupil legal representation at any hearing or investigation which may result in the suspension or expulsion of a child from school. In addition, it was submitted that the functions of the school in that regard, while they were to an extent of a judicial nature, were largely magisterial[121] and so did not involve the obligation to follow legal procedures or procedures akin to a court hearing, but only the obligation of being in general terms fair.

---

[120] Which governed the school at that time.

[121] Adopting the approach in the *Glynn v Keele University* [1971] 1 WLR 487, para **[10.19]** above.

[10.82] Finlay P held that the general school disciplinary scheme,[122] implemented on the day in question, was essentially fair and wise. He considered that the validity of the principal's decision, or the fairness of the methods by which it was reached, was not affected by the absence of one of the prosecutors on the day in question. As to the authority of the principal in these circumstances to effect an immediate suspension, the judge concluded:

> "It would seem an essential power to give to the principal of a school with disciplinary responsibilities and powers over a number of pupils that he or she should be entitled, after a *bona fide* investigation carried out in the informal way which one would expect from a schoolmaster with pupils under his care rather than from a court on the trial of a criminal charge, to make an immediate suspension of one or more pupils in order to maintain peace and discipline within the school ..."

[10.83] Accordingly, Finlay P upheld the decision of the principal to effect an immediate suspending order on both sides of the rival gangs as a minimum responsible decision for a schoolteacher having obligations to maintain discipline and safety within his school. He considered that the school had also acted reasonably having regard to its magisterial responsibility[123] and its duty to enforce and maintain discipline. Not only, he stated, was the board entitled to, in effect, expel the boys from the school but that "they would be failing on their duty to the school and to the other pupils attending it had they not taken that step". Different considerations might well arise, he stated, if the board or the principal had retained some of the "warring parties" in school and had expelled the others.

[10.84] With regard to the obligation falling on the principal or on the board to permit any legal representation at any meeting dealing with the suspension or expulsion, the judge stated:

> "It seems to me inherent in the general provision for the discipline of a school and indeed in the interests of pupils of a school and the relationships which should exist between them and the school authorities and between their parents and the school authorities that communication should, in the first instance at least, be direct and should not preferably, and certainly not as a right, be through legal representatives."[124]

Having satisfied himself that the suspension arrangements complied with the draft articles of management in the school, Finlay P considered that this was a proper, just and equitable arrangement in regard to the management of a school

---

[122] The draft articles of management in the draft deed of trust of Community Schools.
[123] Which Cassell's English Dictionary defines as "pertaining to a master or a magistrate".
[124] *The State (Smullen) v Duffy* [1980] ILRM 46 at 52.

and that if properly complied with and implemented in a *bona fide* manner, proceedings or consequences, resulting from it could not be said, under any circumstances, to be contrary to natural justice.[125]

[10.85] There were significant weaknesses in the presentation of the prosecutor's case such as the failure of the prosecutor's mother to put in writing her son's account of the material incident. Thus, a situation was permitted to arise in which the board sat without hearing any contradictory account of the material incident other than that of the principal. Neither had any replying affidavit been filed to the principal's affidavit, nor was the Principal cross-examined on his affidavit.

[10.86] In the *Smullen* case, Finlay P was speaking at a time when parental participation in school disciplinary matters was minimalist. Moreover, individual rights have evolved considerably since 1980.[126] Hence, it is conceivable that a court might now hold that the hospitalised boy in the *Smullen* case was entitled to be confronted with the charge against him prior to his long-term suspension. In the setting of denominational schools, however, a court would be unlikely to hold that a student has an entitlement to be legally represented at the board meeting which is deciding his fate although it may be held in the future that legal representation is an entitlement in certain circumstances.

[10.87] If this incident had occurred after the coming into force of Part VI of the Education Act 1998, it would be channelled through the appeals procedure under s 29 of the Act with the ultimate option of seeking judicial review if it remained unresolved.

(4) Expulsions

[10.88] In the case of a small number of pupils, known to the school to be of a violent and aggressive nature, school authorities must choose between the hazards of their presence in school and the possibility of being sued for wrongful deprivation of education rights. The expulsion of pupils from Irish schools is complex because of the duality of administrative control over most schools and because of the scarcity of alternative schooling for those pupils who are expelled. However, the provisions of the Education Act 1998 and of the proposed Education (Welfare) Act 1999, when implemented, should go a long way towards remedying this situation. It will be recalled that in *Fitzgerald v Northcote*,[127] the court considered that the school had not a discretionary power

---

[125] *Smullen* at 50.
[126] See *Flanagan v UCD* [1988] ILRM 724, Barron J although there were significant differences in this case.
[127] (1865) 4 F & F 656.

of expulsion but only for reasonable cause. Expulsion is generally a matter for the board and in some instances, such as in national schools, for the patron. When a student is being expelled, procedural steps should be followed precisely and documented carefully.

[10.89] If the code of discipline or school rules comply with the articles of management and are drawn up in conjunction with parents, they will then be aware of the sanctions the school imposes and of the main instances in which they will be implemented. No code of discipline can cover every eventuality that may occur in a school. Hence, it is prudent to leave some residual discretion to the board to cover certain unforeseen instances of misbehaviour.

Principles of Natural Justice

[10.90] The application of the principles of natural justice is well illustrated in *Flanagan v UCD*,[128] although the facts are quite distinctive from those in the *Smullen* case. Firstly, the applicant in *Flanagan* was a post-graduate student whom, it was alleged, had plagiarised an essay submitted for an examination from a tape recording which had been played to the class during lectures in the respondent college. Secondly, the alleged offence, plagiarism, is one of cheating and constitutes the most serious academic breach of discipline possible, being of a criminal nature, which had grave consequences for the applicant's future life. Thirdly, the applicant was a mature student, an experienced social worker who had submitted other academic work which was of honours standard.

[10.91] The applicant was called before a committee of discipline and was told she could be accompanied only by her dean of residence or an official of the students union or by both. No witnesses were called and the committee was addressed by the applicant and her representatives. It was agreed between the applicant and the committee that the matter should be referred to an independent expert for assessment but the applicant was not involved in his selection. Following lengthy considerations, the disciplinary committee decided that the applicant be "sent down" from university for one year at the end of which she would be allowed to resubmit her essay for the next year's examination. Subsequently, the applicant acquired further expert advice which considered that the plagiarism was neither flagrant nor deliberate. Finally, the applicant sought judicial review and an order of *certiorari* quashing the decision of the committee of discipline.

[10.92] Barron J in the High Court stated that once a lay tribunal is required to act judicially, the procedures to be adopted by it must be reasonable having regard to this requirement and to the consequences for the person concerned in

---

[128] [1988] ILRM 724 *per* Barron J.

the event of an adverse decision.[129] He considered that the principles of natural justice require that the person involved should be aquainted with the complaint made against them and should have an opportunity to prepare and present their case:

> "Matters to be considered are the form in which the complaint should be made, the time to be allowed to the person to prepare a defence, and the nature of the hearing at which the complaint may be presented. In addition, depending upon the gravity of the matter, the person concerned may be entitled to be represented and may also be entitled to be informed of their rights. Clearly matters of a criminal nature must be treated more seriously than matters of a civil nature, but ultimately the criterion must be the consequences for the person concerned of an adverse verdict."[130]

[10.93] Barron J allowed the application holding that as plagiarism constituted a most serious breach of academic discipline being criminal in nature, the disciplinary procedures in determining the charge should be close to those of a court hearing. Accordingly, he ruled that the applicant:

(a) should have received in written form details of the specific charge being made against her and the basic facts alleged to constitute the offence;

(b) should have been permitted to be represented by a person of her own choice and should have been told in sufficient time of that right and any other attendant rights conferred on her under the procedure of the disciplinary tribunal;

(c) should have been permitted to hear evidence of the case against her at the hearing itself, to cross-examine that evidence and put forward her own evidence.

In reply to the contention of the respondent college that the *Smullen* decision was relevant to the situation in *Flanagan*, Barron J disagreed, saying that no element of magisterial responsibility or obligation to enforce or maintain discipline existed in the latter case. Furthermore, he was critical of the failure to apply proper procedures in this case and of the absence of any published college regulations under which the committee purported to act, both being matters which had prejudiced the applicant and led to the outcome in this case.[131]

School Rules and Codes of Discipline

[10.94] It is important that school rules and codes of discipline deal with banned substances, dangerous weapons and bullying. When inter-pupil violence arises

---

[129] [1988] ILRM 724 at 730.
[130] [1988] ILRM 724 at 731.
[131] [1988] ILRM 724 at 732.

which does not constitute serious violence or use of dangerous weapons, the procedures in the Code of Discipline or school rules should be implemented.

[10.95] If the principal or teachers become aware that "controlled" drugs are being brought into the school, they should contact the parents of the pupils involved without delay. Their priority must be the safety of the pupils. Any drugs found on the school premises should be confiscated and any "controlled" drugs ought to be given to the police.[132]

The Test of Reasonableness

[10.96] Any sanction administered in school must pass the test of reasonableness.[133] In *R v Taylor*[134] the Court of Appeal affirmed the conviction of a teacher who threw a copy book at a twelve year old pupil "occasioning actual bodily harm". Nolan J stated: "Reasonable chastisement involved a controlled, if not entirely cool, response and the throwing of an exercise book could not come within that category".

Bullying Behaviour

[10.97] When instances of abuse or bullying occur, or where reasonable suspicion of such abuse or bullying arises, the principal ought to act promptly to deal with the situation. Failure to act, which results in causal injury to a pupil or teacher may result in a breach of the duty of care. The law relating to bullying in schools is evolving both here and in England and settlements out of court have been made in both countries.[135] In a recent Irish case, the parents of a five year-old boy, who alleged that he was bullied at his Dublin primary school, finally dropped their claim against the school.[136] In the Circuit Court, the parents accepted a "without prejudice" offer of £1,200. The judge indicated, however, that the boy would be capable of recovering "substantial" damages if he were able to prove liability on the part of the school. Some lawyers are also of the view that teachers may also be under a duty of care to safeguard pupils from the psychological effects of bullying by fellow pupils.[137] The significance of an anti-bullying policy in this setting is obvious.

---

[132] Barrell and Partington, *Teachers and the Law* (1985), Methuen, pp 637-8.

[133] *Scorgie v Lawrie* (1883) 10 R Ct of Sessions 610.

[134] The Times, 28 December 1983.

[135] Beamish, 'Schoolboy injured in attack by bully boy', Irish Times 31 January 1998, in which an unprovoked attach on a secondary school pupil by another boy, who was previously a prefect, resulted in a £10, 000 settlement out of court was approved by the court; Cramb, 'Woman sues over bullies at her old school', Daily Telegraph, 9 November 1996, 10.

[136] 'Damages claim dropped in case of bullying', Irish Times, 11 October 1994.

[137] See Robinson, 'Damages for academic under performance; pupils as plaintiffs' Education and the Law, 9/2 (1996) 93-101.

Anti-Bullying Policy

[10.98] In demonstrating that it had discharged its duty of care as regards bullying, if would be of considerable assistance to a school to point out that:

(a) it had an adequate and appropriate policy on bullying which was sanctioned by the board of management;

(b) that such policy was formulated in conjunction with parents, teachers and senior pupils and formed part of a school's code of behaviour or school rules which parents had signed;

(c) that such policy was implemented when bullying or suspicions of bullying arose in the school;

(d) that when the principal became aware of the bullying behaviour, both the parents of the pupil who is bullying and of the pupil being bullied, were interviewed, permitted to state their case and received a warning regarding any similar future breaches;

(e) that both parties to the bullying were warned of the course of action which would be taken by the school to prevent further bullying;

(f) that close communication with the board was maintained on the bullying incident; and

(g) that other anti-bullying measures had been adopted by the school to prevent similar problems arising in the future.[138]

[10.99] If the matter has been fully discussed with the offending pupil and parents, due warnings have been given and yet the problem continues, then exclusion, suspension or even expulsion must be considered by the school in accordance with the articles of management, school regulations,[139] and Department Circulars. In the case of long-term suspension and expulsion, it is prudent to inform the Department so that arrangements for alternative education may be put in place for the student.

Home-School Agreements

[10.100] If s 23 of the Education (Welfare) Bill 1999 becomes law, schools will be obliged by law to prepare a code of behaviour with specified elements including the procedures to be followed before a student may be suspended or expelled from the school. Some schools draw up home-school agreements or so-

---

138 Such measures might include (a) an invitation to a guest speaker to speak to parents and pupils on the subject of bullying; (b) the use of pastoral care, guidance counsellors or psychological services to alleviate the problem; or the use of mime or drama to counteract bullying.

139 In primary schools the Patron must be informed of any proposed expulsion.

called "contracts" with parents which brings to the fore the question of their legal status.

[10.101] In England the pupil-teacher relationship is becoming more formalised as a result of the introduction of home-school agreements[140] which include a declaration signed by parents[141] or by pupils.[142] Such agreements stipulate the aims and values of the school and the educational duties of the parent and school and they further set out the expectation of the schools regarding student behaviour. The School Standards and Framework Act 1998 makes it clear, however, that these agreements are not legally binding contracts between the parents and the school authority or the school and parents are not bound to sign them.

Violent Pupils

[10.102] While the level of reported incidents of violence in schools in Ireland is low,[143] there is a common perception in society that such problems are on the increase.

[10.103] The Minister's recent circular "Guidelines on Violence in Schools"[144] articulates his concern regarding incidents of violence against staff and others in second level schools. This circular draws attention to the statutory obligations[145] falling on school management authorities to provide a safe environment for employees and others affected by the work activity in the school. It recommends management authorities to consider, agree and implement procedures in regard to violence in schools and emphasises the necessity for an adequate complaints procedure and good communication between home and school generally.

[10.104] Among the internal organisational issues which the circular includes for the school's consideration and implementation, where appropriate, are:

(a) the raising of awareness among school staff of policies relating to discipline, bullying, health and safety and associated spheres such as the threat of violence, through discussion at staff meetings and at other times:

(b) restriction of access by visitors to the school and its environs;

(c) use of signs in the school grounds and premises;

---

[140] Standards and Framework Act 1998, ss 110-111.
[141] Which is not mandatory.
[142] If they are of an age to understand the import of what they are signing.
[143] See Circular M 18/99.
[144] To: Management Authorities of Second Level Schools, M 18/99: see also Circular 40/97 in the case of primary schools.
[145] Under the Safety, Health and Welfare at Work Act 1989 and the Safety, Health and Welfare at Work (General Application) Regulations, 1993.

(d) use of visitors' badges;

(e) requiring visitors to report to a designated area in the school;

(f) implementing security measures in the school;

(g) restricting access to teachers and structuring an appointments only access system;

(h) structuring parent-teacher meetings according to the School Plan; and

(i) drafting a Code of Discipline in accordance with the suggested Code of Discipline circulated with Circular M 33/91 in which violent behaviour towards a teacher is regarded as serious or gross misbehaviour which may warrant suspension.

This circular further outlines steps which ought to be followed in the event of an alleged assault on any person in the school.

[10.105] School authorities have a statutory duty under the Safety, Health and Welfare at Work Act 1989 to provide a safe environment for their employees and pupils which is discussed in Chapter 11 below.

[10.106] The Report of the Committee on Discipline in Schools (1985) was not implemented and since then problems relating to school discipline have received little formal attention and scant forward planning.[146] The issue of school discipline is closely linked to the problem of early school leaving or drop-out and this liaison is recognised in Article 28.1(e) of the Convention on the Rights of the Child which requires State Parties to "... take measures to encourage regular attendance at schools and the reduction of drop-out rates". While home-school liaison schemes and other innovative schemes have made a significant impact, a coordinated, long-term, nationwide plan is long overdue. This situation will be seriously addressed following the passage of the Education (Welfare) Bill 1999 through the Oireachtas.

Recent Changes in English Law

[10.107] In England and Wales, the legal and professional accountability of teachers has grown substantially and this has been perceived as considerably diminishing the autonomy of teachers generally.[147] Many educational professionals are now of the view that the law seems to have driven a wedge between teacher and pupil by interfering with the well-established, legally

---

[146] See however the report of the then Minister for Education, Niamh Breathnach, TD, on discipline in Schools by Dr Maeve Martin, 1997.

[147] See Department of Education and Employment, Press Notice 206/98, Teachers in Service, 27 April 1998.

recognised, *in loco parentis* relationship that the teacher acts as a quasi-parent to the pupil with corresponding authority, responsibility and autonomy.[148] Harris cites, as an illustration of this approach, the manner in which the teacher is warned, by the Department for Education and Employment, against giving advice on contraceptives to pupils below the age of consent in law without the parents' knowledge, on the grounds that only doctors are permitted to do this.[149] He further observes that in some instances parental rights may make it difficult for a teacher to act as guardian of the child's rights. In this regard, he refers to the unconditional right of parents to withdraw their child from sex education in school, introduced in 1994 when the provision of sex education in schools became compulsory in England.[150] A similar right exists in Irish law which has a much wider ambit.[151]

[10.108] English society has responded, to some degree, to the collective concerns of teachers who feared erosion of their disciplinary authority in schools by introducing a number of important statutory supports for schools. Apart from the Local Government (Miscellaneous Provisions) Act 1982, already mentioned, which included a new offence, that of creating a nuisance or disturbance on the premises of maintained schools, the Education Act 1997 put in place, *inter alia*, a number of significant provisions on school discipline including the making of post school detention lawful, s 5, and conferring powers on members of staff to restrain pupils, s 4. The closing of the legal loophole in regard to post-school detention and the introduction of powers of school staff to restrain pupils are particularly significant measures.

[10.109] Moreover, the School Standards and Framework Act 1998 requires the governing body to ensure that the school formulates a policy for the promotion of good behaviour and discipline among its pupils. These provisions should serve to improve the disciplinary climate of English schools and support teachers and schools in their daily work.

---

[148] Harris, 'The Autonomy of the Teacher: Education Law and Educational Standards in England and Wales' Paper read at European Association for Education Law and Policy, 23 december 1998 in Salzburg, at p 8.

[149] Harris referring to Department for Education and Employment Circular 5/94, *Education Act 1993: Sex Education in Schools*, (1994) London, Department for Education and Employment; see also *Gillick v West Norfolk and Wisbeck Area Health Authority* [1985] 3 All ER 402 (HL) in which Victoria Gillick challenged the legality of the provision of advice about contraceptives by doctors to under-aged girls in the absence of parental consent.

[150] Harris; on this issue see further Thompson, 'Sex education and the law: working towards good practice', in Harris, ed, *Children, Sex Education and the Law*, pp 99-112.

[151] Section 30(2)(d) of the Education Act 1998 provides that the Minister shall not require any student to attend instruction in any subject which is contrary to the conscience of the parent of the student or, in the case of a student who has reached the age of eighteen years, contrary to the conscience of the student.

Conclusion

[10.110] The disciplinary-related provisions of the Education Act 1998 introduce some important structuring into the traditionally informal school disciplinary system in Ireland. The appeals procedure introduced by the Act is particularly welcome, as it will bring regulatory control and some equity into this important sphere of school life. Yet, despite the more participative approach to school discipline envisaged by the Act, schools essentially retain their hierarchical structure. The class teacher is normally responsible for the discipline of pupils in the classroom. When serious problems arise, the help of the principal is enlisted and if such problems persist, matters are then referred to the chairperson of the board of management and ultimately to the board of management or the patron. Deputy-principals, year-heads and other teachers may also have disciplinary duties delegated to them in secondary schools.

[10.111] Because the legal and constitutional constraints are rudimentary, boards of management, principals and teachers retain much lawful latitude in the drafting of rules and in the drawing up of disciplinary codes. However, blatant disregard or lack of knowledge of well settled law or well established legal or constitutional rights or duties are no longer acceptable. School authorities and teachers need to be informed and aware of relevant legal principles and of their application in school life. With the guidance of these principles, they can do much to eliminate the capriciousness often associated with school discipline in former days.

[10.112] It appears that the Irish courts will interfere in the administration of discipline in schools only in the following circumstances:

(a) when school authorities or teachers exceed their powers ie act outside of their Articles of Management, or

(b) when decisions made by the Secretary General under s 29 of the Education Act 1998 are appealed to the courts by way of judicial review, or

(c) if the sanction administered fails to pass the test of reasonableness.

It is no longer acceptable to rely entirely on legal sanctions. New approaches are required while existing schemes which have demonstrated a measure of success should be extended. In maintaining good standards of conduct, schools need societal support which translates into a range of support services to assist them in performing their disciplinary obligations. Some changes in the law, as it stands, may also be necessary so as to buttress schools in their disciplinary authority. In this regard s 24 of the Education (Welfare) Bill 1999 and the other provisions of this Bill are of singular relevance.

[10.113] With regard to provision, at this juncture, the author believes that existing State obligations in education should be discharged prior to the assumption of any further obligations such as universal pre-schooling; the exception to this being free pre-schooling for all officially designated disadvantaged areas.

Chapter 11

Employment Law Relating to Teachers

Introduction

[11.01] By contrast with most European countries, in which the State or one of its sub-levels (province, county or city) employs the teacher,[1] the majority of Irish teachers are employed by a board of management on behalf of the churches while, at the same time, they are classified as public servants.[2]

[11.02] This dual control, which has been a feature of teacher employment in Ireland since 1891 has led to a variety of views on the legal relationships which arise when the teacher signs a contract of employment with the school manager. Chapter 6 above has shown that teachers have statutory duties under the Education Act 1998 and that they will have further statutory obligations, it appears, arising under the Education (Welfare) Bill 1999 when it comes into operation.

Teacher Employment: Dual Controls

[11.03] Because of the non-statutory base of education, until recently changes in the Church-State control of education occurred over time which influenced the employment context of teachers. As was shown in Chapter 2, Stanley's letter envisaged that the schools would be State-owned multi-denominational institutions and that the training of teachers would take place in State-owned colleges. By the end of the nineteenth century, however, the reality was that virtually all schools were Church-owned denominational institutions and teachers were trained in denominational colleges. These changes resulted in a considerable increase in church control over the system generally and specifically over teacher employment.

[11.04] Even before legislative reforms were envisaged, changes were being effected by virtue of the evolution of the role of Minister for Education which is

---

[1] See Verbruggen and Fiers, 'Synthetic and Analytical Overview of the Legal Status of Teachers in Europe' *The Legal Status of Teachers in Europe*, in de Groof, ed, (1995), Uitgeverij Acco, Belgium, p 49 at 53.

[2] *Cf* the position of teachers under European law, above, Ch 7.

traced by the late Seán O'Connor in his book *A Troubled Sky*.[3] In latter years, the role of Minister for Education has moved centre-stage and its contemporary development is perhaps best exemplified in the career of Niamh Bhreathnach TD and in that of the current holder of the office, Micheál Martin TD.

[11.05] As Ireland implements a legislative base for education, greater control of education is moving to the State, although to a lesser degree than that envisaged by the Education Bill 1997. These changes will effect a closer employment relationship between the State and the teacher. Although, it is frequently asserted that "no man can serve two masters",[4] Irish teachers have been required to meet this daunting challenge for many generations.[5]

Contrast with European Norm

[11.06] In other European countries, publicly-funded denominational schools co-exist with, but are separate from, the public school sector whereas in Ireland, denominational education is frequently the only option available for teacher employment. As has been seen in earlier chapters, there is some evidence that this traditional pattern is changing. The chief distinction between teachers in Europe, so far as the legal nature of their contract of employment is concerned, is between those who teach in public sector schools and those employed in private education. In some European countries, the former are employed under a public contract and are classified as civil servants[6] while the latter group are

---

[3] (1986) Educational Research Centre, Drumcondra. O'Connor notes the development in the concept of the ministerial function, as perceived by successive Ministers, from that of "dungaree man" in 1956 (contained in General Mulcahy's speech made in 1956) to that of "captain of the ship" made by Dr Hillery TD, Address to Dublin Chómhairle of Fianna Fáil, 28 February 1964. General Mulcahy's speech stated: "Deputy Moylan has asked me to philosophise, to give my views on educational technique or educational practice. I do not regard that as my function in the Department of Education. You have your teachers, your managers and your churches, and I regard the position as Minister in the Department of Education as that of a kind of dungaree man, the plumber who will make the satisfactory communications and streamline the forces and potentialities of the educational workers and educational management in this country. He will take the knock out of the pipes and link up everything. I would be blind to my responsibility if I insisted on pontificating or lapsed into an easy acceptance of an imagined duty to philosophise here on educational matters.", (1956), Dáil Reports, Vol 159. O'Connor's praise for Mulcahy is nonetheless fulsome, his misfortune being to express publicly "what had always been the accepted viewpoint of previous Ministers and of the Department".

[4] See *Chappell v The Times Newspapers Ltd* [1975] 2 All ER 233 at 239 *per* Lord Denning MR; see 'The relation of master and servant at common law' in Redmond, *Dismissal Law in Ireland*, (1999), Butterworths, p 19; on the public service dimension of a teacher's employment see *McEneaney v Minister for Education* [1941] IR 430 discussed below, para **[11.19]**.

[5] See McCarthy, *The Distasteful Challenge*, (1968), IPA, p 109 for an interesting comment of the influence of the national teacher on Irish society.

[6] Eg, teachers are civil servants in Germany, France and Italy, see *The Legal Status of Teachers in Europe*, De Groof, ed, (1995), Uitgeverij Acco.

employed under a contract governed by the usual labour law rules and regulations.[7] Unlike most of their European counterparts, who are paid directly by their employers, teachers in Ireland are paid directly by the State[8] rather than by their employing board of management. As a result of these unique features, this branch of employment law is highly complex.

Industrial Relations Acts

[11.07] While the Industrial Relations Acts 1946-1990 make statutory provision for collective bargaining generally, national teachers, secondary teachers, officers of a VEC and those who are employed "by or under the State" are excluded from the scope of this legislation as they are not classified as "workers" under the Acts.[9] Practical reasons for this exclusion, Forde suggests, may include the need to uphold public authority and the indispensable character of the education services.[10] In any event, separate conciliation and arbitration machinery for teacher pay has been established and new schemes are currently being negotiated which will apply to all teaching sectors.

The Sources of Employment Law

[11.08] Apart from their contractual rights and duties, since the 1970s, teachers, like other employees, are protected by a growing body of individual employment rights, deriving from modern employment legislation. These statutes constitute a basic statutory minimum for all employees, which cannot lawfully be excluded by an employer.[11] This chapter is necessarily selective as it deals only with the legislation which is of particular relevance to teachers. The role of the Constitution is also germane to this branch of law as the employing bodies, teachers and their representative organisations, as well as the pupils, have constitutional rights which influence employment law. Furthermore, Ireland's membership of the EC has resulted in growing protection for employees deriving from a number of Community Directives.

---

7   See Verbruggen and Fiers, 'Synthetic and Analytical Overview of the Legal Status of Teachers in Europe' *The Legal Status of Teachers in Europe*, in de Groof, ed, (1995), Acco, Belgium, p 52.

8   Although in the primary sector, payment is made conditionally as the Rules for National Schools require that the chairperson of the board sign on the monthly "returns" to the Department that the school has implemented the said Rules.

9   Section 23(1) of the 1990 Act.

10 Forde, *Industrial Relations Law*, (1991), Round Hall Press, p 192 and generally Ch 7; Fennell and Lynch, *Labour Law in Ireland*, (1993) Gill & MacMillan.

11 See Meenan, *Working Within the Law*, (1994), Oak Tree Press, Part 2.

Contracts of Employment

[11.09] The parties to the contract of employment in teacher employment comprise the school authorities (boards of management, VECs, limited companies, private individuals, boards of governors - depending on the school type), on the one hand, and the teacher, on the other.

[11.10] There is *privity of contract* between the employer and the employee and a stranger to the contract cannot lawfully interfere in this relationship. It is standard practice that the employer pays a salary or wage to the employee who undertakes to work for him. However, the teacher's contract of employment constitutes an exception to normal privity doctrine. In this respect, the legal position is most unusual in that a third party, the Department of Education and Science, remunerates the teacher out of moneys voted by the Oireachtas.[12] Furthermore, the Department significantly influences the context in which the teacher's contract is made. Hence, the public service dimension of teacher employment can scarcely be denied as a Department of State:

(a) pays teachers' salary and superannuation benefits;

(b) issues salary cheques and payslips to the teacher;

(c) sets terms and conditions of teacher employment;

(d) determines teacher qualifications;

(e) sanctions teacher appointments and promotional posts in recognised schools; and

(f) inspects the professional work of teachers.

[11.11] Moreover, notice of tax free allowances and tax free certificates for teachers all indicate that the Department of Education is the teacher's employer in this regard. By virtue of recent legislation such as the Education Act 1998, teachers will have new provisions inserted into their contracts of employment, by operation of law, under Part V of that Act, when it comes into force. Clearly, the employment relationship between the State and the teacher is becoming more formalised and the teacher may yet be considered as having joint employers, the board of management and the State.

Entering into a Contract of Employment

[11.12] When a teacher accepts a teaching post in a school, he enters into a contract of service[13] with the board of management and agrees to be bound by the Rules for National Schools, in the primary sector. This contract may be written or oral. The law, however, encourages written contracts of employment,[14]

---

[12] *Maunsell v Minister for Education* [1940] IR 213 at 221 *per* Gavan Duffy J.

[13] *Leyden v AG* [1926] IR 334; *Ryan v Madden* [1944] IR 154; *Cox v Ireland* [1992] 2 IR 503.

[14] Terms of Employment (Information) Act 1994, s 3.

and they are now commonly in written form. Letters of appointment or acceptance may also be considered as part of the contract which may later be confirmed by the signing of a Standard Form Contract or Memorandum of Agreement. Contracts normally fall into one of the following categories:

(a) *written or oral contracts* for continuous employment;

(b) *fixed-term contracts* (for a fixed period where, at the time of their making, the date of commencement and termination are known);

(c) *specified purpose contracts* (contracts where at the time of their making, are for a limited period only, but are not capable of exact ascertainment at that time).[15]

[11.13] When a contract for a fixed term expired under the common law, this would not constitute a dismissal as the contract had expired in accordance with its terms.[16] It is now clear, however, that, under the Unfair Dismissals Acts 1977-1993 (UDAs) such terminations are regarded as dismissals and these dismissals may be classified as unfair dismissals unless the employer (the board) can establish substantial grounds justifying the dismissal.[17] If the employer wishes to exclude the application of the UDAs in fixed term contracts and in specified purpose contracts, when these contracts terminate, then he must comply strictly with the requirements of s 2(2)(b) of the UDAs.[18] Section 3 of the Unfair Dismissals (Amendment) Act 1993 amended s 2 of the 1977 Act by inserting a proviso that where:

(a) following dismissal consisting only of the expiry of the term of a fixed term contract,

(b) the employee concerned is re-employed by the employer concerned within 3 months of the dismissal under another fixed term contract of similar nature to the prior contract, and

(c) then the employee is dismissed by reason of the expiry of the second or later fixed term contract, the term of all the contracts will be added together and shall be deemed to be continuous service,

(d) This provision will operate only on condition that in the opinion of the rights commissioner, the Tribunal or the Circuit Court, as the case may be, the entry by the employer into the subsequent contract was wholly or partly for the avoidance of liability under this Act.

---

[15] See further Meenan, *Working within the Law*, (1994), Oak Tree Press, Chs 2 and 3; Forde, *Employment Law*, (1992), Round Hall Press; Redmond, 'Beyond the Net - Protecting the Individual Worker', (1983) JISLL 1; and Redmond, *Dismissal Law in Ireland*, (1999), Butterworths, paras 22.73-22.104.

[16] Madden and Kerr, *Unfair Dismissals: Cases and Commentary* (2nd ed, 1996), Irish Business and Employers Association, p 65 *et seq.*

[17] See *Fitzgerald v St Patrick's College, Maynooth* UD 244 1978.

[18] See further Meenan, p 42; Madden and Kerr, p 65 and Redmond, paras 22.38-22.41.

The Primacy of the Contract

[11.14] Although the employment relationship is also subject to European Union law, constitutional provisions, tort law and a growing body of employment legislation, the individual contract of employment remains at the centre of the employment relationship and the respective rights and duties of the parties and disputes arising are largely governed by the terms of the contract. Although, the contract is the pivot of this relationship, collective bargaining and collective agreements are, in practice, the primary source of regulation.

Collective Agreements

[11.15] There does not appear to be any authority on the question of what constitutes a collective agreement and arguably, it would be a mistake for the courts to attempt to define this term. The Anti-Discrimination Pay Act 1974 defined this term as "an agreement relating to terms and conditions of employment made between parties who are or represent employers and parties who are or represent employees." Clearly, one of the essential elements of collective agreements is that there is a collectivity at work at least on the part of the workers and it takes place in the setting of a firm and continuing relationship between the parties.[19]

[11.16] In practice, however, employing bodies, teacher unions, and the State remain free to negotiate and regulate their respective rights and conduct subject to certain sets of informal rules and regulations made by the Department[20] or by the school[21] or by the agreement of the parties.

The Teacher as Public Servant

[11.17] The exception to the above-mentioned privity doctrine gives rise to a complex tripartite legal relationship described by Gibson J, when construing the Rules for National Schools in *Fox v Higgins*.[22] He stated that the fair inference is that the National Board [of Commissioners], the manager and the teacher are "put together in a kind of triangular pact ...".[23] As the matter at issue in the *Fox* case was the contractual relationship between the manager and the teacher,

---

[19] See further, Von Prondzynski and McCarthy, *Employment Law in Ireland*, (2nd ed, 1989), Sweet and Maxwell, p 24 applied in *O'Cearbhaill v Bord Telecom Éireann,* Supreme Court, unrep, 20 December 1993 at p 18.

[20] Rules for National Schools, (1965) Gov Pubs; Community Schools and Colleges, see Articles of Management contained in Deeds of Trust for Community Schools and Colleges in the Archdiocese of Dublin, 1982.

[21] In the voluntary secondary school sector see *A Manual for Boards of Management of Catholic Schools*, published by the Council of Managers of Catholic Secondary Schools, 1991.

[22] (1912) ILTR 222.

[23] (1912) ILTR 222 at 224.

Gibson J did not find it necessary to further elucidate the legal relationship between the State and the teacher.

[11.18] The triangular nature of the teacher's employment agreement again arose for consideration in the High Court in *Maunsell v Minister for Education.*[24] In that case, Gavan Duffy J held that, on its true construction, the agreement means that both parties sign (the contract) on the understanding that the teacher, so long as his salary is not withdrawn, is to receive from the central authority the remuneration appropriate under the code for a teacher of his class and standing. He found that while there was in terms no express contract between the Board and the teacher, there was at least an implied contract to pay (the teacher), and had there been none, the board would have been bound by estoppel.[25] In his incisive analysis of the managerial system, Gavan Duffy J recognised:

(a) that the Department of Education of which the Minister is the head, was expressly entrusted with primary education by a statute of Saorstát Éireann in 1924;[26]

(b) that the status of a national teacher entering the service under the agreement (contract) had not "the precarious tenure of an officer who can be dismissed at pleasure";

(c) that the teacher's status is that of a pensionable public servant[27] entitled to fair procedures; and

(d) that in the absence of fair procedures, the teacher's salary had been unlawfully withdrawn.[28]

[11.19] Three years later in *McEneaney v Minister for Education,*[29] Gavan Duffy J in the Supreme Court[30] confirmed that, while the Minister is not in terms a party to the teacher's contract, the plaintiff entered into his successive contracts as a condition precedent to the receipt of salary out of public funds entrusted to the board or to the Minister who is at the head of primary education by virtue of statute[31] and a Transfer of Functions Order.[32] Even if it were a tenable

---

[24] [1940] IR 213 (HC).

[25] (1912) ILTR 222.

[26] The Minister and Secretaries Act 1924.

[27] *Maunsell v Minister for Education* [1940] IR 213 at 228.

[28] *Maunsell v Minister for Education* [1940] IR 213 at 234. Such procedures are detailed as (a) that the plaintiff had fair notice that an inquiry was to be held to determine his fate; (b) that the plaintiff had fair notice of the case against him; and (c) that the plaintiff had a fair opportunity to meet the allegations made against him.

[29] [1941] IR 430 439 SC which was a 3:2 decision.

[30] At pp 436-7.

[31] The Minister and Secretaries Act 1924.

[32] *McEneany v Minister for Education* [1941] IR 430 at 433.

proposition in law, he stated, to treat the contract between the manager and the teacher as a matter in which the Department had no concern, it would be quite at variance with reality, but that it is not so.[33] Murnaghan J, who gave the main judgment on behalf on the court, stated that:

(a) the contract between the manager and the teacher does not comprise the entire relationship;

(b) the provision of primary education for more than a century has been recognised as a national obligation;

(c) the manager does not own the school but is in the position of a trustee of an educational trust;

(d) teachers are protected against changes which depend upon new qualifications for the individual teacher; and

(e) the Department is not, in the case of teachers appointed under one set of rules, entitled to modify those rules to the detriment of individual teachers who may not reach special standards devised from time to time.[34]

[11.20] In practice, therefore, the teachers had finally established their status as public servants. Moreover, the Minister could not unilaterally alter a rule in the Rules for National Schools with adverse retrospective effect on a teacher's entitlement. Possibly because of the delicate Church-State interests involved, in *Crowley v Ireland*[35] the Supreme Court took a minimalist view of the State's role in primary education. Apart from stating that the relationship between the State and the teacher was non-contractual,[36] the court did not clarify the precise nature of that important relationship. So, despite the clear advances achieved in *Maunsell* and *McEneaney*, the nature of that relationship remains ambiguous although it will, of course, be fundamentally altered by the Education Act 1998 when fully operational. Some cases coming before the Rights Commissioners or employment tribunals have considered the relationship between the State and the teacher in the context of modern employment legislation.

Modern Employment Law Decisions

[11.21] In *McGovern v Department of Education*,[37] the Employment Appeals Tribunal (EAT) held that the claimant, a national teacher, was not excluded from

---

[33] *McEneany v Minister for Education* [1941] IR 430 at 433.

[34] *McEneany v Minister for Education* [1941] IR 430 at 439 citing *Fox v Higgins* (1912) 46 ILTR 222.

[35] [1980] IR 102.

[36] *Crowley v Ireland* [1980] 102 at 126 *per* Kenny J.

[37] Case No UD 553/89.

bringing a claim under the Unfair Dismissals Act 1977 as, for the purposes of this Act, it considered that the board acted as the agent of the Minister in providing competent teachers to perform the functions devolved on the Minister by the Constitution.[38] Although this approach would not accord with the Supreme Court's findings relating to the system of education in *Crowley v Ireland*,[39] this case was not appealed.

[11.22] It was held in *Candon v Department of Education*,[40] that the Department was the employer for the purposes of the Anti-Discrimination Pay Act 1974. In *Dunphy v Scoil Eoin Phóil*,[41] counsel for the complainant argued before the rights commissioner that his client had two employers for the purposes of the Payment of Wages Act 1991 and that, as she had discharged the duties she had undertaken, she was entitled to be paid for them. The rights commissioner held that the deductions made from the complainant's salary over a ten week period, should not have been made and ordered the Department to pay £184.80 (gross) to the teacher and to recover 20% of that sum from the school.

[11.23] Once again, in *O'Sullivan v Department of Education*,[42] which was an appeal to the EAT against the decision of a rights commissioner, the Department of Education was recognised as the employer for the purposes of the Payment of Wages Act 1991 (the 1991 Act) and not just as "a paying agent" as argued by the Department. The complainant was a secondary school teacher who alleged that she had been paid an incorrect rate of degree allowance since her employment commenced and that this amounted to an unlawful deduction under the 1991 Act. The EAT considered that, in all the circumstances of the case, it was satisfied there were sufficiently close ties and controls exercised by the Department in relation to individual teachers so as to establish that the Department is the employer for the purposes of the 1991 Act and that the deductions were unlawful deductions within the meaning of the 1991 Act.[43]

[11.24] The public service dimension of teacher employment is also manifested in the centralised bargaining process in which teachers collectively participate through their unions and professional bodies.

---

[38] At p 4 of the decision.
[39] [1980] IR 102.
[40] DEP 387.
[41] Rights Commissioners, CW 616/96, 19 June 1996. The complainant, a national teacher, contended that she had discharged extra duties in school and that the Department made unlawful deductions from her pay over a 10 week period in 1995. The school, however, considered that the teacher had been correctly paid.
[42] (1998) ELR, Vol 9, No 4.
[43] See also Case No ST/604/94, *Ni Dhubháin v Scoil Iognáid and Department of Education*, recommendation of Rights Commissioner, 24 June 1994, *Payment of Wages Act 1991*.

Centralised Agreements with the State

(i) Revised Management Structures

[11.25] A revision of management structures for all schools has been implemented as part of the Programme for Competitiveness and Work (PCW) agreement. From the employment perspective, these arrangements are significant as they introduced much needed promotional prospects into school management. They are grounded in new contracts thus indicating the growing formalisation of the teaching profession. These structures include new posts of:

    (a) Deputy principal (formerly vice-principal);

    (b) Assistant principal; and

    (c) Special duties teachers.[44]

The principal, deputy principal and special duties teachers form the in-school management team of the schools.[45] Specific duties have been allocated to these categories and, on appointment, principals, deputy principals and post-holders are required to enter into appropriate contracts.[46] In the case of VEC schools and colleges, the relevant Chief Executive Officer is also required to certify that the principal, deputy principal or teacher concerned is undertaking assigned duties in compliance with the terms of the Circular.[47]

(ii) Remuneration

[11.26] With regard to, *inter alia*, remuneration in the past decade centralised bargaining with the State has given rise to a number of national programmes, in which teaching representative bodies participate such as:

    (a) Programme for National Recovery (PNR);

    (b) Programme for Economic and Social Progress (PESP);

    (c) Programme for Competitiveness and Work (PCW);

    (d) Partnership 2000 for Inclusion and Competitiveness.[48]

The objective of this social partnership is to achieve joint ownership by management, unions and staff of the entire process. In this development,

---

[44] See Department of Education, National Schools, Circulars 6/97, 9/97; Secondary Schools, 3/98, 5/98, 6/98 and 7/98; Community and Comprehensive schools, Circulars 23/98, 24/98, 25/98, Vocational schools and Vocational Colleges, Circulars 20/98, 21/98 and 22/98.

[45] See Circular 5/98.

[46] Specimen contracts have been included in the relevant Circulars sent out to schools.

[47] Circular 20/98.

[48] (1996), Gov Pubs, see Education, p 22. Partnership 2000 contained "Action for Greater Social Inclusion" with a significant focus on education together with a Draft Agreement on Pay and Conditions between the ICTU and employer bodies.

education is envisaged as having a pivotal role to play. Provision was also made in the centralised bargaining process for discussion of redeployment arrangements for comprehensive and community schools and for voluntary early retirement.

[11.27] Not all agreements are made with the State, however and some important collective agreements, negotiated with the bishops, are still in contemporary use. One of these is the Maynooth Agreement.

Collective Agreements with the Bishops: National Teachers

[11.28] Prior to the establishment of the INTO in 1868, national teachers could be dismissed by the manager without notice or cause assigned.[49] Following the recommendations of the Powis Commission Report (1870),[50] a period of three months' notice of dismissal provision was implemented through the introduction of four forms of contract or agreement in 1873. The power of dismissal was absolute in Form No 2 alone and this was the form chosen by virtually all managers. This form commonly referred to as "the green form"[51] is the contract form still signed by the majority of national teachers today, although now substantially altered by implied constitutional and statutory terms. When the teacher signed Form No 2, he could still be dismissed at any time, without cause assigned, by the payment of three months' salary or by the service of three months' written notice. The teacher could, of course, also be dismissed without notice at any time for misconduct or other substantial reason. Since the passing of the Unfair Dismissals Act 1977, notice is no longer a defence to an unfair dismissal.

First Maynooth Agreement or Resolution (1894)

[11.29] The first Agreement was adopted by the bishops in Maynooth in 1894. It provided that no three months' notice of dismissal might be served on a teacher by a Catholic clerical manager until the manager had made the patron (his bishop) aware of his intention to do so and until he had secured the assent of the bishop to serve such notice, the teacher having the right to be heard in his own defence. This fundamentally flawed agreement failed to cover the case of summary dismissal without notice or salary[52] and so dismissals continued,

---

[49] See further O'Connell, *100 Years of Progress*, (1968), INTO, p 43.

[50] *Report of the Commissioners appointed to enquire into the nature and extent of the instruction afforded by the several institutions in Ireland for the purpose of Elementary or Primary education; also in the practical working of the system of National Education in Ireland etc* HC 1870 (c 6) XXVIII, p 1; see also Norman, *The Catholic Church and Ireland in the Age of Rebellion*, (1865), London, p 432.

[51] See Finlay P's reference to it in *Cotter v Ahern* [1996-7] ILRM 248 at 263.

[52] O'Connell, pp 44-60.

leading in time to the successful challenge in *O'Sullivan v Hunt*[53] against the summary dismissal of a teacher in a Leixlip school in 1897 following a disagreement over the conduct of girls in the school choir. The four day hearing before Palles J and a jury in May 1898 gained considerable media attention bringing increased pressure on the bishops to remedy the situation to the satisfaction of the teachers.

The Maynooth "Statute" (1927)

[11.30] In 1898, the Maynooth Resolution was amended in order to rectify the flaw in the original version.[54] In 1927 the resolution was incorporated into a church "statute" in the National Synod of Maynooth. The relevant section of the "statute" reads as follows:

> To avoid prejudice against the managership of schools, a clerical manager is forbidden to appoint any teacher or assistant, male or female, in National Schools until he shall have consulted, and obtained the approval of the Bishop; likewise a clerical manager shall not dismiss any teacher or assistant, male or female, or give notice of dismissal, until the Bishop be notified, so that the teacher, if she/he will, may be heard in her/his own defence by the Bishop.

[11.31] The procedures followed in implementing the Maynooth "Statute", which bound all members of the Catholic church both clerical and lay, closely resembled those adopted in a court of law.[55] This collective agreement, which is grounded in contract law, has provided a considerable degree of protection for Catholic teachers over the years as it incorporated the natural justice principle *audi alteram partem*.[56] The mechanism established by the Maynooth Agreement is still used by contemporary teachers despite the availability of the statutory remedy provided by the Unfair Dismissal Acts 1977-1993.[57]

Redundancy Arrangements

[11.32] The redundancy or redeployment arrangements which exist for primary schools and voluntary secondary schools were described in Chapter 3 above in the constitutional context and further discussed in the setting of European Community law in Chapter 7. It was noted that while no legal challenge has been

---

[53] High Court, May 1898, Palles CB. For full details of this case, see O'Connell, *One Hundred Years of Progress*, p 45 *et seq*. In his address to the jury, Palles CB pointed out that as the law stood, a manager could dismiss a teacher employed by him without cause assigned by giving three months' notice or three months' salary. Furthermore, no matter how exemplary the teacher's conduct or how high his or her educational standard, the teacher's continuance in his or her position, for that period of three months, depended solely on the will of the manager.

[54] O'Connell, p 56.

[55] O'Connell, p 43.

[56] See below, para **[11.76]**.

[57] See below, para **[11.201]**.

taken against the primary school arrangements, the scheme in secondary schools was held to be constitutional in *Greally v The Minister for Education, AG and the ASTI*.[58] Furthermore, the conclusion was drawn in Chapter 7 that these schemes are unlikely to constitute indirect discrimination in Community law as they do not seem to prejudice the practical effectiveness of the EC Treaty itself.

Custom and Practice

[11.33] Certain customs and practice common in the profession may be implied as terms of the employment contract. These constitute rules of conduct which have become common as a result of long usage which if valid would acquire the force of law. If the alleged custom or practice is to be recognised as valid and achieve contractual status, it must meet with four requirements. It must be notorious, certain, reasonable and must not be contrary to statute law.[59]

[11.34] It has been held that a custom cannot be implied into a written contract unless it was so notorious or universal that no employee could have entered into the employment without having regarded it as part of the contract.[60]

The Ethos of Schools

[11.35] Clearly, an employer's interests may be non-financial and may embrace the maintenance of a particular ethos or characteristic spirit.[61] This is particularly true in the context of the largely denominational Irish education system where teachers who encounter ethos-related difficulties have virtually no alternative employment options available to them in the teaching sector.

[11.36] Apart from the common law's recognition of the ethos of denominational schools, the Constitution impliedly supports this concept.[62] Any attempt in protective employment legislation, therefore, to fetter ethos-related rights in denominational schools would be constitutionally vulnerable. Tensions may arise, therefore, between two legally established sets of rights:

(a) that of the religious employing authority to carry on its educational mission in its school(s) according to its religious beliefs and practices; and

(b) that of the individual teacher to freedom from discrimination in employment.

---

[58] High Court, unrep, 29 January 1999 *per* Geoghegan J.

[59] Forde, *Employment Law*, p 58.

[60] See *Devonald v Rosser and Sons* [1906] 2 KB 728 at 741; *Mills v Mayor of Colchester* (1867) LR 2 CP 567.

[61] See Redmond, *Dismissal Law in Ireland*, (1999), Butterworths, p 305, para 18.05.

[62] In Articles 42 and 44, above, Ch 2; *Crowley v Ireland* [1980] IR 102; *Campaign to Separate Church and State v Minister for Education* [1996] 2 ILRM 241.

[11.37] The dilemma which may result, when these two sets of interests conflict, was well illustrated when the internationally recognised author John McGahern was dismissed from his post as a primary teacher following the publication of *The Dark* in 1965. This book had been banned by the Censorship Board established under the Censorship Act 1946 as "indecent or obscene".[63] The author who was dismissed on the instructions of Doctor McQuaid, then Archbishop of Dublin, was no longer dependent on his teaching career as his potential as a writer was by then gaining recognition[64] so no litigation ensued. When Owen Sheehy Skeffington brought the matter up on the adjournment in the Seanad, he was informed that "no Ministerial responsibility was involved" as the Minister had no right to intervene when a teacher is dismissed for non-professional reasons. As the matter concerned the ethos of the school, the State had no jurisdiction over this sphere of teacher employment.[65] Matters relating to school ethos arose again in the 1980s in the case of *Flynn v Power*,[66] which is considered below under unfair dismissal.[67] That a teacher's career may also be vulnerable from a political standpoint, is clear from the case of *Cox v Ireland*[68] which is also discussed later.[69]

Statutory Provision: The Education Act 1998

[11.38] The Education Act 1998 provides for a range of matters relating to rights and duties in regard to education other than third level education. The Act formalises the relationship between the State and teachers in recognised schools by placing that relationship on a statutory basis for the first time in the history of the State.[70] While some of the provisions of the Act have come into effect,[71] Part

---

63   A further reason for the dismissal, it seems, was that Mr McGahern had, during a career break, married a non-Catholic in a registry office.

64   I am indebted to Mr McGahern for the interview he accorded me to discuss his dismissal, see further Owen Sheehy Skeffington, 'McGahern Affair', *Censorship*, June-September 1966 in which the writer states of that period; "We have one of the most successful educational systems in the world, its aim is to prevent the children from thinking for themselves. In all too many cases it is eminently successful ..." (p 30).

65   This matter is further discussed in an interview with the Mr McGahern in *My Education*, Townhouse Pubs, which is an edited version of much acclaimed radio broadcasts made by Radio Éireann between 1991-1996. This interview was later published in the Leitrim Guardian, 1998, p 79 with the kind permission of John Quinn and Townhouse Publishers.

66   [1985] ILRM 336.

67   At para **[11.223]**.

68   [1992] 2 IR 503.

69   At para **[11.235]** *et seq*.

70   With the exception of VEC teachers who already had a statutory framework in the VEC Acts 1930-1970.

71   Sections 2, 3, 4, 5, 6, 13, 25, 26, 36 37 and Parts VIII and IX of the Act are in operation, see Education Act 1998, Commencement Order 1991 (SI 29/1999).

V, which deals with the functions of principals and teachers, has not at the time of writing, come into effect. When Part V becomes operative, ss 22, 23 and 24 will be inserted by operation of law into the contracts of employment of teachers in recognised schools. VEC teachers, however, will not be bound by s 24.

Part V: The principal and Teachers

[11.39] Section 22(1) lays down the joint functions of principals and teachers. It provides that, in a recognised schools, the principal and teachers, under the direction of the principal, are responsible for the instruction of students in the school and that they shall contribute to their education and personal development.

[11.40] The functions of principals and teachers include the following duties, they must:

(a) encourage and foster learning in students,

(b) regularly evaluate students and periodically report the results of the evaluation to the students and their parents,

(c) collectively promote co-operation between the school and the community which it serves, and

(d) subject to the terms of any applicable collective agreement and their contract of employment, carry out those duties that -

    (i) in the case of teachers are assigned to them by or at the direction of the principal, and,

    (ii) in the case of the principal, are assigned to him or her by the board.[72]

[11.41] This provision builds on existing practice in schools.[73] Section 22(d) carries over and confers statutory protection on the existing contracts of employment of teachers and on any applicable collective agreements. Apart from the above-mentioned provisions in s 22, the following section (s 23) applies to the principal, who is also a teacher under the Act (s 2).

The principal

[11.42] Section 23(1) provides that the board of management shall appoint the principal in accordance with procedures to be agreed between the Minister, the patron, recognised school management bodies, teacher unions and staff associations, subject to terms and conditions determined by the Minister with the consent of the Department of Finance. Together with the functions laid down in s 22, the principal is responsible for the day to day management of the school, including the guidance[74] and direction of the teachers and other school staff and

---

[72] Section 22(2).

[73] See *dictum* of McCarthy J in *Murtagh v Board of Management of St Emer's National School* [1991] 2 ILRM 549 cited above, Ch 9, para **[9.10]**.

[74] *Cf* the word "guidance" with that of "control" which was in s 47(2) of the Education Bill 1997.

is accountable to the board for that management. This provision follows the thrust of the common law which cast the responsibility for the day to day running of the school on the principal and considered that teachers were subject to the reasonable directions of the principal provided such directions were within the scope of the contract of employment.

[11.43] The principal is also responsible, under this subsection, for the day to day management of the school for:

(a) providing leadership;

(b) for creating an environment which promotes learning and fosters the professional development of the teachers;

(c) for setting and monitoring school objectives and for encouraging parental participation in the education of the students and in the achievements and objectives of the school.

Again, this provision builds on the *status quo* which existed in schools with the addition of the obligation falling on the principal to set and monitor school objectives and to encourage the participation of parents in school life.

[11.44] Subsection (3) buttresses the role of the principal for it provides that he or she shall have all such powers as are necessary to carry out his functions under the Act in accordance with s 33 and the policies of the board of management.

[11.45] Under sub-s (4), the principal is entitled to become a member of any and every committee appointed by a board. Subsection (5) provides that, where before the commencement of the Act, the employer of a post-primary Principal is a body other than a board of management, that body shall, after the commencement of the Act, have the role outlined above, for the board of management in relation to the appointment of the principal. Subsection (6) provides that in carrying out his functions, a Principal shall consult, wherever practicable, with teachers and other staff. Although this provision views consultation with staff as generally desirable, it takes account of situations where this may be impossible or unattainable.

[11.46] For the most part, the Education Act 1998 puts into statutory form the practice which had been evolving in schools particularly since 1975. It recognises the fact that the principal's role is an integral part of the management of a school and that, although the principal is a teacher under the Act, his status is distinctive from that of other teachers in the school. The principal's functions are linked in some instances to ministerial functions and in others to the powers and potentialities of the governing body of the school.

[11.47] Section 23 stresses the accountability of the principal to the board for the management of the school generally, and specifically for specified areas of school life. While this section clearly envisages a spirit of consultation at least in certain spheres of school life, this is realistically qualified by the words "wherever practicable".

Provisions relating to school staff

[11.48] Section 24 applies to all recognised teachers, with the exception of teachers and other staff employed by VEC who are covered by the Vocational Education Acts 1930-1970.[75] It provides that a board may appoint as many teachers and other staff as are necessary for the performance of its functions under the Act but that the numbers, qualifications and remuneration of staff paid out of public funds are subject to the Minister's approval, with the concurrence of the Minister for Finance.

[11.49] Subsection (3) provides that the board shall appoint teachers and other staff, who are to be paid out of public funds, and that the board may suspend or dismiss such teachers and staff in accordance with procedures agreed between the Minister, the patron, recognised school management bodies and recognised trade unions and staff associations or other staff.

[11.50] Existing appointment, suspension and dismissal procedures are to remain in place pending agreement being reached as provided for in sub-s (3).

[11.51] Subsection (5) provides that the rates of remuneration and pension, which are to be paid out of Exchequer funds, shall be determined by the Minister from time to time with the concurrence of the Minister for Finance. Where before the commencement of the 1998 Act, the employer of staff in a post-primary school is a body other than a board of management, that body will, after the commencement of the 1998 Act, have the role outlined above, for the board of management in relation to staff.

Constitutional Provisions

The Constitutional Right to Dissociate

[11.52] The right to dissociate appears to derive from Article 40.6.1°(iii) and its guarrantee of freedom to form associations and unions. Two Supreme Court decisions, *Educational Co Ltd v Fitzpatrick*[76] and *Meskell v CIE*,[77] have

---

[75] See VEC Acts 1930-1970.
[76] (No 2) [1961] IR 345.
[77] [1973] IR 121.

confirmed the existence of a right not to be coerced into becoming a member of a trade union.

[11.53] In *Cotter v Ahern*,[78] the High Court, applying *Meskell* held that the defendant union's efforts to prevent the appointment or promotion of a national teacher as part of a nationwide strategy to seek to ensure that the plaintiff, and all other national teachers in any specific area or countrywide, would become and remain members of a trade union, was an actionable conspiracy as it sought to coerce the plaintiff into waiving his constitutional right to dissociate.

[11.54] In view of the implied constitutional right of all children to receive free primary education,[79] the question which comes to the fore is "in what circumstances may national teachers take lawful industrial action including strike action?"

The Right to Take Industrial Action

[11.55] A strike[80] is clearly one of more extreme types of industrial action resulting in concerted action by employees and cessation of work.[81] The scope of industrial action, which includes strikes, extends to bans on overtime, go-slows and working to rule. A further distinction arises from the fact that a strike usually results in the withdrawal of wages or salary from the employee[82] while other forms of industrial action may be resorted to without loss of wages or salary.[83]

[11.56] No legislation preventing strikes exists in the State although legal restrictions against strike action are implemented in certain parts of the public sector. Forde believes that some specific types of strike action may be unlawful even in the private sector.[84] In *Bates v Model Bakery Ltd*,[85] the Supreme Court affirmed the reasoning it had applied in *Becton, Dickinson Co Ltd v Lee*[86] that there is an implied term in every contract of employment acknowledging some freedom to resort to industrial action following proper notice.[87] Clearly there are

---

[78] High Court, unrep, 25 February 1977, Finlay P.

[79] *Crowley v Ireland* [1980] IR 102.

[80] For statutory definitions of "strike" see Redundancy Payments Act 1967 s 6 for the purposes of the 1967 Act and the Minimum Notice and Terms of Employment Act 1973.

[81] Kerr and Whyte, *Irish Trade Union Law*, (1985), Professional Books Ltd, Ch 6.

[82] Kerr and Whyte, p 205,

[83] See Redmond, *Dismissal Law in Ireland* (1999), Butterworths, p 384 *et seq.*

[84] Forde, *Industrial Relations Law*, (1991) Round Hall Press, p 102 and generally Ch 5.

[85] [1993] ILRM 22.

[86] [1973] IR 1.

[87] See further Forde, *Industrial Relations Law*, (1991) Round Hall Press, p 104 *et seq*; Byrne and Binchy, *Annual Review of Irish Law 1992*, pp 403-405.

some instances in which a court may find that this implied term does not exist or the contract may include a special term having the opposite effect. Case law indicates that judicial response to strike action alters depending on the means and purpose of strike action as the case of *Nolan Transport (Oaklands) Ltd v Halligan, Nolan, Ayton and SIPTU* illustrates.[88]

The Right of National Teachers to Strike

[11.57] It will be recalled that the case of *Crowley v Ireland*[89] arose out of strike action taken by the INTO on behalf of its members in the Drimoleague schools. The plaintiffs' claim against the INTO was for damage sustained by the plaintiffs arising out of an alleged conspiracy to deprive them of their constitutional right to free primary education. In the High Court, McMahon J was doubtful as to whether the refusal to enrol the children from neighbouring schools was the exercise of a constitutional right. Assuming, without so deciding, that the union members were exercising a constitutional right in refusing to enrol these children, he stated:

> "The character of an act depends on the circumstances in which it is done and the exercise of a constitutional right for the purpose of infringing the constitutional rights of others is an abuse of that right, which in my opinion, can be restrained by the Courts. The teachers who refused to enrol the Drimoleague schoolchildren in adjoining schools did not act primarily for the purpose of exercising a right to work or not to work. In my view their purpose was to deprive the Drimoleague children of primary education in order to exert pressure on Fr Crowley; what was done amounted to the use of unlawful means to deprive the Drimoleague children of their constitutional right."[90]

[11.58] However, the trial judge left open the question as to whether any of the plaintiffs were entitled to damages. The teachers' union did not appeal any part of the judgment and the appeal to the Supreme Court was taken by the State against the finding of liability against it. Delivering the judgment for the majority in the Supreme Court, Kenny J stated that the circular to the adjoining schools[91] was the foundation of the proceedings against the union and its central executive committee. He concurred with the trial judge, who held that the circular was an unlawful interference with the constitutional rights of the infant plaintiffs to free primary education which he considered "a most serious matter, particularly when carried out by this organisation of teachers".[92] This latter

---

[88] [1998] ELR 117.
[89] [1980] IR 102.
[90] *Crowley v Ireland* [1980] IR 102 at 110.
[91] Issued by INTO on 20 August 1976.
[92] *Crowley v Ireland* [1980] IR 102 at 128.

phrase implies that the pupil-teacher relationship was a pivotal factor in this decision as it is grounded in trust arising from the traditional *in loco parentis* principle. With regard to the right of the teachers to refrain from teaching, O'Higgins CJ stated:

> "I do not accept that such teachers had any constitutional right to do what they did. However, if they had any such right to refrain from teaching it was not a right which could be exercised for the purpose of frustrating, infringing or destroying the constitutional rights of others."

[11.59] With regard to the withdrawal of services by teachers, Kenny J stated:

> "The State cannot by laws compel teachers to teach when they do not wish to do so, though it may and should protect their right to teach when they wish to do so and others want to prevent them."[93]

In order to establish whether this particular strike was lawful, the courts balanced the constitutional rights of the pupils to free primary education with the rights of the teachers to strike or withdraw services in the specific circumstances of the case. Once the union sought to exercise such rights without regard to the rights of the pupils and to the harm that accrued to them, then the Court held that became "an abuse and not the exercise of a right given by the Constitution". Thus, it was the issue of the directive by the union on 20 August 1976 which was unlawful together with its implementation by the teachers in outlying schools. While the issue of liability was determined in the *Crowley* decision, the assessment of damages was a matter which was dealt with in subsequent related cases.

Assessment of Damages

[11.60] In *Conway v INTO*[94] Barron J awarded the plaintiff, whose education was adversely affected by the Drimoleague schools' strike, £10,000 for general loss and the loss of career prospects together with £1,500 for exemplary damages. When dismissing the appeal in the Supreme Court, Finlay CJ set down in detail the principles which apply to the granting of damages for tort or breach of constitutional right under three headings:

> (1) Ordinary compensatory damages;[95]

---

[93] *Crowley v Ireland* [1980] IR 102 at 130.

[94] [1991] 2 IR 305; see also *Sheehan v INTO* [1997] 2 IR 327 and *Hurley v INTO* [1991] 2 IR 328.

[95] Being sums calculated to recompense a wronged plaintiff for physical injury, mental distress, anxiety, deprivation of convenience, or other harmful effects of a wrongful act and/or for monies lost and/or expenses incurred or to be incurred by reason of the commission of the wrongful act.

(2) Aggravated damages;[96]

(3) Punitive or exemplary damages.[97]

[11.61] In deciding whether it is available to a court in assessing damages for a wrong comprising the breach of a constitutional right such as the right to a free primary education to grant exemplary damages,[98] the Supreme Court relied on *The State (Quinn) v Ryan*.[99] In particular it noted the statement of O'Dálaigh CJ, that the courts were the custodians of the fundamental rights of the citizens and that its powers in that regard were "as ample as the defence of the Constitution requires".

[11.62] Turning to the defendants in *Conway*, the court considered that the intended consequence of their acts had been to directly deprive the plaintiff of her constitutional right to free primary education together with the special relationship which the defendants bore to the general rights of the pupils to free primary education. The Court was satisfied that the instant case was an appropriate one in which it should mark its disapproval of the defendants' conduct as the right breached in this instance was one expressly vested in a child by the Constitution and it was a right of supreme and fundamental importance, the breach of such right was intended as distinct from an inadvertent result of the defendant's conduct and it must be presumed that the defendants were conscious of that importance.

---

[96] Being compensatory damages increased by reason of:
    (a) The manner in which the wrong was committed, involving such elements as oppressiveness or outrage or
    (b) the conduct of the wrongdoer after the commission of the wrong, such as a refusal to apologise or to ameliorate the harm done or the making of threats to repeat the wrong, or
    (c) conduct of the wrong-doer and/or his representative in the defence of the claim of the wronged plaintiff, up to and including the trial of the action.
Such a list of the circumstances which may aggravate compensatory damages until they can properly be classified aggravated damages is not intended to be in any way finite or complete. The circumstances which may properly form an aggravating feature in the measurement of compensatory damages must, in many instances, be in part a recognition of the added hurt or insult to a plaintiff who has been wronged, and in part also a recognition of the cavalier or outrageous conduct of the defendant.

[97] Arising from the nature of the wrong which has been committed and/or the manner of its commission which are intended to mark the court's particular disapproval of the defendant's conduct in all the circumstances of the case and its decision that it should be publicly be seen to have punished the defendant for such conduct by awarding such damages, quite apart from its obligation, where it may exist in the same case, to compensate the plaintiff for the damage which he has suffered.

[98] See *Rooks v Barnard* [1964] AC 1129.

[99] [1965] IR 70.

[11.63] Further judicial clarification on the right of national teachers to strike emerges from *Hayes v Ireland*,[100] another of the related cases which arose out of the *Crowley v Ireland*[101] case. In *Hayes*, Carroll J considered the union's argument that this was a classic trade union dispute in which it sought to prevent discrimination against a member, whom it suspected was being victimised on account of his trade union activities: Holding that the defendant's arguments could only be taken into account in deciding whether exemplary or punitive damages should be awarded, the judge found that, as such damages were not sought by the plaintiff, he was entitled to recover full damages for the injuries he could prove to have been sustained by him. Manifesting some judicial sympathy for the dilemma in which the union found itself, Carroll J stated:

> "However the union made an error of judgment in the method they chose. It is unfortunate for them and even more unfortunate for the isolated group of children involved that the method they chose was so discriminatory. Perhaps if the INTO had chosen the wider non-discriminatory weapon of a countywide strike which would have affected all the children of the State, they would probably not be here today. In a very difficult and frustrating situation they came to the wrong decision."[102]

Had the union chosen to withdraw its members in a nationwide strike affecting all the children of the State, it would most likely have been a lawful strike as the issue of the unlawful circular would not have arisen in such circumstances.

[11.64] From the above cases, it may be concluded that although national teachers have an implied term in their contracts of employment to some freedom to resort to industrial action, that right is constrained by virtue of the constitutional right of all children to a free primary education in that the teachers may not utilise their right in such a manner as to damage the children's right. The vulnerability of the national teachers' right to strike appears to arise largely from the implied constitutional right of the child to free primary education and from the special status of the teacher as a professional employee whose relationship is grounded in trust.

Deductions from Pay during Industrial Action

[11.65] As Forde observes, it has never seriously been contended that employees are legally entitled to be paid while they are on strike.[103] However, if teachers use other forms of industrial action, short of outright strike and are partially

---

[100] [1987] ILRM 651.
[101] [1980] IR 102.
[102] *Hayes v Ireland* [1987] ILRM 651.
[103] *Industrial Relations Law*, (1991), Round Hall Press, p 112.

performing their contractual duties, the question of whether they are lawfully entitled to full remuneration or part pay arises.

[11.66] General case law suggests that, where an employee has partially performed his contractual duties, that he is entitled to be paid on a *quantum meruit* basis for the work he had done.[104] When it comes to professional employees such as teachers, because their professional obligations are not set down in detail, specific problems may arise as the English case of *Sim v Rotherham MBC*[105] illustrates. This case dealt with an alleged breach of contract by second level teachers in England when they refused to "cover" for their absent colleagues as part of a campaign of industrial action. Scott J stated that he had no doubts as to the status of teaching as a profession.[106] Accordingly, he ruled that a head teacher and other advisory teachers were required to discharge the skill and care of professionals; in this instance, a reasonable head teacher and a reasonable advisory teacher.

[11.67] He noted that the contractual obligations of individuals employed in a professional capacity such as teachers were, (at that time), "defined largely by the nature of their professions and the obligations incumbent on those who follow those professions". Essentially, he indicated that because of the character of the teaching profession, in which many obligations are undefined, (as they then were in England at that time),[107] certain obligations are implied into that profession which are distinctive from those normally implied into the contracts of other non-professional employees. With the achievement of professional status comes professional accountability as equity requires one who enjoys a benefit (professional status) to carry a corresponding burden (professional liability for negligence).

[11.68] While Scott J accepted the premise, that teachers taking industrial action, short of strike, were entitled to the agreed pay, he ruled that the employer is also entitled to set off against such pay the loss sustained by him arising from the teachers' breach of contract. Because the teachers, who had refused to "cover" for absent colleagues during school hours as part of their industrial action, had breached an implied term in their contracts, Scott J held that their

---

[104] See *Miles v Wakefield Council* [1987] AC 539 at 561.

[105] [1986] 3 All ER 387.

[106] In the *Hampshire* appeal (one of "the education appeals") to the House of Lords cited as *X (Minors) v Bedfordshire County Council Appeals* [1995] ELR 404, HL, Lord Browne-Wilkinson also emphasised that teachers were professionals.

[107] The law in England was substantially changed with the coming into operation of the Teacher's Pay and Conditions Act 1991; the Education (School Teachers' Pay and Conditions) Order 1998 and School Teachers Pay and Conditions Document.

employer was acting lawfully when it reduced the teachers' monthly pay by a sum of money representing the damage sustained as a result of those breaches.

[11.69] With reference to vocational teachers, Farry, referring to *Miles v Wakefield Council*[108] and the fact that such teachers are salaried holders of an office, is of the view that deductions may lawfully be made from salary for breach of statutory obligations.[109] However, teachers, for their part, are entitled to avail of the protection of the Payment of Wages Act 1991 as illustrated in *O'Sullivan v Department of Education*,[110] *Dunphy v Scoil Eoin Phóil*[111] and *Ní Dhubhain v Scoil Iognáid and Department of Education*.[112]

Fair Procedures: Natural and Constitutional Justice

[11.70] It is well settled that a person who may be adversely affected by a decision relating to his rights should not be condemned without a hearing but must be given every opportunity to state his case.[113] Fair procedures can assist in ensuring that discipline is maintained in the place of work and that disciplinary measures are applied in a fair and consistent manner.[114] Natural justice principles, in Ireland, are further supported by constitutional justice and in particular the right to fair procedures.[115]

[11.71] One of the earliest Irish decisions on the right of public servants, (in this instance a national teacher), to fair procedures in the case of dismissal was *Maunsell v Minister for Education*.[116] The Minister had ceased the payment of

---

[108] [1985] AC 539 (HL).

[109] See *Vocational Teachers and the Law*, (1998), Blackhall Pubs, p 92.

[110] (1998) ELR, Vol 9, No 4.

[111] Rights Commissioners, CW 616/96, 19 June 1996. The complainant, a national teacher, contended that she had discharged extra duties in school and that the Department made unlawful deductions from her pay over a 10 week period in 1995. The school, however, considered that the teacher had been correctly paid.

[112] Case No ST/604/94, recommendation of Rights Commissioner, 24 June 1994 under Payment of Wages Act 1991.

[113] One of the oldest cases is *Bagg's Case* (1615) 11 Co Rep 936. Among the plaintiff's misdeeds was that of turning the hinder part of his body in an inhuman and uncivil manner towards the aforesaid Thomas Fowens, scoffingly, contemptuously and uncivilly, with a loud voice saying "come and kiss". Baggs, who was a freeman of the borough was disenfranchised but the court granted a *mandamus* for his restoration because it was not shown that he had been permitted to defend himself. Cited in Wade and Forsyth, *Administrative Law*, (7th ed, 1994), see generally Part V, natural justice, Ch 13, the rule against bias, Ch 14 and the right to a fair hearing, Ch 15.

[114] Redmond, *Dismissal Law in Ireland*, (1999), Butterworths, para 13.14.

[115] *McDonald v Bord na gCon* [1965] IR 217 SC; *East Donegal Co-operative v AG* [1970] IR 317 SC; *Re Haughey* [1971] IR 217; *Glover v BLN Ltd* [1973] IR 388 SC; *Gleeson v Minister for Defence* [1976] IR 280 SC; *O'Cearbhaill v Bord Telecom Éireann* Supreme Court, unrep, 20 December 1993 which distinguished *Glover*.

[116] [1940] IR 213.

the plaintiff's salary when enrolments at his school dropped below the required number. Investigations were carried out by the Department without any express notice to the teacher that he had a case to meet. In the High Court, Gavan Duffy J held the plaintiff was entitled to express notice in view of the fact that the Department was about to determine whether or not to put an end to his career:

> "The principle is long and firmly established; it is elementary justice; it applies even where the person affected has no merits; it applies though the enactment does not seem to have contemplated notice; and it applies to everybody having authority to adjudicate upon matters involving civil consequences to individuals."[117]

The court held the plaintiff was entitled to fair notice that an enquiry was to be held to determine his fate together with fair notice of the case against him and a fair opportunity to meet it.[118] Accordingly, it ruled that the plaintiff's salary had not been lawfully withdrawn.

Fair Procedures and Dismissal

[11.72] When it comes to dismissal, fair procedures may be overlooked by the employer at his peril unless there exist grounds which the law considers sufficient to justify the dismissal. The Unfair Dismissals (Amendment) Act 1993 underscores this point as it provides that in determining if a dismissal is unfair dismissal, regard may be had, if the rights commissioner, the EAT or the Circuit Court so decide, to the reasonableness or otherwise of the employer's conduct in regard to the dismissal.[119]

[11.73] The significance of fair procedures was illustrated in *Malloch v Aberdeen Corporation*,[120] a Scottish case which came before the House of Lords in 1971. The plaintiff, who was one of the 37 teachers who refused to join the Teachers Council, had been absent from the meeting which decided to dismiss him. Lord Reid was of the view that, had the plaintiff been present, there was a strong possibility that he might have influenced a sufficient number of the members to prevent a two-thirds majority from voting for his dismissal. In a majority decision, the court held for the teacher stating that if an employer failed to take the preliminary steps, which the law regarded as essential, he had no power to dismiss and any purported dismissal was a nullity.[121]

---

[117] *Maunsell v Minister for Education* [1940] IR 213 at 234.

[118] See also *Collins v Co Cork VEC*, High Court, unrep, 26 May 1982; affirmed, SC, 18 March 1983.

[119] See further Redmond, *Dismissal Law in Ireland* (1999), Butterworths, pp 55-59. Section 5(b) of the 1993 Act which amends s 6(7) of the 1977 Act.

[120] [1971] 2 All ER 1278.

[121] For a number of dismissal cases in England, see Barrell and Partington, *Teachers and the Law,* (1985) Methuen, p 143 *et seq*.

[11.74] Once again, in *R v Secretary of State, ex p Prior*,[122] the English High Court ruled that, where dismissal proceedings were not conducted fairly and in accordance with the law, any decisions arrived at would be invalid and of no effect. That this is also the law in Ireland is clear from *The State (Gleeson) v The Minister for Defence*[123] in which Gleeson successfully brought *certiorari* proceedings to quash his dismissal from the Defence Forces. Gleeson had been dismissed without being furnished with any reason for his discharge, and without being charged with any offence under military or civil law.

[11.75] Where a decision results in patent unfairness, it appears the Irish courts will not hesitate to quash the decision even if it is that of a Minister. In *The State (McMahon) v Minister for Education*,[124] the prosecutor was a community schoolteacher who had been appointed by a selection board to a post of responsibility within the school[125] in accordance with the Draft Deed of Trust for Community schools,[126] although, there was no Deed of Trust or other law, governing the management of the school at the material time. All parties, however, were agreed that the school was in fact managed in accordance with the Draft Deed of Trust. The selection board, which appointed the prosecutor, included a nominee of the Minister. Yet, when the Minister, possibly desirous of avoiding an inter-union dispute,[127] refused to approve the post, the prosecutor sued both the Minister and the board.

[11.76] In refusing to approve the prosecutor's post, the Minister took the view that the post in fact did not exist.

[11.77] Barrington J held the Minister was wrong in this decision as she did not apply her mind to the correct issue which was the prosecutor's suitability for the post for which the board, on which a nominee of the Minister sat, had recommended him. By order of *certiorari*, Barrington J quashed the Minister's decision and made an order for *mandamus* directing the Minister to consider in accordance with law the question of whether she should approve the appointment of the prosecutor to the post of responsibility.

---

[122] High Court, unrep, QBD, 21 December 1993, reported in 'Head Teacher's Briefing', No 47, *The Head's Legal Guide*, Croners Pubs, p 6.

[123] [1976] IR 280 SC.

[124] High Court, unrep, 21 December 1985, Barrington J, as he was then.

[125] These posts have since been replaced by the recent revised management structures under the PCW.

[126] Para 7A(c)(ii).

[127] There were two unions representing teachers in the school. The ASTI took the view that these posts should be filled on the basis of seniority while the TUI was of the view that the criterion used should be merit.

[11.78] In Irish law, there is a wider context to the redress available because of the development of constitutional justice.

Constitutional Justice

[11.79] Constitutional justice or constitutional "due process" derives from the common law, albeit the common law as later "subsumed or illuminated by constitutional provisions".[128] The expression "constitutional justice" appears to have originated in the Supreme Court in *McDonald v Bord na gCon*,[129] where the Court ruled that, in the context of the Constitution, natural justice might be more suitably termed constitutional justice and must be understood to import more than the two well settled principles *nemo iudex in causa sua* (that no man shall be judge in his own cause), and *audi alteram partem,* (hearing the other party's side of the story). Because of the wide ambit of constitutional guarantees, decisive acts and procedures may be impugned for a variety of reasons depending on the circumstances of the case.

[11.80] The Supreme Court in *Re Haughey*[130] held that Article 40.3 is a guarantee to the citizen of basic fairness of procedures.[131] Two years later, the Court, in *Glover v BLN Ltd*,[132] emphasised that public law and the dictates of constitutional justice require that statutes, regulations and agreements establishing machinery for making decisions which may affect rights or impose liabilities, should be construed as providing for fair procedures.

[11.81] In *East Donegal Co-operative v AG*,[133] the Supreme Court ruled that the presumption of constitutionality embodied the implication that all proceedings, procedures and directions, discretions and adjudications which were permitted or prescribed by the Livestock Marts Act 1967, were intended by the Oireachtas to be directed in accordance with the principles of natural justice. By analogy, it can be argued that all proceedings, procedures and discretions permitted or prescribed by the Education Act 1998 were intended by the Oireachtas to be directed in accordance with the principles of natural justice.

[11.82] The Supreme Court in *Gleeson v Minister for Defence*[134] made it clear that if a person brings proceedings seeking to have condemned as invalid a

---

128 *McDonald v Bord na gCon* [1965] IR 217.

129 [1965] IR 217 SC.

130 [1971] IR 217.

131 One of the issues in that case, was whether the plaintiff was allowed defend his good name when questioned in the Dáil by the Public Account's Committee in regard to funds.

132 [1973] IR 388 SC.

133 [1970] IR 317 SC.

134 [1976] IR 280 SC.

decision or a decisive process on the grounds that it is incompatible with the Constitution, it is essential for him to plead and prove that:

(a) the application in the circumstances of the case of an express or implied constitutional right;

(b) that the decision or decisive process has infringed that right; and

(c) that the plaintiff stands aggrieved by that infringement.

Disciplinary Procedures

[11.83] The necessity for disciplinary procedures and the need to ensure that their purpose, function and terms are known and understood by management, employees and trade unions is emphasised in the Labour Relations Commission's Code of Practice on Disciplinary Procedures (the Code).[135] The Code stresses the importance of an internal appeal mechanism and emphasises the need for fair, clear, rational, well-defined procedures to comply with the principles of natural justice and fair procedures.[136] While this code is made under the Industrial Relations Act 1990, which does not apply to teachers, it may be useful to those schools who have not yet negotiated agreed procedures in this area.

[11.84] The Code indicates that the details of alleged complaints must be brought to the attention of the employee concerned who must also be provided with the opportunity to defend himself. The employee concerned must be given the opportunity to avail of representation and must have the right to a fair and impartial determination of the matters being investigated. These principles may also require that the allegations or complaints be in written form, that the source of such complaints or allegations be supplied, or that the employee concerned may be permitted to question witnesses. It is generally accepted that efforts should be made to resolve a disciplinary matter privately at the lowest level, ie between the employee and his or her immediate superior.

[11.85] In primary and secondary schools, teachers generally have negotiated disciplinary procedures with the relevant management bodies and these are included in their respective union handbooks. All employees should receive copies of the disciplinary procedure including those on an induction programme for new teachers. The results of a departure from rules and requirements should

---

[135] Code of Practice: Disciplinary Procedures, Dept of Enterprise and Employment; see an Order declaring this Code to be a Code of Practice for the purposes of the Industrial Relations Act 1990 (SI 117/1996).

[136] *Moran v Bailey Gibson Ltd* UD 69/1977; *Garrett v CIE* UD 177/1980; see further Forde, *Employment Law*, (1992), Round Hall Press, Ch 7 and in particular 'Dismissal Procedures' p 166-172.

be lucidly set out especially in regard to breaches of discipline which if substantiated, would warrant suspension or dismissal.

[11.86] With regard to the dismissal of a teacher, the principles of natural justice and constitutional justice would apply unless the dismissal is for serious misconduct, in which case no notice is necessary. Misconduct may encompass a wide range of activities from embezzlement of school funds to the use of physical violence. There may be instances in which a teacher would be the subject of immediate or summary suspension or dismissal eg where a teacher sexually assaults a student. In such circumstances, a teacher would normally be suspended on full pay pending the result of an investigation into the alleged complaints or breaches of discipline. In *Vogler v Hertfordshire County Council*[137] a headmaster who summarily dismissed a teacher, who had sexual relations with his 16-year-old student, had the dismissal upheld by an Industrial Tribunal as fair, even though he had no authority to dismiss the teacher. Criminal activity on the part of the teacher may also be held to have repudiated the contract of employment and fragmented the employment relationship.[138]

[11.87] Another important element in effective disciplinary procedures is the maintenance of adequate records.

[11.88] In *Dismissal Law in Ireland*,[139] Redmond emphasises the importance of warnings:

> "With the exception of cases of gross misconduct, serious ill-health, or other circumstances entitling an employer to dismiss without notice, an employer is normally expected to give a final formal warning before dismissing an employee although, as a matter of law, the omission of a warning will not render a dismissal unfair. Where a warning, if duly given, is likely to influence the result, its omission may make a dismissal unfair."[140]

[11.89] In the case of a poorly performing teacher, however, he should be advanced carefully through the full disciplinary procedure and be given every opportunity to avail of further training and assistance (eg the services of a teacher welfare officer and or counselling). Care ought to be taken to advise the teacher on any methods which might improve his professional performance.[141] The dismissal process should move forward step by step through:

---

[137] The Times, 7 and 8 November 1975 cited in Barrell and Partington, *Teachers and the Law*, (1985) Methuen, p 146.

[138] See *Nottinghamshire County Council v Bowly* [1978] IRLR 252; *R v Powys County Council, ex p Smith* [1983] 81 LGR 342; see further *The Head's Legal Guide*, Croner, 2-116-117.

[139] (1999), Butterworths, p 212, para 13.63.

[140] Citing *O'Reilly v Dodder Management* UD 311/1978.

[141] See *The Head's Legal Guide*, 2-107-2-117.

    (a) an oral warning;

    (b) a written warning;

    (c) a final written warning;

    (d) suspension;

    (e) transfer to another task or section of the enterprise;

    (f) demotion;

    (g) another appropriate disciplinary action short of dismissal; to

    (h) dismissal.[142]

[11.90] The body which makes the decision to dismiss must be free from bias in its constitution and it must act in an unbiased manner.[143] It is important that the teacher be made aware of his right to be represented, and that he be informed of the next step in the procedure if no improvement occurs. It should also be brought to the teacher's attention that if his performance does not improve within a specified period, that he will be dismissed.[144] Most schools have agreed procedures in this sphere and these should be carefully implemented by the school authorities.

[11.91] Section 24(4) of the Education Act 1998 provides that, pending the agreement of procedures provided for in s 3, the procedures applied in the appointment, suspension and dismissal of teachers or other staff immediately before the commencement of this section, shall continue to apply. Thus, the adjudicating body will be entitled to expect that any existing union management agreed procedures will have been implemented by both parties.[145]

Modern Employment Legislation

[11.92] Since the 1970s, modern employment legislation has provided employees with a framework of legal safeguards together with access to free and informal tribunals. These statutes have inserted implied terms into employees' contracts of employment which bind both parties. The contract, however, continues to be of central importance as both the courts and the tribunals refer to contractual principles in construing and implementing the statutes.[146] This section is concerned with the impact of this legislation on teacher employment. In some circumstances, teachers have negotiated better conditions than those

---

[142] In Code of Practice: Disciplinary Procedures, Department of Enterprise and Employment (SI 117/1996), pp 6-7.

[143] *The Head's Legal Guide*, 2-107-2-117.

[144] *The Head's Legal Guide*, 2-107-2-117.

[145] See further Forde, *Employment Law*, p 215 *et seq*.

[146] Von Prondzynski and McCarthy, *Employment Law*, (2nd ed, 1989) Sweet & Maxwell, p 47 *et seq*.

guaranteed as a statutory minimum, while in ethos related areas of their employment they appear to have less protection than other employees.

Juries Act 1976

[11.93] Under the Juries Act 1976, teachers, among others, who are on the Dáil Electoral Register,[147] may be called for jury service during the school year. They, like other employees, are entitled to receive their salary when discharging this important function. Principals of schools and colleges are among the exempted categories for jury service. It is one of the duties of the County Registrar to choose persons for jury service and those who fail to attend, on foot of a summons, without reasonable cause, are liable to a fine not exceeding £50.[148]

[11.94] Accordingly, a board or principal is under a legal duty to permit teachers to attend for jury service. If difficulties arise because of the character of a teacher's work or because of the time of year (eg examination time, admission of infant classes) or otherwise, the principal may choose to write to the County Registrar explaining these problems and may seek to have the teacher excused from jury service. If the County Registrar refuses to accede to this request, a teacher may then appeal to the relevant court and the court's decision is final.[149] A teacher who has served, or who has attended court to serve on a jury in the preceding three years, may be excused from attending by the County Registrar. A judge may also excuse jurors, at the end of a trial, for a specific period of time or for life. Having attended for service, jurors may not be required to serve but may be excused by the court at approximately 11 am on any day of such service.

Payment of Wages Act 1991

[11.95] The Payment of Wages Act 1991 (the 1991 Act) provides a body of rights for employees. By virtue of the 1991 Act, all teachers, *inter alia*, are entitled to a readily negotiable mode of salary payment, a written statement of gross pay, and itemised deductions from such pay. If salaries are paid by credit transfer, the statement of pay should be given to the teacher soon after the operation of the credit transfer.

[11.96] Deductions from salary may not be made unless they are statutorily required (eg PAYE or PRSI), provided for under a term in the contract of employment (eg occupational pension deductions) or made with the written

---

[147] Such persons aged from 18 years to 70 years.
[148] Section 34(1).
[149] Section 9 of the Act; see further Meehan, *Working Within the Law,* (1994), Oak Tree Press, pp 58-59; Kerr, *Irish Law Statutes Annotated, Worker Protection (Regular Part-Time) Employees Act, 1991,* Sweet and Maxwell.

consent of the employee (eg health insurance deductions or trade union membership subscriptions).

[11.97] There are special restrictions under the 1991 Act falling on employers in regard to deductions made from the wages or salaries of employees and payments received by employers from employees.[150] An employer may not make deductions from an employee's wages or salary or receive any payment from an employee unless they are statutorily required (eg PAYE or PRSI); provided for under a term in the contract of employment (eg occupational pension deductions); or made with the written consent of the employee (eg health insurance deductions or union membership subscriptions).

[11.98] Employees are entitled, within six months of an alleged breach of the Act, to make a complaint to a rights commissioner who will investigate any unlawful deduction or payment on his behalf. The recommendation of the rights commissioner may be appealed to the EAT. As mentioned earlier, teachers have availed of the protection of the 1991 Act in a number of cases and it is notable that the Department of Education and Science has been recognised in these cases as the employer for the purposes of the 1991 Act. These cases, already mentioned are *O'Sullivan v Department of Education*,[151] *Dunphy v Scoil Eoin Phóil*[152] and *Ní Dhubháin v Scoil Iognáid and Department of Education*.[153]

Minimum Notice and Terms of Employment Act 1973

Teachers' contractual notice

[11.99] The majority of employees have a contractual right to a period of notice before they can be lawfully dismissed except where they are being summarily dismissed for misconduct, neglect of duty or unfitness.[154] The teacher's contract of employment normally provides for three months' notice by both parties.[155] In *McDonnell v Minister for Education*,[156] a teacher was given the contractual notice ie three months' notice to terminate on the last day of July. However,

---

[150] Section 5 of the 1991 Act.

[151] (1998) ELR, Vol 9, No 4.

[152] Rights Commissioners, CW 616/96, 19 June 1996. The complainant, a national teacher, contended that she had discharged extra duties in school and that the Department made unlawful deductions from her pay over a ten week period in 1995. The school, however, considered that the teacher had been correctly paid.

[153] Case No ST/604/94, recommendation of Rights Commissioner, 24 June 1994 under Payment of Wages Act 1991.

[154] Forde, *Employment Law*, (1992), Round Hall Press, p 188.

[155] See *Leopard Security Ltd v Campbell* [1997] ELR 227 in which the resignation of an employee who failed to give statutory notice to his employer was held to have breached s 6 of the 1973 Act.

[156] [1940] IR 316.

O'Byrne J held that the only reasonable date on which this employment should terminate was at the close of the school year. He considered that any notice of less than six months' duration would be unreasonable and insufficient to terminate the teacher's employment. The Supreme Court, on appeal, did not agree that notice should terminate at any specific time but only on the date which may be express or implied in the contract of employment.

[11.100] Although teachers in permanent employment have an entitlement to three months' notice, the statutes requiring minimum notice are relevant to a considerable number of teachers ie those teachers who are legally classified as regular part-time employees (ie those teachers who have worked for thirteen continuous weeks for the same employer and are normally expected to work for eight hours per week).

Minimum statutory notice

[11.101] Section 4 of the Minimum Notice and Terms of Employment Act 1973[157] (the 1973 Act) confers on employees under the Act[158] a right to a minimum period of paid notice of dismissal which cannot lawfully be excluded in the contract. The 1973 Act sets down minimum periods of notice, which vary with the length of service, which the board must give to the teacher before it may dismiss him or her. The periods of notice are as follows:

Length of Service	Minimum Notice
13 weeks - 2 years	1 week
2 years - 5 years	2 weeks
5 years - 10 years	4 weeks
10 years - 15 years	6 weeks
15 years upwards	8 weeks

[11.102] An employer or employee may waive the right to notice or they may accept payment in lieu of notice. The 1973 Act (as amended) provides that employees, who are in continuous service with the same employer for 13 weeks, are entitled to notice of not less than one week.

---

[157] As amended by the Worker Protection (Regular Part-Time Employees) Act 1991. The 1973 Act was amended in 1984 to effect a reduction from 21 hours per week to 18 hours per week and again in 1991 so as to bring regular part-time employees within its scope and reduce the weekly threshold to 8 hours per week.

[158] Defined in s 1 of the 1973 Act.

[11.103] In *Sinclair v City of Dublin VEC*[159] a graduate part-time teacher was employed, in a temporary capacity, by the respondent from September 1981 to the end of the 1984/85 academic year. Although the claimant appeared to be fulfilling her duties in a satisfactory manner, on 28 August 1985 she was informed that her services were no longer required by the respondent as an administrative decision was made by the VEC to transfer another full-time teacher to the claimant's post. When her case came before the EAT, it held, in a majority decision, that the claimant was entitled to two weeks notice less three days and so she received 1.4 times her average weekly salary being £207.20 by way of compensation in lieu of notice. As no grounds justifying unfair dismissal were established in evidence, a majority decision also found that the claimant had been unfairly dismissed and was entitled to compensation of £2, 250.[160]

"Permanent and Pensionable"

[11.104] The meaning of the phrase "permanent and pensionable" was considered in the context of a vocational teacher's contract of employment in *Carr v City of Limerick VEC*.[161] As the teacher's contract of employment provided for three months' notice, Murphy J held it was unrealistic for the plaintiff to submit that she was contracted to teach for the remainder of her life. Murphy J held that the words "permanent and pensionable" bore the meaning that the contract was not merely a temporary one being subject to the notice specified in one of its terms, ie three months' notice. Sections 7 and 8 of the VEC (Amendment) Act 1944 which governed the plaintiff's employment in this instance, did not confine the employer to removing the employee on the grounds of misconduct or unfitness as these provisions specified. The judge ruled that the parties were permitted to add other terms, such as notice, so long as these additional terms did not conflict with the statutory provisions.[162]

Misconduct

[11.105] Section 8 of the 1973 Act as amended provides "Nothing in this Act shall affect the right of any employer or employee to terminate a contract of employment without notice because of the misconduct of the other party". The question arises as to "what constitutes misconduct"? The High Court in

---

[159] UD 349/1986.

[160] See further Madden and Kerr, *Unfair Dismissal: Cases and Commentary* (2nd, ed 1996), Fed of Irish Employers, p 129.

[161] High Court, unrep, 22 May 1987 and 31 July 1987 *per* Murphy J; see also *Walsh v Dublin Health Board* 98 ILTR 82.

[162] See further Byrne and Binchy, *Annual Review of Irish Law 1987*, Round Hall, Sweet & Maxwell, p 229.

Brewster v Burke and the Minister for Labour[163] recognised a UK definition of that term:

> "It has long been part of our law that a person repudiates the contract of service if he wilfully disobeys the lawful and reasonable orders of his master. Such a refusal fully justifies an employer in dismissing an employee summarily."[164]

[11.106] This point was further clarified in *Purcell v The Board of Management of Tallaght Community School*.[165] The claimant was employed to manage the respondent's sports complex at the school. The claimant met with the management committee to discuss expressed concerns regarding the running of the complex in 1987. He was requested to close a specific management account and to ensure that tax and PRSI deductions were made for all staff members. However, the claimant failed to close the said account and proceeded to hold a staff meeting arising from which a new club was established to avoid tax and PRSI. Moreover, without the knowledge of the management committee, a new bank account was opened and operated by the claimant. The EAT concluded that the claimant's dismissal was not unfair as he had misled the management committee as to the tax and PRSI deductions and had acted contrary to their instructions which amounted to misconduct warranting dismissal.

Terms of Employment (Information) Act 1994

[11.107] The Terms of Employment (Information) Act 1994 (the 1994 Act), provides for the implementation of Council Directive No 91/533/EEC[166] on an employer's obligation to inform employees of the conditions applicable to the contract of employment relationship, to amend the 1973 Act and to provide for related matters. Sections 9 and 10 of the 1973 Act are repealed by the 1994 Act. The 1994 Act applies to virtually all teachers working under a contract of employment or apprenticeship including teachers employed by a VEC. However, the 1994 Act does not apply to employment in which an employee is normally expected to work for an employer for less than eight hours per week or employment in which the employee has been in the continuous service of the employer for less than one month.[167]

Written statement

[11.108] One of the most important provisions of the Act is s 3 which provides that an employer shall, not later than two months after the commencement of an

---

[163] 61 (1985) 4 JISLL 98.
[164] See Redmond, *Dismissal Law in Ireland*, (1999), Butterworths, p 55.
[165] [1990] ELR 218.
[166] Of 14 October 1991, OJ No L 288, 18-10-91.
[167] Section 2(1)(a) and (b).

employee's employment, give or cause to be given to the employee a statement in writing containing certain specified particulars of the terms of the employee's employment. This statement must be signed and dated by, or on behalf of, the employer and a copy ought to be retained during the period of the employee's employment and for one year thereafter. The written statement must contain the following:[168]

(a) the full names of the employer and employee,

(b) the address of the employer in the State or, where appropriate, the address of the principal place of the relevant business of the employer in the State or the registered office (within the meaning of the Companies Act, 1963,

(c) the place of work or, where there is no fixed or main place of work, a statement specifying that the employee is required or permitted to work at various places,

(d) the title of the job or nature of the work for which the employee is employed,

(e) the date of commencement of the employee's contract of employment,

(f) in the case of a temporary contract of employment the expected duration thereof or, if the contract of employment is for a fixed term, the date on which the contract expires,

(g) the rate or method of calculation of the employee's remuneration,

(h) the length of the intervals between the times at which remuneration is paid, whether a week, a month or any other interval,

(i) any terms or conditions relating to hours of work (including overtime),

(j) any terms or conditions relating to paid leave (other than paid sick leave),

(k) any terms or conditions relating to -

(i) incapacity for work due to sickness or injury and paid sick leave, and

(ii) pensions and pension schemes,

(l) the period of notice which the employee is required to give and entitled to receive (whether by or under statute or under the terms of the employee's contract of employment) to determine the employee's contract of employment or, where this cannot be indicated when the information is given, the method for determining such period of notice,

(m) a reference to any collective agreements which directly affect the terms and conditions of the employee's employment including, where the employer is not a party to such agreements, particulars of the bodies or institutions by whom they were made.

Form of written statement

[11.109] The particulars set down in sub-s 3(1), paragraphs (g)-(l) inclusive may be given to employees in the form of relevant references to the provisions of statutes, secondary law or other laws, collective agreements or administrative

---

[168] 1994 Act, s 3(1).

provisions, which the employee has reasonable opportunity of reading during the course of his employment or which are reasonably accessible. However, this written statement is not *per se* a contract or a copy of a contract of employment but rather a statement of the main terms or legal obligations in the contract.

Time limits

[11.110] In the case of contracts of employment negotiated on or following 16 May 1994 (the commencement date of the 1994 Act), the written statement of particulars must be given, or cause to be given, by the employer, within two months of the commencement of employment whereas in the case of employees, whose employment commenced prior to 16 May 1994, the written statement must be given, or cause to be given by the employer within two months of being requested to do so by the employee.

[11.111] The employer must also notify the employee of any changes contained in the written statement within one month from the date the change takes effect. Section 4 requires the employer to furnish a statement (under s 3 of the Act together with additional details under s 4) if the employee is required to work outside the State for a period of not less than one month.

Complaints and appeals

[11.112] The 1994 Act includes a provision which gives a right of complaint to a rights commissioner if the employer fails to comply with the provisions of the Act. This complaint must be made within six months beginning on the date of termination of the relevant employment. Either party may appeal to the EAT from a recommendation of a Rights Commissioner within six weeks of the date on which the relevant recommendation was communicated to the party. If the employer fails to comply with the determination of the EAT, it may be enforced by the District Court in which the employer ordinarily resides or carries on any profession, business or occupation.

Maternity Protection Act 1994

[11.113] The Maternity Protection Act 1994, provides a statutory right to unpaid maternity leave[169] (14 consecutive weeks being the minimum leave). In introducing protective legislation in this sphere, Ireland gave effect to Directive 89/391/EEC and Directive 92/85/EEC on the introduction of measures to encourage improvements in the safety and health of pregnant workers and workers who have recently given birth or are breastfeeding. Accordingly, the 1994 Act[170] repeals and re-enacts with amendments the Maternity Protection of

---

[169] The employer is not obliged to pay the employee during maternity leave but the employee is entitled to a maternity allowance under the Social Welfare Acts 1993-1995.

[170] See Maternity Protection (Time-Off for Ante-Natal and Post-Natal Care) Regulations 1981 (SI 358/1981).

Employees Acts 1981-1991. Henceforth, women suffering medically certified illness or health risks during pregnancy will be entitled to full leave from work, if necessary, in addition to existing statutory provision (see "health and safety" leave in Part III of the Act).

[11.114] The 1994 Act also protects the right to unpaid time off for ante-natal and post-natal care and other associated rights provided written notification is given to the employer of the date and time of the appointment at least two weeks in advance. The employee has the right to return to work following maternity leave or to be allocated suitable alternative employment on her return. As a consequence of the statutory protection, no break occurs in the employee's continuity of service and both contractual rights and statutory rights are protected by the Acts. Various significant amendments are made in the 1994 Act to the Unfair Dismissals legislation.

Restrictions during maternity leave

[11.115] Certain restrictions fall upon the employer during maternity leave. The employer may not lawfully serve notice of termination of employment or terminate employment during maternity leave, or serve a disciplinary suspension on an employee during maternity leave or on time-off. Ireland's statutory provision of 14 consecutive weeks, however, seems minimal by comparison with such leave in other Member States.

The necessity to give written notice

[11.116] The employee's rights under the Acts are, however, dependant upon the service of written notice by the employee on the employer at least four weeks prior to the commencement of maternity leave and this should be accompanied by a medical certificate or other appropriate certificate confirming the fact of pregnancy and the expected date of confinement. The precise dates of maternity leave may be at the discretion of the employee provided the period covers the four weeks prior to the confinement and the four weeks following the confinement.

[11.117] The right to return to work under s 22 was, under earlier legislation, subject to the employee giving written notice to the employer of her intention to do so, not later than four weeks prior to the date on which she intended to return to work. Furthermore, the employee had to confirm this written notification of her intention to return to work between four and two weeks prior to the date on which she expected to return to work. The EAT decision in *Murphy v Clarkes of Ranelagh Ltd*[171] underscored the significance of this notification as the tribunal

---

[171] (1983) UD 822/1982. See also *Ski-line Ltd* [1988] IR 399.

held that the failure to give notice deprived the employee of her statutory right to return to work.

[11.118] This aspect of the legislation has been improved on and the simplified notification procedures in the 1994 Act have eliminated many of the ambiguities in the earlier legislation and in particular s 22.

Application to teachers

[11.119] Section 4(2) of the 1994 Act permits more favourable arrangements to be made between employer and employee than the statutory minimum. Accordingly, teachers covered by the 1994 Act have secured, through negotiation, paid maternity leave which extends to those who are in permanent employment and to those teachers who have at least 14 weeks to run from the first day of leave and the end of their contract of employment. Such teachers are entitled to the following rights:

   (a) 14 consecutive weeks maternity leave;

   (b) Extended maternity leave without pay for a maximum period of 4 consecutive weeks, including weekends, or

   (c) Additional leave without pay to the end of the school year (with the consent of the Board),

   (d) Extra leave in lieu of holidays eg when a teacher whose 14 weeks maternity leave coincides with holiday leave, that teacher will be entitled to leave in lieu with pay and with entitlement to substitute cover for a period up to a maximum of 27 extra school days in a calendar year (not including weekends).

   (e) right to time off for ante-natal and post-natal care (in the case of post-natal care, time off is paid during the 14 weeks immediately following the birth).[172]

[11.120] Employees are protected by these statutes from the first day of their employment with the exception of regular part-time employees, ie those who are normally expected to work for 8 hours per week and have 13 weeks service with the same employer. The Maternity Acts have applied to regular part-time employees since 17 June 1991. As Redmond points out, s 6(2)(f) of the Unfair Dismissals Act 1977 has been substantially amended by European law and so most pre-1993 maternity leave decisions are unreliable.[173]

---

[172] See Department of Education Circulars 21/97, 22/97 and 1/99 and booklet published by the Department entitled 'Maternity, Adoptive and Parental Leave', ndg.

[173] *Dismissal Law in Ireland*, (1999) Butterworths, pp 229-232, para 14.11 and n 16: see in particular para 22.81 "Covering for employees on protection leave or natal care absence" and the necessity for the employer to inform the substitute teacher in writing, that the employment will end on the return to work of the permanent teacher.

Adoptive Leave Act 1995

[11.121] Under the Adoptive Leave Act 1995 (1995 Act), employees in permanent employment and those who are on fixed term contracts with at least ten weeks left to run, are entitled to be paid adoptive leave which commences on the date of adoption. The 1995 Act provides for an extra four weeks unpaid adoptive leave. It is important to note that the 1995 Act provides separately for the entitlements of the adopting mother, or sole male adopter, and for the entitlement of the adopting father to adoptive leave, or for additional adoptive leave in certain circumstances.

[11.122] As with the notification requirements for the Maternity Protection Act 1994, the giving of notice by the employee is pivotal. The first day of leave must commence with the date of placement of the adopted child. Four weeks' written notice must be given by an employee who is seeking such leave and this must include the anticipated date of placement. Within four weeks of placement, the employee must show evidence of placement (ie the certificate of placement) to the employer (in a teacher's case the board of management). In accordance with s 4(4), some sectors may negotiate more favourable treatment with the employer. Teachers have acquired paid adoptive leave.

[11.123] When a teacher's adoptive leave coincides with normal school holiday leave, he is entitled to leave-in-lieu of such holidays as overlap, with pay, for the holidays overlapped (including bank holidays and church holidays) to a maximum of 19 days. Should a teacher wish to avail of the extra consecutive four weeks unpaid leave, immediately following paid leave or leave-in-lieu, if any, then four weeks' written notice to the board is necessary before the end of the paid leave. Furthermore, an employee's right to return to work is subject to the serving of at least four weeks' written notice on her employer before the date she expects to return to work. Special provisions are included in the Act to cover foreign adoption and such circumstances as the death of the adoptive mother. Any disputes arising under the 1995 Act may be referred to a rights commissioner or the EAT generally within a six month period[174] from the date of placement. The determination of the EAT may be appealed to the High Court on a point of law or the EAT may make such a referral on a point of law. Up to 20 weeks' pay may be awarded as compensation for breach of the 1995 Act. As with maternity leave, the employer shall inform the substitute teacher in writing, when the employment commences, that the employment will end when the teacher on adoptive leave returns to work following adoptive leave or additional adoptive leave.

---

[174] With special provisions for extension in certain circumstances.

Parental Leave Act 1998

[11.124] The Parental Leave Act 1998 (the 1998 Act) transposes into Irish law Council Directive 96/34/EC of 3 June 1996 on the framework agreement on parental leave.[175] A principal objective of the 1998 Act is the promotion of reconciliation of work and family life and of equal opportunities and equal treatment between men and women. While the Directive lays down minimum standards for parental leave, it leaves considerable discretion to the Member States as to the elements of its parental leave schedules. In Ireland, by contrast with seven other European countries,[176] the leave is unpaid.

[11.125] The 1998 Act makes provision for an entitlement on the part of parents to unpaid parental leave to facilitate them in caring for their children of tender years.

[11.126] The legislation also provides for limited paid leave for employees in times of family emergencies which is termed *force majeure* leave.[177] This comprises three days annual paid leave (up to a maximum of five days every three years) to facilitate parents in coping with emergencies emanating from injury or illness to a close member of the family.

[11.127] With regard to the transposition of the Directive into Irish law, the Department of Justice, Equality and Law Reform sought and was granted a six month postponement period as the legislation was due to be enacted in June 1998.[178] Accordingly, thousands of parents, it appears, who were lawfully entitled to such leave were denied it. Action may be taken against Ireland in this regard and so it may be necessary to amend the 1998 Act. The central elements in the 1994 Act are as follows:

    (a) the leave is applicable to -

        (i) parents of children who were born on or after 3 June 1996 or

        (ii) parents of children in whose case an adoption order was made on or after 3 June 1996;

    (b) the leave is unpaid;[179]

    (c) the leave must be availed of -

        (i) before a child reaches its fifth birthday or

---

[175] Concluded by UNICE, CEEP and the ETUC.

[176] Where some type of payment is made by the employer, the up-take of the leave by men is very low, with the exception of Sweden, see Kerr, 30-02.

[177] See further Byrne and Binchy, *Annual Review of Irish Law*, 1998 30-01 *et seq*.

[178] This delay was sought because of anticipated problems for employers in implementing the legislation within a short time-frame. See further Seanad Debates, 155 Col, 1410.

[179] See reasons for this Seanad Debates 155 Col 1408.

　(ii) in the case of an adopted child who is aged 3 years or more and less than 8 at the date of the adoption order, the leave may be taken within 2 years from the date of the adoption order.

　(iii) the leave may be taken as a continuous block or by agreement between the employer and employee in separate weeks, days or hours or by reduced working hours.[180]

　(iv) each parent is entitled to 14 weeks leave for such child.

[11.128] An employee is required to give at least six weeks' written notice of his intention to take such leave. Each parent has the right to separate parental leave which may not be transferred between the parents. The entitlement to parental leave under the 1998 Act is subject to the employee having completed one year's continuous employment with the employer from whose employment the leave is taken. Although the leave is unpaid, the 1998 Act provides in s 14 that employees will be treated for the purposes of all employment rights, except the right to remuneration and superannuation benefits, as if they had remained at work. Accordingly, time spent on such leave will count as service for the purpose of promotions, annual leave, increments etc.

Appeals

[11.129] There is a right of appeal to a rights commissioner under the 1998 Act. Where either party is dissatisfied with the decision of a rights commissioner, he may appeal to the EAT. The EAT may refer a question of law arising in proceedings before it to the High Court. Likewise, a party to the proceedings may appeal the determination of the EAT to the High Court on a point of law.

Tobacco (Health Promotion and Protection) Act 1988

Smoking in the Workplace

[11.130] Section 2(1) of the Tobacco (Health Promotion and Protection) Act 1988 (the 1988 Act) provides that the Minister may, by regulations, either prohibit or restrict the consumption of tobacco products in a designated area or a designated facility. "Designated area" means a place or building specified in

---

[180] In the case of a teacher this may be as follows:
　(a)　One continuous 14 week period or
　(b)　Two separate blocks of 7 continuous weeks; or
　(c)　a maximum of 5 separate leave blocks comprises as follows or any combination thereof:
　　(i)　one continuous 7 week period;
　　(ii)　3 periods of 2 consecutive weeks
　　(ii)　one single week
See further *Maternity, Adoptive and Parental Leave*, Department of Education and Science and Circular 12/97, 22/97 and 1/99.

regulations made under s 2 of the Act as being an area in which the consumption of tobacco products is either prohibited or restricted. Subsection (2) permits the Minister for Health, without prejudice to the generality of sub-s (1), to *inter alia:*

(b) prohibit or restrict the consumption of tobacco products in such part of a school, as may be specified.

[11.131] The Tobacco (Health Promotion and Protection) Regulations 1990[181] were made by the Minister for Health under the authority of the 1988 Act. They prohibit smoking in primary and secondary schools, including the school yard. Under the Regulations, a person is not permitted to consume a tobacco product in designated areas which include:

any part of a primary or secondary school (including the school yard), save that smoking may be permitted where specific facilities, other than classrooms or recreation rooms, are provided for staff to smoke.

[11.132] As the term "recreation rooms" would most likely be construed as being inclusive of staff rooms or common rooms, smoking may, it appears, be permitted only in a room specifically designated for that purpose if such is available in the school.

[11.133] Apart from staff and pupils, other persons who use the school premises are also bound by the Regulations while on the school premises. Such persons would include those attending parent-teacher meetings, bridge sessions, art classes, sales of work, senior citizen groups etc. Primary responsibility for the enforcement of the Regulations remains with the owner, manager or other person in charge, eg the board or the principal acting on its behalf.

[11.134] Persons in charge of schools who fail to discharge their duty together with those who smoke are liable to prosecution under the Regulations. On conviction, provision is made for imprisonment and the imposition of heavy fines for failure to ensure compliance with the Regulations.

Passive smoking and negligence claims

[11.135] There is another dimension to this issue which is worthy of mention. In view of pending litigation based on alleged personal injury to employees (barmen) arising out of passive smoking, school authorities could be faced with similar negligence claims in the future. Accordingly, they would be well advised to implement the provisions of the Regulations in schools. Employers have a duty of care to employees to provide a safe place of work free from any risk to health, safety and welfare.

---

[181] SI 39/1990, which came into effect on 1 May, 1990.

Employment Equality

EC Directives

[11.136] Article 141 (ex Article 119) of the EC Treaty, which has "direct effect" in the Member States, supports the principle that men and women should receive equal pay for equal work. Accordingly, it prohibits sex discrimination in pay. Member States are required to introduce into their legal systems all necessary measures to implement this principle. Two Directives are germane to the issue of employment equality law in Ireland. Council Directive 75/117/EEC gave effect to the principle of equal pay contained in Article 119 (now Article 141), and Council Directive 76/207/EEC gave effect to the principle of equal treatment.[182] The influence of Article141 (ex Article 119) and the EC Directives will not be lessened in any manner by the operation of the Employment Equality Act 1998 which will come into operation in September 1999. The 1998 Act repeals the Anti-Discrimination (Pay) Act 1974 and the Employment Equality Act 1977.

The Employment Equality Act 1977

[11.137] The Anti-Discrimination (Pay) Act 1974, which predates Directive 75/117/EEC, prohibits direct and indirect discrimination in pay on grounds of sex.

[11.138] The Employment Equality Act 1977 (the 1977 Act) applies, *inter alia*, to all teachers including vocational teachers.[183] It prohibits direct and indirect discrimination in treatment on the grounds, of sex and marital status.[184] It will be noted that the latter grounds are re-enacted in the 1998 Act[185] and that the term "marital status" in the 1998 Act is much wider, encompassing single, married, separated, divorced or widowed persons.

Direct Discrimination

[11.139] In effect, direct discrimination means less favourable treatment. If, for instance, a female teacher wished to establish that she had been directly discriminated against on the basis of gender, it would be necessary for her to show that she had been treated less favourably than a male teacher in comparable circumstances; and that such treatment was because of her gender.

[11.140] Of course, the claimant in such circumstances may be male as is clear from *Limerick VEC v Cotter*.[186] In that case Mr Cotter alleged that the VEC had

---

[182] "... that there shall be no discrimination whatsoever on grounds of sex either directly or indirectly by reference in particular to marital or family status."

[183] Section 1 of the 1977 Act which defines the term "employee" broadly.

[184] See, however, s 2(c) and (d) of the 1977 Act.

[185] Section 6(2)(a) and (b).

[186] Case EE/11 1989.

discriminated against him on grounds of marital status by transferring him to another school within its jurisdiction. Mr Cotter was a single man while a more junior female teacher on the staff, who taught the same subject, was married. The equality officer found that the VEC had discriminated against the complainant who was granted damages of £1,500 in regard to distress and injured feelings and a recommendation was also made that he be transferred back to his original post.

[11.141] There is a considerable body of case law relating to schools which shows that the issue of discrimination has arisen in a wide variety of circumstances such as:

(a) in short-listing for teaching posts,[187]

(b) at interview for teaching posts,[188]

(c) in promotion within the school,[189]

(d) in class allocation within the school,[190]

(e) in transfers within the VEC system,[191]

(f) in allocation of duties to persons of the same sex but of a different marital status,[192] and

(g) in interviews for principalship.[193]

(h) in denial of appointment to a teaching post.[194]

If an unsuccessful female candidate could establish that she was better qualified than the male appointee or *vice versa*, this raises a presumption of discrimination which may have to be explained by the board of management.[195]

---

[187] *The Management of Fynborough National School v A Teacher,* EE 10/80 where two male teachers were chosen from a list of five men and four women, discrimination was found to have occurred even though the interview board had chosen a man, whom it considered to be the most suitable candidate.

[188] *Board of Management of St Fergal's National School v A Teacher* EE 2/1987 and EE 3/1987; see also EE 85/13, EE 2/1987, EE 85/4.

[189] *Teacher v Scoil Mhuire, Navan* EE 5/83 and DEE 3/83, *Teacher v Scoil Mhuire, Tallow Co Waterford* EE 9/92 and DEE 1692.

[190] *Teacher F v St Brigid's BNS Foxrock,* EE 3/79.

[191] See *Limerick VEC v A Teacher* EE/11 1989.

[192] *Teacher v The Principal of St Catherine's National School,* Bishopstown, Cork, EE 12/80.

[193] *Culloo v The Board of Management of the Model School, Limerick,* High Court, unrep, 11 May 1989, Costello P.

[194] *Teacher v Moylough National School* EE 03/1994 in which the EO recommended that the teachers discriminated against be offered the teaching post which was already filled by another teacher. The EO recommended the creation of a temporary post and awarded damages of £2,000 for stress.

[195] See *Humphreys v St George's School* [1978] ICR 546.

[11.142] The importance of assessing work experience and qualifications for a post cannot be overlooked. In *Higgins v Co Laois VEC*[196] the equality officer and the Labour Court found that the defendants, in failing to appoint a teacher to an "A" post of responsibility in the school, had discriminated against her on grounds of sex as in reaching its decision the interview board had failed to consider the claimant's superior work experience and qualifications. The pivotal significance of assessing work experience and qualifications, and of following proper procedures for board of management meetings, had already been emphasised by Costello P in *Culloo v Board of Management of the Model School, Limerick*,[197] the leading equality case in teacher employment.

[11.143] In the *Culloo* case, the judge held that the interview board discriminated against the plaintiff on grounds of sex thus denying her access to Principalship.

[11.144] The Department planned to amalgamate the boys' and girls' schools, (both Model schools and therefore State schools), into one co-educational school, the respective principals being the sole applicants for the post of principal in the new school. Following the interview board's recommendation, the male principal was appointed to the post.

[11.145] Acting on behalf of the complainant (Ms Culloo), the INTO referred a case of discrimination against her to the Labour Court. The Equality Officer found that Ms Culloo had higher professional qualifications than the male appointee and that the interview board had failed to address the question of the candidates' qualification and experience as specifically required by Department of Education Circular 30/84. The equality officer concluded that the interview board's reasoning was flawed and biased as against the complainant and awarded her £11,000 compensation for discrimination. Two improperly constituted, out of time, appeals were later lodged to the Labour Court[198] which disallowed both appeals.

[11.146] On appeal to the High Court, on a point of law, Costello P referred to the many inconsistencies and procedural deficiencies at the meeting of the board of management which lodged the appeal to the Labour Court. Having examined the evidence before him, he concluded that the appeal did not emanate from a properly constituted meeting of the board of management. In dismissing the

---

[196] EE 15/1996.

[197] High Court, unrep, 11 May 1989.

[198] One appeal was lodged by the Department inspector who was chairman of the board of management; the other was lodged by the Chief State Solicitor on behalf of the board. Neither appeal, it seems, was properly authorised by the board of management.

appeal, he ruled that the Labour Court was entitled to arrive at the decision it had reached.

Indirect Discrimination

[11.147] In *Conlon v University of Limerick*,[199] the exclusion from interview for a post of professor in the university at "senior academic level" was at issue.

[11.148] The phrase "senior academic level" was later interpreted by the college to mean experience at senior lecturer level and this effectively excluded the claimant from interview. As the percentage of women at senior lecturer level was relatively small, the claimant contended that this requirement indirectly discriminated against women. In the Labour Court, the senior academic criterion was found to be "essential". However, the court does not appear to have applied the principles laid down by the Supreme Court in *Nathan v Bailey Gibson*[200] or adopted the stricter approach to objective justification laid down by the European Court of Justice in a number of cases.[201] On appeal to the High Court, McCracken J held that the Labour Court had applied the principles in regard to indirect discrimination correctly. Although he was critical of other aspects of the decision, he held that the Labour Court viewed the disputed criterion as "objectively essential" in the circumstances of the case.

[11.149] Article 6 prohibits discrimination relating to vocational training. Thus, any person or educational or training body offering a course of vocational training[202] to persons over the age of 15 years, may not discriminate against such a person in regard to the terms on which any such course or related facility is offered by refusing or omitting to afford access to any such course or facility, or in the manner in which any such source or facility is provided.

[11.150] Although the 1998 Act will not come into effect until September 1999, it is considered in this chapter from the perspective of its impact on particular areas of life in schools. This is a long and complex Act containing 105 provisions. Hence, it is advisable to study the provisions of the Act closely and to seek professional advice should one need to take proceedings arising under the Act. The Equality Authority will replace the Employment Authority Agency

---

[199] DEE 11/97.

[200] EE1/90; DEE 1/91; (1993) ELR 106 HC, Murphy J; Supreme Court, February 1996. This case was remitted to the Labour Court which gave a second determination, see DEE 7/97.

[201] The approach of the ECJ to indirect discrimination may be seen in the following cases; *Bilka-Kaufhaus v Weber von Hartz* 1986 IRLR 317; *Nimz v Freie und Hansestadt Hamburg* [1991] IRLR 222; *Enderby v Frenchay Health Authority and Secretary of State for Health* [1993] IRLR 591; *Kording v Senator fur Finanzen* [1997] IRLR 710; *Gerster v Freistaat Bayern* [1997] IRLR 699.

[202] See s 6(2) of the 1977 Act for definition.

when the 1998 Act comes into operation. The 1998 Act also establishes the office of Director of Equality Investigations,[203] which will also have functions, it appears, in relation to the proposed Equal Status legislation.

The Employment Equality Act 1998

Purpose of the Act

[11.151] The purpose of the Employment Equality Act 1998 (the 1998 Act) is to further extend the grounds on which discrimination in regard to employment, vocational training, and membership of certain special bodies can be shown to repeal the Anti-Discrimination (Pay) Act 1974 and the Employment Equality Act 1977 and to provide for an express provision on employer liability, an express prohibition on harassment in employment and in the workplace, including gender and non gender harassment. The 1998 Act will also provide for the change of name and constitution of the Employment Equality Agency and for the administration by that body of various matters pertaining to the 1998 Act.

[11.152] The achievement of the purpose of this legislation necessitated a balancing by the legislature of various constitutional rights which were the subject of considerable public interest when the 1996 Bill was referred by President Robinson to the Supreme Court to test its constitutionality in *Re Article 26 of the Constitution of Ireland and In the Matter of the Employment Equality Bill 1996*.[204] Following the fall of that Bill, it was redrafted and subsequently passed into law as the Employment Equality Act 1998. At the time of writing, the Equal Status Bill 1998 is passing through the Oireachtas.

[11.153] The 1998 Act, which has major implications for employers and employees generally, applies to all teachers including VEC teachers who, for the purposes of the Act, are deemed to be employees of the VECs under a contract of service.[205] As will be seen, the 1998 Act takes account of and makes special provision for the ethos of religious schools which comprise the vast majority of schools in Ireland.

Major Changes to be effected by the 1998 Act

[11.154] When the 1998 Act comes into effect, there will be nine discriminatory grounds. The Act will make provision for express exemptions for certain institutions under the direction or control of a body established for religious purposes. Express prohibitions of gender harassment and non-gender harassment will be included and an implied gender equality clause will be

---

[203] And other officers under s 75 of the Act.
[204] [1997] 2 IR 321.
[205] Section 6(1).

inserted into all contracts by law. The 1998 Act contains express provision on vicarious liability of employers for discrimination by their employees and for defences by the employers in this regard. It places an express ban on discriminatory advertisements, repeals existing equality legislation and introduces quality reviews and action plans. The 1998 Act changes the name and constitution of the Employment Equality Agency to the Employment Equality Authority.

Discrimination

[11.155] One of the main objectives of the 1998 Act is to prohibit discrimination, which for the purposes of the Act shall be taken to occur "where on any of the grounds in sub-s 6(2), one person is treated less favourably than another is, has been or would be treated. This definition is considerably wider than that contained in s 2 of the Employment Equality Act 1977 which refers to circumstances in which a person *is* treated less favourably on the grounds of sex or marital status.

[11.156] As between any two persons, "the discriminatory grounds" in the 1998 Act are as follows:

  (a) that one is a woman and the other is a man (in this Act referred to as "the gender ground"),

  (b) that they are of different marital status (in this Act referred to as "the marital status ground"),

  (c) that one has family status[206] and the other does not (in this Act referred to as the "family status ground"),

  (d) that they are of different sexual orientation (in this Act referred to as "the sexual orientation ground"),

  (e) that one has a different religious belief from the other, or that one has a religious belief and the other has not (in this Act referred to as "the religion ground"),

  (f) that they are of different ages, but subject to subsection (3) (in this Act referred to as "the age ground"),

  (g) that one is a person with a disability and the other either is not or is a person with a different disability (in this Act referred to as "the disability ground"),

  (h) that they are of different race, colour, nationality or ethnic or national origins (in this Act referred to as "the ground of race"),

---

[206] "Family status" means responsibility (a) as a parent or as a person *in loco parentis* in relation to a person who has not attained the age of 18 years, or (b) as a parent or the resident primary carer in relation to a person of or over that age with a disability which is of such a nature as to give rise to the need for care or support on a continuing, regular or frequent basis.

   (i)   that one is a member of the travelling community and the other is not (in this Act referred to as "the traveller community ground").

In order to establish direct discrimination, a comparison must be made as set out in s 6(2) of the 1998 Act. For example, in gender discrimination, the comparison must be between a man and a woman; in discrimination on the religious ground, the comparison must be between an individual with a religious belief and one who does not have such a belief or holds a different religious belief. In disability discrimination, the comparison must be between an individual with a disability and another who has not or is an individual with a different disability and so forth.

[11.157] The 1998 Act also prohibits discrimination in specific areas as follows in:

   (a) access to employment,

   (b) conditions of employment,

   (c) training or experience for or in relation to employment,

   (d) promotion or regrading, or

   (e) classification of posts.[207]

The 1998 Act provides that it is unlawful for an employer to discriminate on any of the above-mentioned "discriminatory grounds" against an employee or prospective employee. Neither may an employer have rules or instructions which would discriminate against an employee or class of employee in regard to any of the matters set out in (b) to (e) above or operate a practice which would result or be likely to result in any such discrimination.[208]

Exemptions from Discrimination

[11.158] While the 1998 Act prohibits discrimination as outlined above, it contains a number of exemptions from such prohibition, such as the exemption on age grounds in s 6(3) and the exemption on the grounds of religion in ss 12(4) and (5) and 37, both of which relate particularly to the school setting. Section 6(3) provides that where a person has attained the age of 65 years or has not attained the age of 18 years, then, subject to s 12(3), treating that person more favourably or less favourably than another shall not be regarded as discrimination on the age ground.

Constitutionality of the age ground

[11.159] The provisions of the Employment Equality Bill 1996 were considered by the Supreme Court as a result of a presidential referral in *Re Article 26 of the*

---

[207] Section 8(1).

[208] Section 8(4)(a) and 8(b).

Constitution of Ireland and the Employment Equality Bill 1996.[209] The Supreme Court provided for a hearing on behalf of the State (Attorney General) and counsel assigned by the Court. Amongst other matters, it was submitted by counsel assigned on behalf of the Court that "the age ground" provision in the Bill was discriminatory, without rational justification and a violation of Article 40.1.

[11.160] The Court held that the enactment by the Oireachtas of a measure which discriminates between groups of persons in the community is not of itself a violation of the guarantee of equality contained in Article 40.1.[210] It ruled that Article 40.1 expressly permits the recognition in legislation of differences of capacity, physical and moral, and of social function. Having considered the relevant constitutional provisions and germane case law,[211] the Court held that the enactment by the Oireachtas of legislation, intended to promote equality between employed persons, necessitates the balancing by the legislature of different constitutional values, in the instant case, the guarantee of equality, the citizen's right to work and earn a livelihood and the citizen's property rights.

[11.161] This exercise was, the Court stated, peculiarly within the province of the Oireachtas.[212] Hence, it should not interfere with the resolution of that body relating to the competing constitutional rights involved "unless, objectively judged, that resolution was so contrary to reason and fairness as to constitute an unjust attack on the constitutional rights of the citizen".[213] It was beyond argument, the Court stated, that not to permit employers to make any discrimination on the ground of age would be entirely unjust and impracticable. Furthermore, the fixing of the relevant ages at 18, in the case of young people, and at 65 in the case of older citizens, simply reflected a choice by the Oireachtas of generally accepted median age limits for entry into and departure from the work place.

[11.162] Regarding the exclusion for the Defence Forces, the Garda Síochána or the Prison service, the court held that, given the distinctive requirements for these three branches of the public service, and the particular importance attached to ensuring a high level of physical and mental fitness, it could scarcely be said that the decision of the Oireachtas to exclude them from the ambit of this

---

[209] [1997] 2 IR 321.

[210] Citing *DPP v Quilligan (No 3)* [1993] IR 305 at 321.

[211] *Quinn's Supermarket v AG* [1972] IR 1 at 13; *DPP v Quilligan (No 3)* [1993] IR 305 at 312; *Murtagh Properties v Cleary* [1972] IR 330; *Cox v Ireland* [1992] 2 IR 503; *Re Article 26 of the Constitution and the Regulation of Information (Termination of Pregnancies) Bill 1995* [1995] IR 1.

[212] *Tuohy v Courtney* [1994] 3 IR 1 at 47.

[213] At pp 29, 30 of the unreported judgment.

particular measure, whether correct or not, is unrelated to a permissible legislative objective or irrational or unfair.[214] Thus, the Court declared itself satisfied that it had not been established that the provisions relating to this group of public servants were repugnant to the provisions of the Constitution.

Providers of vocational training and religious institutions

[11.163] The term "vocational training" is broadly defined in s 12(2) of the 1998 Act to mean:

> "any system of instruction which enables a person being instructed to acquire, maintain, bring up to date or perfect the knowledge or technical capacity required for the carrying on of an occupational activity and which may be considered as exclusively concerned with training for such an activity".

Clearly, this definition extends to the education and training of teachers and nurses who have traditionally received their professional education and training in denominational institutions.[215]

[11.164] Section 12 of the 1998 Act provides that, subject to sub-s 7,[216] any person, including an educational or training body, who offers a course of vocational training, shall not in regard to any such course offered to persons over the maximum age at which those persons are statutorily obliged to attend school (currently 15 years),[217] discriminate against a person in s 16:

(a) in the terms on which any such course or related facility is offered,

(b) by refusing or omitting to afford access to any such course or facility, or

(c) in the manner in which any such course or facility is provided.

[11.165] However, s 12(4) provides:

> For the purposes of ensuring the availability of nurses to hospitals and teachers to primary schools which are under the direction or control of a body

---

[214] At p 38 of the unreported judgment.

[215] See McCarthy, *The Distasteful Challenge*, (1968), IPA, pp 109-110. The late Charles McCarthy notes that the national teacher, who was trained in a residential training college which was conducted on remarkably authoritarian lines, was a key figure in the shaping of Irish culture. He states, "the special stamp which is so noticeable in Irish culture was largely the work of these very able man and women who were prepared for teaching in this strict and authoritarian way."

[216] Which provides that nothing in sub-s (1) shall make unlawful discrimination on the age ground or on the ground of race in regard to any course of vocational training offered by a vocational or training body where it provides different treatment in regard to fees for admission, attendance or allocation of places at any such course attended by Irish citizens or other EU citizens or if it offers assistance to particular categories of person by way of reasonably justifiable sponsorships, scholarships, bursaries or other awards having regard to traditional or historical considerations.

[217] Shortly to be raised to 16 years, Education (Welfare) Bill 1999.

established for religious purposes or whose objectives include the provision of services in an environment which promotes certain religious values, and in order to maintain the religious ethos of the hospitals or primary schools, the prohibition of discrimination in subsection (1), in so far as it relates to discrimination on the religion ground, shall not apply in respect of *inter alia*:

(b) places in a vocational training course specified in an order made under subsection (5).

Thus, certain bodies which were established for religious purposes, such as primary schools and certain hospitals, are permitted to discriminate on the grounds of religion, in certain circumstances laid down in s 12, in order to allow them to promote religious values and to maintain their religious ethos. Hence, a College of Education, or other educational or training body may apply to the Minister for Education and Science for an order permitting it to reserve places in a vocational training course offered by it. The Minister may, by order, permit that body to reserve places in such numbers as seem reasonably necessary to him to meet the purposes set down in sub-s (4). An order under sub-s (5) may be revoked by a further Ministerial order containing safeguards for those who acted on the earlier order. This provision permits the religious denominations to ensure that the annual cohort of trainee teachers entering Colleges of Education are of a particular religion. However, some colleges now also make provision for the training and education of other teachers who are exempt from the obligation to study or teach religious instruction and these teachers teach mainly in the multi-denominational schools.

[11.166] Further safeguards for religious institutions are contained in s 37 of the 1998 Act which provides:

(1) A religious, educational or medical institution which is under the direction or control of a body established for religious purposes or whose objectives include the provision of services in an environment which promotes certain religious values shall not be taken to discriminate against a person for the purpose of this Part or Part II if -

(a) it gives more favourable treatment, on the religion ground, to an employee or a prospective employee over that person where it is reasonable to do so in order to maintain the religious ethos of the institution, or

(b) it takes action which is reasonably necessary to prevent an employee or a prospective employee from undermining the religious ethos of the institution.

(2) Nothing in this Part or Part II applies to discrimination against C in respect of employment in a particular post if the discrimination results from preferring D on the ground that the relevant characteristic of D is or amounts to an occupational qualification for the post in question.

The constitutionality of the religion ground

[11.167] The constitutionality of the religion ground was considered by the Supreme Court when the Employment Equality Bill 1996 was referred to the Supreme Court in *Re Article 26 of the Constitution of Ireland and the Employment Equality Bill 1996.*[218]

[11.168] Counsel for the Court submitted that these provisions were repugnant to the Constitution and that, if enacted into law, they would purport to legalise religious discrimination contrary to the provisions of Articles 40.1, 44.2 and to endow certain religions contrary to Article 44.2.2°. He contended, *inter alia,* that this would have the effect of making religion a criterion for employing people, dismissing people and for admission to vocational training. The result, he submitted, would be to undermine in an unconstitutional manner, the right of citizens who are members of a minority religious denomination or who have no religion, to earn a livelihood. The main submissions of counsel assigned by the Court were that the religion ground in Article 37 breached the guarantees of freedom of conscience and free practice of religion in Article 44.2.1° and that it breached the State guarantee not to impose any disabilities or make any discriminations on the ground of religious profession, belief or status.

[11.169] Counsel for the Court further submitted that the Oireachtas had failed to achieve a proper balance between the rights of the different religious denominations and the rights of other citizens to equality before the law to earn a livelihood. He maintained that if these provisions passed into law, they would constitute an unjust and disproportionate attack on the rights of these other citizens.

[11.170] Counsel for the State submitted that insofar as the Bill purported to authorise a religious discrimination or distinction, this was a form of positive discrimination (and no more than was necessary) to give effect to the provisions of Article 44. He denied that the Bill in any manner authorised the endowment of any religion. Further, he pointed out that State aid to religious and charitable institutions, referred to in the challenged provisions, are religious, educational and medical institutions under the direction or control of a body established for religious purposes or whose objectives include the provision of services in an environment which promotes certain religious values. While counsel acknowledged that a tension exists between the right to equality guaranteed by Article 40.1, the right to free profession and practice of religion guaranteed by Article 44.2 and the right to earn a livelihood in Article 40.3, he stated that the sections under discussion manifested a balanced attempt by the Oireachtas to resolve these tensions.

---

[218] [1997] 2 IR 321.

[11.171] Having heard the arguments of both sides, the Court summed up the relevant constitutional provisions which require the State to respect and honour religion and permit the State to support denominational schools.[219] It noted that Article 44.2.5° which guarantees protection to the right to maintain institutions for religious and charitable purposes. In order to analyse the meaning of "religious denomination", the Court turned to Article 44.1.2°[220] (since deleted).[221] It concluded that this was a generic term sufficiently broad to cover the various churches, religious congregations and religious societies under whatever name they assumed. These various religious denominations, the Court noted, may control religious, educational or medical institutions either directly or through a board of guardians or trustees. These are the religious, educational and medical institutions referred to in s 37(1) of the 1996 Bill, it appeared to the Court. Furthermore, these institutions are also governed by the phrase "institutions for religious and charitable purposes" in Article 44.2.5°.[222] With reference to "charitable purposes", the Court stated that the term "charity" in its legal sense, has four different divisions:

(1) trusts for the relief of poverty;

(2) trusts for the advancement of education;

(3) trusts for the advancement of religion; and

(4) trusts for other purposes beneficial to the community.

[11.172] The Court reiterated that it is not generally permissible to make any discrimination or distinctions between citizens on the grounds of religious profession, belief or status. However, it accepted that occasions may arise, when it becomes necessary to make distinctions "in order to give life and reality to the constitutional guarantee of the free profession and practice of religion". This principle was recognised both in Irish law[223] and in American law.[224] It noted that

---

[219] At 45-7.

[220] Which referred to the special position of the Holy Catholic Apostolic and Roman Church as guardian of the faith professed by the great majority of the citizens. It also provided: "The State also recognises the Church of Ireland, the Presbyterian Church in Ireland, the Methodist Church in Ireland, the Religious Society of Friends in Ireland, as well as the Jewish congregations and the other religious denominations existing in Ireland at the date of the coming into operation of this Constitution".

[221] By the 5th Amendment of the Constitution in 1972.

[222] *Re Article 26* at 47-8.

[223] *Re Article 26* at 50 citing *Quinn's Supermarket Ltd v AG* [1972] IR 1; *Mulloy v Minister for Education* [1975] IR at 88 *per* Walsh J; *McGrath and O'Ruairc v Trustees of Maynooth College* [1979] ILRM at 166.

[224] See *Corporation of the Presiding Bishop of the Church of Jesus Christ of the Latter Day Saints v Amos* 483 US 327 in which the plaintiff, who was employed by the Mormon church for 16 years was dismissed because he failed to produce a certificate to confirm that he was a member of a Mormon church and eligible to attend its temples.

the American Civil Rights Act 1964 banned religious discrimination in employment. However, para 702 of that Act exempted religious organisations from that prohibition. Hence, the Court did not find s 37 of the 1996 Bill unconstitutional.

Implied Gender Equality Clause in Contracts

[11.173] Section 21 of the 1998 Act provides for the insertion of a gender equality clause into contracts of employment if such contracts do not expressly, or by reference to a collective agreement or otherwise, already include such a term. Section 21(2) provides:

> A gender equality clause is a provision relating to the terms of a contract of employment, other than a term relating to remuneration or pension rights, which has the effect that if -
>
> (a) A is employed in circumstances where the work done by A is not materially different from that done by B in the same employment, and
>
> (b) at any time A's contract of employment would (but for the gender equality clause):
>
> > (i) contain a term which is or becomes less favourable to A than a term of a similar kind in B's contract of employment, or
> >
> > (ii) not include a term corresponding to a term in B's contract of employment which benefits B,
>
> then the terms of A's contract of employment shall be treated as modified so that the term in question is not less favourable to A or, as the case may be, so that they include a similar term benefiting A.

Discriminatory Advertisements

[11.174] Discriminatory advertising relating to employment is prohibited by s 10 of the 1998 Act and the court may grant an injunction preventing the appointment of any person to any post to which a discriminatory advertisement relates until a decision of the Director is made in that regard or until the court otherwise orders.

[11.175] Thus, if a school publishes *or displays* or causes to be published *or displayed* a discriminatory advertisement, the appointment of a teacher could be delayed for a considerable time and the Court may grant an injunction preventing the appointment of any person to any post to which the advertisement relates for a period.[225] The word "display" under this section may be interpreted as placing on a notice-board within the school. Section 10 does not, in any way, prohibit an advertisement which specifies a requirement, restriction or other matter *which relates to employment* and which it would not be unlawful for an

---

[225]Section 10(5).

employer to impose having regard to any other provision of the 1998 Act. So, if a school wishes to appoint a teacher with special expertise in games and sports, there is nothing in the 1998 Act preventing it from stating that requirement when it invites applications from suitably qualified men and women for the post, even though it is most likely that more men could comply with that requirement.

Vicarious Liability of Employers

[11.176] Under the 1977 Act, there is no express provision dealing with the vicarious liability of employers for the discriminatory acts of their employees.[226]

[11.177] The concept of vicarious liability of employers relates to two main areas in the 1998 Act:

    (a) vicarious liability for discriminatory acts of employees; and

    (b) vicarious liability for harassment of employees.

[11.178] The relevant sections are ss 15, 23 and 32. Applying the provisions of s 15(1)-(3) to the school situation, it appears that anything done by a teacher in the course of his employment shall be treated in any proceedings brought under the 1998 Act as done also by the board of management, and that this remains so whether or not it was done with the board's knowledge or approval. In such circumstances, however, sub-s (3) provides that it shall be a defence for the employer (the board) to show that it took reasonably practicable steps to prevent the teacher from doing that act or similar acts in the course of his employment.[227] For example, if a teacher employee, nominated by the board to sit on the selection committee or interview board with a view to interviewing candidates for a post within the school, inadvertently breaches the 1998 Act, normally the board will carry responsibility for such breaches. However, if the board can show that, prior to the interviews, it had instructed the teacher or caused him to be instructed, in the application of the 1998 Act to the conduct of interviews, then it may well be a good defence for the board in any resulting proceedings. This brings to the fore the importance of carefully drafted policies and procedures for discriminatory acts of employees and for both gender and non-gender harassment which should be drawn up by the employer or his legal representative.

[11.179] Much will depend on the employer's response to harassment,[228] discrimination and bullying by employees and on the policies imposed by the employer in these areas of growing importance in the workplace. This presupposes that an employer has informed, educated and instructed his

---

[226] See, however, *BC v A Health Board* (1994) 5 ELR 27.
[227] Section 15(1)-(3).
[228] On this point see *Allen v Dunnes Stores Ltd* [1996] ELR 203.

employees about sexual harrassment,[229] non-gender harassment, and bullying and that adequate policies have been drafted and implemented by the employer. Clearly, such policies will go well beyond mere prohibition of harassment, bullying etc and that they will include: procedures for the investigative process; a range of penalties commensurate with the offence;[230] the follow-on measures which will be set in motion by the employer in the event of a positive finding; and professional advice and/or pastoral care, which may be required for the alleged harasser,[231] bully or perpetrator of the discrimination. The indications are that sexual harassment is already an evolving area of law.[232] The term "sexual harassment" has been defined in statute law for the first time in the 1998 Act, s 23(3) and indications are[233] that this will be an developing area of law in the future.[234]

[11.180] Redmond, in *Dismissal Law in Ireland,*[235] discusses such matters as absenteeism,[236] double-jobbing, loyalty and fidelity,[237] grooming and personal hygiene,[238] alcohol-related conduct and drugs[239] and refusal to obey lawful orders, all of which may, on occasion, be relevant to teacher employment.

Qualifications and Proficiency in the Irish Language

[11.181] In the 1998 Act, due regard is taken of the constitutional status of the Irish language as the national language and the first official language[240] and of the right of the State to provide by law for any one or more official purposes in that regard.[241] Account is taken of established State policy which requires all teachers, both primary and post-primary, to have some knowledge of the Irish language.

[11.182] Section 36(3) makes provision for statutory protection of State policy in this regard for the first time. It provides that nothing in Part II or Part IV of the 1998 Act shall make unlawful the application of any provision (whether in

---

[229] *Regan v Killarney Hotels Ltd UD* 786/1993.

[230] *Allen v Dunnes Stores Ltd* [1996] ELR 203.

[231] See Redmond, *Dismissal Law in Ireland,* (1999) Butterworths, para [16.69].

[232] See *Annual Report of the Employment Equality Agency 1995.*

[233] See *Annual Report of the Employment Equality Agency 1995* and in particular data on sexual harrassment.

[234] See *Health Board v (C) B and the Labour Court* [1994] ELR 27.

[235] Butterworths, (1999).

[236] At pp 281-282.

[237] At p 284 *et seq.*

[238] At p 287.

[239] At pp 282-284.

[240] Article 8(1) of the Constitution.

[241] Article 8(3) of the Constitution.

the nature of a requirement, practice or otherwise) in relation to proficiency in the Irish language with regard to teachers in primary and post-primary schools. While the rationale behind this provision is undoubtedly the lawful protection and promotion of the Irish language,[242] in effect, it may deprive "the ground of race" in s 6(2)(h) of much of its potential in so far as the teaching profession is concerned as very few persons "of different race, colour, nationality or ethnic or national origins" would be likely to reach the standard required by the State of its teachers in relation to the Irish language. In this matter, the State can rely on the decision in *O'Sheil v Minister for Education and Science*[243] and on the Community law decision in *Groëner v Ireland.*[244]

[11.183] It is clear from the provisions of s 36(4) that nothing in Part II or Part IV of the 1998 Act shall make it unlawful for an employing board of management to require in regard to a particular post that a person holds a specified educational, technical or professional qualification which is generally accepted in the State for such posts. Neither is a board precluded from requiring the production and evaluation of information about any qualification other than such a specified qualification. Thus, if a teacher candidate for a post in a school claims to have skills over and above the normal requirements and specifications for the post, such as Grade VII as a pianist, the board may require the production and evaluation of such information. Likewise an employer is entitled to ensure that a person wishing to enter the teaching profession holds the required qualifications. However, nothing in s 36 renders discrimination on "the gender ground" lawful.

[11.184] From s 36(5), it is also clear that nothing in Part II or Part IV of the 1998 Act will make it unlawful for a body controlling the entry to, or carrying on of a profession, vocation or occupation (such as a Teaching Council, if it comes into existence) to require an individual wishing to enter or carrying on that profession, vocation or occupation to holds a specified educational, technical or other qualification which is suitable in the circumstances.

Exclusion of Discrimination on Religion Grounds

[11.185] Section 37(1) provides that a religious, educational or medical institution which is under the direction or control of a body set up for religious purposes, or whose objectives include the provision of services in a setting which promotes certain religious values, shall not be considered to discriminate against a person under Part II or Part IV in two instances. The first of these

---

[242] See *Groener v Minister for Education and the City of Dublin VEC* [1989] ECR 3967, for further discussion of this case, see above paras **[7.71]-[7.74]**.

[243] High Court, unrep, 16 April 1999, Laffoy J.

[244] [1989] ECR 3967.

instances is, if it reasonably confers more favourable treatment, on the religious ground, on an employee or prospective employee over another, so as to maintain the religious ethos of the institution. The second instance is where it takes action, which is reasonably necessary to prevent an employee or a prospective employee from undermining the religious ethos of the institution. These exceptions would permit a Catholic school board, *inter alia*, reasonably to give preference to a Catholic candidate at interview for a teaching post in the school or reasonably to dismiss a teacher or trainee teacher who persisted in undermining the religious ethos of the school.

[11.186] Section 37(1) is in line with the Rules for National Schools,[245] with the obligations falling on the boards of management of voluntary secondary schools[246] and with the Articles of Management of Community Schools Deeds of Trust which state "A teacher shall not advertently and consistently seek to undermine the religious belief or practice of any pupil in the school".[247]

[11.187] Furthermore, with regard to Part II and Part IV of the 1998 Act, a board may lawfully discriminate between two teachers at interview provided the preferment of the chosen teacher derives from an occupational qualification for the teaching post. So, if a primary school wishes to appoint a teacher with music or choir skills, it would not constitute discrimination under Part II or Part IV if the board favoured a male teacher, with the required expertise, over a female teacher lacking such expertise as the requirement arose from an occupational qualification. Ideally, the advertisement for the post should specify that the board invites applications from suitably qualified men and women teachers with expertise in the required area. It would appear prudent for the principal to bring to the notice of the board (and later to the interviewing body) the requirements of the post at the outset of the appointment procedure.

Obligations of Employers

[11.188] Section 16 provides that nothing in the 1998 Act shall be construed so as to require any person to recruit or promote an individual to a position, or to retain in his employment, or to provide training or experience to an individual in relation to a position if that individual -

    (a) will not undertake (or, as the case may be, continue to undertake) the duties attached to that position or will not accept (or, as the case may be, continue to accept) the conditions under which those duties are, or may be required to be, performed, or

---

[245] Chapter IX, rules 68 and 69.
[246] *A Manual for Boards of Management of Catholic Secondary Schools*, p 12.
[247] Para 7C.

(b) is not, (or as the case may be, is no longer) fully competent and available to undertake, and fully capable of undertaking, the duties attached to that position, having regard to the conditions under which those duties are, or may be required to be, performed.

Neither is anything in the 1998 Act to be construed as requiring an employer to recruit, retain in employment or promote a person if the employer is aware, on the basis of a criminal conviction of the person, or other reliable information, that the person engages, or has a propensity to engage in, any form of sexual behaviour *which is unlawful*. An employer may not discriminate on the grounds of an employee's sexual orientation.[248]

[11.189] However, s 16(6) goes on to provide:

Without prejudice to the generality of subsection (5), that subsection applies in particular where the employment concerned involves access to minors or to other persons who are vulnerable.

In the event of proceedings relating to the above situation, in the school context, the Equality Authority would be likely to resolve the conflict arising between the employer's interests and the individual rights of the teacher in favour of the employing board. One must conclude, therefore, that the rights conferred on Irish teachers by s 6(2)(d) of the 1998 are vulnerable in the context of a school. An English school teacher, who is a lesbian, has recently taken her case to an Industrial Tribunal. She claimed that she was forced to give up her position because of constant name-calling from pupils and that she suffered continuous harassment as a result of the failure of the school to take action, thereby causing her to suffer stress.[249]

Sexual Harrassment

[11.190] While the 1977 Act did not contain any express provision on the vicarious liability of an employer for the sexual harassment actions of employees of co-employees, the case law indicated an assumption of employer liability until *BC v A Health Board*.[250]

[11.191] Section 23(3) of the 1998 provides a definition of sexual harassment in legislation for the first time in Irish law. It provides (where A is the complainant) that for the purposes of the 1998 Act -

(a) any act of physical intimacy by B towards A,

---

[248] Section 6(2)(d).

[249] The Telegraph, 16 March 1999.

[250] (1994) 5 ELR 27 which involved a case of serious sexual assault by another employee. Costello P held that, under common law principles, the sexual assault was not an act for which the employer was vicariously liable.

(b) any request by B for sexual favours from A, or

(c) any other act or conduct of B (including, without prejudice to the generality, spoken words, gestures or the production, display or circulation of written words, pictures or other material).

shall constitute sexual harassment of A by B, if the act, request or conduct is unwelcome to A and could reasonably be regarded as sexually, or otherwise on the gender ground, offensive, humiliating or intimidating to A.

[11.192] This definition is quite widely drafted and includes the display and circulation of written words, pictures or other material which accords with the case law and with the European Code of Practice on the Dignity of Women and Men at Work which is repeated in the Irish Code.

[11.193] The circumstances in which harassment will amount to discrimination are widely drawn and so the alleged harasser may be another employee, the employer or a client, customer or business contact of the employer with whom A's employer might reasonably expect A to come in contact in the workplace or otherwise in the course of A's employment. Section 32(5) contains a definition of non-gender harassment.

Redress which may be Ordered

[11.194] Section 82 of the 1998 provides for redress which may be given by the Director of Equality Investigations:

(a) an order for compensation in the form of arrears of remuneration ... in respect of so much of the period of employment as begins not more than 3 years before the date of referral under section 77(1) which led to the decision,

(b) an order for equal remuneration from the date of referred to in paragraph (a),

(c) an order for compensation for the effects of acts of discrimination or victimisation which occurred not earlier than six years before the date of the referral of the case under section 77,

(d) an order for equal treatment in whatever respect is relevant to the case; and

(e) an order that a person or persons specified in the order take a course of action which is so specified.

An appeal lies from a decision of the Director to the Labour Court.

Part-Time Workers

[11.195] The Worker Protection (Regular Part-Time Employees) Act 1991 (the 1991 Act) provides the protection of seven employment statutes[251] to regular

---

[251] Minimum Notice and Terms of Employment 1973; Holidays (Employees) Act 1973 on a modified basis; The Unfair Dismissals Acts 1977-1993; Worker Protection Enterprises Act 1977-1978; Maternity Protection of Employees Acts 1981-1994.

part-time employees ie those who have been in the continuous service of the same employer for not less than 13 weeks and are normally expected to work at least 8 hours per week. All employees covered by the 1991 Act acquire a statutory minimum of rights including the benefits of the Unfair Dismissals Acts 1977-1993.

[11.196] The law holds that if an employee has continuous employment with the same employer for more than one year, he has rights unless the employee has complied with the requirements of s 2(2)(b) of the Unfair Dismissals Act 1977 (the 1977 Act).

Excluding the Unfair Dismissals Act

[11.197] Section 2(2)(b) of the 1977 sets down the terms upon which a contract of employment can be entered into without coming under the provisions of the Act.

[11.198] Section 2(2)(b) provides that the Act shall not apply to a dismissal in the following two cases:

    (a)   where the employment was made under a contract of employment for a fixed term,[252] or

    (b)   where the employment was made under a contract of employment for a specified purpose[253] of limited duration which could not be ascertained exactly at the time the contract was made[254] provided that:

        (i)   the contract is in writing;

        (ii)   the contract was signed by both parties; and

        (iii) the contract contained a clause stating that the Act shall not apply to such a dismissal.

Application to School Context

[11.199] If a school employs a teacher under a *fixed term contract*, the contract will terminate on the end-date specified, without the necessity of giving notice. If the end-date is permitted to pass, however, and the teacher continues to teach, the contract automatically acquires the status of a *contract for an indefinite*

---

[252] At the time of making a contract, if the commencement date and the termination date can be ascertained, then it is a fixed term contract, eg a one year career break contract.

[253] At the time of making the contract the period of the contract is limited but its exact duration is unknown eg, when a substitute teacher is taking the place of a teacher who is on sick leave, see further Redmond, *Dismissal Law* p 433 *et seq.*

[254] See *Coras Iompar Éireann v Herbert*, Circuit Court, 1985 *per* Clarke J cited in Madden and Kerr, *Unfair Dismissal*, IBEC, pp 33-4.

term.[255] The teacher's rights under the 1977 Act may be excluded if he complies with the procedure outlined in s 2(2)(b).

Unfair Dismissal Acts 1977-1993

[11.200] The purpose of the Unfair Dismissals Act 1977 (the 1977 Act) is to safeguard employees from being unfairly dismissed from their employment by laying down criteria by which dismissals are deemed unfair and by establishing an adjudication system and redress for an employee whose dismissal has been deemed unjustified.[256] From the date the 1977 Act came into force, (15 April 1977), the onus fell upon the employer to show that he dismissed fairly. In other words, the 1977 Act gave rise to a presumption that every dismissal of an employee is deemed to be unfair unless the employer can show substantial grounds justifying the dismissal, except where dismissal is not in dispute, eg where the claimant is alleging constructive dismissal or where issues relating to jurisdiction are at issue. A number of Acts have amended the 1977 Act including the Worker Protection (Regular Part-Time Employees) Act 1991 and the Unfair Dismissals (Amendment) Act 1993. The 1991 Act extended the ambit of the 1977 Act to include regular part-time employees. The Unfair Dismissals (Amendment) Act 1993[257] made a number of significant amendments to the 1977 Act which are discussed below.

Remedies for Unfair Dismissal

[11.201] Although, it has been recognised by the EAT[258] and others[259] that an employee has a species of property right to his job, the statutory initiative to create a legal entitlement to remain in one's post has not been successful in Ireland. However, redress for unfair dismissal includes re-instatement in the original position, re-engagement in the original position or in a suitable alternative position which the adjudicating body deem reasonable, or financial compensation with a maximum of two year's gross remuneration. An employee adjudged to be unfairly dismissed who has endured no financial loss may be awarded up to one month's pay or may receive *nil* damages.

---

[255] See Kerr, *Termination of Employment Statutes* (1995), Sweet and Maxwell, pp 160-164.

[256] See Forde, *Employment Law*, (1992), Round Hall Press, Ch 7; Kerr and Madden, *Unfair Dismissals Cases and Commentary*, Federation of Irish Industry, 1996; Meenan, *Working Within the Law* (1994), Oak Tree Press, Ch 17; Redmond, *Dismissal Law in the Republic of Ireland*, (1982), Incorporated Law Society generally.

[257] Which came into force on the 1 October 1993.

[258] *O'Connor v Heat Recovery Ltd* UD 105/1980; *McBride v Midland Electrical Co Ltd* UD 37/1979.

[259] See *Wynes v Southrepps Hall Broiler Farm Ltd* (1968) ITR 407 at 8; see further Redmond, 'The Law and Worker's Rights', in *Industrial Relations in Ireland,* p 225; Redmond, *Dismissal Law in Ireland* (1999), Butterworths, pp 445-6 and generally Ch 23.

Time Limits

[11.202] An employee seeking redress under the Unfair Dismissals Acts, must within 6 months of the date of dismissal (this period may be extended to 12 months in exceptional cases), give formal notice of their claim in writing either to:

(i) a rights commissioner, or to

(ii) the Employment Appeals Tribunal.

From 1 October 1993 the duty of furnishing a copy of the employee's claim to the employer falls on the rights commissioner or on the EAT as the case may be.

Written Notice of Dismissal Procedures

[11.203] Section 14(1) of the 1977 Act requires an employer to give a notice in writing to each employee setting down the procedure which he will observe before and for the purpose of dismissing the employee. This notice must be given to the employee not later than 28 days after he enters into a contract of employment with the employer.[260]

Application to Teachers

[11.204] Teachers generally are protected by the 1977-1993 Acts provided they have at least one year's continuous service with the same employer. The one year's continuous service, necessary to acquire protection for unfair dismissal, is not required where the dismissal is for pregnancy or for trade union membership or activity or for exercising rights acquired by the employee under the Maternity Protection of Employees Act 1994.

[11.205] In *O'Reilly v EAT, Hand and the Minister for Education*,[261] the teacher applicant had less than the requisite one year's employment with the employing board of management. However, it was successfully argued before the EAT and in the High Court that the EAT must hear all of the evidence in order to establish whether there was a fair dismissal and if so whether the employer was justified in failing to give the three months' contractual notice which would have brought the teacher within the ambit of the legislation.

[11.206] Vocational teachers, who are officers of a VEC, are specifically excluded from the benefit of s 2(1) of the 1977 Act, as amended by s 3(a) of the 1993 Act which provides that the Act shall not apply to:

---

[260] See Education Act 1998, s 24(3) and s 24(4).
[261] High Court, unrep, November 1997 *per* Shanley J.

(j) officers of a health board (other than temporary officers) or a vocational education committee established by the Vocational Education Act 1930.[262]

Farry points out, however, that the provisions of the Unfair Dismissals Act apply to employees such as Eligible Part Time Teachers (EPTs) or hourly part-time vocational teachers who are not officers of a VEC.[263]

Justifying a Dismissal as Fair

[11.207] In order to justify a dismissal, the board of management would have to show that such dismissal resulted wholly or mainly from one or more of the following:

(a) the capability, competence, or qualification of the employee for performing work of the kind which he was employed by the employer to do;

(b) the conduct of the employee;

(c) the redundancy of the employee; and

(d) the employee being unable to work or continue to work in the position which he held without contravention (by him or his employer) of a duty or restriction imposed by or under any statute or instrument made under statute.

If a board has dismissed a teacher, if requested, it must supply in writing within 14 days, the principal grounds for dismissal.

Probation or Training

[11.208] The 1977 Act does not apply in relation to the dismissal of an employee during a period of probation or training, if his contract of employment is in writing and the duration of the probation or training is one year or less and is so specified in the contract.[264]

[11.209] In the case of *Stevenson v Dalton Secondary Preparatory Schools (1976) Ltd,*[265] the claimant worked as a teacher for a probationary period from 1 October 1975 to 31 July 1976. He was informed by the employer in April 1976 that he would continue to be employed as a probationary teacher until 31 July 1977, the date on which he was dismissed. The respondents contended that the claimant's employment was, *inter alia,* excluded from the 1977 Act as being (a)

---

[262] The Unfair Dismissals (Amendment) Act 1993, s 3 amends s 2 of the 1977 Act by substituting a new paragraph (j) thereby inserting the words "other than temporary officers" thus extending the protection of the Acts to temporary officers in health boards.

[263] *Vocational Teachers and the Law,* (1998), Blackhall Pubs, p 78.

[264] Section 3(1) of the 1977 Act.

[265] UD 10/1978.

based on a contract for a fixed term made prior to 16 September 1977 without being renewed and as being a probationary contract. The respondents further argued that there were substantial grounds justifying the dismissal such as the capacity, competence or qualifications of the claimant as a teacher and redundancy.

[11.210] The EAT determined that the claimant's employment was not excluded from the 1977 Act. His original contract was renewed on the same or substantially the same terms and the renewal extended his employment to a period greater than one year. It further found that the claimant's capability, competence and qualifications were of such a standard so as not to justify unfair dismissal and the claimant was not dismissed wholly or mainly because of redundancy. Hence, his dismissal was held to be unfair and the appropriate remedy was reinstatement.[266]

Substantial Grounds for Dismissal

[11.211] In *Fitzgerald v St Patrick's College, Maynooth*,[267] the EAT found that the applicant had been unfairly dismissed from her lecturing post in the respondent college. The EAT concluded that:

(i) if an employer dismisses an employee to whom the Act applies, he ought to have substantial grounds for doing so;

(ii) if an employer cannot establish such grounds, then the dismissed employee is entitled to redress;

(iii) the definition in the Act of "dismissal" on which the applicant relied implied that where the Act is concerned, an employer is deemed to terminate a contract of employment when, on the expiry of the fixed term contract, he fails to renew it;

(iv) if an employer does not renew a fixed term contract of employment on its expiry, he ought to be able to establish substantial grounds for the non-renewal;

(v) substantial grounds are deemed by s 6(4) of the Act to exist where the dismissal results wholly or mainly from the capability, conduct or redundancy of the employee; but there may be other substantial grounds under s 6(6);

(vi) an example of such other substantial ground for the non-renewal of a fixed term contract would be as follows: if a teacher falls ill and is likely to remain ill for a school year, a substitute teacher may be employed for that school. The substitute's contract may be a fixed

---

[266] The case of a third level teacher was considered in *March v UCD*, UD 27/1977 in an appeal against the decision of a rights commissioner.

[267] UD 244/1978.

term contract. If on its expiry, the permanent teacher has made a full recovery so as to be capable of resuming teaching, there will be no further need for the susbstitute's further employment. The non-renewal of the substitute's fixed term contract will be justified by the permanent teacher's return to work.

(vii)   In the example given in (vi), the employment on the fixed-term contract can be traced to and justified by a special set of circumstances which constitute an emergency. If the emergency has passed at the time of the expiry of the fixed-term contract, the situation no longer requires the renewal of the fixed-term contract. The cessor of the emergency by the time of the expiry of the fixed term is the justification for the non-renewal of the fixed term contract, the substantial ground for the "dismissal" under the Act.[268]

[11.212] The EAT stated that the evidence showed that special circumstances had arisen in the *Fitzgerald* case, the arising of a vacancy for a permanent lecturer in the English Department in Maynooth College in 1976 and its continuance throughout 1977, which gave rise to the appointment of the applicant in 1976 and in 1977 on a fixed term contract. On the expiry of the latter contract, the special circumstances still existed. No permanent appointment was made. The respondent college had the option of renewing the applicant's contract for a further year. It did not do so. By not doing so and because the respondent, when making a contract with the applicant had omitted to avail of the provisions of s 2(2) of the Act, it was deemed in effect and for the purposes of the 1977 Act to have dismissed her. As the EAT established that there were no substantial grounds for the applicant's dismissal, it was deemed to be unfair dismissal. However, the remedies of reinstatement and re-engagement were considered inappropriate and as there was no evidence before the EAT that the applicant suffered any financial loss,[269] the applicant was awarded *nil* damages for the unfair dismissal. In the workplace generally, the EAT has found that a poor attitude on the part of the employee may give rise to a fair dismissal if the employer's business or the morale of fellow workers or the employee's record of performance, suffer as a consequence.[270]

The School Context: the Leonard *Case*

[11.213] In *Leonard v BOM Loreto Secondary School*,[271] it was alleged by the claimant that she had been unfairly dismissed from her position as a teacher in a secondary school. This case, which came before the EAT, dealt with the totality

---

[268] See further Madden and Kerr, *Unfair Dismissal*, IBEC 1966, p 113.

[269] See s 7(3).

[270] *Dermott v Lightstar Catering Ltd* UD 349/1991.

[271] Case UD/996/97.

of the duties of a teacher, prior to dismissal including class discipline, class management and the handling of students. The dismissal, *per se,* was not in dispute.

[11.214] The claimant was employed as an art teacher in the respondent school from 1992-1997 when she was dismissed from her permanent post on foot of a decision of the board of management (the board hereafter) following a disciplinary hearing. The substance of the complaints made against the claimant comprised a considerable volume of written complaints from parents and some limited instances of complaints from pupils. The evidence of the school Principal was augmented at the EAT hearing by the direct evidence of two of the claimant's pupils.

[11.215] For a number of years prior to the dismissal, it appears, difficulties had arisen pertaining to the teacher's professional duties including alleged bullying and intimidation of pupils. However, it should be stated, no worthwhile evidence was found by the EAT to upset the conclusion that the claimant's work as an art teacher was of a standard of excellence. The catalyst in the principal's decision to refer the matter to the board arose from complaints made about the claimant following an art trip in which the claimant and her class (of 14 to 15 year-old students) visited a photographic exhibition in January 1997.

[11.216] The subject matter of some of the pictures, it was accepted by all parties in this appeal, comprised photographs which were of an explicitly sexual nature which were unsuitable viewing for children of that age. No report of the visit to the gallery was given by the claimant to the school authority.

[11.217] In May 1997, the claimant was supplied with copies of the letters of complaint against her and the following August she was suspended pending an investigation of the whole matter. It was brought to the attention of the claimant that there would be a disciplinary hearing which would take place at board level and that a full hearing would follow at which the claimant could have complainants present to cross-examine them. The claimant was represented by a solicitor and counsel at the disciplinary hearing at board level at which she supplied a detailed written response to the alleged complaints against her and she did not, it appears, request the board to call any witnesses.

[11.218] It was argued by the claimant that the hearing procedure was fatally flawed, in that the board did not call any of the complainants to give evidence and merely relied upon the written complaints and the principal's notes in regard to her meetings with the claimant and in regard to the documentation of verbal complaints by her. Ten days later, on foot of a unanimous decision of the board, the claimant was dismissed. It was further submitted by the claimant that one of the board members, who was present at an earlier meeting, should have absented herself from the meeting which made the decision to dismiss her and that another board member, who made an allegedly biased remark against the claimant at the decision-making meeting, should have done likewise.

[11.219] The EAT made the following findings of fact:

(a) The complaints made against the claimant on a sustained basis for nearly two years were in substance true;

(b) The truth of those complaints and in particular the allegation relating to the bullying and intimidation of pupils in an isolated part of the classroom known as "the dark corner" was found to be established on the basis of the direct evidence of one of the pupils who appeared before the EAT. The veracity of this witness's evidence was not challenged in cross-examination;

(c) The failure of the claimant to report to the principal or to anyone in authority in the school after the art trip was "a gross dereliction of her duty to both the pupils under her care and the school who had entrusted her with that care";

(d) The claimant's behaviour at the art gallery, when informed of the unsuitable nature of the material, was a matter of utter misjudgement and was exacerbated by her failure, neglect or refusal to inform the school authorities on her return;

(e) The referral of the complaints to the board of management by the principal upon the discovery of the art trip by written complaints was entirely appropriate given the consequential erosion of her confidence in the claimant as a teacher;

(f) The blanket denial by the claimant of the complaints over a period of almost two years deprived all of the parties concerned of an opportunity to remedy the situation;

(g) The claimant's assertion that she constantly asked for an inspector to be brought in to monitor her ability was disputed by the respondent and no finding was made in relation to this assertion;

(h) The decisions of certain board members not to stand down from the board of management did not deprive the claimant of her right to fair procedures;

(i) As regard a warning, it was accepted from the evidence by the EAT that there was no written or oral warning to the claimant that her job was on the line. The first indication that this would be a possibility was contained in a letter of 21 May 1997 to the claimant. This failure to give a formal warning deprived the claimant of any opportunity to improve her performance;

(j) The employer having decided to hold a disciplinary hearing failed to conduct that hearing in a fair manner;

(k) The refusal of the board to call oral evidence was a decision taken in the light of having afforded the claimant the right to have any of the complainants present and as a consequence the claimant was not prejudiced by this.

[11.220] The EAT determined that the claimant was unfairly dismissed but that she had contributed to the dismissal to a very significant degree by her conduct in the matters complained of. Although the claimant sought re-instatement as her redress this was deemed in the circumstances to be entirely inappropriate as was also the remedy of re-engagement. The sum of £1,000 damages was awarded to the claimant under the Unfair Dismissals Acts 1977-1993.

Claims for unfair dismissals may be taken to a rights commissioner, with two exceptions[272] or before the EAT. When the rights commissioner's recommendation has not been implemented by the employer, the employee may appeal to the EAT. The Unfair Dismissals (Amendment) Act 1993, s 11(1) provides for an appeal to the Circuit Court from a determination of the EAT within six weeks of the date of the communication of the determination to the parties. Furthermore, case law[273] indicates that an appeal lies from cases that have been commenced in the EAT to the High Court. Well drafted disciplinary procedures are pivotal when dealing with such matters as employee dismissal so as to ensure that natural justice and constitutional justice procedures are implemented.

Dismissal for Failure to uphold the Ethos of the School

[11.221] As has been seen, denominational school authorities have implied constitutional rights, established common law rights and statutory entitlements to protect the ethos of their schools. Meanwhile, the rights of employees are increasingly finding expression in modern employment legislation. Nowhere is the unease between employer and employee's rights more manifest than in teacher employment as the vast majority of schools are denominational. It is in this sphere that the individual teacher may face a dilemma, by virtue of his personal life, in upholding the religious ethos of the school.

---

[272] Section 8(3) and s 5 of the 1977 Act as amended.

[273] In particular see *Commissioners of Irish Lights v Noel Sugg* [1994] ELR 97; *McCabe v Lisney and Son,* High Court, unrep, 16 March 1981; see generally Redmond, *Dismissal Law in Ireland,* (1999), Butterworths, Ch 24 "Procedural Aspects of Unfair Dismissal", p 477.

[11.222] Irish teachers, it seems are not generally expressly bound by their contracts obliging them to uphold the school ethos. Whether the courts would imply a term into teachers' contracts obliging them to do so, is a question which has not yet received any detailed consideration by the Irish courts although Costello P referred to the matter briefly in *Flynn v Power*.[274]

Flynn v Power

[11.223] Section 6(2)(f) of the 1977 Act[275] provides that a dismissal resulting "wholly or mainly" from the pregnancy of the employee or matters connected therewith shall be deemed to be an unfair dismissal.[276] In *Flynn v Power*[277] the claimant was a teacher in a voluntary secondary school who alleged that she had been unfairly dismissed from her post as a result of matters arising "wholly or mainly" from her pregnancy. At the material time, the claimant was residing with, and had become pregnant by, a married man in a country town. Prior to the pregnancy, the claimant had been requested to end the relationship as the employing school authority (a religious order) stated that the parents of some of the students had submitted complaints about the plaintiff's "lifestyle". The EAT considered that the dismissal was not unfair.[278]

[11.224] When the matter reached the High Court on appeal, the appellant argued that her private life was a matter for herself and that she had not overtly rejected the norms of the school.

[11.225] Costello J ruled that the plaintiff was not dismissed for reasons arising from her pregnancy but rather because her lifestyle did not accord with the ethos of the school and the norms of behaviour and the ideals which the school existed to promote. The High Court distinguished a secular school from a religious school having long established and well recognised aims and objectives. Costello J held that an employee's behaviour in sexual matters may justify dismissal if it is capable of damaging the employer's business. In this instance it was held that the plaintiff's conduct might damage the school's efforts to promote certain norms of behaviour and religious principles which it was established to foster. Deciding the case solely on the basis of the Unfair Dismissals Act, Costello J ruled that the plaintiff was fairly dismissed.

---

[274] [1985] ILRM 336.
[275] Amended by the 1993 Act.
[276] See, however, some exceptions in s 6(2)(f) as amended.
[277] [1985] IR 648; [1985] ILRM 336.
[278] With the Chairman dissenting.

Canada: The Caldwell Case

[11.226] In Canadian Catholic schools in British Columbia, teachers' contracts, by contrast with those of their Irish counterparts, contain "a Catholicity clause" requiring them to exhibit at all times conduct and way of life consistent with Catholic denominational standards. Costello J, in *Flynn v Power* among other cases, referred to *Caldwell v Stuart*[279] which came before the Canadian Supreme Court in 1985. The nett issue in the *Caldwell* case was whether or not it was contrary to the British Columbia Human Rights Code (the Code)[280] for a denominational school to refuse to continue to employ a teacher who had personally disregarded Church teachings. The plaintiff's transgression was that, when employed as a teacher in a Catholic school, she had married a divorced man in a civil ceremony contrary to Church teaching. The Supreme Court explicitly recognised the right of employers in the province of British Columbia to establish and run a denominational school according to Roman Catholic concepts of education. It was unequivocal in deciding that the teachers were contractually bound: "The teaching of doctrine and the observance of standards by the teachers form part of the Contract of Employment of the Teachers".[281] The Court balanced the two sets of legally established rights that of the individual to freedom from discrimination in employment and that of a religious group to carry on its activities in the operation of its denominational school according to its religious beliefs and practices.

[11.227] Finally, the Canadian Supreme Court resolved the conflict between the two positions in favour of the respondent school stating:

> "As has been pointed out, the Catholic school is different from the public school. In addition to the ordinary academic programme, a religious element which determines the true nature and character of the institution is present in the Catholic school. To carry out the purposes of the school, full effect must be given to this aspect of its nature and teachers are required to observe and comply with the religious standards and to be examples in the manner of their behaviour in the school so that students see in practice the application of the principles of the Church on a daily basis and thereby receive what is called a Catholic education."[282]

[11.228] In short, the Court held that the school's religious or doctrinal nature and the unique role played by its teachers, through their example in attaining its legitimate objects, were essential to a finding that religious conformity was a

---

[279] *Caldwell & Director, Human Rights Code of British Columbia v Stuart & the Catholic Schools of Vancouver Archdiocese & the AG of British Columbia* (1985) 1 WWR 620 (SCS).
[280] RSBC 1979, c 186, s 8.
[281] SC, Vol, 2, 1984 at 603-630 at 628.
[282] At pp 633-4 of the judgment.

bona fide qualification for employment. Thus, it held that the plaintiff had deprived herself of such a qualification through her breach of Canon Law. Consequently Ms Caldwell was not, it ruled, protected by the provisions of s 8 of the Code of Human Rights.

[11.229] Relating *Caldwell* to the Irish context, one significant difference is apparent, that, unlike their British Columbian counterparts, Irish teachers do not generally have an express term in their contracts to uphold the ethos of the school. Whether a court would imply such a term into teachers' contracts of employment must await a judicial decision. However, Costello J's comments in the *Flynn* case indicated, without so deciding, that he considered the plaintiff was impliedly bound by her contract (to act as the respondents required of her):

> "... the appellant knew from her own upbringing and previous experience as a teacher the sort of school in which she sought employment, and should have been well aware of the obligations she would undertake by joining its staff."[283]

It is arguable, however, that this part of Costello J's decision is merely *obiter* and as such would not be binding on later courts.

The Marian Regional High School Case

[11.230] The British Columbia Industrial Relations Council[284] (the Council hereafter) followed the decision in *Caldwell* and upheld the decision of a Vancouver Catholic School Board in its closure of Marian Regional High School following a dispute with the teachers' Union. The Board and the Union failed to agree over a requirement that "teachers exhibit at all times conduct and way of life consistent with Catholic denominational standards." (commonly termed "a Catholicity clause"). Such a clause is included in the personal service contract signed by all teachers in the 41 schools operated by the Archdiocese of Vancouver. Apparently the Union in *Marian High School* contemplated a Catholicity clause covering "school hours only" and it also proposed that disputes relating to the interpretation, application and administration of that clause would be referred to a third party neutral arbitrator as was the norm in other matters. The school authority disagreed and insisted on the inclusion of the 24 hour Catholicity clause in the teachers' contracts. When no agreement was forthcoming, the school authorities closed the school on the advice of the Archbishop.

---

[283] At p 12 of the judgment.

[284] *Marian Regional High School Education Committee (the Employer) v Catholic Secondary School Teachers' Association (the Union)*, 4 November 1988, Industrial Relations case, reported by Reverend Hawkswell, 'IRC decision on Marian Regional High School', (20 November 1988), *The British Columbia Catholic*, pp 8-9.

[11.231] The Council relied on *Caldwell v Stuart*[285] and found the Board did not violate its statutory duty to bargain in good faith by closing the school and that it was it not guilty of unfair labour practices by so doing. The evidence before the Council established that the employer's "business" was intrinsically unique and distinctly different from the operation of secular schools by virtue of its special doctrinal nature. Furthermore, it found that the school closure did not comprise an illegal lockout. Rather, it concluded that in the absence of the commitment, freely given by the teachers in the Catholicity clause, the school was not viable as a Catholic institution.

The Contract: Excluding the Unfair Dismissals Acts

[11.232] A teacher's rights, *inter alia*, under the Unfair Dismissals Acts 1977-1993 may be excluded under s 2(2) as follows:

(a) in a fixed term contract, under which the teacher is let go when the contract ends, or

(b) in a specified purpose contracts,[286] under which the teacher is let go when the purpose ceases,

provided the contract is in writing and provided it contains an exemption clause, signed by both parties, that the Unfair Dismissals Acts 1977-1993 do not apply.[287]

[11.233] Since 1 October 1993,[288] if a series of two or more of these contracts, between which there was no more than a three month break, is deemed to have existed for the purpose of avoidance by the employer of liability under the Acts, then the two periods of employment will be added together to calculate continuous service of an employee under the Acts. Any provision in an agreement, whether a contract of employment or otherwise, to exclude or limit the application of the Acts is void. If an employer is to require special standards of his employees, then these should be set down in written form so as to avoid ambiguity and litigation at a later date.[289]

Disqualification under Statute

[11.234] A vocational teacher who is convicted of an offence specified in s 3(a) of the Vocational Education (Amendment) Act 1947 may be disqualified from

---

[285] (1985) 1 WWR 620 (SCS).

[286] Being a purpose of such a kind that the duration of the contract was limited but was, at the time of its making incapable of precise ascertainment.

[287] Section 2(2)(b) as amended; see *CIE v Herbert*, judgment delivered 12 February 1986.

[288] The date the Unfair Dismissals (Amendment) Act 1993 came into force.

[289] See *O'Brien v Good Shepherd Convent* UD 342/1991; see further Redmond, *Dismissal Law in Ireland*, (1999), Butterworths, p 206, para 13.42.

his office or employment by s 6(6)(b) of that Act. Thus, if such a person knowingly makes or allows to be made a false statement for the purpose of obtaining payment under this section for himself or another, he may be disqualified, fined or imprisoned.[290]

[11.235] Prior to the decision in *Cox v Ireland*,[291] a teacher could also be disqualified under the Offences Against the State Act 1939 (the 1939 Act) which deals only with criminal and quasi-criminal matters. Section 34(3)(a) of the 1939 Act imposed penalties on those within its ambit[292] providing that:

> Every person who is convicted by a Special Criminal Court of an offence which is, at the time of such conviction, a scheduled offence for the purposes of Part V of this Act, shall be disqualified (a) for holding, within seven years after the date of such conviction, any office or employment remunerated out of the Central Fund or moneys provided by the Oireachtas or moneys raised by local taxation or in or under or as a paid member of a board or body established by or under statutory authority.

[11.236] The plaintiff, a qualified second level teacher, was employed in a County Longford community school from November 1974 to February 1988.[293] He was arrested in November 1987 and charged before the Special Criminal Court with certain firearms offences under the Firearms Acts 1925-1971 which are scheduled offences under Part V of the 1939 Act. The plaintiff pleaded guilty to certain of the firearms offences and spent two years in prison. Allowing for remission, he was released on 18 August 1989. While the plaintiff was in prison, a substitute teacher was employed to replace him.

[11.237] For his part, the Minister sought to enforce s 34 of the 1939 Act against the plaintiff as a result of which his post in his school was vacated and he was ineligible for re-employment at the school or any school funded by the State for seven years from the date of his conviction. Furthermore, the plaintiff's pension rights were forfeited and he lost his rights to PAYE benefits for a like period.

[11.238] In judicial review proceedings Barr J held that the penalties imposed by s 34 of the 1939 Act were "patently unfair and capricious in nature" and were an unreasonable and unjustified interference with the plaintiff's personal rights guaranteed by Article 40.3. Accordingly, Barr J gave a declaration that the provisions of ss 1-4 of s 34 of the 1939 Act were unconstitutional and void. He further held that the plaintiff was entitled to damages as against the State, that issue to stand adjourned for plenary hearing.

---

[290] See further Farry, *Vocational Teachers and the Law*, (1998), Blackhall Pubs, Ch 8.

[291] [1992] 2 IR 503.

[292] But not on those who are outside the scope of s 34.

[293] As a teacher of physical education and geography.

[11.239] On appeal to the Supreme Court, which dealt only with the validity of the impugned section of the 1939 Act, the Court held that the provisions of s 34 of the 1939 Act potentially constituted an attack on the unenumerated constitutional right of that person to earn a living, on certain property rights protected by the Constitution such as the right to a pension, gratuity or emolument already earned and on the right to the advantages of a subsisting contract of employment. Essentially, the Court was concerned with whether, in enacting s 34, the Oireachtas had acted fairly and even-handedly by imposing penalties on those persons within its scope (eg teachers or public servants) but not on others (such as those in private employment). The Court stated:

> "The State has a right to impose conditions of employment by statute, even outside the public sector, in the interests of the common good, eg, as to the maximum daily working hours or annual holiday entitlement. But these must apply to every employee or to all within specific categories and intervention by the State into the relationship of master and servant must be fair and even-handed. The provisions of section 34 do not satisfy that test. The fact that it applies to, for example, a lorry driver employed by Kerry County Council or the ESB but not to a comparable driver employed in the private sector does not have any logical justification and its operation in practice seems to be capricious."[294]

[11.240] The Supreme Court considered that the penalties imposed by s 34 on those within its ambit are "patently unfair and capricious in nature" and that its operation was itself against the common good which requires consistency and fairness in the application of the law. Accordingly, the Court disallowed the appeal and declared the provisions of s 34 of the 1939 Act to be unconstitutional and void in its entirety. By reason of s 34, the plaintiff was deprived of his teaching post and so the Court held he was entitled to damages and also to the declaration which he sought at paragraph 2 of his claim.[295]

[11.241] Following a consent agreement in the High Court, on 30 April 1993, between the plaintiff and the Department, Mr Cox resumed work at his original school having given an undertaking to refrain from any subversive activities and from teaching any subversive doctrines, to uphold the Constitution, to desist from any criminal activities and to attend a professional refresher course at his personal expense.[296] Finally it should be noted that the courts in certain instances have granted injunctions restraining dismissal.[297]

---

[294] *Cox v Ireland* [1992] 2 IR 503.

[295] *Cox v Ireland* [1992] 2 IR 503.

[296] See further Farry, *Vocational Teachers and the Law*, (1998), Blackhall Pubs, p 99.

[297] *Phelan v BIC Zrl Ltd* [1994] ELR 208; *Bolan v Phoenix Shannon plc* [1997] ELR 113; *Courtenay v Radio 2000 Ltd* [1992] ELR 198; *Maher v Irish Permanent plc (No 1)* [1998] 5 ELR 77; *Mooney v An Post* [1998] 5 ELR 238. In *O'Malley v Aravon School Ltd* High Court, unrep, 13 August 1997, it was held that the principal was not entitled to an injunction as trust had broken down between the parties.

Safety, Health and Welfare at Work Act 1989

Employers' Duties

[11.242] First and second level educational institutions in Ireland employ approximately 48,000 persons.[298] Together with their duties under the common law,[299] employers have further duties under the Safety, Health and Welfare at Work Act 1989 (the 1989 Act) and regulations made thereunder[300] to ensure "so far as is reasonably practicable" the safety, health and welfare at work of all its employees.[301]

[11.243] This means that the board as employer must provide a working environment that is "so far as is reasonably practicable" safe and without risks to health together with adequate facilities for the employee's welfare at work. That these are not absolute duties is clear from the qualifying phrase "so far as is reasonably practicable" which was interpreted in *Edwards v National Coal Board*[302] and in *West Bromwich Building Society v Townsend*[303] as meaning that the employer may balance the degree of risk involved, as against the sacrifice involved in time, expense or trouble to put the matter right.

[11.244] A further statutory duty on the board extends to the provision and maintenance "so far as is reasonably practicable" of:

    (a) safe plant and machinery;

    (b) safe systems of work; together with

    (c) handling systems and transportation; and

    (d) storing methods of substances and articles that are safe and without risk to health.[304]

[11.245] Further duties falling on the employer are in regard to the provision of systems of work that are planned, organised, performed and maintained, so as to be "so far as reasonably practicable" safe and without risk to health.[305] This latter duty is relevant to a number of areas of school life such as:

---

[298] The Report of the Advisory Committee on Occupational Safety and Health at First and second Levels in the Educational Sector, Health and Safety Authority, 1995, p 3.

[299] See Brazier, *Street on Torts* (8th ed, 1988), Ch 17.

[300] See in particular Safety, Health and Welfare at Work Act 1989; Control of Specific Substances and Activities) Regulations 1991; Safety, Health and Welfare at Work (General Application) Regulations 1993 (SI 44/1993); Safety, Health and Welfare at Work Act (Carcinogens) Regulations (SI 80/1993).

[301] Safety, Health and Welfare at Work Act 1989 s 6(1).

[302] [1949] 1 KB 704.

[303] [1983] ICR 257.

[304] See Safety, Health and Welfare at Work (General Application) Regulations 1993.

[305] Section 6(2)(d).

(a) supervision of students generally in accordance with articles of management, regulations, circulars and internal school rules;

(b) procedures for assembly, egress and fire drills; [306]

(d) arrangements and policy formulation for school tours;

(e) codes of discipline including anti-bullying policies;[307]

(f) Anti-smoking policies;

(g) Manual handling including training of all staff in lifting and transportation of equipment;

(h) Stress prevention policies and anit-violence policies.[308]

[11.246] In instances where it is not reasonably practicable for the board to control or eliminate hazards, a further duty lies in regard to the provision of, and maintenance of, suitable protective clothing or equipment that is necessary to ensure the safety and health at work of the employees is required by the Act. In the setting of a school, this latter provision might include, *inter alia*, the provision of such items as non-slip mats, protective gloves for the administration of first aid, oven gloves for domestic economy classes, guards and goggles for machines and white coats for science classes. While prosecutions in the general workplace, under the 1989 Act, are not unusual, prosecutions in schools are much less frequent. Failure to comply with the provisions of the 1989 Act and the Regulations made thereunder may, however, lead to a criminal prosecution against the school and may also be relevant in compensation cases.

[11.247] In 1992, however, County Kerry VEC was held to have breached s 48(17) of the 1989 Act and the 1993 General Applications Regulations. The VEC was fined £400 by the Health and Safety Authority (HSA) for failing to ensure that a woodworking machine in one of its community colleges was fitted with a riving knife as a result of which a student suffered personal injury.[309] More recently, the matter of the required standard of the storage and usage of hazardous chemicals in schools was at issue in proceedings involving a County Galway vocational school following a gas explosion at the school as a result of which the caretaker and some students were injured. In this instance, the employing VEC was served with a summons relating to breaches of the 1989

---

[306] See Fire Services Act 1981.

[307] See Circular M 33/91.

[308] See Circular 40/97 (Primary Schools) and Circular M 18/99 (Guidlines on Violence in Schools. See also Byrne, 'Health and Safety Requirements for Primary Schools: A 1999 Update', lecture delivered in Trinity College Law School, 27 March 1999.

[309] See further Dowling Maher, 'The Safety, Health and Welfare at Work Act, 1989 with Particular Reference to an Effective Policy for Science Laboratories', (1996), unpublished thesis, M Sc, Trinity College, Dublin, p 99.

Act including failure to have a safety statement and failure to instruct and train its caretaker in health and safety matters. In the District Court[310] the VEC was fined £2,400 relating to these breaches. The court also held that the VEC had failed in its obligation to instruct the caretaker regarding his duties in the school. Civil proceedings may also follow.

Consultation and Training

[11.248] One of the duties falling on the board is the provision of information, instruction, training and supervision to ensure, "so far as it reasonably practicable" the health and safety at work of employees.[311] This duty pervades almost all work activities in the school including the supervision of students. While the Report of the Advisory Committee on Occupational Safety and Health at First and Second Levels in the Education Sector to the HSA[312] (the 1995 Report) concluded that, the education sector does not present acute risk,[313] it noted an element of non-compliance in schools with health and safety legislation in the following areas:

    (a) consultation with employees;

    (b) the production of Safety Statements; and

    (c) accident reporting.[314]

[11.249] The consultation and training of employees is clearly a duty falling on the employer.[315] However, the teacher unions have commenced a major training programme for safety representatives which should greatly assist the implementation of the 1989 Act in schools. The obligation on the employer to draft and implement a Safety Statement is unqualified.[316] A further finding of the 1995 Report was that, although progress had been made in many schools in relation to the development of legally mandatory safety statements, confusion often reigns in regard to the contents of such statements. Failure to report certain accidents may result in breaches of the 1993 Regulations which require employers to report occupational accidents to the HSA which result in an

---

[310] Loughrea District Court on 23 March 1998.

[311] Section 6(2)(e) of the 1989 Act.

[312] Health and Safety Authority 1995, p 3. The survey had a response rate of 57%.

[313] The 1995 Report, at p 5, noted that employer liability claims were at a relatively low level, averaging 23 per year between 1989-1993. The majority of claims arose from defective plant or machinery, defective premises and slips and trips. Public liability claims, on the other hand, averaged 169 per annum over the same period with the majority of claims arising from slips and trips.

[314] *Report of the Advisory Committee on Occupational Safety and Health at first and second Levels in the Education Sector to the HSA*, pp 6-10.

[315] The 1989 Act s 6(2)(e).

[316] Section 12.

employee's absence from work for more than three days, which requires treatment from a registered medical practitioner or treatment in a hospital, and when an accident results in the death of an employee.

First Aid

[11.250] Prior to November 1989, there was no statutory requirement concerning first aid in schools and colleges. Part IX of the 1993 Regulations places a general duty on employers to make, or ensure that there is made, adequate first aid provision for their employees if they are injured or become ill at work.[317] "First-aid" in this context means:

(a) in a case where a person requires treatment from a registered medical practitioner or a registered general nurse, treatment for the purpose of preserving life or minimising the consequences of injury or illness until the services of such a practitioner or such a nurse are obtained, or

(b) in a case of a minor injury which would otherwise receive no treatment or which does not need treatment by a registered medical practitioner or registered general nurse, treatment of such an injury.[318]

[11.251] Section 56 requires an employer (the board) to make provision for first-aid equipment,[319] and to provide or ensure the provision at each place of work under his control such number of occupational first-aiders[320] as is necessary to render first-aid at the place of work concerned, taking account of the size or hazards or of the undertaking or establishment or both. It is highly desirable that some teachers on a staff attend a first-aid course and that they acquire a certificate in first aid. Teachers and pupils ought to be familiar with the names of first-aiders so that they can call on their assistance in a crisis situation. However, if there is no such expertise in the school, school policy should indicate that, rather than have a teacher who is unskilled in first-aid treat a child, they should summon competent aid immediately.[321]

Summoning an Ambulance

[11.252] On the question of giving priority to a parent's presence or calling an ambulance, Cassells J in *Felgate v Middlesex County Council*[322] had little doubt as to the correct procedure:

---

[317] Sections 56, 57, see First Aid Regulations 1993.
[318] Section 54.
[319] Suitably marked and easily accessible.
[320] Section 54 provides that an "occupational first-aider" means the person who is the holder of a certificate in first aid, issued within the immediately preceeding period of three years, by a person who is recognised as an occupational first aid instructor by an approved person."
[321] See further *The Head's Legal Guide*, Croners, 3-115.
[322] This unreported 1954 decision is cited in *The Head's Legal Guide*, Croners, para 3-115.

"If a child is injured to such an extent that it is quite clear to those who are in authority at the school that skilled treatment, possibly hospital treatment is necessary, then I think the ambulance should be sent for at once. It may be that some parents would raise objection if they were not sent for at the same time, but I think authorities need not fear any criticism of any kind if they have taken the appropriate steps to summon the ambulance for attendance at the earliest possible moment. Children are happier if they have their mothers with them, but I think the presence of the mother before the ambulance is summoned is not nearly so important as the summoning of the ambulance."

[11.253] An important school related provision is included in s 23 of the Non-Fatal Offences Against the Person Act 1997 which is relevant to this topic. It provides that a pupil who has reached the age of 16 years may give consent to any surgical, medical or dental treatment. The phrase "surgical, medical or dental treatment" includes any procedure undertaken for the purposes of diagnosis and such procedure includes the administration of an anaesthetic which is ancillary to any treatment as it applies to that treatment. However this provision may be constitutionally vulnerable.

Health and Welfare Facilities

[11.254] As in other workplaces, there is a duty on schools to provide and maintain facilities for the welfare of teachers and pupils such as toilet and washing facilities, first aid facilities, seating facilities and facilities suitable for pregnant women and breastfeeding mothers.[323]

Violent Pupils or Other Violent Persons

[11.255] While normally, the problem of violence in schools[324] is to be determined by reference to the law of trespass and the criminal law of assault, it has relevance also to the area of health and safety. In discharging its obligation to ensure a safe working environment, so far as is reasonably practicable, a school has a duty to take reasonable precautions to ensure that pupils and teachers are protected from violent pupils or other such persons on the school premises. Counsel's contention in *West Bromwich Building Society v Townsend*[325] that the risk of injury from criminals was beyond the scope of the employer's obligations under the English Health and Safety at Work Act 1974, was rejected by O'Neill J. Although he was referring to the absence of a "bandit screen" in a building society in that case, an analogy may be drawn with the school context and the absence of a panic button in circumstances where danger is reasonably foreseeable.

---

[323] Byrne, Lecture delivered in Trinity College Law School, 27 March 1999, p 8 of the handout.
[324] See HSA Guide on Stress on Workplace Violence (1992).
[325] [1983] ICR 257.

[11.256] For example, if a board becomes aware that a pupil or a parent or other person has a dangerous propensity, it is expected to take precautions to lessen the risk arising to teachers and pupils from that child. This might involve the installation of a panic button in the principal's office and/or in individual classrooms where danger is reasonably foreseeable. Further measures might include seeking counselling, remedial teaching, teacher aid assistance or other support services for the student in question. The sanctions of exclusion or suspension can also be utilised in such circumstances. Finally, it may be necessary for the board to suspend or even, in extreme cases, expel the child, which decision may be appealed under s 29(1) of the Education Act 1998 provided any procedure established under s 28 by a school or patron has been concluded or exhausted. The Department had recently issued guidelines to second level schools on *Violence in Schools* and the necessity to implement procedures to counter such violence has been emphasised.

Serious Risk to Safety

[11.257] As the *dicta* of Finlay P in the *The State (Smullen) v Duffy*[326] indicate, there may be circumstances in a school in which the giving of an immediate suspension order against the pupils may constitute a duty falling on the principal or the board. Where physical violence is causing danger to other pupils or to teachers, it may be necessary to use immediate suspension or even expulsion. The *Smullen* case was concerned with the immediate suspension by the principal of eight boys following a gang fight outside the school in which one of the participating boys was stabbed. Having considered the draft Articles of Management[327] in this regard, Finlay P held that this was "a minimum responsible decision for a schoolteacher with obligations to maintain discipline and safety within his school."

[11.258] School policies ought to point out that classrooms are accessible only to those who seek permission through the principal's office in advance and that appointments must be made to see an individual teacher. Troublesome parents may also be prohibited from coming on the school grounds by the board of management or by the principal. In England, the Local Government (Miscellaneous Provisions) Act 1982 introduced a new statutory offence, that of creating a nuisance or disturbance on the premises of maintained schools. The police and the Local Education Authorities (LEAs) have the right to prosecute

---

[326] [1980] ILRM 46 at 51. See M/99 Guidelines on Violence in Schools and the earlier circulation to primary schools, 40.97.

[327] *The State (Smullen) v Duffy* [1980] ILRM 46; the judge held that the draft Articles of management were "a proper, just and equitable arrangement in regard to the running and management of a school, whose procedures if properly applied in a *bona fide* manner would not be contrary to natural justice."

under this Act. Those who have no lawful right to be on the school premises and who are creating a disturbance or nuisance on such premises may be removed by the police and by those authorised by the LEAs, using such force as is reasonable in the circumstances. This power extends to any individual who has been told to leave, including an aggressive parent or a formally suspended pupil.

[11.259] While an action in negligence will not normally lie against the parent of a pupil who has caused injury to a teacher, there are some circumstances in which such a parent may be liable. Where, for example, a parent ordered or sanctioned the offending action or it would not have taken place but for the negligence of the parent, then an action against the parent may succeed.[328] If a parent knows or ought to be aware of a dangerous propensity in his child, and he fails to safeguard others from it, then he may be liable. However, as McMahon and Binchy note, some decisions seem to require something close to *scienter* on the part of the parent.[329]

The Obligation to Report Accidents

[11.260] The Report of the Advisory Committee on Occupational Safety and Health[330] observed that it was constrained in attempting to quantify the current level of occupational accidents in the education sector by the lack of data in this sphere. The 1989 Act and the 1993 Regulations require the employer to put in place general health and safety provisions including the use of work equipment, provision of personal protective clothing, manual handling of loads,[331] first aid, display screen equipment and notification of accidents and dangerous occurrences. The school authority is required to provide systems of work that are planned, organised, performed and maintained in such a manner as to be, so far as is reasonably practicable, safe and without risk to health.

Employees' Duties

[11.261] Section 9(1) of the 1989 Act, *inter alia,*[332] requires an employee to take reasonable care for his own safety and for that of any other person who may be affected by his acts or omissions while at work, eg pupils and parents. Employees are also required to co-operate with their employers and others in the implementation of the 1989 Act and to report without undue delay any defects in plant, equipment, place and system of work which might endanger safety and

---

[328] For a discussion of a number of cases involving violent pupils in England, see Barrell and Partington, *Teachers and the Law*, (1985) Methuen, pp 464-467.

[329] At p 295 citing *Streifel v Stroz* 11 DLR (2d) 667 (BC SC), Whittaker J, 1957.

[330] HSA 1995, op cit, pp 3-5.

[331] See Manual Handling of Loads Regulations 1993; Part VI of the General Application Regulations 1993.

[332] See also the Regulations made under the 1989 Act.

health. An important duty falling on employees is to use any protective clothing or equipment provided by the employer to ensure their safety and not to interfere with or misuse anything provided by the employer to safeguard safety, health and welfare at work.[333]

[11.262] In 1986 an English science teacher was fined £500 under the Health and Safety at Work Act 1974 as he had failed to ensure that his students used goggles, which were provided by the school authority, to protect the safety and health of his pupils during a science experiment in which a number of pupils were injured.[334] The same principle governs any protective article or safety equipment provided by the school authority in other classes in compliance with its obligations under the 1989 Act.[335]

Who is Responsible in the School?

[11.263] Clearly, the hierarchical structure of a school's authority would indicate that the patron, board of management and the principal teacher would have responsibility in this regard. However, in some instances, a teacher could be prosecuted eg where they fail to use whatever has been provided by the board for their protection or for the protection of the students or if he fails to exercise reasonable care for himself or his students. In view of the fact that when s 14 of the Education Act 1998 comes into effect, boards of management will be corporate bodies with power to sue and be sued in their corporate names, prosecutions against schools may become more common, for as Byrne points out,[336] prosecutions against corporate bodies, such as companies or local authorities, are the most common type of prosecution brought by the HSA.

Protections for Persons Reporting Child Abuse Act 1998

[11.264] The Protections for Persons Reporting Child Abuse Act 1998 (the 1998 Act)[337] aims to provide protection from civil liability for persons who report child abuse in certain circumstances and to protect to such persons from penalisation by their employers, to provide for an offence in respect of the false reporting of child abuse and to provide for related matters. This most welcome Act is relevant to the school setting as teachers previously felt particularly vulnerable when reporting any form of child abuse. The term "child abuse" in the 1998 Act includes sexual abuse, assault, ill-treatment, neglect and impairment or neglect of a child's health, development or welfare. The term

---

[333] Section 9.
[334] Times Educational Supplement, 21 November 1986.
[335] See further Brierley, 'School Sports' Bulletin, *The Head's Legal Guide*, 9 March 1994.
[336] Byrne, lecture delivered in Trinity College, 27 March 1999, handout, p 13.
[337] See Appendix B.

"welfare" in relation to a child means comprises moral, intellectual, physical, emotional and social welfare of the child.

[11.265] Section 3 of the 1998 Act provides:

(1) A person who, apart from this section, would be so liable shall not be liable in damages in respect of the communication, whether in writing or otherwise, by him or her to an appropriate person of his or her opinion that-

    (a) a child has been or is being assaulted, ill-treated, neglected or sexually abused, or

    (b) a child's health, development or welfare has been or is being avoidably impaired or neglected,

unless it is proved that he or she has not acted reasonably and in good faith in forming that opinion and communicating it to the appropriate person.

[11.266] An employee is protected by s 4 of the Act from penalisation by his employer for having formed an opinion of the kind referred to in s 3 of the 1998 Act and for having communicated that opinion in writing or otherwise to an appropriate person "if the employee has acted reasonably and in good faith in forming that opinion and communicating it to an appropriate person". An "appropriate person" means a designated officer (ie an officer of a health board established under the Health Act 1970) or a member of the Garda Síochána.

[11.267] In proceedings brought before a rights commissioner or the EAT in regard to a complaint made that s 4(1) has been breached, it shall be presumed, until the contrary is proved, that the employee acted reasonably and in good faith in forming the opinion and in making the communication concerned.[338] An employee may present a complaint to a rights commissioner regarding the contravention of s 4(1) by his employer and the rights commissioner shall give a decision in writing and communicate the decision to both parties.[339] A decision of a rights commissioner under s 4(4) shall do one of the following:

(a) declare that the complaint was or, as the case may be, was not well founded,

(b) require the employer to comply with subsection (1) of this section,

(c) require the employer to pay to the employee compensation of such amount (if any) as is just and equitable having regard to all the circumstances, but not exceeding two years remuneration in respect of the employee's employment.

[11.268] Regarding the false reporting of child abuse, a person who states to an appropriate person that a child has been or is being assaulted, ill- treated, neglected or sexually abused, or that a child's health, development or welfare has

---

[338] Section 4(2) of the Act.
[339] Section 4(4).

been or is being avoidably impaired or neglected, knowing that statement to be false, shall be guilty of an offence.[340]

[11.269] A person guilty of an offence under s 5 of the 1998 Act will be liable -

    (i)   on summary conviction, to a fine not exceeding £1,500 or to imprisonment for a term not exceeding 12 months or to both,

    (ii)   on conviction on indictment, to a fine not exceeding £15,000 or to imprisonment for a term not exceeding 3 years or to both.[341]

[11.270] Summary proceedings for an offence under the 1998 Act may be instituted within 12 months from the date of the offence.[342]

---

[340] Section 5(1).

[341] Section 5(2).

[342] Section 5(3). Guidelines for the Reporting of Child Abuse are available form the Department of Health 1987, the Department of Education and Science, 1991 and the Child Abuse Prevention Programme, Cherry Orchard Hosptial, Dublin. New guidelines will be issued by the Department of Education and Science shortly.

Chapter 12

Freedom of Information: Access to Records in Schools

Introduction

[12.01] Schools retain a considerable body of information on others including references, testimonials, reports and examination results.[1] The Department of Education, among other public bodies, also has in its possession various records and information relating to the public and in particular on teachers and students. This chapter will be concerned with Data Protection Act 1988 (the 1988 Act), the Freedom of Information Act 1997 (the 1997 Act) and the Education Act 1998 (the 1998 Act) and the obligations which they impose. Because many of the provisions of the 1988 Act and the 1997 Act have not yet been judicially considered or have not been the subject of the Commissioners' decisions, it is only possible to speculate as to the likely outcome in some of these spheres. Likewise, at the time of writing, only a limited number of provisions of the Education Act 1998 are in operation, none of which have been considered by our courts. As will be appreciated, it will not be possible to give an exhaustive treatment of these Acts in one chapter. Accordingly, this chapter will be limited to certain important elements of these Acts as they may relate to the school context.

Freedom of Information

[12.02] The campaign for freedom of information has gained momentum in many countries in recent decades, Sweden being the pioneer having introduced the right of access to official documents in 1766.[2] The global growth in freedom of information has been reflected in Ireland by demands for greater openness in public affairs generally and also in State agencies and public bodies.[3] The enactment of the Freedom of Information Act 1997 is a significant democratic

---

[1]   See further Barrell and Partington, *Teachers and the Law*, (1985), Methuen, Ch XX, 'In Confidence', p 595.

[2]   The USA introduced freedom of information in 1966. Other European countries followed; Norway (1970), Denmark (1970), France (1978), Greece (1986), Italy (1990), the Netherlands (1991), Belgium (1991), Spain (1992), Portugal (1993), see McDonagh, *Freedom of Information Law in Ireland*, (1998), Round Hall Press, p 4 *et seq.*

[3]   See Smyth and Brady, *Democracy Blindfolded: The Case for a Freedom of Information Act in Ireland*, Undercurrent Series, O'Toole, ed, (1994) Cork University Press, Cork; Ryan, *Keeping us in the Dark: Censorship and Freedom of Information in Ireland*, (1995), Gill and Macmillan; *Annual Report of the Ombudsman 1995*, Gov Pubs, pp 14-17.

landmark as Ireland moves from a tradition of deeply embedded secrecy both in political life and in public administration.[4] Perhaps, nowhere was that culture of secrecy more obvious than in the Department of Education,[5] for as the late Sean O'Connor, who was Secretary of that Department for many years, admitted, it was "the long-standing practice of the Department never to reveal the nature of the action taken".[6] Against this background, statutory access to information represents an immense challenge to the cultural traditions of centuries. Mirroring the covert nature of the wider society in which they exist, schools were reluctant to share information with parents in the past.[7] However, in latter years, administrative practices and State agencies have shown a clear commitment to partnership in the workplace which has come of age with the enactment of the 1997 Act.

Access to Information

[12.03] Prior to the coming into effect of the Freedom of Information Act 1997 (the 1997 Act), on 21 April 1997, there was no general right of access to information. A right existed in regard to automatically processed personal data by the Data Protection Act 1988 and as regards certain decisions made under An Bord Pleanála and relating to environmental issues. Moreover, the parties to an action could seek access to relevant documents from the High Court in a procedure commonly known as "discovery of documents".[8]

[12.04] In *Campbell v Tameside MBC*,[9] "discovery" was granted to an English teacher who wished to ascertain whether the school authority (the LEA), whom he was suing for negligence, knew that a particular pupil, who had assaulted

---

[4] See Farrell, 'Cagey and Secretive: Collective Responsibility, Executive Confidentiality and the Public Interest', in *Modern Irish Democracy: Essays in Honour of Basil Chubb*, Hill and Marsh, eds, (1993), Irish Academic Press, p 82.

[5] See Hyland, 'The Irish Educational System and Freedom of Information' in *Ireland: A Journal of History and Society*, special ed (1995); Irish Democracy and the Right to Freedom of Information, p 103.

[6] *A Troubled Sky*, (1986), Education Research Centre, St Patrick's College, p 27; The Department's reluctance to explain the rationale behind its actions which led up to the legal challenge in *Crowley v Ireland* [1980] IR 102, O'Higgins J in the Supreme Court stated: "It is strange that the appointment of Mr McCarthy should have been sanctioned despite the express terms upon which he was appointed to the temporary position. It is stranger still that no explanation of why it was done has ever been given." However, O'Higgins CJ had, at p 116 of the judgment, indicated that the manager of the school, Fr Crowley, claimed to be acting on behalf of his bishop, Dr Lucey.

[7] *Dáil Reports,* vol 207, col 408, 15 February 1964.

[8] An order of the Court compelling the parties to an action to reveal to each other, on affidavit, all relevant documents in their possession or control, Murdoch, *A Dictionary of Irish Law*, (1988), Topaz, p 161.

[9] [1982] 2 All ER 791.

him, had a propensity to violence. On the other hand, the Court refused to grant discovery in the Northern Ireland case of *McGroarty v McKendry*[10] where an alleged wrongdoer sought to obtain access to his victim's educational records in order to minimise his potential liability in damages.

[12.05] Another avenue of access to information was available when an employer was seriously interfering with the rights and liabilities of others in response to natural justice[11] requirements. Thus, if the employer was attempting to dismiss an employee, the law recognised an obligation on the employer to supply the employee with all germane information so as to enable the latter to know and meet the case against him. For example, when an English probationary teacher sought access to inspector's reports on him and the head teacher refused to grant him access, the court held it was a failure in natural justice on the part of the head teacher not to communicate to the probationary teacher "the gist of adverse confidential reports on him prepared by school inspectors so as to have an opportunity to answer them".[12] Similarly a student being expelled from a school would be entitled to certain information regarding the reasons for that decision in order that fair procedures would apply.

Access to Information in Schools

[12.06] In addition to the above mentioned avenues of access, the law has conferred statutory rights on the person who is the subject of automatically processed or computerised data. All schools in Ireland have computers and, if they retain automated personal data, they are regulated by the provisions of the Data Protection Act 1988[13] (the 1988 Act). Likewise, the Freedom of Information Act 1997 has important implications for schools which are discussed below. When ss 9(g), 20, 21, 22(b) and 27 of the Education Act 1998 come into force, schools will be subject to further statutory regulation of certain forms of information which will give rise to a number of rights and obligations relating to records, plans, procedures and evaluations.

Data Protection Law

Background to Data Protection Law

[12.07] By the 1970s, the capacity of computers for the speedy storage, retrieval, processing and global transfer of data of a personal nature, gave rise to official

---

[10] [1981] NI 71.

[11] And constitutional justice.

[12] The Times, 23 November 1982.

[13] For an interesting discussion on the right to privacy and generally, see Clark, *Data Protection Law in Ireland*, (1990), Round Hall Press, Ch 1; *Gascin v Liverpool County Council* [1981] WLR 1549; *D v NSPCounty Council* [1978] AC 171.

concern regarding the potential abuse of such facilities. Abuses could arise from the use of inaccurate or incorrect personal data or from the incorrect use of such data.[14] In England, the Lindop Report (1978) took the view that if the law was to cope with speedily evolving information systems, it must lay down flexible rules for the future. It was finally decided that the law on data protection would differ from the law on privacy in that, rather than laying down rights, it would establish a framework which would balance the competing interests of the data subject, the data user and the wider community.[15]

The Data Protection Act 1988

[12.08] The 1988 Act[16] regulates the keeping of automatically processed or computerised personal data. The Act confers rights on persons in regard to automated personal data and imposes obligations on individuals or bodies who keep automated personal data. The objectives of the Act are to give effect to the Council of Europe Data Protection Convention and to regulate the collection, processing, keeping, use and disclosure of personal information that is processed automatically. Clark outlines the background to the evolution of the Act and sets its proper context by examining it against the backdrop of the law of privacy, legal professional privilege, vicarious liability and implied constitutional protection.[17]

Interpretation

[12.09] For the purposes of the Act:

(a) the term *data* means information in a form in which it can be processed automatically;

(b) *Data subject* means an individual who is the subject of personal data;

(c) *Data controller* is a person who, either alone or with others, controls the contents and use of personal data; and

(d) *Data processors* are persons who process personal data on behalf of a data controller but this term does not include an employee of a data controller who processes such data in the course of employment;

(e) *Personal data* means data relating to a living individual who can be identified either from the data or from the data in conjunction with other information in the possession of the data controller.

---

[14] Clark, *Data Protection Law in Ireland*, (1990), Round Hall Press, pp 12-13 and generally Ch 1.
[15] See England: *Report of the Committee on Data Protection* 7341 Cmnd.
[16] Which came fully into force on 13 April 1989.
[17] Clark, *Data Protection Law in Ireland*, (1990), Round Hall Press, Ch 1.

Scope of the 1988 Act

[12.10] The Act casts a duty on both data controllers and data processors to protect the data they keep and imposes upon them a special duty of care in relation to the individuals about whom they keep such data.[18] The Act does not extend to personal information kept on manual files but, as will be show, other statutes are germane to this sphere. Section 2 of the 1988 Act lays down principles which, among other things, require that personal data:

(a) shall have been obtained and processed fairly;

(b) shall be relevant, accurate and up to date;

(c) shall be kept for no longer than is necessary;

(d) shall be kept only for one or more specified and lawful purpose;

(e) shall have appropriate security measures taken to protect it.

Right of Access to Personal Data

[12.11] The 1988 Act confers rights on every individual, on whom personal data is kept regardless of nationality or residence, as follows:

(a) to establish the existence of personal data;

(b) to have access to any such data relating to him;

(c) to have inaccurate data rectified or erased;

(d) to have personal data removed from a direct marketing or direct mailing list; and

(e) to have the right to complain to the Data Protection Commissioner.

The 1988 Act requires data controllers to ensure that the computerised data is collected in a fair manner, is accurate and up-to-date, is kept for lawful purposes only and is not used or disclosed in any manner incompatible with those purposes. Any person, about whom personal data is kept, is entitled to a copy of the data retained on him following the making of an access request to the data controller.

Formal Access Requests

[12.12] There are specific rules applying to access requests[19] which include the requirement that the application must be in writing; that the applicant must supply the data controller with certain details so as to facilitate the accessing of

---

[18] Section 7 provides: "For the purposes of the law of torts and to the extent that that law does not so provide, a person being a data controller or a data processor, shall, so far as regards collection by him of personal data or information intended for inclusion in such data or his dealing with such data, owe a duty of care to the data subject concerned ...."

[19] Section 4.

the data; and if the data controller requires an access fee, it must be paid but currently it may not exceed £5.

Formal Access Requests in Schools

[12.13] It is conceivable that there may be some areas of a teenager's life which may not be readily accessible by parents because of statutory intervention. Section 23 of the Non-Fatal Offences Against the Person Act 1997 which provides that a minor, who has attained the age of 16 years, may give an effective consent to any surgical, medical or dental treatment and so parental consent no longer appears necessary in these areas. Nevertheless, the teenager is still a minor under the Age of Majority Act 1985[20] until his eighteenth birthday and, by virtue of parental powers deriving from the Constitution,[21] the family/parent would still appear to retain over-arching control of the teenager until the age of majority is attained by him. Hence, s 23 of the Non-Fatal Offences Against the Person Act 1997 appears constitutionally vulnerable as the Constitution now stands.

[12.14] It will be recalled that in *Gillick v West Norfolk and Wisbech Area Health Authority*,[22] the House of Lords stated:[23]

> "Having regard to the reality that a child became increasingly independent as it grew older and that parental authority dwindled correspondingly, the law did not recognise any rule of absolute parental authority until a fixed age. Instead, parental rights were recognised by the law only as long as they were needed for the protection of the child and such rights yielded to the child's right to make his own decisions when he reached a sufficient understanding and intelligence to be capable of making up his own mind. Accordingly, a girl under 16 did not, merely by reason of her age, lack legal capacity to consent to contraceptive advice and treatment by a doctor."[24]

[12.15] The *Gillick* case is not binding on an Irish court, but it may be persuasive. Parental access to sensitive information relating to teenagers between 16-18 years may be refused as the Data Commissioner may decide that

---

[20] Section 2.

[21] Article 41 and Article 42.

[22] [1985] 3 All ER 402 at 403.

[23] Lord Templeman dissenting.

[24] *Gillick v West Norfolk and Wisbech Area Health Authority* [1985] 3 All ER 402 at 405 e, 416 c to e and 428 d to e; In such circumstances, the *Gillick* case indicates, that a parent who wishes to proceed against a public authority to protect what he or she alleges to be his or her parental rights against a threatened infringement by the authority is entitled, because of the private law content of the claim, to proceed by way of an ordinary action rather than by way of judicial review; *O'Reilly v Mackman* [1982] 3 All ER 1124 distinguished; see also *City of Akron v Akron Reproductive Center for Reproductive Health*, the US Supreme Court struck down any laws that give parents the sole power to authorise an abortion for a minor.

it is accessible to the teenager alone. When the student has reached his or her eighteenth birthday, there is no ambiguity as the right of access vests in the student and disclosure of information will be made to the student alone unless otherwise authorised by him. For their part, school authorities will need to approach this area of life with due care and they should seek expert advice should the need arise.

Response to Access Request

[12.16] When an individual makes a formal access request, the data controller must respond to that request by:

    (a) supplying the information to the person within 40 days after compliance with the access request under s 4 of the Act (60 days in the case of examinations data);

    (b) providing the information in a format which will be intelligible to the average person (eg any codes must be explained);

    (c) ensuring that personal information is given only to the individual concerned or to someone acting on his or her behalf. If the latter has reached the age of 18 years, then personal information may only be given with their authority.

The data controller is not obliged to refund any fee paid for dealing with the access request if he or she discovers that he does not retain any relevant data. However, such fee must be refunded if the data controller does not comply with the request for personal information, or if he has to rectify, erase or supplement the relevant personal data.

Requests in regard to Examination Results

[12.17] Section 4(6)(a) of 1988 Act provides that a request by a person under sub-s 1 of this section in regard to the results of an examination, at which he or she was a candidate, shall be deemed to be made on the date of the first publication of the results of the examination, or the date of the request, whichever is the later. In this instance, the time limit for responding to an access request is extended to 60 days. In this subsection, the term "examination" means "any process for determining the knowledge, intelligence, skill or ability of a person by reference to his performance in any test, work or other activity". Thus, the duty to disclose in schools would appear to extend to public examinations, house examinations, objective tests or other school tests which constitute *data*.

Powers of Commissioner

[12.18] The 1988 Act provides for the establishment of the office of Data Protection Commissioner[25] (the Commissioner) whose remit is to ensure that

---

[25] Section 9.

those who retain personal information on computer comply with the provisions of the Act. The Commissioner has wide powers of enforcement including the serving of legal notices compelling a data controller to provide information or to compel him to enforce the 1988 Act. The Commissioner may also investigate complaints and authorise officers to enter premises for the purpose of inspecting personal data retained on computers.

[12.19] Where a complaint is made to the Commissioner under paragraph 10(1)(a), he must investigate the complaint or cause it to be investigated unless he is of the view that it is frivolous or vexatious. The Commissioner must then notify the individual in writing of his decision and, if aggrieved by that decision, that individual may appeal it to the Circuit Court under s 26 of the 1988 Act,[26] within 21 days of the receipt of the notification.

The Public Register

[12.20] The Commissioner maintains a register of persons or bodies, to whom the duty to register[27] applies and this register is open to the public. The public register contains:

(a) the name and addresses of the person keeping the information;

(b) a short description of the type of information kept;

(c) the purposes for which the information is used; and

(d) a list of those to whom the information is disclosed.

The register, which does not include the information itself but only describes such information, may be inspected in the Data Commissioner's Office during normal office hours. The Commissioner has a wide range of powers to investigate complaints made to him and he will initiate appropriate action against any person or body who is failing to comply with the Act.

The Duty to Register

[12.21] Data controllers, who are public authorities, such as the VECs, have a duty to register with the Commissioner[28] and they generally register on behalf of all the schools under their jurisdiction. The duty to register also falls on all data controllers, if they keep personal data relating to any of the following areas of "sensitive information":

(a) racial origin;

(b) political opinion;

---

[26] Section 26 sets down four grounds for appeal.

[27] Under s 16 of the Act.

[28] Third Schedule, s 6.

(c) religious or other beliefs;

(d) physical or mental health;

(e) sexual life; or

(f) criminal convictions.

[12.22] If schools keep such details on students or others, they must be registered. If a school should be registered, it is an offence under the 1988 Act not to be registered. Fines under the 1988 Act range up to £50,000 on conviction or indictment. If a school is in doubt as to whether it should be registered, it should contact the Data Commissioner's Office.[29]

[12.23] In compliance with the registration process, a data controller must nominate a person to whom enquiries are to be addressed. This would normally be the principal, or other person of authority and experience in the school, who can exhort other members of staff to comply with the Act. The prohibitions on use, source, disclosure or transfer of the data apply to employees or agents of a registrable data controller and accordingly to all school staff. Infringements of s 19 results in any person who infringes being liable if they are registrable under the 1988 Act.

Disclosure of Personal Data in Certain Cases

[12.24] Any restrictions imposed by the 1988 Act on the disclosure of personal data do not apply in a number of circumstances outlined in s 8. Under this section an access request may be made to the school by, and with the consent of, a former student who is now an adult, through another person acting on his behalf. As this is not a formal access request, the school has a discretion to disclose the information or to refuse to do so. Clark discusses the possibility of the employer being liable in contract[30] if he fails to observe the requirements of the Act as well as the criminal offences[31] and civil breaches[32] of the Act which may be committed by registrable data controllers.

Legal Obligations on Employees

[12.25] Even if the employee is neither a data controller nor a data processor, the Act still imposes obligations on him. If a teacher retains personal data on data equipment at home so as to perform school-related work, they may be considered as data controllers for the purposes of the 1988 Act and they may, in

---

[29] Whose address is Block 4, Irish Life Centre, Talbot Street, Dublin 1.

[30] See *Data Protection Law in Ireland* (1990), Round Hall Press, Ch 10.

[31] Section 19 of the Act, see Clark, *Data Protection Law in Ireland* (1990), Round Hall Press, Ch 9.

[32] Section 7 of the Act, see Clark, *Data Protection Law in Ireland* (1990), Round Hall Press, Ch 9.

certain instances be obliged to register or they may be required to disclose information to data subjects.[33]

The Disclosure Principle

[12.26] The disclosure principle in s 2 would be infringed by a teacher if he were to discuss personal data held by the school on a student as a matter of gossip outside the school. However, the passing on of personal data, either directly or indirectly by a data controller (eg the board or the principal) to another teacher, to enable them to discharge their professional duties, would not constitute a disclosure under s 2. Neither would the passing on of personal data from one teacher to another, for professional purposes, be likely to infringe the disclosure principle although the Act is silent on this issue. If the disclosure principle is breached, the non-registrable data controller (eg the teacher who keeps personal data on students at home which is not of a sensitive nature) is subject to the enforcement procedures set down under ss 10(2) and 10(3) of the 1988 Act.

Enforcement Procedures

[12.27] By virtue of registration, it is conceivable that an employee (eg the principal or another teacher or member of staff) could be identified as the person responsible for breaches of the 1988 Act under s 2.

[12.28] If non-registrable data controllers and employees fail to comply with s 2(1), that does not *per se* result in a criminal breach of the 1988 Act. However, if the Commissioner issues an enforcement notice and the employee fails or refuses to respond to that notice, without reasonable cause, then this could result in criminal liability under ss 10 and 12 of the 1988 Act.[34]

Vicarious Liability

[12.29] An employee of the board, (a principal or teacher) may discharge contractual duties in a manner which breaches the data protection principles by:

   (a) disclosing personal data to someone not entitled to see it; or by

   (b) keeping data which is inaccurate, misleading or out of date.

If, as a result of these infringements, or indeed of criminal breaches of the 1988 Act,[35] another person suffers loss, damage or distress, can that person sue the school board in tort even though the board was not negligent, did not authorise the act or gain any advantage from the outcome of the act? If the act was done by the teacher "in the course of employment", then the doctrine of vicarious

---

[33] Clarke, *Data Protection Law in Ireland,* (1989), Round Hall Press, p 143 *et seq.*

[34] See further, Clark, *Data Protection Law in Ireland,* (1989), Round Hall Press, pp 143-5 and in particular 'Miscellaneous Criminal Offences', p 145.

[35] See ss 10 and 12.

liability applies and the board is liable for the teacher's wrongs.[36] If, however, the teacher was prohibited from doing those specific acts, or from doing them in a particular fashion, then the board could conceivably avoid vicarious liability.

[12.30] In view of the fact that school boards, with the exception of those under the control of the VECs, will shortly be corporate bodies, pursuant to s 14 of the Education Act 1998, s 29 of the 1998 Act has important implications for schools. Section 29 provides:

> (1) Where an offence under this Act has been committed by a body corporate and is proved to have been committed with the consent or connivance of or to be attributable to any neglect on the part of a person, being a director, manager, secretary or other officer of that body corporate, or a person who was purporting to act in any such capacity, that person, as well as the body corporate, shall be guilty of that offence and be liable to be proceeded against and punished accordingly.

> (2) Where the affairs of a body corporate are managed by its members, subsection (1) of this section shall apply in relation to the acts and defaults of a member in connection with his functions of management as if he were a director or manager of the body corporate.

It seems that under this section, the chairperson and individual members of the board could conceivably be personally liable for breaches of the Act in the circumstances outlined above in s 29(1). Thus, indemnification of board members in these spheres seems pivotal.

Freedom of Information

The Freedom of Information Act 1997

[12.31] The Freedom of Information Act 1997 (the 1997 Act) is a complex piece of legislation which will, when the public becomes more familiar with its potential, bring much greater openness into Irish life.[37] However, as the Ombudsman and Information Commissioner, Kevin Murphy, has recently pointed out, the Act does not set out to confer on requesters a complete and unfettered right of access to all records held by public bodies.[38]

---

[36] See *Lloyd v Grace, Smith and Co.* [1912] AC 716; *Johnson and Johnson v CP Security* [1986] ILRM 559, HC, Egan J; McMahon and Binchy, *Irish Law of Torts*, (2nd ed, 1990), p 759.

[37] For the background and history of the 1997 Act, see McDonagh, *Freedom of Information Law in Ireland*, (1998), Round Hall Sweet and Maxwell, Ch 2.

[38] Paper entitled 'FOI - The Commissioner's Experience of the First Year' delivered at a conference in Dublin Castle on 13 April 1999 entitled 'Freedom of Information-One Year On' hosted by Department of Law, University College, Cork and Department of Finance, FOI Central Policy Unit.

[12.32] The 1997 Act was enacted on 21 April 1997 and entered into force for central government departments and a number of significant public bodies on 21 April 1998. The Act has applied to local authorities and health boards since 21 October 1998. The term "local authority" in the Act means a local authority for the purposes of s 2(c) of the Local Government Act 1941, which does not include VECs. Hence, vocational schools are not, at the time of writing, public bodies for the purpose of the 1997 Act. The term "the Minister" in the Act means the Minister for Finance.

[12.33] The 1997 Act applies to "public bodies," a term which is defined in the First Schedule of the Act and includes the Department of Education, Government Departments and State Offices, local authorities and health boards. Certain important public sector bodies are not yet within the scope of the Act, eg schools and colleges, the Garda Síochána and voluntary hospitals. It is most likely that the Minister will prescribe a wide range of bodies, which are funded or partly-funded from State funds, so as to bring them within the scope of the Act within the next year or two. It appears that the 1997 Act will become effective in regard to voluntary hospitals in Autumn 1999.[39]

Application to Schools

[12.34] At the time of writing, the 1997 Act does not apply to schools and there is no time frame as to when schools will become subject to the Act. However, it is envisaged that schools will be subject to the 1997 Act at a later date in accordance with the new spirit of openness and accountability to parents. Thus, the ambit of the 1997 Act may be broadened so as to encompass certain other bodies by regulation, with the agreement of the Minister responsible for that sector. Section 1(5) of the First Schedule includes a list of the bodies which may be brought within the scope of the Act by regulation. Section 1 provides:

> Each of the following shall be a public body for the purposes of this Act: ...
>
> (5)(b)(1) a body, organisation or group established -
>
> > (i) by or under any enactment (other than the Companies Act 1963 to 1990) or any scheme administered by a Minister of the Government, or
> >
> > (ii) under the Companies Act 1963 to 1990, in pursuance of powers conferred by or under another enactment, and financed wholly or partly ... by means of moneys provided, or loans made or guaranteed, by a Minister of the Government ...

---

[39] See McDonagh, *Freedom of Information Law in Ireland,* (1998), Round Hall Sweet and Maxwell for an insightful analysis of the relevant law.

[12.35] These two provisions would embrace schools, including the multi-denominational schools established under the Companies Acts, and accordingly schools can be prescribed by the Minister for Finance with the consent of the Minister for Education and Science. When schools are prescribed by the Minister, schools will become public bodies for the purpose of the 1997 Act and the Act will apply in full to them.

Main Aims of the 1997 Act

[12.36] The 1997 Act aims to create:

(a) a general right of access to specific government records on foot of the making of a request subject to some exceptions;

(b) a right of access for individuals to personal information or files in the possession of public bodies and to have such information corrected and brought up-to-date;

(c) a statutory right to be furnished with reasons by public bodies for decisions affecting an individual; and

(d) a right to receive assistance in enabling individuals to exercise their rights including the publication of a booklet informing the public of certain information about them including its appeals procedures.

[12.37] The Act also provides for the independent review of decisions of public bodies relating to the above rights and for the operation of the 1997 Act generally. Furthermore, it provides for the amendment of the Official Secrets Act 1963, for the establishment of the new Office of Information Commissioner, for the definition of its functions and for other related purposes.

Meaning of "Personal Information"

[12.38] The term "personal information" indicates the kind of information to which the person to whom the information relates generally has a right of access and that third parties do not have any right of access in this regard. Under the 1997 Act, the term "personal information" means information about an identifiable individual that -

(a) would, in the ordinary course of events, be known only to the individual or members of the family, or friends, of the individual, or

(b) is held by a public body on the understanding that it would be treated by it as confidential.

Examples of personal information, subject to the generality of the foregoing, include -

(i) information relating to the educational, medical, psychiatric or psychological history of the individual,

(ii)   information relating to the financial affairs of the individual,

(iii)   information relating to the employment or employment history of the individual,

(iv)   information relating to an individual falling under s 6(6)(a) - a personnel record ie a record relating to one or more of the following; the competence or ability of the individual in his or her capacity as a member of staff of a public body or his employment or employment history or an evaluation of the performance of his or her functions generally or a particular such function as such member,

(v)   information relating to the criminal history of the individual,

(vi)   information relating to the religion, age, sexual orientation, or marital status of the individual,

(vii)   a number, letter, symbol, word, mark or other thing assigned to the individual by a public body for the purpose of identification or any mark or other thing used for that purpose,

(viii) information relating to the entitlement of the individual under the Social Welfare Acts as a beneficiary,

(ix)   information required for the purpose of assessing the liability of the individual in respect of a tax, duty or other payment owed or payable to the State or other public body,

(x)   the name of the individual where it appears with other personal information relating to the individual, or where the disclosure of the name would, or would be likely to, establish that any personal information held by the public body concerned relates to the individual,

(xi)   information relating to the property of the individual including the nature of the individual's title to any property, and

(xii)   the views or opinions of another person about the individual.

The above information is "personal" to the individual to whom it refers and he or she generally has a right of access to such information and a right to have it amended if it is inaccurate, incomplete or out of date.

Access to Students' Records

[12.39] Section 28(6)(a) of the 1997 Act permits the Minister to provide by regulations for a grant of a request under s 7 where "... the requester concerned is the parent or guardian of the individual ...".[40] Apart from any constitutional or common law right a parent may have in this regard, therefore, when schools are prescribed and s 28 of the Act becomes operational, parents or guardians will

---

40   Section 28(6)(a).

have a statutory right of access to their children's records in schools, in the Department of Education and Science and in other public bodies. Likewise, a teacher has access to personal information held by the Department on him and will have such rights in relation to schools when they are prescribed.

Refusals to Grant Access to Personal Information

[12.40] There are some instances, however, under which a head of a public body may refuse to grant a request for access under s 7. Under s 28(3) access to medical, psychiatric or social work type records may be refused if in the opinion of the head concerned, disclosure of the relevant information to the requester might be prejudicial to their physical or mental health, well-being or emotional condition. This section could include such matters as medical reports and other reports having serious implications for the requester eg psychological, psychiatric or social work related reports in certain instances. On foot of such a refusal by the head, however, if the requester requests it, a health professional with expertise in the subject-matter of the record must be given access in accordance with s 8(3).

The General Right of Access

[12.41] Section 6 of the 1997 Act provides a general right of access to any record in the possession or control of a public body. This is a right of access to records other than those relating to the individual himself or herself, which are covered elsewhere, and it is a central pillar of freedom of information legislation generally. By contrast with the earlier approach to disclosure of official documentation, those who posses such records no longer have a discretion to argue that they belong to the institution and will not be disclosed and those seeking access, pursuant to the Act, need not demonstrate any particular interest in the records sought in order to achieve access.[41]

Manner of Access to Records

[12.42] Rather than giving a definition of "access", the 1997 Act lists a number of methods by which access may be granted to a requester as they may be supplied with:

(a) a copy of the record;

(b) a transcript of the relevant information;

(c) a computer disk or other electronic device containing the information;

(d) a reasonable opportunity of inspecting the record;

---

[41] McDonagh, *Freedom of Information in Ireland,* (1998), Round Hall Sweet and Maxwell, p 29.

(e) where the record is of sound or visual images, a reasonable opportunity to hear or view the record;

(f) if the record is in shorthand or other code, the information in decoded form;

(g) the information in such other form as may be determined; or

(h) the information in a combination of any two or more of the foregoing.

In cases in which a record is partly exempt and partly non-exempt, the requester must be informed that they are merely getting part of the record.

Records

[12.43] A "record" includes:

> any memorandum, book, plan, map, drawing, diagram, pictorial or graphic work or other document, any photograph, film or recording (whether of sound or images or both), any form in which data (within the meaning of the Data Protection Act 1988) are held, any other form (including machine-readable form) or thing in which information is held or stored manually, mechanically or electronically and anything which is part or a copy, in any form, of any of the foregoing or is a combination of two or more of the foregoing ...[42]

Scope of the 1997 Act

[12.44] The right of access is limited by virtue of certain exclusions. At the time of writing, the 1997 Act applies to the public bodies set down in the First Schedule, to Local Authorities and Health Boards but, as has been seen, may yet embrace other State-funded institutions by virtue of the Minister's powers to prescribe such bodies in sub-s 5 of the First Schedule.[43] The 1997 Act applies to "records" and not to information and thus clearly excludes all verbal information or unrecorded knowledge. Furthermore, the 1997 Act applies to specific "records" only which fall into two categories, personal and non-personal records as indicated in Part II of the Act:

(1)(a) personal records no matter where created and access to such records is available solely to the individual to whom they refer;

(b) personal records created within a 3-year period before the commencement of the Act, unless these records are used or are proposed to be used in a manner that affects or will or may affect adversely the interests of the person to whom the records relate in which instance they will be accessible even though they were created before the 3-year limit;

(2)(a) non-personal records created following the commencement of the Act;

---

[42] Section 2 of the 1997 Act.

[43] See further McDonagh, *Freedom of Information Law in Ireland*, (1998), Round Hall Sweet and Maxwell, pp 29-30 *et seq.*

(b) non-personal records created prior to the commencement of the Act where such are necessary in order to understand records created after such commencement.[44]

Date of Commencement

[12.45] The date of "commencement of the Act" means the time at which this Act (other than subparas (3) and (4) of para 1 of the First Schedule) comes into operation. As the 1997 Act may come into operation on different days for various public bodies, the date of commencement would be the date the Act became operational for the relevant public body. Thus, if schools were to be made subject to the 1997 Act on 1 September 2000, that would be the date of commencement for schools. Because of the retrospective effect of the Act, as indicated at (b) above, personal records currently being made ie those within the three-year period, and earlier in some instances, will be accessible by those to whom they relate. This fact alone underscores the need for school staff to become familiar with the requirements of the Act as a matter of some urgency.

Exercising the Right to Access

[12.46] An individual who wishes to exercise his right to access makes a request for access in writing, or some other determined form, to the head of the public body concerned for access to the records concerned.[45] In the school context, this would normally be the principal. However, s 4 permits the head to delegate in writing to a member of staff of the public body any of the functions under this Act. Accordingly, the decision to grant or refuse access may be made by a staff member rather than by the head of the public body. As for the requester, he must state that the request is made under the Act and it must contain sufficient particulars to enable the record to be identified by the taking of reasonable steps. If the requester is seeking access in a particular form or manner, in accordance with s 12, then that must also be specified.

[12.47] The head, or person to whom these duties are delegated, having received such a request, must acknowledge receipt of it within two weeks and that notification must include a summary of the provisions of s 41 and particulars of the rights of review under the Act. If the head does not hold the record requested, but is aware that one or more other public bodies do hold it, then he/she must pass on the request to that public body or bodies not more than two weeks after the receipt of the request.

---

[44] Sections 6(5) and 6 (6) of the 1997 Act.
[45] Section 8 of the 1997 Act.

The Right of the Public Body to Refuse Access

[12.48] A head, to whom a request is made pursuant to s 7 of the 1997 Act may refuse to grant access if:

    (a) the record does not exist or cannot be found following the taking of all reasonable steps;

    (b) the request fails to comply with s 7(1);

    (c) in the opinion of the head, granting the request would require "a substantial and unreasonable interference with or disruption of the other work of the public body concerned";

    (d) publication of the record is required by law and is intended to be effected not later than twelve weeks following the receipt of the request by the head;

    (e) the request is, in the opinion of the head, frivolous or vexatious;

    (f) a fee or deposit payable under s 47 has not been discharged.

[12.49] Decisions relating to requests for access to records must normally be given "as soon as may be" and in any event, no later than four weeks after the receipt of a request under s 7.[46] A decision may be refused, deferred, or granted fully or in part. When making a decision whether to refuse or accede to a request, the head is required by the 1997 Act to disregard any reason that the requester supplies for the request together with any belief or opinion they may have as to what reasons the requester had for making the request. The 1997 Act requires that the requester be notified of the decision taken by the head within four weeks. Provision is also made for extending time in certain instances.

[12.50] If the request is refused wholly or in part, then the reasons for the refusal must be given to the requester.[47]

Right to have a Statement of Reasons Provided by Public Bodies

[12.51] Section 18 of the 1997 Act provides that the head of a public body, on receipt of a written application, shall, not later than four weeks after the receipt of the application, cause a statement, in writing or in such other form as may be determined, to be given to that person of the reasons for the act, and of any findings of any material issues of fact made for the purposes of the act.

[12.52] The right to a statement of reasons in s 18 is restricted. Firstly, it applies in regard to an act, which includes a decision other than a decision under the 1997 Act,[48] of a public body which is listed in the First Schedule of the Act (eg

---

[46] Section 8(1) of the 1997 Act.
[47] Section 8(2)(d)(i) and section 8(2)(d)(ii).
[48] Section 18(6) of the 1997 Act.

the Department of Education and Science). No express right to a statement of reasons exists in the case of a public sector body. Secondly, the right to be furnished with a statement of reasons applies only in the case of a person who is affected by an act of the public body and has a material interest in a matter affected by the act or relating to the act. In order to be entitled to a statement of reasons, a person would be required to establish that they were aggrieved by the act, by contrast with others generally, or by contrast with a sizeable class of persons of which the person is a member.[49] Moreover, there are four exceptions to the requirement that public bodies must furnish a statement of reasons:

(a) the giving to a person of information contained in an exempt record;[50]

(b) the disclosure of the existence or non-existence of a record if the non-disclosure of its existence or non-existence is required by this Act;

(c) a decision of the Civil Service Commissioners under the Civil Service Commissioners Act 1956, not to accept a person as qualified for a position thereunder; or to

(d) a decision made by the Local Appointments Commission made under the Local Authorities (Officers and Employees) Act 1926 not to recommend a person to a local authority for appointment to an office referred to in that section.

Exempt Records

[12.53] Part III of the 1997 Act provides that certain records are exempt from access. These are mainly government-related and include certain functions, deliberations and negotiations of public bodies and such areas as law enforcement, public safety, security, defence and certain Parliamentary, court and other matters. Furthermore, it should be noted that, by virtue of s 18(6), decisions under the 1997 Act are not included in the right to be given reasons for administrative acts and decisions under s 18. As has been seen, separate provision for furnishing reasons for decisions to refuse access to records is made under s 8(2)(d).

Reviews

[12.54] As s 14 provides, internal review applies only when the original maker of the decision on access was a delegate of the head of the public body eg deputy principal or year head in the school context. Furthermore, internal review is restricted to certain decisions which are set out in s 14.[51] The head may review a

---

49 Section 18(5) of the 1997 Act.

50 Section 18(2)(a).

51 See further McDonagh, *Freedom of Information Law in Ireland*, (1998), Round Hall Sweet and Maxwell, p 348 *et seq*.

decision to which this section applies and they may affirm or vary or annul the decision or make such other decision as they consider proper.

[12.55] Internal review is not available in certain circumstances such as in the case of:

    (a) the review of a decision relating to third party consultation requirements;

    (b) extensions under s 9; and

    (c) in the case of deferral of access under s 11(1)(b) and s 11(1)(c).

Appeals

[12.56] The 1997 Act provides for an appeal relating to the right to be given reasons for the contents of a statement[52] and the refusal of an application. If the decision to refuse was taken by another staff member to whom such duties were delegated, then the appeal initially would be to the head of the public body[53] or to a staff member of a higher grade than the initial decision-maker.[54] The decision of the head may be appealed to the Information Commissioner.[55] The failure of public bodies to comply with s 18 could conceivably lead to the applicant seeking an order of *mandamus* to compel the public body to discharge its statutory obligation under the 1997 Act.[56]

Fees and Deposits

[12.57] Under s 47, appropriate fees must be charged by the relevant public body, and be paid by the requester, in regard to the provision of access to records. Such charges are a common element of Freedom of Information legislation.[57] The public body may impose fees solely for the estimated cost of the search and retrieval of the relevant record, and the estimated cost of any copy of the record made by the public body concerned for the relevant requester.

[12.58] The above fees are based on an hourly rate which is prescribed by regulations (Freedom of Information Regulations 1998[58]) and currently stands at £16.50 per hour in respect of the time that was spent, or ought in the opinion of the relevant head to have been spent, in carrying out the search and retrieval

---

52 Section 14(1)(f).

53 Section 14(1)(f).

54 Sections 4(1) and 14(3).

55 Section 34(1)(a).

56 See Hogan and Morgan, *Administrative Law in Ireland*, (2nd ed, 1991), Round Hall Sweet and Maxwell, pp 720-722.

57 See further McDonagh, *Freedom of Information Law in Ireland*, (1998), Round Hall Sweet and Maxwell, p 76 *et seq.*

58 SI 139/1998.

efficiently.[59] The cost of reproducing copies is also prescribed by the said regulations and currently stands at 3p per photocopy; 40p for computer diskette; and £8 for a CD-ROM. These fees should act as a considerable disincentive to frivolous or vexatious claims. Where, in the opinion of the head concerned, the estimated cost of the search for and retrieval of a record, is likely to exceed £40, provision is made for the payment of a deposit, not being less than 20% of such cost.

Personal Information

[12.59] When access is sought to personal information, there is no fee charged for search and retrieval unless the grant concerned relates to "a significant number of records".[60] Provision is made in s 47(4)(b) for waiver of fees, if in the opinion of the head concerned, it would be unreasonable, having regard to the means of the requester and the nature of the record concerned, to include the cost.

Publication of Information: Reference Books

[12.60] One of the most pivotal provisions of the 1997 Act is the obligation falling on public bodies to publish two reference books under ss 15 and 16. The purpose of these books is to assist members of the public in ascertaining and exercising their rights under the 1997 Act.[61] The Department of Education complied with this requirements in April 1998 and its booklets, which are of a high standard, are available to the public[62] and on the Internet.[63] However, it would be of great assistance to the general public if the relevant Circulars were included in the s 16 book and on the website also. Section 16(2)(d) requires the updating of this reference book every three years.

Obligations under Sections 15 and 16

[12.61] When schools are prescribed, ss 15 and 16 will apply to them. Section 15 of the 1997 Act requires public bodies to cause to be prepared, published and made available in accordance with sub-s 7, a reference book which must contain:

---

[59] Section 47(3)(a).

[60] Section 47(4)(a).

[61] Section 15(3).

[62] Department of Education and Science: Guide to the Functions and Records of the Department: Freedom of Information Section 15 Reference Book, April 1998 and Department of Education and Science: Rules and Practices: Freedom of Information Section 16 Reference Book, April 1998.

[63] www.irlgov.ie.

(a) a general description of its structure, organisation, functions, powers and duties, services provides and procedures by which these may be accessible by the public;

(b) a general description of the classes of records held by the public body as the particulars as are reasonably necessary to exercise the right to access;

(c) a general description of matters referred to in s 16(1)(a) and (b);

(d) the arrangements made by the public body -

   (i) to facilitate access to records held by the body;

   (ii) to facilitate application for amendment of such records that relate to personal information;

   (iii) to facilitate persons applying under s 18(1).

(e) the names and designations of staff members responsible for giving access to records (unless the head of the body reasonably believes that publication of that information could threaten the physical safety of well-being of the persons;

(f) the address or addresses at which requests under s 7 or applications under ss 17 or 18 should be given;

(g) appropriate information relating to any right of review or appeal in regard to decisions made by the body and the appeal procedure and decisions under the 1997 Act and any related time limits;

(i) any other information that the head considers relevant for the purpose of facilitating the right to access;

(j) information relating to other matters, if any, which may be prescribed.

Under s 15(4), a public body is required to supply a summary of its reference book to the Minister for Finance, who is required to publish a reference containing all the summaries.

[12.62] Section 16 of the 1997 Act obliges public bodies to publish their rules, procedures, practices, guidelines and interpretations and an index of any precedents kept by the body for the purpose of making decisions, determinations or recommendations.

Role of the Information Commissioner

[12.63] The Office of Information Commissioner[64] is established by the 1997 Act and the Commissioner is independent in the performance of his functions.[65]

---

[64] Part IV of the 1997 Act.
[65] Section 33.

In contrast with his role as Ombudsman pursuant to the Ombudsman Act 1980,[66] the Commissioner has authority to issue legally binding decisions. Nonetheless, the Commissioner's role is inquisitorial and not adversarial. He may review a variety of decisions, make his own decisions, review the operation of the 1997 Act and carry out investigations as required. The Commissioner's powers include a right to carry out an investigation into the practices and procedures adopted by public bodies for the purposes of enabling persons to exercise the rights the 1997 Act confers and to facilitate the exercise of those rights. Under s 37, he has power to enter the premises of public bodies and to require that he be furnished with records and examine and take copies of same. As of 23 April 1999, the Commissioner had dealt with 330 cases which represents less than 10% of all requests. The fact that 90% of all requests are dealt with without reference to the Commissioner's office would indicate that the 1997 Act is operating reasonably satisfactorily although the figure of 5% or less seems to be the average figure in other jurisdictions.[67]

Case Law

[12.64] No formal education-related decisions have been made by the Commissioner's Office. There have, however, been a number of settlements relating to education and currently, there are fifteen reviews on hand. One of the more notable decisions of the Commissioner related to the overturning of the decision of the Revenue Commissioners to release the names of approximately 5,500 charities to the media.

[12.65] Another controversial issue, which has not yet reached resolution, centres on the application made by the Sunday Times, The Sunday Tribune and the Kerryman to release the examination results for the year 1998.[68] The Department of Education and Science claimed exemption under s 10 of the 1997 Act stating that this would lead to administrative difficulties due to the number and nature of the records and information concerned, thus causing "substantial and unreasonable interference with or disruption of other work of the public body concerned". Essentially, the media argues that parents are "consumers" of the education services while the Department contends that the examinations

---

[66] See s 6(3) of that Act which confers on the Ombudsman the right to recommend certain courses of action at the end of his or her investigation.

[67] From a Paper entitled 'FOI - The Commissioner's Experience of the First Year' delivered by the Commissioner, Kevin Murphy, at a conference in Dublin Castle on 13 April 1999 entitled 'Freedom of Information-One Year On' hosted by Department of Law, University College, Cork and Department of Finance, FOI Central Policy Unit. Commissioner, Kevin Murphy, FOI-The Commissioner's Experience of the First Year' at p 1.

[68] In the case of the Kerryman, it is understood that it sought merely access to the said result in County Kerry while the Sunday Times, in particular, sought sought access to much wider information.

were not designed with this objective in mind and that, presumably, the State is acting, in its constitutional capacity as "guardian of the common good" under Article 42.3.2°. The Commissioner consulted the partners in education, two principal teacher groups and other experts in the field. Furthermore, he sought submissions from academic or research sources which were supplied by both parties. To date, no decision has been reached by the Commissioner.

[12.66] Meanwhile, Part IX, *inter alia*,[69] of the Education Act 1998 has come into operation which includes s 53. Section 53 confers a certain discretion on the Minister for Education and Science:

> Notwithstanding any other enactment, the Minister may -
>
> (a) refuse access to any information which would enable the compilation of information (that is not otherwise available to the general public) in relation to the comparative performance of schools in respect of the academic achievement of students enrolled therein, including without prejudice to the generality of the foregoing -
>
>> (i) the overall results in any year of students in a particular school in an examination, or
>>
>> (ii) the comparative overall results in any year of students in different schools in an examination, and
>
> (b) refuse access to information relating to the identity of the examiners.

[12.67] By virtue of this section, the Minister for Education and Science has statutory authority to make a decision under this section. It would lead to quite a dilemma if the Commissioner and the Minister were not *ad idem* on this issue. At the time of writing, neither party has made any decision. However, it seems most likely that both will refuse to grant access to these documents. Such a decision would, of course, be open to a judicial review challenge and this intractable issue, which looks set to run for some time, may well be finally decided in the High Court.

Sanctions under the 1997 Act

[12.68] A person who fails or refuses to comply with such requirements under this section, or who hinders or obstructs the Commissioner in the performance of these functions shall be guilty of an offence and will be liable on summary conviction to a fine of not more than £1,500 or to imprisonment for not more than six months or both.[70] The Commissioner is required to foster publication of

---

[69] Together with ss 2-6 inclusive, 13, 25, 26, 36, 37 and Part VIII, SI 29/1999 which came into effect on 5 April 1999.

[70] Section 37(7).

information by public bodies,[71] to publish commentaries of practical application and to prepare annual reports.[72]

Facilitating Change

[12.69] Snell makes the point that the key policy dynamic associated with "the right to know legislation" is how a radical cultural change for officials is to be implemented and maintained in compliance with the legislation.[73] Like Nader,[74] he believes that this culture change can only eventuate if there are universities, law reviews, public interest law firms, citizen groups, newspapers, magazines, or the electronic media who systematically follow through the courts on denials of agency information. Accordingly, the successful operation of this legislation depends to a large degree on the determination of the people.

School Records and the Education Act 1998

The Education Act 1998

[12.70] The Education Act 1998 (the 1998 Act) contains provisions relating to:

    (a) the keeping of records;[75]

    (b) access to records;[76]

    (c) procedures for informing parents of students in the school of matters relating to the operation and performance of the school;[77]

    (d) the publication of a school plan;[78]

    (e) evaluating and reporting the results of the evaluation to students and their parents;[79] and

    (f) establishing and maintaining procedures for the purposes of keeping students informed of the activities of the school.

---

[71] Section 39.

[72] Section 40.

[73] Rick Snell, teaches law at the Law School, University of Tasmania, and has been editor of the *FOI Review* for the past five years. He delivered a Paper entitled "Administrative Compliance and Freedom of Information in Three Jurisdictions" (Australia, Canada and New Zealand) to a conference in Dublin Castle on 13 April 1999 entitled "Freedom of Information - One Year On" hosted by Department of Law, University College, Cork and Department of Finance, FOI Central Policy Unit.

[74] Nader, 'Freedom From Information: The Act and the Agencies' (1970) 5(1) Harvard Civil Rights-Civil Liberties Law Review, 14.

[75] Section 9(g).

[76] Section 9(g).

[77] Section 20.

[78] Section 21.

[79] Section 22(b).

The School Plan

[12.71] When s 21 of the 1998 Act comes into force, boards and principals will be required to make arrangements for the preparation of a plan (the "school plan") which will be regularly reviewed and updated.[80] The school plan must state the objectives of the school in regard to equality of access to and participation in the school, and the measures the school proposes to adopt to achieve those objectives including equality of access to and participation in the school by students with disabilities or who have other special educational needs. The board must make arrangements for the circulation of the school plan to the patron, parents, teachers and other staff of the school.[81]

Access to Student Records

[12.72] Furthermore, when s 9 of the 1997 Act becomes operational, a recognised school will be required to "ensure that parents of a student, or in the case of a student who has reached the age of eighteen years, the student, have access, in the prescribed manner, to records kept by that school relating to the progress of that student in his education."[82] Presumably the "prescribed manner of access" to such records will be detailed in regulations or circulars.

Type of Record to be Disclosed

[12.73] As to the type of record to which the right of access adheres in s 9(e), (those relating to the progress of that student in his or her education), at first glance, this appears to mean "curricular records" only and not "other educational records" such as psychological or psychiatric records or "a teacher's record". However, it should be borne in mind that other avenues of access are available under the Data Protection Act 1988, if such records are computerised and constitute "personal data" or under the Freedom of Information Act 1997 as under s 2 "personal information" is defined as "information relating to the educational, medical, psychiatric or psychological history of the individual ...".

[12.74] The extent of the duty to disclose[83] under the 1998 Act is a matter which will most likely be clarified in regulations or in circulars which will spell out the detail of the Act. Even if the right of access was broadened to include "other educational records", it would necessarily have to contain a number of exceptions where, for example disclosure might militate against the welfare of

---

[80] Section 21.

[81] Section 21(4).

[82] Section 9(g).

[83] In England the regulations state that an "entitled person" may, on making a request in writing, view a pupil's record and make a copy of it provide they are willing to defray the cost of production.

the child; a principle now firmly established in Irish law and in human rights law.[84] Although there is a duty falling on schools to establish or maintain contacts with other schools and at appropriate levels throughout the community served by the schools,[85] there is no duty on schools to transfer student records from one school to a new school when a child moves school, or from primary schools to second level schools. In the author's opinion, this is a significant omission in the 1998 Act.

Evaluation of Students

[12.75] When s 22(2)(b) of the 1998 Act comes into effect, one of the duties falling on the principal and teachers will be:

> to regularly evaluate students and periodically report the results of the evaluation to the students and their parents.[86]

It will be noted that the right to be evaluated in this section adheres to the student while the right to receive periodic reports of the results of such evaluation vests in the students as well as the parents. The 1998 Act is silent on the form of reporting and the frequency of such reporting matters which will, no doubt, be clarified later in regulations or circulars.

Student Information and Participation

[12.76] When s 27 of the 1998 Act comes into force, a board will be required to establish and maintain procedures with the objective of informing students in a school of the school activities. Such procedures shall facilitate student involvement in the operation of the school, taking account of their age and experience in association with their parents and teachers.[87] Under this section, there is also an obligation on the board to encourage the establishment of a student council in post-primary schools and to facilitate and assist such councils where they are in operation.[88]

Admissions Policy

[12.77] When s 15(2)(d) of the 1998 Act comes into effect, a recognised school will be required to publish the policy of the school concerning admission to the school and participation in the school including:

> (a) the school's policy in relation to the expulsion and suspension of students; and

---

[84] See UN Convention on the Rights of the Child, Article 3(1).
[85] Section 9(1).
[86] Section 22(2)(b).
[87] Section 22(2)(b).
[88] Section 27(3)-(6).

    (b) the policy of the school in regard to the admission to and participation by students with disability or other special educational needs.

Clearly, the school's policy on admissions cannot be read in isolation from the remaining functions of the board in s 15. Hence, in its admission policy, the school must ensure that the following principles are respected:

    (a) principles of equality, democracy and diversity;

    (b) the right of parents to send their children to a school of their choice;

    (c) directions made from time to time by the Minister;

    (d) the characteristic spirit of the school;

    (e) the constitutional rights of all persons concerned; and

    (f) the efficient use of resources including making reasonable provision for students with a disability or special educational needs.

Thus, in the school's admission policy, tensions may arise between the intersecting rights of the child, the family or parents, the school and the State in its role as "guardian of the common good". In particular, the ethos of the school is a concept that can never be overlooked especially in the setting of denominational schools which are impliedly constitutionally protected. There will, no doubt, be particular concerns among minority denominational schools that the ethos, which their schools were specifically established to promote, may be diluted by an unduly open admission's policy.

[12.78] It will be recalled[89] that, in regard to an admission's policy, the primacy of the right of a voluntary aided school was recognised in England in *Choudhury v Governors of Bishop Challoner Roman Catholic Comprehensive School*[90] in 1992. The court accepted that the very *raison d'etre* of this school was to provide education on Christian and specifically Roman Catholic principles. Accordingly, it held that in circumstances where the number of parental preferences for application exceeded the number of places available, the school was lawfully entitled to discriminate, in its admission policy in favour of Christians and specifically Roman Catholics. Hence, it was not unlawful for the school to have this aim in mind when refusing to facilitate the parental preferences of Muslim and Hindu parents under the Education Act 1980, s 6.[91]

---

[89] See Ch 3.

[90] [1992] 3 All ER 277.

[91] Section 6(6) of this Act, enables the Governing bodies of Roman Catholic (RC) schools to agree with the Local Education Authority (LEA) a limit of the non-RC children who may be admitted and some others provide that no non-RC children may be admitted.

Enrolment Policy: A Legal Challenge

[12.79] As the case of *O'Huallacháin v Burke*[92] illustrates, a school may encounter problems as a result of a poorly drafted admissions policy. On the other hand, further difficulties may arise from an overly-rigid policy which may limit the board in the application of the discretion which it is its duty to exercise. In the *O'Huallacháin* case, the applicants were a group of eight parents who unsuccessfully sought to have their children enroled in a County Dublin Community School. Subsequently, the applicants sought an order of *certiorari* to quash certain decisions of the first-named respondents,[93] whereby applications made by the applicants for places for the year 1987/88 were rejected by them. The grounds on which the order of *certiorari* was sought were:

(a) that the board did not possess power to impose criteria whereby children would be selected for entry to the school from a number of applicants which exceeded the number of places available in the school;

(b) if the board had such an implied power, then, as a matter of law, they were bound to ensure that the criteria issued should be lawful and fair and that due notice of the existence of such criteria should have been furnished to each and every person who had a child eligible for admission to the school and that the criteria should have been properly and fairly applied and without any discrimination or bias in favour of any child or group of children.

[12.80] The school was established in 1979. It executed a deed of trust in 1981 and appointed a board of management which was responsible for the general direction of the conduct and curriculum of the school. Not only had the board an implied right to limit the intake of pupils to 165 as it had done, but perhaps, the judge stated, it had a duty to do so as it would be irresponsible of the board to admit an excessive number of students as to do so would involve a decline in educational standards and a danger to health and safety in the school. In limiting the pupil intake, he was satisfied that some elimination process had to be applied, however regrettable. He made it clear, however, that the court could not become involved in the substance of the decision which was a matter for the board:

> "There are no circumstances in which this court could substitute its judgment for that of the board of management in a matter such as this. The court's only function is to check had the decision of the Board a fair and rational basis. That is fully vindicated."

---

[92] High Court, unrep, 7 August 1987.
[93] Raphael Burke TD and GB Wright TD and Others.

[12.81] The criteria applied by the board in September 1987 had been formulated by a sub-committee of the board and were, following some amendments, unanimously agreed by the board. These criteria were then applied as follows:

   (a) Students living in the area prior to 1981 whose brother(s) or sister(s) attended the school.

   (b) Children of one parent families living in the area;

   (c) Remaining places to be drawn from a list which included:

      (i) pupils living in the area who are the eldest in the family;

     (ii) brother(s)/sister(s) of the remaining pupils in the school who are living in the area.

[12.82] Commenting on the criteria for selection of students, the judge stated that there was nothing to prevent the board having regard to the following selection criteria:

   (a) educational or family circumstances;

   (b) sibling preference;[94]

   (c) length of residence in the area;

[12.83] As regards the lottery, he was of the view that although it "may seem a crude or naive device", the applicants appeared to be unable to suggest any alternative or any more rational means of dealing with the problem presented. However, the judge remarked that the criteria for selection in the enrolment policy were badly drafted as the draftsman did not see fit to include as a criterion that intending applicants should live in the area. Hence, the obvious was overlooked. In the application of the criteria, however, the judge noted that all applicants who lived in the area were, in practice, included in the ballot if they were not already elected under the first category. Notwithstanding some inconsistencies, he concluded that the intake of students was arrived at in accordance with the said criteria, that he was absolutely satisfied of the fairness and integrity of the board members in discharging their functions and that he was also satisfied that that they had applied the criteria without bias or favour of any kind.

[12.84] Accordingly, he dismissed the application. This case underscores that in the event of aspiring numbers of students, who exceed the number of places available in a school, in the absence of any statutory provisions, as was then the case, there may be a duty on a board to draft and implement an adequate

---

94 Giving preference to brothers or sisters of existing students already in the school.

enrolment procedure for the school and a further duty to apply such procedure in a proper, just and equitable manner.

The Position in England

[12.85] In England the obligation on LEAs and school governing bodies to publish detailed particulars annually in regard to various forms of information about schools, came into effect as a result of the Education Act 1980.[95] The duty to keep and transfer records came into force on 1 September 1989 under the Education (School Records) Regulations 1989 while the provisions concerning disclosure became operative on 1 September 1990. However, the 1989 Regulations applied only to a pupil's "curricular record"[96] while the obligation to disclose extended to "other educational records including "a teacher's record".[97] Section 20 of the Education Act 1997 makes provision for information about individual pupil's performance. The substance of what must be included in head teacher's reports to parents, school leavers and pupils' new schools is detailed in circulars.[98]

Defamation

[12.86] If a student or teacher gains access to their file and it contains information about them which is false, it is conceivable that an action for defamation could follow. In *Kirkwood-Hackett v Tierney*,[99] the plaintiff, a student at University College Dublin, had been wrongfully accused of obtaining a money-order by false pretences. The court held the plaintiff had been defamed.

[12.87] The tort of defamation[100] consists in the wrongful publication of a defamatory statement about a person, without lawful justification.[101] A

---

[95] Regulations made pursuant to s 8 require the publication of various kinds of information about schools and the admissions policy; the Education Reform Act 1988 *s* 31(2) required grant-maintained schools to include in their Governing Articles a requirement that details of admissions and appeal procedures be published.

[96] "A formal record of a pupil's academic achievement, his or her other skills and abilities and his/her progress at school," reg 4 (1).

[97] See Circular 17/89; see generally Harris, *The Law Relating to Schools*, (1990), Fourmat, Ch 4.

[98] See Circular No 1/97, February 1997 'Reports on Pupils' Achievements in Primary Schools in 1996/97'; Circular No 2/97, February, 1997 'Reports on Pupils' Achievements in Secondary Schools in 1996/97'.

[99] [1952] IR 185.

[100] See *Gately on Libel and Slander*, (1995), Sweet and Maxwell, p 59 *et seq*; McMahon and Binchy, *Irish Law of Torts*, (2nd ed, 1990), Ch 34, p 609; McDonald, *Irish Law of Defamation*, (1989), Round Hall Press in association with Irish Academic Press; Murdock, *A Dictionary of Irish Law*, (2nd ed, 1993), Round Hall Sweet and Maxwell, p 151.

[101] Heuston and Buckley, *Salmond and Heuston on the Law of Torts* (21st ed, 1996), Sweet and Maxwell, p 143.

defamatory statement is an untrue statement which tends to lower that person in the eyes of right thinking members of society or tends to hold that person up to hatred, ridicule or contempt, or causes that person to be shunned or avoided by right thinking members of society generally.[102] Publication, an essential element of the tort of defamation,[103] means communication to a third party which may occur when an individual makes a statement, circulates a statement or repeats a statement to a third person. Clearly, no action will lie if the statement is communicated by private correspondence or by telephone to the plaintiff.[104] Neither can a statement be defamatory if it is true.

A Defamatory Statement: Slander and Libel

[12.88] A defamatory statement may constitute a libel or a slander which have two main distinguishing features.[105] Slander is defamation arising from spoken words which is a civil injury and is generally actionable only on proof of special damage.[106]

[12.89] Section 14(2) of the Defamation Act 1961 provides that any reference to words shall be construed as including a reference to visual images, gestures and other methods of signifying meaning. However, slander is actionable without proof of special damage in certain circumstances, in the case of words spoken and published imputing:

(a) unchastity or adultery to any woman or girl;[107]

(b) a criminal offence punishable by death or imprisonment;[108]

(c) a contagious venereal disease;

(d) words calculated to disparage the plaintiff in any office, profession, calling, trade or business.[109]

Since the Defamation Act 1961 came into operation, it is not necessary to prove special damage when slander of professional reputation occurs as this is actionable *per se*.[110] However, if this occurs in the school setting, it would be

---

[102] *Sim v Stretch* (1936) 52 TLR 669-671 *per* Lord Atkin.

[103] *Powell v Gelston* [1916] 2 KB 615, 619.

[104] See *Keogh v Incorporated Dental Hospital of Ireland* [1910] 2 IR 166, 171, 577.

[105] McMahon and Binchy, *Irish Law of Torts*, (2nd ed, 1990), Butterworths, pp 612-615.

[106] Such as the loss of a contract, a sale, a benefit or a friendship which arises directly from the words complained of.

[107] Defamation Act 1961, s 16.

[108] Hence, for a teacher to call a student "a thief" may be slander, if it is untrue as it is in a category which is actionable without proof of special damage.

[109] Defamation Act 1961, s 19; see McMahon and Binchy, *Irish Law of Torts*, (2nd ed, 1990), pp 615-620.

[110] Section 19.

prudent for teachers to seek professional advice rather than rush headlong into legal proceedings which they may later have cause to regret.

Libel

[12.90] Libel, on the other hand, is defamation in a permanent form such as in written form, in the form of a wireless broadcast,[111] or being included in a film. Libel is not only an actionable tort, it may also be a crime in certain circumstances[112] and it is actionable *per se*. However, such a statement must be untrue and be published to a third party in order to be actionable. Hence, the person who publishes a defamatory statement about another does so at his peril, and is liable if this statement later proves to be untrue, no matter that he acted both honestly, carefully or mistakenly.[113]

[12.91] This principle is subject to a number of significant exceptions which are collectively termed "privilege" in which the right of free speech is permitted wholly or partially to gain mastery over the right of reputation.[114] The principles of free speech dictate that statements made in certain settings will not be defamatory, however false or maliciously made, as they are protected by a special right of immunity termed privilege which may be absolute or qualified. Some circumstances are protected by absolute privilege and so cannot ground a defamation action.

Absolute Privilege

[12.92] Absolute privilege confers an immunity which is a complete defence to a defamation action. In the limited circumstances in which absolute privilege applies, total freedom of speech is valued so highly by society that words spoken in these special circumstances cannot constitute defamation regardless of the motivation involved. Thus, even though the statement complained of is published with the knowledge that it is false and with the intention of damaging another, it will still not give rise to defamation proceedings. Absolute privilege has been conferred by law in the interest of public policy, free speech and the common good of society. The main instances in which absolute privilege applies are:

(a) Parliamentary privilege which protects any utterance made in either House of the Oireachtas wherever published and all official reports and

---

[111] Defamation Act 1961, s 15.
[112] See Part II of the Defamation Act 1961; Heuston and Buckley, *Salmond and Heuston on the Law of Torts*, (21st ed, 1996), Sweet and Maxwell, pp 144-145.
[113] Heuston and Buckley, pp 164-165.
[114] Heuston and Buckley, p 207.

publications of the Oireachtas or of either House (Articles 15.12 and 15.13 of the Constitution);[115]

(b) Judicial proceedings and this protection extends to statements made by judges, counsel,[116] solicitors or parties.[117]

(c) Presidential privilege within the context of Article 13.8.1°.

(d) Newspaper and broadcast reports of proceedings in court under s 18(1) of the Defamation Act 1961.[118]

The protection of qualified privilege,[119] however, is of application to teachers.

Qualified Privilege

[12.93] There are some instances in which the law recognises the right of individuals to communicate freely so long as this is not done with malice and in such circumstances, qualified privilege operates.[120] An occasion of qualified privilege arises where a person who makes a communication has a duty, legal, social or moral, or an interest to make it to the person to whom it is made, and the person to whom it is made, has a corresponding duty to receive it.[121] The production of a routine school report on a student is an example of the operation of an occasion of qualified privilege, because the teacher is discharging a moral, social or legal duty in providing the report and the parent is under a duty to receive it.

[12.94] When s 22(2)(b) of the Education Act 1998 comes into operation, principals and teachers, in recognised schools, will have a legal duty "to evaluate students and periodically report the results of the evaluation to students and their parents". These reports must be made honestly and fairly and must not be the outcome of any improper motive. The teacher responsible for preparation of school records or reports is protected by "qualified" privilege and will be liable in defamation only if the student can establish that in making the report, the teacher was actuated by malice.[122] If malice on the part of the teacher is established, the defence of "qualified" privilege is lost.

---

[115] This immunity would also appear to extend to discussions at meetings of the Government, see *AG v The Sole Member of the Beef Tribunal* [1993] ILRM 81 SC.

[116] *Munster v Lamb* (1883) 11 QBD 588.

[117] *Royal Aquarium and Summer and White Garden Society Ltd v Parkinson* [1892] 1 QB 431 at 451, *per* Lopez L J.

[118] See further McMahon and Binchy, *Irish Law of Torts* (2nd ed, 1990), Butterworths, p 641 *et seq.*

[119] *Bridgeman v Stockdale* [1953] I WLR 704.

[120] McMahon and Binchy, *Irish Law of Torts* (2nd ed, 1990), Butterworths, p 647 *et seq.*

[121] *Hynes-O'Sullivan v O'Driscoll* [1989] ILRM 349 (SC 1988).

[122] See *Bridgeman v Stockdale* [1953] I WLR 704; see further Poole, Colemen and Liell, *Butterworths Education Law,* (1997), London, p 231.

Malice

[12.95] In the context of defamation, malice is a wrong or improper motive or even gross or unreasoning prejudice.[123] While it is difficult to prove malice, a sustained practice of libelling the plaintiff[124] or a record of confrontation between the parties can contribute to a finding of malice.[125] The defendant teacher who acts rashly or stupidly, however, is protected provided he or she acts *bona fide* but not if he or she uses a privileged occasion for any other purpose other than that for which it was intended.[126] Accordingly, any such reports, references and testimonials emanating from a school ought to be factual, fair, objective, accurate, and be concerned solely with the student's school life. Furthermore, they ought to be limited to areas upon which the teacher is professionally qualified to comment.[127] Sometimes it may be the teacher who has been defamed.[128]

Defamation of Teachers

[12.96] In *Hume v Marshall*[129] Cockburn CJ held, in an action for defamation, that a report, concerning the drunkenness of an assistant teacher, made by a deputy headmaster to the headmaster and school governors, was privileged, having been made *bona fide* and without malice. However, as there was some evidence of ill feeling on the part of the defendant towards the plaintiff, the judge did not withdraw the question of malice from the jury who found for the plaintiff granting him forty shillings damages.

[12.97] It is the occasion which is privileged and not the circumstance as is clear from *Goslett v Garment*.[130] The plaintiff Goslett, a teacher, who had taught at Watford Collegiate College for 18 months had left on good terms with the school. Some time later, the headmaster went to visit the home of some absentee pupils who had been corrected by Y, Goslett's successor in the school, in the defendant's (Garment) home. During this visit, Garment, among other matters,

---

[123] *Horrocks v Lowe* [1975] AC 135.

[124] *Barrett v Long* (1851) 3 HLC 395 at 414 (Parke B).

[125] *McCarthy v Maguire* [1899] 2 IR 802.

[126] *Coleman v Kearns* (1946) Ir Jur Rep 5; also McMahon and Binchy, *The Law of Torts*, (2nd ed, 1990), Butterworths, p 616.

[127] See Barrell and Partington, *Teachers and the Law*, (1986), Methuen, p 590.

[128] See McDonald, *Irish Law of Defamation*, (1989), Round Hall Press in association with Irish Academic Press, pp 35-6; Poole, Coleman and Liell, *Butterworths Education Law*, (1997), Dublin, p 231; see in the English context, *Reeve v Widderson* (1929) The Times, 24 April; *M'Carrogher v Franks* (1964) The Times 25 November; *Ripper v Rate* The Times, 17 January 1919; *Jones v Jones* [1916] 2 AC 481; *Baraclough v Bellamy* The Times, 18 July 1928.

[129] [1878] The Law Times, Vol xxxvii, (ns) 711.

[130] QBD (1897) 391-2.

made the following comment: "Fine set of masters you have. I have seen one master on a Sunday drunk in the street," naming Mr Goslett as that master.

[12.98] Cave J held that if those words had been spoken of Y, then there was privilege, as the head teacher had gone to the home of his pupils to enquire as to why they had absented themselves from school. So long as Y was under discussion the communication was privileged. Moreover, if no name had been mentioned, the communication was still privileged. As Goslett had left the school, however, the matter was no longer privileged. The fact that the defendant had an honest *bona fide* belief did not make the occasion privileged and so the plaintiff was held entitled to £25 for damages for slander.

[12.99] The facts in *Bridgeman v Stockdale*,[131] arose out of an examination on a trade course during which an invigilator remarked to the class that one of the trainees, a qualified engineer, had "cribbed". The invigilator later repeated this comment to the trainee's employer who summarily dismissed the trainee. In an action for slander, the plaintiff claimed that the original remark, and the alleged repetition of it, was each a separate slander of him, as he was a professional person, and he pleaded his dismissal as special damage. The defendants pleaded, *inter alia*, that the words were spoken on a privileged occasion and without malice, and that no action lay. Malice was not pleaded in reply.

[12.100] The court held that the occasion was privileged, it being the common interest of the invigilator and all the class that the examination should manifestly be conducted in a fair and proper manner. In any event, the remark was not something said of him in the way of his business or profession but was simply a remark as to his character, so that in the absence of special damage the action failed.

[12.101] It would be defamatory to falsely accuse an author of plagiarism.[132] It has also been held defamatory falsely to attribute to a widely-known teacher and lecturer, an article which attributed to him statements which manifest complete ignorance on the subject on which he holds himself out to have skills as a teacher or lecturer.[133] With regard to a professor, it has been held defamatory of him to state that he was unfit for his duties, which he neglected, and that his class was in a state of insubordination.[134]

[12.102] In the Irish context, it has been held to be defamatory to write of a school principal that he did not cooperate with the parents of the students or with

---

[131] [1953] 1 WLR 704.
[132] See *Gately on Libel and Slander*, p 59, para 2.36; with regard to alleged plagiarism on the part of a student, see *Flanagan v UCD* [1988] ILRM 724, *per* Barron J.
[133] *Ben Oliel v Press Publishing* 167 NE 432 (NY 1929).
[134] *Alexander v MacDonald* (1826) 4 Murr 94.

the board of management and that certain aspects of his life had been the subject of criticism.[135] It has also been held as defamatory to state that a teacher had robbed banks and post-offices and shot innocent people and to add "You are nice people in the parish of Bekan that you have such a blackguard ... to train children".[136]

Slander of Professional Reputation

[12.103] Section 19 of the Defamation Act 1961 provides:

> In an action for slander in respect of words calculated to disparage the plaintiff in any office, profession, calling, trade or business held or carried on by him at the time of the publication, it shall not be necessary to allege or prove special damage, whether or not the words are spoken of the plaintiff in the way of his office, profession, calling, trade or business.

The above section alters the common law position which was the law prior to the coming into force of the Defamation Act 1961. Prior to that, in order for the slander to be actionable *per se*, it had to disparage the plaintiff in his office, profession, calling, trade or business, and the words spoken had to be about his office. Hence, to state of a school teacher that he had committed adultery with the school cleaner, was not actionable without proof of special damage, for, although these words might disparage the teacher in his office, the words were not spoken about his office.[137]

[12.104] In order for words spoken to be actionable *per se,* the law requires that the words spoken disparage the plaintiff in his office, they need not be about the plaintiff's office. Accordingly, to falsely state of a teacher or office holder[138] at the time of publication, that he is incompetent in his employment or office, may not lower such persons in the estimation of others but these words will, nonetheless, be defamatory because of the injury to reputation in his profession or office by virtue of s 19 of the Defamation Act 1961.

Verbal Abuse

[12.105] Defamatory statements require to be distinguished from abusive statements, however, the former being actionable as they may injure reputation, dignity and pride while abusive statements hurt only dignity and pride and are not actionable.[139]

---

[135] *Coffey v Irish Times*, 14 May 1977 cited in McDonald, *Irish Law of Defamation* (1989) Round Hall Press in association with Irish Academic Press.

[136] *McDonagh v Tarpey* [1933] IR 666.

[137] *Jones v Jones* [1916] 2 AC 481; see further McMahon and Binchy, p 616 *et seq.*

[138] Such as a VEC teacher.

[139] McDonald, *Irish Law of Defamation* (1989) Round Hall Press in association with Irish Academic Press, p 26.

Teacher Assessment: Records and Reports

[12.106] Principals are frequently requested to write references or testimonials for staff or ancillary staff and teachers often write references for students. There are a number of distinctions between a reference and a testimonial. Barrell and Partington, who consider these documents in some detail, state: "Whereas testimonials are general appraisals of an individual in either a professional or personal capacity, references are confidential letters of recommendation".[140] It has been held that, if an employer refuses to grant a certificate of character to an employee leaving the employment, no action shall lie against the employer.[141] However, if an employer furnishes a reference knowing it to be untrue to a potential employer, then he may be liable in negligence, for negligent misstatement, or in deceit.[142] References become the property of the individual to whom they are addressed and they are usually more detailed and explicit than testimonials.[143] A testimonial, on the other hand, is a more general assessment of an individual in their professional competence and it becomes the property of the individual to whom it refers once it is given to him.[144] It appears there is no obligation on a principal to write a testimonial for an assistant teacher or on a teacher to write one for a pupil. If they undertake to do so, however, it must be a fair one. Testimonials and references should be accurate, factual, fair, free from malice.[145]

[12.107] If a testimonial, honestly given, is likely to disadvantage the recipient then it may be wiser not to give it.[146] Barrell and Partington suggests there is no need to give a reason for declining to give a testimonial, and considers it is unwise to do so, but advises that the principal should point out that this does not necessarily indicate that had the testimonial been given it would be unfavourable. If a testimonial is refused, Barrell suggests, it is reasonable to supply a certificate of service which sets down the period and capacity in which the writer has known the applicant.[147] The advice of one's professional association should be sought as the threat of defamation may follow the refusal. Actions arising from testimonials may emanate from two directions:

   (a) from the recipient who may allege that the testimonial is malicious and sue for libel;

---

[140] Barrell and Partington, *Teachers and the Law*, (1985), Methuen, p 611 and generally 606-613.

[141] *Lint v Johnson* (1894) 28 ILTR 16.

[142] Murdock, *A Dictionary of Irish Law*, p 426.

[143] Barrell and Partington, p 607

[144] Barrell and Partington, *Teachers and the Law*, Methuen, p 607.

[145] See McDonald, *Irish Law of Defamation* (1989) Round Hall Press in association with Irish Academic Press, p 26.

[146] Barrell and Partington, *Teachers and the Law*, (1985), Methuen.

[147] *Roche v Pielow* [1986] ILRM 189.

(b) from a subsequent employer who relies on an over- generous or inaccurate testimonial and thereby suffers loss, he may sue for damages.[148]

Careless Statements: Liability for Negligent Misstatement

[12.108] The courts normally require that individuals who claim special skills must use such skill as is usual in the profession. Since 1963 the House of Lords in a unanimous decision, *Hedley Byrne & Co Ltd v Heller & Partners Ltd*,[149] held that a duty to take care in making statements arises whenever a special relationship exists between the parties, and there has been no disclaimer of responsibility.

[12.109] In Irish law,[150] it has also been established that certain circumstances may give rise to a relationship between two parties in which, if one party seeks information from the other and receives it, that other is under a duty to take reasonable care to ensure that the information given is correct.[151] Thus, if a careers teacher or guidance counsellor undertakes to show professional skill and care to a student who relies on such skill and suffers damage as a result of such reliance, then he may sue the teacher or counsellor in negligence for failure to show due skill and care.[152] This situation could conceivably arise when a teacher or counsellor is giving advice to a student in regard to the student's choice of career or the student's choice of subjects for the purposes of filling the Central Applications Office form. As with other professions, it is important for teachers to keep up to date with the developments in their profession and to note any changes in the requirements for entrance to university or other institution that may occur from year to year. In the absence of any specific contractual provision imposing a more onerous duty, a teacher would be required by the court to exercise reasonable care and skill in rendering his services to a student in such circumstances unless, unusually, the somewhat higher professional standard of care is applied as had been the case in some recent English cases.[153]

---

[148] *Roche v Pielow* [1986] ILRM 189.

[149] [1964] AC 465.

[150] *Securities Trust Ltd v Moore and Alexander Ltd* [1964] IR 417 *per* Davitt J. HC.

[151] *Securities Trust Ltd v Moore and Alexander Ltd* [1964] IR 417 *per* Davitt J HC at 421; see further McMahon and Binchy, 'Hedley Byrne in Ireland', p 150-155.

[152] In the English context, see *Christmas v Hampshire County Council* [1995] ELR 404 HL; see Cohen, 'Some Legal Issues in Counselling and Psychotheraphy' in British Journal of Guidance and Counselling, Vol 20, No I, January 1992, pp 10-27.

[153] See the *Dorset, Hampshire and Bromley* appeals ("the education appeals") to the House of Lords (cited as *X (Minors) v Bedfordshire County Council and Appeals;*) these included the following cases; *X (Minors) v Bedfordshire County Council; M (a Minor) v Newham LBC; E (a Minor) v Dorset County Council; Christmas v Hampshire County Council; Keating v Mayor and Burgesess of the London Borough of Bromley* [1995] ELR 404, HL already discussed in Ch 9, para **[9.102]**.

[12.110] If the teacher can show that he followed "good standard and approved practice," with no inherent defects, then he would, most likely, have a good defence. It would not be sufficient for him to have followed such practice mindlessly, however. Likewise, if counsellors can establish that they acted in accordance with a responsible body of competent professional opinion in the circumstances of the case, (eg the Institute of Guidance Counsellors), they would, most likely be able to establish that they were not negligent in following that opinion provided such professional opinion had no inherent defects.[154]

---

[154] *Roche v Pielow* [1986] ILRM 189 as in the circumstance of solicitor's negligence.

Appendices

Appendix A

Education Act, 1998

Number 51 of 1998

ARRANGEMENT OF SECTIONS

Part I

PRELIMINARY AND GENERAL

Part II

SCHOOLS

Part III

THE INSPECTORATE

Part IV

BOARDS OF MANAGEMENT

Part V

THE PRINCIPAL AND TEACHERS

Part VI

MISCELLANEOUS

Part VII

NATIONAL COUNCIL FOR CURRICULUM AND ASSESSMENT

Part VIII

EXAMINATIONS

Part IX

BODIES CORPORATE

Schedule 1

THE COUNCIL

Schedule 2

EXAMINATIONS

ACTS REFERRED TO

Adoption Acts, 1952 to 1998	
Children Acts, 1908 to 1989	
Child Care Act, 1991	1991, No. 17
Civil Service Commissioners Act, 1956	1956, No. 45
Civil Service Regulation Acts, 1956 to 1996	
European Parliament Elections Act, 1997	1997, No. 2
Guardianship of Children Acts, 1964 to 1997	
Health Act, 1970	1970. No. 1
Health Acts, 1947 to 1996	
Intermediate Education (Ireland) Act, 1878	1878, 41 & 42 Vic. c. 66
Intermediate Education (Ireland) Acts, 1878 to 1924	
Local Government Act, 1941	1941, No. 23
Ministers and Secretaries (Amendment) Act, 1956	1956, No. 21
Public Service Management Act, 1997	1997, No. 27
Trade Union Acts, 1871 to 1990	
Vocational Education Act, 1930	1930, No 29

AN ACT TO MAKE PROVISION IN THE INTERESTS OF THE COMMON GOOD FOR THE EDUCATION OF EVERY PERSON IN THE STATE, INCLUDING ANY PERSON WITH A DISABILITY OR WHO HAS OTHER SPECIAL EDUCATIONAL NEEDS, AND TO PROVIDE GENERALLY FOR PRIMARY, POSTPRIMARY, ADULT AND CONTINUING EDUCATION AND VOCATIONAL EDUCATION AND TRAINING; TO ENSURE THAT THE EDUCATION SYSTEM IS ACCOUNTABLE TO STUDENTS, THEIR PARENTS AND THE STATE FOR THE EDUCATION PROVIDED, RESPECTS THE DIVERSITY OF VALUES, BELIEFS, LANGUAGES AND TRADITIONS IN IRISH SOCIETY AND IS CONDUCTED IN A SPIRIT OF PARTNERSHIP BETWEEN SCHOOLS, PATRONS, STUDENTS, PARENTS, TEACHERS AND OTHER SCHOOL STAFF, THE COMMUNITY SERVED BY THE SCHOOL AND THE STATE; TO PROVIDE FOR THE RECOGNITION AND FUNDING OF SCHOOLS AND THEIR MANAGEMENT THROUGH BOARDS OF MANAGEMENT; TO PROVIDE FOR AN INSPECTORATE OF SCHOOLS; TO PROVIDE FOR THE ROLE AND RESPONSIBILITIES OF PRINCIPALS AND TEACHERS; TO ESTABLISH THE

NATIONAL COUNCIL FOR CURRICULUM AND ASSESSMENT AND TO MAKE PROVISION FOR IT, AND TO PROVIDE FOR RELATED MATTERS. [23rd December, 1998]

BE IT ENACTED BY THE OIREACHTAS AS FOLLOWS:

Part I

PRELIMINARY AND GENERAL

1. Short title and commencement

(1) This Act may be cited as the Education Act, 1998.

(2) Subject to subsection (3), this Act shall come into operation on such day or days as, by order or orders made by the Minister under this section, may be fixed either generally or with reference to any particular purpose, function provision or class of school, and different days may be so fixed for different purposes, functions or provisions of this Act or different classes of schools.

(3) This Act shall come into operation in respect of any purpose, function, provision or class of school, with reference to which the Minister has not made an order under subsection (2), two years from the date of its passing.

(4) As soon as practicable after the end of the first and second years following the date of passing of this Act, the Minister shall prepare a report on the implementation of the Act and shall cause copies of the report to be laid before each House of the Oireachtas.

(5) The Intermediate Education (Ireland) Acts, 1878 to 1924 and this Act may be cited together as the Education Acts, 1878 to 1998, and shall be construed together as one.

2. Interpretation

(1) In this Act, except where the context otherwise requires-

"articles of management" means any instruments, relating to the operation and management of schools, as are in operation on the commencement of this Act and as shall be agreed from time to time by patrons of schools, national associations of parents and recognised trade unions and staff associations representing teachers;

"board" means a board of management established under section 14;

"centre for education" means a place, other than a school or a place providing university or other third level education, where adult or continuing education or vocational education or training, is provided and which is designated for that purpose under section 10(4);

"characteristic spirit" means the characteristic spirit referred to in section 15(2)(b);

"Council" means the body established under section 39;

"curriculum" shall be construed in accordance with section 30;

"disability" means

(a) the total or partial loss of a person's bodily or mental functions, including the loss of a part of the person's body, or

(b) the presence in the body of organisms causing, or likely to cause, chronic disease or illness, or

(c) the malfunction, malformation or disfigurement of a part of a person's body, or

(d) a condition or malfunction which results in a person learning differently from a person without the condition or malfunction, or

(e) a condition, illness or disease which affects a person's thought processes, perception of reality, emotions or judgement or which results in disturbed behaviour;

"educational disadvantage" has the meaning assigned by section 32(9);

"examination" has the meaning assigned to it by section 49;

"functions" includes powers and duties;

"Gaeltacht area" means an area for the time being determined to be a Gaeltacht area by order made under section 2 of the Ministers and Secretaries (Amendment) Act, 1956;

"Inspector" means a member of the Inspectorate;

"Inspectorate" means the Inspectorate appointed under section 13;

"Minister" means the Minister for Education and Science;

"national association of parents" means an association or other body of persons established by parents with objects which include representing the views and interests of parents with regard to education and assisting parents in exercising their rights and role in the process of the education of their children, that is

(a) established and organised on a national basis and has a membership distributed over a substantial part of the State, and

(b) for the time being recognised by the Minister for the purposes of this Act, including the National Parents Council Primary and the National Parents Council (Post-Primary) Limited, being bodies for the time being so recognised;

"National Council for Curriculum and Assessment means the body established in accordance with section 39;

"parent" includes a foster parent, a guardian appointed under the Guardianship of Children Acts, 1964 to 1997, or other person acting *in loco parentis* who has a child in his or her care subject to any statutory power or order of a court and, in the case of a child who has been adopted under the Adoption Acts, 1952 to 1998, or, where the child has been adopted outside the State, means the adopter or adopters or the surviving adopter;

"parents' association" means an association to which section 26 applies;

"patron" has the meaning assigned to it by section 8;

"prescribed" means prescribed by regulations made by the Minister and cognate words shall be construed accordingly;

"Principal" means a person appointed under section 23;

"recognised school" means a school which is recognised by the Minister in accordance with section 10;

"recognised school management organisations" means those bodies as may be established for the purpose of representing the interests of persons engaged in the management of schools and which are recognised by the Minister for the purposes of this Act;

"unrecognised trade union" means a trade union licensed under the Trade Union Acts, 1871 to 1990, that stands recognised for consultation purposes;

"school" means an establishment which -

(a) provides primary education to its students and which may also provide early childhood education, or

(b) provides post-primary education to its students and which may also provide courses in adult, continuing or vocational education or vocational training,

but does not include a school or institution established in accordance with the Children Acts, 1908 to 1989, or a school or institution established or maintained by a health board in accordance with the Health Acts, 1947 to 1996, or the Child Care Act, 1991;

"school plan" has the meaning assigned to it by section 21(1);

"school week" means the period of time during a week when a school is open for the reception of students;

"school year" means such twelve month period commencing on a day that falls between the first day of July and the first day of October in any year as may be prescribed from time to time by the Minister, either generally or in respect of any school or class of schools;

"special educational needs" means the educational needs of students who have a disability and the educational needs of exceptionally able students;

"student", in relation to a school, means a person enrolled at the school and in relation to a centre for education, means a person registered as a student in that centre;

"support services" means the services which the Minister provides to students or their parents. schools or centres for education in accordance with section 7 and shall include any or all of the following:

(a) assessment of students;

(b) psychological services;

(c) guidance and counselling services;

(d) in technical aid and equipment, including means of access to schools, adaptations to buildings to facilitate access and transport, for students with special needs and their families;

(e) provision for students learning through Irish sign language or other sign language, including interpreting services;

(f) speech therapy services;

(g) provision for early childhood, primary, post-primary, adult or continuing education to students with special needs otherwise than in schools or centres for education;

(h) teacher welfare services;

(i) transport services;

(j) library and media services;

(k) school maintenance services;

(l) examinations provided for in Part VIII;

(m) curriculum support and staff advisory services, and

(n) such other services as are specified by this Act or considered appropriate by the Minister;

"teacher" includes a Principal;

"vocational education committee" means a committee established by section 7 of the Vocational Education Act, 1930.

(2) (a) In this Act a reference to a Part, section or a Schedule is a reference to a Part or section of or a Schedule to this Act, unless it is indicated that a reference to some other Act is intended.

(b) In this Act a reference to a subsection, paragraph or subparagraph is a reference to a subsection, paragraph or subparagraph of the provision in which the reference occurs, unless it is indicated that a reference to some other provision is intended.

(3) A reference in this Act to the performance of functions includes, with respect to powers and duties, a reference to the exercise of powers and the carrying out of duties.

3. Expenses

Any expenses incurred by the Minister in the administration of this Act shall, to such extent as may be approved of by the Minister for Finance, be paid out of monies provided by the Oireachtas.

4. Services of notices.

Where a notice, direction or other document is authorised or required by or under this Act or regulations made thereunder to be served on a person, it shall unless otherwise specified in this Act, be addressed to the person and shall be served on or given to the person in one of the following ways -

(a) where it is addressed to the person by name, by delivering it to the person, or

(b) by leaving it at the address at which the person ordinarily resides or, in a case in which an address for service has been furnished, at that address, or

(c) by sending it by ordinary prepaid post addressed to the person at the address at which the person ordinarily resides, or in a case in which an address for service has been furnished, at that address.

5. Laying of regulations and orders

Every regulation and every order made under this Act shall be laid before each House of the Oireachtas as soon as may be after it is made and, if a resolution annulling the regulation or order is passed by either such House within the next 21 days on which that House has sat after the regulation or order is laid before it, the regulation or order shall be annulled accordingly, but without prejudice to the validity of anything previously done thereunder.

6. Objects of Act

Every person concerned in the implementation of this Act shall have regard to the following objects in pursuance of which the Oireachtas has enacted this Act:

(a) to give practical effect to the constitutional rights of children, including children who have a disability or who have other special educational needs, as they relate to education;

(b) to provide that, as far as is practicable and having regard to the resources available, there is made available to people resident in the State a level and quality of education appropriate to meeting the needs and abilities of those people;

(c) to promote equality of access to and participation in education and to promote the means whereby students may benefit from education;

(d) to promote opportunities for adults, in particular adults who as children did not avail of or benefit from education in schools, to avail of educational opportunities through adult and continuing education;

(e) to promote the right of parents to send their children to a school of the parents' choice having regard to the rights of patrons and the effective and efficient use of resources;

(f) to promote best practice in teaching methods with regard to the diverse needs of students and the development of the skills and competences of teachers;

(g) to promote effective liaison and consultation between schools and centres for education, patrons, teachers. parents, the communities served by schools, local authorities, health boards, persons or groups of persons who have a special interest in, or experience of, the education of students with specie! educational needs and the Minister;

(h) to contribute to the realisation of national educational policies and objectives;

(i) to contribute to the realisation of national policy and objectives in relation to the extension of bi-lingualism in Irish society and in particular the achievement of a greater use of the Irish language at school and in the community;

(j) to contribute to the maintenance of Irish as the primary community language in Gaeltacht areas;

(k) to promote the language and cultural needs of students having regard to the choices of their parents;

(I) to enhance the accountability of the education system, and

(m) to enhance transparency in the making of decisions in the education system both locally and nationally.

7. Functions of Minister

(1) Each of the following shall be a function of the Minister under this Act:

(a) to ensure, subject to the provisions of this Act, that there is made available to each person resident in the State, including a person with a disability or who has other special educational needs, support services and a level and quality of education appropriate to meeting the needs and abilities of that person,

(b) to determine national education policy, and

(c) to plan and co-ordinate

    (i) the provision of education in recognised schools and centres for education, and

    (ii) support services.

(2) Without prejudice to the generality of subsection (1), each of the following shall be a function of the Minister:

(a) to provide funding to each recognised school and centre for education and to provide support services to recognised schools, centres for education, students, including students who have a disability or who have other special educational needs, and their parents, as the Minister considers appropriate and in accordance with this Act;

(b) to monitor and assess the quality, economy, efficiency and effectiveness of the education system provided in the State by recognised schools and centres for education, having regard to the objects provided for in section 6 and to publish, in such manner as the Minister considers appropriate, information relating to such monitoring and assessment;

(c) to lease land or buildings to any person or body of persons for the purpose of establishing a school without prejudice to the establishment by patrons of schools which are situated on land or in buildings which are not leased to them by the Minister, the extension and further development of such schools when established and the recognition of such schools in accordance with section 10;

(d) to provide support services through Irish to recognised schools which provide teaching through Irish and to any other recognised school which requests such provision;

(e) to perform such other functions as are specifically provided for by this Act or any other enactment, and

(f) to do all such acts and things as may be necessary to further the objects for which this Act is enacted.

(3) The Minister shall have all such powers as are necessary or expedient for the purpose of performing his or her functions.

(4) In carrying out his or her functions, the Minister

(a) shall have regard to -

(i) the resources available,

(ii) the provision for education and training made by other agencies with funds provided by the Oireachtas,

(iii) the need to reflect the diversity of educational services provided in the State, and

(iv) the practices and traditions relating to the organisation of schools or groups of schools existing at the commencement of this Part and the right of schools to manage their own affairs in accordance with this Act and any charters, deeds, articles of management or other such instruments relating to their establishment or operation,

and

(b) shall make all reasonable efforts to consult with patrons. national associations of parents, parents' associations in schools, recognised school management organisations, recognised trade unions and staff associations representing teachers and such other persons who have a special interest in or knowledge of matters relating to education, including persons or groups of persons who have a special interest in, or experience of, the education of students with special educational needs, as the Minister considers appropriate.

Part II

SCHOOLS

8. Patron of school

(1) (a) The person who, at the commencement of this section, is recognised by the Minister as the patron of a primary school, and

(b) the persons who, at the commencement of this section, stand appointed as trustees or as the board of governors of a post-primary school and, where there are no such trustees or such board, the owner of that school, shall be deemed to be the patron for the purposes of this Act and the Minister shall enter his, her or their name, as appropriate, in a register kept for that purpose by the Minister.

(2) In any case other than that provided in subsection (1), the patron of a recognised school shall be the person who requested recognition of the school or a nominee of such person and the name of that person shall be entered in the register.

(3) The Minister may amend the register in respect of any school on the application of the person who stands for the time being registered as the patron or of the successor to that person.

(4) In the case of a school established or maintained by a vocational education committee that committee shall be the patron of the school for the purposes of this Act.

(5) Where two or more persons exercise the functions of a patron they may be registered as joint patrons.

(6) The patron of a school shall carry out the functions and exercise the powers conferred on the patron by this Act and such other functions and powers as may be conferred on the patron by any Act of the Oireachtas or instrument made thereunder, deed, charter, articles of management or other such instrument relating to the establishment or operation of the school.

(7) In this section -

"person" includes a body of persons;

"school" includes a proposed school.

9. Functions of a school

A recognised school shall provide education to students which is appropriate to their abilities and needs and, without prejudice to the generality of the foregoing, it shall use its available resources to

    (a)   ensure that the educational needs of all students, including those with a disability or other special educational needs, are identified and provided for,

    (b)   ensure that the education provided by it meets the requirements of education policy as determined from time to time by the Minister including requirements as to the provision of a curriculum as prescribed by the Minister in accordance with section 30,

    (c)   ensure that students have access to appropriate guidance to assist them in their educational and career choices,

    (d)   promote the moral, spiritual, social and personal development of students and provide health education for them, in consultation with their parents, having regard to the characteristic spirit of the school,

    (e)   promote equality of opportunity for both male and female students and staff of the school,

    (f)   promote the development of the Irish language and traditions, Irish literature, the arts and other cultural matters,

    (g)   ensure that parents of a student, or in the case of a student who has reached the age of 18 years, the student, have access in the prescribed manner to records kept by that school relating to the progress of that student in his or her education,

    (h)   in the case of schools located in a Gaeltacht area, contribute to the maintenance of Irish as the primary community language,

(i)   conduct its activities in compliance with any regulations made from time to time by the Minister under section 33,

(j)   ensure that the needs of personnel involved in management functions and staff development needs generally in the school are identified and provided for,

(k)   establish and maintain systems whereby the efficiency and effectiveness of its operations can be assessed, including the quality and effectiveness of teaching in the school and the attainment levels and academic standards of students,

(l)   establish or maintain contacts with other schools and at other appropriate levels throughout the community served by the school, and

(m)   subject to this Act and in particular section 15(2)(d), establish and maintain an admissions policy which provides for maximum accessibility to the school.

10. Recognition of schools

(1) On a request being made for that purpose, the Minister may from time to time designate a school or a proposed school to be a school recognised for the purposes of this Act.

(2) The Minister may designate a school or a proposed school to be a school recognised for the purposes of this Act where the Minister, on a request being made for that purpose by the patron of a school or a proposed school, is satisfied that -

(a)   the number of students who are attending or are likely to attend the school is such or is likely to be such as to make the school viable,

(b)   in the case of a proposed school, and having regard to the desirability of diversity in the classes of school operating in the area likely to be served by the school, the needs of students attending or likely to attend the school cannot reasonably be met by existing schools,

(c)   the patron undertakes that the school shall provide the curriculum as determined in accordance with section 30,

(d)   the patron agrees to permit and co-operate with regular inspection and evaluation by the Inspectorate,

(e)   the school complies, or in the case of a proposed school shall comply, with health, safety and building standards as are determined by law and any further such standards as are determined from time to time by the Minister, and

(f)   the patron agrees that the school shall operate in accordance with such regulations as may be made by the Minister from time to time under section 13 and with this Act and with any other terms and conditions as may reasonably be attached to recognition by the Minister.

(3) A school that, on the commencement of this section, is in receipt of funds provided by the Oireachtas in respect of -

(a)   the education activities for students of that school, or

(b)   the remuneration of teachers in that school,

shall be deemed to be a school recognised in accordance with this section.

(4) The Minister may from time to time designate a place to be a centre for education.

11. Withdrawal of recognition

(1) Where the Minister is satisfied that the requirements for recognition of a school as provided for in section 10(2) are not being met by a school, including a school recognised in

accordance with section 10(3), or that the functions of a school are not being effectively discharged and is of the opinion that recognition should be withdrawn from that school, the Minister shall inform the board, the patron, the teachers, the student council where one exists and the parents of students in that school by notice in writing of that opinion and the reasons for the opinion.

(2) If, after the expiration of three months from the date of the notice issued under subsection (I), and, after consideration of any representations made to the Minister by the board or the patron of the school, the teachers or the parents or the student council where one exists, the Minister remains of the said opinion, the Minister may withdraw recognition from the school by notice in writing addressed to the board and the patron of the school, and such notice shall be effective on and from the last day of the school year following the school year in which the notice was addressed to the board or such later date as the Minister may determine.

(3) It shall be the duty of the Minister in respect of a school from which recognition has been withdrawn to arrange to make alternative and appropriate education facilities available for those students who were enrolled in the school on the date of such withdrawal and who require those facilities.

(4) Where the Minister is satisfied that a school from which recognition has been withdrawn satisfies the requirements for recognition of a school as provided for in section 10, and that the functions of the school will be effectively discharged, the Minister may restore recognition to that school, provided that such restoration of recognition shall not entitle that school or any person employed in the school to receive any payment out of monies provided by the Oireachtas in relation to the period subsequent to the withdrawal of recognition and prior to the restoration of recognition.

12. Annual funding

(1) The Minister, with the concurrence of the Minister for Finance shall determine and publish in each school year criteria by which any class or classes of recognised schools or centres for education are to be funded in the following school year from monies provided by the Oireachtas and such criteria shall allow for the payment of additional monies to recognised schools having regard to the level of educational disadvantage of students in the schools.

(2) Except as otherwise provided by this Act, the Minister shall, in each school year by such date or dates as shall be determined by the Minister, make to each recognised school or centre for education a grant or grants, which accords with the criteria determined pursuant to this section, from monies provided by the Oireachtas in accordance with this Act, for the purposes of carrying or, that school or centre for education.

(3) A grant or grants shall not be made unless the school is a recognised school at the date that such grant or grants are to be made.

(4) Except as otherwise provided in this Act, where, on the commencement of this section, arrangements are in place whereby grants are provided by the Minister to a body of persons which disburses such grants to two or more recognised schools, then nothing in this Act shall operate to alter such arrangements except with the agreement of that body or its successor.

(5) Where subsection (4) applies, the Minister shall, from monies provided by the Oireachtas, make such grant or grants to the body referred to in that subsection or its successor of an amount equal to the amount which, but for this subsection, would have been made to schools

under subsection (2) and any such grant or grants shall be applied by that body for the benefit of students in those schools.

Part III

THE INSPECTORATE

13. The Inspectorate

(1) The Minister shall appoint a Chief Inspector and such and so many Inspectors as the Minister considers appropriate and the Chief Inspector and Inspectors collectively shall be known and are referred to in this Act as the "Inspectorate".

(2) The Minister shall include amongst those he or she appoints as Inspectors under subsection (1) persons who hold qualifications as psychologists or who have other expertise, including expertise in the education of students with special educational needs.

(3) The functions of an Inspector shall be:

    (a) to support and advise recognised schools, centres for education and teachers on matters relating to the provision of education and, without prejudice to the generality of the foregoing, an Inspector -

        (i) shall visit recognised schools and centres for education on the initiative of the Inspectorate, and, following consultation with the board, patron, parents of students and teachers, as appropriate, use any or all of the following:

            (I) evaluate the organisation and operation of those schools and centres and the quality and effectiveness of the education provided in those schools or centres, including the quality of teaching and effectiveness of individual teachers;

            (II) evaluate the education standards m such schools or centres;

            (III) assess the implementation and effectiveness of any programmes of education which have been devised in respect of individual students who have a disability or other special educational needs;

            (IV) assess the implementation of regulations made by the Minister, and

            (V) report to the Minister, or to the board, patron, parents of students and teachers, as appropriate, and as prescribed, on these matters or on any other matter relating to the activities of those schools or centres and the needs of students attending those schools or centres,

        (ii) may conduct assessments of the educational needs of students in recognised schools and advise those students, their parents and the schools as appropriate in relation to the educational development of those students,

        (iii) shall advise teachers and boards in respect of the performance of their duties. and, in particular, assist teachers in employing improved methods of teaching and conducting classes, and

        (iv) shall advise parents and parents' associations;

    (b) to evaluate the quality and effectiveness of the provision of education in the State. including comparison with relevant international practice and standards, and to report thereon to the Minister;

    (c) to conduct research into education and to provide support in the formulation of policy by the Minister;

(d) to promote excellence in the management of, teaching in and the use of support services by schools and in the procedures for consultation and co-operation within and between schools and centres for education;

(e) to disseminate information relating to -

(i) the performance by the Inspectorate of the functions provided for in this section, and

(ii) successful educational initiatives which have been implemented by schools and centres for education

and promote informed debate on those matters;

(f) to evaluate the effectiveness of the teaching, development promotion and use of Irish in schools and centres for education and to report to the Minister on those matters;

(g) to advise the Minister on any matter relating to education policy and provision. including the curriculum taught in recognised schools. assessment and teaching methods, and

(h) to perform such functions relating to the preparation and marking of the school examinations which are conducted in the State as the Chief Inspector shall determine, the monitoring and evaluation of the content and standards of those examinations and to report thereon to the Minister.

(4) Without prejudice to the generality of subsection (3) an Inspector to whom subsection (2) applies shall have the following functions:

(a) in consultation with parents to assess the psychological needs of students in recognised schools and to advise as appropriate those students, their parents and the schools in relation to the educational and psychological development of such students;

(b) to advise recognised schools on policies and strategies for the education of children with special educational needs;

(c) to advise the Minister on any matter relating to the psychological needs of students in recognised schools;

(d) in collaboration with parents and the Principal and teachers in recognised schools, to assist in the creation of a school environment which prevents or limits obstacles to learning which students may experience, and

(e) to advise the Minister on any matter relating to the linguistic needs of deaf students in recognised schools.

(5) Where an Inspector has carried out an evaluation or an assessment under subsection (3)(a)(i), he or she may make recommendations to the Minister in respect of improvements that he or she considers appropriate.

(6) The Minister may, if a teacher and the board consent, second that teacher to the Inspectorate for such period as the Minister shall determine, to carry out any or all of the functions conferred on an Inspector.

(7) An Inspector shall have all such powers as are necessary or expedient for the purpose of performing his or her functions and shall be accorded every reasonable facility and co-operation by the board and the staff of a school or centre for education.

(8) An Inspector, including the Chief Inspector, shall carry out his or her functions in accordance with such procedures for, and criteria of, inspections as may be determined by the Minister from time to time, following consultation with patrons, school management organisation recognised trade unions and staff associations representing teachers and such other persons as the Minister considers appropriate. and such directions as may be given by the Minister from tine to time.

(9) A teacher or the board of a school may request the Chief Inspector to review any inspection carried out by an Inspector which affects the teacher or the school and the Chief Inspector shall review the inspection in accordance with such procedures as the Chief Inspector shall determine.

(10) A person who immediately before the commencement of this Part holds an office as Chief Inspector, Inspector or Inspector of Guidance Service/Psychologist or who is seconded to the Inspectorate shall on the commencement of this Part continue to hold that office or be so seconded as appropriate and this section shall apply to any such person.

(11) The Civil Service Commissioners Act, 1915, and the Civil Service Regulation Acts. 1956 to 1996, shall apply to Inspectors.

(12) The Minister shall appoint Inspectors or second teachers to the Inspectorate, in accordance with this section, with the concurrence of the Minister for Finance.

Part IV

BOARDS OF MANAGEMENT

14. Establishment and membership of management

(1) It shall be the duty of a patron, for the purposes of ensuring that a recognised school is managed in a spirit of partnership, to appoint where practicable a board of management the composition of which is agreed between patrons of schools, national associations of parents, recognised school management organisations, recognised trade unions and staff associations representing teachers and the Minister.

(2) A board established in accordance with subsection (1) shall fulfil in respect of the school the functions assigned to that school by this Act, and, except in the case of a school established or maintained by a vocational education committee, each board shall be a body corporate with perpetual succession and power to sue and may be sued in its corporate name.

(3) Pending the establishment of a board as provided for by subsection (1) the persons who have responsibilities under the structures and systems in place in a school for the management of that school at the commencement of this Part, including boards of governors, shall, as appropriate, discharge the functions of a board under this Act.

(4) The members of a board shall, except where articles of management otherwise provide, be appointed by the patron of the school.

(5) When making appointments to a board established in accordance with subsection (1) the patron shall comply with directions given by the Minister in respect of an appropriate gender balance and the Minister, before giving any such directions, shall consult with patrons, national associations of parents, recognised school management organisations and recognised trade unions and staff associations representing teachers.

(6) The Minister, with the agreement of the patron, national associations of parents. recognised school management organisations and recognised trade unions and staff

associations representing teachers, shall prescribe matters relating to the appointment of a board.

(7) Except as provided by this Act, no action shall lie against a member of a board in respect of anything done by that member in good faith and in pursuance of this Act or any regulations made by the Minister under this Act.

(8) Where a patron determines that the appointment of a board in accordance with subsection (1) is not practicable, the patron shall inform the parents of students, the teachers and other staff of the school and the Minister of that fact and the reasons therefor at the time of such determination and, thereafter, if a board is not so appointed, the patron shall, from time to time or as requested by the Minister, inform the parents, teachers and other staff and the Minister of the reasons therefor.

15. Functions of a board

(I) It shall be the duty of a board to manage the school on behalf of the patron and for the benefit of the students and their parents and to provide or cause to be provided an appropriate education for each student at the school for which that board has responsibility.

(2) A board shall perform the functions conferred on it and on a school by this Act and in carrying out its functions the board shall

   (a)   do so in accordance with the policies determined by the Minister from time to time,

   (b)   uphold, and be accountable to the patron for so upholding, the characteristic spirit of the school as determined by the cultural, educational, moral, religious, social, linguistic and spiritual values and traditions which inform and are characteristic of the objectives and conduct of the school, and at all times act in accordance with any Act of the Oireachtas or instrument made thereunder, deed, charter, articles of management or other such instrument relating to the establishment or operation of the school,

   (c)   consult with and keep the patron informed of decisions and proposals of the board,

   (d)   publish, in such manner as the board with the agreement of the patron considers appropriate, the policy of the school concerning admission to and participation in the school, including the policy of the school relating to the expulsion and suspension of students and admission to and participation by students with disabilities or who have other special educational needs, and ensure that as regards that policy principles of equality and the right of parents to send their children to a school of the parents' choice are respected and such directions as may be made from time to time by the Minister, having regard to the characteristic spirit of the school and the constitutional rights of all persons concerned, are complied with,

   (e)   have regard to the principles and requirements of a democratic society and have respect and promote respect for the diversity of values, beliefs, traditions, languages and ways of life in society,

   (f)   have regard to the efficient use of resources (and, in particular, the efficient use of grants provided under section 12) the public interest in the affairs of the school and accountability to students, their parents, the patron, staff and the community served by the school, and

   (g)   use the resources provided to the school from monies provided by the Oireachtas to make reasonable provision and accommodation for students with a disability or other special educational needs including, where necessary alteration of buildings and provision of appropriate equipment.

(3) For the avoidance of doubt, nothing in this Act shall confer or be deemed to confer on the board any right over or interest in the land and buildings of the school for which that board is responsible.

16. Dissolution by a patron

(1) Subject to this section and to the consent of the Minister, the patron may -

(a) for good and valid reasons stated in writing to a member of a board of management remove that member from that office, or

(b) if satisfied that the functions of a board are not being effectively discharged, dissolve that board.

(2) Where a patron proposes to remove a member of a board from that office or to dissolve a board, the patron shall inform that member or board by notice in writing of his or her intention and the reasons therefor.

(3) If, at the end of a period of one month after the date of the notice provided for in subsection (2), the patron, having considered any representations made to him or her by or on behalf of the member or the board, remains of the view that the member should be removed from office or that the board should be dissolved then the patron may, subject to the approval of the Minister, by notice in writing and stating the opinion of the patron and the reasons there for, remove the member from office or dissolve the board as appropriate.

(4) A copy of every notice issued under this section and any representations made to the patron shall be delivered to the Minister as soon as may be after it has been made.

(5) Whenever the patron dissolves a board, the patron may, subject to the approval of the Minister, appoint any person or body of persons as the patron thinks fit to perform the functions of the board.

(6) Where a patron removes a member of a board the resulting vacancy shall be filled in accordance with regulations made under section 14(6).

(7) The patron shall provide, in accordance with section 14 for the reestablishment of a board dissolved under subsection (1) not later than six months following the dissolution or such longer period as the patron, with the consent of the Minister, considers appropriate and when the new board has been established the functions of the dissolved board shall be revested in the new board and shall cease to he functions of the person or body of persons, if any, appointed under subsection (5).

17. Dissolution by patron at request of Minister

(1) Where -

(a) the Minister is satisfied that the functions of a board are not being effectively discharged, or

(b) a board willfully neglects to comply with any order, direction or regulation of the Minister given or made under this Act, or

(c) a board fails to comply with any judgment or order of any court of competent jurisdiction.

the Minister may, by notice in writing, require the patron to dissolve the board for reasons stated in such notice and the patron shall dissolve the board accordingly as soon as may be after the date of such notice.

(2) Before the Minister serves a notice as provided for in subsection (1), he or she shall inform the board and the patron of his or her intention to do so and shall consider any representations made to him or her by or on behalf of the board or the patron within one month of informing the board and the patron.

(3) Whenever the patron dissolves a board under this section, subsections (5) and (7) of section 16 shall apply.

18. Keeping of accounts and records

(1) Except in the case of a school established or maintained by a vocational education committee a board shall keep all proper and usual accounts and records of all monies received by it or expenditure of such monies incurred by it and shall ensure that in each year all such accounts are properly audited or certified in accordance with best accounting practice.

(2) Accounts kept in pursuance of this section shall be made available by the school concerned for inspection by the Minister and by parents of students in the school, in so far as those accounts relate to monies provided in accordance with section 12.

19. Report on operation of board

(1) Where the Minister or the patron is of the opinion that the functions of a board are not being effectively discharged, the Minister or the patron, as the case may be, shall inform the board of that opinion and the reasons therefor.

(2) Having considered any representations by the board the Minister or the patron, as the case may be, may authorise any person or persons as the Minister or the patron may deem appropriate to report to the Minister or the patron or both the Minister and the patron on any matter arising from or relating to the operation of that board.

(3) Any person appointed to prepare a report under this section shall be entitled at all reasonable times to enter any premises occupied by the school concerned and shall be afforded every facility and co-operation by the board, the teachers and other staff of the school, including access to all records, to perform his or her functions.

(4) A Principal or board shall supply the patron and the Minister with such information regarding the performance of the board's functions as the patron or the Minister, as the case may be. may from time to time require.

(5) Where either the Minister or a patron proposes to exercise functions under this section then -

    (a)   the Minister shall inform the patron, or

    (b)   the patron shall inform the Minister,

as appropriate, of the proposed course of action.

20. Report and information

A board shall establish procedures for informing the parents of students in the school of matters relating to the operation and performance of the school and such procedures may include the publication and circulation to parents, teachers and other staff and a student council where one has been established of a report on the operation and performance of the school in any school year, with particular reference to the achievement of objectives as set out in the school plan provided for under section 21.

21. The school plan

(1) A board shall, as soon as may be after its appointment, make arrangements for the preparation of a plan (in this section referred to as the "school plan") and shall ensure that the plan is regularly reviewed and updated.

(2) The school plan shall state the objectives of the school relating to equality of access to and participation in the school and the measures which the school proposes to take to achieve those objectives including equality of access to and participation in the school by students with disabilities or who have other special educational needs.

(3) The school plan shall be prepared in accordance with such directions, including directions relating to consultation with the parents, the patron, staff and students of the school, as may be given from time to time by the Minister in relation to school plans.

(4) A board shall make arrangements for the circulation of copies of the school plan to the patron, parents, teachers and other staff of the school.

Part V

THE PRINCIPAL AND TEACHERS

22. Functions of Principal and teachers

(1) The Principal of a recognised school and the teachers in a recognised school, under the direction of the Principal, shall have responsibility, in accordance with this Act, for the instruction provided to students in the school and shall contribute, generally, to the education and personal development of students in that school.

(2) Without prejudice to subsection (1), the Principal and teachers shall -

    (a) encourage and foster learning in students,

    (b) regularly evaluate students and periodically report the results of the evaluation to the students and their parents,

    (c) collectively promote co-operation between the school and the community which it serves, and

    (d) subject to the terms of any applicable collective agreement and their contract of employment, carry out those duties that -

        (i) in the case of teachers, are assigned to them by or at the direction of the Principal, and

        (ii) in the case of the Principal, are assigned to him or her by the board.

23. The Principal

(1) A board shall, in accordance with procedures agreed from time to time between the Minister, the patron, recognised school management organisations and any recognised trade union or staff association representing teachers, appoint to the school in a whole-time capacity a person to be Principal of that school subject to such terms and conditions as may be determined from time to time by the Minister with the consent of the Minister for Finance.

(2) In addition to the functions of a Principal provided for in section 22, the Principal shall -

(a) be responsible for the day-to-day management of the school, including guidance and direction of the teachers and other staff of the school, and be accountable to the board for that management,

(b) provide leadership to the teachers and other staff and the students of the school,

(c) be responsible for the creation, together with the board, parents of students and the teachers, of a school environment which is supportive of learning among the students and which promotes the professional development of the teachers,

(d) under the direction of the board and, in consultation with the teachers, the parents and, to the extent appropriate to their age and experience, the students, set objectives for the school and monitor the achievement of those objectives, and

(e) encourage the involvement of parents of students in the school in the education of those students and in the achievement of the objectives of the school.

(3) For the purpose of carrying out his or her functions under this Act, a Principal shall have all such powers as are necessary or expedient in that regard. and shall carry out his or her functions in accordance with such policies as may be determined from time to time by the board and regulations made in accordance with section 33.

(4) The Principal shall be entitled to he a member of any and every committee appointed by a board.

(5) Where, at the commencement of this section, the employer of the Principal in a post-primary school is a person or body of persons other than the board of the school then subsection (1) shall apply as if the person who or the body which. at such commencement and from time to time thereafter, is such empower, is substituted for the board as therein referred to.

(6) Wherever practicable, the Principal shall, in exercising his or her functions under this section, consult with teachers and other staff of the school.

24. Provisions relating to staff

(1) Subject to this section, a board may appoint such and so many persons as teachers and other staff of a school as the board from time to time thinks necessary for the performance of its powers and functions under this Act.

(2) The numbers and qualifications of teachers and other staff of a school, who are to be paid from monies provided by the Oireachtas, shall be subject to the approval of the Minister, with the concurrence of the Minister for Finance.

(3) A board shall appoint teachers and other staff, who are to be paid from monies provided by the Oireachtas, and may suspend or dismiss such teachers and staff, in accordance with procedures agreed from time to time between the Minister, the patron, recognised school management organisations and any recognised trade union and staff association representing teachers or other staff as appropriate.

(4) Pending the agreement of procedures provided for in subsection (3), the procedures applied in the appointment, suspension and dismissal of teachers or other staff immediately before the commencement of this section shall, after such commencement, continue to be applied.

(5) The terms and conditions of employment of teachers and other staff of a school appointed by a board and who are to be paid from monies provided by the Oireachtas shall be determined by the Minister, with the concurrence of the Minister for Finance.

(6) Where all or part of the remuneration and superannuation of teachers and other staff of a school is paid or is to be paid from monies provided by the Oireachtas, such remuneration or superannuation shall be determined from time to time by the Minister, with the concurrence of the Minister for Finance.

(7) Where, at the commencement of this section the employer of the teachers or other staff in a post-primary school is a person or body of persons other than the board of the school, then subsections (1), (3) and (5) shall apply as if the person who or the body which, at such commencement and from time to time thereafter, is such employer, is substituted for the board as therein referred to.

(8) Except in the case of an agreement as provided for in subsection (3), nothing in this Act shall have the effect of altering, after the commencement of this Act, the terms and conditions of teachers and other staff of a school under which they were employed before such commencement.

(9) This section shall not apply to teachers or other staff of a school which is established or maintained by a vocational education committee.

Part VI

Miscellaneous

25. School year, week day

The Minister may from time to time, following consultation with patrons, national associations of parents, recognised school management organisations and recognised trade unions and staff associations representing teachers, prescribe -

(a) the minimum number of days in a school year during which a school shall be open to receive students and provide them with instruction,

(b) the minimum number of hours of instruction in a school day or in a school week, and

(c) any matters related to the length of the school year, the school week or the school day and the organisation and structure of such year, week or day.

26. Parents' association

(1) The parents of students of a recognised school may establish, and maintain from among their number, a parents' association for that school and membership of that association shall be open to all parents of students of that school.

(2) A parents' association shall promote the interests of the students in a school in co-operation with the board, Principal, teachers and students of a school and for that purpose may

(a) advise the Principal or the board on any matter relating to the school and the Principal or board, as the case may be, shall have regard to any such advice, and

(b) adopt a programme of activities which will promote the involvement of parents, in consultation with the Principal, in the operation of the school.

(3) The board shall promote contact between the school, parents of students in that school and the community and shall facilitate and give all reasonable assistance to parents who wish to establish a parents' association and to a parents' association when it is established.

(4) (a) A parents' association shall, following consultation with its members, make rules governing its meetings and the business and conduct of its affairs.

(b) Where a parents' association is affiliated to a national association of parents, the rules referred to in paragraph (a) shall be in accordance with guidelines issued by that national association of parents with the concurrence of the Minister.

27. Information to students and student council

(1) A board shall establish and maintain procedures for the purposes of informing students in a school of the activities of the school.

(2) The procedures established and maintained under subsection (1) shall facilitate the involvement of the students in the operation of the school, having regard to the age and experience of the students, in association with their parents and teachers.

(3) Students of a post-primary school may establish a student council and, without prejudice to the generality of subsection (1), a board of a post-primary school shall encourage the establishment by students of a student council and shall facilitate and give all reasonable assistance to -

(a) students who wish to establish a student council, and

(b) student councils when they have been established.

(4) A student council shall promote the interests of the school and the involvement of students in the affairs of the school, in co-operation with the board, parents and teachers.

(5) The rules for the establishment of a student council shall be drawn up by the board, in accordance with such guidelines as may be issued by the Minister from time to time, and such rules may provide for the election of members and the dissolution of a student council.

(6) A student council, following consultation with the board, may make rules governing its meetings and the business and conduct of its affairs.

28. Grievance and other procedures

(1) The Minister, following consultation with patrons of recognised schools, national associations of parents, recognised school management organisations and recognised trade unions and staff associations representing teachers, may from time to time prescribe procedures in accordance with which -

(a) the parent of a student or, in the case of a student who has reached the age of 18 years, the student, may appeal to the board against a decision of a teacher or other member of staff of a school,

(b) grievances of students, or their parents, relating to the students' school (other than those which may be dealt with under paragraph (a) or section 29), shall be heard. and

(c) appropriate remedial action shall, where necessary, be taken as a consequence of an appeal or in response to a grievance.

(2) In prescribing procedures for the purposes of this section the Minister shall have regard to the desirability of determining appeals and resolving grievances in the school concerned.

29. Appeals to Secretary General

(1) Where a board or a person acting on behalf of the board -

(a) permanently excludes a student from a school, or

(b) suspends a student from attendance at a school for a period to be prescribed for the purpose of this paragraph, or

(c) refuses to enroll a student in a school, or

(d) makes a decision of a class which the Minister, following consultation with patrons, national associations of parents, recognised school management organisations, recognised trade unions and staff associations representing teachers, may from time to time determine may he appealed in accordance with this section,

the parent of the student, or in the case of a student who has reached the age of 18 years, the student, may, within a reasonable time from the date that the parent or student was informed of the decision and following the conclusion of any appeal procedures provided by the school or the patron, in accordance with section 28, appeal that decision to the Secretary General of the Department of Education and Science and that appeal shall be heard by a committee appointed under subsection (2).

(2) For the purposes of the hearing and determination of an appeal under this section, the Minister shall appoint one or more than one committee (in this section referred to as an "appeals committee") each of which shall include in its membership an Inspector and such other persons as the Minister considers appropriate.

(3) Where a committee is appointed under subsection (2) the Minister shall appoint one of its number to be the chairperson of that committee and who, in the case of an equal division of votes, shall have a second or casting vote.

(4) In hearing and determining an appeal under this section an appeals committee shall act in accordance with such procedures as may be determined from time to time by the Minister following consultation with patrons, national associations of parents, recognised school management organisations and recognised trade unions and staff associations representing teachers and such procedures shall ensure that -

(a) the parties to the appeal are assisted to reach agreement on the matters the subject of the appeal where the appeals committee is of the opinion that reaching such agreement is practicable in the circumstances.

(b) hearings are conducted with the minimum of formality consistent with giving all parties a fair hearing, and

(c) appeals are dealt with within a period of 30 days from the date of the receipt of the appeal by the Secretary General, except where, on the application in writing of the appeals committee stating the reasons for a delay in determining the appeal, the Secretary General consents in writing to extend the period by not more than 14 days.

(5) On the determination of an appeal made under this section, the appeals committee shall send notice in writing of its determination of the appeal and the reasons for that determination to the Secretary General.

(6) Where -

(a) an appeals committee upholds a complaint in whole or in part, and

(b) it appears to the appeals committee that any matter which was the subject of the complaint (so far as upheld) should be remedied,

the appeals committee shall make recommendations to the Secretary General as to the action to be taken.

(7) As soon as practicable after the receipt by the Secretary General of the notice referred to in subsection (5), the Secretary General -

   (a)   shall, by notice in writing, inform the person who made the appeal and the board of the determination of the appeals committee and the reasons therefor, and

   (b)   in a case to which subsection (6) applies, may in such notice give such directions to the board as appear to the Secretary General (having regard to any recommendations made by the appeals committee) to be expedient for the purpose of remedying the matter which was the subject of the appeal and the board shall act in accordance with such directions.

(8) The Minister, in consultation with patrons of schools, national associations of parents, recognised school management organisations and recognised trade unions and staff associations representing teachers, shall from time to time review the operation of this section and section 28 and the first such review shall take place not more than two years from the commencement of this section.

(9) In the case of a school which is established or maintained by a vocational education committee an appeal against a decision of the board of such school shall lie, in the first instance, to the vocational education committee and thereafter to the Secretary General in accordance with subsection (1).

(10) The Minister shall, from time to time, following consultation with vocational education committees, national associations of parents and recognised trade unions and staff associations representing teachers, prescribe -

   (a)   the procedures for appeals under this section to vocational education committees. and

   (b)   which appeals shall inquire into whether the procedure adopted by a board in reaching a decision or conducting an appeal was fair and reasonable and which appeals shall be by way of a full rehearing.

(11) The Secretary General may, in accordance with sections 4(1)(i) and 9 of the Public Service Management Act, 1997, assign the responsibility for the performance of the functions for which the Secretary General is responsible under this section to another officer of the Department of Education and Science.

(12) For the purposes of subsection (1)(c), "student" means a person who applies for enrolment at a school and that person or his or her parents may appeal against a refusal to enroll him or her in the same manner as a student or his or her parents may appeal a decision under this section.

30. Curriculum

(1) The Minister may, from time to time, following such consultation with patrons of schools, national associations of parents, recognised school management organisations and recognised trade unions and staff associations representing teachers, as the Minister considers appropriate, prescribe the curriculum for recognised schools, namely -

   (a)   the subjects to be offered in recognised schools,

   (b)   the syllabus of each subject,

   (c)   the amount of instruction time to be allotted to each subject, and

   (d)   the guidance and counselling provision to be offered in schools.

(2) Without prejudice to the generality of subsection (1), the Minister -

   (a)   shall have regard to the desirability of assisting schools to exercise their powers as provided for under subsection (4),

(b) shall have regard to the characteristic spirit of a school or class of school in exercising his or her functions under this section,

(c) may give directions to schools, where he or she considers it appropriate, to ensure that the subjects and syllabuses pursued in those schools are appropriate and relevant to the educational and vocational needs of the students in those schools.

(d) shall ensure that the amount of instruction time to be allotted to subjects on the curriculum as determined by the Minister in each school day shall be such as to allow for such reasonable instruction time, as the board with the consent of the patron determines, for subjects relating to or arising from the characteristic spirit of the school, and

(e) shall not require any student to attend instruction in any subject which is contrary to the conscience of the parent of the student or in the case of a student who has reached the age of 18 years, the student.

(3) The Minister may -

(a) consult with the National Council for Curriculum and Assessment and such other persons or bodies of persons as the Minister considers appropriate on any matter relating to the curriculum for recognised schools, and

(b) establish, as the Minister considers appropriate, such bodies of persons to conduct research and to advise him or her on matters relating to his or her duties under this section.

(4) A school, may, subject to the requirement that the curriculum as determined by the Minister is taught in that school, provide courses of instruction in such other subjects as the board considers appropriate.

31. Teaching through Irish

(1) The Minister shall establish a body of persons -

(a) (i) to plan and co-ordinate the provision of textbooks and aids to learning and teaching through Irish.

(ii) to advise the Minister on policies relating to the provision and promotion of education through the medium of Irish in recognised schools generally and in schools located in a Gaeltacht area.

(iii) to provide support services to those schools through the medium of Irish, and

(iv) to conduct research into any or all matters to which this paragraph applies, and

(b) to plan and co-ordinate the provision of textbooks and aids to the learning and teaching of Irish and to conduct research into and to advise the Minister on strategies which have as their objective the enhancement of the effectiveness in the teaching of Irish in recognised schools and centres for education.

(2) The Minister may by order, made with the consent of the Minister for Finance, delegate any of his or her functions in respect of the matters referred to in subsection (1) to the body established in accordance with that subsection which shall carry out those functions under the direction and control of the Minister.

(3) The body established in accordance with subsection (1) -

(a) shall, with the consent of the Minister, establish a committee to assist it in the performance of the functions conferred on it under subsection (1)(b), and

(b) may, with the consent of the Minister, at any time dissolve a committee appointed under this subsection or remove a member of a committee from such membership.

(4) The body established in accordance with subsection (1) shall, from time to time, as it considers appropriate, advise the National Council for Curriculum and Assessment on matters relating to -

(a) the teaching of Irish,

(b) the provision of education through the medium of Irish, including matters relating to the curriculum for primary and post-primary schools which provide education through the medium of Irish and assessment procedures employed in those schools, and

(c) the educational needs of people living in a Gaeltacht area,

and the National Council for Curriculum and Assessment shall have regard to any such advice in the exercise by it of its functions.

(5) The Minister may by order amend or revoke any order made under this section, including an order made under this subsection.

(6) In each financial year the Minister, with the concurrence of the Minister for Finance, out of monies provided by the Oireachtas, may make to the body appointed in accordance with subsection (1) a grant or grants for the purposes of expenditure by that body in the performance of its functions.

(7) The Minister may provide such secretarial and administrative support to a body established under this section as the Minister considers necessary.

32. Educational disadvantage

(1) The Minister shall by order, following consultation with patrons, national associations of parents, recognised school management organisations, recognised trade unions and staff associations representing teachers and such other persons as the Minister considers appropriate, establish a committee, hereinafter referred to as the "educational disadvantage committee", to advise him or her on policies and strategies to be adopted to identify and correct educational disadvantage.

(2) Subject to subsection (3), the Minister shall appoint persons to be members of an educational disadvantage committee for such period not exceeding three years as he or she thinks fit and may renew such appointments as he or she thinks fit.

(3) Up to half of the membership of the educational disadvantage committee shall be appointed from nominees of such voluntary and other bodies which have objects which the Minister considers relevant to the work of the committee.

(4) The Minister may by order amend or revoke any order made under this section, including an order made under this subsection.

(5) The educational disadvantage committee may, as soon as is practicable after it has been established and, thereafter, from time to time as it considers appropriate, prepare and submit to the Minister a statement containing -

(a) proposed policies and strategies for the identification and correction of educational disadvantage, relating to such period as it considers appropriate, and

(b) the areas of activity to which the committee accords priority.

514

(6) In preparing a statement as provided for in subsection (5), the educational disadvantage committee shall have regard to -

(a) the resources, including the financial resources, available, and

(b) the public interest in ensuring that the resources available are applied in an effective and efficient manner.

(7) In each financial year the Minister, with the concurrence of the Minister for Finance. out of monies provided by the Oireachtas, may make to the educational disadvantage committee a grant or grants for the purposes of expenditure by that committee in the performance of its functions.

(8) The Minister may provide such secretarial and administrative support to the educational disadvantage committee as the Minister considers necessary.

(9) In this section "educational disadvantage" means the impediments to education arising from social or economic disadvantage which prevent students from deriving appropriate benefit from education in schools.

33. Regulations

The Minister, following consultation with patrons, national associations of parents, recognised school management organisations and recognised trade unions and staff associations representing teachers. may make regulations for the purpose of girths effect to this Act and, without prejudice to the generality of the forgoing, the Minister may make regulations relating to all or any of the following matters:

(a) the recognition of schools and the withdrawal of recognition from schools;

(b) the making of grants by the Minister to schools and centres for education;

(c) the appointment and qualifications of persons who are to be employed as teachers in schools or centres for education;

(d) the inspection of schools;

(e) the building, maintenance and equipment of schools;

(f) the length of the school year, school week and school day;

(g) admission of students to schools;

(h) access to schools by school attendance officers and other persons;

(i) access to schools and centres for education by students with disabilities or who have other special educational needs, including matters relating to reasonable accommodation and technical aid and equipment for such students;

(j) procedures for the promotion of effective liaison and co-operation by schools and centres for education with -

    (i) other schools and centres for education,

    (ii) local authorities (within the meaning of the Local Government Act, 1941),

    (iii) health boards (within the meaning of the Health Act, 1970), and

    (iv) voluntary and other bodies which have a special interest in education. in particular, education of students with special educational needs:

(k) appeals, and

(l) the curriculum of schools.

34. Financial year

In this Act "financial year" means such period of 12 months as may be prescribed by the Minister.

35. Amendment of Intermediate Education (Ireland) Act 1878

(1) Section 5 of the Intermediate Education (Ireland) Act, 1878, is hereby amended in subsection (4) by the deletion of "; provided that no examination shall be held in Any subject of religious instruction. nor any payment made in respect thereof".

(2) Without prejudice to the application of the Intermediate Education (Ireland) Act, 1878, to both male and female students, section 6 of that Act is hereby amended by the repeal of subsection (4).

36. Amendment of Vocation Education Act, 1990

The Vocational Education Act, 1930, is hereby amended -

 (a) in section 105(1) by the substitution of "a person" for "an officer of the Minister", and

 (b) in sections 106 and 107 by the substitution of "a person" for "an officer" wherever it occurs.

37. Education support centres

(1) In this section "education support centre" means a place in which services are provided for schools, teachers, parents, boards and other relevant persons which support them in carrying out their functions in respect of the provision of education which is recognised for that purpose by the Minister in accordance with subsection (2).

(2) The Minister may recognise a place as an education support centre and where the Minister so recognises a place he or she shall cause the name and address of that centre to be entered in a register maintained by the Minister and available for inspection by members of the public during normal working hours.

(3) An education support centre shall have a management committee, to manage the business and staff of that centre.

(4) A committee established in accordance with subsection (3) shall be a body corporate with perpetual succession and with power to sue and may be sued in its corporate name and no action shall lie against a member of a board in respect of anything done by that member in good faith and in pursuance of their functions as such members.

(5) The Minister may withdraw recognition from an education support centre.

(6) The Minister may, from time to time, make regulations relating to all or any of the following matters:

 (a) procedures for the appointment of management committees;

 (b) the appointment and remuneration of staff;

 (c) the making of grants to education support centres;

 (d) the provision of information to the Minister on any matter relating to the operation of education support centres;

 (e) access to an education support centre and to the financial and other records of that education support centre by persons appointed by the Minister; and

 (f) such other matters relating to the operation of such centres as the Minister considers appropriate.

Part VII

NATIONAL COUNCIL FOR CURRICULUM AND ASSESSMENT

38. Establishment day

The Minister shall by order appoint a day to be the establishment day for the purpose, of this Part.

39. Establishment of National Council for Curriculum and Assessment

(1) There shall stand established on the establishment day a body to be known as the National Council for Curriculum and Assessment, or in the Irish language An Chomhairie Náisiúnta Curaclaim agus Measúnachta (in this Act referred to as "the Council") to perform the functions assigned to it by or under this Act.

(2) The Council shall be a body corporate with perpetual succession and an official seal and shall have power to sue and may be sued in its corporate name and, with the consent of the Minister to acquire, hold and dispose of land or an interest in land and to acquire, hold and dispose of other property.

(3) Schedule 1 shall apply to the Council.

40. Composition and appointment

(1) The composition of the Council shall be determined by order, made by the Minister following consultation with patrons, national associations of parents, recognised school management organisations, recognised trade unions and staff associations representing teachers and with such other persons or bodies of persons as the Minister considers appropriate.

(2) In determining the composition of the Council, the Minister shall ensure that, as far as is practicable, the membership of the Council -

- (a) is representative of bodies and persons involved in the education system at early childhood and primary and post-primary levels, in particular national associations of parents, recognised school management organisations and recognised trade unions and staff associations representing teachers, and

- (b) includes other persons who

  - (i) have experience or skills, including experience of and skills in business and industry, which in the opinion of the Minister are relevant to the work of the Council and would complement the experience and skills of the persons appointed in accordance with paragraph (a),

  - (ii) have a special interest in, or experience of, the education of students with a disability or other special educational needs, or

  - (iii) are representative of Irish language organisations,

  as the Minister considers appropriate.

(3) The Minister may by order, amend or revoke an order made under this section, including an order made under this subsection.

(4) The members of the Council shall be appointed by the Minister in accordance with regulations drawn up by the Minister following consultation with patrons, national associations of parents, recognised school management organisations, recognised trade

unions and staff associations representing teachers and with such other persons or bodies of persons as the Minister considers appropriate.

41. Objects and functions

(1) The object of the Council shall be to advise the Minister on matters relating to -

    (a) the curriculum for early childhood education, primary and post-primary schools, and

    (b) the assessment procedures employed in schools and examinations on subjects which are part of the curriculum.

(2) Without prejudice to the generality of subsection (1), it shall be a function of the Council:

    (a) from time to time to review the curriculum, or any part of the curriculum, for schools and the syllabuses taught and to advise the Minister;

    (b) to advise the Minister on appropriate methods for the assessment of the effectiveness of the education provided in schools, with particular regard to mechanisms whereby students who have problems achieving their potential may be identified as early as practicable and assisted;

    (c) to advise the Minister on strategies which will assist students to make a successful transition from primary school to post-primary school;

    (d) from time to time to advise the Minister on the standards of knowledge and skills which students at various age levels should attain and on the mechanisms for assessing the achievement of such standards, having regard to national and international standards and good practice in relation to such assessment;

    (e) from time to time to review the in-service training needs of teachers, including needs arising from the introduction of new curricula, subjects or syllabuses in schools, and to advise the Minister in relation to those needs;

    (f) to advise the Minister on the requirements, as regards curriculum and syllabuses, of students with a disability or other special educational needs;

    (g) to advise the Minister on strategies which have as their objective the enhancement of the effectiveness in the teaching and use of the Irish language in schools;

    (h) to maintain manage, administer and invest all the money and assets of the Council;

    (i) to promote research and development in education and to conduct or commission such research and development where appropriate to its objects and functions;

    (j) to promote equality of access to education generally and to instruction in any particular subjects between male and female students;

    (k) to accept gifts of money, land or other property upon such trusts and conditions, if any, as may be specified by the donors, provided that nothing in any trust or condition is contrary to this Act, and

    (l) to do all such acts and things as may be necessary to further the objects of the Council, including such functions in relation to review and reform of the curriculum in schools and the assessment of the outcomes of the education provided in schools as the Minister shall from time to time direct.

(3) In carrying out its functions the Council shall -

    (a) have regard to the implications of its advice for the resources, including financial resources, available and shall quantify, as far as practicable, the resources necessary to give effect to any of its proposals,

(b) have regard to the desirability of achieving equality of access to, participation in and benefit from education,

(c) act in accordance with such directions as may from time to time be given to the Council by the Minister, including directions as to the priority to be accorded to the exercise by it of its different functions, and

(d) have regard to the practicalities of implementation of any advice which it proposes to give to the Minister.

42. Consultation with designated bodies

(1) The Minister may, for the purposes of this section, by order designate persons who, or organisations which, have a special interest in the exercise by the Council of its functions and the persons or organisations so designated are hereinafter referred to as "designated bodies".

(2) The Council shall, from time to time as it considers appropriate, consult with designated bodies and shall consult with such bodies when requested to do so by the Minister.

(3) A designated body may at any time, as it considers appropriate, make representations to the Council on any matter relating to the functions of the Council and the Council shall consider such representations and shall inform the designated body of the outcome of that consideration.

(4) The Council shall give to each designated body a copy of each publication issued by it as soon as may be after it has been issued.

43. Chief executive officer

(1) The Minister shall, from time to time, appoint to the Council in a whole-time capacity a chief executive officer who shall carry on, manage and generally control the administration of the Council and shall manage and control the staff of the Council.

(2) The person who, immediately before the day on which the chief executive officer is appointed under subsection (1), holds the office of chief executive officer of the body of persons known as National Council for Curriculum and Assessment, being an unincorporated and non-statutory body of persons appointed by the Minister shall, if he or she so consents, be appointed as the first chief executive officer of the Council.

(3) The chief executive officer shall he employed by the Minister in accordance with such terms and conditions, which may include secondment from another office or employment, and receive such remuneration as the Minister, with the consent of the Minister for Finance, from time to time determines.

44. Staff

(1) The Minister, with the consent of the Minister for Finance, may appoint such and so many persons to assist the Council in the performance of its functions as the Minister considers appropriate.

(2) The persons appointed in accordance with subsection (1) shall be employed in accordance with such terms and conditions, which may include secondment from another office or employment, and receive such remuneration as the Minister, with the consent of the Minister for Finance, from time to time determines.

(3) The Minister may provide such administrative and secretarial support to the Council as he or she considers necessary.

(4) The Civil Service Commissioners Act, 1956, and the Civil Service Regulation Acts, 1956 to 1996, shall apply to full-time, permanent employees of the Council.

45. Grants

In each financial year the Minister, with the concurrence of the Minister for Finance, out of monies provided by the Oireachtas, may make to the Council a grant or grants for the purposes of expenditure by the Council in the performance of its functions.

46. Accounts and information

(1) The Council shall keep, in such form as may be approved of by the Minister, with the concurrence of the Minister for Finance, all proper and usual accounts and records of all monies received or expenditure incurred by it and, in particular, shall keep in such form as aforesaid such special accounts and records as the Minister may, with the concurrence of the Minister for Finance, from time to time direct.

(2) Accounts kept in pursuance of this section shall be submitted annually by the Council to the Comptroller and Auditor General for audit on a date not later than the thirtieth day of April in the year following the year to which the accounts relate, or on such other date as the Minister may from time to time determine, and, immediately after the audit, a copy of the accounts and of such other accounts, if any, as the Minister has directed to be kept, together with a copy of the report of the Comptroller and Auditor General on the accounts shall be presented by the Council to the Minister.

(3) The Minister shall cause copies of the accounts presented to him or her under this section by the Council, together with copies of the report of the Comptroller and Auditor General thereon, to be laid before each House of the Oireachtas.

(4) The Council shall provide the Minister with such information regarding the performance of its functions as the Minister may from time to time require.

47. Committees

The Council may -

    (a)   establish committees, consisting either wholly or partly of persons who are members of the Council, to assist it in the performance of its functions,

    (b)   delegate to a committee appointed under this section any of its functions that may be better or more conveniently performed by a committee, and

    (c)   at any time dissolve a committee appointed under this section or remove a member of a committee from such membership.

48. Annual Report

As soon as may be after the end of each year, the Council shall prepare and submit to the Minister, in such form as may be determined by the Minister, a report on the performance of the Council in that year.

Part VIII

EXAMINATIONS

49. Interpretation

In this Part -

"candidate" means a person who, in accordance with procedures determined from time to time by the Minister, is registered to present himself or herself for an examination;

"examiner" means a person who is employed by the Minister for the purpose of

(a) the preparation of examination papers or other examination materials,

(b) the marking of such papers or other such materials, or

(c) the carrying out of any other functions in respect of the conduct of examinations;

"examination" means an examination relating to post-primary, adult and vocational education and vocational training as may from time to time be conducted in accordance with procedures determined by the Minister or by a body of persons established by the Minister and to which this Part applies in accordance with section 50;

"examination paper" includes any paper, plan, map, drawing, diagram, pictorial or graphic work or other document and any photograph, film or recording (whether of sound or images or both) -

(a) in which questions are set for answer by candidates as part of an examination or which are related to such questions, or

(b) in which projects or practical exercises are set which candidates are required to complete as part of an examination or which are related to such projects or exercises.

50. Examinations

(1) This Part shall apply to the examinations set out in Schedule 2.

(2) In addition to the examinations set out in Schedule 2, the Minister may from time to time prescribe such other examinations as he or she considers appropriate to which this Part shall apply.

51. Regulations

(1) The Minister may make regulations as he or she from time to time considers appropriate for the effective conduct of examinations and in particular, without prejudice to the generality of the aforesaid may make regulations relating to

(a) the preparation of an examination paper and other examination materials.

(b) procedures at places where examinations are conducted, including the supervision of examinations,

(c) the marking of work presented for examination.

(d) the issuing of results of examinations,

(e) the charging and collection of fees for examinations,

(f) the terms under which candidates may appeal against the results of an examination and the procedure for such appeals,

(g) the penalties to be imposed on a person who acts in breach of regulations made by the Minister or who otherwise misconducts himself or herself in respect of an examination, and

(h) the designation of places where examinations may be held.

(2) The Minister may from time to time appoint a person or a body of persons to advise him or her on any matter relating to the examinations or to supervise or review any part of the conduct of the examinations, including appeals by candidates against the results of examinations.

52. Offences

(1) A person who -

(a) knowingly and without lawful authority publishes an examination paper or part of such paper to any other person prior to the holding of the examination concerned,

(b) has in his or her possession without lawful authority an examination paper or part of such paper prior to the holding of the examination concerned,

(c) carries out any duties relating to the preparation of examination papers and knowingly and without lawful authority provides a candidate for an examination or any other person with information concerning the material prepared by him or her in the course of those duties with the intention of conferring an advantage upon a candidate over other candidates,

(d) knowingly and wilfully credits a candidate with higher marks than the marks to which that candidate was entitled with the intention of conferring an advantage on that candidate over other candidates,

(e) knowingly and maliciously credits a candidate with lower marks than the marks to which that candidate was entitled,

(f) personates a candidate at an examination or knowingly allows or assists a person to personate a candidate at an examination,

(g) knowingly and maliciously destroys or damages any material relating to an examination,

(h) knowingly and maliciously obstructs any candidate or a person engaged in the conduct of an examination or otherwise interferes with the general conduct of an examination,

(i) knowingly and without lawful authority alters any certificate or any other record, including a record in machine-readable form, containing the results of an examination, or

(j) knowingly issues or makes use of any certificate or other document which purports to be a document issued by the person or body under whose authority the examination was conducted and to contain the results of an examination knowing that those results are false,

shall be guilty of an offence.

(2) A person who knowingly aids, abets, counsels or procures another person to commit any offence under subsection (1) or conspires with another person for the commission of any such offence shall be guilty of an offence.

(3) A person who is guilty of an offence under this section shall be liable -

(a) on summary conviction, to a fine not exceeding £1,500 or (at the discretion of the court) to imprisonment for a term not exceeding six months, or to both such fine and such imprisonment, or

(b) on conviction on indictment, to a fine not exceeding £5,000 or (at the discretion of the court) to imprisonment for a term not exceeding two years, or to both such fine and such imprisonment.

(4) No action shall lie against an examiner in respect of anything done by him or her in good faith and in pursuance of his or her functions as an examiner.

53. Refusal of access to certain information

Notwithstanding any other enactment the Minister may -

(a) refuse access to any information which would enable the compilation of information (that is not otherwise available to the general public) in relation to the comparative performance of schools in respect of the academic achievement of students enrolled therein, including, without prejudice to the generality of the foregoing -

    (i) the overall results in any year of students in a particular school in an examination, or

    (ii) the comparative overall results in any year of students in different schools in an examination,

and

(b) refuse access to information relating to the identity of examiners.

Part IX

BODIES CORPORATE

54. Establishment of bodies to provide services related to education

(1) The Minister, with the concurrence of the Government, may from time to time by order (in this Act referred to as an "establishment order") establish a body to perform, subject to subsection (2), functions in or in relation to the provision of support services.

(2) The performance of functions by a body established under subsection (1) shall be subject to the determination of matters of policy by the Minister.

(3) A body established under subsection (1) shall be known by such title as may be specified in the establishment order.

(4) A body so established shall be a body corporate with perpetual succession and a seal and with power to sue and be sued in its corporate name and to hold land.

(5) The Minister may from time to time by order amend an establishment order or an order made under this subsection.

(6) The person appointed as principal officer of a body established under subsection (1) shall be accountable to the Minister in carrying out the functions referred to in that subsection.

(7) Before making an order under this section the Minister shall consult, as the Minister considers appropriate, with persons directly affected by the proposed order or with trade unions or associations representing such persons.

(8) Notwithstanding section 5, the Minister shall not make an order under this section unless he or she has first caused to be laid before each House of the Oireachtas a draft of the proposed order and a resolution approving of the draft has been passed by both Houses.

55. Membership and staff

(1) Every establishment order shall contain such provisions as the Minister considers appropriate in relation to -

(a) the number of members of the body established by the order, the method, terms and conditions of their appointment and their tenure of office, and

(b) the number, grades, qualifications, method of appointment (including secondment), conditions of service, tenure of office and the remuneration and superannuation of the persons employed in or by the body so established.

(2) A person seconded or transferred to a body established under section 54, shall not, while in the service of that body, receive less remuneration or be subject to less beneficial conditions of service than the remuneration to which that person was entitled and the conditions of service to which that person was subject prior to such secondment or transfer.

56. Functions

An establishment order shall contain such provisions as the Minister considers appropriate defining the functions of the body established by the order and the manner in which and the conditions under which the body so established may perform the functions so defined.

57. Administration

An establishment order shall contain such provisions relating to the administration generally of the body established by the order as the Minister considers appropriate including provisions relating to -

    (a) the meetings of the body so established and the procedure at such meetings,

    (b) the use and authentication of its seal,

    (c) the regulation of its finances and the keeping and auditing of its accounts, and

    (d) the furnishing to the Minister by such body from time to time of information regarding the performance of its functions, and the furnishing of such information to the Minister at any time at his or her request.

58. Grants

In each financial year the Minister, with the concurrence of the Minister for Finance, out of monies provided by the Oireachtas, may make to a body appointed under section 54 a grant for the purposes of expenditure by that body in the performance of its functions.

59. Revocation of establishment order

(1) The Minister may at any time by order revoke an establishment order.

(2) A revoking order shall contain such provisions as the Minister thinks necessary or expedient consequential on the revocation, and, in particular, may make provision for -

    (a) the dissolution of the body established by the establishment order and the transfer or distribution of the property, rights and liabilities thereof to any of the following -

        (i) the Minister, or

        (ii) any one or more than one other body established by an establishment order,

    (b) the preservation of continuing contracts made by the dissolved body,

    (c) the continuance of pending legal proceedings,

    (d) notwithstanding any restriction in any other Act, the transfer of the holder of any office under the dissolved body to -

        (i) the Department of Education and Science, or

        (ii) any other body established by an establishment order.

SCHEDULE 1
Section 39

THE COUNCIL

1. (1) As soon as may be after its establishment the Council shall acquire and retain in its possession a seal.

(2) The seal of the Council shall be authenticated by the signature of the chairperson or a member of the Council authorised by the Council to act in that behalf and by the signature of an officer of the Council authorised to act in that behalf.

(3) Judicial notice shall be taken of the seal of the Council and every document purporting to be an instrument made by the Council and to be sealed with the seal (purporting to be authenticated in accordance with this Schedule) of the Council shall be received in evidence and shall be deemed to be such instrument without proof unless the contrary is shown.

2. (1) The Minister shall appoint the chairperson of the Council.

(2) The chairperson may, at any time, resign from office as chairperson by letter addressed to the Minister and the resignation shall take effect from the date on which the letter is received.

3. The term of office of a member (including the chairperson) shall not be greater than five years.

4. (1) If a member of the Council dies, resigns, becomes disqualified, is removed from office or for any other reason ceases to hold office, the Minister may appoint a person to be a member of the Council to fill the casual vacancy so occasioned and the person so appointed shall be appointed in the same manner as the member of the Council who occasioned the casual vacancy.

(2) A person appointed to be a member of the Council in accordance with this paragraph shall hold office for the remainder of the term of office of the member who occasioned the casual vacancy he or she is appointed to fill and shall be eligible for re-appointments a member of the Council.

5. (1) The Minister may, at any time, remove a member of the Council from office if he or she has committed stated misbehaviour or if his or her removal appears necessary to the Minister for the effective performance by the Council of its functions.

(2) The Minister may, at any time for reasons stated in writing to the members of the Council, remove all such members from office.

(3) A member may, at any time, resign from office as such member by letter addressed to the Minister and the resignation shall take effect from the date on which the letter is received.

(4) A member of the Council who is absent from all meetings of the Council for a period of six consecutive months, unless such absence was due to illness or was approved by the Council, shall be disqualified at the expiry of such period from continuing to be a member of the Council for the remainder of that person's term of office.

(5) A member (including the chairperson) whose term of Office expires by effluxion of time shall be eligible for re-appointment.

6. (1) The Council shall, from time to time as occasion requires, appoint from amongst its members (other than the chairperson) two members to be deputy-chairpersons of the Council

(2) A deputy-chairperson of the Council shall, unless that member sooner resigns, hold office until the expiration of that member's period of office as a member of the Council.

7. (1) Where a member of the Council (including the chairperson) -

    (a) accepts nomination as a member of Seanad Éireann, or

    (b) is elected as a member of either House of the Oireachtas or as a representative in the European Parliament, or

    (c) is regarded pursuant to Part XIII of the Second Schedule to the European Parliament Elections Act, 1997, as having been elected to the European Parliament to fill a vacancy, or

    (d) is adjudged bankrupt or makes, under the protection or procedure of a court a composition or arrangement with creditors, or

    (e) is sentenced to a term of imprisonment by a court of competent jurisdiction,

that member shall thereupon cease to be a member of the Council.

(2) A person shall not be eligible to be a member of the Council if that person -

    (a) is for the time being entitled under the Standing Orders of either House of the Oireachtas to sit therein, or

    (b) is for the time being a member of the European Parliament, or

    (c) is an undischarged bankrupt, or

    (d) within the immediately preceding three years has, under the protection or procedure of a court, made a composition or arrangement with creditors, or

    (e) within the immediately preceding five years, has been sentenced to a term of imprisonment by a court of competent jurisdiction.

8. A member of the Council including the chairperson who has -

    (a) any interest in any company or concern with which the Council proposes to make any contract, or

    (b) any interest in any contract which the Council proposes to make,

shall disclose to the Council the fact of the interest and the nature thereof and shall take no part in any deliberation or decision of the Council relating to the contract, and the disclosure shall be recorded in the minutes of the Council.

9. The chairperson and members of the Council shall be paid, out of funds at the disposal of the Council, such allowances for expenses as the Minister, with the approval of the Minister for Finance, may decide.

10.(l) The Council shall hold such and so many meetings and at such time as the chairperson deems necessary.

(2) A chairperson shall convene a meeting of the Council whenever requested to do so by not less than six members.

(3) The quorum for a meeting of the Council shall be one third of the total number of members, rounded up to the next whole number, plus one.

11. At a meeting of the Council

    (a) the chairperson shall, if present, be the chairperson of the meeting,

    (b) if and so long as the chairperson is not present or if the office of chairperson is vacant, the deputy-chairperson who is present or if both deputy-chairpersons are present the deputy-chairperson as chosen by the members of the Council who are present shall, be chairperson of the meeting,

(c) if and so long as the chairperson is not present or the office of chairperson is vacant, and a deputy-chairperson is not present or the offices of deputy-chairperson are vacant, the members of the Council who are present shall choose one of their number to be chairperson of the meeting.

12. Every question at a meeting of the Council shall be determined by a majority of the votes of members present and voting on the question and, in the case of an equal division of votes, the chairperson of the meeting shall have a second or casting vote.

13. Subject to paragraph 10 (3), the Council may act notwithstanding one or more than one vacancy among its members.

14. Subject to this Act, the Council shall regulate, by standing orders or otherwise, its procedure and business.

SCHEDULE 2
Section 50

EXAMINATIONS

Leaving Certificate Examination

Junior Certificate Examination

Technological Certificate Examination

Trade Certificate Examination

Certificate in Commerce Examination

Ceardteastas Gaeilge Examination

Teastas i dTeagasc na Gaeilge Examination

Typewriting Teachers Certificate Examination

Commercial Instructors Certificate Examination

Appendix B

Protections for Persons Reporting Child Abuse Act, 1998

Number 49 of 1998

ARRANGEMENT OF SECTIONS

Section

1. Interpretation.
2. Designated officers.
3. Protection from civil liability of persons who have reported child abuse.
4. Protection of employees from penalisation for having reported child abuse.
5. False reporting of child abuse.
6. Saving.
7. Short title and commencement.

ACTS REFERRED TO

Health Act, 1970	1970, No. 1
Petty Sessions (Ireland) Act, 1851	14 & 15 Vict., c. 93
Terms of Employment (Information) Act, 1994	1994, No. 5
Unfair Dismissals Act, 1977	1977, No. 10
Unfair Dismissals Acts, 1977 to 1993	

AN ACT TO PROVIDE PROTECTION FROM CIVIL LIABILITY TO PERSONS WHO REPORT CHILD ABUSE IN CERTAIN CIRCUMSTANCES, TO PROVIDE PROTECTION TO SUCH PERSONS FROM PENALISATION BY THEIR EMPLOYERS, TO PROVIDE FOR AN OFFENCE IN RESPECT OF THE FALSE REPORTING OF CHILD ABUSE AND TO PROVIDE FOR RELATED MATTERS. [23rd December, 1998]

BE IT ENACTED BY THE OIREACHTAS AS FOLLOWS:

1. Interpretation

(1) In this Act, unless the context otherwise requires -

"the Act of 1994" means the Terms of Employment (Information) Act, 1994;

"appropriate person" means a designated officer or a member of the Garda Síochána;

"child" means a person who has not attained 18 years of age;

"designated officer" means an officer of a health board appointed under section 2 of this Act to be a designated officer for the purposes of this Act;

"employee" and "employer" have the same meaning as they have in the Act of 1994;

"health board" means a health board established under the Health Act, 1970;

"the Minister" means the Minister for Health and Children;

"welfare", in relation to a child, comprises the moral, intellectual, physical, emotional and social welfare of the child.

(2) In this Act a reference to any enactment shall, unless the context otherwise requires, be construed as a reference to that enactment as amended, adapted or extended by or under any subsequent enactment including this Act.

2. Designated officers

(1) The chief executive officer of each health board shall -

    (a)   immediately upon the commencement of this Act, and

    (b)   thereafter from time to time as occasion may require (including a case in which a direction is given under this section),

appoint one or more officers of the board to be a designated officer or designated officers for the purposes of this Act; in making any such appointment the chief executive officer shall comply with any direction under this section for the time being in force.

(2) The Minister may give a direction in writing to the chief executive officer of a health board requiring him or her to appoint to be designated officers each person falling within a category or categories of officer of the board specified in the direction.

(3) The Minister may give a direction in writing to the chief executive officer concerned amending or revoking a direction given to him or her under this section (including a direction under this subsection).

(4) In this section "chief executive officer" includes a person acting as deputy chief executive officer in accordance with section 13 of the Health Act, 1970.

3. Protection from civil liability of person who have reported child abuse

(1) A person who, apart from this section, would be so liable shall not be liable in damages in respect of the communication whether in writing or otherwise, by him or her to an appropriate person of his or her opinion that -

    (a)   a child has been or is being assaulted, ill-treated, neglected or sexually abused, or

    (b)   a child's health, development or welfare has been or is being avoidably impaired or neglected,

unless it is proved that he or she has not acted reasonably and in good faith in forming that opinion and communicating it to the appropriate person.

(2) The reference in subsection (1) of this section to liability in damages shall be construed as including a reference to liability to be the subject of an order providing for any other form of relief.

4. Protection of employees from penalisation for having reported child abuse

(1) An employer shall not penalise an employee for having formed an opinion of the kind referred to in section 3 of this Act and communicated it, whether in writing or otherwise, to an appropriate person if the employee has acted reasonably and in good faith in forming that opinion and communicating it to the appropriate person.

(2) In proceedings under this section before a rights commissioner or the Employment Appeals Tribunal in relation to a complaint that subsection (1) of this section has been contravened, it shall be presumed, until the contrary is proved, that the employee concerned acted reasonably and in good faith in forming the opinion and making the communication concerned.

(3) If a penalisation of an employee, in contravention of subsection (1) of this section, constitutes a dismissal of the employee within the meaning of the Unfair Dismissals Acts, 1977 to 1993, relief may not be granted to the employee in respect of that penalisation both under this section and under those Acts.

(4) An employee may present a complaint to a rights commissioner that his or her employer has contravened subsection (1) of this section in relation to him or her and, if he or she does so, the commissioner shall give the parties an opportunity to be heard by the commissioner and to present to the commissioner any evidence relevant to the complaint, shall give a decision in writing in relation to it and shall communicate the decision to the parties.

(5) A decision of a rights commissioner under subsection (4) of this section shall do one or more of the following:

(a) declare that the complaint was or, as the case may be, was not well founded,

(b) require the employer to comply with subsection (1) of this section, and, for that purpose, require the employer to take specified steps,

(c) require the employer to pay to the employee compensation of such amount (if any) as is just and equitable having regard to all the circumstances, but not exceeding 104 weeks remuneration in respect of the employee's employment calculated in accordance with regulations under section 17 of the Unfair Dismissals Act, 1977,

and the references in the foregoing paragraphs to an employer shall be construed, in a case where ownership of the business of the employer changes after the contravention to which the complaint relates occurred, as references to the person who, by virtue of the change, becomes entitled to such ownership.

(6) For the purposes of this section -

(a) subsections (3) to (6) and subsection (7)(a) of section 7 of the Act of 1994 shall apply in relation to a complaint presented under this section as they apply in relation to a complaint presented under subsection (1) of that section 7, with the following modifications, namely -

    (i) the deletion in that subsection (3) of all the words from "if it is presented" to the end of that subsection and the substitution of "unless it is presented to him within the period of 12 months beginning on the date of the contravention to which the complaint relates or (in a case where the rights commissioner is satisfied that exceptional circumstances prevented the presentation of the complaint within the period aforesaid) such further period, not exceeding 6 months from the expiration of the said period of 12 months, as the rights commissioner considers reasonable",

    (ii) the substitution in that subsection (6) of a reference to a decision for the reference to a recommendation, and any other necessary modifications,

(b) sections 8 to 10 of the Act of 1994 shall apply as they apply for the purposes of that Act, with the following modifications, namely -

    (i) the substitution in those provisions of references to a decision for references to a recommendation,

    (ii) the addition to section 8 of the following subsection:

        "(7) Proceedings under this section before the Tribunal shall be heard otherwise than in public.",

(iii) the substitution in section 9 of the Act of 1994 of -

    (I)   references to the Circuit Court for references to the District Court, and

    (II)   the following subsection for subsection (3):

"(3) An application under this section to the Circuit Court shall be made to the judge of the Circuit Court for the circuit in which the employer concerned ordinarily resides or carries on any profession, trade or business.",

and any other necessary modifications.

(7) For the avoidance of doubt nothing in subsection (6) of this section operates to confer on the Minister any of the functions of the Minister for Enterprise, Trade and Employment under the Act of 1994 and those functions shall be performable by the Minister for Enterprise, Trade and Employment for the purposes of the provisions of the Act of 1994, as applied by that subsection (6), to the like extent as they are performable by him or her for the purposes of the Act of 1994 and the provisions of the Act of 1994 (including section 11) shall apply accordingly.

5. False reporting of child abuse

(1) A person who states to an appropriate person that -

    (a)   a child has been or is being assaulted, ill-treated, neglected or sexually abused, or

    (b)   a child's health, development or welfare has been or is being avoidably impaired or neglected,

knowing that statement to be false shall be guilty of an offence.

(2) A person guilty of an offence under this section shall be liable -

    (a)   on summary conviction, to a fine not exceeding £1,500 or to imprisonment for a term not exceeding 12 months or to both,

    (b)   on conviction on indictment, to a fine not exceeding £15,000 or to imprisonment for a term not exceeding 3 years or to both.

(3) Notwithstanding section 10(4) of the Petty Sessions (Ireland) Act, 1851, summary proceedings for an offence under this Act may be instituted within 2 years from the date on which the offence was committed or, if later, 2 years from the date on which evidence that, in the opinion of the person by whom the proceedings are brought, is sufficient to justify the bringing of the proceedings comes to that person's knowledge.

(4) For the purposes of subsection (3) of this section, a certificate signed by or on behalf of the person bringing the proceedings as to the date on which the evidence referred to in that subsection relating to the offence concerned came to his or her knowledge shall be prima facie evidence thereof and in any legal proceedings a document purporting to be a certificate issued for the purpose of this subsection and to be so signed shall be deemed to be so signed and shall be admitted as evidence without proof of the signature of the person purporting to sign the certificate.

6. Saving

Section 3 of this Act is in addition to, and not in substitution for, any privilege or defence available in legal proceedings, by virtue of any enactment or rule of law in force immediately before the passing of this Act, in respect of the communication by a person to another (whether that other person is an appropriate person or not) of his or her opinion that -

    (a)   a child has been or is being assaulted, ill-treated, neglected or sexually abused, or

    (b)   a child's health, development or welfare has been or is being avoidably impaired or neglected.

7. Short title commencement

(1) This Act may be cited as the Protections for Persons and Reporting Child Abuse Act, 1998.

(2) This Act shall come into operation one month after its passing.

Appendix C

Education (Welfare) Bill, 1999

As initiated

ARRANGEMENT OF SECTIONS

Part I

PRELIMINARY AND GENERAL

Part II

NATIONAL EDUCATIONAL WELFARE BOARD

Part III

EDUCATIONAL WELFARE AND COMPULSORY SCHOOL ATTENDANCE

27. Duty on Board to make reasonable efforts to ensure certain children receive prescribed minimum education.
28. Supply of personal data etc. to prescribed bodies.
29. Amendment of Protection of Young Persons (Employment) Act, 1996.

Part IV

PROVISIONS RELATING TO FINANCE AND STAFF OF BOARD

30. Grants to Board.
31. Accounts and audits.
32. Reports and information.
33. Gifts.
34. Chief Executive.
35. Staff.
36. Remuneration of staff.
37. Performance of functions of Board by members of staff.
38. Transfer of staff.
39. Superannuation.

Schedule

NATIONAL EDUCATIONAL WELFARE BOARD

ACTS REFERRED TO

Companies Act, 1990	1990, No. 33
Companies Acts, 1963 to 1990	
Data Protection Act, 1988	1988, No. 25
Education Act, 1998	1998, No. 51
Employment Agency Act, 1971	1971, No. 27
European Parliament Elections Act, 1997	1997, No. 2
Health Act, 1970	1970, No. 1
Holiday (Employees) Acts, 1973 and 1991	
Medical Practitioners Act, 1978	1978, No. 4
Minimum Notice and Terms of Employment Acts, 1973 to 1991	
Protection of Young Persons (Employment) Act, 1996	1996, No. 16
Redundancy Payments Acts, 1967 to 1991	
Regional Technical Colleges Act, 1992	1992, No. 16
School Attendance Acts, 1926 to 1967	
Unfair Dismissals Acts, 1977 to 1993	
Vocational Education Act, 1930	1930, No. 29
Youth Work Act, 1997	1997, No. 30

AN ACT TO PROVIDE FOR THE ENTITLEMENT OF EVERY CHILD IN THE STATE TO A CERTAIN MINIMUM EDUCATION, AND, FOR THAT PURPOSE, TO PROVIDE FOR THE REGISTRATION OF CHILDREN RECEIVING EDUCATION IN PLACES OTHER THAN RECOGNISED SCHOOLS, THE COMPULSORY ATTENDANCE OF CERTAIN CHILDREN AT RECOGNISED SCHOOLS, THE ESTABLISHMENT OF THE NATIONAL EDUCATIONAL WELFARE BOARD, THE COORDINATION OF ITS ACTIVITIES AND THOSE OF CERTAIN OTHER PERSONS IN SO FAR AS THEY RELATE TO MATTERS CONNECTED WITH SCHOOL ATTENDANCE, THE

IDENTIFICATION OF THE CAUSES OF TRUANCY ON THE PART OF CERTAIN CHILDREN AND THE ADOPTION OF MEASURES FOR ITS PREVENTION, TO REPEAL THE SCHOOL ATTENDANCE ACTS, 1926 TO 1967, TO PERMIT THE SUPPLY OF DATA RELATING TO A PERSON'S EDUCATIONAL HISTORY TO CERTAIN PERSONS, TO PROVIDE FOR THE AMENDMENT OF THE PROTECTION OF YOUNG PERSONS (EMPLOYMENT) ACT, 1996, AND TO PROVIDE FOR MATTERS CONNECTED THEREWITH.

BE IT ENACTED BY THE OIREACHTAS AS FOLLOWS:

Part I

PRELIMINARY AND GENERAL

1. Short title and commencement

(1) This Act may be cited as the Education (Welfare) Act, 1999.

(2) This Act shall come into operation on such day or days as the Minister may appoint by order or orders either generally or with reference to any particular purpose or provision and different days may be so appointed for different purposes or different provisions.

2. Interpretation

(1) In this Act, except where the context otherwise requires -

"the Act of 1997" means the Youth Work Act, 1997;

"the Act of 1998" means the Education Act, 1998;

"authorised person" has the meaning assigned to it by section 15;

"the Board" means the National Educational Welfare Board established by section 9;

"board of management" means a board of management appointed in accordance with section 14 of the Act of 1998;

"Chief Executive" means the Chief Executive Officer of the Board appointed under section 34;

"child" means -

(a) a person resident in the State who has reached the age of 6 years and who -

   (i) has not reached the age of 16 years, or

   (ii) has not completed 3 years of post-primary education,

   whichever occurs later, but shall not include a person who has reached the age of 18 years, or

(b) any other person to whom this Act for the time being applies by virtue of an order made by the Minister under section 3;

"educational welfare officer" shall be construed in accordance with section 11;

"health board" means a board established under section 4 of the Health Act, 1970;

"inspector" means an inspector appointed under section 13(1) of the Act of 1998 and includes the Chief Inspector appointed thereunder;

"the Minister" means the Minister for Education and Science;

"national association of parents" has the same meaning as it has in the Act of 1998;

"National Council for Curriculum and Assessment" means the body established by section 39 of the Act of 1998;

"National Youth Work Advisory Committee" means the committee appointed under section 10 of the Act of 1997;

"parent" has the same meaning as it has in the Act of 1998;

"prescribed" means prescribed by regulations, and cognate words shall be construed accordingly;

"prescribed minimum education" has the meaning assigned to it by section 14(1),

"principal" shall be construed in accordance with section 23 of the Act of 1998, and includes any person, for the time being, performing the functions of principal, in relation to a recognised school, under that Act;

"recognised school" means -

(a)   a school designated by the Minister under subsection (1) of section 10 of the Act of 1998 to be a school recognised for the purposes of that Act, or

(b)   a school deemed to be a school recognised in accordance with the said section 10;

"recognised school management organisations" has the same meaning as it has in the Act of 1998;

"recognised trade union or staff association" means a trade union or staff association recognised by the Board for the purposes of negotiations that are concerned with the remuneration, conditions of employment, or working conditions of employees;

"registered medical practitioner" has the same meaning as it has in the Medical Practitioners Act, 1978;

"school day" shall be construed in accordance with regulations under section 25 of the Act of 1998;

"school year" has the same meaning as it has in the Act of 1998;

"vocational education committee" means a committee established by section 7 of the Vocational Education Act, 1930;

"youth work" has the meaning assigned to it by section 2 of the Act of 1997.

(2) In this Act, a reference to a Part, section or Schedule is a reference to a Part or section of, or a Schedule to, this Act unless it is indicated that reference to some other enactment is intended.

(3) In this Act, a reference to a subsection, paragraph or subparagraph is a reference to the subsection, paragraph or subparagraph of the provision (including the Schedule) in which the reference occurs, unless it is indicated that a reference to some other provision is intended.

(4) In this Act, a reference to any enactment shall be construed as a reference to that enactment as amended, adapted or extended, whether before or after the commencement of this subsection, by or under any subsequent enactment.

3. Extension of application of Act

(1) The Minister may by order apply this Act to any person who has not reached the age of 18 years and who, but for the making of such an order, would not be a child for the purposes of this Act.

(2) The Minister may by order amend or revoke an order under this section.

4. Orders and Regulations

Every order or regulation under this Act shall be laid by the Minister before each House of the Oireachtas as soon as may be after it is made and, if a resolution annulling the order or regulation is passed by either such House within the next 21 days on which that House sits after the order or regulation is laid before it, the order or regulation shall be annulled accordingly but without prejudice to the validity of anything previously done thereunder.

5. Expenses

The expenses incurred by the Minister in the administration of this Act shall, to such extent as may be sanctioned by the Minister for Finance, be paid out of monies provided by the Oireachtas.

6. Service of documents

(1) A notice or other document under this Act shall be addressed to the person concerned by name, and may be served on or given to the person in one of the following ways:

(a) by delivering it to the person,

(b) by leaving it at the address at which the person ordinarily resides or, in a case in which an address for service has been furnished, at that address, or

(c) by sending it by post in a prepaid registered letter to the address at which the person ordinarily resides or, in a case in which an address for service has been furnished, to that address.

(2) For the purposes of this section, a company within the meaning of the Companies Acts, 1963 to 1990, shall be deemed to be ordinarily resident at its registered office, and every other body corporate and every unincorporated body shall be deemed to be ordinarily resident at its principal office or place of business.

7. Offences

(1) Summary proceedings for an offence under this Act may be brought and prosecuted by the Board.

(2) Where an offence under this Act is committed by a body corporate and is proved to have been so committed with the consent or connivance of or to be attributable to any neglect on the part of any person being a director, manager, secretary or other officer of the body corporate, or a person who was purporting to act in any such capacity, that person, as well as the body corporate, shall be guilty of an offence and shall be liable to be proceeded against and punished as if he or she were guilty of the first-mentioned offence.

8. Repeals

The School Attendance Acts, 1926 to 1967, are hereby repealed.

Part II

NATIONAL EDUCATIONAL WELFARE BOARD

9. Establishment of National Welfare Board

(1) There is hereby established a body to be known as the National Educational Welfare Board or in the Irish language An Bord Náisiúnta Leasa Oideachais (in this Act referred to as "the Board") to perform the functions assigned to it by this Act.

(2) The provisions of the Schedule shall have effect in relation to the Board.

10. Functions of Board

(1) The general functions of the Board shall be to ensure the provision of a prescribed minimum education to each child, whether in a recognised school or otherwise, and to assist in the formulation and implementation of policies and objectives of the Government for the time being concerning the education of children and, for those purposes, but without prejudice to the generality of the foregoing -

(a) to promote and foster in society, and in particular in families, an appreciation of the benefits to be derived from education, in particular as respects the physical, intellectual, emotional, social and moral development of children, and of the social and economic advantages that flow therefrom,

(b) to promote and foster, in recognised schools, an environment that encourages children to attend school and participate fully in the life of the school,

(c) to conduct and commission research into the reasons for truancy on the part of students and into strategies and programmes designed to prevent it,

(d) to disseminate to recognised schools the findings of research conducted or commissioned pursuant to paragraph (c), and to advise such schools on matters relating to the prevention of truancy, and the good conduct of students generally,

(e) to assist recognised schools in so far as is practicable to meet their obligations under this Act,

(f) to advise and assist the parents of children who exhibit problems relating to attendance at school,

(g) to monitor, and assess the effectiveness of, strategies and programmes aimed at preventing truancy in recognised schools,

(h) to co-operate with such persons as the Board considers appropriate, and to co-ordinate the activities of the Board with the activities of those persons in so far as they relate to preventing truancy in recognised schools,

(i) to assess the adequacy of training and guidance provided to teachers relating to matters of school attendance and good discipline on the part of students, and to make recommendations to the Minister in relation thereto,

(j) to advise the National Council for Curriculum and Assessment as respects aspects of the curriculum provided in recognised schools that in the opinion of the Board can lead to increased truancy or improved school attendance, and

(k) to advise the Minister on any matter to which this Act relates.

(2) The Board shall have all such powers as it considers necessary for the performance of its functions under this Act.

(3) The Board shall, in giving advice or making recommendations to the Minister under this section, have regard to the cost of measures that would have to be taken if the Minister were to take such advice or implement such recommendations.

(4) The Board may, with the consent of the parent of the child concerned, arrange for a child to be given a psychological examination.

(5) The Board may, in the performance of its functions, consult with such persons as it considers appropriate.

11. Educational welfare officers

(1) Subject to section 35, the Board may appoint such persons or classes of persons as it considers appropriate to be educational welfare officers for the purposes of this Act.

(2) A person appointed under subsection (1) shall, on his or her appointment, be furnished by the Board with a warrant of his or her appointment and when exercising a power conferred by this Act shall, if requested by any person thereby affected, produce such warrant to that person for inspection.

(3) An educational welfare officer shall, in addition to the functions conferred on him or her by this Act, perform such additional functions as may be assigned to him or her by the Board.

12. Liaison officer

(1) The Board shall, for the purposes of ensuring that, so far as is practicable -

(a) the activities of the Board, and those of a relevant authority, in so far as they relate to a function of the Board, are coordinated, and

(b) the policies of the Board, and those of a relevant authority, in so far as they relate to a function of the Board, are consistent,

designate one or more of its officers, not below such rank as the Minister shall determine (who or each of whom shall be known as and is referred to in this section as a "liaison officer"), to liaise with such persons as are designated under subsections (2) and (3), and an officer so designated shall for those purposes, perform such functions as are assigned to him or her by the Board.

(2) A relevant authority (other than a health board, a vocational education committee, the National Council for Curriculum and Assessment or the National Youth Work Advisory Committee) shall for the purposes specified in subsection (1), designate one of his or her officers or a member of his or her staff, as may be appropriate, not below such rank as the Minister shall, after consultation with the relevant authority concerned, determine, to liaise with a liaison officer, and an officer or member of staff so designated shall for those purposes, perform such functions as are assigned to him or her by the relevant authority concerned.

(3) The Chief Executive Officer of a relevant authority (other than a relevant authority to which subsection (2) applies) shall for the purposes specified in subsection (1), designate an officer or member of staff, as may be appropriate, of the relevant authority concerned, not below such rank as the Minister shall, after consultation with the Chief Executive Officer concerned, determine, to liaise with a liaison officer, and an officer or member of staff so designated shall for those purposes, perform such functions as are assigned to him or her by the Chief Executive Officer concerned.

(4) A person designated under this section by a relevant authority shall provide the Board with such information as to the policies and activities of the relevant authority concerned in so far as they relate to a function of the Board, as the Board requests or, where the Board has not requested such information, as the relevant authority considers appropriate.

(5) For the purposes of this section, each of the following shall be a relevant authority, that is to say:

(a) the Minister for Health and Children;

(b) the Minister for Social, Community and Family Affairs;

(c)   the Minister for Justice, Equality and Law Reform;

(d)   the Minister for Enterprise, Trade and Employment;

(e)   the Commissioner of the Garda Síochána;

(f)   a health board;

(g)   a vocational education committee;

(h)   the National Council for Curriculum and Assessment;

(i)   the National Youth Work Advisory Committee; and

(j)   such other persons as may be prescribed by the Minister.

13. Board Directions of Minister

(1) The Minister may give a direction in writing to the requiring it to comply with policy decisions made by the Minister in relation to the functions of the Board.

(2) The Minister may by direction in writing amend or revoke a direction under this section (including a direction under this subsection).

(3) The Board shall comply with a direction under this section.

Part III

EDUCATIONAL WELFARE AND COMPULSORY SCHOOL ATTENDANCE

14. Minimum standard of education

(1) The Minister may, after consultation with, the National Council for Curriculum and Assessment and such other persons (if any) as the Minister considers appropriate, prescribe a minimum education to be provided to each child (in this Act referred to as a "prescribed minimum education").

(2) Regulations under subsection (1) may prescribe different minimum standards of education in respect of children of different ages or of different capacities (including physical, mental and emotional capacities).

15. Register of children receiving education in a place other than school

(1) The Board shall, as soon as may be after the commencement of this section, cause to be established and maintained a register of all children in receipt of education in a place other than a school recognised school (hereafter in this section referred to as "the register").

(2) Where a parent chooses to educate, or have educated, his or her child in a place other than a recognised school he or she shall, in accordance with this section, apply to the Board to have the child concerned registered in the register.

(3) An application under this section shall -

(a)   be in writing,

(b)   specify the times and place at which the child receives the education to which the application relates, and

(c)   comply with such requirements (if any) as may be prescribed by the Minister.

(4) As soon as is practicable after an application under this section is received by the Board, the Board shall, for the purpose of determining whether the child is receiving a prescribed minimum education, and with the consent of the parent of the child to whom the application relates, cause an authorised person to -

(a) enter the place at which the child is being educated and observe the child receiving such instruction as forms part of the education being provided to him or her,

(b) inspect such premises, equipment and materials as are used in the provision of education to the child concerned, and

(c) carry out an assessment of the child concerned as to his or her intellectual, emotional and physical development, which shall include an assessment of his or her knowledge and understanding of such subjects, and proficiency in such exercises and disciplines, as the authorised person considers appropriate,

and the performance of any or all of the functions referred to in paragraphs (a), (b) and (c) are hereafter referred to in this section as an "assessment".

(5) An authorised person may, in respect of a registered child, carry out assessments at such intervals (if any) as may be specified by the Board, and accordingly subsection (4) shall apply with the necessary modifications.

(6) An authorised person shall, as soon as may be after completing an assessment under this section, prepare and submit to the Board a report of his or her findings in relation to such assessment.

(7) The Board shall serve a copy of a report received by it under this section on the parent of the child to whom the report relates and shall invite such parent to make representations to the Board concerning the matters to which the report relates.

(8) As soon as may be after considering a report submitted under this section in respect of a child to whom an application under this section relates, and any representations made to it by the parent of the child concerned the Board shall -

(a) if satisfied that the child concerned is receiving a prescribed minimum education, register the child concerned in the register, or

(b) if not so satisfied -

    (i) register the child in the register subject to the parent of the child undertaking to comply with such requirements of the Board as in its opinion will ensure that the child receives a prescribed minimum education,

    or

    (ii) refuse to register the child concerned in the register.

(9) An undertaking to which paragraph (b)(i) of subsection (8) applies shall be in writing and shall be given within such period as may be specified by the Board.

(10) After considering a report submitted under this section in respect of a registered child, and any representations made to it by the parent of the child concerned, the Board shall -

(a) if not satisfied that the child is receiving a prescribed minimum education -

    (i) remove the child's name from the register, or

    (ii) require the parent of the child to undertake in writing to comply with such conditions as, in the opinion of the Board, will ensure that the child receives a prescribed minimum education, or

(b) if not satisfied that the parent of the child is abiding by an undertaking given pursuant to paragraph (b)(i) of subsection (8), or paragraph (a)(ii) or complying with a requirement under section 16(6)(c), remove the child's name from the register.

(11) Where the parent of a child fails or refuses -

    (a) to give his or her consent to the carrying out, within such period as may be specified by the Board, of an assessment in accordance with subsection (4) or (5), or

    (b) to give an authorised person such assistance as he or she may require for the purpose of carrying out an assessment, the Board shall -

        (i) in the case of an application to have that child registered in the register, refuse to so register the child, or

        (ii) in the case of a registered child, remove his or her name from the register maintained under this section.

(12) Where the Board decides to register a child under paragraph (a) or (b) (i) of subsection (8) it shall cause the name of the child and such other particulars as may be prescribed by the Minister to be entered in the register and the child shall thereupon be registered for the purposes of this section.

(13) The parent of a registered child shall, if a particular entered in the register in accordance with subsection (12) ceases to be correct, so inform the Board as soon as may be.

(14) The Board shall not remove a child's name from the register solely on the ground that the child concerned is prevented from receiving a prescribed minimum education due to illness, whether of a permanent or temporary nature.

(15) The Board shall, as soon as may be after registering under paragraph (a) or (b)(i) of subsection (8) a child who is registered at a recognised school, so inform by notice in writing the principal of that school, and the principal concerned shall, on receipt of such notification, remove the child's name from the register maintained under section 20 in respect of the school concerned.

(16) This section does not apply to -

    (a) a child who is being educated at a school outside the State, or

    (b) a child who is participating in a programme of education, training, instruction or work experience prescribed by the Minister.

(17) In this section -

"authorised person" means an inspector, educational welfare officer or a person appointed by the Board to perform the functions of an authorised person under this section;

"registered child" means a child who, for the time being, is registered in accordance with this section.

16. Appeal against decision of Board

(1) Where the Board -

    (a) refuses, in accordance with paragraph (b)(ii) of subsection (8) of section 15, to register a child in the register maintained under that section,

    (b) agrees to register the child in that register in accordance with paragraph (b)(i) of the said subsection (8),

    (c) removes a child's name from that register in accordance with subsection (10) of that section, or

(d) requires the giving of an undertaking in accordance with paragraph (a)(ii) of the said subsection (10)

(hereafter in this section referred to as a "decision"), it shall so inform the parent of the child concerned by notice in writing and the parent of the child concerned may appeal against the decision and for that purpose shall serve a notice of appeal on the Minister within 21 days of his or her receiving the first-mentioned notice.

(2) A notice of appeal under subsection (1) shall be in writing and shall be in such form (if any) as may be prescribed by the Minister.

(3) The Minister shall within 14 days of receiving a notice of appeal under subsection (1) appoint a committee to hear and determine an appeal under this section (hereafter in this section referred to as an "appeal committee").

(4) An appeal committee shall consist of such judge of the District Court as shall be nominated by the President of the District Court, such inspector and such other person (other than an officer of the Minister) as may be appointed thereto by the Minister.

(5) An appeal committee shall invite the parent of the child concerned and the authorised person who prepared and submitted the report under subsection (6) of section 15, to make submissions to it concerning the matters to which the appeal relates.

(6) The appeal committee shall, having considered any submissions made to it pursuant to subsection (5) and the report referred to in that subsection -

(a) affirm the decision of the Board,

(b) require the Board to register the child concerned in the register maintained under section 15, or

(c) require the Board to register the child concerned in the said register subject to the parent of the child undertaking to comply with such requirements as the appeal committee considers appropriate.

(7) The Board shall comply with a requirement of an appeal committee under subsection (6).

17. Parent to cause child too attend school

(1) Subject to subsection (2), the parent of a child shall cause the child concerned to attend on each school day a recognised school.

(2) A child shall not be required to attend a recognised school where -

(a) he or she is registered in the register maintained under section 15, or a decision in respect of an application to be so registered or an appeal against a refusal of the Board to register the child in that register is pending,

(b) the child is temporarily attending a school outside the State and the parent of the child has notified the school at which the child is registered of the reason for his or her non-attendance at the second-mentioned school,

(c) he or she is a child referred to in subsection (16) of section 15, or

(d) there exists some other sufficient cause for his or her not so attending.

18. Notification of child's absence from school

(1) Where a child is absent from the school at which he or she is registered during part of a school day or for a school day or more than a school day the parent of such child shall, as soon as is practicable but not later than 3 school days after the child's last attendance at the school concerned, notify the principal of the school of -

(a) the reasons for the child's absence, and

(b) where the child is absent due to illness, the nature of the illness.

(2) A notification under subsection (1) shall be made in writing or by such other means as may be agreed to by the principal of the school concerned.

19. Admission of child to recognised school

(1) The board of management of a recognised school shall not refuse to admit as a student in such school a child, in respect of whom an application to be so admitted has been made, except where such refusal is in accordance with the policy of the recognised school concerned published under section 15(2)(d) of the Act of 1998.

(2) The parent of a child who has made an application referred to in subsection (1) shall provide the recognised school concerned with such information as may be prescribed by the Minister.

20. School registers

(1) The principal of a recognised school shall, as soon as may be after the commencement of this section, cause to be established and maintained a register of all students attending that school.

(2) The principal of a recognised school shall, as soon as may be after a parent has accepted an offer from the board of management of the school concerned to admit his or her child as a student therein, enter the name of the child and such particulars as may be prescribed by the Minister in the register maintained in respect of that school under this section, and the child concerned shall, for the purposes of this Act, be deemed, as on and from the date of entry of his or her name in the said register, to be registered in that school.

(3) The principal of a recognised school shall, as soon as may be after entering in the register maintained under this section in respect of that school the name of a child who is registered in another recognised school, so inform by notification in writing the principal of the second-mentioned school.

(4) The principal of the second-mentioned school referred to in subsection (3) shall, on receipt of a notification under that subsection, remove the name of the child concerned from the register maintained under this section in respect of the said second-mentioned school.

(5) The principal of a recognised school shall, on receiving a notification under subsection (3) in relation to a child, notify the principal of the first-mentioned school referred to in that subsection of any problems relating to school attendance which the child concerned had while attending the second-mentioned school referred to in the said subsection.

(6) The principal of a recognised school shall not remove a child from the register other than -

(a) in accordance with subsection (4), or

(b) where he or she has received a notification in writing from the Board that the child concerned is registered in the register maintained under section 15.

21. School attendance records

(1) The principal of a recognised school shall cause to be maintained in respect of each school year a record of the attendance or non-attendance on each school day of each student registered at that school.

(2) A record maintained under subsection (1) shall specify the following, that is to say:

(a) where a student attends at the school concerned on a school day, the fact of his or her attendance, or

(b) where a student fails to so attend, the fact of his or her failure and the reasons for such failure.

(3) A record to which this section applies shall be maintained at the recognised school concerned and shall be in such form as may be specified by the Board.

(4) Where -

(a) a student is suspended from a recognised school for a period of not less than 6 days,

(b) a student is expelled from a recognised school,

(c) the aggregate number of school days on which a student is absent from a recognised school during a school year is not less than 11,

(d) a student's name is, for whatever reason, removed from the register referred to in section 20 by the principal of the school concerned, or

(e) a student is, in the opinion of the principal of the recognised school at which he or she is registered, not attending school regularly,

the principal of the school concerned shall forthwith so inform an educational welfare officer.

(5) The board of management of a recognised school shall not later than 6 weeks after the end of each school year submit a report to the educational welfare officer who has been assigned functions under this Act in relation to that school on the levels of attendance at that school during the immediately preceding school year.

(6) A report under subsection (5) shall be in such form and comply with such requirements as may be prescribed by the Minister.

(7) An educational welfare officer may during any school day enter a recognised school and inspect the register maintained at that school under section 20 or a record to which this section applies.

22. School attendance strategies

(1) The board of management of a recognised school shall, after consultation with the principal of, teachers teaching at, parents of students registered at, and the educational welfare officer assigned functions in relation to, that school, prepare and submit to the Board a statement of the strategies and measures it proposes to adopt for the purposes of fostering an appreciation of learning among students attending that school and encouraging regular attendance at school on the part of such students (hereafter in this section referred to as a "statement of strategy").

(2) Without prejudice to the generality of subsection (1), a statement of strategy shall provide for -

(a) the rewarding of students who have good school attendance records;

(b) the identification at an early stage of students who are at risk of developing school attendance problems;

(c) the establishment of closer contacts between the school concerned and the families of students to which paragraph (b) applies;

(d) the fostering, promoting and establishing of contacts by the school with other schools that provide primary or post-primary education, and with bodies engaged in the provision of youth work programmes or services related thereto, or engaged in the organising of sporting activities;

(e) in so far as is practicable, the coordination with other schools of programmes aimed at improving discipline among students and encouraging regular attendance at school by students, and the exchanging of information relating to matters of discipline and school attendance with such schools;

(f) the identification of aspects of the operation and management of the school and of the curriculum at the school that may contribute to truancy on the part of certain students and the removal of those aspects in so far as they are not necessary or expedient for the proper and effective running of the school.

(3) The board of management of a recognised school shall, in preparing a statement of strategy, have regard to such guidelines issued by the Board regarding the preparation and carrying into effect of statements of strategy.

(4) A statement of strategy prepared and submitted by the board of management of a recognised school, in accordance with subsection (1), shall be carried out by that board of management in accordance with its terms.

(5) The board of management of a recognised school may, with the consent of the Minister, and for the purpose of giving effect to a statement of strategy prepared and submitted by it in accordance with this section, appoint such and so many teachers employed by it, as it considers appropriate, to liaise with the parents of students registered at the school concerned and to give such assistance to the families of those students as the board of management concerned considers appropriate.

(6) The Board shall issue guidelines to boards of management of recognised schools for the purposes of this section.

23. Discipline policy

(1) The board of management of a recognised school shall, after consultation with the principal of, the teachers teaching at, the parents of students registered at, and the educational welfare officer assigned functions in relation to, that school, prepare, in accordance with subsection (2), a code of behaviour in respect of the students registered at the school, (hereafter in this section referred to as a "code of discipline").

(2) A code of discipline shall specify -

(a) the types of behaviour on the part of a student that may require disciplinary measures to be taken in relation to him or her;

(b) the nature of the measures referred to in paragraph (a);

(c) the procedures to be followed before a student may be suspended or expelled from the school concerned;

(d) the grounds for removing a suspension imposed in relation to a student;

(e) the steps that will be taken to ensure that a student who is expelled will receive a prescribed minimum education.

(3) The board of management of a recognised school shall, in preparing a code of discipline, have regard to such guidelines as may be issued by the Board regarding the preparation and carrying into effect of codes of discipline.

(4) The principal of a recognised school shall, on registering a child as a student at that school in accordance with section 20, provide the parents of such child with a copy of the code of discipline in respect of the school concerned.

(5) The principal of a recognised school shall, on a request being made by a student registered at the school or a parent of such a student, provide the student or parent, as the case may be, with a copy of the code of discipline in respect of the school concerned.

24. Employment of children

(1) A person shall not employ under a contract of employment or engage under a contract for services a child -

    (a) during a school day, or

    (b) in the case of a child registered under section 15, where the employment interferes or is likely to interfere with the child's ability to receive a prescribed minimum education.

(2) A person who contravenes this section shall be guilty of an offence and shall be liable on summary conviction to a fine not exceeding £1,500, or to imprisonment for a term not exceeding 6 months, or to both such fine and imprisonment.

(3) A person guilty of an offence under subsection (3) shall, on each day after having been convicted of such offence on which the contravention to which that offence relates is continued by him or her, be guilty of an offence and shall be liable on summary conviction to a fine not exceeding £200, or imprisonment for a term not exceeding one month, or to both such fine and imprisonment.

(4) This section shall not apply in respect of employment that forms part of a programme of education, training, instruction or work experience referred to in section 15(16)(b).

(5) In this section "contract of employment" means -

    (a) a contract of service,

    (b) a contract of apprenticeship (that is not entered into for the purpose of participating in a programme prescribed by the Minister under section 15(16)(b)),

    (c) any other contract whereby an individual agrees with another person, who is carrying on the business of an employment agency within the meaning of the Employment Agency Act, 1971, and is acting in the course of that business, to do or perform personally any work or service for a third person (whether or not the third person is a party to the contract),

whether the contract is express or implied, and if it is express, whether it is oral or in writing.

25. School attendance notice

(1) Where the Board is of opinion that a parent is failing or neglecting to cause his or her child to attend a recognised school in accordance with this Act, other than in circumstances to which section 17(2) applies, the Board shall serve a notice (hereafter in this section referred to as a "school attendance notice") on such parent -

    (a) requiring him or her on the expiration of such period as is specified in the notice, to cause his or her child named in the notice to attend such recognised school as is specified in the notice, and there to attend on each school day that the notice is in force, and

(b) informing him or her that if he or she fails to comply with a requirement under paragraph (a) he or she shall be guilty of an offence.

(2) A school attendance notice under this section shall remain in force for such period as may be specified in the notice or until it is revoked by the Board.

(3) Before making a school attendance notice the Board shall, in such manner as it considers appropriate, make all reasonable efforts to consult with the parents of the child concerned and shall, when specifying a recognised school under subsection (1)(a), have regard, as far as is practicable, to the preference (if any) expressed by the parents of the child.

(4) A person who contravenes a requirement in a school attendance notice shall be guilty of an offence and shall be liable on summary conviction to a fine not exceeding £500, or to imprisonment for a term not exceeding one month, or to both such fine and imprisonment.

(5) A person guilty of an offence under subsection (4) shall, on each day after having been convicted of such offence on which he or she continues to contravene a requirement in the school attendance notice to which that offence relates, be guilty of an offence and shall be liable on summary conviction to a fine not exceeding £200, or to imprisonment for a term not exceeding one month, or to both such fine and imprisonment.

(6) In proceedings for an offence under this section it shall be a defence for a parent to show that he or she has made all reasonable efforts to cause the child to whom the proceedings relate to attend a recognised school in accordance with this Act.

(7) In proceedings for an offence under this section the burden of proving that -

(a) the person to whom the prosecution relates is not a child,

(b) under section 17(2)(b) or (d) the child to whom the prosecution relates is not required to attend a recognised school, or

(c) the child to whom the prosecution relates is being educated outside the State,

shall be on the defendant.

(8) Where a parent, who is convicted of an offence under this section, or in proceedings for such an offence, shows, in accordance with subsection (6), that he or she has made all reasonable efforts to cause the child to whom the proceedings relate to attend a recognised school in accordance with this Act, the Board shall forthwith so inform in writing the health board for the area in which the parent concerned resides.

26. Right of Board to appeal etc decision of board of management under section 29 of Act of 1998

(1) The Board may appeal a decision to which paragraph (a) or (c) of subsection (1) of section 29 of the Act of 1998 applies and accordingly a reference in the said subsection (1) to "parent of the management under student'; or "student" shall be construed as including a reference to the board.

(2) Section 29 of the Act of 1998 is hereby amended by the insertion of the following subsection:

"(4A) The National Educational Welfare Board may, at the hearing of an appeal brought by a parent or student against a decision to which paragraph (a) or (c) of subsection (1) applies, make such submissions (whether in writing or orally) to the appeals committee, as it considers appropriate."

27. Duty on Board to make reasonable efforts to ensure certain children receive prescribed minimum education

(1) Where a decision to which paragraph (a) or (c) of section 29 of the Act of 1998 applies is upheld by an appeal committee appointed under that section or where no appeal is brought against such a decision the Board shall make all reasonable efforts to have the child to whom the decision concerned relates enrolled in another recognised school.

(2) Where the Board having made all such reasonable efforts as are referred to in subsection (1), fails to have the child concerned enrolled in another recognised school it shall, with the consent of the Minister, make such other arrangements as it considers appropriate to ensure that the child receives a prescribed minimum education.

28. Supply of personal data etc to prescribed bodies

(1) The data controller of a prescribed body may supply personal data kept by him or her, or information extracted from such data, to the data controller of another prescribed body If he or she is satisfied that it will be used for a relevant purpose only.

(2) The data controller of a prescribed body may, for a relevant purpose only, keep and use personal data supplied to him or her under this section.

(3) In this section -

"data controller" and "personal data" have the meanings assigned 5 to them by the Data Protection Act, 1988;

"prescribed body" means a body prescribed by the Minister;

"relevant purpose" means the purpose of -

    (a)   recording a person's educational or training history or monitoring his or her educational or training progress in order to ascertain how best he or she may be assisted in availing of educational or training opportunities or in developing his or her full educational potential, or

    (b)   carrying out research into -

        (i)   the extent to which persons in receipt of, or who have received, a prescribed minimum education present for examinations to which Part VIII of the Act of 1998 applies, and into the performance in such examinations of persons who so present,

        (ii) the extent to which persons who have received a prescribed minimum education participate further in programmes of education, training or instruction, or

        (iii) the general effectiveness of educational or training programmes.

29. Amendment of Protection of Young Persons(Employment) Act, 1996

The Protection of Young Persons (Employment) Act, 1996, is hereby amended by the insertion of the following section:

"11A. (1) The Board shall, as soon as may be after the commencement of section 29 of the Act of 1999, cause to be established and maintained a register of young persons (hereafter in this section referred to as 'the register').

(2) Any young person may apply to the board to be registered in the register.

(3) Any child who will, at the end of a school year (within the meaning of the Act of 1999), cease to be a child for the purposes of that Act may, during that school year, apply to the Board to be registered in the register.

(4) An application under this section shall be in such form and contain such particulars as may be prescribed.

(5) The Board shall, upon receiving an application under this section, register the young person concerned in the register, and shall, as soon as may be thereafter, issue a certificate of registration to the young person concerned (hereafter in this section referred to as a 'certificate') which shall contain such particulars as are prescribed by the Minister.

(6) An employer shall not employ a young person on any work unless the young person is the holder of a certificate.

(7) An employer shall, as soon as practicable but in any case not later than one month after the young person concerned has commenced employment with the employer, so inform the Board by notice in writing.

(8) A notice under subsection (7) shall contain such other particulars as shall be prescribed by the Minister.

(9) Before prescribing anything under this section, the Minister shall -

    (a)   consult the Minister for Enterprise, Trade and Employment;

    (b)   consult such representatives of employers and representatives of employees as the Minister, with the concurrence of the Minister for Enterprise, Trade and Employment, considers appropriate, and

    (c)   publish in such manner as the Minister thinks fit, notice of his or her intention to so prescribe, and permit, within 21 days of such publication, the making of representations by any person in relation to the proposed regulations.

(10) As soon as practicable after the Board has issued a certificate to a young person the Board shall, after consultation with the young person concerned, his or her parents, his or her employer, and such other persons as the Board considers appropriate, prepare a plan for the purpose of assisting that young person to avail of educational and training opportunities, and shall give all such other assistance to such young person, his or her parents or his or her employer as it considers appropriate, for the purpose of carrying out such plan.

(11) This section does not apply to a young person who -

    (a)   is registered at a recognised school,

    (b)   is engaged in, or has completed (having attained such standard as may be prescribed), a course of study (within the meaning of the Regional Technical Colleges Act, 1992), or

    (c)   is engaged in, or has completed (having attained such standard as may be prescribed), a prescribed programme of education, training or instruction.

(12) In this section -

'the Act of 1999' means the Education (Welfare) Act, 1999;

'the Board' means the National Educational Welfare Board established by the Act of 1999;

'parent' has the same meaning as it has in the Act of 1999;

'prescribed' means prescribed by regulations made by the Minister for Education and Science, and cognate words shall be construed accordingly;

'young person' means a person (other than a child) who is of a prescribed age but shall not include a person who has reached the age of 18 years.".

Part IV

PROVISIONS RELATING TO FINANCE AND STAFF OF BOARD

30. Grants to Board

The Minister may, with the consent of the Minister for Finance, advance to the Board out of moneys provided by the Oireachtas such sums as the Minister may determine.

31. Accounts and audits

(1) The Board shall keep, in such form as may be approved of by the Minister with the consent of the Minister for Finance, all proper and usual accounts of all moneys received or expended by it and all such special accounts (if any) as the Minister, with the consent of the Minister for Finance, may direct.

(2) Accounts kept in pursuance of this section shall be submitted, not later than the 30th day of April in the year immediately following the accounting period to which they relate or on such other date as the Minister may, from time to time, specify, by the Board to the Comptroller and Auditor General for audit and, immediately after the audit, a copy of the accounts, and of such other (if any) accounts kept pursuant to this section as the Minister, after consultation with the Minister for Finance, may direct and a copy of the Comptroller and Auditor General's report on the accounts shall be presented to the Minister who shall cause copies thereof to be laid before each House of the Oireachtas.

32. Reports and information

(1) The Board shall not later than the 31st day of March in each year prepare and submit to the Minister a report on its activities in the immediately preceding year and the Minister shall, as soon as may be, cause copies of the report to be laid before each House of the Oireachtas.

(2) The Board shall furnish the Minister with such information regarding the performance of its functions as the Minister may from time to time require.

33. Gifts

(1) The Board may accept gifts of money, land or other property upon such trusts or conditions (if any) as may be specified by the donor.

(2) The Board shall not accept a gift if the trusts or conditions attached to it would be inconsistent with its functions.

34. Chief Executive

(1) There shall be a chief executive of the Board (who shall be known and is referred to in this Act as "the Chief Executive").

(2) The Chief Executive shall carry on and manage, and control generally, the administration and business of the Board and perform such other functions (if any) as may be determined by the Board.

(3) The Chief Executive shall be appointed and may be removed from office by the Board, with the consent of the Minister.

(4) The Chief Executive shall hold office upon and subject to such terms and conditions (including terms and conditions relating to remuneration and allowances) as may be determined by the Board with the consent of the Minister given with the approval of the Minister for Finance.

(5) The Chief Executive shall be ex officio a member of the Board.

35. Staff

(1) The Board shall appoint with the consent of the Minister and the Minister for Finance such and so many persons to be members of the staff of the Board as it may from time to time determine.

(2) The terms and conditions of service of a member of the staff of the Board shall, with the consent of the Minister and the Minister for Finance, be such as may be determined from time to time by the Board.

(3) There shall be paid by the Board to the members of its staff such remuneration and allowances as, from time to time with the consent of the Minister and the Minister for Finance, the Board determines.

36. Remuneration of staff

The Board, in determining the remuneration or allowances for expenses to be paid to members of its staff or the other terms or conditions subject to which such members hold or are to hold their employment, shall have regard to Government or nationally agreed guidelines which are for the time being extant and to Government policy concerning remuneration and conditions of employment which is so extant and, in addition to the foregoing, the Board shall comply with any directives with regard to such remuneration, allowances, terms or conditions which the Minister may give to the Board with the consent of the Minister for Finance.

37. Performance of functions of Board by members of staff

The Board may perform any of its functions through or by any member of the staff of the Board duly authorised in that behalf by the Board.

38. Transfer of staff

(1) Every person who immediately before the commencement of this Act is a school attendance officer shall be transferred to and become a member of the staff of the Board.

(2) Save in accordance with a collective agreement negotiated with any recognised trade union or staff association concerned, a person referred to in subsection (1) shall not, while in the service of the Board be brought to less beneficial conditions of service (including conditions in relation to tenure of office) or of remuneration than the conditions of service (including conditions in relation to tenure of office) or remuneration to which he or she was subject immediately before the commencement of this section.

(3) In relation to persons transferred to the Board under subsection (1), previous service in a local authority shall be reckonable for the purposes of, but subject to any exceptions or exclusions in, the Redundancy Payments Acts, 1967 to 1991, the Holidays (Employees) Acts, 1973 and 1991, the Minimum Notice and Terms of Employment Acts, 1973 to 1991, and the Unfair Dismissals Acts, 1977 to 1993.

39. Superannuation

(1) As soon as may be after its establishment, the Board shall prepare and submit to the Minister a scheme or schemes for the granting of superannuation benefits to or in respect of such of its staff (including the Chief Executive) as the Board shall think fit.

(2) Every such scheme shall fix the time and conditions of retirement for all persons to, or in respect of whom superannuation benefits are payable under the scheme, and different times and conditions may be fixed in respect of different classes of persons.

(3) The Board may at any time prepare and submit to the Minister a scheme amending a scheme previously submitted and approved under this section.

(4) A scheme or amending scheme submitted to the Minister under this section shall, if approved by the Minister with the consent of the Minister for Finance, be carried out by the Board in accordance with its terms.

(5) If any dispute arises as to the claim of any person to, or the amount of, any superannuation benefit in pursuance of a scheme under this section, such dispute shall be submitted to the Minister who shall refer it to the Minister for Finance whose decision shall be final.

(6) No superannuation benefit shall be granted by the Board to or in respect of any of its staff (including the Chief Executive) who are members of a scheme under this section, nor shall any other arrangement be entered into for the provision of any superannuation benefit to such persons on their ceasing to hold office, other than in accordance with such scheme or schemes submitted and approved under this section.

(7) The Minister shall cause every scheme submitted and approved under this section to be laid before each House of the Oireachtas as soon as may be after it is approved, and if either House, within the next twenty-one days on which that House has sat after the scheme is laid before it, passes a resolution annulling the scheme, the scheme shall be annulled accordingly, but without prejudice to the validity of anything previously done thereunder.

Schedule

NATIONAL EDUCATIONAL WELFARE BOARD

1. (1) The Board shall be a body corporate with perpetual succession and a common seal and a power to sue and be sued in its corporate name and, with the consent of the Minister given with the approval of the Minister for Finance, to acquire, hold and dispose of land or an interest in land, and to acquire, hold and dispose of any other property.

(2) The seal of the Board shall be authenticated by the signature of the chairperson of the Board or by the signatures of both an ordinary member and a member of the staff of the Board authorised by the Board to act in that behalf.

(3) Judicial notice shall be taken of the seal of the Board and every document purporting to be an instrument made by and to be sealed with the seal of the Board (purporting to be authenticated in accordance with this paragraph) shall be received in evidence and be deemed to be such instrument without proof unless the contrary is shown.

2. (1) The Board shall consist of the following members, that is to say a chairperson and 6 ordinary members (including the Chief Executive).

(2) The chairperson of the Board shall be appointed by the Minister from among persons who, in his or her opinion, have a special interest and expertise in matters relating to the functions of the Board.

(3) The ordinary members of the Board shall be appointed by the Minister, after consultation with the Minister for Health and Children, the Minister for Justice, Equality and Law Reform, the Minister for Social, Community and Family Affairs, the Minister for Enterprise, Trade and Employment and the Minister for Tourism, Sport and Recreation, from among persons who, in his or her opinion, have a special interest and expertise in matters relating to the functions of the Board.

(4) The chairperson of the Board shall hold office for a period of 5 years from the date of his or her appointment.

(5) An ordinary member of the Board (other than the Chief Executive) shall hold office for a period of 3 years from the date of his or her appointment.

(6) A member of the Board whose term of office expires by the effluxion of time shall be eligible for reappointment to the Board.

3. (1) The Minister may at any time remove from office a member of the Board.

(2) A member of the Board may resign from office by notice in writing given to the Minister and the resignation shall take effect on the date on which the Minister receives the notice.

(3) A member of the Board shall cease to be qualified for office and shall cease to hold office if -

    (a) he or she is adjudicated bankrupt,

    (b) he or she makes a composition or arrangement with creditors,

    (c) he or she is convicted of any indictable offence in relation to a company,

    (d) he or she is convicted of an offence involving fraud or dishonesty, whether in connection with a company or not,

    (e) he or she is the subject of an order under section 160 of the Companies Act, 1990, or

    (f) he or she is sentenced to a term of imprisonment by a court of competent jurisdiction.

(4) A member of the Board shall, subject to the provisions of this Act, hold office upon such terms and conditions (including terms and conditions relating to remuneration and allowances) as may be determined by the Minister, with the consent of the Minister for Finance.

4.(1) If a member of the Board dies, resigns, ceases to be qualified for office and ceases to hold office or is removed from office, the Minister may appoint a person to be a member of the Board to fill the casual vacancy so occasioned.

(2) A person appointed to be a member of the Board pursuant to this section shall hold office for that period of the term of office of the member who occasioned the casual vacancy concerned that remains unexpired at the date of his or her appointment and shall be eligible for reappointment as a member of the Board on the expiry of the said period.

5. The chairperson and each ordinary member of the Board shall be paid by the Board such remuneration (if any) and such allowances for expenses as the Minister, with the approval of the Minister for Finance, may determine.

6.(1) The Board shall hold such and so many meetings as may be necessary for the due fulfilment of its functions.

(2) At a meeting of the Board -

    (a) the chairperson of the Board shall, if present, be the chairperson of the meeting, or

    (b) if and so long as the chairperson of the Board is not present or if that office is vacant, the members of the Board who are present shall choose one of their number to be chairperson of the meeting.

(3) Every question at a meeting shall be determined by a majority of the votes of the members of the Board present and voting on the question and, in the case of an equal division of votes, the chairperson of the meeting shall have a second or casting vote.

(4) The Board may act notwithstanding one or more vacancies among its members.

(5) Subject to the provisions of this Act, the Board shall regulate its procedure by rules or otherwise.

(6) The quorum for a meeting of the Board shall unless the Minister otherwise directs be 4.

7.(1) Where a member of the Board is -

    (a) nominated as a member of Seanad Éireann,

    (b) elected as a member of either House of the Oireachtas or to be a representative in the European Parliament, or

    (c) regarded pursuant to Part XIII of the Second Schedule to the European Parliament Elections Act, 1997, as having been elected to that Parliament,

he or she shall thereupon cease to be a member of the Board.

(2) Where a member of the staff of the Board is -

    (a) nominated as a member of Seanad Éireann, or

    (b) elected as a member of either House of the Oireachtas or to be a representative in the European Parliament, or

    (c) regarded pursuant to the said Part XIII, as having been elected to that Parliament,

he or she shall thereupon stand seconded from employment by the Board and shall not be paid by, or be entitled to receive from, the Board any remuneration or allowances in respect of the period commencing on such nomination or election, or when he or she is so regarded as having been elected (as the case may be), and ending when such person ceases to be a member of either such House or a representative in such Parliament.

(3) A person who is for the time being entitled under the Standing Orders of either House of the Oireachtas to sit therein or who is a representative in the European Parliament shall, while he or she is so entitled or is such a representative, be disqualified for membership of the Board or for employment in any capacity by the Board.

(4) A period mentioned in subparagraph (2) shall not, for the purposes of any superannuation benefit, be reckoned as service with the Board.

8. (1) Where at a meeting of the Board any of the following matters arise, namely -

    (a) an arrangement to which the Board is a party or a proposed such arrangement, or

    (b) a contract or other agreement with the Board or a proposed such contract or other agreement, then, any member of the Board present at the meeting who otherwise than in his or her capacity as such a member has an interest in the matter shall -

    (i)   at the meeting disclose to the Board the fact of such interest and the nature thereof,

    (ii) neither influence nor seek to influence a decision to be made in relation to the matter,

    (iii) absent himself or herself from the meeting or that part of the meeting during which the matter is discussed,

    (iv) take no part in any deliberation of the Board relating to the matter, and

    (v) not vote on a decision relating to the matter.

(2) Where an interest is disclosed pursuant to this section, the disclosure shall be recorded in the minutes of the meeting concerned and, for so long as the matter to which the disclosure relates is being dealt with by the meeting, the member by whom the disclosure is made shall not be counted in the quorum for the meeting.

(3) Where at a meeting of the Board a question arises as to whether or not a course of conduct, if pursued by a member of the Board, would constitute a failure by him or her to comply with the requirements of subparagraph (1), the question may be determined by the chairperson of the meeting, whose decision shall be final, and where such a question is so determined, particulars of the determination shall be recorded in the minutes of the meeting.

(4) Where the Minister is satisfied that a member of the Board has contravened subparagraph (1), the Minister may, if he or she thinks fit, remove that member from office and, in case a person is removed from office pursuant to this subparagraph, he or she shall thenceforth be disqualified for membership of the Board.

9. (1) Where a member of the staff of the Board has an interest, otherwise than in his or her capacity as such a member, in any contract, agreement or arrangement, or proposed contract, agreement or arrangement, to which the Board is a party, that person shall -

    (a) disclose to the Board his or her interest and the nature thereof,

    (b) take no part in the negotiation of the contract, agreement or arrangement or in any deliberation by the Board or members of the staff of the Board in relation thereto, and

    (c) neither influence nor seek to influence a decision to be made in the matter nor make any recommendation in relation to the contract, agreement or arrangement.

(2) Subparagraph (1) shall not apply to contracts or proposed contracts of employment of members of the staff of the Board with the Board.

(3) Where a person contravenes this paragraph the Board may make such alterations to the person's terms and conditions of employment as it considers appropriate or terminate the person's contract of employment.

10. (1) A person shall not disclose confidential information obtained by him or her while performing duties as a member or member of the staff of, or an adviser or consultant to, the Board unless he or she is duly authorised by the Board to do so.

(2) A person who contravenes subparagraph (1) shall be guilty of an offence and shall be liable on summary conviction to a fine not exceeding £1,500 or to imprisonment for a term not exceeding 12 months or to both such fine and imprisonment.

(3) In this section "confidential information" includes -

(a) information that is expressed by the Board to be confidential either as regards particular information or as regards information of a particular class or description, and

(b) proposals of a commercial nature or tenders submitted to the Board by contractors, consultants or any other person.

11. (1) The Board may establish committees to advise it in relation to the performance of any of its functions and may determine the terms of reference and regulate the procedure of any such committee.

(2) The Board shall, as soon as is practicable after the commencement of this paragraph, establish a committee to advise it in relation to the performance of its functions, the members of which shall be appointed by the Board for such terms as may be determined by the Board and shall include -

(a) not less than one person appointed from among persons nominated by the national association of parents,

(b) not less than one person appointed from among persons nominated by recognised school management organisations, and

(c) not less than one person appointed from among persons nominated by trade unions and staff associations representing teachers.

(3) A committee established under this paragraph may include persons who are not members of the Board.

(4) A committee established under this paragraph (including a committee established under subparagraph (2)) shall, where the Chief Executive considers it appropriate, include the Chief Executive or such other person as may be nominated by the Chief Executive.

(5) A member of a committee established under this paragraph may be removed from office at any time by the Board.

(6) The Board may at any time dissolve a committee established under this paragraph (other than a committee established under sub paragraph (2)).

(7) The Board may appoint a person to be chairperson of a committee established under this paragraph.

(8) There may be paid by the Board to members of a committee established under this paragraph such allowances for expenses (if any) incurred by them as the Board may, with the consent of the Minister and the Minister for Finance, determine.

Appendix D

Code of Practice: Disciplinary Procedures

An Order (S.I. No. 117 of 1996) declaring this Code to be a Code of Practice for the purposes of the Industrial Relations Act, 1990 was made by the Minister for Enterprise and Employment on the 6 May, 1996 (Appendix 1).

Other Codes of Practice available from the Department of Enterprise and Employment:

Code of Practice on Dispute Procedures, including procedures in Essential Services (S.I. No. 1 of 1992).

Code of Practice on Duties and Responsibilities of Employee Representatives and the Protection and Facilities to be afforded them by their Employer (S.I. No. 169 of 1993).

Introduction

1. Section 42 of the Industrial Relations Act 1990 provides inter alia for the preparation of draft codes of practice by the Labour Relations Commission for submission to the Minister for Enterprise and Employment and for the making by him of an order declaring that a draft code of practice received by him under section 42 and scheduled to the order shall be a code of practice for the purposes of the said Act (Appendix 1).

2. The main purpose of this code of practice is to set out for the guidance of employers, employees and their representatives the general principles which should apply in the operation of disciplinary procedures. For the purposes of this code of practice, "employee representative" includes a colleague of the employee's choice and an authorised trade union but not any other person or body unconnected with the enterprise.

3. In any enterprise or organisation, it is important that procedures of this kind exist and that the purpose, function and terms of such procedures are known and clearly understood by management, employees and trade unions.

General

4. This code of practice contains general guidelines on the application of disciplinary procedures and the promotion of best practice in giving effect to such procedures.

5. The principles and procedures of this code of practice should apply unless alternative agreed procedures exist in the workplace which conform to its general provisions for dealing with disciplinary issues.

Importance of Procedures

6. Procedures are necessary to ensure both that discipline is maintained in the workplace and that disciplinary measures can be applied in a fair and consistent manner. Apart from considerations of equity and natural justice, the maintenance of a good industrial relations atmosphere at workplace level requires that acceptable procedures be in place and be observed.

7. Such procedures serve a dual purpose in that they provide a framework which enables management to maintain satisfactory standards and employees to have access to procedures whereby alleged failures to comply with these standards may be fairly and sensitively addressed.

561

General Principles

8. The essential elements of any procedure for dealing with disciplinary issues are that they be rational and fair, that the basis for disciplinary action is clear, that the range of penalties that can be imposed is well-defined and that an internal appeal mechanism is available.

9. Procedures should be reviewed and up-dated periodically so that they are consistent with changed circumstances in the workplace, developments in employment legislation and case law, and good industrial relations practice generally.

10. The procedures applied must comply with the general principles of natural justice and fair procedures which include:

    (i)   that details of the allegations or complaints be put to the employee concerned;

    (ii)   that the employee concerned be given the opportunity to respond fully to any such allegations or complaints;

    (iii) that the employee concerned is given the opportunity to avail of representation;

    (iv) that the employee concerned has the right to a fair and impartial determination of the issues being investigated, taking into account the allegations or complaints themselves, the response of the employee concerned to them, any representations made by or on behalf of the employee concerned and any other relevant or appropriate evidence, factors or circumstances.

11. These principles may require that the allegations or complaints be set out in writing, that the source of the allegations or complaint be given or that the employee concerned be allowed to confront or question witnesses.

12. As a general rule, an attempt should be made to resolve a disciplinary issue between the employee concerned and his or her immediate manager or supervisor. This could be done on an informal or private basis.

Disciplinary Procedures

13. In the interest of good industrial relations, disciplinary procedures should be in writing and presented in a format and language which is easily understood. Copies of the procedures should be given to all employees and should be included in any induction programme for new employees. The consequences of a departure from rules and employment requirements should be clearly set out, particularly in respect of breaches of discipline which if proved would warrant suspension or dismissal.

14. Disciplinary action may include:

    (a) an oral warning

    (b) a written warning

    (c) a final written warning

    (d) suspension without pay

    (e) transfer to another task, or section of the enterprise

    (f) demotion

    (g) some other appropriate disciplinary action short of dismissal

    (h) dismissal

Generally, the steps in the procedure will be progressive, for example, an oral warning, a written warning, a final written warning, and dismissal. However, there may be instances where more serious action, including dismissal, is warranted at an earlier stage.

An employee may be suspended on full pay pending the outcome of an investigation into an alleged breach of discipline.

15. Procedures should set out clearly the different levels in the enterprise or organisation at which the various stages of the procedures will be applied.

16. Warnings should be removed from an employee's record after a specified period and the employee advised accordingly.

17. The operation of a good disciplinary procedure requires the maintenance of adequate records. It also requires that all members of management, including supervisory personnel and all employees and their representatives be familiar with and adhere to the terms of the procedure.

Appendix 1

Industrial Relations Act, 1990, Code of Practice on Disciplinary Procedures (Declaration) Order, 1996 (S.I. No. 117 of 1996)

WHEREAS the Labour Relations Commission has prepared a draft code of practice on disciplinary procedures;

AND WHEREAS the Labour Relations Commission has complied with subsection (2) of section 42 of the Industrial Relations Act, 1990 (No. 19 of 1990), and has submitted the draft code of practice to the Minister for Enterprise and Employment;

NOW THEREFORE, I, Richard Bruton, Minister for Enterprise and Employment, in exercise of the powers conferred on me by subsection (3) of that section, the Labour (Transfer of Departmental Administration and Ministerial Functions) Order, 1993 (S.I. No. 18 of 1993) and the Industry and Commerce (Alteration of Name of Department and Title of Minister) Order, 1993 (S.I. No. 19 of 1993), hereby order as follows:

1. This Order may be cited as the Industrial Relations Act, 1990, Code of Practice on Disciplinary Procedures (Declaration) Order, 1996.

2. It is hereby declared that the code of practice set out in the Schedule to this Order shall be a code of practice for the purposes of the Industrial Relations Act, 1990 (No. 19 of 1990).

Given under my Official Seal,

this 6 day of May, 1996.

RICHARD BRUTON

Minister for Enterprise and Employment

Appendix II

Codes of Practice:

Section 42 of the Industrial Relations Act, 1990 states:

(1) The Commission shall prepare draft codes of practice concerning industrial relations for submission to the Minister, either on its own initiative or at the request of the Minister.

(2) Before submitting a draft code of practice to the Minister, the Commission shall seek and consider the views of organisations representative of employers and organisations representative of workers, and such other bodies as the Commission considers appropriate.

(3) Where the Minister receives a draft code of practice from the Commission he may by order declare that the code, scheduled to the order, shall be a code of practice for the purposes of this Act.

(4) In any proceedings before a court, the Labour Court, the Commission, the Employment Appeals Tribunal, a rights commissioner or an equality officer, a code of practice shall be admissible in evidence and any provision of the code which appears to the court, body or officer concerned to be relevant to any question arising in the proceedings shall be taken into account in determining that question.

(5) A failure on the part of any person to observe any provision of a code of practice shall not of itself render him liable to any proceedings.

(6) The Minister may at the request of or after consultation with the Commission by order revoke or amend a code of practice.

(7) Every order made under this section shall be laid before each House of the Oireachtas as soon as may be after it is made and, if a resolution annulling the order is passed by either House within the next twenty-one days on which that House has sat after the order has been laid before it, the order shall be annulled accordingly, but without prejudice to the validity of anything previously done thereunder.

Appendix E

Press Releases

The Ombudsman Kevin Murphy has upheld a complaint from the mother of the child with disabilities about the school transport service offered by the Department of Education and Science (DES). In an investigation report published today, Kevin Murphy recommended that the child involved be awarded £6,800 in compensation for the inadequate transport service he was offered. The Ombudsman also recommended that the DES publish a fair school transport scheme catering for children with disabilities. The DES has accepted Kevin Murphy's recommendations and has promised to implement them without delay. The Department of Finance has also accepted his recommendations.

Kevin Murphy's four recommendations were that:

1. Compensation be paid to Mrs X for the hardship caused for the period September 1994 to 29 November 1996. The amount of £6,800 was calculated on the basis of the cost of a taxi service to the school for each school day.

2. The Department of Education and Science devise and publish a school transport scheme for children with special needs and that this include details of the transport grants.

3. Cases involving exceptional circumstances should be dealt with on their merits and not by reference to arbitrary financial restrictions.

4. The published school transport scheme for children with special needs should include:

    (i) a provision that children with special needs will not, as for as possible, be disadvantaged by their distance from schools or by their isolation from other such children;

    (ii) details of the rules by which the schemes, including payment of transport grants, is administered;

    (iii) provision for a right of appeal to an official or authority other than the initial decision-maker;

    (iv) guidelines used by DES in making provision for exceptional cases;

    (v) provision that the level of transport grants be related to the actual cost of travel by road.

The Child ("Y"), whose name is not being released for reasons of confidentiality, is a child with spine bifida and uses a wheel chair. He started attending a special school recommended by the DES in September 1994. His mother ("Mrs X") complained that the transport arrangements offered by the DES were unsatisfactory in that her child was to be picked up by a school bus at a point 2.3 miles from his home. Most other children attending the school were provided with a transport service from their homes. The DES offered an annual grant of £240 towards the cost of private transport to and from the pick up point for the child, but Mrs X rejected this as inadequate. Mrs X felt that her son was not being treated fairly and complained to the Ombudsman, Kevin Murphy. She pointed out that she had two other children in the family who had to be brought to a national school and that the pick up arrangement was too difficult for her to manage. After Y's first week in school, Mrs X drove him there and back, a distance of 36 miles a day.

During the Ombudsman's detailed investigation of the case, the DES reviewed Y's transport arrangements and provided, in November 1996, a service for Y from 200 yards from his home.

In his investigation report the Ombudsman notes that Y was penalised because he was the only child with disabilities in his particular area; Kevin Murphy says that the school transport scheme must address the needs of children with disabilities living in isolated areas or at a distance from the school they need to attend. He also notes that Y was refused transport from his home because the DES could not arrange it within the expenditure limit of £9.00 per day and that the basis for this figure is unclear. Procedures for dealing with cases which exceeded this limit were ill-defined; this, coupled with the fact that the transport scheme itself was unpublished, was contrary to fair and sound administration, and could lead to discrimination and different treatment for children in similar circumstances.

The Ombudsman findings included the following:

1 It was unfair of the DES not to provide Y with transport from as close as possible to his home from September 1994. The service offered to him at that time did not meet Y's needs and the DES delayed unduly in arriving a solution to the case.

2. The transport grant system operated by the DES was inadequate because the grants were not related to the cost of travel by road.

3. The school transport scheme for children with special needs made no provision for special consideration of children like Y, who lived in isolated areas and could lead to improper discrimination against them. The scheme as it applied to these children did not meet the requirements of fair and sound administration because it was undocumented and unpublished and could therefore lead to an inconsistent approach to individual cases.

The text of the published investigation report is available on the Office of the Ombudsman web site - http://www.irlgov.ie/ombudman/

Enquiries about the investigation report or about this press release should be addressed to:

Office of the Ombudsman
at telephone number' +353 1 678 5222
Fax number: +353 1 6610570
E-mail ombudsman@ombudsman.irlgov.ie
11 February 1998

II. HISTORIC MOVE IN STATE FUNDING FOR SCHOOL BUILDINGS

Micheál Martin, T.D,

Minister for Education and Science

"CHANGES WILL RELIEVE SIGNIFICANT FUNDRAISING PRESSURES ON LOCAL COMMUNITIES"

Sunday 10 January 1999

An historic move in the way Government funds school building projects was announced in Cork today by Education Minister Micheál Martin. As a result of this move, which will see the State meet the entire cost of new sites and a significantly greater proportion of renovation costs, the fundraising pressures on many local communities will be greatly reduced.

Explaining the background to the announcement, the Minister said that the cost of new schools and major renovations required schools and communities throughout the country to raise a large amount of money to meet the current local contribution requirements. Existing regulations require the patrons of most schools to fully fund the purchase of school sites and up to 15% of the cost of all building work. These costs can be particularly high for smaller schools and schools in areas where the price of land is high.

"What I am announcing today is the most significant change in the State funding of school capital projects since independence. I have agreed with the Minister for Finance that the State will offer to provide the full costs of sites for all new schools at both primary and second level. In addition, the level of local contribution requited for building projects will be reduced significantly and will be capped at a low level."

Specifically nearly all schools, at both levels, will, from now on, have their contribution to the cost of new school reduced to 5% and capped at £50,000 and their contribution to the cost of renovations, including extensions, will be reduced to 10% and capped at £25,000.

There will be even further benefits for special schools and schools which are designated as serving areas of significant disadvantage where the local contribution for building work will be set at 5% and capped at £10,000.

The changes will have a particular impact for the Multi-denominational schools movement which has often struggled to meet the high cost of land and buildings in and close to major urban areas. This has resulted from their lack of a parochial or diocesan support structure to help them with fundraising. Schools in smaller communities, who have a very limited fundraising base, will also be major beneficiaries.

In recent years local contributions of up to £1 million including the cost of sites have been required of schools. The Minister praised the work of school managements in particular in meeting the challenge of this fundraising through the years and noted that the scale of the funds to be raised had clearly put unreasonable pressures on many management authorities.

The current funding arrangements for new schools for Gaelscoileanna will be maintained for Gaelscoileanna which have either permanent or provisional recognition from the Department of Education & Science. The local contribution from Gaelscoileanna for renovations and extensions will be reduced to the new 10% and £25,000 limits.

The new local contributions and site funding arrangements wild come into effect immediately. The new schools provided under these changes will be in the ownership of the state and be leased to the patrons under a lease or deed of trust, The Minister stated that discussions will be held with all interested parties on the operational arrangements.

PRIMARY SCHOOLS

Type of School	Present arrangement re site	Proposed arrangement re site	Present arrangement re building	Proposed arrangement re building
Denominationl/ Multi Denominationl	Patron provides full cost of site.	State to offer to provide full cost of site.	*New building* Patron provides up to 15% of capital cost.	*New building* Patron to provide 5% of capital cost subject to ceiling of £50k.
			Renovation Patron provides 15% of capital cost.	*Renovation* Patron to provide 10% of capital cost subject to ceiling of £25k.
	Patron owns site.	State to own site.	Patron owns building.	State to own building (in case of "new" only).
Special/ Disadvantaged Schools	Patron provides full cost of site.	State to offer to provide full cost of site.	*New buildings & Renovation* Patron usually provides 5% of capital cost.	*New building & Renovation* Patron to provide 5% of capital cost subject to ceiling of £10k.
	Patron owns site.	State to own site.	Patron owns building.	State to own building (in case of "new," only).
Gaelscoileanna	State provides full cost of site.	State to provide full cost of site.	*New building* State provides full cost.	*New building* Patron to provide 5% of capital cost subject to ceiling of £50k.**
			Renovation Patron provides 15% of capital costs.	*Renovation* Patron to provide 10% of capital. cost subject to ceiling of £25k.
	State owns site.	State to continue to own site.	State owns building.	State to continue to own building.

**current arrangements to apply to all Gaelscoileanna with either permanent or temporary recognition.

SECOND LEVEL SCHOOLS

Type of School	Present arrangement re site	Proposed arrangement re site	Present arrangement re building	Proposed arrangement re building
Secondary Schools	School provides full cost of site.	State to offer to provide full cost of site.	*New building & Renovations* Patron provides up to 10% of capital cost.	*New building* Patron to provide 5% of capital cost subject to ceiling of £50k. *Renovation* Patron to provide 10% of capital cost subject to ceiling of £25k.
	Patron owns site.	State to own site.	Patron owns building.	State to own building (in case of "new" only).
Community & Comprehensive	State provides full cost of site.	State to provide full cost of site.	*New building* Trustees Religious/VECs provide 5% of capital cost each. *Renovation* State provides full cost.	*New buildings* Trustees to provide 5% of capital cost subject to ceiling the capital cost of £50k. *Renovation* State to provide full cost.
	State owns site.	State to continue to own site.	State owns building.	State to continue to own building.
VEC Schools	State provides full cost of site.	State to continue to provide full cost of site.	*New building & Renovation* State provides full cost fo site.	*New building & Renovation* State to continue to provide full cost of site.
	State owns site.	State to continue to own site.	State owns building.	State to continue to own building.

Appendix F

Historical Documents

I. THE STANLEY LETTER

Copy of a Letter from the Chief Secretary for Ireland, to His Grace the Duke of Leinster, on the Formation of a Board of Commissioners for Education in Ireland; this, the so called 'Stanley Letter' became the basis of the system of primary education in Ireland; two versions of this letter exist, see Report of the Powis Commission 1831/2, Vol XXIX, p 757, reprinted 1837 Vol IX p 585.

Irish Office, London, October, 1831.

My Lord - His Majesty's Government having come to the determination of empowering the Lord Lieutenant to constitute a Board for the Superintendence of a System of National Education in Ireland, and Parliament having so far sanctioned the arrangement as to appropriate a sum of money in the present year as an experiment of the probable success of the proposed system, I am directed by His Excellency to acquaint your Grace that it is his intention, with your consent, to constitute you the President of the new Board: And I have it further in command, to lay before your Grace the motives of the Government in constituting the Board, the powers which it is intended to confer upon it, and the objects which it is expected that it will bear in view, and carry into effect.

The Commissioners, in 1812, recommended the appointment of a Board of this description to superintend a system of education, from which should be banished even the suspicion of proselytism, and which, admitting children of all religious persuasions, should not interfere with the peculiar tenets of any. The Government of the day imagined that they had found a superintending body, acting upon a system such as was recommended, and intrusted the distribution of the National grants to the care of the Kildare street Society. His Majesty's present Government are of opinion that no private society deriving a part, however small, of their annual income from private sources, and only made the channel of the munificence of the Legislature, without being subject to any direct responsibility, could adequately and satisfactorily accomplish the end proposed; and while they do full justice to the liberal views with which that society was originally instituted, they cannot but be sensible that one of its leading principles was calculated to defeat its avowed objects, as experience has subsequently proved that it has. The determination to enforce, in all their schools, the reading of the Holy Scriptures without note or comment, was undoubtedly taken with the purest motives; with the wish at once to connect religious with moral and literary education, and, at the same time, not to run the risk of wounding the peculiar feelings of any sect by catechetical instruction, or comments which might tend to subjects of polemical controversy. But it seems to have been overlooked that the principles of the Roman Catholic Church (to which, in any system intended for general diffusion throughout Ireland, the bulk of the pupils must necessarily belong) were totally at variance with this principle; and that the indiscriminate reading of the Holy Scriptures without note or comment, by children, must be peculiarly obnoxious to a Church which denies, even to adults, the right of unaided private interpretation of the sacred volume with respect to articles of religious belief.

Shortly after its institution, although the society prospered and extended its operations under the fostering care of the Legislature, the vital defect began to be noticed, and the Roman Catholic system to which they were on principle opposed, and which they feared might lead in its results to proselytism, even though no such object were contemplated by its promoters. When this opposition arose, founded on such grounds, it soon became manifest that the system could not become one of National Education.

The Commissioners of Education, in 1824-5, sensible of the defects of the system, and of the ground, as well as the strength of the objection taken, recommended the appointment of two teachers in every school, one Protestant and the other Roman Catholic, to superintend separately the religious education of the children; and they hoped to have been able to agree upon a selection from the Scriptures, which might have been generally acquiesced in by both persuasions. But it was soon found that these schemes were impracticable; and, in 1828, a Committee of the House of Commons, to which were referred the various Reports of the Commissioners of Education, recommended a system to be adopted which should afford, if possible, a combined literary and a separate religious education, and should be capable of being so far adapted to the views of the religious persuasions which prevail in Ireland, as to render it, in truth, a system of National Education for the poorer classes of the community.

For the success of the undertaking much must depend upon the character of the individuals who compose the Board; and upon the security thereby afforded to the country, that while the interests of religion are not overlooked, the most scrupulous care should be taken not to interfere with the peculiar tenets of any description of Christian pupils.

To attain the first object, it appears essential that the Board should be composed of men of high personal character, including individuals of exalted station in the Church, to attain the latter that it should consist of persons professing different religious opinions.

It is the intention of the Government that the Board should exercise a complete control over the various schools which may be erected under its auspices, or which, having been already established, may hereafter place themselves under its management, and submit to its regulations. Subject to these, applications for aid will be admissible from Christians of all denominations; but as one of the main objects must be to unite in one system children of different creeds, and as much must depend upon the co-operation of the resident clergy, the Board will probably look with peculiar favour upon applications proceeding either from -

1st   The Protestant and Roman Catholic clergy of the parish; or
2nd   One of the clergymen, and a certain number of parishioners professing the opposite creed; or
3rd   Parishioners of both denominations.

Where the application proceeds exclusively from Protestants, or exclusively from Roman Catholics, it will be proper for the Board to make inquiry as to the circumstances which lead to the absence of any names of the persuasion which does not appear.

The Board will note all applications for aid, whether granted or refused, with the grounds of the decision, and annually submit to, Parliament a Report of their proceedings.

They will invariably require, as a condition not to be departed from, that local funds shall be raised upon which any aid from the public will be dependent.

They will refuse all applications in which the following objects are not locally provided for:

1st A fund sufficient for the annual repairs of the school-house and furniture.

2nd A permanent salary for the master, not less than   pounds.

3rd A sum sufficient to purchase books and school requisites at half-price.

4th Where aid is sought from the Commissioners for building a school-house, it is required that at least one-third of the estimated expense be subscribed, a site for building, to be approved of by the Commissioners, be granted for the purpose, and that the school-house, when finished, be vested in trustees, to be also approved of by them.

They will require that the schools be kept open for a certain number of hours, on four or five days of the week, at the discretion of the commissioners, for moral and literary education only, and at the remaining one or two days in the week be set apart for living, separately, such religious education to the children as may approved of by the clergy of their respective persuasions.

They will also permit and encourage the clergy to give religious instruction to the children of their respective persuasions, either before or after the ordinary school hours, on the other days of the week.

They will exercise the most entire control over all books to be used in the schools, whether in the combined moral and literary, or separate religious instruction; none to be employed in the first except under the sanction of the Board, nor in the latter, but with the approbation of those members of the Board who are of the same religious persuasion with those for whose use they are intended. Although it is not designed to exclude from the list of books for the combined instruction, such portions of Sacred history or of religious or moral teaching as may he approved of by the Board, it is to he understood that this is by no means intended to convey a perfect and sufficient religious education, or to supersede the necessity of separate religious instruction on the day set apart for that purpose.

They will require that a register shall be kept in the schools, in which shall be entered the attendance or non-attendance of each child on Divine Worship on Sundays.

They will, at various times, either by themselves or by their Inspectors, visit and examine into the state of each school, and report their observations to the Board.

They will allow to the individuals or bodies applying for aid, the appointment of their own teacher, subject to the following restrictions and regulations:

1st He (or she) shall be liable to be fined, suspended, or removed altogether, by the authority of the Commissioners, who shall, however, record their reasons.

2nd He shall have received previous instruction in a model school in Dublin, to be sanctioned by the Board.

NB It is not intended that this regulation should apply to prevent the admission of masters or mistresses of schools already established, who may be approved of by the Commissioners

3rd He shall have received testimonials of good conduct, and of general fitness for the situation, from the Board.

The Board will be intrusted with the absolute control over the funds which may be annually voted by Parliament, which they shall apply to the following purposes:

1st Granting aid for the erection of schools, subject to the conditions hereinbefore specified.

2nd paying Inspectors for visiting and reporting upon schools.

3rd Gratuities to teachers of schools conducted under the rules laid down, not exceeding pounds each.

4th Establishing and maintaining a model school in Dublin, and training teachers for country schools.

5th Editing and printing such books of moral and literary education as may be approved of for the use of the schools, and supplying them and school necessaries, at not lower than half-price.

6th Defraying all necessary contingent expenses of the Board.

I have thus stated the objects which His Majesty's Government have in view, and the principal regulations by which they think those objects may be most effectually promoted: and I am directed by the Lord Lieutenant to express His Excellency's earnest wish that the one and the other may be found such as to procure for the Board the sanction of your Grace's name, and the benefit of your Grace's attendance.

A full power will of course be given to the Board to make such regulations upon matters of detail, not inconsistent with the spirit of these instructions, as they may judge best qualified to carry into effect the intentions of the Government and of the legislature. Parliament has already placed at his Excellency's disposal a sum which may be available even in the course of the present year; and as soon as the Board can be formed, it will be highly desirable that no time should be lost, with a view to the estimates of the ensuing year, in enabling such schools, already established, as are willing to subscribe to the conditions imposed, to put in their claims for protection and assistance; and in receiving applications from parties desirous to avail themselves of the munificence of the Legislature in founding new schools under your regulations.

I have the honour to be, &c.

(Signed) E C Stanley.

II. The O'Neill Letter

Extract from a letter from Seosamh O'Neill, Secretary of the Department of Education, dated the 2nd July 1934. This letter is contained in the De Valera Papers, File No 1074 and also in the State Papers' Office File s 2979.[1]

Re Article 10

Article 10 has never bee fully invoked, and we have not so far obtained a legal interpretation of it, or of the obligation which it imposes.

The present position is that elementary education is free except in a few of the Model schools, and in these schools the practice of charging fees is being gradually terminated and in a few years it will have disappeared.

Apart however from the obligation that elementary education should be free, there are other claims which might possibly be made under the Article in question. These include

(1) Whether a small number of children, say two, three or four, living on an island, or at a long distance from a National School: could successfully claim the right to be transported daily to a National School; or to have a school established for their own use;

(2) Whether the Article could be construed to put an obligation on the State not only to pay the teachers but also to build, equip and maintain schools and provide free books and requisites for the schoolchildren.

In my opinion the present position is that the principle underlying the Article is fundamental and should be preserved if possible, but in the absence of a clear definition of the State's obligation under the Article, it would be undesirable to put it in such a position as to make it more difficult to deal by legislation with any problem which might arise thereunder.

---

[1] Thie letter is reprinted by the kind permission of the Franciscan Fathers.

Glossary

Ab initio	From the beginning.
Certiorari	An order of the High Court granted in exercise of its general superintending and correctiv jurisdiction over orders of inferior courts for the purpose of bringing up orders for review.
Data:	The term data means information in a form in which it can be processed automatically; Data subject means an individual who is the subject personal data; Data controller is a person who, either alone or with others, controls the contents and use of personal data; and Data processors are persons who processes personal data on behalf of a data controller but this term does not include an employee of a data controller who processes such data in the course of employment. Personal data means data relating to a living individual who can be identified either from the data or from the data in conduction with other information in the possession of the data controller.
Corpus	A body of law.
Denominational Schools	The mainstream schools which are owned by the various churches in which the patron (usually the bishop) has traditionally provided the full cost of the site and up to 15% towards building costs. This is the dominant form of education in the State.
Imprimatur	Let it be printed, a licence to publish or print a book.
In loco parentis	In the place of a parent, a person to whom parental duties are delegated eg a teacher during the course of the school day.
Inter-Denominational School	Currently there is only one such school in which Catholic and Protestants children are educated together.
Irish Medium Schools	Referred to in this book as "gaelscoileanna" in which all teaching is in the Irish language and Irish is the spoken language of the school.
Locus standi	A place of standing before a court ie the right to be heard before a court.

Multi-Denominational Schools	The first multi-denominational school was established in Dalkey in 1978 to cater for parents who do not wish to have a specifically religious ethos for their children or who wish to have their children educated with those of other religions or none.
Obiter Dictum	A saying by the way, an observation by a judge in a case, based on facts that were not present or were not at issue, in the case, or which arose in such a manner as not to require a decision. The obiter dictum is not binding on future cases but may be persuasive.
Occupier's Liability	The liability which falls on the occupier of premises under the Occupier's Liability Act 1995.
Per se	By itself.
Prima Facie	Of first appearance, on the face of it, a first impression. A *prima facie* case is one in which there is sufficient evidence given to ground a party's allegation to require an answer from his/her opponent.
Private Schools	These are independent schools of which there are approximately 80 at primary or national school level.
Ratio Decidendi	The reason for a judicial decision which forms the precedent for other similar cases.
Recognised School	A school recognised by the Minister for Education and Science in accordance with s 10 of the Education Act 1998.
Reductio Ad Absurdum	An absurd conclusion.
School Ethos	The characteristic spirit of the school.
Second Level Teacher	All teachers who teach in second level schools ie voluntary secondary teachers, vocational teachers, community and comprehensive school teachers. The various categories of school are explained in Chapter 2.
Secondary schools	Voluntary secondary schools only (ie those schools run by religious orders and diocesan authorities)
Secondary teacher	a member of staff who teaches in a secondary school.
Special Educational Needs	The educational needs of students who have a disability.
Special Schools	These schools cater for children with a variety of special educational needs such as those children with disabilities, those who are emotionally disturbed, who have a specific learning difficulty, who are at risk, or who are young offenders .

Tort	A civil wrong independent of contract which arises from a breach of duty imposed by law, the main remedy for which is damages. The most common torts are trespass, nuisance, negligence and defamation.
Tortfeasor	A person who commits a tort.
Via Media	A middle way, a mean between extremes.
Vicarious Liability	The liability which falls on one person as a consequence of an action of another eg employer for civil wrongs of employees.

Bibliography

Books

Akenson, *A Mirror to Kathleen's Face: Education in Independent Ireland 1922-1960*, (1975) McGill and Queen's University Press

Akenson, *Education and Enmity: The Control of Schooling in Northern Ireland, 1920-1950*, David and Charles, Newtown Abbot, 1973

Akenson, *The Irish Education Experiment*, (1970) Routledge and Keegan Paul

Alvey, *Irish Education: The Case for Secular Reform*, (1991), Church and State Books

Atkinson, *Irish Education*, (1969), Allen Figgis

Auchmuty, *Irish Education: a Historical Study*, (1937), Hoggis Figgis

Bacik and O'Connell, *Crime and Poverty in Ireland*, (1988), Round Hall Sweet and Maxwell

Balfour, *The Educational Systems of Great Britain and Ireland*, (2nd ed, 1903), Clarendon Press

Barrell and Partington, *Teachers and the Law*, (6th ed, 1985) Methuen

Beaumont and Moir, *The European Communities (Amendment) Act 1993 with the Treaty of Rome (as amended): Text and Commentary*, (1994), Sweet and Maxwell

Beddard, *Human Rights and Europe*, (3rd ed, 1993), Grotius Publications

Berlin, *Four Essays on Liberty*, (1969), Oxford

Birrell and Murie, *Policy and Government in Northern Ireland: Lessons of Devolution*, (1980), Gill and Macmillan

Boyle and Greer, *New Ireland Forum: The Legal Systems North and South*, (1983), Government Publications

Breen, Hannan, Rottman and Whelan, *Understanding Contemporary Ireland*, (1990), Gill and Macmillan

Brennan, *Schools of Kildare and Leighlin AD 1775-1835*, (1935), Gill and Son

Brownlie, *Basic Documents on Human Rights* (3rd ed, 1992) Oxford

Burke, *Teaching: Retrospect and Prospect*, (1992), Government Publications

Byrne and Binchy, *Annual Review of Irish Law 1992*, Round Hall Sweet and Maxwell

Byrne, *Transfer of Undertakings*, (1999), Blackhall Publications

Carleton, *Traits and Stories of the Irish Peasantry*, (1843/44) Dublin

Casey, *Constitutional Law in Ireland*, (1987), Sweet and Maxwell

Charlesworth and Percy on Negligence, (1997), Sweet and Maxwell

Clark, *Data Protection Law in Ireland*, (1990), Round Hall Press

Coolahan, *Irish Education: History and Structure*, (1981), Institute of Public Administration

Coolahan, *The ASTI and Post-Primary Education in Ireland*, 1909-1984, (1984), ASTI

Corcoran, State Policy in Irish Education 1536-1836, (1916), Dublin

Corish, *The Irish Catholic Experience: a Historical Survey*, (1985), McGill and MacMillan

Corpus Iuris Civilis written by Byzantine lawyers in 534 AD

Coyne, *Ireland: Industrial and Agricultural*, (1902), Brown and Nolan

Croker, *Researches in the South of Ireland*, (1824), London

Crowe, *The Changing Profile of the Natural Law*, (1977), The Hague

Cullen, *Girls Don't Do Honours: Irish Women in Education in the 19th and 20th Centuries*, (1987) Women's Educational Bureau

De Groof and Penneman, *The Legal Status of Pupils in Europe*, 1998, Klumer Law International

De Groof, *Subsidiarity and Education: Aspects of Comparative Educational Law*, (1994), Acco

De Groof, *The Legal Status of Teachers in Europe*, (1995), Acco

De Witte, *European Community Law of Education* (1989), Baden-Baden

Dowling, *A History of Irish Education: a Study in Conflicting Loyalties*, (1971), Mercier

Dowrick, *Human Rights, Problems, Perspectives and Texts*, (1979) Saxon House

d'Entreves, *Medieval Contribution to Political Thought*, (1939), Oxford

d'Entreves, *Natural Law: An Introduction to Legal Philosophy*, (1970), Hutchinson

Edmund Spenser, *View of the State of Ireland*, (1809), Dublin

Essays in Memory of Alexis Fitzgerald, (1987), Incorporated Law Society

Farragher, *Dev and His Alma Mater*, (1984), Dublin

Farry, *Education and the Constitution*, (1996), Round Hall, Sweet and Maxwell

Farry, *Vocational Teachers and the Law* (1998), Blackhall Publications

Fennell and Lynch, *Labour Law in Ireland*, (1992), Gill and MacMillan

Finnis, *Natural Law and Natural Rights*, (1980), Clarendon Press

Forde, *Employment Law*, (1993), Round Hall Press

Forde, *Industrial Relations Law*, (1991) Round Hall Press

Foster, *Modern Ireland 1600-1972*, (1989), Penguin

Gately on Libel and Slander, (1995), Sweet and Maxwell,

Ginsberg, *On Justice in Society*, (1965), Penguin

Good News Bible, Proverbs, (1976), Fontana

Grayson, *Sport and The Law*, (1995), Butterworths

Green, Hartley and Usher, *The Legal Foundations of the Single European Market*, (1991), Oxford University Press

Hall's Ireland, (1843), Vol 3, London

Harris, *The Law Relating to Schools*, (1990) Fourmat Publications

Hogan and Morgan, *Administrative Law in Ireland*, (2nd ed, 1991), Round Hall Sweet and Maxwell,

Hyland and Milne, eds, *Irish Educational Documents* (1987), Church of Ireland College of Education

Jacobs, *The European Convention on Human Rights* (1975), Clarendon Press

Jarman, *Landmarks in the History of Education*, (1963), London

John and Mary Hanlon, *A Journey with Gavan: Coping with Autism*, (1996) published by the authors Leixlip, Co Kildare

Joyce, *A Handbook of School Managment* (4th ed, 1872), McGlashan and Gill

Kelly, *Fundamental Rights in the Irish Law and Constitution*, (1967), Allen Figgis

Keogh, *Ireland and the Vatican*, (1995), Cork University Press

Keogh, *The Vatican, the Bishops and Irish Politics, 1919-1939* (1986), Cambridge

582

Keogh, *Twentieth Century Ireland: Nation and State*, (1994), Gill and Macmillan
Kerr and Whyte, *Trade Union Law*
Kerr, ed, *The Acquired Rights Directive*, (1996), Irish Centre for European Law
Kerr, *Irish Law Statutes Annotated, Worker Protection (Regular Part-Time) Employees Act, 1991*, Sweet and Maxwell
Levi-Strauss, *Structural Anthropology*, (1969), translated by Jackson and Grundfest, Penguin
Liell and Saunders, eds, *The Law of Education*, (9th ed, 1987) Butterworth
Little, *Malachi Horan Remembers*, (1976), Dublin
Longford and O'Neill, *Eamon de Valera*, (1970), Hutchinson
Madden and Kerr, *Unfair Dismissals: Cases and Commentary* (2nd ed, 1996), IBEC
Mahon, *Negligence and the Teacher*, (1995) Ennis Teachers' Centre
Maine, *Ancient Law*, (1961), Routledge
Manners and Customs of the Native Irish, (1873), Dublin
Maritain, *The Rights of Man and Natural law*, (1944), London
McCarthy, Kennedy and Matthews, *Focus on Residential Child Care in Ireland*, (1996) Focus Ireland
McCarthy, *The Distasteful Challenge*, (1968), Institute of Public Administration
McDonagh, *Freedom of Information Law in Ireland*, (1998), Round Hall, Sweet and Maxwell
McDonald, *Irish Law of Defamation*, (1987), Round Hall, Sweet and Maxwell in association with Irish Press
McMahon and Binchy, *Irish Law of Torts*, (2nd ed, 1990), Butterworths
McMahon and Murphy, *European Community Law in Ireland*, (1989), Butterworths
Meenan, *Working Within the Law* (1994), Oak Tree Press
Murdoch, *A Dictionary of Irish Law*, (2nd ed, 1993), Round Hall, Sweet and Maxwell
Neave, *The EEC and Education*, (1984), Stoke-on-Trent
Norman, *The Catholic Church and Ireland in the Age of Rebellion*, (1865), London
O'Buachalla, *Educational Policy in Twentieth Century Ireland*, (1988), Wolfhound
O'Connell, *A History of the INTO*, (1968), INTO
O'Connell, MP, *Memoir on Ireland*, (1844), Dublin
O'Connell, *One Hundred Years of Progress*, INTO
O'Connor, *A Troubled Sky: Reflections on the Irish Educational Scene 1957-1968*, (1968), Drumcondra Teachers' Centre
O'Donnell, *Wordgloss*, (1990), Institute of Public Administration
O'Flaherty, *Management and Control in Irish Education: The Post-Primary Experience*, (1992), Drumcondra Teachers' Centre,
O'Rahilly, *Thoughts on the Constitution* (1937), Brown and Nolan
Poole, Colemen and Liell, *Butterworths Education Law*, (1997), London
Porter, *The Life and Times of Henry Cooke*, (1871), London
Quinn, McDonagh and Kimber, *Disability Discrimination Law in the United States, Australia and Canada*, (1993) Oak Tree Pres
Redmond, *Dismissal Law in Ireland*, (1999), Butterworths
Redmond, *Dismissal Law in the Republic of Ireland*, (1982), Incorporated Law Society
Redmond-Howard, *The New Birth of Ireland* (1913), Collins Press

Roberston, *Human Rights in Europe*, (2nd ed, 1977) Manchester University Press

Rudden and Wyatt, *Basic Community Laws*, (1993), Oxford University Press

Ryan, *Keeping us in the Dark: Censorship and Freedom of Information in Ireland*, (1995), Gill and Macmillan

Salmond and Heuston on the Law of Torts, (21st ed, 1996) , Sweet and Maxwell

Sex Education in Schools, (1994) London, Department for Education and Employment

Shaw, *European Community Law*, (1993), Macmillan

Short Guide to the Convention on Human Rights (1991) Council of Europe

Sister Randles, *Post-Primary Education in Ireland 1957-1970*, (1975), Dublin

Smyth and Brady, *Democracy Blindfolded: The Case for a Freedom of Information Act in Ireland*, Undercurrent Series, O'Toole, ed, (1994) Cork University Press, Cork

Street on Torts, Brazier & Murray eds, (19th, ed 1999)

Szabo, *Cultural Rights*, (1974) Leiden

Teigten, *Collected Edition of the Travaux Preparatoires of the European Convention on Human Rights*, Council of Europe, 1985

The Documents of Vatican II, Abbott, ed, (1966), New York

The Educational Structures in the Member States of the European Community, (1989), Luxembourg, Office for Official Publications of EC

The Head's Legal Guide, (1998), Croner

The Papal Encyclicals 1740-1878, (1981), Raleigh, McGrath Publications

Titley, *Church, State and the Control of Schooling in Ireland 1900-1944*, (1983), Gill and MacMillan

Van Bueren, *International Documents on Children*, (1993) Dordrecht

Vocational Teachers and the Law, (1998), Blackhall Publications

Von Prondzynski and McCarthy, *Employment Law in Ireland*, (2nd ed, 1989), Round Hall Sweet and Maxwell

Wade and Forsyth, *Administrative Law*, (7th ed, 1994) , Oxford University Press

Walters, *The Story of a Hedge School Master*, (1974), Mercier

Weatherill and Beaumont, *European Community Law*, (1994), Penguin

Articles

An American looks at Irish Education' Address to AGM of Conference of Convent Secondary Schools, 23 June 1960. Published in Report of CCSS 1959-1960

Barbas Homen, 'Right to Education and Minorities, Portuguese Report' in *The Legal Status of Minorities in Education*, de Goof and Fiers, eds, (1996) Acco, Leuven

Barrington, 'Article Forty-Four-1', *Studies* 80 (1952)

Beales, 'John Henry Newman' in *Pioneers of English Education*, Judges, ed, (1952), Faber and Faber

Beamish, 'Schoolboy Injured in Attack by Bully Boy', Irish Times 31 January 199

Beckmann, 'Creating a Legal Framework to Support the Provision of High Quality Education in South Africa', Education and the Law 9 (1997) 2 123. 63

Binchy, 'Abortion Ruling one of the most significant legal decisions since foundation of the State', Irish Times, 15 May 1995

Binchy, 'Schools Liability in Negligence', 78 Incorporated Law Society of Ireland Gazette (1984) 153

Buckley, 'The Administration of National Schools-Aspects of the Legal and Constitutional Background' in *A Proposal for Growth; The Administration of National Schools*, (1980), INTO

Byrne, 'Health and Safety Requirements for Primary Schools: A 1999 Update', lecture delivered in Trinity College Law School, 27 March 1999

Carolan, "P v S and Cornwall County Council: The European Court of Justice, The Equal Treatment Directive, and Transsexuality," (1998), ILT, No 9

Clancy, 'Participation of the Socially and Economically Disadvantaged', UCD and the HEA

Clarke, 'Freedom of Thought and Educational Rights in the European Convention', (1987) Ir Jur

Clarke, 'Freedom of Thought in Schools: A Comparative Study', 35 (1986) ICLQ 271

Clarke, 'The Role of Natural law in Irish Constitutional Law' (1982) 17 Ir Jur (ns) 187

Costello, 'The Natural Law and the Irish Constitution' *Studies* (1956) 45

Cramb, 'Woman sues over bullies at her old school', Daily Telegraph, 9 November 1996

Cullen, 'New certification body will be set up', Irish Times, 13 January 1995

Currall, 'Education Rights under the EC Treaty' in *Mobility of People in the European Community*, (1989), ICEL

Dahl, 'The Right to Education: The Legal Position of Minorities in Education in Norway' in The *Legal Status of Minorities in Education*, de Goof and Fiers eds, (1996) Acco, Leuve

De Blacam, 'Justice and Natural Law', (1997), Ir Jur, Vol 32

De Witte, 'Educational Equality for Community Workers and their Families' in *European Community Law of Education*, (1989), Baden-Baden

De Witte, 'Introduction' in *European Community Law of Education*, (1989), Baden-Baden, Nomos

Dillon-Malone, 'Individual Remedies and the Strasbourg System in an Irish Context', in Heffernan, *Human Rights: A European Perspective* 1994, Round Hall Press

Dowling Maher, 'The Safety, Health and Welfare at Work Act, 1989 with Particular Reference to an Effective Policy for Science Laboratories', (1996), unpublished thesis, M Sc, Trinity College, Dublin

Duncan, 'The Constitutional protection of Parental Rights' in *Report of the Constitution Review Group*, (1996), Government Publications

Edward Grayson, 'Breaking new ground in schools', NLJ, 29 July 1988

Emilou (1992), "Subsidiarity: an effective barrier against the enterprises of ambition?", 17 ELR

Fahey, 'Nuns in the Catholic Church in Ireland in the Nineteenth Century', in *Girls Don't Do Honours*, Cullen, ed, (1987), Women's Bureau

Fankhauser, 'Development of Education Law on Schools in Austria (1993-1996), Part 1: Schools', in *European Journal for Education Law and Policy*, (1997) Kluwer Law International

Farrell, 'Cagey and Secretive: Collective Responsibility, Executive Confidentiality and the Public Interest', in *Modern Irish Democracy: Essays in Honour of Basil Chubb*, Hill and Marsh, eds, (1993), Irish Academic Press

Farrell, 'Ireland out of step on European rights', Irish Times, 29 December 1997

Farrell, 'The Drafting of the Irish Free State Constitution: I (1970) 5 Ir Jur, 115

Faughnan, 'The Jesuits and the Drafting of the Irish Constitution' *Irish Historical Studies*, (1988) No 101

Flynn, 'Vocational Training in Community law and Practice', *Yearbook of European Law*, 1988

Frisby and Beckham, 'Developing School Policies on the Application of Reasonable Force', 122 Ed Law Rep 27

Glendenning and Whelan, 'Irish Educational Structures' in *The Legal Status of Teachers in Europe: Mobility and Education*, de Groof, ed, (1995), Acco

Glendenning, 'The Role of the State in First and Second Level Education in Ireland: Retrospect and Prospect', PhD dissertation, Law School, Trinity College, Dublin 1996

Gould, 'Equality of Access to Education', (1989) 52 MLR, 540

Harris, 'The Autonomy of the Teacher: Education Law and Educational Standards in England and Wales' Paper read at European Association for Education Law and Policy, 23 December 1998

Hawkswell, 'IRC decision on Marian Regional High School', (20 November 1988), The British Columbia Catholic

Hennis, 'Access to Education in the European Communities', (1990) 3 Leiden Journal of International Law

Hogan, 'Constitutional Interpretation' in *The Constitution of Ireland 1937-1987*, Litton, ed, (1988)

Hogan, 'Constitutional Issues Raised in the Educational Bill, 1997', The Bar Review, Vol 2

Hyland 'The Multi-Denominational Experience in the National School System' *Irish Educational Studies* Vol 8

Hyland, "Recognition of Qualifications of Migrant Workers-The Irish Situation" in *Free Movement of Workers in Ireland*, forthcoming, Irish Centre for European Law

Hyland, 'The Irish Educational System and Freedom of Information' in *Ireland: A Journal of History and Society*, special ed (1995)

Keogh, 'The Irish Constitutional Revolution: The Making of the Constitution: an Historical Analysis' in *The Constitution of Ireland 1937-1987*, Litton, ed, (1988), Vol 35

Kimber, 'Disability Discrimination Law in Canada' in *Disability Discrimination Law*, (1993)

Kirp, 'Introduction: The Fourth R: Reading, Writing, 'Rithmetic-and Rules'; in *School Days, Rule Days, The Legalization and Regulation of Education*, Kirp and Jensen, eds, (1986) The Falmer Press

Kiss, 'La Protection internationale Du Droit de L'enfant a L'education', *Droits de l'Homme*, (1973)

Lane, 'The Use of the Least Restrictive Environment Principle in Placements Decisions Affecting School-Age Students with Disabilities', (1992) 69 Univ of Detroit, Mercy L Rev 291

Lauterpacht, 'The UN Declaration of Human Rights' in British Yearbook of International Law, 25 (1948)

Lenaerts, 'Subsidiarity and Community Competence in the Field of Education' in de Groof, *Subsidiarity and Education: Aspects of Comparative Educational Law*, (1994), Acco

Linehan, 'The Schoolteacher and the Law of Negligence' (1965) 31 Ir Jur 38

Lonbay, 'Education and Law: the Community Context', 14 ELR (1989)

Macbeth, 'The Child Between', *Studies*, (1984), Office for Official Publications

McDonagh, 'Disability Discrimination Law in Australia' in Disability Discrimination Law, (1993)

McGlade-Cooney, 'Educational Malpractice Suits - Another American Import?', (1991), The Irish Student Law Review

McNeill, 'Guidelines for an Irish Educational Policy' (1979) 14 Ir Jur (ns) 378

Meredith, 'Education Legislation in England and Wales', in *European Journal for Education Law and Policy*, (1997), Kluwer Law International

Meredith, 'Recent Educational Disputes and the Courts', ACE Bulletin, 26 November/ December 198

Mooney, 'A Lesson from Church Schools', The Times, 22 January 1999

Murphy, 'Democracy, Natural Law and the Irish Constitution', (1996) ILT Vol 14

Murray, 'Educational Segregation "Rite" or Wrong', in *Ireland: A Sociological Profile*, Clancy, Drudy, Lynch and O'Dowd, eds, (1986), Institute of Public Administration

Neal and Kirp, 'The Allure of Legalization Reconsidered: The Case of Special Education' in Law and Contemporary Problems, (1985), Vol 48

Neville Harris, 'The Autonomy of the Teacher: Education Law and Education Standards in England and Wales', Paper delivered to Education Law Association, Salzburg, 19 December 1998

Newell, 'The Beaters Beaten', Times Educational Supplement, 14 August 1987

Osborough, 'Irish Law and the Rights of National Teachers' (1979) 15 Ir Jur 36-60

Osborough, 'Education in the Irish Law and Constitution' (1978) 13 Ir Jur (ns) 145

O'Cleary, 'Sex abuse, rape "are common" in Republic, says US State Department' Irish Times, 3 February 1995

O'Hanlon, 'Natural Rights and the Irish Constitution' (1993) 11 ILT 8

O'Keefe, 'Judicial Interpretation of the Public Service Exception to the Free Movement of Workers' in *Constitutional Adjudication in European Community and National Law*, Curtain and O'Keefe, eds, (1992) Butterworths

Parkes, 'University Education', in *Irish Education Documents*, Hyland and Milne, eds, (1987), Vol 1

Perteck, 'Free Movement of Professionals and Recognition of Higher Diplomas' in *Yearbook of European Law*, Bard and Wyatt, eds, (1992), Oxford University Press

Pollack, Education Correspondent, 'FÁS gets a mixed Euro-fund report' in Education and Living, Irish Times, 2 February 1999

Potgieter, 'The Right to Education and the Protection of Minorities in South Africa: a Preliminary Perspective' in *The Legal Status of Minorities in Education*, de Goof and Fiers, ed, (1986), Acco

587

Power, 'Human Rights and the EEC' in Heffernan with Kingston, *Human Rights: a European Perspective*, (1994), Round Hall Press in association with Irish Centre for European Law

Ramsey, 'Educational Negligence and the Legislation of Education' (1988), University of New South Wales Law Journal

Redmond, 'Beyond the Net-Protecting the Individual Worker', (1983) JISLL 1

Redmond, 'The Law and Worker's Rights', in *Trade Unions and change in Irish Society* ed, Nevin, (1980), Dublin

Robinson, 'Damages for Academic under Performance; Pupils as Plaintiffs' Education and the Law, (1996)

Robinson, 'Special Educational Needs, the Code and the New Tribunal' in Education and the Law, (1996)

Ryan, 'Mum who educated autistic son gets £30,000', Irish Independent, 16 November 1996

Shaw, 'Education and the Law in the European Community', Journal of Law and Education (1992)

Smith, 'Irish-qualified teachers benefit from EU directive on professions', Irish Times, 22 February, 1996

Thompson, 'Sex Education and the Law: Working towards Good Practice', in Harris, ed, Children, Sex Education and the Law

Twomey, 'The Death of the Natural Law?' (1995) ILT (ns) 270

Van Bueren, 'Education: Whose Right is it Anyway?' in Heffernan, *Human Rights, A Europrean Perspective*, (1994) Round Hall Press

Verbruggen and Fiers, 'Synthetic and Analytical Overview of the Legal Status of Teachers in Europe' in *The Legal Status of Teachers in Europe*, de Groof, ed, (1995), Acco

Verbruggen, 'European Community Educational Law A Short Overview' in *Subsidiarity and Education: Aspects of Comparative Educational Law*, de Groof, ed, (1994), Acco

Walsh, 'Legal Challenge to integration of Religious Studies', Irish Times, 17 September 1991

Walsh, 'The Constitution and Constitutional Rights' in *The Constitution of Ireland 1937-1987*, Litton, ed, (1988), Institute of Public Administration

Walsh, 'The Judicial Power, Justice and the Constitution of Ireland', in *Constitutional Adjudication in European and National Law*, (1992), Butterworths

Warbrick, 'Rights, the European Convention on Human Rights and English Law' ELR, Vol 19, (1994)

Whelan, 'Constitutional Amendments in Ireland: The Competing Claims of Democracy', *Justice and Legal Theory in Ireland*, Quinn, Ingram and Livingstone, eds, (1995)

Whyte, 'Constitutional Adjudication, Ideology and Access to the Courts' in *Law and Liberty in Ireland*, Whelan, ed, (1993), Dublin

Whyte, 'Education and the Constitution,' in *Religion, Education and the Constitution*, Lane, ed, (1992), The Columba Press

Whyte, 'Education and the Constitution: Convergence of Paradigm and Praxis', (1990/92) 25-27, Ir Jur (ns) 69

Whyte, 'Natural Law and the Constitution' (1996) 14 ILT (ns), 8

Index